(Mùa đông) 1992

2/19/92

# THE ILLUSTRATED HISTORY OF
# ANTIQUES

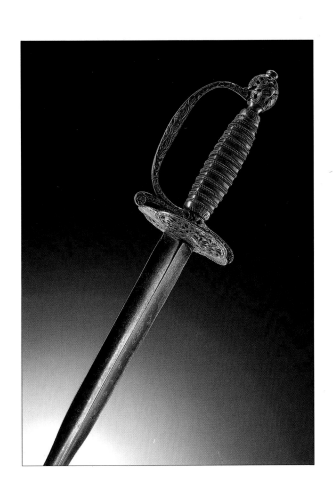

# THE ILLUSTRATED HISTORY OF
# ANTIQUES

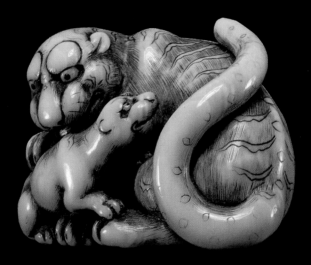

## THE ESSENTIAL REFERENCE FOR ALL ANTIQUE
## LOVERS AND COLLECTORS

*General Editor · Huon Mallalieu*

RUNNING PRESS
PHILADELPHIA, PENNSYLVANIA

9 8 7 6 5 4 3 2 1
Digit on the right indicates the number of this
printing

Library of Congress Cataloging-in-Publication
Number 91 - 52790

ISBN 0-89471-888-6

This book was designed and produced by
Quarto Publishing plc
6 Blundell Street
London N7 9BH

**Senior Editor** Cathy Meeus
**Editor** Paul Szuscikiewicz
**Copy Editors** Tony Whitehorn, Patricia Bayer

**Designer** Allan Mole
**Illustrator** David Kemp

**Picture Researchers** Jane Lambert, Donna Thynne
**Picture Research Manager** Sarah Risley

**Art Director** Moira Clinch
**Publishing Director** Janet Slingsby

Typeset in Great Britain by
ABC Typesetting Ltd, Bournemouth and
Bookworm Typesetting, Manchester.
Manufactured in Singapore by Chroma Graphics
(Overseas) Pte. Ltd
Printed in Singapore by Tien Wah Press (Pte.) Ltd

Quarto would like to thank the following for their
help in the preparation of this book:
Ann-Marie Benson, Philip Chidlow, Stefanie Foster,
Karen Evans, Katie Klitgaard, Jane Parker,
Debbie Sumner, Peter Waldron.

This book may be ordered by mail from the
publisher. Please include $2.50 for postage and
handling. *But try your bookstore first!*

Running Press Book Publishers
125 South Twenty-second Street
Philadelphia, Pennsylvania 19103

# CONTENTS

## INTRODUCTION

## 1
## FURNITURE

## 2
## CARPETS AND RUGS

## 3
## TEXTILES AND COSTUME

## 4
## CLOCKS AND WATCHES

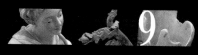

# 10
# GLASS
PAGE 466

# 11
# COINS AND MEDALS
PAGE 504

# 12
# ARMS AND ARMOR
PAGE 528

# 13
# TOYS
PAGE 554

# 14
# BOOKS, MANUSCRIPTS, AND MAPS
PAGE 588

# GLOSSARY
PAGE 622

# INDEX
PAGE 631

# CONTRIBUTORS

## General Editor

**Huon Mallalieu** is a respected authority on antiques. He was formerly the Sale Room writer for *Country Life*. He was general editor and coordinator of *The Popular Antiques Yearbook*, and was cataloguer of watercolours at Christie's in London. He has contributed articles to many general and trade publications, including *The Antiques Trade Gazette, House & Garden* and *Connoisseur*.

## The Contributors

**Dr Charles Avery** formerly was deputy keeper of sculpture at the Victoria and Albert Museum in London for 12 years.

**Claire Ayres** is a member of Christie's valuation department at their South Kensington, London, salerooms. She has a general interest in all antiques.

**David Battie** started a career in antiques as a porter at Sotheby's in 1967. He became a director in 1976. He has written price guides to both *19th-Century British Pottery* and *Porcelain* and is the editor of *Sotheby's Encyclopedia of Porcelain*. He appears on BBC Television's *Antiques Road Show*.

**Patricia Bayer** is a freelance writer, editor and consultant specializing in late-19th- and early-20th-century decorative arts.

**Ian Bennett** is a consultant to Sotheby's and a collector of Oriental rugs and carpets.

**Simon Castle** has been dealing in treen for 15 years.

**John K.D. Cooper** is a freelance lecturer and consultant on silver, design and fine art. He is a freeman of London's Goldsmith's Company.

**Aileen Dawson** is curator of medieval and later antiquities at the British Museum.

**Richard Falkiner** is a dealer and consultant in coins and medals, and ancient and medieval art.

**Richard Garnier** was for 15 years head of the clock and watch department at Christie's, London. He is now head of the antique clock department at Garrard & Co, the Crown Jewellers.

**Michael German** has been a specialist dealer in walking sticks for 20 years, and is now the leading authority on the subject.

**Julia Harris** does valuation and cataloguing work for the Phillips Collectors Centre in London. Her publications include *The History of Twentieth Century Collectibles* (Letts and Co.), published in 1990.

**Malcolm Haslam** worked for some years as an antique dealer before becoming a lecturer and writer specializing in the decorative arts. He is the author of several books including *In the Nouveau Style* and *Arts and Crafts Carpets*.

**Stephen Helliwell** is head of the silver and objects departments at Christie's, and is an associate director of the company. His book *Collecting Small Silverware* was published in 1988.

**John Hope-Falkner**, a collector and dealer in Oriental art, has been involved in the art and antiques world all his working life.

**Peter Hornsby** is author of *Pewter, Copper and Brass* and *Collecting Antique Copper and Brass*. He has been a consultant to London's three main auction houses – Christie's, Phillips and Sotheby's – as well as the Museum of London.

**Peter Johnson** is a prolific contributor to magazines on the subjects of antiques and collecting.

**Caroline Knight** is a freelance lecturer in the history of art and architecture, with a special interest in houses and their furnishings.

**Sebastian Kuhn** is a specialist in European ceramics working for Sotheby's in Zürich.

**Gordon Lang**, a leading authority on Oriental ceramics, is senior tutor and deputy director of Sotheby's education department.

**Lori Lang** is a freelance writer.

**Martin Levy** is the fourth generation of his family in the London antique dealers H. Blairman & Sons. He was a contributor to the exhibition catalogue *George Bullock Cabinet-Maker* (1988) and has written for various journals including *Apollo, Country Life* and *Furniture History*.

**Arthur Middleton** runs his own shop in London's Covent Garden, specializing in scientific instruments. He is a committee member of the Scientific Instruments Society.

**David Miles** is an antique dealer, consultant and collector of antique musical instruments and books.

**Brian Morgan** was for many years a director of Bluett and Sons, to whom he is still a consultant.

**Susan Newell** is assistant keeper of applied and fine art at the Tyne & Wear Museum. She was formerly senior museum assistant at the Wallace Collection.

**Mark Newstead** is deputy director of Sotheby's European ceramics department.

**Felicity Nicholson** is director in charge of the antiquities department at Sotheby's.

**Catherine Parry-Wingfield** is course tutor for the Study Centre for the History of the Fine and Decorative Arts, London.

**Peter Philp** trained as a furniture designer. His books include *Furniture of the World* and *Antiques Today*.

**Jonathan Potter** runs one of the world's leading antiquarian map sellers located in London's Mayfair. His *The Country Life Book of Antique Maps* is one of the most popular introductions to the subject.

**Sarah Potter** works for Barling of Mount Street Ltd, specialists in early Chinese furniture.

**Noël Riley** has written extensively on the decorative arts and antiques. She wrote *The Victorian Design Source Book* (Phaidon, 1989) and was a contributor to *Sotheby's Concise Encyclopedia of Furniture*.

**Diana Scarisbrick** is the author of *Ancestral Jewels* (André Deutsch 1990), and the forthcoming *Jewellery in Britain* (Michael Russell) and *Cartier* (Hamlyn).

**Ken Swift** has been dealing in prints, maps and books since 1973.

**Kerry Taylor** works for Sotheby's, where her responsibilities have ranged from toys and dolls to European costume and textiles – all subjects on which she has written books and numerous articles.

**Lars Tharp** is currently a director of Sotheby's in Sussex, England. His interest in the history and material culture of China and Japan developed during his studies at Gonville and Caius College, Cambridge. He was a contributor to *Sotheby's Concise Encyclopedia of Porcelain*.

**Susan Ward** is a freelance editor and specialist writer on American art and antiques. Her most recent book is *A Catalog of Antiques*.

**Judy Wentworth** is a partner in the Antique Textile Company, which she founded with Sarah Franklyn in 1981. She lives and works in London, and writes and lectures on textiles.

**John Whitehead** is a specialist dealer in French furniture and Sèvres porcelain. He is currently working on a survey of French 18th-century interior decoration and decorative arts.

**Frederick Wilkinson** is a consultant to Sotheby's arms and armour department and works for the Royal Armouries at the Tower of London. He is a Fellow of the Royal Society of Arts.

**Peter Williams** is head of the ceramics department at Sotheby's Chester saleroom. For several years he worked in Sotheby's European ceramics department in London.

**Perran Wood**, formerly of Sotheby's, London, is a founder-fellow of the Corning Museum of Glass in Corning, New York.

# INTRODUCTION

E xcept for the purposes of customs duties for which it is defined as an artefact that is over 100 years old, "antique" is not a precise term; many things are avidly collected which are not antiques and in a more general sense never will be. Around 1800 the English water-colourist Thomas Rowlandson hit this point in a drawing of an auctioneer offering a chamber pot: "What am I to bid for tomorrow's antique?" Confusion of nomenclature and terminology continues, since some call more modern artefacts "collectables" and others "collectibles", while still others think both versions inelegant but cannot coin anything better.

This has made the task of deciding what should have a place here and what should be excluded both invigorating and invidious. With

This one-day weight-driven shelf clock dating from 1870, was made by the Set Thomas Clock Co in the USA. Such clocks are among America's chief contribution to modern collecting; the growth of the industry there, especially in New England, is a classic example of how art and craft came together to satisfy a market need. (*Above*)

This Spanish shaving-dish and ewer were made in Madrid in 1768. The man who originally purchased them was undoubtedly a high ecclesiastic – note the bishop's mitre and initials engraved on the body of the ewer. The oval shaving dish is similarly engraved. It was common custom at the time to personalize such items; for today's collector, this can add to the value of such a piece, both in terms of interest and in the sale room. (*Left*)

This marquetry and mahogany side cabinet dates from around 1900. By this time, the collecting mania, which had become a 19th-century obsession, was at its height; along with this went a pride in craftsmanship, which characterized the approach of the leading furniture-makers of the time. Turn-of-the-century furniture is extremely collectable today. (*Right*)

unlimited space and time, all would be covered. However, while there are inevitable omissions, even within the constraints of this volume the range of artefacts covered is wide.

We have imposed a dateline of our own that varies according to the sense of each subject, since in some fields it is not yet possible to know what recent products will have an enduring appeal. Obviously "flat art", or more politely, the fine as opposed to the plastic arts – pictures, drawings and, where they are separate from books, prints – are not our concern here.

Interest in accumulating artefacts of beauty and/or curiosity has been a preoccupation of individuals since the earliest civilizations. In Imperial Rome there were auctions of works of art, beginning with the booty of war, and these were accompanied by flourishing art dealers and a thriving industry supplying fakes and forgeries. In Medieval Europe, the chief hoarders and accumulators were the Church and the emergent monarchies. In the 15th century not only the Princes of Renaissance Italy with the Medici of Florence at their head, but also the great nobles of France and Burgundy understood their political duty to be patrons of the arts; in Machiavelli's words: "A prince should also show his esteem for talent, actively encouraging able men, and paying honour to eminent craftsmen." Some of these noble collectors were artists themselves, such as René of Anjou, or that fine poet Charles, duc

In late-19th-century Russia, the Fabergé factory became renowned for its production of exquisite miniature artefacts, ranging from the celebrated imperial Easter eggs made for the Romanovs down to cigarette cases. All are extremely collectable. This tiny sedan chair, in which Tsarina Catherine the Great is being carried, is a fine example of the work in which Fabergé excelled. (*Above*)

d'Orlèans, who like his uncle Jean, the duc de Berry of the famous illuminated manuscript, the "Très Riches Heures", and their Burgundian cousins, realized that patronage and collecting, and cultural eminence were as essential to their position as military prowess. In Charles' case they were actually much more essential, since he spent the quarter century after Agincourt as a prisoner in England.

Among the treasures listed in the inventory taken at the death of Lorenzo Medici (the Magnificent) in 1492, along with a painting by van Eyck and the great trio of the battle of San Romano by Uccello, are the horn of a unicorn, examples of Chinese porcelain and an extensive collection of ancient cameos. Of them all, by far the most highly prized was the horn. It was valued at 6,000 florins against 30 for the van Eyck and about 300 for the three paintings by Uccello. Such accumulations of treasure and bric à brac by the great nobles were still to a large extent manifestations of the glory of the state, but leavened and informed by personal taste and connoisseurship. The tradition survived on through the 17th century in the *Wunderkammern* (cabinets of curiosities) of the princes, which were emulated by true private collectors, especially in the Netherlands and Great Britain.

In such collections, anything might find a place – porcelain, cameos, jewels, scientific instruments, busts and statues in serried ranks, blue and white porcelain in heaps, clocks, mermaids, Aztec headdresses, lacquers and silks, maps, shells, medals, ivory-handled pistols, Limoges

A German gold beaker, made in Dresden around 1750, probably for a royal court. In the hands of an expert, such a piece can tell its own story. (*Above*)

This Turkish weft-faced, flat-weave, all wool kilim comes from the Ushak region of western Anatolia and dates from the 17th century. It is one of only a very small number of known examples of Ushak village kilims – approximately ten are known to exist. This scarcity value makes them extremely attractive to collectors. The majority feature horizontal bands of floral designs, as here, though the yellow warps are an unusual feature. It is also less finely woven than most of the other known kilims of this type. (*Below*)

An oak centre table, dating from the mid 19th century, shows how the Victorian revival of the medieval Gothic style penetrated every area of design, down to tables, chairs and other items of household furniture. The stark simplicity of this table is truly Gothic; it would have fitted well into an early fortified manor house or the refectory of a monastery. (*Above*)

enamels. When in 1842, long after his death, the contents of Strawberry Hill, Horace Walpole's "Gothic mouse-trap", were sold off, *The Times* sneered that there was "nothing for which a good judge would have travelled a step out of his road", although Queen Victoria and the many other buyers disagreed. However, the description is still a good one of the contents of a magpie cabinet of curiosities: "suits of mail standing like ghosts in armour here and there, fantastic carvings bought from monkish cloisters, rusty weapons of various kinds, distorted figures in china and wood and iron and ivory: tapestry and strange furniture that might have been designed in dreams." There was Renaissance as well as French 18th-century furniture, Anne Boleyn's historically dubious clock (bought by Queen Victoria) as well as the products of Walpole's private printing press. By Walpole's time most collectors were more methodical than he, but "a cabinet of curiosities" in the sense of Walpole's heterogeneous collections might well provide a fitting secondary title for this book.

The 19th century, of course, was obsessed and enchanted by things. Lord Briggs, in his book *Victorian Things* (1988), explains how seriously the Victorians treated collecting in the middle years of the century. "By a coincidence it was in the year of the Great Exhibition, 1851, that Captain Henry Lane-Fox...began collecting fire arms before going on to collect almost everything else from all parts of the world, including utensils, machines, ornaments, dress and 'any other ponderable object produced or used at home.' His purpose was not to select 'unique specimens' but to assemble examples of what was 'ordinary and typical', and he went on to trace in an elaborate system of classification of things 'the succession of ideas by which the minds of men...have progressed from the simple to the complex, and from the homogeneous to the heterogeneous." In his collection a case labelled

This green glazed tripod jar was made in China during the period of Tang rule from AD 618 to 906. The fine quality of the glaze and the precision of the potting are typical of the best examples from that period. The shape is derived from metalwork, with even small details, such as the rivets in the cover, being faithfully copies by the Tang craftsmen. European interest in things Chinese dates back to before the days of the medieval explorer Marco Polo. (*Above*)

French "gorge de pigeon" scent bottles and toilet jar (second from left), dating from around 1825. During the 19th century, the craftsman gradually became an artist, a process culminating in the achievements of such masters of style as Lalique. The fine workmanship displayed here is the reason why utilitarian objects have become recognized as works of art in their own right. (*Right*)

Matthaus Bäur made this solid-looking silver teapot in Augsburg in around 1690. For Europeans of the time, taking tea was just as much a social ritual as it still is for the Japanese, and for the well-to-do fine silverware was an essential adjunct. Bäur emphasized tea's links with the east in the decoration; you can see a beturbanned Turk, succinctly labelled Ottomanus (Ottoman), on the side. (*Above*)

These wind meters date from the late 19th century and reflect solid Victorian values in their down-to-earth, well made, matter-of-fact styling. Scientific instruments are just as collectable as any other antiques; scientists themselves, in fact, have been among the greatest collectors. (*Right*)

"religious emblems and ritual objects" contained such unlikely companions as a medieval crucifix, a Chinese geometric compass and a set of divining bones from Nigeria.

Although they would have been thought a complete contrast at the time, the crowded contents of "that wonderful place", as *Harper's Weekly* called Menlo Park, Thomas Edison's laboratory in New Jersey, would to us form a continuum with Lane-Fox's assemblage. There were many new things and miracles of modern science, but also fragments of old machines, and the gap was bridged by a stuffed eagle which presided there. It had been bought at the 1889 Paris Exhibition, and it had an electric bulb in its head to give fire to the eyes. These 18th- and 19th-century collectors were trying to do with their objects what we have aimed at on a still vaster scale in words with this book.

Our intention is to place types of things and individual objects in their historical and social context. Just as it is foolish to look at historical events and processes through distorting layers of subsequent experience, or to judge our ancestors as if they thought and reacted as we do, so it is important for a full enjoyment of antiques to know something of the cultures and conditions that produced them. It is as well to remember, too, that many things we now think of as treasures were often simply utilitarian objects to their makers and first possessors. Relatively speaking, many would have been considered as disposable as the throw-away incidentals of our own day.

However, we have concentrated throughout upon quality, and where relevant, upon the greatest artists and craftsmen, many of whose

Tetradrachm from the period of the Egyptian Pharaoh Ptolemy I. For historians, the way in which such coins are decorated can provide a valuable insight into the way of life of the society in which they were first minted. For numismatists, who are among the most dedicated of collectors, fine coin collections have an intrinsic value of their own, especially when carefully preserved. (*Above*)

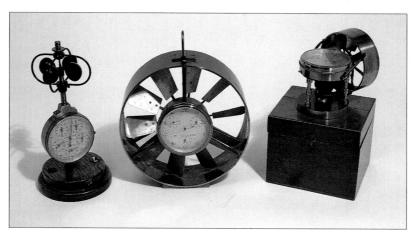

Rugs from what was once the Ottoman empire provided its rulers with a major export and have always been prized by connoisseurs. This village rug (wool pile on all-wool foundation), comes from the Konya region of central Anatolia and dates from the 15th-16th centuries. Now in the Alexander Collection, California, it is one of the greatest Turkish rugs in any Western exhibit, public or private. Together with other early Anatolian examples, it provides a valuable insight into the quality and diversity of weaving before the onset of Ottoman "court" art in the 16th century. (*Below*)

styles and characteristics are featured in special boxes. These are matters in which one should learn to judge by the standards of the best whenever possible.

Just occasionally true quality is irrelevant, when the point of an object or a collection is association, rather than intrinsic merit. The face powder brush used by Anne Boleyn on the morning of her execution, and a string of pearls worn by Marie Antoinette shortly before hers, which now lie side by side in a private family's collection of royal souvenirs, both have a value of their own as ivory or pearls, but it is as nothing to the value of their associations.

I would like to think that this book can be enjoyed in as many ways as a *Wunderkammer* or a great miscellaneous collection. Some may wish to make their entrance on the first page, and not emerge again until they have seen everything that it contains. Others may wish to start with just one chapter dealing with a single category of antiques.

A late 17th-century Kakiemon tiger. The Japanese made Kakiemon porcelain primarily for export to the West; the finest collection was assembled by the Elector Frederick Augustus I of Saxony, who also founded the Meissen factory.

The book should be a pleasure to browsers, but also invaluable to those who wish to study seriously. With practical reference features such as the glossary of terms, I hope that it will be as much an aid to those who like to provide themselves with background when they visit museums as it will be a security to those who are embarking on an actual purchase. The numerous specialist contributors have, by supplying suggestions for further reading in each field, attempted to open doors to more in-depth research for those whose interest has been kindled in a particular area.

Huon Mallalieu

# CHAPTER 1

# FURNITURE

EARLY EUROPEAN FURNITURE•
17TH-CENTURY ENGLAND•
18TH-CENTURY ENGLAND•
REGENCY•VICTORIAN REVIVALS•
FRANCE•ITALY•SPAIN AND PORTUGAL•
GERMANY, AUSTRIA, AND EASTERN EUROPE•
RUSSIA•SCANDINAVIA•THE NETHERLANDS•
BRITAIN AND EUROPE 1860–1920•
AMERICA•ORIENTAL FURNITURE

MALCOLM HASLAM
CAROLINE KNIGHT
MARTIN LEVY
CATHERINE PARRY-WINGFIELD
PETER PHILP
SARAH POTTER
NOËL RILEY
JOHN WHITEHEAD

This page: **ITALIAN EBONY AND** *PIETRE DURE* **CABINET,**
c. 1700 (detail).

# FURNITURE

**T**HE STYLISTIC VARIETY AND WIDE RANGE OF DIFFERENT PIECES MAKE THIS ONE OF THE MOST IMPRESSIVE CATEGORIES OF ANTIQUES. **A**RTISTIC AND TECHNICAL DEVELOPMENTS HAVE TURNED FURNISHINGS INTO SYMBOLS OF STATUS, AS WELL AS ATTRACTIVE ITEMS IN THEIR OWN RIGHT.

**CIRCULAR DINING TABLE**
*English*
Rosewood with floral marquetry of various woods; **c. 1830**

Tables such as this, with tops that tipped sideways for easy storage, made room arrangement conveniently flexible.

Unified schemes of interior decoration – that is, harmony between architecture, ornamental features, furniture and upholstery – first began to appear during the Renaissance. In the 17th century such carefully contrived effects were quite usual among the beau monde in France, the Netherlands and England. By the end of the century those who wanted to be fashionable had design books to guide them.

Books of engraved patterns and ornament and of architectural styles had been available since the 16th century. The earliest furniture pattern book was *Différents Pourtraicts de Menuiserie* (*c*. 1588) by Hans Vredeman de Vries (1527– after 1604), and this was followed by another major work, *Oficina Arcularia* (1621) by Crispin de Passe. Early design books were mainly concerned with architecture, or with architectural features such as chimney-pieces or decorated ceilings, but increasingly furniture was included.

Most engraved pattern books were published in early centres of the printing industry, such as Nuremberg, Augsburg, Amsterdam and Utrecht, but many of the late-17th- and early-18th-century productions were produced in Paris: whereas in the early 17th century architects and designers had looked to Italy for their models and Italian craftsmen were enticed all over Europe to add Italian decorative refinements to the most luxurious schemes, by the late 17th century the French had secured the lead both in design and craftsmanship. French sophistication, embodied in the splendours of Versailles, but manifest in many lesser projects too, became the goal of the fashion-conscious throughout Europe, and France remained the most potent influence on interior design throughout the 18th century.

THE SPREAD OF FASHIONS

Design books were one means of disseminating fashions. The movement of craftsmen and designers around Europe was another. The

**STOOL**
*French*
Carved giltwood, knotted
pile upholstery; **late 17th
century**

At this period, stools were
as much used as chairs for
seating, and were often
made in matching sets with
rich upholstery. The French
royal carpet factory, known
as the Savonnerie, founded
in 1627, was the most
important producer of fine
carpets and upholstery
(such as on this stool) in
17th and 18th century
Europe.

Italian Domenico Cucci (*c.* 1640–1705) and the Flemings Pierre Golle
(1620–84) and Daniel Marot (1663–1752) were merely the most celebrated of many outstanding foreigners who were attracted to Paris in
the 17th century. After the Revocation of the Edict of Nantes in 1685
those who were Huguenots were forced to flee, taking their skills – and
French styles – to Protestant-friendly countries such as England, the
Netherlands and Germany.

Ambitious princes sent designers and craftsmen to Paris to assimilate the latest refinements so that they could introduce them in the
purest possible form at home, and French or French-trained architects
and furniture designers found enthusiastic clients for their services in
all parts of Europe. Prime examples are the attachment of Marot to
the court of the English king William III, of François Cuvilliès
(1695–1768) to those of the Electors of Bavaria, and of Nicholas
Pineau (1684–1754) to that of Peter the Great in Russia.

Those sufficiently eager for the latest designs from Paris could
receive them within two or three weeks, even if they lived as far afield

**COMMODE**
*François Cuvilliés, Bavaria*
Painted and silvered wood
with marble top; **1739**

This piece, from the
Hunting Room at the
Amalienburg, Schloss
Nymphenburg, shows the
palatial Rococo at its most
extreme.

**GAMES AND WRITING TABLE**

*Attributed to Giuseppe Maggiolini*

Tulipwood and fruitwood with marquetry decoration; **late 18th century**

Pictorial marquetry panels – in this case a hunting trophy and sewing utensils surrounded by a band of flowerheads and husks – employing many different woods, are typical of the work of Maggiolini, the leading Neo-Classical cabinet maker of late–18-century Milan. (*Above*)

as Poland or Sweden. This desire of the rich everywhere to adopt newly fashionable styles as soon as possible ensured the rapid spread of artistic movements such as the Baroque, Rococo and Neo-Classical. These tended to have few national variations as long as they remained in the hands of those high on the social scale. As soon as they percolated downwards through the social strata they became first nationalized, then regionalized.

The downward filtering of styles can be seen most markedly in the way the Rococo was adopted around Europe. Developing in Paris during the early 18th century, it was soon taken up in an extravagant way at the courts of German princes such as Maximilian Emanuel of Bavaria and Augustus the Strong of Saxony. When it was adopted in England and the Netherlands, rather later, Rococo became a style of the *nouveaux riches* rather than aristocrats and emerged in a nationally identifiable form. It was not long before rococo elements – asymmetric C-scrolls and curlicues, cabriole (double-curved) and bombé (bulging lower front) shapes – filtered into the regional furniture forms of all the countries in Europe.

The adoption of the Neo-Classical style followed a similar pattern. The first manifestations were the most aggressively "new" and pure; within 20 years or so the style had become watered down for the masses and modified according to national tastes and forms.

## DESIGN AND PATTERN BOOKS

Design books played a major part in this process, particularly in mid-18th-century England, where volumes specifically devoted to furniture rather than to predominantly architectural styles began to appear. Influential though such books as *De la Distribution des Maisons de Plaisance* (1737–8) by Jacques-François Blondel on the development of rococo decoration in smaller houses or *Antiquities of Athens* (1762) by James Stuart (1713–88), on the adoption of Neo-Classical forms

**COMMODE**

*French*

Marble top, marquetry decoration and applied ormolu mounts; **last quarter of the 18th century**

The skills of the *ébénistes* and the *chiseleurs* – which were rigidly separated by the French guild system – have been sumptuously united in this Neo-Classical commode. The symmetrically disciplined form and decoration of the piece, together with the technical virtuosity of its craftsmanship, give it a dignified grandeur.

**BED**
*Probably made by James Norman to designs by Matthias Lock*
**Carved and gilded wood, hung with red damask; c. 1765**

Matthias Lock was one of the leading exponents of the Rococo in England and this bed, with its domed top and gilded cornice, represents a late flowering of the style. The upholstery is embellished at the foot and the head and on the valance above with applied ornaments and with knotted fringe.

and motifs, were, it was the distillation of the styles in furniture pattern books that did most to ensure their usage by the gentry.

The pattern books, largely produced by designers who were also working carvers and cabinet-makers, translated the styles into practical methods of application for other craftsmen. Among the first were books of engravings in the Rococo style produced by Matthias Lock, including *Six Sconces* (1744), *Six Tables* (1746), *The Principles of Ornament* (undated, *c.* 1748) and *A New Book of Ornaments* (1752), in collaboration with the engraver Henry Copland. Another rococo carver, Thomas Johnson, issued *Twelve Girandoles* (1755) and in subsequent years other designs, which were collected in 1761 as *One Hundred and Fifty New Designs*; these were for mirror and picture frames, pier tables, chimney-pieces, clock cases and other items.

Thomas Chippendale (1718–79) took things a stage further than his predecessors with his *The Gentleman and Cabinet-Maker's Director*, first published in 1754, with subsequent editions in 1755 and 1762 (and a French edition in the same year); its comprehensive attention to all branches of furniture and comprehensive designs, measurements and instructions for finishing each piece ensured its instant success. The most influential of the later furniture pattern books, notably, with the *Universal System of Household Furniture* (1762) by William Ince and John Mayhew, *The Cabinet-Maker and Upholsterer's Guide* (1788) by George Hepplewhite (d. 1786) and *The Cabinet-Maker and Upholsterer's Drawing Book* (1791–4) by Thomas Sheraton (1751–1806) followed a similar pattern. The two latter, with their elegant but practical interpretations of the Neo-Classical style, influenced middle-class furniture all over Europe and North America.

## UPHOLSTERY

Two threads, those of status and comfort, weave their way throughout the history of furniture. Status could be embodied in the importance

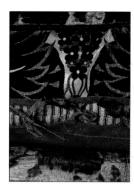

**ARMCHAIR**
*English*
**c. 1730**

This chair, with its deep, comfortable squab cushion, is one of a pair of "love-seats" from a set of seat furniture also comprising 18 upholstered side chairs and a settee. They represent the increasing comfort of opulent interiors in the early 18th century. This detailed view of the chair shows the bright colours of the red and green Spitalfields "Genoa" velvet in unfaded condition.

as well as the modishness of furniture: it was certainly often reflected in its cost. Comfort was also related to status: the most wealthy paid attention not just to changes in style but to developments in comfort and convenience. The increase in the numbers and specific functions of small tables during the 18th century represented an aspect of this, but the evolution of upholstery was an even more important consideration.

The part played by the upholsterer in interior design is an often neglected aspect of its history. Architects may have laid down the shapes of rooms, their style of decoration and sometimes their furniture, but it was upholsterers who had the last word in the finished effect. The 18th-century "upholder", was concerned not just with seat upholstery and bed hangings but with wall and floor coverings, window blinds and curtains, and was usually responsible for the arrangement of furniture in a room.

Because textiles are so much more perishable than furniture, and as a consequence have rarely survived, emphasis placed on them in the interiors of the 17th, 18th and 19th centuries can easily be forgotten. Hangings for beds invariably cost much more than the bed frames themselves; seat furniture was often made expressly to set off embroidery; and the sums spent on curtains, hangings and textile wall coverings in many instances far exceeded expenditure on woodwork. The very term furniture was, in the 18th century, used as much for hangings and coverings as for movables. This supremacy of the upholsterer

**PAIR OF ARMCHAIRS**
Mahogany; *c.* 1760

These chairs, with their crisply carved cabriole legs, were probably made by an Irish cabinet-maker. Their fine needlework upholstery of tent- and cross-stitched classical scenes in wool and silk are thought to have been worked by the Countess of Mornington, mother of the 1st Duke of Wellington. It was quite usual for ladies to undertake major needlework projects of this kind in the first half of the 18th century.

over other furniture craftsmen was often enhanced by his direct contact with the client rather than, as was usually the case with other members of the furnishing team, with the client's agent. Indeed, the upholsterer's perceived superiority was often a cause of friction with architects, who felt their control over total schemes to be threatened.

The most powerful cabinet-makers were those, such as Thomas Chippendale, William Vile (d. 1767), John Cobb (d. 1778) and Samuel Norman, whose business embraced both cabinet-making and upholstery. Chippendale, for example, supplied his important clients not only with furniture but with wallpapers and borders, curtains and blinds, bedding, carpets and other household equipment.

Curtains, cushions and rich wall hangings were in widespread use among the status- and comfort-conscious nobility of Europe during the medieval period, but upholstered chairs, with stuffing and fabric fixed to their frames, did not come into use until the 16th century and were not adopted widely until the 17th. The typical farthingale (joined and upholstered) chair of this period had a stuffed back as well as seat, with covers of leather, patterned Turkey-work or embroidery, and with added embellishment in the form of fringes or brass-headed nails.

In its early stages the technique of upholstery was still relatively primitive, with luxurious effects achieved through the use of rich and colourful fabrics rather than through any particular artistry in applying them, but from the late 17th century the upholsterer in France emerged as a craftsman establishing standards of excellence that were maintained throughout the next two centuries all through Europe and America with surprisingly little change.

## NEW CHAIR TYPES

Forms of seating more luxurious than the farthingale chair were soon designed: tall-backed wing chairs (with wing-like side projections),

**TWO STAGES IN UPHOLSTERING A CHAIR**
Engraving from Denis Diderot's *Encyclopédie*; 18th century

In this French design a reinforcing hair-filled roll is attached to the front edge before the curled hair is laid on the webbing of the seat base. English chairs would have narrower webbing, forming a lattice, and an extra layer of hessian as a basis for the seat stuffing.

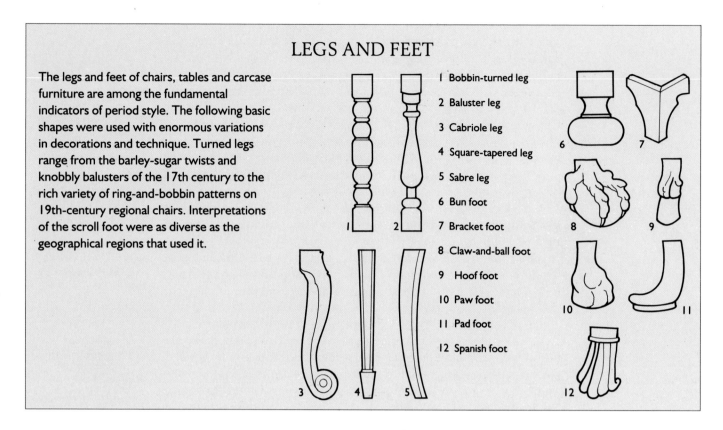

# LEGS AND FEET

The legs and feet of chairs, tables and carcase furniture are among the fundamental indicators of period style. The following basic shapes were used with enormous variations in decorations and technique. Turned legs range from the barley-sugar twists and knobbly balusters of the 17th century to the rich variety of ring-and-bobbin patterns on 19th-century regional chairs. Interpretations of the scroll foot were as diverse as the geographical regions that used it.

1 Bobbin-turned leg
2 Baluster leg
3 Cabriole leg
4 Square-tapered leg
5 Sabre leg
6 Bun foot
7 Bracket foot
8 Claw-and-ball foot
9 Hoof foot
10 Paw foot
11 Pad foot
12 Spanish foot

some with adjustments for reclining; sofas with down-filled cushions and arms padded with horsehair; and chairs (having plain wooden arms or none at all) with upholstered seats and full-length backs. Even cane-seated chairs of the early 18th century were generally made more comfortable with mattress-like tufted squabs tied on with tapes. From the mid 18th century tufting was used to secure the square-edged, even shape of English upholstered chair seats. At this time French chairs differed in having domed stuffed seats, and it was not until the 1780s, when the Neo-Classical period was well advanced, that the French generally adopted squarer forms of stuffing to harmonize with the linear Neo-Classical style.

For trimming the edges of upholstered chairs, fringes gave way to braids, often home-made by the ladies of the household; but the most

**SIDE TABLE**
*Duncan Phyfe*
**Mahogany; c. 1815**

The bold carving and the use of high quality mahogany are typical of the Scottish-born cabinet-maker Duncan Phyfe, whose ability to distil English and French Neo-Classical styles with equal confidence to an increasingly prosperous New York clientele ensured booming business in his lifetime.

usual form of chair edging during the second half of the 18th century was decorative brass nailing. Loosely fitting cotton covers were placed over upholstery to protect precious materials from sunlight and dust when a room was not in formal use for grand occasions. Such attention to conservation has ensured the survival of a number of important suites of upholstered furniture.

During the 19th century upholstery grew more luxuriously thick, and tufting on chairs and sofas was increasingly replaced by buttons, which secured the horsehair padding inside more firmly. Upholstery reached its deep-buttoned peak of comfort, if not elegance, during the 1840s, by which time coiled springing had also come into widespread use. The French *crapaud* (toad chair) and the English Chesterfield sofa epitomize the overstuffed technique of upholstering in which no vestige of the seat frame is left visible.

### THE INTERIOR DECORATOR

By this time the 18th-century upholsterer had turned into the interior decorator, who was now in charge not only of the supply and co-ordination of furnishings and decoration but also of the planning and design of schemes. In England Morris & Co. (founded by William Morris) was an important example, and the earlier-established firm of Crace was also influential. The work of the latter at Chatsworth, Longleat and several Astor residences in the late 19th century showed a thoroughgoing approach to historical revivalism (including extensive research), providing designs for ornament, furniture and upholstery as well as having them made up, and even collecting (and restoring) antique furnishings where these were appropriate. In this last function they heralded the practice of early 20th-century decorating firms such as Lenygon & Morant, who were also antique dealers. Purposeful collecting of antique furniture in the 19th century (much stimulated by antiquarianism), rather than its mere accumulation by families, meant that interior decoration henceforth was concerned as much with antique furnishings as with new.

**BEDROOM**
**Lithograph; mid 19th century**

In this design, the grandeur of the festoon curtains is contrasted with the homely sprigged wallpaper. The furniture is in a restrained neo-rococo style.

THE STURDY, SIMPLE FURNITURE OF THE MIDDLE AGES WAS

TRANSFORMED DURING THE RENAISSANCE INTO MORE HEAVILY WORKED,

PIECES THAT WERE HIGHLY DECORATIVE IN THEIR DOMESTIC SETTING.

# EARLY EUROPEAN FURNITURE

After the fall of the Roman Empire in the 5th century AD, many of the skills and luxurious materials used in the furniture of the ancient world disappeared. From the 11th to the 15th century, however, furniture slowly regained its importance. The study of it during this early period is very largely based on paintings, sculpture and illuminated manuscripts; but some early pieces do survive in museums, private collections and churches. They are, however, often damaged or much changed from their original appearance by repairs and particularly by the loss of the bright colours with which much furniture was once decorated.

Furniture throughout this period was sparse, even in great households. Types of furniture were limited to meeting the basic needs of eating, sleeping, sitting, storage and to a lesser extent, in an age of very limited literacy, reading and writing. Furniture did, however, have the additional function of expressing rank in society or status within the household, and this was done mainly through the use of luxurious textiles. Oak was the most commonly used wood for furniture at this time. Spain and Italy also had abundant supplies of walnut, cypress and fruitwoods, and conifers were plentiful in the Alpine regions. Carved decoration was based on architectural motifs, first the Romanesque with its classically-inspired round-headed arches, then, in the 14th and 15th centuries, the Gothic, with its pointed arches, buttresses, crockets and tracery.

## CHESTS

By far the most numerous pieces of early furniture were chests of varying sizes, and these, because of the strength of their construction, survive most frequently. Chests were immensely useful, used not only for storage and securing valuables but also as seats, tables or even beds. The earliest kind of chest was made from a hollowed-out tree trunk (giving one

**DESCO DA PARTO**
*Workshop of Apollonio di Giovanni*
Tempera on panel with gilt gesso border; **c. 1460**

This Florentine workshop was known for its high-quality marriage chests and decorative trays like this one, which celebrated births in important families. Petrarch's *Triumph of Love* was the source for the painted decoration: Eros escorted by figures in courtly dress against a Tuscan landscape. (*Right*)

**CASSONE**
*Italian*
Intarsia, walnut and other woods; **c. 1500**

The two coats of arms suggest that this was a marriage chest. The geometric inlay is similar in design to that of the *certosina* work of Lombardy and the Veneto, though it is executed entirely in different coloured woods without the mother-of-pearl or silver popular in those areas. (*Below*)

of the alternative names for a chest), with iron bands for strength. By the 13th century construction was a little more refined: chests were made from planks split or sawn lengthways down a log and joined together in a box form by nails or oak pins. They were made secure not only by ironwork, now often decoratively scrolled, but also by locks. The second half of the 15th century saw the development of framed construction, in which lighter panels sit in the grooves of a mortise-and-tenon frame.

All houses of the Middle Ages were cold and damp, whatever the rank of the occupant, and furniture needed to be raised above floor level to prevent rotting. For this reason, from the 12th century onwards, chests often had stiles

**THE BIRTH OF THE VIRGIN**
*School of the Veneto*
Tempera on panel; **c. 1480**

This room is very sparsely furnished, as was common in the 15th century. St Anne sits up in a bed which has simple chests placed in pairs around it, all set on a low dais. The chests were useful for storage and doubled as seats or tables. The bed itself is of box form, with panels of equal height forming head- and foot-boards, which are decorated with ball finials. The tightly swaddled baby is being washed from a small tub, made by the coopering method used for barrels.

(uprights) projecting downwards to provide legs. Decoration was often done by chip carving, a simple technique using gouge and chisel to chip out Romanesque arcades in relief across the front panel.

In the Gothic period carving, like architecture, became much more elaborate, and the front surfaces of chests were carved with pointed arches and tracery; some examples even had small "buttresses", fixed to the stiles with wooden pins. In the prosperous Low Countries, where there was a thriving wool and cloth trade and merchants' houses were well-furnished, carving became particularly fine. Many 15th century English inventories record "Flaunders chests" made in the Low Countries, which were often carved with a linenfold motif (a stylized representation of folded linen). The so-called Tilting chests produced in France and England in the 14th and early 15th centuries are carved in relief with figures of armour-clad knights jousting.

In Italy simple chests were not only used for storage but were placed in pairs around a bed dais – as a step up to the bed and as a seat and a table. Certain areas of Italy excelled in the production of marriage chests as objects of great status, painted with the arms of the two families and scenes of courtly love. Specialized workshops flourished; one of the best known was that of Apollonio di Giovanni in Florence. The front panels were painted in tempera ( a mixture of pigment and egg yolk), the same technique as that used on contemporary altarpieces. They showed appropriately romantic scenes, such as the meeting of Solomon and Sheba, often set within architectural vistas that reflected Renaissance interest in perspective.

The walls of grand rooms in Italian palaces were often decorated with panels painted to imitate costly tapestries. Similar painted decoration was used on *desci da parto* (trays commemorating the births of new babies). Another important form of decoration that evolved in Italy at this time, and that was used on cupboard as well as chest panels, was *intarsia* (inlay). In this a design was gouged out of a carcase wood (often walnut), then filled in with different coloured woods – for example, fruitwoods, yew and olive. The designs were often pictorial and frequently demonstrate skill in depicting perspective.

## BEDS

Few beds survive from this early period, largely because they depended on perishable textiles for their grand appearance. That beds played a significant role in expressing status is evident from pictorial sources, and the rich nature of their hangings – furs, silks, tapestries – is shown by medieval inventories. At this period the state bed emerges as the most costly piece of furniture in a great household, often intended less for sleep than for show.

Like chests, northern European beds required raising from the damp floors. Those of the Romanesque period often had low railings, joining the four short bedposts, with a lower section in the middle of one side to allow the occupant to get in. Burgundian carvings in the 12th-century cathedral of Autun clearly show a simple type of wooden bed frame of a type known as far back as ancient Egypt, with a hide lashed to the frame with leather thongs.

By the 13th century northern Europe had begun to seek greater sleeping comfort, and beds were made with warm hangings, which could be detached and packed in chests when a great household travelled. Such beds were of two main types. One was the sparver, or tent bed: a conical, textile-covered softwood bowl was suspended from the ceiling above a couch bed and to it were attached rich hangings that were pulled around the bed in tent-like fashion. The other type of bed is often shown in the work of Netherlandish artists, who used opulent bourgeois interiors as settings for religious paintings. Its hangings were suspended from a rectangular canopy, where they ran on iron rails, and were drawn up by day into pear-shaped bundles. The rich embroidery of the backcloth added to

the prestigious nature of the whole piece. Another improvement in comfort can be seen in the feather beds and plump pillows that are increasingly depicted in paintings and manuscripts from the 15th century onwards.

In Italy the warmer climate made bed hangings less necessary; privacy was obtained by curtaining off part of the room. The characteristic bed was of a box type, with end panels heightened to form head and foot boards. As in other Italian furniture, the end panels were often decoratively treated, either painted or inlaid.

## SEAT FURNITURE

The X-framed chair and stool have the oldest pedigree, traceable back through antiquity to Ancient Egypt. Roman magisterial seats were also of this form, and the X-framed chair thus became associated with authority, which could be reinforced by the extra height of a dais and the addition of a canopy of state. This type was used throughout Europe in the Middle Ages, with distinctive regional variations; the Italian version is popularly known as a Savonarola chair (after the 15th-century social reformer). The earliest X-framed stools were of a folding type,

with brightly painted leather slung between the side rails to form a seat. The addition of a back support formed a fixed chair, and greater comfort was achieved with the use of padding, cushions and a footstool.

The X-framed chair was still being made in the 17th century, as a utilitarian seat in the Netherlands but in England, France and Germany retaining a ceremonial function.

A few throne-like chairs, like the famous 14th-century coronation chair in Westminster Abbey, were also made. They were often constructed on the same box-like principles as the chest, upward projections forming back and sides, and were commonly decorated with architectural motifs, such as pinnacles and crockets. A third type of chair was the barrel chair, the most primitive kind being quite literally made from part of a barrel with the addition of a few boards to form a seat.

Stools were probably the only form of seating in humble households. They were made from a circular or triangular slab of wood with three or four turned or square legs driven into the seat and secured by pegs. In some cases the back leg was elongated upwards and given a curving back rail to form a very simple chair. As an alternative to a solid seat, rushes were sometimes woven round the seat rails. Rather more sophisticated rectangular-seated, slab-ended stools were also made, their solid supports sometimes enlivened with Gothic ogee (S-sided) arches cut into the bottom. In some examples the seat had a circular hole with a cross bar cut into it for easy carrying.

Benches were either slab-ended, like stools, or solid and chest-like, when they were known as settles. These had a hinged lid, and were cushioned.

### TABLES, CUPBOARDS, MIRRORS

Dining tables were crude trestle tables consisting of a long, narrow softwood board resting on easily movable square-cut V- or A-shaped supports. Fixed tables seem to have been rare.

Early cupboards were simply shelves attached to the wall, to hold cups. By the 15th century small chests with doors and long legs were being made, and also livery (food) cupboards with doors pierced for ventilation, often in Gothic patterns. To keep out vermin, small hanging livery cupboards were also made. Some larger dressers for linen storage also

**THE LAST SUPPER**
*Anon. Portuguese artist*
Oil on panel; **c. 1480**

Dignity is given to the figure of Christ by the cloth of honour, a traditional mark of rank, hung behind him. The linen-covered table would have been a simple trestle. The disciples sit on a variety of typical 15th-century stools; on the left is one with turned legs, in the centre there is a fine X-framed example and on the right is a cruder stool with square-cut legs. (*Above*)

**FRENCH PROVERBS**
*Pieter Bruegel the Younger*
Oil on panel; **c. 1610**

This detail shows the interior of a modest Netherlandish house. The triangular stool has turned legs and a wooden seat. The simple chair behind it derives from the same shape, with a curved rail to support the back. (*Below*)

appeared in the 15th century. A few survive in churches.

Both hanging and hand mirrors of polished steel or crystal were known in the 14th and 15th centuries.

### THE LOW COUNTRIES 1500–1650

The Low Countries (the modern Netherlands and Belgium) passed from Burgundian to Habsburg rule in 1493. The largely Protestant Northern Provinces broke away in 1579, leaving the Catholic Southern Netherlands under Spanish rule.

In the Low Countries Grotesque ornamentation, originating in Renaissance discoveries of Roman decoration in a supposed grotto, assumed an increasingly exaggerated character in the hands of Antwerp designers. One, the prolific Hans Vredeman de Vries (1527–1604), who strongly influenced English craftsmen, produced designs of fantastic architectural vistas, cartouches (shields or tablets) of strapwork (interlacing bands) and variations on the classical orders. He was also the author of an influential furniture pattern book, one of the first produced.

Cabinet-making was as prized in the Low Countries as elsewhere in Europe, and in the early 17th century both Antwerp and Amsterdam emerged as major centres of the craft. There was an increasing use of exotic woods, particularly ebony, which was mainly used as a veneer or as decorative mouldings, especially on mirror and picture frames. Tortoiseshell, coloured on the back, was also used as a veneer. Inside, cabinets often had painted panels and stacks of small drawers.

In the early 17th century both X-framed and rectangular chairs were made more comfortable in the Low Countries by fixed padding and upholstery. Chairs were often covered with velvet or with tooled and gilt leather fixed with large decorative brass-headed nails. The traditional carved-lion finial continued to be used on chair backs. Stretchers (horizontal struts

**DETAIL OF MERODE ALTARPIECE**
Oil on panel; **c. 1426**

St Joseph is shown in his workshop, using a breast-drill. Other tools and a mousetrap are set out on a simple workbench. (*Above*)

**ALLEGORY OF PRUDENCE AND VANITY**
*Giovanni Bellini*
Oil on panel; **c. 1490**

Shows a convex mirror of blown glass. The Venetians developed flat mirrors in around 1500. (*Left*)

**THE GAME OF BACKGAMMON**
*Dirck Hals*
Oil on canvas; **c. 1650**

Shows upholstery of fringed textile and brass-studded leather and, in the centre, simple rush-seating.

connecting legs) were in double rows to give strength and the legs were turned to resemble balusters.

## ITALY 1500–1700

Italy was renowned for the splendour of its decorative arts, but furniture remained sparse, even in the grandest *palazzi*. In the 16th century the production of fine chests flourished, their craftsmen being considered superior in rank to makers of more rudimentary pieces. The gilded and painted *cassoni* (chests) of the late 15th century were superseded in the 16th by a richly carved type, with the front panel often decorated with high-relief scenes of battles or triumphs (such carving began to become Mannerist, with contorted poses and elongated figures). Some chests were also decorated with gilded gesso (plaster base) designs in relief, their motifs usually Grotesque.

The *cassapanca* (settle) derived from the *cassone* by raising its back and sides to form supports for the back and arms, in the same way that northern European settles evolved. However, the sarcophagus form of the *cassapanca* gave it its own distinctively antique appearance.

In the early 17th century there evolved a distinctively Italian type of chair that was taken up by the English, who erroneously called it a *sgabello*. It rested on cartouche-shaped supports front and back and the backrest was also often of cartouche shape, though examples of shell backs are also known.

In the 16th century the ancient Roman technique of *pietre dure* (hard-stone inlays) was revived, the most famous workshop, the *Opificio delle Pietre Dure*, being founded in Florence in 1588. The craft involved cutting hard stones, such as lapis lazuli, porphyry and agate, and laying them out in interlocking, mosaic-like (often strapwork) patterns. These were used on table tops, which at this time had supports in the form of lions, griffins, sphinxes or human figures.

Scagliola, imitation marble made from mixing powdered selenite with size, was also developed in 16th-century Italy. Skilful craftsmen were able to imitate costly *pietre dure* work in this cheap material, and in the following century the technique slowly spread throughout Europe.

During the 17th century Venice became famous for its imitation oriental lacquer. It was applied to standard Italian softwood furniture

types, which were then decorated with raised areas of gesso, painted in gold and other colours. The whole was then varnished to give it a high gloss.

## GERMANY 1500–1700

In the 15th century the predominantly Catholic southern German cities of Augsburg and Nuremberg, already flourishing artistic centres, became famous for their woodcuts and engraved designs. Peter Flötner, Augsburg-trained but working in Nuremberg from *c.*1522, had visited Italy and some of his designs relate closely to the decorative painting of Raphael at the Villa Madama in Rome in the use of Grotesque motifs, acanthus scrolls and putti. His furniture designs also incorporate architectural forms, as several of his extant pieces reveal.

Augsburg craftsmen and designers became noted for the exuberance and virtuosity of their productions, as particularly exemplified by inlay work based on the designs of Lorenz Stöer, who added a Mannerist twist to Renaissance interest in ancient architecture and perspective by producing designs of ruined buildings in deliberately distorted perspective. These often included strapwork, which, developed by Italian stuccoists at the French palace of Fontainebleau to form a border to their compositions, was taken up with great enthusiasm by the designers of northern Europe. The skills of the inlay worker and the carver combined in the production of extravagantly decorated cabinets, using not only woods of various colours but also amber and precious metals. These cabinets were at first placed on tables and later on stands. The *Kunstkammer*, a cabinet for displaying precious

**TABLE CABINET**
*Italian*
Scagliola with ebonized and parcel-gilt mouldings; **Mid 17th century**

In the 16th century the Grand Dukes of Tuscany revived the Roman craft of making scagliola, a composition material of ground marbles, gypsum, plaster of Paris and glue. This was applied like paint and, when dry, was polished. It was so like marble and *pietre dure* that it was known as "counterfeit marble". The style of this cabinet, with its architectural treatment of the central cupboard and its ripple mouldings, is similar to that of other cabinet-making centres, but the scagliola decoration of birds and flowers and the geometric patterns on the side panels have their origins in the designs used in the distinctively Italian craft of *pietre dure*.

objects, replaced the earlier *Wunderkammer,* in which merely bizarre objects were put on show.

The mainly Protestant north of Germany retained its strong Gothic tradition of vigorous wood carving, but this was often combined with the use of Renaissance architectural motifs.

### SPAIN AND PORTUGAL 1500–1700

During the 16th century the arts flourished in both Spain and Portugal. The vocabulary of the decorative arts was enriched by the *mudéjar* (Moorish) style, which in furniture took the form of geometric inlay, often using as a ground wood the walnut in which Spain was so rich. (The influence of this Moorish decoration can be seen both in Italian *certosina* work, particularly popular in Venice, where inlays of mother-of-pearl enlivened the surface, and in the geometric mouldings of late 16th- and early 17th-century Dutch furniture.) In Spain *mudéjar* decoration co-existed with Renaissance ornament and other types of Islamic decoration.

Spanish territorial acquisitions in the New World were rich in precious metals, and the most grand furniture was inlaid with silver. Exotic woods, such as ebony and mahogany, were also used. The common 16th-century chair known in England as a backstool may have originated in Spain, where its name is *sillón de fraileros* (monk's chair). Early Spanish types were strongly constructed, with square-cut legs and hefty stretchers. Covers were of velvet, damask or the tooled and painted leather (another Moorish craft) associated particularly with the city of Cordoba. In the 17th century this type of chair took on the French-inspired characteristics of elaborate spiral-turned uprights and stretchers, but the distinctive Spanish use of leather continued.

The rise of the cabinet as a display piece was as marked in Spain as elsewhere in Europe. The *vargueño* (a 19th-century term) was a cabinet whose distinctive characteristic was a drop front resting on slides drawn out from a decorative stand, often of arcaded form. Exteriors were often relatively plain but interiors could be highly ornamented with *mudéjar* motifs, silverwork-style reliefs or inlay. In the 17th century *vargueños* continued to be popular as luxury objects, but were superseded as high fashion in mid-century by the *papeleira,* a type of cabinet lacking the characteristic Spanish drop front and closer in style to Dutch and French pieces.

Spanish cabinets on stands at this time are remarkable for their rich veneers, usually of ebony and tortoiseshell and sometimes of carved ivory.

### ENGLAND 1500–1600

England's geographical isolation from the rest of Europe was reinforced in the 16th century by the cultural isolation resulting from Henry

**TOBIAS AND SARAH**
Stained glass; 16th century

The northern need for bed-hangings as draught-excluders is shown in this German image. There is comfort in the stacks of pillows, but also rich housing for bedbugs. (*Above*)

**TABLE**
*Spanish*
Walnut with iron stretchers; c. 1600

The legs are elaborately bobbin-turned, for which walnut was a particularly suitable wood. The S-shaped iron stretchers and loosely mortised top are removable, allowing the table to be folded away. (*Left*)

VIII's break with Rome. One result of this was that the Italian artists who had helped to embellish Henry's palaces departed. Of the luxurious pieces that furnished these buildings only a few survive, such as Henry VIII's writing box in the Victoria and Albert Museum, London, its bright colours a reminder that much 16th-century furniture was painted. Oak was the most commonly used wood, but imported walnut was used for the grandest pieces, particularly beds.

Portraits of Tudor monarchs show the continuing English use of the ceremonial X-framed chair and canopy. In most ordinary households chairs were few in number, benches and stools still being the most usual type of seating. In the 1520s the decoration of heavy box-chairs, constructed like a chest and often having a hinged seat, sometimes combined Gothic linenfold carving on the panels of the base with Renaissance Grotesque motifs or romayne heads (profile heads in medallions) on the stiles or rails of the panelled back. The French-inspired *caqueteuse* (gossip-chair) evolved in the 1530s; this had a seat narrower at the back than the front, a tall back and, in place of the side panels of the box-chair, splayed arms. Later in the century the backstool developed: this had upholstered square seats and rectangular backs, and straight-cut or turned legs joined by stretchers.

The use of fixed sturdy bedposts and wooden headboard and tester (canopy) made the 16th-century bed more ponderous than its predecessors. In the century's latter part the bedposts were often carved with a bulbous ornamentation known as cup-and-cover.

Standing tables of joined construction with a strong underframing were used for dining; trestle tables were still used for the main body of the household. Table supports in the 1580s were carved with cup-and-cover decoration. Draw tables, with extendable leaves supported on slides, became popular from the 1540s, and small tables were in use by the end of the century, the inlays of some denoting the table's use in their designs, such as cards, musical instruments and games boards. The use of inlay spread during the Elizabethan period with the arrival of immigrant German craftsmen in London in the 1580s.

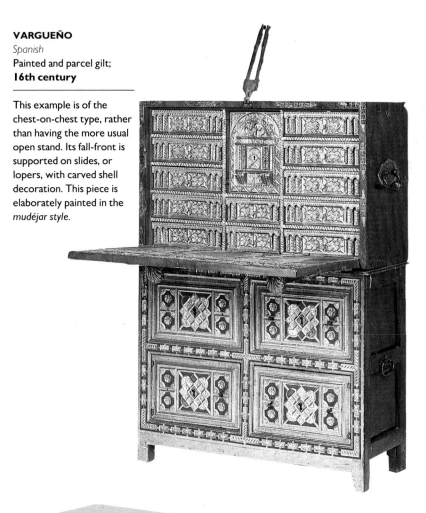

**VARGUEÑO**
*Spanish*
Painted and parcel gilt;
**16th century**

This example is of the chest-on-chest type, rather than having the more usual open stand. Its fall-front is supported on slides, or lopers, with carved shell decoration. This piece is elaborately painted in the *mudéjar style*.

**JOINT STOOL**
*English*
Oak; **c. 1580**

This piece derives its strength from its material and from its construction with sturdy mortise-and-tenon joints. The legs have been carved in the form of fluted columns supporting the arcaded rail, which still has traces of the original infilling of carved shell ornament, now worn away by constant handling. Although architectural ornament is the source of the decoration, the handling and proportions show English dependence on pattern-books, rather than first-hand knowledge of antiquity or of Renaissance Italy.

"THE FURNITURE OF OUR HOUSES…IS GROWN IN MANNER TO EVER PASSING DELICACY," WROTE WILLIAM HARRISON IN 1598. BUT THE CHANGES OVER THE NEXT CENTURY WERE TO BE EVEN MORE STRIKING.

# 17TH CENTURY ENGLAND

The Stuart kings James I (1603–25) and Charles I (1625–49) introduced continental standards of luxury to England: vast sums were spent on royal palaces, and agents abroad sent back paintings and sculpture, or lured foreign artists to work in England. But all this was swept away by the Civil War of 1642–9. Country houses were ransacked by troops, families fled into exile, and after the execution of Charles I in 1649 his goods were systematically sold off. It is difficult to envisage the palaces and grand houses of pre-1640: practically all the exquisite pieces made for the king and court have disappeared.

In 1660 the monarchy was restored under Charles II (1660–85), and palaces and the gentry's houses were rebuilt and refurnished. This, combined with the massive rebuilding of City houses after the Fire of London in 1666, provided a large market for good-quality furniture in fashionable styles.

New pieces of furniture, increasingly specialized in use, were developed. At first these were based largely on Dutch models; later, in the reigns of James II (1685–8) and of William and Mary (1689–1702), French fashions predominated. The Huguenots, Protestant refugees fleeing from persecution in France, brought their considerable skills – in cabinet-making, metalwork and silk-weaving – to London, and raised the levels of craftsmanship to continental standards.

### THE EARLY 17TH CENTURY
In the first half of the century the great hall of a house retained its role as entrance, but was no longer used as a dining room. It was traditionally furnished with a long, heavy oak table and benches. Leading off the hall was the parlour, furnished more comfortably with tables, one or two chairs, stools and perhaps a chest or cupboard. The main, or "state", rooms were usually on the first floor. Chief among them was the great chamber, which served as both state

**X-FRAME CHAIR OF STATE**
c. 1610

This is a rare survival of a traditional type. The surface of the wood is completely covered, either painted or encased in fabric, and the chair is richly upholstered in cut velvet. The tasselled cushion and heavy fringe add to the opulent effect.

**DAY-BED**
Giltwood with original upholstery; c. 1695

This magnificent day-bed is upholstered in Genoese silk velvet and has a tasselled fringe.

dining and reception room and had the finest furniture: a draw-table, armchairs, stools and cupboards displaying silver dishes and flagons.

The bed, together with its hangings, was by far the most expensive item in the house. Otherwise, bedroom furniture was similar to that in other rooms. The long gallery was sparsely furnished, with chairs and stools against the walls, a few small tables and chests, perhaps a cabinet, and paintings. The most private room was the closet, which might contain a day-bed, a small writing table and a cabinet for papers or precious objects.

Very few furniture types were used in the early 17th-century house: tables, chairs and stools, chests, coffers and cupboards, and beds. Most of these had hardly changed since the late 16th century, and were made with the same woods – oak, and occasionally walnut – and using the same construction techniques.

### THE LATE 17TH CENTURY

In the second half of the century the picture changed. An imposing staircase led from the entrance hall up to a saloon (the old great chamber), on either side of which were apartments, sets of rooms consisting of an anteroom, bedchamber and closet, some with the addition of a withdrawing room and presence chamber for royal use. For these splendid rooms the finest furniture was made: tables, looking glasses and

**CHAIR**
*Style of Daniel Marot*
**Carved walnut; c. 1695**

The high back, scrolled legs and upholstered seat are all fashionable features of the 1690s. The rich carving of the back and stretcher show the influence of the French designer Daniel Marot.

torchères (candlestands) set against the piers (spaces between tall windows), lavishly upholstered beds and chairs, exquisite cabinets and writing desks. Furniture became increasingly specialized, with chests of drawers, bookcases and other pieces made for specific purposes. Walnut replaced oak as the standard material, and other woods – laburnum, kingwood, ebony

## MARQUETRY

Marquetry is a decorative technique in which a thin veneer, 1.6–3.2mm ($^1/_{16}$–$^1/_8$ in) thick, of differently coloured woods or other materials is glued to the carcase of a piece of furniture. It became popular in England in the late 17th century, when it was practised as part of the new craft of cabinet-making.

The most popular type of marquetry was the floral panel, depicting a vase or spray of flowers. At first made of contrasting light and dark woods, such as sycamore or box on walnut, floral panels later became brilliantly coloured by the use of ivory or bone stained green for leaves or red for the exotic birds sometimes incorporated into the panel. This emphasis on decoration influenced the design of furniture: large flat areas were needed for the increasingly elaborate marquetry panels. Table tops provided ideal surfaces, as did the double doors of cabinets. Occasionally,

especially in Dutch pieces, marquetry covered the entire surface, but typically it was contained within an oval panel, with the spandrels (spaces between the panel and the corners of the surface) decorated with a simpler design in marquetry.

Seaweed marquetry, which became fashionable in the 1690s, consisted of small-scale stylized, arabesque designs, usually of yellow sycamore wood contrasted with a darker walnut background. A difficult and expensive technique, it was used mainly on fine pieces of furniture, such as small writing-tables or small longcase clocks.

**WRITING CABINET**
Walnut with floral marquetry; c. 1690

**GATE-LEG TABLE**
Oak; *c.* 1670

When not in use, the two table flaps and the "gate" supporting them can be folded against the central part, and the table placed against a wall. The baluster leg is typical of the Charles II period (1660–85). (*Left*)

**DUTCH TABLE, PIER GLASS AND CANDLESTANDS**
Painted and gilded wood; *c.* 1680

The painted decoration is derived from contemporary Dutch flower paintings and is here enriched with carved and gilded wood. (*Below*)

– were used for exotic effects. Oriental lacquer and its European imitations were fashionable, and their dark tones contrasted with carved and gilded wood. Textiles lost their importance.

Different crafts developed to make these new styles. Joiners, who had made most early 17th-century furniture, were now rivalled by carvers and gilders, and, most importantly, by cabinet-makers, who used marquetry (thin, decorative wood veneers).

These craftsmen, working in London, made the finest pieces of furniture. Of course plenty of furniture continued to be made using traditional methods and materials and ignoring new fashions. Simple oak chairs, stools, chests and tables were made well into the 18th century; the details of a chair back or the panels of a chest might differ from 17th-century examples, but the basic type altered little. Regional variations continued too, and a chair or chest from Wales or the north-west of England would have decorative motifs peculiar to that area. Although often attractive and always useful, these pieces were not stylistically important: it was the furniture made for the royal palaces and great houses that set new trends.

### NEW FASHIONS IN TABLES

For dining, the draw-table, whose two ends could be drawn out, gradually replaced the long, heavy oak table. Most draw-tables were of oak, but some were of walnut. The legs were bulbous, perhaps shaped as Ionic capitals, a decoration sometimes continued on the frieze.

Gate-leg tables, introduced in the 16th century, were popular throughout the 17th. They had a folding top, which could be opened out and supported on the "gate-leg". By the 1660s

**SMOKER'S CHAIR**
*Lancashire*
Oak; **Late 19th century**

This plain provincial chair has a drawer for pipes and tobacco.

unknown), some of black marble, some of white, some inlaid. Later in the century marble-topped tables became rarer, but were used sometimes for dining rooms.

### PIER TABLES

After the Restoration the most striking new furniture arrangement was the side table with a looking glass over it, placed against a pier and often flanked by a pair of matching candlestands. Pier tables were rectangular and small. In the 1660s a walnut veneer was usual – sometimes inset with panels of oyster veneer or parquetry (both veneers with geometric patterns) – and the legs were spiral and connected by flat stretchers. By the 1670s panels of floral marquetry (see box, p.35) decorated the top of the table and sometimes its frieze, which occasionally had a shallow drawer; the legs formed S-scrolls and had serpentine stretchers. Other tables were made of ebony, sometimes with plaques of embossed silver, and a few were of imported lacquer or japanned. In the 1690s French fashion dictated a straight tapering leg with a gadrooned capital (that is, one edged with alternately convex and concave carving) and scrolled stretchers that rose in the centre to an urn shape. By the end of the century, these tables were of carved and gilded wood and their tops had elaborate carved or punched designs.

### CHAIRS AND COUCHES

In the 17th century armchairs were symbols of status: the great chair and its footstool were reserved for the head of the household, with perhaps one other for his wife or an important guest. By *c.* 1610 in any aristocratic household an upholstered chair would have replaced the earlier wooden one, and was usually made *en suite* with a footstool, armless chairs, and stools. "Joint stools" – that is, made by joiners – often known today as farthingale chairs, were the most common upholstered chairs. They had a padded back and seat, with a gap between that enabled women wearing a farthingale (hooped whalebone petticoat) to sit comfortably. The covering was of turkeywork (imitation Turkish carpet), cloth or leather.

Caning for the backs and seats of chairs was introduced from the Netherlands in the 1660s. Early caning was of wide mesh. The front stretcher, the supports flanking the cane panel of the back and the cresting rail (joining the two supports) were all carved, and cushions covered the cane seat. By the 1670s the mesh had

walnut gate-leg tables with spiral, turned legs were replacing draw-tables for dining.

Also used were small, movable tables, made of pine or oak and covered with leather or textiles, or occasionally of much finer quality – of carved and silvered wood, or possibly overlaid with embossed metal. Marble-topped tables on stone baluster stems or strong wooden frames were made in the early 17th century, some by the sculptor Nicholas Stone (1587–1647). Charles I owned several such tables (makers

## ARMCHAIR
Walnut, with caned back and seat; **c. 1670**

The wide-mesh caning of the seat would have been covered by a cushion. The spiral turned supports of the legs and back later gave way to scroll legs and carved decoration. In this transitional chair, the cresting, back panel frame and front stretcher are treated as decorative areas. (*Left*)

become finer and the height of the back had increased, reaching an extreme by the century's end. The earlier straight stretcher and cresting rail were replaced by pierced and arched forms.

Armchairs were solidly upholstered and lost their farthingale gap; the most comfortable were wing chairs. Most late-17th-century armchairs were of walnut, but some were of beechwood painted black, or "ebonized", to resemble the expensive imported wood.

*Sgabello* chairs (carved wooden chairs with two solid supports in place of legs) usually made of walnut, often partly gilded, were made in England in the 1630s as well as imported.

**Day beds and couches** Day beds, dating mainly from the second half of the century, have a cane seat and single caned end, a carved cresting rail and eight legs, united by stretchers. Later

## KNEEHOLE BUREAU
Burr-walnut veneer; **c. 1700**

This bureau originated in the sloping-topped writing box of the 16th century and the chest of drawers. The recessed kneehole makes it comfortable to sit at, and there is plenty of storage space. The deep area above the drawers is a well, accessible only when the writing flap is down. The burr-walnut veneer is cross-banded into contrasting walnut, and the area between the drawers is embellished with a half-round moulding. The elaborate escutcheons, the pear-drop handles and the bun feet are all characteristic of the late 17th century. (*Right*)

**BOOKCASE**
Oak; *c. 1670*

Glazed doors protect the books, and finely carved mouldings separate the upper and lower stages and form a deep cornice. This design continued into the 18th century. (*Above*)

were bound with iron; most were panelled, some had carved decoration. The style of chests was less affected by changing fashions than that of any other piece of furniture, and in the following century provincial chests still resembled those made a hundred years earlier. The coffer was a type of chest with a domed lid and wood encased in leather or fabric and was made by cofferers, who belonged to the Leathersellers' Company. Large coffers were used as travelling trunks. They had leather covers held in place by brass studs arranged in decorative patterns, and their corners were strengthened by metal mounts. Small coffers, covered in velvet or embroidered silk, were decorative enough to sit on dressing tables and were used as jewel boxes.

### CUPBOARDS AND BOOK CASES

By the early 17th century, the cupboard, an open-fronted storage piece, consisted of three shelves with a decorated frieze, on carved supports. (One type, known as the court cupboard, had an enclosed upper section.) Cupboards were used in the hall, parlour or great chamber to display silver; at the end of the previous century William Harrison had observed that in "the houses of knights, gentlemen and merchantmen" he had seen "costly cupboards of plate, worth five or six hundred or a thousand pounds" (a reference to the plate, not the furniture, which was of negligible value).

The press, practical rather than decorative, was an oak cupboard enclosed by doors, with shelves and pegs for clothes inside.

Bookcases hardly existed in the early 17th century: a set of hanging shelves or a chest were considered sufficient. However, as book-buying increased, so did the need for efficient and accessible storage. In 1666 Samuel Pepys noted in his *Diary* that he had ordered bookcases from a joiner, and they still survive, as do similar examples. They have a bold cornice (moulded projection at the top), glazed doors and adjustable shelves.

### CHESTS OF DRAWERS

The 17th century, a period of few innovations in British furniture-making, did, however, see the development of a compact, practical new piece, the chest of drawers. Early examples were massive and heavy, usually of oak, occasionally with an inlay of bone or mother-of-pearl. Some had double doors which opened to reveal the drawers inside; others had one very deep drawer at either top or bottom (the stan-

ones have a padded seat and end. Couches, the ancestors of modern sofas, have two ends and a back. By the 1690s they were comfortably padded and had a high, shaped back.

### CASE FURNITURE

In the 17th century, chests – made by joiners and usually of oak – were the traditional form of storage for all sorts of objects, from books and papers to linen and clothes. Some were cased entirely in iron and had massive locks, for use as strong-boxes; others, only slightly less secure,

dard arrangement of the deepest drawer at the bottom and graduated shallower ones above had not yet been introduced). The drawer fronts had Flemish-inspired decoration, either with faceted panels or with geometric mouldings and applied baluster decoration, in which sections of turned wood were split vertically and glued to the surface. Handles were simply small wooden knobs.

From the 1660s, the design of chests of drawers was refined. Oak was replaced by walnut, drawers acquired little brass drop handles and, by the end of the century, when the chest of drawers became known as the commode, panels of floral or seaweed marquetry (see box, p.35) were applied to the sides and front, making it an expensive and decorative piece as well as a useful one. Some examples were built on stands and, with their spiral, turned legs and curved stretchers, resembled cabinets.

## CABINETS

The cabinet on stand was the most fashionable new piece of furniture of the 17th century. In the preceding century a cabinet was simply a small portable box with either two doors or a fall front, which was placed on a table in the closet or study and served as a container for jewels, miniatures or papers. The cabinet on

**CHEST OF DRAWERS**
Oak, inlaid with holly and bog oak; **c. 1660**

The drawer fronts have contrasting coloured woods inlaid into the oak carcase in simple foliage designs. The side panels have applied baluster decoration of a type used in the early 17th century on beds and tables. (*Above*)

**CABINET ON STAND**
Walnut with marquetry veneer; **c. 1680**

The walnut background is of oyster veneer, and a contrasting band of pale wood encloses the marquetry panels. In these, the ebony background sets off the light brown and green colours of the birds, foliage and flowers. (*Left*)

stand, used to furnish bedrooms, great chambers and long galleries, was much more substantial and highly decorative.

In the 1620s and 1630s most cabinets were imported from Europe. Paris specialized in ebony veneers (so much so that cabinet-makers in France were called *ébénistes*), as did Augsburg in Germany, where the veneer was enriched with silver mounts (handles, corner pieces and so on). Other fine cabinets came from Italy. The English diarist John Evelyn (1620-1706) possessed a particularly splendid one made in Florence. It is inlaid with panels of *pietre dure* (coloured hard stones) and decorated with gilt-bronze mounts. Evelyn's cabinet is unusual in not having outer doors enclosing the small drawers, which by mid-century had become the standard design. In the later 17th century, a cornice formed another, handle-less drawer.

### VENEERING AND LACQUER

After the Restoration, production of cabinets increased. Usually they were made with a matching stand, which had six legs and stretchers. The design of the leg developed from spiral-turned to scrolled to tapered. Some cabinets were of walnut, either oyster-veneered or with inset panels of floral marquetry (see box); others were of exotic woods or of other native woods, such as laburnum, which, cut in trans-

verse sections, produced a strongly contrasted pattern of light and dark.

The fashion for lacquer (a hard glossy finish, often black with gold decoration) originated with cabinets and screens imported from China and Japan. By the 1670s this fashion had become a craze, supply could not match demand, and a substitute process for lacquer was introduced – japanning, which produced a similar effect. Lacquer and japanned cabinets were usually set, not on matching stands, but on richly carved and gilded stands and sometimes with matching cresting rails above the cabinet.

The escritoire (writing desk) was a development of the cabinet. Usually veneered in walnut, it had the same arrangement of small drawers as the cabinet but had a fall front to write on.

### ELABORATE FRAMEWORKS
The bed was the single most valuable item in a 17th-century house, because of its expensive hangings. Grand beds had a tester (wooden canopy supported on posts) and curtains; and some had a carved headboard and two bedposts

**CABINET ON STAND**
Laburnum wood with silver mounts; **c. 1670**

The strong markings of oyster-veneered laburnum make a dramatic pattern; only the spiral turned legs are plain. The silver mounts of this piece are a particularly fine feature. (*Above*)

**MODEL OF THE QUEEN'S BEDROOM AT HAM HOUSE, SURREY**, as in **c. 1680**

The bed area is raised slightly above the surrounding floor and is protected by a balustrade. The tester bed has rich hangings, and ostrich plumes set in vases form four finials. On either side is a pair of chairs, covered *en suite*, and on the left is an ivory cabinet on stand, **c. 1650**. (*Right*)

**PIER GLASS**
*Verre églomisé* with carved and gilded wood; **c. 1700**

This elongated pier glass is typical of the end of the century, and the carved cresting has the Baroque outline of continental furniture designs. The *verre églomisé* makes a striking and colourful surround. (*Below*)

**MIRROR**
Needlework, with walnut frame; **c. 1660**

Wide and decorative frames were used even on small mirrors. This example has figures of Charles II and his queen worked in coloured silks on an ivory silk background. Raised leaves worked in metal thread encircle the central compartments, and the whole is framed in a half-round walnut veneer. (*Above*)

left visible at the foot. But such beds were superseded by the more fashionable French bed, which had no visible woodwork.

After the Restoration in 1660, beds became increasingly elaborate and costly. The neat exterior of the French bed acquired a richly decorated, deeply fringed valance round the tester. One of the finest surviving examples, probably by the joiner Thomas Robins, is a state bed made for James II, now at Knole, Kent. It was made *en suite* with a pair of armchairs and six stools, all covered in Genoese cut velvet. Bed and seats have giltwood legs carved with putti (cherubs) and the royal coat of arms.

By the 1690s beds, like chair backs and looking glasses, had become impressively high. The Melville Bed (now in the Victoria and Albert Museum, London), is, with a height of 4.6m (15ft) and its elaborate draperies, a remarkable survival of this style.

### MIRRORS

Some glass was manufactured in England in the early 17th century, but it was of poor quality and many houses had only mirrors of polished steel. Mirror glass, usually imported from Italy, was a luxury. In the 1630s, it was fashionable to frame it in ebony cut into wave-moulding to give a rippling effect. By the time of the Restoration mirror frames were decorated with raised figures in stumpwork (a form of embroidery).

In 1663 the establishment of the Vauxhall glassworks made mirror glass more widely available. The most characteristic frame in the 1660s and 1670s was the cushion frame, which was a wide, convex-profiled, rectangular frame, veneered usually in walnut. Other frames were also veneered, the simplest in walnut, others in ebony or tortoiseshell.

Pier glass frames might be japanned or lacquered or made of ebony with silver mounts or entirely of silver. By the 1690s pier glasses had become taller: the cresting was replaced by a second plate of framed mirror. Frames were of carved giltwood, or coloured glass or of *verre églomisé* (gold-engraved glass). Overmantel mirrors were sometimes fixed into panelling.

### PICTURE FRAMES

Picture frames were made by the same craftsmen as mirror frames, and tended to be similar. Wave-moulded ebony frames were a standard frame in the early 17th century. Other frames of the time were made of carved giltwood or of tortoiseshell edged with ebony. Some were decorated with silver.

## GRINLING GIBBONS (1648-1721)

Born in Rotterdam of English parents, and trained as a sculptor, Gibbons left Holland when he was 19 and came to England, where he was to become renowned for his ornate, detailed, naturalistic woodcarving. The diarist John Evelyn claimed to have discovered him and introduced him to Charles II and Sir Christopher Wren, for both of whom he executed many commissions, some of them in stone.

From 1677 Gibbons worked at Windsor Castle, where some of his finest carving is in the private dining room: around a painting over the chimney piece, dead game, fruit and flowers are arranged in festoons above bunches of ribbons. He was also employed at Hampton Court and Kensington Palace. At the latter his work includes the gilded Baroque frames for the two overmantel mirrors in the Queen's Gallery, carved to represent draperies, trumpets and festoons of foliage.

His brilliant technique enabled him to achieve remarkably realistic effects, such as on his carving of a lace cravat at Chatsworth, Derbyshire.

**GRINLING GIBBONS CARVING, PETWORTH HOUSE, SUSSEX**
Limewood; *c.* 1690

THE GROWTH OF A WEALTHY MIDDLE CLASS RESULTED IN AN INCREASE
IN GOOD QUALITY, UNPRETENTIOUS FURNITURE, THAT WAS OFTEN
RESTRAINED IN DECORATION BY COMPARISON WITH ITS CONTINENTAL
COUNTERPARTS.

# 18TH CENTURY ENGLAND

**ESCRITOIRE**
Walnut; **early 18th
century**

Like much furniture of the
period, this piece relies on
its well-figured walnut
veneers and crossbandings
for its decoration.

Trends in English furniture during the late
17th century – the emergence of an Anglo-
Dutch style, the consolidation of cabinet-making and upholstery skills, and the predominating
use of walnut – continued during the reigns
of Anne (1702–14) and George I (1714–27).
Unpretentiousness became a hallmark of the
furniture of this time and continued to be so
throughout the century. There was, however,
no shortage of colour – this was the great period
of the upholsterer, and seat furniture was lavishly covered with needlework, damasks, silks
and velvets. Windows and beds were hung with
them. In the early years of the century japanning
(imitation lacquer) was still fashionable and was
applied to small items like dressing mirrors,
ladies' cabinets and corner cupboards as well as
to major show-pieces like cabinets on stands.

### EARLY 18TH CENTURY FORMS

Among turn-of-the-century developments was
the evolution of the chest on a stand, by way of
the chest-on-chest (or tallboy), into the large
bureau cabinet. Some examples of this were
double-domed, while others had a straight cornice (moulded projecting top). The disposition
of storage space also varied: a kneehole arrangement of drawers with a central recessed cupboard was one departure from the most usual
arrangement of three or four drawers below the
fall-front bureau section. Above, there might be
a pair of mirror doors (on narrow cabinets a
single door) concealing shelves or small compartments, or there might be plain veneered (or
japanned) doors.

Such items, designed to grace the saloons of
fashionable houses, were given the most lavish
cabinet-making treatment: veneers of strongly
figured (grained) or burr (knotted) woods, such
as mulberry, walnut, elm or laburnum, were
used, and japanning in brilliant red or lustrous
black, with gold chinoiseries (Chinese-style ornamentation) in relief, was popular.

Bun feet (slightly flattened ball feet) were
usual for cabinets and chests in the early 18th
century, but they gradually gave place to
bracket feet (shaped like a right-angled bracket), which continued until the 19th century.
The chest-on-chest also continued as a storage
piece, evolving by mid-century into the gentleman's wardrobe, an arrangement of drawers
below, and shelves within a cupboard above.

What has come to be known as the Queen
Anne style is most closely associated with the
evolution of the cabriole (double-curved) leg.
The H-shaped stretchers (horizontal struts
uniting the legs) of the earliest cabriole-legged

## 18TH-CENTURY LONDON CABINET-MAKING FIRMS

| | | |
|---|---|---|
| **JENSEN, Gerrit** | 1680–1715 | M▮▮▮▮▮ ▮or Charles II, William and Mary and Queen Anne, and members of the ar▮▮▮▮▮uced intricate metal marquetry mixed with dark and light woods and t▮▮▮▮▮▮ter furniture was decorated with wood marquetry. |
| **GUMLEY, John, and MOORE, James, firm of** | 1714–26 | Supplied looking glasses and gilded tables. Moore specialized in gilded furniture. |
| **GRANGER, Hugh, firm of** | 1692–1706 | High-quality case furniture, veneered in walnut and burr woods. |
| **BENNETT, Samuel** | 1695–1741 | High-quality veneered furniture. |
| **COXED & WOSTER, firm of** | 1700–36 | High-quality veneered furniture. |
| **GRENDEY, Giles, firm of** | 1726–c. 1770 | Worked in walnut and mahogany. Exported japanned goods. |
| **GOODISON, Benjamin** | c. 1700–67 | Royal cabinet-maker. Produced furniture that was part of an overall architectural design. |
| **CHIPPENDALE, Thomas** | 1718–79 | Produced consistently high-quality furniture: rectangular, squat chair backs, flared at top, carved organic forms, scrolled feet, tables and chairs made in many designs. Published the *Director*, a catalogue of all available styles. |
| **CHANNON, John** | 1711–c. 1783 | Specialized in large-scale carcase pieces with ingenious hidden gadgetry and richly chiselled ormolu mounts; brass-inlaid writing tables and cabinets. |
| **VILE, William and COBB, John, firm of** | fl. 1751–64 | High-quality, stylish pieces in Adam style. Supplied royalty and aristocracy. |
| **HALLETT, William** | c. 1707–c. 1781 | High-quality furniture. |
| **NORMAN, Samuel** | fl. 1746–67 | High-quality furniture. |
| **WHITTLE, James** | fl. 1731–59 | High-quality furniture. |
| **LINNELL, John & William, firm of** | 1749–63 | High-quality furniture. |
| **INCE, William and MAYHEW, John, firm of** | 1758–1804 | High-quality furniture. |

chairs were soon dispensed with, and tables and chairs stood on gently serpentine legs terminating in pad feet. More robust curves developed later, and the knees or bulges at the tops of the legs were often carved with shell medallions; by George I's reign feet were usually of the lion's paw or ball and claw variety. The backs of Queen Anne and early Georgian chairs were also serpentine in outline, with vase-shaped splats (central uprights) of well-figured walnut or with carved shells at the top: these were occasionally partially gilt. Upholstered seats added colour. (Japanned chairs, of roughly similar outline, more often had a caned seat and back.)

Still more colourful – and comfortable – were the sets of chairs now favoured for gentlemen's houses: side chairs with shaped seats and

**DINING CHAIR**
Walnut; *c.* 1730

The shape of this chair's seat, as well as the vigorous lion masks on the knees of its cabriole legs, are characteristic of the best examples of early Georgian seating. The chair has carved front legs and a vase-shaped splat.

rounded backs upholstered in brightly coloured needlework, sometimes with arms of sinuous walnut; and matching upholstered settees. Most luxurious were the all-over upholstered and cushioned "wing" chairs of the period.

Another feature of the Queen Anne and early Georgian period was a proliferation of small, well-made pieces, such as tables for taking tea, displaying china or needlework. "Claw" (round tripod) tables were made in various styles; while tables with folding tops often had decoratively quartered veneers. Dressing tables, small chests of drawers, known as bachelor's chests, small kneehole desks and small cupboards and cabinets for displaying china were also popular.

In any house, whether grand or humble, the bed was the most costly item. Few "ordinary" beds of the early 18th century have survived: their framework, concealed by the much more valuable hangings, was made of soft wood or beech, easily ravaged by woodworm and rot. Many more state beds have survived from the first half of the 18th century, and these show the influence of the Huguenot decorator and furniture designer Daniel Marot (1663–1752). Most have a tester (canopy) supported by four posts, which were concealed by the rich textile hangings, but others had only a half-tester, projecting from the head of the bed and supported from the ceiling.

Gerrit Jensen (*fl.* 1680–1715) is regarded as the first English cabinet-maker to achieve fame. Well-established before the Revolution of 1688, he is known to have made a table, stands and looking glass for Charles II (1660–85). These have not survived, but examples of the elaborate marquetry he made for William and Mary (1689–1702) and Queen Anne (1702–14) are still in the royal collections. His intricately crafted metal marquetry was undoubtedly influenced by that of the celebrated French cabinet-maker André-Charles Boulle (1642–1732) but it is relatively muted in its opulence, its silver and brass inlays being interspersed with dark and light woods and tortoiseshell. In his later furniture, including some pieces for Queen Anne, Jensen abandoned the use of metal inlays in favour of japanning and seaweed marquetry (patterns resembling fine seaweed leaves) of breathtaking complexity.

The partnership of John Gumley (*fl.* 1691–1727) and James Moore (*c.* 1670–1726) supplied grand looking glasses and lavishly gilded tables and stands to royalty and the nobility. Gumley's looking-glass shop in the Strand

**WRITING BUREAU**
Walnut; **George I (1714–27)**

Veneers of burr walnut are framed by feathered bandings on this writing bureau, and the edges of its drawers are cock-beaded; the sloping fall-front conceals drawers and pigeonholes and is supported on lopers when open. This type of bureau remained a standard shape throughout the 18th century. (*Above*)

**MIRROR**
Walnut veneers and parcel gilding; **c. 1740**

The carved and gilded decoration is in the restrained English Rococo style. (*Left*)

became a fashionable meeting place where people could also buy tables, cabinets, desks and bookcases. Moore specialized in furniture on which low-relief patterns of strapwork (interlacing bands) or leaves were built up in gesso (plaster base) before being gilded. Examples survive both in the royal collection and at Blenheim Palace. Moore's son James (c. 1690–1734) became cabinet- and chair-maker to Frederick, Prince of Wales, and is known to have worked with the architect William Kent (1685–1748).

Kent was one of the first designers to consider furnishings as a total part of a scheme. His furniture is ponderously architectural, with a baroque and gilded grandeur that made it suitable only for palatial interiors, but his influence on subsequent designers and on the emergence in England of the Neo-Classical style later in the century was considerable.

Fashionable, as opposed to regional, furniture can rarely be attributed with any certainty to individuals (it was not obligatory or customary for English makers to stamp their work), and most cabinet-makers who produced good-quality pieces for gentlemen's houses remain anonymous. Of the few who did use trade labels or stamped their names, Hugh Granger, Samuel

**JAPANNED ARMCHAIR**
*Giles Grendey*
**c. 1730**

This comes from a set of cane-seated chairs; the shapes of the cross stretchers (which most English cabinet-makers had dispensed with by this time), the European-looking Chinese figures and the high-quality gilt-and-red japanning are characteristic of Grendey's work, much of which was exported.
(*Right*)

**WRITING TABLE**
*Probably designed by William Kent and made by the carver John Boson*
Mahogany and parcel-gilding; *c.* 1735

This is one of a pair of pier glasses and tables decorated with owls, made for Chiswick House, the Third Earl of Burlington's palladian villa outside London.

Bennett and Coxed & Woster are associated with fine case furniture, mostly veneered in walnut or burr woods, produced 1700–30. Another, Giles Grendey (1693–1780), worked in both walnut and mahogany.

### FROM PALLADIAN TO ROCOCO

The Palladian movement of the 1720s and 1730s (a revival of classic Roman styles) coincided with a gradual transition from walnut to mahogany. The lustre and strength of the latter made it an ideal material for chairs, with their crisply carved ornament, and for the architecturally conceived furniture of William Kent and his contemporaries, of whom the royal cabinet-maker, Benjamin Goodison (c. 1700–67) was the most important.

Even as the Palladians were introducing the sober discipline of classical form into the design and decoration of the English country house, the French Rococo was gaining ground in England. This was hardly surprising in view of the large numbers of immigrant craftsmen working in England and the availability of many engravings and pattern books depicting the work of leading French designers. Engravers such as the French immigrant Hubert Gravelot (1699–1773) were widely influential. The new ideas quickly took root in cabinet-making, and furniture became touched with the fantastical wand of the Rococo, with its restless asymmetrical twists and curves. Carved and gilded woodwork showed waterfalls dripping on to rocky piles amid swishing fronds of palm or acanthus; birds of paradise hovering over flowery garlands; and putti and Chinamen peeping through gilded vistas of shells and foliage.

Of the many English Rococo design books the most influential were those of Thomas Johnson (1714–c.1788) and Matthias Lock (fl. 1740–65), both of whom were teachers and master-carvers as well as designers of great vivacity. By the 1750s the Rococo had embraced Gothic as well as Chinese fantasies and these were added to the design styles purveyed by the pattern books of the 1750s and 1760s, the most important of which was *The Gentleman and Cabinet-Maker's Director* (1754, 1755 and 1759–62), by the cabinet-maker and furniture designer Thomas Chippendale (1718–79).

### THE INFLUENCE OF CHIPPENDALE

Chippendale's *Director* was the first design book to cover all kinds of furniture, and its success in distilling the current styles of decoration into a form both workable for the cabinet-maker and acceptable to his clients ensured the adoption of "Chippendale" as a generic label for mid-18th-century furniture. For posterity the *Director* has been an invaluable guide to the array of decorative styles available to the period's gentry. Practically all the furniture covered alludes to the Rococo: even sober designs for library bookcases in the Palladian architectural idiom have Rococo flourishes as well as Gothic tracery or Chinese fretwork in the glazing bars.

Chair backs had been growing steadily less elongated from the 1720s with the decline in Marot's influence, and by the 1750s they were of a squat rectangular shape, slightly flaring at the top. Both the top rail, which often terminated in projecting "ears", and the pierced back

**SIDE CHAIR**
Mahogany; **c. 1760**

This Chippendale-style chair incorporates both Chinese and Gothic elements in the decoration of the back. (*Above*)

**ARMCHAIR**
**c. 1750**

The well-carved and gilded underframe of this English Rococo chair is in elegant contrast to the smooth lines of its upholstery. (*Left*)

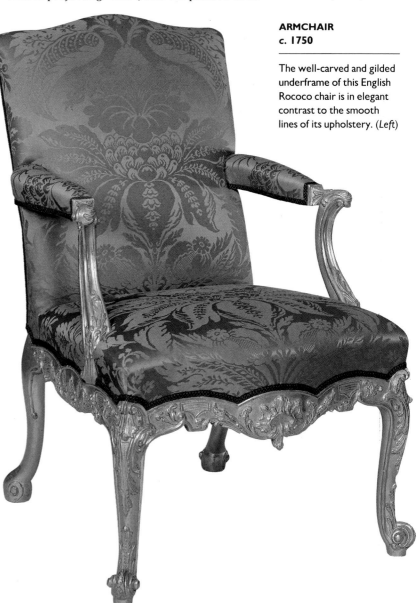

**WRITING AND DRESSING CHEST**
*John Channon*
Mahogany and ormolu;
**c. 1750**

Exeter-born Channon was a London-based cabinet-maker whose work has a flamboyant Germanic flavour. The vigorously curving front and sides of this piece, its rich mahogany veneers and the inlaid brass lines around the drawers – as well as the high quality of the gilt-bronze mounts (see detail above) – are distinctively his. The writing drawer across the frieze is supported on the canted corners, which slide forward with it. Many Channon pieces have hidden opening mechanisms for drawers or doors.

splat were carved into sinuous organic forms, acanthus foliage, ribbons, shells, Gothic arches or geometric Chinese patterns. All these were echoed in the carving on the knees and front cabriole legs; scrolled feet were now more fashionable than ball and claw or pad feet. Some chairs of this period have straight front legs decorated with fluting or carved borders and reinforcing stretchers. Seats were generally upholstered, but narrow-backed "hall" chairs usually had wooden seats.

Chairs with upholstered backs as well as seats were known as French chairs, whether they were of the round-contoured, cabriole-legged variety, with frames carved and gilded in French Rococo style, or of the minimally ornamented, squarish-backed type that we now call Gainsborough chairs. Tables – breakfast, shaving, tea, gaming, sewing, writing, china and "claw" – were made in a profusion of designs, as were beds. China cabinets, stands, mirrors, screens and much else were produced for the growing numbers of the well-to-do.

It was a golden age of cabinet-making: hundreds of craftsmen, greatly helped by design

books, were kept busy in cities all over the country. It was London, however, that remained the chief centre of operations for the furniture trade, and talented craftsmen who wished to better themselves made every effort to set up their workshops there. Among the most successful were John Channon (1711–c.1783), whose speciality – large-scale carcase pieces with ingenious hidden gadgetry and richly chiselled ormolu mounts – reflects a continental influence; and William Vile (c. 1700–67) and John Cobb (c. 1715–78), William Hallett (c. 1707–81), Samuel Norman (fl. 1746–67), James Whittle (fl. 1731–59), William Ince and John Mayhew (fl. 1758–1804), and William (c. 1703–63) and John (1729–96) Linnell, all of whom supplied furniture of superlative craftsmanship in the latest styles.

The fashion-conscious had to move quickly in mid-18th-century England: the Rococo came late and its full glory was relatively brief. No sooner had the smartest houses been fitted up with "French" chairs, lacquered or marquetry bombé (bulging at the sides and front) commodes and fantastically carved and gilded mirrors than the discipline of a new classicism was being urged.

## NEO-CLASSICISM

Classical ideals were already well rooted in England, most recently through the Palladian movement, whose archaeologically based designs remained fundamental to much furniture of the 1750s, however much decked out in rococo ornament they might be. Archaeological discoveries at Herculaneum and Pompeii during the middle of the 18th century coincided with a general flagging of interest in rococo ornament and generated a new fascination with classical antiquity. Engravings like Giambattista Piranesi's evocative visions of Roman ruins, and illustrated books on archaeology fuelled the fire, and a whole new range of ornamental motifs, many of them derived from the wall paintings of Herculaneum and Pompeii, entered the repertoire of architects and furniture-makers. For the remainder of the 18th century and for at least the first decade of the 19th, there was a general striving towards greater archaeological accuracy in classical interpretation.

Among the first exponents of the Neo-Classical style was the architect James "Athenian" Stuart (1713–88), who had spent more than a decade immersed in the ruins of Rome and Athens and who published the important guide *Antiquities of Athens* (vol I 1762). Stuart designed furniture for Kedleston Hall in Derbyshire and Spencer House, London, using carved griffins, fluting, paterae (rosettes), anthemia (stylized honeysuckle forms) and other motifs soon to be adopted by others. Sir William Chambers (1723–96), another inveterate traveller, who had produced the Oriental design book *Designs of Chinese Buildings, Furniture, Dresses, Machines and Utensils* (1757), also contributed to English Neo-Classical development.

No designer, however, was more important or more prolific than Robert Adam (1728–92). Like Stuart and Chambers, Adam had acquired his knowledge of classical design, as well as a wide circle of friendly artists, dilettanti and aristocrats, during his years spent in Italy, and his subsequent employment by many of the most rich and powerful property owners in Britain gave him immense prestige and wide influence. In his all-embracing approach to building schemes (and in partnership with his brother James), he took responsibility for all aspects of interior decoration – the painting of walls and ceilings, stucco-work, furniture, carpets, curtains and lighting – and by so doing gave patronage to some of the best craftsmen of the time. Among the cabinet-makers who collaborated with him were John Linnell, Thomas Chippendale, Ince & Mayhew, Vile & Cobb and Samuel Norman.

The light elegance of the Adam style was well suited to the domestic interior and enhanced the skills of the furniture craftsman, giving unprecedented scope for marquetry decoration. The playful asymmetrical flourishes of rococo plasterwork were translated on furniture into well-regulated borders of anthemia or paterae, scrolled acanthus, looped garlands and graceful arabesques. Painting and gilding were also widely used, and decorative ceramic plaques as well as finely chiselled ormolu mounts were applied to surfaces veneered in finely-figured mahogany or satinwood.

The style was distilled most successfully in *The Cabinet-Maker and Upholsterer's Guide* (1788), the posthumously published design book by George Hepplewhite (d 1786), which took the Adam style not only to the furthest corners of the British Isles but to many parts of Europe and North America. Hepplewhite's express aim "to unite elegance and utility" was fulfilled in "near three hundred different pat-

**DRESSING TABLE**
*Possibly Pierre Langlois*
Tulipwood and ormolu;
**c. 1770**

The front is decorated with marquetry flower panels and the top with a pheasant among flowers. The rising mirror section is flanked by hinged compartments for toilet accoutrements. The piece is in the French style fashionable during the 1760s and 1770s and is attributed to the French immigrant *ébéniste* Langlois, who was famous for "all sorts of curious inlaid work, particularly commodes in the foreign taste".

**CABINET**
*Robert Adam*
Satinwood and ormolu;
**1771**

Designed to hold *pietre dure* panels, the cabinet was made by Ince & Mayhew, with mounts by Matthew Boulton. (*Above*)

**CHIPPENDALE COMMODE**
Satinwood and marquetry of other woods; **1773**

This Neo-Classical piece was made for Harewood House. The roundel of Britannia is on one of its doors. (*Top and above*)

terns for furniture". Forty of them were for chairs, most of which had decorated shield or square backs and upholstered seats. Hepplewhite drew attention to the Adam-inspired fashion for "finishing them with painted or japanned work" and "assorting the prevailing colour to the furniture and light of the room".

Hepplewhite's essentially conservative approach is seen in his retention of the cabriole leg in some instances; serpentine-fronted chests and side tables appear alongside those of half-round Neo-Classical shape. Chairs, small tables and parlour pieces such as tea caddies and trays are given most decorative attention; utilitarian furniture – wardrobes, library bookcases, chests of drawers and pot cupboards – is classically simple. Although large tables were beginning to

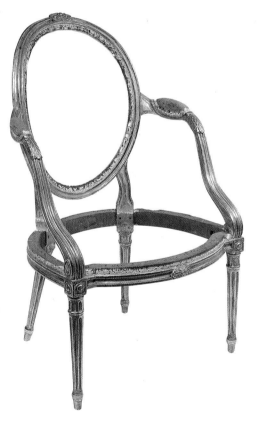

**CHAIR FRAME**
Carved giltwood; **c. 1780**

This Adam period chair is from a drawing-room suite. (*Above*)

**WEEKS CABINET**
Satinwood, sabicu and
ebony; c. 1795

This finely made Sheraton
cabinet, with sabicu panels
and ebony stringing,

comprises a clock inscribed
"Week's Museum,
Tichborne Street", along
with a display case and two
drawers below. One
drawer is a fall-front
secretaire fitted for

writing, the other a well-
equipped dressing table.
Thomas Week's museum of
mechanical curiosities was a
fashionable haunt of turn-
of-the-century Londoners.

appear as permanent fixtures in dining rooms, they did not yet feature in design books. They signalled a more formal approach to dining habits, replacing the movable, multi-purpose tables of smaller but often adjustable sizes that had been used for the past century.

Hepplewhite's *Guide*, and others of the period, such as the anonymous *Cabinet-Maker's London Book of Prices* (1788), reflect the elegant well-made furniture that was being produced in huge quantities by firms such as Gillow (est. *c.*1730) and George Seddon (1753–1868). Gillow's archives survive, providing a detailed source of knowledge about furniture-making practices in the late 18th century and for most of the 19th. The firm's habit of stamping its furniture has enabled many items to be identified.

George Seddon (*c.* 1727–1801) was already regarded as "one of the most eminent cabinet-makers of London" in 1768, and his firm, which continued under his sons and grandsons, was the largest in London. Its name is associated with a wide range of well-made furniture and particularly with fine cabinets and tables in satinwood and mahogany. Some of these had patent mechanical fittings of the type much in vogue during the late 18th and early 19th centuries, a time known in English furniture as the Sheraton period, after the designer Thomas Sheraton (1751–1806).

Relatively little is known of Sheraton's working life. Unlike Chippendale and Hepplewhite, he probably never had a workshop of his own, although he must have been trained as a cabinet-maker. His trade card read: "T. Sheraton/Teaches Perspective, Architecture and Ornaments, makes Designs for Cabinet-makers and sells all kinds of Drawing Books etc." His first pattern book, *The Cabinet-Maker and Upholsterer's Drawing Book* (1791–4) echoes the distinctly francophile Neo-Classicism of the architect Henry Holland (1745–1806), whose work for the Prince of Wales at Carlton House heralded the Regency style of the early 19th century. The *Drawing Book* was seen as a digest of the most refined Neo-Classical taste and, like Hepplewhite's *Guide*, influenced furniture all over Europe as well as in America and Britain. It was followed in 1803 by *The Cabinet Dictionary* (see page 64) and in 1805 by the first part of his most ambitious work, *The Cabinet-Maker, Upholsterer and General Artist's Encyclopedia*, which remained unfinished at his death.

# REGIONAL FURNITURE

During the early 18th century there came into widespread use a type of chair known as the Windsor chair. Characterized by a solid wood seat, simple turned legs and a stick back (one made from turned spindles), this robust form of seating gave rise to a host of regional variants. These Windsor, or stick-back, chairs were only part of a rich rural tradition of chair-making that included the spindle- and ladder-backs of the Midlands and northern England and the button backs of East Anglia. The styles of these chairs were governed more by geography than by period fashions. (Regional variations also played a notable part in the design of Welsh dressers.)

Because new styles eventually percolate downwards through the social strata, regional or traditional chairs often display the characteristic decorative features of "town" furniture, such as pad feet, cabriole legs and vase-shaped splats. Some East Anglian chairs can be associated with Sheraton designs. Even so, most regional chairs were built for durability rather than elegance and their legs are usually reinforced by stretchers.

Other rural pieces, particularly tables and chests, of solid oak, elm or fruitwoods, continued throughout most of the 18th century to be made in earlier styles.

**PORTABLE ANGLO-INDIAN WRITING DESK**
Coromandel wood and ivory; **18th century**
(*Above*)

**"BROAD-ARM" WINDSOR CHAIR**
Yew with elm seats; **first half of 19th century.**
(*Below*)

**WELSH DRESSER**
*Pembrokeshire*
Oak with typical open pot board, unbacked rach and shaped frieze; **c. 1790**
(*Left*)

# IRISH FURNITURE

Very little identifiably pre-18th-century Irish furniture exists. (One notable exception, made about *c.* 1690, is a table with cross-stretchers – X-shaped struts connecting the legs – closely modelled on a French prototype and with carved decoration by James Tabary.) Furniture made after *c.* 1740, however, is readily found. The characteristically Irish pieces and their decoration evolved from English models.

Until *c.* 1775 there was a vogue in Irish furniture for carved decoration, including masks, scallop shells, acanthus and, as a symbol of welcome, a basket of fruit and flowers. Cabriole (double-curved) legs sometimes have a collar beneath the knee and a lappet (small projection) or carved

acanthus above the foot. A common type of foot is the squared, five-toed claw, but faceted pad feet and three-lobed toes appear often. Small, plain ogee (double-curved) brackets are found on both dining and wing chairs (with wing-like side projections at head level) of *c.* 1770–90 when the square, chamfered (bevelled-edged) leg with stretchers enjoyed popularity. Later, during the Regency, period in furniture (*c.* 1800–*c.* 1830), brackets are found running along seat-rails to provide support for the stiles (verticals) of the back.

By the 1780s Neo-Classicism had come into fashion. Pale timbers – satinwood and harewood (stained sycamore) – were inlaid with popular motifs and simulated fluting in

**CARVED SIDE TABLE**
**19th century**

groups of three. A semi-elliptical plan was preferred to the English half-round for card and pier tables and for cabinets and commodes; this is particularly seen in those by Christopher Hearn and William Moore.

Probably the most prized of all Irish timbers was the ebony-black bog oak, and much mid-18th-century Irish mahogany furniture was stained and finished to resemble that native timber. Gilding was much used for mirrors, but the Rococo o. Neo-Classical carving is usually less three-dimensional and balanced than its English counterpart. However, the architectural classicism of Dublin's Francis and John Booker's mirrors is robust and well-drawn.

A well-known Irish piece is the wake table – a gateleg table (one with drop leaves supported by legs that swing out) with shallow hinged leaves. The side table was very popular; it had carved decoration on the often deep frieze, and wooden tops were preferred to marble. Later models were inlaid or had gilded bases and sometimes had inlaid marble tops by Bossi.

Chairs of the mid-18th century are identifiable by various characteristically Irish back shapes, among them corkscrew terminals to top-rails and vase-shaped splats (central uprights) interrupted by a second rail. Some tallboys were made in two pieces, one on top of the other, but others were in a single, narrow piece with six to eight drawers. One uniquely Irish piece was an architect's table or chest of drawers with a fitted top drawer and supported on legs with an integral cabinet top.

Coopered and brass-bound mahogany peat buckets were often decorated with horizontal ribbing – a popular feature from the early 19th century seen on the edges of dining tables, table supports and elsewhere. Another characteristically Irish item is the wine canterbury, a handled tray with divisions to accommodate six to twelve wine bottles. Sometimes the sides are shaped to allow the bottles to be stored horizontally, but they are always raised on legs, usually cabriole, and often have a shell-carved frieze.

As the 19th century progressed, better communications made regional and national

**CURVED-BACK SIDE TABLE**
*Probably by Gillington's, Dublin*
Mahogany with gallery back and carved lion's head and paw supports; 1840s
(*Above*)

**CHESS SET**
Killarney ware (*Right*)

**SIDE TABLE**
Carved decoration; *c.* 1800
(*Above*)

**CHAIR**
Vase-shaped splat and second top-rail (*Below*)

differences less apparent. However, in midcentury, Killarney developed its own idiosyncratic product, usually made from locally-grown arbutus wood. It is characterized by its wood inlay of local flora – such as shamrock, arbutus and fern – and poker-work pictures of local buildings (principally Muckross Abbey). The leading exponents of this style were James Egan and Jeremiah O'Connor.

DESPITE THE MANY INFLUENCES ON FURNITURE MADE IN BRITAIN
BETWEEN 1790 AND 1840, SIMILARITIES JUSTIFY THEIR CATEGORIZATION
UNDER A SINGLE HEADING – REGENCY.

# REGENCY

Regency, as the description of a period of English furniture design, is an imprecise, modern term. Far from being confined to furniture made during the single decade of the historical Regency (1811–20), when the Prince of Wales (later George IV) took over the reins of monarchy from his ailing father George III, it includes furniture produced from about 1790 until the early 1840s.

The earliest pieces of furniture designated Regency are those of the late 18th century that cannot be categorized as a late flowering of the Adam style, such as those inspired by Louis XVI furniture that were included by Thomas Sheraton in *The Cabinet-Maker and Upholsterer's Drawing-Book* (1791–3). At the other end of the period, the last Regency furniture is principally in a somewhat debased Neo-Classical style.

Neo-Classicism, which had replaced Rococo in the 1760s, was dominant throughout the Regency period, but this was an age

**ROLL-TOP SECRETAIRE**
*Attributed to John McLean*
**Rosewood veneers with lacquered bronze mounts; c. 1810**

The form of this chaste and elegant *secrétaire* owes a debt to the work of late 18th-century French cabinet-makers such as Saunier and Weisweiler. The lattice grille of the superstructure, the scrolled surround above the frieze drawers, the handles and the legs are all typical of McLean's work. (*Left*)

of eclectic taste, and there were many other popular styles including chinoiserie, Gothic Revival, Egyptian Revival, Louis XIV Revival and Rococo Revival. A single designer would often produce work inspired by a variety of stylistic traditions.

None of the styles current during the Regency period existed in isolation; they were related to similar trends in architecture, painting, sculpture and the decorative arts. Nor did these styles appear out of the blue; they were the result of such influences as furniture imported from abroad, the presence in London of *émigré* cabinet-makers from Revolutionary France, articles brought back from the Grand Tour, and the availability of foreign pattern books and other source material.

### A CHANGING MARKET
The Regency period saw considerable demographic change. In 1780 the population of Great

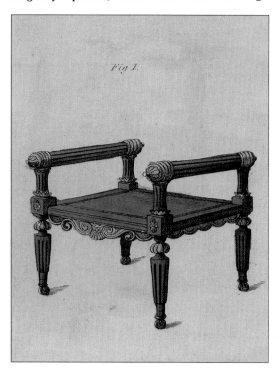

*Fig. 1.*

**WINDOW SEAT**
*Design from J. Stokes, The Complete Cabinet-Maker and Upholsterers' Guide*
**Hand-coloured aquatint; 1829**

Inspired by Roman prototypes, such as those published in 1799 by C.H. Tatham, earlier variants of this model were designed and made by George Bullock in c. 1815 and published by Richard Brown (1822). As late as 1840, another version was available from the cabinet-maker William Smee. (*Bottom left*)

# FURNITURE FORMS

Typical of the small-scale furniture that became popular during the Regency period were Quartetto tables. They were made in sets of four and were (according to Thomas Sheraton) "made to draw out of each other, and may be used separately".

Sofa tables, raised on supports ranging from plain rectangular uprights to lyres and monopodia, were an elongated form of Pembroke table, suitable for one to use while seated on a sofa.

Work tables – with silk bags beneath in which needlework could be kept – were small, multi-purpose "occasional" tables which sometimes contained a reading stand and a games board.

The Davenport was a small writing desk with a sloping top above a set of drawers. It is thought to have taken its name from an example supplied in the late 18th century by the furniture-makers Gillow of Lancaster and London to a Captain Davenport.

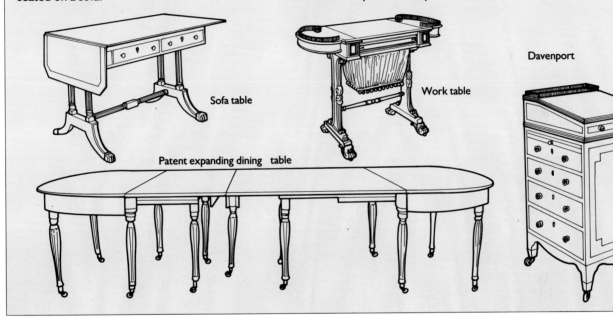

Sofa table

Work table

Davenport

Patent expanding dining table

Britain was perhaps seven-and-a-half million; by 1815 it was about 13 million, and by the 1870s it had doubled again. From 1815 to 1840 there was a move away from the countryside and a vast increase in the urban middle class. Cities such as Birmingham, Glasgow, Leeds and Liverpool at least doubled in size. Some furniture-makers adapted to these changes. While still continuing to cater for wealthy, aristocratic patrons with expensive and luxurious furnishings, at the same time they supplied the new market with solid, serviceable items. These remain as respectable and practical today as when they were first made.

Notable among the manufacturers of the period are Gillow of Lancaster and London (active from c.1730 and throughout the 19th century), Seddon of London (1753–1868), Trotter of Edinburgh (c.1750–1852) and Blain of Liverpool (1830s). Less well known are Wilkinson of London (1808–40) and James

**WRITING TABLE**
Tulipwood veneer, boxwood stringing and ormolu mounts; *c.* 1810

A particular feature of this small table is the lavish use of finely cast and chased ormolu. Lion masks and ring handles were popular throughout the period, but more unusual are the *espagnolettes* (female masks) on the corners, which recall a motif associated with the Régence period in France.

and lotus leaf carving and inlaid brass borders. Kitchen and servants' furniture tended to be made with the emphasis on durability rather than style, but even so it too can have considerable charm.

The principal woods used in commercially produced furniture during the Regency period were mahogany and rosewood. However, the grander early 19th-century pieces were often veneered with rare and exotic woods. Satinwood remained fashionable, as it had been at the end of the 18th century. Amboyna, calamander, ebony and kingwood were also popular, as was zebrawood, although in 1820, according to the novelist Maria Edgeworth, there was "no more of it to be had for love or money". Furniture was, where appro-

Winter of London (1823–40). Their furniture tends to be not particularly distinguished in terms of design and, although well executed, might have escaped identification but for the fact that they often marked their output. During this period – and throughout the 19th century – many firms stamped their name on to the top of a drawer front, the door of a cupboard or the underside of a table or chair.

### DESIGN AND MATERIALS
The two main characteristics of Regency furniture are a strong sense of design and the wide range and high quality of materials that cabinet-makers used.

Design is marked by an archaeological approach, a diligent research into all available sources of styles of the past. Material drawn upon ranged from antique marbles to contemporary publications such as Thomas Hope's *Household Furniture and Interior Decoration* (1807). The resulting furniture included both accurate reproductions of antique forms and stylizations of them. In the work of an able designer, such as George Bullock (see p. 65), furniture that thus revealed its sources of inspiration from the past was yet, at the same time, distinctly of its own period.

Most furniture produced for the middle classes was not produced by leading cabinet-makers and is therefore less distinguished than the major examples pictured here. Even so, much of it shows great elegance in its use of typical Regency features derived from pattern books, such as sabre legs on chairs, turned or reeded (carved with convex parallel lines) legs on tables and chairs, stylized acanthus

**CHAMBER WRITING TABLE**
*Gillow, Lancaster*
Mahogany; 1811

The figured wood, reeded legs and inkwell compartment are typical Gillow features. The table was made for Parlington Hall, near Leeds. (*Above*)

**SIDE CHAIR**
Beech wood, painted to simulate maple; c. 1810

Painted seat furniture was popular throughout the Regency period. The lyre is an attribute of Apollo, god of music and poetry. It is likely that this lyre-back chair was designed for a music room. (*Below*)

priate, embellished with gilt gesso (plaster) mouldings and ormolu (gilt-bronze) and lacquered-brass mounts. Brass inlay was widely used both for inlaid lines and for decorative borders and panels. Also common was painted furniture with landscape vignettes on chair backs. And there was an increased use of indigenous woods such as oak, elm and yew, not just for country-made pieces but also for sophisticated London-made furniture. A leading exponent of this trend was George Bullock.

### FRENCH INFLUENCES

A key figure in the introduction of late-18th-century French Neo-Classicism into English furniture design was the architect and designer Henry Holland (1745–1806). His major commissions during the 1780s and 1790s included work for the Prince of Wales at Carlton House, London, and at the Royal Pavilion, Brighton. He also worked for the 5th Duke of Bedford at Woburn and Samuel Whitbread at Southill, both in Bedfordshire, and for the 2nd Earl Spencer at Althorp, Northamptonshire. Much of the contemporary furniture which survives from these commissions has a distinctly Gallic flavour and some of it was almost certainly designed by Holland himself. The few furniture designs definitely attributable to Holland, such as those at the Royal Institute of British Architects, London, and at the Pierpont Morgan Library, New York, are very much in the late Louis XVI style of a French *ébéniste* (cabinet-maker) such as the German-born Adam Weisweiler (1744–1820).

At Southill there are several low, marble-topped cupboards and bookcases which were probably made from Holland's designs by the Royal cabinet-makers Elward, Marsh and Tatham of London (active 1774–1840). These pieces typify the Anglo-French style of early Regency furniture. The overall appearance of these so-called dwarf-cabinets recalls commodes by Parisian *ébénistes* such as Claude-Charles Saunier (1735–1807), Jean-Henri Riesener (1734–1806) and Weisweiler. The richly figured veneers relieved by delicate ormolu mounts, the gilded columns and the marble tops are all French-inspired.

English dwarf-cabinets of the above type often have doors lined with pleated silk (as shown in contemporary pattern books), and sometimes the door frames contain wire grilles. The dwarf-cabinet remained popular throughout the Regency period, becoming less and less

**ARMCHAIR**
*Marsh and Tatham*
Giltwood; **c. 1800**

Part of a suite made for Powderham Castle, Devon, the chair shows the influence of Louis XVI

chair-makers. The dolphin, an attribute of Neptune, is often found on Regency furniture; here it represents the family crest. (*Above*)

**DWARF CUPBOARD**
Rosewood veneer, gilding and marble; **c. 1800**

This French-inspired cupboard represents a furniture style associated with architect Henry Holland. (*Below*)

elegant towards the middle of the century. The later examples lack the proportion and refinement of their original source of inspiration.

**John McLean** On the evidence of surviving furniture, one of the London cabinet-making firms which most successfully adapted the late – 18th-century French style was John McLean & Son. Their documented furniture can be dated only to 1805–15 but they were probably active 1770–1825. McLean has the distinction of having been singled out by Sheraton in his *Cabinet Dictionary* (1803), to which he was a subscriber. The text to plate 67, a "Pouch Table", comments: "The design...was taken from one executed by Mr M'Lane... who finished these small articles in the neatest manner."

McLean's debt to Louis XVI *ébénistes* is clear in the restrained, somewhat severe form of his small tables and cabinets. His furniture is usually veneered with finely figured rosewood, now faded to a mellow colour (the original dark wood can be seen, protected beneath the handles and other mounts). It is enriched by distinctive lacquered-brass mounts, the design of which seems, in some instances, to be unique to McLean's workshop. There is a *sécrétaire* (writing desk) by McLean in the Victoria and Albert Museum, London, and an exquisite *bonheur du jour* (lady's writing table) by him in the Metropolitan Museum, New York. The latter has typical parcel-gilt (partly gilded) turned legs and the upper part of the piece, which is a book tray, has a fine lacquered-brass grille.

## REGENCY FURNITURE-MAKERS

| | | | |
|---|---|---|---|
| **GILLOW, Firm of** | *fl.* 1730–c. 1900 | Lancaster and London (from 1769) | During the Regency period, their most characteristic furniture was in finely figured mahogany, with turned and fluted legs on tables and chairs. Made complete range of domestic furniture. Often stamped their furniture as GILLOWS LANCASTER. |
| **SEDDON, Firm of** | 1753–1868 | London | Noted for painted satinwood furniture in the late 18th century. Documented furniture in the early 19th century often in mahogany; examples recorded in up-to-date Neo-Classical taste. Furniture sometimes labelled. |
| **WILKINSON, Firm of** | 1808–40 | London | Some furniture in Egyptian taste recorded. Generally plain mahogany furniture, typically: chairs, bookcases, chests of drawers and dining tables etc. Furniture sometimes stamped. |
| **BULLOCK, George** | *fl.* 1804–18 | Liverpool and London | Furniture characterized by use of plant-inspired brass inlay; powerful architectural forms and use of marble slabs for tops to cabinets. Also used oak, sometimes inlaid with holly. Designed furniture made in his workshop. |
| **McLEAN, Firm of** | 1770–1825 | London | During Regency period, noted for rosewood and ormolu mounted tables and cabinets in elegant Louis XVI taste. Documented examples are labelled. |
| **MARSH and TATHAM** | *fl.* 1774–1840 | London | In various forms of partnership, involved in supply of furniture to Prince Regent for Carlton House and Brighton Pavilion. |
| **MORGAN and SANDERS** | 1801–20 | London | Famous as makers of patent and metamorphic furniture. Dining tables with their brass name-plate often found. Also made library chairs which converted into steps and a small writing table which had the appearance, when closed, of a globe on stand. |
| **OAKLEY, George** | *fl.* 1773–1819 | London | Furniture of 1809 identified as by him from Papworth Hall, Cambridge. In mahogany and satinwood, in the "Grecian" taste. Bookcases, small tables and bedroom furniture. |

### THE INFLUENCE OF ANTIQUITY

One valuable source of ideas for Regency furniture-makers was *Etchings, Representing the Best Examples of Ancient Ornamental Architecture; Drawn from the Originals in Rome* (1799) by Charles Heathcote Tatham (1772–1842). For example, one plate in the book, "Antique Seats of White Marble from Originals at Rome", included a representation of a marble stool, and this inspired the manufacture of a pair of similar-looking beech and mahogany stools painted to simulate marble. This type of "reproduction" furniture, based directly on Classical exemplars, would probably have been intended for a formal sculpture gallery or an entrance hall.

Another influential figure who based his designs on models from the antique world was Thomas Hope (1769–1831), who was born into a wealthy Dutch banking family. Hope studied architecture from an early age and, on a Grand Tour which included Egypt, Greece, Sicily and Spain, spent eight years making sketches of architectural remains. He later bought an Adam house in Duchess Street, London, and installed there his collection of antique vases and ancient and modern sculpture in rooms specially created by himself. The furniture and other modern works of art which made up the ensemble were, to a large extent, also designed by Hope and were sophisticated interpretations of mainly Greek, Roman and Egyptian styles, though French Empire was also an influence.

Hope's *Household Furniture and Interior Decoration* (1807), illustrating his pieces at Duchess Street, is perhaps the most significant collection of furniture designs published during the Regency period and greatly influenced commercial cabinet makers.

Hope's furniture exhibits purity of line and appositeness in its use of embellishment – for example, bacchanalian masks on an urn suitable for a dining room and a sleeping greyhound on a day-bed.

**Thomas Chippendale the Younger** Hope's pure style set a standard which few commercial cabinet-makers could follow. One notable exception, however, is the early 19th-century work of Thomas Chippendale the Younger (1749–1822) for Sir Richard Colt Hoare at Stourhead, Wiltshire. This has much of the tension and confidence in design that is associated with Hope's furniture. For example, the mahogany library chairs, with their low curved backs resting neatly on supports like Egyptian caryatids (carved upright figures) for the front

legs, are both original and elegant. Apart from their brass castors, there is no additional embellishment and it is the design and quality of the timber alone which make them outstanding. Equally fine is the large library desk with freestanding sphinx-head caryatids at the ends and similar pilasters at the sides supporting heads of Greek philosophers.

**CENTRE TABLE**
Calamander veneer, ormolu mounts and gilding;
**c. 1810**

Inspired by a Hope design, this table is given great richness by its exotic veneer. Unusual timbers were much prized during the Regency period. (*Right*)

**STOOL**
Mahogany and parcel-gilt;
**c. 1810**

The design of this lion-headed X-frame stool is taken directly from one illustrated in Thomas Hope's *Household Furniture*, 1807. Hope also showed a version with goat heads. (*Left*)

**INKSTAND**
Amboyna, ebony, inlaid brass and ormolu mounts;
**c. 1805**

Regency furniture often drew directly on classical sources; the balanced form of this magnificent inkstand is based on a Roman tomb. It displays a notable use of materials. (*Below*)

GEORGE SMITH

With his book *A Collection of Designs for Household Furniture and Interior Decoration* (published in three parts from 1805, as a single book 1808), George Smith (*c.*1786–1826) was the first designer truly to popularize contemporary Regency taste. Little is known about Smith and, although he is recorded in contemporary trade directories as a cabinet-maker, there is scant evidence of his activity in this field and no surviving documented furniture. Nor has there ever been any substantiation of his claim to be "Upholder [Upholsterer] Extraordinary" to the Prince of Wales (later George IV), to whom, with permission, he dedicated his book.

The furniture designs Smith published are a most attractive collection which, if judged by the considerable number of surviving pieces inspired by them, were highly successful in promoting what he himself termed his "most approved and elegant taste". The designs, far less rigorous than those of Tatham and Hope, are embellished with popular motifs in Classical, Gothic and Chinese style. Many of the 158 plates in the book reveal a delightful sense of fantasy in Smith, although on occasion the furniture is somewhat overladen with ornamentation. Beds are covered with colourful and elaborate upholstery; one is constructed in the form of Roman spears and banners, another has carvings of draped figures holding up the canopy and standing on plinths in the form of candelabra. Chimeras (carved animals) and caryatids support tables, desks, commodes and wardrobes. A "Dwarf Library Bookcase", appropriately inscribed "Homer" and "Virgil", has ends in the form of antique cineraria (urns containing cremation ashes). There are two designs for tables "in the Chinese style" and a scheme for the "Decoration of a Drawing Room in the Chinese taste", complete with painted walls, pagoda fireplace, vases of bamboo shoots and hanging "Chinese" lanterns.

Smith's work in the Gothic vein is typical of that of the early Regency period and, as with 18th-century Gothic, is more concerned with the quaint appearance of its quatrefoils, crock-

**CLOCK**
*Benjamin Vulliamy*
**Black marble and ormolu;**
**1808**

The design of this clock was influenced by drawings made on Napoleon's Egyptian campaign. An identical clock is in the Victoria and Albert Museum, London. Vulliamy (1747–1811) was a major supplier of clocks and metalware to the Prince Regent. (*Below*)

**ARMCHAIR**
Painted and parcel-gilt wood; **c. 1810**

This piece is based directly on a design for "Drawing Room Chairs" in George Smith's *A Collection of Designs for Household Furniture...*, 1808. Classically inspired animal heads and legs regularly appear on Regency furniture. (*Left*)

ets and pointed arches than with historically accurate use of such motifs or with the original forms of medieval English furniture.

CHINOISERIE

The first chinoiserie (objects in Chinese or pseudo-Chinese style) was the 17th-century European furniture, ceramics, silver and textiles influenced by imports from China via the trade routes. In the main (porcelain and pottery being exceptions), chinoiserie produced in England consisted of already fashionable European forms and only their decoration was Chinese. Regency chinoiserie reflected the continuing influence of the East which developed in late-17th-century England and was later popular as part of the Rococo style. In the late 18th and early 19th centuries, the style survived the onset of Neo-Classicism by the use of Chinese

and Japanese lacquer panels, together with European imitations, to decorate ormolu-mounted desks and cabinets.

Undoubtedly the most extraordinary chinoiserie interiors from the Regency period are those at the Royal Pavilion, Brighton.

### ACKERMANN'S *REPOSITORY*

There is no better overview of design during the central years of the Regency period than the furniture designs which appeared in *The Repository of Arts, Literature, Commerce, Manufactures, Fashions and Politics* (1809–28), a series of magazines published by the German-born Rudolph Ackermann (1764–1834).

The first issue of *The Repository* showed two of George Smith's designs: a *chaise-longue* and a window seat. Throughout, Ackermann was apparently able to persuade leading cabinet-makers to provide him with designs.

**BOOKCASE**
*Design from George Smith's A Collection of Designs for Household Furniture...*
**1807**

Smith's Gothic style makes use of arches, crockets, quatrefoils and tracery on otherwise conventional furniture. Later designers showed a greater understanding of Gothic forms and structure. (*Left*)

**CENTRE TABLE**
Lacquer with brass banding;
**c. 1815**

One of a pair, this end standard table was formerly at Warwick Castle. A typical example of Regency chinoiserie, the top is of Chinese lacquer but the frieze and legs are "japanned" in imitation of oriental work. The table is a standard Regency type, variants of which might be found in mahogany or rosewood. (*Right*)

# THE BRIGHTON PAVILION

The outstanding British example of chinoiserie in interior decoration is to be found in the Royal Pavilion, Brighton. It reflects the combined tastes of the architect John Nash (1752–1835), who rebuilt Henry Holland's original in 1815; of the decorators Frederick Crace (1779–1859) and Robert Jones; and of the Prince Regent.

Although much restored, the ground floor has a variety of fantastic schemes. The walls in the principal corridor are decorated with painted bamboo branches and *rocaille* (shell and rock motifs) in blue on a pink ground and the banqueting room has large Chinese figure groups, framed within painted bamboo borders. Both schemes are based on the original decoration. The music room, the *tour de force*, has a gold and red ground decoration of Chinese landscapes and buildings. Throughout, columns turn into palm trees, a cast-iron staircase appears to be made of bamboo and light fittings are clung to by swirling Chinese dragons. Elward, Marsh and Tatham supplied cabinets and chairs in beechwood, carved and painted to simulate bamboo.

Imitation bamboo furniture was popular throughout the period (and indeed for the rest of the century), particularly for bedrooms. Also found are small cabinets and tables with fanciful polychrome chinoiserie scenes, sometimes with *tôle peinte* (painted metal panels). Other typically Regency examples of popular

**THE CORRIDOR**
From John Nash's *Views of The Royal Pavilion Brighton*, 1826
Hand-coloured aquatint;
**c. 1820**

chinoiserie as decoration can be found on tea-caddies, occasional tables, coasters (*papier-mâché* containers for decanters), hand-screens and work-boxes. The decoration is most commonly in gold on a black ground, but other backgrounds include white, red, green and brown. Another form of chinoiserie, found on the same range of pieces, was penwork. In this technique the design was "voided" on the wood, which was often prepared with a coating of gesso. The background was inked in, usually in black, ornamental details on the design were then carried out in fine line work with a pen.

---

Contributions were made by the London cabinet-makers Morgan and Sanders (active 1801–20) and John Taylor (1821–9). Morgan and Sanders are remembered for their metamorphic furniture (adjustable dining tables, portable chairs, collapsible beds and the like) and their patent furniture (pieces that usually incorporated some mechanical device, the invention of which was protected by a patent).

Before setting up on his own, Taylor had provided designs for the cabinet-maker George Oakley (active 1773–1840), recorded at various London addresses. Oakley appears to have had a significant business, but little of his work has been identified. His best known commission, from which a considerable amount of elegant "Grecian-style" furniture has been recorded, was in 1809 for Charles Madryll Cheere of Papworth Hall, Cambridge.

**WRITING AND GAMES TABLE**
*Design from Ackermann's Repository of Arts...*
Hand-coloured aquatint;
**February 1814**

The table was "intended to serve the double purpose of usefulness and pleasure.... it is convenient as a breakfast or sofa table.... a convenient writing table.... for the games of chess, drafts, backgammon &c."

Two other well-known London firms of cabinet-makers who each provided Ackermann with one design were William and Edward Snell (*c*.1788–1839) and Morel and Hughes (1790–1830).

Year by year, the designs which appeared in *The Repository* reflected the developing current taste for such revival styles as Neo-Classical, Egyptian, French Empire and Gothic. The magazine also included designs for patent and metamorphic furniture, as well as a wide range of designs for window curtains, and is a consistently useful guide to methods and materials used in upholstery.

In two instances, Ackermann illustrated the work of designers whose furniture was in the forefront of fashion. Between 1816 and 1822 there were at least 12 designs by the cabinet-maker George Bullock (see next section). And from 1825 to 1827 the magazine published 27 plates of "Gothic Furniture" by A. C. Pugin (1762–1832), perhaps assisted by his son A. W. N. Pugin (1812–52), one of the most influential of all 19th-century architect-designers.

### GEORGE BULLOCK

No cabinet-maker embodies the eclecticism and vigour of Regency design to a greater degree than George Bullock. Beginning to practise as a cabinet-maker in Liverpool, he is first recorded there in 1804, when he was in partnership with William Stokes. In 1814 he moved to London where, with the financial backing of Colonel Charles Fraser, he lived and worked in a prestigious house in Tenterden Street. Modern

**LIBRARY READING CHAIRS**
*Design from Ackermann's Repository of Arts...*
Hand-coloured aquatint;
**September 1810**

———

*(Above)*

**SIDE CHAIR**
*George Bullock*
Mahogany; **c. 1815**

———

*(Right)*

**GOTHIC LIBRARY TABLE**
*From Ackermann's Repository of Arts...*
Hand-coloured aquatint;
**March 1826**

———

*(Below)*

workshops were erected at the end of his garden, fronting on to Oxford Street. Bullock's gregarious nature and artistic personality attracted a sophisticated patronage, which included the novelist Sir Walter Scott. Perhaps his most famous commission was to provide the British government with furniture and household supplies for Napoleon's use in exile on St Helena. Bullock's reputation rests mainly on this brief London period before his untimely death aged 35.

Bullock was a designer of considerable

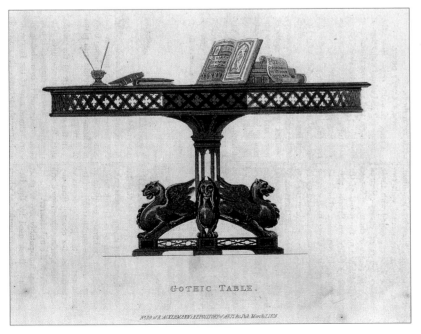

GOTHIC TABLE.

## SHERATON'S *CABINET DICTIONARY*

Thomas Sheraton (1751–1806) trained as a cabinet-maker but from 1793 supported his family by writing. His second book, *The Cabinet Dictionary* (1803), is an important collection of furniture designs and illustrates many characteristic features and motifs associated with Regency furniture

Many of the 500 or so subscribers to the *Dictionary* were cabinet-makers, and this demonstrates how important such pattern books were in disseminating styles. At the back of the book is a list of more than 250 "... Master Cabinet-Makers, Upholsterers and Chair Makers, in and about London, for 1803". This valuable compendium indicates how large the furniture trade was becoming.

The 79 principal plates illustrate a wide range of furniture, including chairs, tables, book-cases, sofas and mirrors. Sheraton's designs include caryatids, sabre legs, lion-masks, animal feet and X-supports for chairs.

**LIBRARY TABLES**
*Design from Thomas Sheraton's The Cabinet Dictionary*
Engraving; 1802

**DEER CANDELABRUM**
Pen and ink with black wash and watercolour;
**February 1819**

Derived from classical sources, probably by Piranesi, the drawing shows a candelabrum by George Bullock. In 1819 an example was sold from his house in Tenterden Street, London. Unlike Sheraton, Bullock did not produce a pattern book.

---

**DESK**
*Design attributed to Thomas Hopper (1776–1856)*
Oak, with limestone top;
**c. 1830**

This Norman Revival desk was made for Penrhyn Castle, North Wales.

talent, capable of working in many styles; the "Tracings by Thomas Wilkinson from the designs of the late Mr George Bullock 1820", provide ample evidence of his ability. Most of his surviving designs and furniture are in Neo-Classical style. However, from 1804–5 he also worked in the Gothic-Revival style, which was developing as the result of growing antiquarian research into Britain's past.

Throughout his career, Bullock supplied fur-

**SIDE CHAIR**
*Design attributed to Edward Blore (1787–1879)*
Ebonized beech; **c. 1830**

This antiquarian chair, based

on a mid-17th-century English example, formed part of the furnishings of Lambeth Palace.

niture appropriate for "Old English Mansions", to quote from the title page of *Furniture with Candelabra* (1826; full edition 1838) published by his collaborator Richard Bridgens (1785–1846). This "Old English" style is exemplified by the oak and painted furniture Bullock supplied to Battle Abbey, Sussex (1816–18).

In its use of flat-pattern ornament based on British plant forms, Bullock's work has a vitality which clearly anticipates later 19th-century designers such as A. W. N. Pugin, Owen Jones and Dr Christopher Dresser.

## BRASS INLAY

The British passion for collecting grand French furniture reached a high point during the first quarter of the 19th century. Massive dispersals of the collections of the French Crown and nobility took place following the French Revolution. The Prince Regent, the writer William Beckford and the Duke of Wellington were among the notable figures who took advantage of the opportunities offered. These three collectors all owned examples of Boulle (tortoiseshell and brass marquetry) furniture (see p. 76) dating from the 17th and 18th centuries; and the appearance in England of pieces ornamented in this style (described at the time as buhl) had a profound effect on the decoration of early 19th century domestic furniture.

Brass inlay was used for furniture decoration in four main ways. The simplest was as stringing (thin lines) or slightly broader strips. In 1803 Thomas Sheraton wrote: "Small lines of brass are now much in use in English

**WRITING TABLE**
*Louis Le Gaigneur*
Ebony, with brass inlay and ormolu mounts; **c. 1815**
(Below)

**SOFA TABLE**
*George Bullock*
Rosewood with brass inlay and ormolu mounts;
**c. 1815**
(Above)

furniture, and looks very handsome in black rose and other dark wood grounds." The second use was to create decorative borders of anthemions (stylized honeysuckle-flower designs), scrolls, Greek-key (maze-like) patterns and other motifs on various types of furniture, including sofas and chair backs.

The third use of brass inlay was as complete boulle panels on cabinet doors and table tops, usually on a wooden ground rather than the tortoiseshell used by the French. Finally, brass inlay was used in French-style brass and tortoiseshell boulle marquetry on a small group of Louis XIV-Revival pieces made by Louis Le Gaigneur of London (c.1814–c.1821), Thomas Parker, also of London (1805–30) and some other cabinet-makers. These near-copies of French prototypes were doubtless produced to make up a shortfall in the supply of imported originals caused by excess demand. The only pieces of this description identified to date are some coffers on stands, writing tables and inkstands.

SURROUNDED BY A FEVERISH PACE OF SCIENTIFIC AND TECHNOLOGICAL
ADVANCES, THE PEOPLE OF VICTORIAN BRITAIN SEEMED TO FIND A
REASSURING FAMILIARITY IN ADOPTING PAST STYLES
FOR THEIR FURNISHINGS.

# VICTORIAN REVIVALS

The seeds of a whole range of historical revivals in furniture had already germinated by the beginning of Queen Victoria's reign (1837–1901), chief among them being Gothic, Elizabethan, Louis Quatorze and Renaissance. Most were stylistically mixed, borrowing elements from one another in a way that appalled contemporary purists but delighted the public, who were not much concerned with historical accuracy.

These revivals fitted in with the needs of an increasingly affluent middle class, who, anxious to display their wealth as conspicuously as possible, made novelty a lodestar of acquisition. In furniture the new was sought not only in design and ornamentation but in material, and exotic woods became increasingly favoured and, through the growth of a colonial empire, increasingly available. Mahogany, satinwood and rosewood continued to be favoured, but even more sought after were elaborately figured (grained) woods, such as walnut and the expensive amboyna, thuja, purplewood (amaranth) and calamander (coromandel). In many instances these were combined with other timbers, both native and imported.

Marquetry became more popular than ever, and metals were increasingly used, both as decoration, in the form of inlaid brass or ormolu (gilt-bronze) mounts, and in their own right, as in cast-iron garden and other mass-produced furniture and brass bedsteads.

Developments in papier-mâché manufacture produced a material of sufficient strength to enable it to be used not just for trays and boxes but, from the 1830s onwards, for tables, chairs and even beds. And its decorative possibilities – it lent itself to being inlaid with pearl shell, gilded, bronzed and painted in brilliant colours on lustrous dark backgrounds – appealed to the exuberant tastes of the Victorians.

Other manufacturing developments played a part in the growth of the florid Victorian style of interior decoration. One was the introduction of the coiled spring in the late 1820s, which led to the bulky upholstery with deep buttoned seating that was characteristic of the Victorian interior. Another development was the use of spirit varnishes, known as French polish, first adopted in the Regency period and now taken up with increasing enthusiasm by furniture manufacturers, who used them to produce a brilliant "piano finish" that far outshone the mellow lustre obtained from beeswax and turpentine. Both coiled springing and French polish were liberally applied to old as well as new furniture, regardless of suitability.

The introduction of wafer-thin machine-cut veneers, and mechanically carved decoration also contributed to the extravagant Victorian style. According to the architectural and horticultural writer J. C. Loudon (1783–1843) all that most people of the time wanted was "to get a display of rich workmanship at as cheap a rate as possible".

### ELIZABETHAN REVIVAL

Mechanical carving was well suited to the production of furniture in the Elizabethan taste, with its panels of open decoration and strapwork (interlacing bands) and profusion of knobs

**BOOKCASE**
Mahogany; **c. 1840**

The foliate decoration and "jewels" on the pilasters, the heavy twist-turned columns, the pierced strapwork and the jewelled lower doors are typically hybrid on this Elizabethan Revival bookcase. (*Right*)

**NEST OF TABLES**
*Papier-mâché; c. 1850*

These tables, with turned supports and gilded decoration on the legs and stretchers, were probably made in Birmingham or Wolverhampton, where English *papier-mâché* production was concentrated. They have painted and gilded tops and inlays of mother-of-pearl. The largest table has a painted farmyard scene after J. F. Herring; the next, a mother-of-pearl inlaid chessboard; and the others two painted scenes of dogs after George Armfield. The production of such high-quality *papier-mâché* furniture was a feature of the middle decades of the 19th century. (*Left*)

**CENTRE TABLE**
*A.W.N. Pugin*
**Rosewood; c. 1835**

This design appears in Pugin's *Gothic Furniture* (1835). Rosewood was an unusual choice, suggesting an individual commission: Pugin's preference was for oak.

crowning a chair) and other decoration typical of a century later.

The strictly classical architect C. R. Cockerell went so far as to criticize Elizabethan Revival as "an imperfect and incongruous imitation of both Grecian and Gothic styles", but its popularity was bolstered by publications such as T. F. Hunt's *Exemplars of Tudor Architecture adapted to Modern Habitations* (1830), Henry Shaw's *Specimens of Ancient Furniture* (1836) and Joseph Nash's *Mansions of England in the Olden Time* (1838–49), and it persisted well into the 1840s.

## GOTHIC REVIVAL

The Elizabethan style and the Gothic had much in common. Both were seen as particularly English and therefore patriotic; both were rooted in the cult of the picturesque; both were adopted by romantics hungry for novelty; and both primarily used native woods, such as oak or walnut.

Gothic architectural embellishments, such as crockets, cusps and pinnacles, were used in Victorian furniture of standard manufacture, but the revival of the Gothic style pursued by the English architect and interior designer A. W. N. Pugin (1812–52) was much more radical. It was a search for historical accuracy and aesthetic purity and in this respect had more in common with Neo-Classicism than with the old romantic associations of the Gothic. In 1835 Pugin published *Gothic Furniture in the Style of the 15th Century* in which his assimilation of medieval forms of construction is evident. However, it was in the solidly simple furniture, its decoration pared to an elegant minimum, that he designed for the House of Lords and for country houses during the 1840s that Pugin most nearly attained his interior design ideals. These pieces clearly exerted a considerable influence on later furniture designers, such as William Burges (1827–81), William Morris (1834–96), Charles Eastlake (1836–1906) and Bruce Talbert (1838–81).

## LOUIS QUATORZE REVIVAL

Louis Quatorze was the label given to the vast array of furniture of more or less French influence that filled the homes of the Victorian middle classes. It actually embraced the Louis Quinze, or Neo-Rococo, style as well, and consequently this type of furniture is often simply referred to as Louis. In the more expensive examples weighty baroque forms were overlaid

and bosses. This was a style associated in the minds of the early Victorians with the "Merrie England" and "Olden Time" romanticized in Sir Walter Scott's novels. Although some of its proponents, such as the architect Anthony Salvin, were serious antiquarians who paid meticulous attention to stylistic accuracy, most producers of Elizabethan Revival furniture mixed genuine Tudor motifs with the barley-sugar turnings, carved crestings (ornamentation

with asymmetrically curvaceous rococo ornament and gilding was often used; but even the relatively unostentatious pieces rarely escaped rococo flourishes such as cabriole (double-curved) legs and C-scrolled borders. Particularly sumptuous were literal copies of French 18th-century marquetry pieces by the finest English craftsmen.

Closely related to the Neo-Rococo was the naturalistic style, which looked back to the early 18th century *genre pittoresque*, characterized by lavish use of plant and animal forms in its decorative motifs.

### RENAISSANCE REVIVAL
During the 1840s classical forms re-emerged in a revived Renaissance, or Italian, style. This was another rag-bag of ornamental ideas, as shown by a contemporary writer's pronouncement that Renaissance design "may contain the classical orders and ornaments combined with conventional Byzantine scrollwork, Moorish tracery and interlacings, scrolled shields, fiddle-shapes, and strap-work, natural imitations of animal or vegetable forms of every description, and the grotesque arabesques."

### OTHER REVIVALS
The furniture displayed at the 1851 Great Exhibition was marked by dazzling craftsmanship and stupendous decorative excess; and most middle-class Victorians continued to feel

**MIRRORED SIDEBOARD**
Wood and marble

The carved ornament is a heady mixture of baroque masks, Elizabethan "jewels", rococo birds and curlicues, and classical borders and pilasters. (*Above*)

**SIDE CABINET**
*Jackson of London*
Ebony, purpleheart, ormolu, lapis lazuli and watercolour; **c. 1855**

This exhibition-quality piece, in the French style of Eugène Prignot, is of the type favoured by the conspicuously rich. (*Right*)

comfortable with lavishly decorated historical pastiches. During the following decade, however, the plainer Old English style came to be favoured, and a little later the Queen Anne, both much influenced by architects of the domestic revival such as Eden Nesfield (1835–88) and Richard Norman Shaw (1831–1912).

**DESIGN FOR A SIDEBOARD**

Made for the prestigious Leeds furnisher, Marsh, Jones & Cribb, the design is for a recessed sideboard in the Victorian Renaissance manner. (*Above*)

Good-quality reproductions of French furniture continued to be made for the affluent by firms such as John Webb, Wright & Mansfield and Edwards & Roberts. At the same time, almost all manufacturers purveyed furniture in the quintessentially English styles of Chippendale, Hepplewhite and, by the end of the century, Sheraton.

**COMBINED SECRETAIRE AND WHATNOT**
Walnut, ebony and brass; **mid 19th century**

The well-figured veneers are contrasted with ebony borders on the drawers and a brass galleried shelf above. A fall-front is disguised as two drawers in this useful, well-made piece, of a type seen in many a comfortable Victorian interior.

## J. C. LOUDON

The work of the architect John Claudius Loudon (1783–1843) embodies Victorian eclectic taste at its best. A man of advanced social views, he welcomed the scientific and technological innovations of his age, and was among the first to emphasize the importance of developments such as wire springing and cast iron for the furniture industry. His *Encyclopaedia of Cottage, Farm and Villa Architecture and Furniture* (1833) included designs inspired by Classical, Gothic, Tudor, Italianate, and even "Hindoo" and Swiss styles. Loudon rejected the indiscriminate contemporary preoccupation with decorative effects and novelty for its own sake. He believed that furniture should have a unity of style and a suitability of purpose, and many of his designs are strikingly simple for their time.

AFTER YEARS OF FOLLOWING THE STYLES OF OTHER EUROPEAN
COUNTRIES, FRENCH FURNITURE-MAKERS OF THE LATE 17TH CENTURY
AND AFTER BECAME THE CONTINENT'S LEADERS IN FASHION.

# FRANCE

When the Renaissance spread from Italy to France at the end of the 15th century and when, as a result, French artists and craftsmen rediscovered classical antiquity, they adopted two features of it in particular. One was the Grotesque style of ornamentation – distorted, fantastical animal, plant and other forms. The other feature was the use of architectural forms – for example, classical columns, cornices and pediments.

In furniture the French Renaissance style can be broadly divided into two periods, one roughly coincident with the reign of Francis I (1515–47), the other beginning with the reign of Henry II (1547–59) and lasting until roughly the 1580s when the French Wars of Religion dis-

### CAQUETOIRE CHAIR
Walnut; **second half of 16th century**

Sparse and elegant architectural forms, including the *trompe-l'oeil* arcade carved on the back, are characteristic of this period, when chairs were not upholstered but would have had removable cushions. (*Right*)

### BUFFET
Walnut with marble inlay; **mid 16th century**

The low relief carving of scrolls and mythological figures, and the inlaid marble plaques, are subordinate to the classical architectural framework of this piece. The maker will have been familiar with the work of Jacques Androuet du Cerceau. (*Left*)

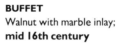

rupted creative activity. In the first period panels of Grotesque carvings cover every available surface and architectural forms are subordinate to decoration. In the second the reverse is the case and graceful proportion predominates over carving, which at the same time becomes more geometric and restrained.

Oak, the principal wood used during the Gothic period, was replaced in French Renaissance furniture by the darker, oilier walnut, easier to carve and producing a high sheen when polished. Carving was supplemented by other decorative techniques: inlays of wood, precious stones, ivory and other materials. But metal mounts (adjuncts such as hinges, handles, locks and corner pieces) were generally eschewed as being too obtrusive.

The principal showpiece of the period was the buffet (sideboard). Typically, this had two compartments, one above the other and each with two doors (but there were other forms). The door panels were carved and framed by architectural features. Tables, supported during the first period by elaborately carved end-pieces, became more elegant by mid-century and stood on legs in the form of slender, turned columns on plain bases. Similarly, chairs at first had a wide, tall back and were supported by side-pieces, but in later chairs, known as *caqueteuses* (gossip chairs), the back became narrower and the side-pieces were replaced by slender columns. Beds, especially their headboards, were often extravagantly carved.

The most important regional style in French Renaissance furniture is that of the Île de France, characterized by refined architectural proportions. Also significant are the styles of Burgundy, marked by massive shapes and bold carving, and of the south, in which painting in many colours and marquetry are prominent.

### THE EARLY 17TH CENTURY

In the reigns of Henry IV (1589–1610) and Louis XIII (1610–43) Spanish, Dutch and German styles, techniques and materials joined those from Italy in influencing French art, particularly that of the court. So well were they assimilated in furniture-making that it is often difficult to determine the country of origin of pieces from this period. At the same time the Renaissance style continued in parallel, but with modifications: the architectural structures and elaborate ornament of the previous century gave way to mouldings (applied strips of carved wood), geometric carving and lathe-turned (rounded) legs, pedestals and so on.

The principal piece of furniture of the early 17th century was the cabinet. This was box-like, with two doors that opened to reveal drawers, and stood on a support of table height with turned legs. The favourite material for decorating cabinets was ebony, an expensive wood of which craftsmen made lavish and clever use. Thick sheets of ebony veneer were decorated

**TABLE**
Walnut; **mid 16th century**

In this table, carving and architectural decoration are equally important. It is provincial in origin. (*Above*)

**CABINET ON STAND**
Ebony; **first half of 17th century**

The carving and mouldings enhance this piece. (*Below*)

### ARMCHAIR
Giltwood; **mid 17th century**

Leaf scroll carving, hairy paw feet and "mutton bone" legs and stretchers are typical of this period, as is the cut velvet upholstery. (*Left*)

### CONSOLE TABLE
Giltwood and red marble; **c. 1715**

Inspired by a design of Nicolas Pineau, the light-hearted motifs such as dolphins, masks of bearded men and hoof feet are typical of the lightening of style at the beginning of the 18th century. (*Below*)

with low-relief carving, then applied to the cheap wood carcass of the piece. The inside was sometimes crafted in ebony to resemble architectural façades with turned columns, pediments and doorways; it might also incorporate tortoiseshell and silver ornaments or classical perspective decoration executed in wood and ivory marquetry.

Large cupboards and buffets were also a feature of this period. Many were of the same basic construction as their Renaissance predecessors but were decorated with heavy mouldings framing panels of geometric carving or, in the case of buffets, with veneer.

Chairs, tables and much decoration for case furniture (cabinets and cupboards) were all made in fruitwood and walnut. The construction of some included complicated lathe turning (a technique now in widespread use), such as spiral twist. Chairs became more comfortable: seats and backs were padded and covered

with brightly coloured embroidered velvet, to match the decoration of the rest of the room.

The engravings of Abraham Bosse, which provide the most vivid views of interiors of this period, show the extent to which textiles were used to cover furniture. Tables were draped with cloth, chairs had their legs covered in the upholstery material of seat and back, and beds (none of which survive, since they were discarded once they were out of fashion) were comprehensively draped to reveal no wood at all. The increased convenience, as well as comfort, of furniture of this period, as depicted by Bosse, is testified to by the large number of small tables that survive. These have oblong or octagonal tops and turned legs.

## LOUIS XIV

The long reign of the "Sun King" Louis XIV (1643–1715) is noted for his absolutism and for the splendour of the king's courts at Versailles and Paris. After Louis's minority, which lasted until 1661, the dominant cultural figure in France was the interior designer Charles Lebrun (1619–90). Lebrun was the first director of the Gobelins tapestry workshop, later named *Manufacture Royale des meubles de la Couronne*, which contained a cabinet-making department run by the Italian Domenico Cucci (*c.*1640–1705). This specialized in elaborate cabinets decorated with panels of Florentine *pietre dure* (coloured hard-stone inlay) and mounted with gilt bronze.

The Dutch cabinet-maker Pierre Golle (1620–84), who worked in Paris from the 1640s onward, belonged to a different tradition: his pieces are a development of the great ebony cabinets of the early 17th century. Golle created court furniture of simple, usually traditional shapes, such as cabinets on stands, tables and kneehole desks, using colourful marquetry of woods, ivory, shell and metals.

As in the first half of the century, *ameublements* (sets of seat furniture), together with matching bed and wall hangings, are found in profusion; but cabinet work is rare. Large chairs and armchairs were carved with scrolls and gilded and were covered with velvet or silk embroidered with gold and silver thread. The giltwood side table first made its appearance at this time. Such tables often have straight, tapering legs, a scroll-shaped stretcher (strut connecting the legs) and a frieze carved with strapwork and other stylized motifs. They were known simply as *pieds de table* (table supports),

since the costly marble top was always considered more important than the comparatively cheap support.

**Case furniture** Cabinets, cupboards and desks of the Louis XIV period are distinguished by their opulence and size. The Gobelins workshop produced cabinets in ebony inlaid with Florentine *pietre dure* panels; gilt bronze was used to frame the panels and also for figural mounts, which supply architectural shape. The Gobelins and others also made cabinets in wood marquetry, with a central door, drawers at the side and often giltwood figural supports. Matching sets (now sometimes known as triads) consisting of a table, two candlestands and a mirror frame, in wood marquetry or lacquer, were extremely popular.

The use of metal and tortoiseshell marquetry, generally known as boulle, after André-Charles Boulle, its prime exponent (see box), had become widespread by the 1680s and is found

**CABINET**
*Attributed to Pierre Golle*
Ebony, gilt-bronze, tortoiseshell, mother-of-pearl, ivory and lacquer;
**c. 1650**

The Flemish tradition is apparent in this piece. Golle used many materials and techniques to create a varied effect.

## BOULLE MARQUETRY

Boulle marquetry is a furniture veneer of brass set in tortoiseshell. It is named not after its inventor, the French cabinet-maker Pierre Gole (*fl.* 1644–84), but after its most noted practitioner, André-Charles Boulle (1642–1732).

The veneer was produced by fastening tightly together a sheet of brass and one of tortoiseshell, placing on top a sheet of paper marked with a pattern, then cutting with a fretsaw around the pattern and through the sheets of material below. The cut-out piece of brass then fitted perfectly into the space left in the tortoiseshell. Much of Boulle's furniture was made in pairs, the piece with the brass-in-tortoiseshell marquetry known as *première partie*, and the other piece, veneered with the "negative" of cut-out tortoiseshell set in brass, called *contre partie*. Sometimes a mixture of both types was used on the same piece.

The marquetry pattern was usually one of scrolled foliage within geometric borders or of fanciful scenes inspired by the work of the decorator and designer Jean Bérain (1640–1711). Brass patterns were usually engraved, with, for example, tendrils or shading to produce a three-dimensional effect; and the tortoiseshell was often coloured, most commonly red or blue, by placing painted paper beneath it on the carcase of the furniture.

In the early years of boulle marquetry – approximately from 1660 to 1680 – pewter, ebony and walnut were also used, but after 1680 brass and tortoiseshell were almost exclusively employed.

**BOULLE MARQUETRY ARMOIRE ;** *Attributed to Noel Gérard ;* **early 18th century**

on various types of furniture. These include the *armoire* (large cupboard) and the *bureau à caissons* (kneehole desk), later known as the *bureau Mazarin*. This desk is the most commonly surviving piece of Louis XIV furniture. It usually has eight legs, either square and tapering or scroll-shaped, each set of four being joined by an X-shaped stretcher. There are three or four drawers at each side and one long, shallow drawer above the kneehole. In a variation called a *bureau brisé* (folding desk) the top folds back in the centre to reveal further small drawers inside and a writing surface.

**New designs** Towards the end of Louis' reign, André-Charles Boulle (see box) experimented with new furniture shapes and created two designs which were to prove more popular in the next century than any other: the *bureau plat* (writing table) and the commode (chest of drawers). The *bureau plat* is large, stands on four legs and has three drawers in the frieze at the front, usually genuine at one side and dummies at the other. Much more than the chest of drawers we know now, the finely ornamented commode was the focal point of a room, often being placed at the centre of the longest wall.

Both these pieces were originally decorated with boulle marquetry, but by the king's death this had been replaced by simpler geometric wood veneers.

### RÉGENCE AND LOUIS XV

After Louis XIV's death in 1715 the reaction against the grandiose that had set in towards the end of the king's reign continued under the regency by which France was ruled for the next eight years, during the minority of Louis XV (1715–74). The style of this period (roughly 1700–30), known as Régence, is less heavy and more graceful than that of the previous 40 years. In furniture plain wood veneer replaced boulle marquetry and gilt-bronze ornamentation was simplified.

Louis XV furniture continued this rejection of the weighty by introducing a rococo exuberance in which curves replaced angularity. Curvilinear motifs, such as water, plants, dragons and shells proliferated in carved wood, marquetry and gilt bronze, and the structure of pieces became all but invisible. On a Louis XV chair, for example, the legs, arms, seat and back all contribute to a single flowing curve, interrupted only by an occasional carving of, say, a leaf or rococo scroll.

Seat furniture and architectural furniture (furniture that forms part of the wall decoration), such as console tables (tables with no back legs, attached to a wall by brackets) and mirrors, were made of beech or walnut, joined and pegged invisibly and gilded or painted to

**COMMODE**
*Charles Cressent*
**Kingwood and gilt-bronze;
c. 1735-40**

This is a good example of Cressent's bold mounts. (*Above*)

**PAIR OF FAUTEUILS**
*Attributed to Nicolas Heurtaut*
**Giltwood; mid 18th century**

The flat-back armchair was designed to stand against a wall. (*Below*)

harmonize with the rest of the room. Case furniture, whose carcasses were often made cheaply from pine but sometimes constructed of oak, was veneered with exotic woods in geometric patterns known as parquetry, because of their resemblance to parquet floors.

By the 1740s flower marquetry had become popular. One technique consisted of tinting the inlays with dyes or in hot sand; the other, producing finer results, used inlays cut from across the grain of a wood whose grain itself formed the desired pattern. Veneering was sometimes carried out with lacquer, either Japanese, Chinese or a French imitation known as Vernis Martin. Case furniture also incorporated gilt-bronze mounts as adornment on projecting corners and on feet, as handles and as frames for marquetry panels.

**New furniture forms** Many new types and shapes of furniture appeared during the Louis XV period. The *fauteuil* (armchair), the most common type of chair, had a scrolled, heart-shaped seat and back and curved legs and arm rests; if the back was flat it was called *à la reine*, if curved *en cabriolet*. The *bergère* (easy chair) was large and comfortable and had upholstery under as well as on top of the arm rests. Console tables stood on exaggeratedly curved legs decorated with carvings – foliage on the legs themselves, a basket of flowers or a rococo scroll on the stretchers.

The commode was the principal piece of case furniture of this period. It had a curved front, sides and legs, and either two or three rows of drawers. The *bureau plat* competed with various new types of desk, such as the *secrétaire à*

*abattant* (fall-front writing desk), which had two doors and a writing-surface flap that when pulled down revealed small drawers inside.

Enchanting small *tables à écrire* (writing tables), with one drawer at the side, and sometimes a slide under the top, survive in all shapes and sizes. One is the *bonheur du jour* (small writing table with a recessed superstructure). Another, the *bureau à cylindre* (cylinder-top desk) reveals a writing surface when its quarter-cylindrical cover is slid back.

*Tables à transformations*, a speciality of German cabinet-makers, contained intricate locking devices, drawers, flaps and recesses, suitable for many uses, such as writing, hiding secret papers, needlework or (some drawers being convertible into kneelers) even praying.

### THE LATE 18TH CENTURY

Towards the end of Louis XV's reign, between about 1760 and 1770, the Rococo style that had long been favoured in interior design began gradually to be replaced by an emergent

## MENUISIERS AND EBENISTES

Until the Revolution in 1789 all furniture-makers in France belonged to the guild of woodworkers (which also included carpenters and coachbuilders). Furniture-makers consisted of two distinct categories: the *menuisier*, who made chairs, tables and other plain items; and the *ébéniste*, who made cabinets and other case furniture which was usually veneered (*ébéniste* derives from the early use of ebony as a veneer). Each was a specialized activity and a craftsman would work in one or the other.

Strict legislation governed furniture-making: *a maître* (master craftsman) had to serve a lengthy apprenticeship, produce a *chef d'oeuvre* (masterpiece) and pay a considerable sum of money before he could practise under his own name; he had to mark each piece with his own name (a procedure which has made establishing the provenance of French furniture relatively straightforward); officers of the guild held periodic quality checks and stamped approved pieces with the guild mark JME (*Juré des Menuisiers-Ébénistes*); and the practice of stamping furniture as a guarantee of quality was enforced by an edict of 1751.

**PAIR OF *FAUTEUILS***
*Stamped by Jean-Baptiste Sené*
Giltwood; *c.* 1780

The spirally fluted legs, shield-shaped back and delicate carving are characteristic of the work of Sené, one of the greatest of the Neo-Classical chair-makers.

Neo-Classicism. This was characterized by the use of Classical architectural forms and motifs, such as straight lines, symmetry, pilasters, fluting, rosettes, lion masks and leaf or bead mouldings. The gradual modification of the Rococo by the Neo-Classical, before the latter became dominant, is known as the Transitional style.

At the start of the transitional period furniture was still curvilinear in the Rococo manner but was acquiring Neo-Classical ornamentation. Then furniture shapes also began to incorporate Neo-Classical elements. For example, the commode retained its curved legs but its body became rectilinear. And in seat furniture a heart-shaped back was now often supported by fluted, tapering straight legs. These Neo-Classical shapes became increasingly decorated in the same style. The body of the commode, for example, was adorned with formal flower marquetry and a severe scroll frieze; gilt-bronze corner mounts were sometimes modelled on the triglyph (a three-grooved tablet in the Doric frieze) and mounts on the apron (the lower front edge of a piece) modelled on a smoking cassolette (incense vessel).

By 1770 Neo-Classicism had almost completely superseded the Rococo. Classical forms and motifs were, however, not applied to interior decoration with any solemnity but were used in a fanciful way that produced an elegant style well suited to the light architectural interiors of the day.

**Louis XVI** During the reign of Louis XVI (1774–92) few new types of furniture appeared; adaptations were simply made to the large number of pieces developed earlier. Seat

# FRENCH FURNITURE-MAKERS

| | | |
|---|---|---|
| **DE CERCEAU, Jacques** | c. 1515–c. 1585 | Architect, designer and engraver. From 1559 he published numerous series of decorative designs which were widely used by cabinet-makers as inspiration for shapes and decoration. |
| **BOSSE, Abraham** | c. 1605–76 | Architect, designer and engraver. Best known for his engraved representations of French interiors of the first half of the 17th century. |
| **LEBRUN, Charles** | 1619–90 | Architect and designer. Co-ordinator of the decoration of the Royal palaces from 1661 to 1683. He was responsible for the architectural aspect of early Louis XIV furniture. |
| **GOLE, Pierre** | c. 1620–84 | Ebéniste. Worked for the king from the 1650s to his death, producing cabinets, tables, desks, stands, cupboards, in marquetry of wood, ivory, or metal and tortoiseshell, as well as in lacquer. His style was influenced by his Dutch origin. |
| **BOULLE, André-Charles** | 1642–1732 | "Ebéniste, ciseleur, doreur, et sculpteur du Roi". Made famous the technique of marquetry in metal and tortoiseshell, employing it on bold, architecturally inspired pieces lavishly mounted in gilt-bronze. Worked for members of the royal family and sometimes for Louis XIV. |
| **CRESSENT, Charles** | 1685–1768 | Ebéniste. Trained originally as a sculptor. His cabinetwork, principally commodes, cabinets and bureaux plats, is decorated with bold sculptural mounts. |
| **VANRISAMBURGH, Bernard** | 1696–1766 | Ebéniste. The greatest cabinet-maker of the Louis XV period. He made commodes, small tables, secretaires and bureaux plats of gracious rococo shape, in end-cut flower marquetry or lacquer, decorated with finely chiselled fanciful gilt-bronze mounts. |
| **TILLIARD, Jean-Baptiste** | 1685–1766 | Menuisier. His pieces are distinguished by their generous shape, firm rococo scrolls and carving of flowers. |
| **OEBEN, Jean-François** | 1721–63 | Ebéniste. Produced marquetry commodes and "meubles à transformations" in the late Louis XV style; he was among the first to incorporate Neo-Classical detail in his furniture. |
| **RIESENER, Jean-Henri** | 1734–1806 | Ebéniste du Roi. Probably the most successful of all French 18th-century cabinet-makers. His huge quantity of work for the royal palaces is well known, in very fine marquetry, with gilt-bronze mounts chiselled to a perfection never before attained. |
| **WEISWEILER, Adam** | 1744–1820 | Ebéniste. Worked for the marchands-merciers, including Dominique Daguerre, producing furniture in rare materials such as Japanese lacquer and Sèvres porcelain, with gilt-bronze slender columns and applied arabesque frieze mounts. |
| **JACOB, Georges** | 1739–1814 | Menuisier. Established himself as the leading chairmaker in France. His work for Marie-Antoinette consisted of richly carved sets of chairs, with elaborate details such as legs shaped like quivers full of arrows. When Georges retired in 1796 his two sons took over the business. They filled Napoleon's palaces with lavish pieces, in mahogany with gilt-bronze. |
| **WERNER, Jean Jacques** | 1791–1849 | The principal furniture-maker of the Empire period. He took part in the industrial exhibitions of the day and received many official orders. He used local woods such as ash in veneering. |
| **FOURDINOIS, Alexandre-Georges, and Henri-Auguste** | 1799–1871 1830–1907 | Suppliers of furniture to the Empress Eugénie. They worked in the Louis XVI style, but their speciality was the Renaissance. |

furniture lost all traces of the Rococo: legs were turned, tapered and fluted, the joint between legs and rails was made in the form of a cube with a rosette, and the square backs and seat frames were moulded and decorated with Classical friezes, such as ribbon twist. Beds and console tables had slender, fluted column uprights and architectural friezes.

Case furniture also acquired an angular look. Commodes were often square, though sometimes incorporating a breakfront façade (in which the centre part of the facade is shaped as a projecting panel) or half-moon shape. The *bureau plat, bonheur du jour, table à écrire* and

**TABLE**
*Signed by Martin-Guillaume Biennais*
Gilt-bronze and scagliola;
**late 18th century**

The top is decorated with scenes inspired by archaeological finds in Italy. (*Right*)

**SECRETAIRE À ABATTANT**
*Stamped by Martin Carlin*
Japanese lacquer and gilt-bronze; **c. 1780**

Carlin worked almost exclusively for the *marchand-merciers*. This piece belonged originally to Mlle Laguerre, a notorious Parisian opera singer and courtesan who died in 1782, at the age of 28, "épuisée par des excès de tout genre" ("worn out by excessive living").

*secrétaire* were all made with a square shape and straight, tapering, turned or square legs. They usually had a Grecian frieze in the upper part and gilt-bronze mouldings framing the main panel. The *console d'ébénisterie*, among the few new types of furniture to originate at this time was supported by column legs.

Pictorial marquetry continued to be used on case furniture. Common motifs were ruins in landscapes, exotic objects, such as Chinese tableware, and complex geometric forms. Gradually, however, plain veneer, especially in mahogany, began to supplant marquetry. Well-figured woods (woods with a distinctive grain), outlined with finely chiselled gilt bronze, were used, as was oriental lacquer. Panels of *pietre dure* or boulle marquetry, often scavenged from decrepit Louis XIV furniture, were often fixed to commodes and cabinets and given surrounds of ebony veneer. Plaques of Sèvres porcelain

were also applied to case furniture.

**Marchands-merciers** In the 18th century there emerged a group of dealers called *marchands-merciers* whose function was to supply furniture and decorative objects to a rich clientele. Through their position the *merciers* exerted considerable influence not just on the marketing of furniture but also on its design. Lazare-Duvaux, one of the most famous *merciers* of the reign of Louis XV, had a considerable hand in the design of the pieces he provided for the king's mistress Mme de Pompadour and others. Eventually, *merciers* came to control the work of all the specialists involved in the manufacture of a piece of furniture. Dominique Daguerre, the greatest *mercier* of the late 18th century, commissioned drawings, ordered plaques of specific shape and decoration from the Sèvres porcelain factory, bought lacquer cabinets to be dismantled for their panels and arranged for gilt-bronze mounts to be made by leading metal-workers. This left only the making of the carcass and the final assembly to the *ébéniste*, who was thus reduced from designer to mere executant.

### DIRECTOIRE AND EMPIRE

The years following the Revolution in France were turbulent ones – anarchy, the Reign of Terror (1793–4), the Directorate (1795–9), its overthrow by Napoleon as consul (1799–1804) and finally his rule as emperor (1804–14). This political upheaval was mirrored by an artistic one. In furniture-making the dissolution of the guilds had a dramatic effect, opening up the trade to anyone who wished to practise it and ending the centuries-old specializations. In addition, the difficult economic conditions of the times imposed austerity on a hitherto luxurious craft. Elaborate veneered and gilt-bronze-mounted pieces were no longer commercially possible; as a result, much simple painted furniture was produced and the only veneers used were of plain mahogany.

**Directoire** The style of design prevalent from approximately 1793 to 1804 is named Directoire, after the Directorate. Its principal characteristic was the use of arabesque and Etruscan forms and motifs – for example, fanciful animals, sea lions, eagles, serpents, lozenges and palmettes (stylized palm leaves).

Furniture shapes were simpler than under Louis XVI, and there was less variety than before. Commodes were plain, often with paw feet. For the first time dining tables, of mahogany, were made to be seen and not hidden under a cloth. Seat furniture, usually painted in light colours, is perhaps the most original and graceful feature of the period. Legs were often shaped like sabres or cornucopias or were turned and tapering (but not fluted); backs were usually openwork with the top rail curling over like a scroll.

**Empire** The personal influence of the Emperor Napoleon upon the arts was considerable. To lend the regime an aura of strength and stability, he encouraged the development of a monumental style, based on massive, solid shapes and bold decoration. An enormous quantity of furniture was made for the imperial palaces and much surviving Empire furniture closely resembles known imperial commissions.

The main source of inspiration for the Empire style was the heavy, carved marble outdoor furniture of the Greco-Roman world. But

**DESIGN FOR MARCHEPIEDS (STOOLS) Early 19th century**

This appeared in the influential publication, *Meubles et Objets de Goût*, published by Pierre de la Mésangère from 1802 to 1835. (*Below*)

**DESIGN FOR TWO ARMCHAIRS AND A SECRETAIRE BOOKCASE**
**early 19th century**

These pieces, in mahogany and gilded and patinated bronze, show the influence of ancient furniture on Empire decoration. The figures on the *secrétaire* are of Egyptian inspiration. The design appeared in Pierre de la Mésangère's *Meubles et Objects de Goût*.

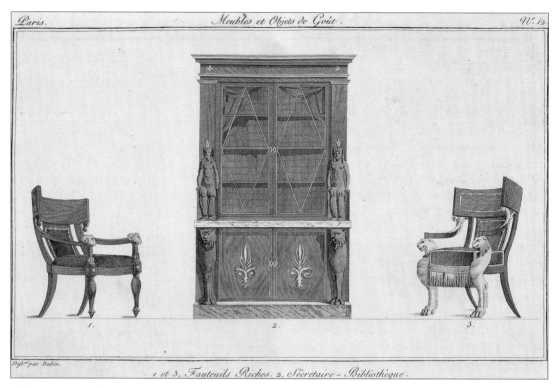

Paris.      Meubles et Objets de Goût.      N.º 12.

*Dess.ᵉ par Babin.*

*1 et 3, Fauteuils Riches. 2, Sécretaire - Bibliothèque.*

Egypt was another major influence: Napoleon's expedition to the country in 1799 had included artists who recorded what they saw, and this began a craze in France for anything Egyptian. As a result, decorative motifs on furniture began to include winged scarabs, mummies, sphinxes and hieroglyphs.

Empire seat furniture was made either of mahogany or giltwood. With their square backs and boldly carved front legs rising to form the supports of the arm rests, such seats appear to have been designed more to fit in with an imposing interior than with the sitter in mind. Large stools also survive, often with an X-frame construction in the shape of crossed sabres. Sets of commodes and *secrétaires* were often made with matching beds, dressing tables and looking glasses. Their fine mahogany veneers set off elaborate gilt-bronze mounts, pierced plaques or panels with military motifs. Large writing tables stood on massive carved end supports.

Adding to the generally sombre effect created by these heavy pieces were large bookcases of architectural shape. An innovation of this period is the psyche (cheval mirror).

## RESTORATION

The final downfall of Napoleon in 1815 saw the restoration of the Bourbon monarchy: Louis XVIII (1815–24), Charles X (1824–30) and Louis-Philippe (1830–48). This period coincided with the start of the Industrial Revolution

**PAIR OF *FAUTEUILS***
*Bois clair;* **c. 1825**

More comfortable forms are used for these chairs with flowing curves, executed in light-coloured wood with a darker inlay. The upholstery is stamped with Neo-Classical motifs.

and the rise of the middle classes, and the output of decorative furniture increased considerably to cater for the newly prosperous.

During the Restoration antiquity ceased to be the sole source of artistic inspiration. Interest in the art of many nations, brought about by easier foreign travel, and the rediscovery of a glorious national past through the historical fiction of Hugo and others led to what is known as the Romantic Revival. One aspect of this was the popularity of the Gothic; furniture incorporated such design elements as pointed arches, trefoils and clustered columns. The search for novelty in design led to the use of many different shapes and decorative motifs without any consistent underlying theme, an eclecticism furthered by the effect on designers of the various industrial exhibitions staged during this period.

There was no immediate break with the Empire style (for example, Louis XVIII retained Napoleon's furniture, simply replacing the imperial bees with the royal fleur-de-lis). But gradually a less grandiose, more domestic style developed. Finely grained walnut, yew and maple veneer were inlaid with darker woods, such as rosewood or ebony, and vice versa. Gilt-bronze mounts gradually disappeared and were replaced by inlaid decoration and the greater use of wood-carving.

In seat furniture comfort replaced pomp as the guiding principle: pieces became smaller and curves were reintroduced, rounded seats and backs sweeping down to legs carved with scrolls. Turned legs were also used, the back ones often being sabre-shaped. Sofas and *chaises-longues* were made in many different shapes. The *pommier* was a cross between the two, with one arm rest the same height as the back and the other lower.

Case furniture became more fussy yet utilitarian to meet middle-class needs. Desks of *bonheur du jour* shape, often standing on clustered-column end-supports, were made with many small drawers. *Etagères* (two- or three-tiered open cabinets used as bookcases or repositories for knick-knacks) were constructed with fretwork side panels and galleries and in an

**CONSOLE TABLE**
*Jacob-Desmalters*
Amboyna, gilt and patinated bronze; **early 19th century**

One of a pair, this table derives from designs by the architect Charles Percier. These are in the robust style of antiquity.

astonishing range of shapes. Commodes and *secrétaires* abounded but even so they were now outnumbered by a variety of new functional pieces, such as jardinières, small screens, side tables and, for the first time, the piano as an item of furnishing.

## SECOND EMPIRE

The monarchy was replaced in 1848 by the Second Republic, but four years later its first president, Louis Napoleon, Bonaparte's nephew, declared himself emperor as Napoleon III. This Second Empire lasted until 1871, when it was replaced by the Third Republic. This time there was no imperial style imposed from above; nor even was there any clearly defined Second Empire style at all. Artists and craftsmen of the period merely interpreted and adapted a wide range of styles from the past and from all over the world. And sometimes designers even used several styles for one piece. What was new, however, was a technical perfection made possible by modern mechanical processes.

The Renaissance style was especially popular with furniture-makers, and great cabinets were made, incorporating a profusion of carving, marquetry and other techniques. The 17th and 18th centuries also provided inspiration. The Empress Eugénie was nostalgically attracted to Louis XVI's queen consort Marie Antoinette, and many pieces were made in imitation of the Louis XVI style. These were often in marquetry inlaid with fake Sèvres porcelain plaques, or in ebony inlaid with *pietre dure* panels.

The Louis XIV style was also copied: much boulle marquetry case furniture was made, often with a red tortoiseshell background, as well as Louis XIV chairs, beds and other pieces. It was usually the finest or most elaborate pieces that were imitated; their detail was exaggerated and painstakingly executed. Lacquer was used extensively. Usually black, and decorated with painted and gilt detail and mother-of-pearl inlay, it was applied to spindly chairs, tables, cabinets, screens, inkstands, caskets and many other objects. Some of these articles were made of papier mâché, a cheap process which permitted mass production.

It became fashionable to design whole rooms in a specific style and often to design the different rooms in a house each in its own style – perhaps a Renaissance dining room, a Gothic library and a Louis XV drawing room. Every possible shape and technique in furniture-making was employed, with the emphasis on the intricate and lavish. Porcelain, marble, *pietre dure*, rare woods, patinated and gilt bronze, silver, cast and wrought iron, pewter and other metals, ivory and tortoiseshell were all used profusely. Upholstery was equally complex; for example, typical furnishings for the centre of a room were huge buttoned pouffes (a cross between a bench and a stool), with plants growing out of them. Among the more fanciful designs of the period was a stool standing on giltwood legs carved to resemble twisted rope.

**THE EMPRESS EUGENIE'S STUDY AT ST CLOUD**
*Baptiste Fortuné de Fournier*
**Watercolour; 1860**

This room is a good example of the eclecticism of the Second Empire, wherein earlier furniture is mixed with modern, comfortable and useful pieces. The study reflects the Empress's nostalgia for Marie-Antoinette.

# FRENCH PROVINCIAL FURNITURE

French provincial furniture can be attributed stylistically to particular regions, but most pieces are anonymous, since the Paris guilds did not hold sway in the provinces, and very few country craftsmen stamped their names on their products. Distinctive styles are restricted to the period 1650–1850, although precise dating can be difficult, because popular forms continued to be made for a long time, as part of a living tradition.

Regional furniture was seldom veneered. It was made by the *menuisier*, who worked in solid, native timber – oak, walnut, chestnut, poplar, elm, pine, beech, birch and fruitwoods – producing any or all of the following pieces.

**Armoire:** cupboard or wardrobe, usually matching the *boiserie* (panelling and other fixed woodwork) of the room. Constructed in sections and assembled with pegs driven into holes, it was easily dismantled. A Louis XIII/XIV type with geometric mouldings remained popular in central France until replaced about 1750 by the Louis XV type with asymmetrical rococo panels.

**Bonnetière:** small version of the armoire, known in Normandy as a *coëffière*; usually only one door, enclosing an interior fitted with shelves to hold the wide-brimmed hats favoured by countrywomen.

**Buffet-bas:** waist-high cupboard, used as sideboard; doors with rococo panels on pin hinges, two or three drawers above.

**Buffet-vaisselier** or **dressoir:** buffet with rack of shelves above. Typical Auvergne versions have restrained decoration, those in Brittany have turned spindles forming plate-guards on shelves, Normandy examples are rich in well-carved detail, many in Alsace are painted with flowers.

**Buffet-à-deux-corps:** buffet with cupboard above. Doors of upper section may be panelled or glazed. Some mid-19th-century examples are very large and include a weight-driven clock in the upper stage.

**Coffre:** lidded chest or coffer, usually oak. In some areas continued being made to 16th- and 17th-century designs well into the 18th century. The Lorraine type has a panelled front carved with floral motifs.

**DOUBLE-DOME ARMOIRE**
Cherrywood with carved decoration; *c.* 1790

*(Above)*

**COMMODE**
Cherrywood with carved frieze and *arc-en-arbalète* front; *c.* 1740

*(Below)*

Medieval-looking Auvergne and Basque types sometimes prove to be 19th-century.

**Commode:** chest-of-drawers. Very few provincial types have the full *bombé* shape (a bulging lower front) of the sophisticated Louis XV commode, but many are shaped from side to side in serpentine or *arc-en-arbalète* (crossbow) form. Some are richly carved, others – especially those in the Louis XVI style – relatively plain. The top is usually wood, not marble.

**Lit clos:** "cupboard" bed. Those of 17th-century style persisted in rural areas, Brittany especially, until the late 19th century; the panelled doors are pierced for ventilation, the vents being made into decorative features with turned spindles. Others resemble Louis XV armoires.

**Panetière:** small food cupboard, usually fixed to the wall, composed mainly of turned members to allow maximum ventilation while protecting the food from domestic animals. The turnings are socketed into horizontal rails that, in good Provençale examples, are fancifully shaped and carved.

**Sièges:** country seat furniture, usually with wooden or rushed seats.

# ITALY

The motley collection of city states, principalities and duchies that during the 17th century made up what is now Italy exerted its influence on furniture-making throughout Europe, and Florence, Venice, Genoa, Rome and Naples were major centres of the craft.

Many of the furniture forms developed during the Renaissance persisted into the 17th century but with more and more elaborate embellishment, in keeping with the Baroque style that was flourishing in other arts in Italy at the time. Chests, chairs and table supports were massively carved with such motifs as negro and caryatid figures, putti and gods, eagles and dolphins, fruit and plants in sumptuous garlands, supported by volutes (spiral scrolls) and shells. Beds were magnificently gilded and hung with silk or velvet. And table tops were made of exotically coloured marble.

The leading practitioners of these sculptural effects were Andrea Brustolon (1662–1732) in Venice, Domenico Parodi (1668–1740) in Genoa and Antonio Corradini (1668–1752),

**ARMCHAIR**
Venice
**17th century**

This chair is in the manner of the sculptor Andrea Brustolon (1662–1732), whose heavily carved furniture with figure supports established a showy tradition for Venetian *palazzo* furniture.

**CHAIR**
*Probably Antonio Corradini*
Carved and gilt; **c. 1730**

This chair, from the Ca' Rezzonico in Venice, shows the florid sculptural style at its most extravagant.

who took the full-blown sensuality of the Venetian Baroque into the 1730s. Their furniture represented the peak of the grand effect for which many aristocrats strove. The wealthy citizens of Rome, Genoa, Florence and Turin made sure that their state rooms reflected their worldly success: galleries with painted ceilings had antique statues ranged along the walls, interspersed with carved and gilded console tables, throne-like chairs and fantastically decorated cabinets.

Such cabinets were designed not only to house the collections of curiosities owned by all rich connoisseurs of the time but just as much to display virtuoso craftsmanship in their own right: gilded bronze sculptures on the drawers and borders, carvings in boxwood or lignum vitae (a dense, dark West Indian wood) or panels of tortoiseshell. Most, and particularly those made in the *Opificio delle Pietre Dure* in

Florence, were inset with naturalistic birds and flowers in *pietre dure* (coloured hard-stone). These cabinets were commissioned not only by Italian tycoons but by royal and aristocratic patrons all over Europe; unmounted panels of *pietre dure* or scagliola (imitation marble), which could be used for cabinets or table tops, were snapped up by rich Grand Tourists.

By the end of the 17th century the leading stylist of hard-stone furniture was Giovanni Battista Foggini (1652-1725), a sculptor who set off flat hard-stone panels with elaborate gilt bronze mounts. Equally exuberant were the three-dimensional swags of fruit and leaves with which he provided a colourful foil for ponderously Baroque ebony furniture.

In contrast to the show rooms of Italian *palazzi*, their living rooms were, like those of middle-class houses, much more sparsely and simply furnished with solid pieces usually of walnut. But few could resist decoration of some sort, and inlays of ivory, pewter and mother-of-pearl were favoured for the more important carcase pieces made in the Venice and Lombardy areas. Like much Italian furniture, they are crudely constructed compared with similar pieces from northern Europe, but their decoration has a pleasing vivacity.

Venice was famous all over Europe for the production of mirror glass, and until France and England developed their own industries in the late 17th and early 18th centuries, the city effectively enjoyed a monopoly. The manufacture of elaborately carved and gilded frames to complement looking glasses was an important industry in both Venice and Florence, and Venetian mirrors were regarded as essential in any well-appointed Italian room.

In 18th-century Italy greater attention was paid to the furnishing of smaller rooms in houses and palaces, and a range of furniture types was introduced from north of the Alps. These included the long sofa, upholstered or caned; chairs from France; and the bureau bookcase from England and the Netherlands. Chests of drawers became much more widely used. Whereas in northern Europe the emphasis was on good craftsmanship and solid quality, many of the Italian pieces are colourfully embellished but shoddily constructed.

The enthusiasm for oriental lacquer imported to Europe through the East India companies was also shared by the Italians, who, in the face of difficulty and expense in acquiring the genuine variety, not only adopted japanning

**BOMBE COMMODE**
*North Italian*
Walnut, ivory, mother-of-pearl, pewter and gilt-metal; **mid 18th century**

The exuberant inlays of flowers and grotesques belong to a style already popular in the late 17th century. Along with the elaborate handles and escutcheons, they illustrate the enthusiasm for decorative effects – sometimes at the expense of sound construction – among Italian furniture makers. (*Above*)

**LOOKING GLASS**
*North Italian*
Carved and gilt; **1730s**

This mirror is in the lighter Rococo style. Venice had maintained a virtual monopoly of mirror-glass production until the late 17th century and continued to export looking glasses all over Europe, even after plate glass was being produced elsewhere. (*Right*)

as an alternative but developed their own method of imitating its effect. *Lacca povera (or lacca contrafatta)* involved pasting cut-out and painted pictures – chinoiserie or rustic scenes usually – on to a painted furniture surface and then lavishly coating the whole with varnish. The resulting decoration resembles the texture and sometimes also the colour of japanning, though it rarely deceives. Painting – of landscapes, flowers or figure scenes – was another much favoured form of decoration for such furniture as chests, tables and cupboards.

In Turin the Sicilian architect Filippo Juvarra (1676–1736) gathered together a group of outstanding craftsmen for work at the Palazzo Reale in the 1730s. They included the sculptor Francesco Ladatte (1706–87) and the cabinet-maker Pietro Piffetti (*c.*1700–77). Together, they produced some of the most unrestrained

ornamentation on furniture ever devised, even in Italy, but at least it was well made.

## THE ROCOCO STYLE

Piffetti's confections of inlaid ivory, mother-of-pearl and exotic woods, with their finely chiselled bronze mounts, were among the earliest manifestations of the lightening of the Baroque style into the Rococo in Italy. Rococo was much favoured for the still showy but less grandiose furnishings of living rooms and led to an enthusiastic adoption of bombé (rounded, convex) fronts and serpentine shapes. These taxed the abilities of many Italian craftsmen, but they camouflaged any defects in workmanship with gay painting or *lacca* and with lavish gilding.

The bombé front took different forms, ranging from a full-bosomed curve high in the carcase of Venetian chests to the almost

**WALL SCONCE**
*Italian*
**Papier-mâché; 18th century**

The sconce is in a Rococo-style gilded frame surrounding a still life.

# ITALIAN FURNITURE MAKERS

| | | | |
|---|---|---|---|
| **BRUSTOLON, Andrea** | 1662–1732 | Venice | Expert carver and leading exponent of Baroque. Famous especially for his chairs. |
| **PARODI, Domenico** | 1668–1740 | Genoa | Produced extravagantly decorated furniture in Baroque style. |
| **CORRADINI, Antonio** | 1668–1752 | Venice | Worked in Baroque style. Known for his chair and console frames in carved and gilded wood. |
| **FOGGINI, Giovanni Battista** | 1652–1725 | Florence | A sculptor. Produced extravagantly decorated hardstone and ebony furniture in Baroque style. |
| **PIFFETTI, Pietro** | *c.*1700–77 | Turin | Cabinet-maker who produced pieces with surfaces highly decorated with precious materials – exotic woods, ivory, mother-of-pearl etc. |
| **BONZANIGO, Giuseppe Maria** | 1745–1820 | Turin | A wood sculptor whose furniture contains elements of rococo and Neo-Classical styles. Demonstrated his skill in carved and gilded decoration. Painted decoration was also a characteristic of his work. |
| **MAGGIOLINI, Giuseppe** | 1738–1814 | Milan | Produced rectilinear pieces with no carving, decorated with marquetry panels using many different woods. |
| **SOCCHI, Giovanni** | *fl. c.*1809–15 | Florence | Produced restrained furniture in the Empire style. Made furniture for the Palazzo Pitti, Florence, commissioned by Napoleon's sister, the Grand Duchess of Tuscany. |
| **PALAGI, Pelagio** | 1775–1860 | Turin | An artist/sculptor who produced highly sculptural pieces – chairs, tables, sofas – in the Empire style. Provided furniture for the Palazzo Reale, Turin. |

**WRITING DESK**
*Pietro Piffetti*
Inlaid with precious woods
and ivory; 1741

Piffetti's furniture for the
Palazzo Reale in Turin took
the Italian Rococo to its
most fantastic extreme.

restrained undulation low down in the sides
of those made in Lombardy. The cabriole
(double-curved) legs of chairs, tables and commodes were more exaggeratedly curved
in Italy than elsewhere in Europe. Other Rococo
expressions, such as cartouches (ornate tablets
or shields), leafy flourishes and shell forms,
were in widespread use.

## NEO-CLASSICISM

In the mid 18th century, Italy, and specifically
Rome, attracted archaeologists, artists and designers from all over Europe in search of "the
antique" and became the chief source of Neo-
Classical ideas and models. Despite this, in the
development of Neo-Classical style in furniture,
Italy lagged behind France and England. Straight
lines and disciplined ornament were clearly
alien to Italian natural exuberance and it was not
until later in the century that Neo-Classicism
was adopted. Even then, the less grand furniture
often retained Rococo elements in carved,
marquetry or scagliola decoration.

The work of Giuseppe Maria Bonzanigo
(1745–1820), for palaces in and around Turin in
the late 18th century, shows elements of both
Neo-Classical and Rococo styles. Although he

**FIRE SCREEN**
*Giuseppe Bonzanigo*
Carved and gilt; 1775

Featuring painted
decoration by Michele
Rapous, the fire screen was
made for the Palazzo Reale
in Turin. It represents the
showy form of Neo-
Classicism favoured in Italy
at this time.

used rectilinear shapes and classical motifs, his own superlative skill as a wood sculptor is seen in the elaborate carved and gilded decoration of his pieces. Painted decoration, usually of Rococo-style flowers, was also a hallmark of his work, and his furniture for the Sardinian royal family in particular is unmistakably Italian in its florid delicacy.

When the French-inspired version of the Neo-Classical style was eventually adopted in the state rooms of the most fashionable *palazzi*, it was dominated by a handful of giants, headed by Giuseppe Maggiolini (1738–1814) in Milan. No curving or carving are to be seen in his severely rectilinear commodes and cupboards; instead he relied on a vast array of different woods (as many as 86 in 1795) for pictorial marquetry panels of astonishing virtuosity, many of them designed by painters.

Close to Maggiolini in the production of high-quality furniture in Italy were Ignazio (b. 1756) and Luigi (b. 1776) Revelli, father and son, who worked in Turin. Noted for their half-rounded commodes, the Revelli's also specialized in marquetry decoration.

### THE EMPIRE STYLE
The full-blown Napoleonic Empire style was established in Italy by various members of the Bonaparte family, not least Napoleon's sister Eliza Baciocchi, who, as Grand Duchess of Tuscany, employed the cabinet-maker

**CHAIRS**
*Florence*
**Carved and gilt wood;
c. 1800**

There are no traces of Rococo elements in these two stylish Neo-Classical chairs with red damask upholstery, which come from a set of four.

Giovanni Socchi (*fl. c.* 1809–15) to make furniture for the Palazzo Pitti in Florence. His style is exemplified in a series of drum-shaped cupboards with marble tops, pine-cone feet and gilded wood mounts, of a tasteful restraint reminiscent of Biedermeier (informal 19th-century German) furniture, but he is most celebrated for ingenious pieces, a good example of which is a hefty oval chest on legs, standing on a plinth that slides open into an elegant writing desk with raised inkstand and a chair.

A little earlier, the Sienese architect Agostino Fantastici had designed Neo-Classical furniture of similar restraint, veneered in walnut with ebony bandings and with a minimum of decoration. Some of his most celebrated work, made for Giuliano Bianchi Bandinelli, an influential advocate of Neo-Classicism, shows a distinct quirkiness of style.

The Empire style endured in Italy long after the fall of Napoleon, especially for palatial decoration. In furniture it was interpreted in its most ponderously heroic form by Pelagio Palagi (1775-1860), who in the 1830s provided highly sculptured pieces for the Palazzo Reale in Turin, including candelabra, stools, sofas, chairs and the gilt-bronze table in the Council Chamber, with its massive winged caryatids supporting a deep frieze of anthemion (stylized honeysuckle motif) and scrolls. Palagi worked in the Gothic style too, when he felt it was appropriate. Both Gothic Revival and Renaissance Revival appeared in Italy, notably in a native manifestation known as Dantesque. This style was characterized by X-frame chairs, uncomfortable stools and heavily carved tables.

### REGIONAL FURNITURE

Everyday furniture was produced by household carpenters in various regional styles and was often extremely robust. The furniture of northern Italy was much influenced by that of southern France, and that of both regions was predominantly of local walnut. The area was traditionally famous for intarsia work (inlays of differently coloured woods). Painted furniture was typical of the Alpine regions, where japanning and *lacca* were also practised, as in many parts of Italy; Alpine and Genoese embellishment of this kind as well as furniture forms themselves, were of a more restrained design than those of the Venetian region.

Genoa, as one of the chief ports of the Mediterranean, was considerably influenced by Spain, and imported woods such as pali-

sander were used alongside walnut in its high-quality furniture. The same influence can also be seen in Sicilian ivory-inlaid ebony cabinets, modelled on the Spanish *vargueño*. The furniture of Tuscany, also most commonly of walnut, tends to have a solidity both of form and decoration that contrasts strongly with the exuberant shapeliness and shallow decoration of Venetian pieces.

The furniture of Emilia Romagna, the region south of Venice, was also of a solid character (oak was used as well as walnut), but its most conspicuous feature was its geometric ornamentation of metal studs and roundels applied to the fronts of chests and cupboards alongside interestingly turned wooden knobs.

Like most furniture built for the comfort and convenience of ordinary people rather than for fashionable display, Italian regional furniture is almost impossible to date. Styles were handed down by practical rather than bookish tradition and persisted for centuries with little change.

**COMMODE**
*Ferrara*
Walnut; **first half of 18th century**

This small piece features three drawers and a serpentine front. Its widely flaring cornice and base, as well as chunky bracket feet, are typical regional characteristics of furniture from Ferrara.

THE FURNITURE MADE FOR THE COURT IN MADRID PUSHED FASHIONS FORWARD IN SPAIN, ALTHOUGH, AS HAPPENED IN PORTUGAL, ENGLISH IMPORTS HAD STRONG INFLUENCE.

# SPAIN AND PORTUGAL

The furniture of 18th-century Spain and Portugal was rich in references to colonial expansion and cultural cross-currents. In Spain, the dominant influences were from France and Italy: both were dynastically linked to the Spanish kings. However, the Moorish past, with its decorative forms, lived on in provincial and country furniture.

Philip V's palace of La Granja at Segovia was the most sophisticated manifestation of the French-inspired Rococo in Spain. The Rococo fashion for console and side tables, heavily carved and gilded, and complemented by ornate mirrors, was particularly appropriate for lofty Spanish rooms, and led to the establishment of a mirror factory at San Ildefonso in 1736.

The *vargueño* (cabinet) was gradually replaced by the commode as a show-piece. Although the commode originated in France, its shape and decoration in Spain were Italianate, particularly after the Neapolitan decorator, Matias Gasparini, became director of the royal workshops in Madrid in 1768. Later in the 18th century, however, Spanish Neo-Classical furniture acquired extravagant severity all its own. Marquetry was generally detailed and delicate; painting and gilding were also used, but metal mounts rarely.

Imported English furniture in the first half of the 18th century also influenced Spanish design, particularly that of chairs. Japanned pieces were a popular import, and the English cabinet-maker Giles Grendey sent a huge consignment of scarlet japanned furniture to the Duke of Infantado in the 1730s. Early Georgian and Thomas Chippendale designs were translated by the Spanish into walnut or poplar and given carved and gilded Rococo ornamentation and H-form stretchers (horizontal struts connecting legs). Later the Hepplewhite and Sheraton designs were echoed, but less obviously.

In 1808 Napoleon's invasion of Spain began a period of political tumult for the country that continued until the 1830s. Furniture tended to follow the French Empire style. The sumptuous Fernandino style was marked by the use of applied ornament in gilded bronze or "antique" classical motifs in carved and gilded wood.

### PORTUGAL

In Portugal, where the riches of the South American colonies were more obviously enjoyed – at least, at court – English influence was most powerful. When the widowed consort of Charles II, Catherine of Braganza, returned to her native Portugal in 1693, she took English furniture with her. The fashion she thus introduced was later reinforced by mercantile

**CHAIR**
*Spanish*
**Wood and painted leather;
c. 1840**

From a suite of furniture, this chair shows a bizarre combination of classic Rococo and Baroque elements in the strongly sculptural carving of the legs and back. The painted-leather upholstery is a characteristically Spanish product associated with Toledo.

**CHAIR**
*Portuguese*
**Walnut; c. 1730**

From a set of five, the chair
has an interlacing
strapwork splat, carved legs
with ball-and-claw feet and
a drop-in seat. English
influence is evident, but the
stretchers and low-slung
effect of the exaggerated
cabriole front legs are
distinctly Portuguese.
(*Right*)

**COMMODE**
*Portuguese*
**Marquetry; late 18th
century**

The piece is known as a
Donna Maria commode,
typified by its linear design,
finely crafted marquetry,
deep apron and marble top.
(*Below*)

of late 18th-century Portugal. Chairs and settees made in sturdy versions of the Hepplewhite
and Sheraton styles, many of them beautifully
painted, suggest a familiarity with English
design books of the period.

Nineteenth-century styles in Portugal were
governed by successive outside influences: early
in the century the French Empire style gave rise
to some chunky classical interpretations; after
the expulsion of Napoleon in 1811 furniture
followed English designs; and after 1820 the
Biedermeier style.

treaties between the two countries that resulted in large consignments of English furniture
finding their way into Portuguese homes.

Japanned pieces were popular, as in Spain,
and the Portuguese also carried out their own
imitations of oriental lacquer. English styles
were reflected most often in Portuguese chairs,
but these were generally more exuberantly
carved than the originals and usually had H-
shaped stretchers, which were discarded
in England in the early 18th century. In many
examples, English taste merges with French
Rococo influence, but interpretations are distinctively Portuguese and often carried out in
non-European woods such as the hard dark
jacaranda, imported from Brazil.

In commodes and beds the Portuguese gave a
distinctive and original interpretation to the
Rococo, with an emphasis on embellishment in
carved wood rather than applied metalwork.
Portuguese commodes were taller than those of
other European countries, nearly always with a
depth of four drawers.

After the disastrous Lisbon earthquake of
1755, and the subsequent restructuring of the
Portuguese economy by the Marquess of
Pombal, much fine furniture was produced to
complement the Neo-Classical architecture.

Cylinder-topped commodes and bureaux
with well-crafted marquetry and parquetry decoration, as well as a profusion of occasional and
games tables and matching mirrors and console
tables, also reflected the comfort and prosperity

# GERMANY, AUSTRIA, AND EASTERN EUROPE

Strong regional differences are discernible in the furniture made throughout central and eastern Europe. Like Italy, Germany was a collection of more or less independent states rather than a unified nation. Italian influence was strong in the predominantly Catholic south, Dutch influence in the Protestant north. The patronage of princely bishops and other ecclesiastics was often as lavish as that of secular princes, especially in western Germany. In the north much furniture was produced to reflect the wealth of rich merchants from flourishing city states like Danzig, Hamburg and Lübeck.

Nuremberg and Augsburg continued their long tradition of fine furniture craftsmanship, producing cabinets richly decorated with ivory, ebony, tortoiseshell, metals and semi-precious stones. They were works of art in their own right and were exported to rich connoisseurs all over Europe. Towards the end of the 17th century these two towns also became known for the publication of ornamental engravings of interiors and of books of designs for furniture and interior decoration. In the early 18th century, the influence of French courtly fashions was to be seen in the engraved and embossed silver furniture produced in Augsburg for export to the more flamboyant courts of Germany. Very little survives.

### THE BAROQUE STYLE

Munich was also a major centre of furniture craftsmanship, particularly in the Italian-inspired Baroque style of the later 17th century; tables with inlaid marble tops and robustly carved figure supports were among the most lavish pieces and were produced there under the influence of architects and artists from Turin.

Towards the end of the 17th century, the inspiration of Paris, and particularly of the cabinet-maker André-Charles Boulle is apparent in much of the furniture produced in southern Germany. A leading exponent of

**BUREAU-CABINET**
*German*
Walnut with marquetry inlays and crossbandings of walnut, pear and ebony;
*c.* 1740

---

Probably made in Würzburg or Mainz, this piece of furniture is of the type known as a *Tabernakel-Schreibkommode*. It includes Rococo elements – the bombé shape of the *Tabernakel* section and the rocaille scrolls and carved cresting – but its mood is still ponderously Baroque.

boulle marquetry was H. D. Sommer (*fl.* 1666–84), of Kunzelsau in Swabia whose materials included ebony, brass, tortoiseshell, pewter and ivory. The Augsburg partnership of Esser and Wolfhauer combined boulle marquetry with marble mosaic.

The solid magnificence of the Baroque style found a ready acceptance all over Germany and persisted well into the 18th century. It was embodied most often in the *Schrank* (large cupboard) which graced the hall or landing of every wealthy burgher's house. Heavy cornices (overhanging moulded projections), architectural pilasters (flat columnar projections) and panelling were usually embellished with carving; often this was in the fleshy, ear-like style known as *knorpelwerk*, for which designs were pub-

# GERARD DAGLY

The late 17th- and early 18th-century enthusiasm for japanning was as strong in Germany as it was in the rest of Europe. One of the most skilled exponents of the technique was Gerard Dagly (*fl.* 1687–1714), who was employed in Berlin, first by the Elector Frederick William of Brandenburg and later by King Frederick I of Prussia (1701–13). Dagly was a native of Spa, in what is now Belgium, where japanning flourished for most of the 17th and 18th century. His output of finely decorated cabinets, clocks, keyboard-instrument cases and stands, produced while he served as *Directeur des Ornements* to the royal court, surpassed almost all other European japanning in its quality. He created fine work in black and gold, but his most characteristic pieces, japanned in bright greens, reds and other colours on a creamy white ground, are more reminiscent of porcelain than furniture decoration.

**CABINET**
*style of Gerard Dagly, possibly Berlin;* Lacquered; **early 18th century**

lished by the Frankfurt cabinet-maker Friedrich Unteutsch among others. By the end of the 17th century decoration on these still massive cupboards more often consisted of arabesque patterns, ripple-moulded panels and bobbin-turned columns.

Smaller cupboards included the *Geschirrschrank* (china cupboard) and the *Stollenschrank* (cabinet-on-stand), both of which were architectural in concept and relied for their embellishment on carved or moulded panels. The *Tabernakel* was a cupboard enclosing drawers, which by the 18th century had become part of a multi-purpose piece consisting of the *Tabernakel* above and a slope-fronted desk with a three-drawer chest beneath.

*Knorpelwerk* had found its way on to chairs in the 17th century. The plank-seated, splayed-legged variety – with carving on what must have been a punishingly uncomfortable back – progressed to upholstered chairs that later had very tall carved backs. By the early 18th century, chairs produced in northern Germany showed evidence of Dutch and English influence, with cabriole legs, shaped backs, and caning in seats and back panels.

Germany's long tradition of wood carving was to continue in much of the furniture pro-

duced during the 18th and 19th centuries, but from the early 18th century veneers of walnut, ebony and other woods were also increasingly used. By this time the seeds of the Rococo were being sown by certain princes in Germany, even though the Baroque showed little sign of fading from favour for the majority. Contributing to this late continuance of the Baroque in Germany were the widely influential designs of Johann Jacob Schübler, published in Nuremberg and Augsburg in the 1720s and 1730s; in these furniture of ingenious gadgetry was dressed in the Baroque ornament of 50 years earlier.

During the first two decades of the 18th century, great palaces continued to be built in the Baroque style, culminating in the grandeur of the Schloss Pommersfelden, built for Lothar Franz von Schönborn, Prince Bishop of Bamberg, and largely furnished in the Louis XIV style by Ferdinand Plitzner (1678-1724). The palace, with Plitzner's *Spiegelkabinett* (mirror room), survives.

### EARLY ROCOCO

The *Residenz* of the Electors of Mainz, the magnificent Palace of Würzburg, was begun in 1720 in the Baroque style, but the furnishing and dec-

## GERMAN, AUSTRIAN AND EAST EUROPEAN FURNITURE MAKERS

| | | | |
|---|---|---|---|
| **DAGLY, Gerard** | fl. 1687–1714 | Spa and Berlin | Skilled at japanning. His most characteristic pieces were japanned in bright colours on a creamy ground. Worked for Friedrich Wilhelm, Elector of Brandenburg. |
| **PLITZNER, Ferdinand** | 1678–1724 | Bamberg | Exponent of Baroque style. Provided furniture in Louis XIV style for Schloss Pommersfelden, including the mirror room. |
| **MATTERN, Carl Maximilian** | fl. 1733–70 | Würzburg | Early Rococo. Pieces embellished with elaborate decoration and marquetry. |
| **SCHUMACHER, Martin** | 1695–1781 | Ansbach | Early Rococo. Work characterized by restrained linearity. Pieces sometimes veneered with mahogany. |
| **SPINDLER, Johann Friedrich and Heinrich Wilhelm** | 1726–c.1799 1738–c.1799 | Bayreuth and Berlin | Rococo. Worked for the sister of Frederick the Great, and then for Frederick himself. |
| **SCHNELL, Martin** | fl. 1703–40 | Berlin and Dresden | A pupil of Dagly. He was lacquer-maker to the royal court. Produced pieces richly decorated with relief lacquer and gilded figures. |
| **HOPPENHAUPT, Johann Michael and John Christian** | 1709–c.1755 1719–86 | Berlin and Potsdam | Rococo. Furnished the palaces of Charlottenburg, Potsdam and Sanssouci. Work characterized by rich veneers of exotic woods and decoration in ivory, mother-of-pearl, silver, etc. |
| **NAHL, Johann August** | 1710–73 | Berlin, Potsdam and Kassel | Designer and carver in Rococo style. Produced gilded stucco decorations at palaces of Charlottenburg, Potsdam and Sanssouci. |
| **ROENTGEN, Abraham and David** | 1711–93 1743–1807 | Neuwied | Abraham made speciality of marquetry. Their work was characterized by complex mechanisms – locks, secret drawers, etc. |
| **VON KLENZE, Leo** | 1784–1864 | Munich | Classical designer who worked in the Empire style. Made pieces for the Prussian royal family. |
| **SCHINKEL, Karl Friedrich** | 1781–1841 | Berlin | Court architect in Berlin who designed furniture in Empire style. |
| **DANHAUSER, Josef** | 1780–1829 | Vienna | Foremost designer of Biedermeier. Work known for high quality craftsmanship and abstract, curving forms. |
| **LEISTLER, Carl** | 1805–57 | Vienna | Extravagant Neo-Rococo style in reaction against Classicism. Made Neo-Gothic bookcase for Great Exhibition of 1851. |
| **THONET, Michael** | 1796–1871 | Boppard-am-Rhein and Vienna | Famous for his bentwood chairs and other bentwood furniture – the first mass-produced furniture. |

oration embodied the finest manifestations of the early Rococo in Germany. Among the craftsmen who contributed were Franz Anton Schlott of Bamberg, the four Guthmann brothers of Munich, Johann Wolfgang van der Auvera, Carl Maximilian Mattern (fl. 1733–70), Johann Georg Nestfell and Johann Kohler. Their elaborate confections of virtuoso marquetry, with lavish use of carving and gilding, look clumsy in the light of later Rococo pieces, but they are of consummate craftsmanship and certainly served their purpose of princely ostentation.

The *Residenz* at Ansbach was another influential gathering place for purveyors of the early Rococo, as was the *Residenz* of Bamberg. One of the chief Ansbach cabinet-makers was Martin Schumacher (1695–1781), whose furniture, restrained, linear, sometimes veneered in mahogany, has a peculiarly English resonance.

The Rococo flourished at Bayreuth, home of the Markgraf Friedrich and his wife Wilhelmine (sister of Frederick the Great), who were both enthusiastic builders of palaces. The most important cabinet-makers they patronized were the Spindler brothers, who later worked for Frederick the Great.

Augustus the Strong, Elector of Saxony (1694–1733) and King of Poland (1697–1733), favoured English-inspired designs, especially early on, for writing cabinets and chairs, but the influence of the French rococo supervened before long, and from the 1720s onwards much of the furniture for his court at Dresden was strongly French in flavour. Among the more distinctively Saxon pieces were writing cabinets with mirrors in the upper doors. Martin Schnell (*fl.* 1703–40), lacquer-maker to the royal court, produced japanned work of the greatest richness, decorated with relief figures of lacquered and gilded copper.

The most extreme Francophile manifestations of the Rococo in Germany were without doubt those undertaken for the Electors of Bavaria in Munich. The Elector Maximilian Emmanuel (1662–1726), formerly exiled at the court of Louis XIV, introduced the most advanced French taste into his surroundings at Munich. His chief architects and designers, first Joseph Effner (1687–1745) and later François Cuvilliès the Elder (1695–1768), both Paris-trained, decorated the Munich *Residenz* and the Palace of Nymphenburg in airy, dazzling Rococo style. Cuvilliès published his designs for ornament, panelling and furniture, which became known all over Europe, and continued to dominate Rococo design in Germany until his death.

An altogether beefier Rococo than that of Cuvilliès was that produced for Frederick the Great (1740–86) at Berlin and Potsdam. At first under the direction of Frederick's superintendent of palaces, Georg Wenzeslaus von Knobelsdorff (1699–1753), and later under their own steam, a gathering of consummate craftsmen, led by the brothers Johann Michael

**SECRETAIRE-CABINET**
*Attributed to Franz Anton Hermann, Mainz*
**Walnut with wood and bone inlays, ormolu; 1738**

The elaborate inlays as well as the gilt-bronze mounts, are typical of Mainz productions. (*Above right*)

**CONSOLE TABLE**
*Francois Cuvilliès*
**Carved and gilt; 1739**

In the full-blown Rococo style, the table was made for the Amalienburg hunting lodge at Schloss Nymphenburg, Munich. (*Right*)

(1709–c.1755) and John Christian Hoppenhaupt (1719–86), Johann August Nahl (1710–73), Johann Melchior Kambli (1718–73) and the brothers Johann Friedrich (1726–c.1799) and Heinrich Wilhelm Spindler (1738–c.1799), filled the palaces of Charlottenburg, Potsdam and Sans-Souci with boldly curvaceous furniture of unparalleled magnificence. Commodes, veneered with tortoiseshell or exotic timbers or decorated with marquetry of wood, mother-of-pearl, ivory and even silver, were profusely ornamented with gilt-bronze mounts made in Kambli's workshops, and chairs of painted or gilded softwood were carved with often Italianate confidence.

All this courtly extravagance had a varying effect on the styles of furniture further down the German social scale. Regional characteristics were preserved, especially in the design of the *Schrank* which remained an important symbol of household affluence. On the whole the Hanseatic towns and the free cities of the north showed the greatest conservatism. The *Schrank* as interpreted in Brunswick, for example, was still in the mid 18th century an essentially Baroque piece, with an architectural cornice, classical pilasters and symmetrical door panels of intarsia. The cupboards of Frankfurt and Hamburg also kept their solidly Baroque character until the mid 18th century. On the other hand, the solid oak cupboards of Aachen, like those of Liège, were carved with *boiseries* (leafy carving) of surprising lightness.

In Mainz, the Rococo was embodied in a particularly elaborate, three-stage *Schreibkommode* (form of writing bureau), a speciality of the cabinet-maker Peter Schuss. The serpentine-fronted commode section in the base was surmounted by a concave-shaped, sloping-topped bureau and above this was a two-door cupboard, all decorated with marquetry. The canted corners, the cornice above and the apron below were all carved into volutes and twists, with asymmetrical cartouches and mouldings wherever opportunity offered; and in the most extravagant examples some of these carved appendages were gilded. The fine craftsmanship lavished on these pieces cannot, however, overcome their ungainly shape.

Other southern German bureau-cabinets were less elaborate in their carved detail but still impressive: walnut with marquetry of other woods, often in geometric designs, was usual; canted corners and concave fronts for the drawers in the base and a *Tabernakel* section on top

gave a solidity to many such pieces. In these areas of Germany and Austria the influence was predictably Italian, and many pieces of carcase furniture around the mid 18th century borrowed Italian elements like exaggeratedly stumpy cabriole legs and well-fattened bombé shapes. However, most pieces made for the middle-class market were relatively restrained and solid.

In the areas to the south and east of the region, traditional painted furniture continued to be produced: relatively simple forms and construction were enhanced by an uninhibited use of colour and pattern.

English and Dutch influence was apparent in the north, particularly on chairs. The tall, straight-backed form with H-shaped stretchers, and often caned seat and back, associated with the early 18th century in England, was still popular in central and eastern Europe in mid-century. Alongside this, cabriole-legged chairs of English and French derivation were usual.

At a higher level, the two most influential cabinet-makers of the second half of the 18th century were Abraham Roentgen (1711–93) and his son David (1743–1807), from whose workshops in Neuwied-am-Rhein furniture of the most exquisite virtuosity and complexity emanated. Through Abraham's experience in the Netherlands and England and, later, David's travels throughout Europe, the Roentgens cultivated an international, largely royal clientele and bridged the Rococo and the Neo-Classical. Their marquetry was unsurpassed, and the complex internal mechanisms (locks, secret drawers, clocks and so on) of many pieces earned David Roentgen in France the title of *ébéniste-méchanicien du Roi et de la Reine* (cabinet-maker-mechanic to the King and Queen).

### THE NEO-CLASSICAL STYLE

The elegance of David Roentgen's late-18th-century writing tables and cabinets in the Neo-Classical style contrasts markedly with the ostentation of his earlier, essentially Rococo pieces. Marquetry now took the form of graceful flowers, leaves, beribboned festoons or writing or musical instruments, rather than the earlier colourful elaborate architectural scenes; and furniture forms lost their curves to become elegant interpretations of the Louis XVI style.

Other cabinet-makers in Germany were less eager to adopt the austere lines of Neo-Classicism, and in some transitional pieces of the 1770s Rococo curves co-exist with straight tapered legs and rectangular carcase shapes. In others Neo-Classical ornament is superimposed on old forms. By the end of the 18th century, however, classical straight-lined discipline of form and decorative motifs had been accepted in furniture that reflected both English and French influence. Nowhere was such elegant Neo-Classicism more successfully exhibited than at the court of the Emperor Joseph II (1780–90) in Vienna, and it was Vienna that was to become the focus of the new

**CIRCULAR CENTRE TABLE**
*German*
**Mahogany; early 19th century**

The table has a swivelling top and four spring-loaded drawers. Its ebonized and parcel-gilt decoration includes Neo-Classical motifs and masonic symbols. (*Above*)

**DESIGN FOR A WALL**
*Heinrich Asmus, Berlin*
**1844**

Taken from *Neue Ornamente von Heinrich Asmus*, this design is for "the upper part of a richly decorated wall". It exemplifies the lingering enthusiasm for the florid Grecian style in mid-19th-century Germany.

and distinctive Empire style of the Napoleonic years in the early 19th century.

The fully-fledged Empire style was too short-lived, and perhaps too austerely academic, to become a style of the people. It was seen in the furniture of palaces, like that designed by Johann Valentin Raab for the Würzburg *Residenz*, Leo von Klenze (1784–1864) in Munich and Karl Friedrich Schinkel (1781–1841) for the Prussian royal family in palaces in and around Berlin.

## BIEDERMEIER

The most pervasive development of the classical influence was the Biedermeier style which flourished in and around Vienna about 1815–1848 and spread through German-speaking Europe. This plain but comfortable style (*bieder* means "plain", *Meier* is a common German surname) evolved in response to the authoritarianism in Austria after the Congress of Vienna. Discouraged from political activity, the people concentrated on commerce, home life and a bourgeois culture of elegant simplicity. In furniture-making there was a new comfort-led practicality and the use of colourful textiles and figured woods. Different timbers were used

with great effect: mahogany, rosewood, walnut, fruitwoods, maple, sycamore and poplar. Inlaid patterns of ebony or black-stained fruitwood were sometimes used as a concession to embellishment. Lines were clean, but as often rounded as straight.

The ostentatiously large items of furniture of former years tended to give way to smaller pieces designed for specific functions. These included ladies' writing desks, sewing tables, cheval mirrors (a recent introduction) and bookcases. Particular ingenuity was shown in the design of small tables. Every well-furnished parlour now had a piano, and many had a china cabinet too. Emphasis was placed on comfortable seating: well-upholstered sofas with upswept sides were complemented by deep armchairs and a range of side chairs with upholstered seats and boldly shaped backs, standing on square tapered or turned legs with the minimum of embellishment. To meet the demand for such pieces many town-based joiners' workshops grew up.

In northern Germany the Biedermeier style was interpreted with less colour and variety, most often in mahogany with upholstery of black horsehair; shapes were reminiscent of

**BIEDERMEIER DRAWING ROOM**
*German*
Watercolour; **c. 1830**

This anonymous work shows the cosy informality that was a hallmark of the Biedermeier style. Comfortable as well as upright chairs are arranged around the centre table; personal mementoes sit on the side table; and a piano (possibly harpsichord) provides evidence of the period's enthusiasm for domestic music. The grandness of the tasselled curtains, with their gilded pelmets and tiebacks, is offset by the profusion of potted plants. (*Below*)

early 19th-century English furniture designs.

The pure designs of Biedermeier were inevitably displaced by the romantic, anti-classical spirit that emerged in the 1830s and 1840s all over Europe, unleashing its historical hotchpotch. The epitome of the new extravagance was reached by Carl Leistler (1805–57) of Vienna, who, having completely refurnished the breath-taking entertainment rooms of the Palais Liechtenstein with his wondrously carved Neo-Rococo splendours, went on to produce a monumental Gothic bookcase for the Great Exhibition of 1851.

## BENTWOOD FURNITURE

Leistler did not completely fill the Liechtenstein Palace with his own work: the chairs in the ballroom were provided by the Prussian-born Michael Thonet (1796–1871), whose bentwood (steam-curved wood) style is famous, not just for its elegance but because it represents the first mass-produced, universally available furniture. Thonet subsequently exported it all over the world. All types of pieces were sold, in parts, to be assembled with a few screws at their destination.

**AN ARTIST'S ROOM**
*Ludwig Hild*
Watercolour; 1841

Pictures and ornaments jostle for space in this extremely informal room. While the room's decoration is in the Neo-Rococo taste, most of the furniture in it, such as the chairs, table, mirror and lectern-shaped display case on the right, are Neo-Gothic. However, the desk on the left is pure Biedermeier and the small table in the window beyond is Neo-Classical. (*Above*)

**BIEDERMEIER SOFA**

Well-made furniture of solid proportions but unpretentious decoration such as this was characteristic of the Biedermeier style. (*Below*)

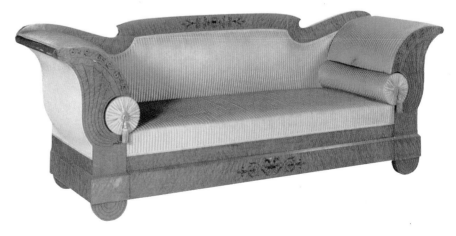

THE PROVERBIALLY IMMENSE WEALTH OF THE RUSSIAN ARISTOCRACY IN
THE DAYS OF THE TSARS DEMONSTRATED ITSELF IN THE SHOWY PIECES
WITH WHICH THEY FURNISHED THEIR GRAND HOMES.

# RUSSIA

In Russia the most fashionable European fur-niture styles were enthusiastically adopted for palaces and country houses. What sort of furnishings the masses enjoyed is not well docu-mented, but they were probably more starkly contrasted with those of the aristocracy than in any other European country. Russian cabinet-makers themselves were customarily bound to particular houses as serfs and were not free to seek their fortunes as elsewhere.

In the late 17th century, Russia began im-porting fine-quality pieces and having them copied by local craftsmen in native woods. The ambitions of Peter the Great (1672–1725) to establish a great cultural and economic centre at St Petersburg (founded 1703) prompted him to send cabinet-makers to England and the Netherlands to study the styles and techniques of the best craftsmen there. Thus an interesting blend of mid-European styles and peculiarly Russian characteristics developed during the 18th century and into the 19th.

### FRENCH AND GERMAN INFLUENCES

It was the French Rococo that made the most direct impact on the furnishing of Russian palaces. Between 1716 and 1726 the French sculptor and woodcarver Nicolas Pineau (1684-1754), one of the leading exponents of Rococo design, worked in Russia, introducing carved

*boiseries* into Peter the Great's study. The import of fashionable French furniture and the published designs of other leading practitioners of Rococo were additional factors in the adop-tion of a highly developed form of the style in Russia. Later, Count Bartolommeo Francesco Rastrelli (*c.*1700–71), son of an Italian sculptor, became chief architect at the Russian court, and introduced a florid and Germanic style of deco-ration to the Imperial residence Tsarskoe Selo and the Winter Palace at St Petersburg.

Neo-Classicism in Russia took an equally sumptuous form. It was introduced by the Scottish architect Charles Cameron (*c.*1743–1812), who worked for Catherine the Great (1729–96) from the late 1770s and pro-vided decorations and furnishings for many of the royal residences. The furniture was supplied by the most fashionable Parisian *ébénistes*.

David Roentgen was also a major influence on the development of Neo-Classicism in Russia. He visited St Petersburg several times and supplied Catherine with no less than seven consignments of furniture. Many of the most-respected cabinet-makers working in Russia were German migrants imbued with the crafts-manship ideals of the Roentgens' Neuwied-am-Rhein workshop. One of these was Christian Meyer; another was Heinrich Gambs (1765–1831), who designed furniture for

**WRITING CABINET**
*Russian*
**Karelian birch and poplar veneer; early 19th century**

This piece is some 280 cm (9 ft 2 in) high, but only 94 cm (37 in) wide.

## RUSSIAN FURNITURE MAKERS

| | | | |
|---|---|---|---|
| **RASTRELLI, Bartolommeo Francesco** | *c.*1700–71 | St Petersburg | Chief architect at the Russian court. Produced large-scale, Rococo-style furniture with vigorous carved decoration and strong colours. |
| **CAMERON, Charles** | *c.*1743–1812 | St Petersburg | Scottish architect; introduced Neo-Classicism into Russia. Worked for Catherine the Great and produced richly gilded interiors. |
| **GAMBS, Heinrich** | 1765–1831 | St Petersburg | The most important cabinet-maker of the period. Designed furniture for Catherine's successor, Paul I. |

## THE STEEL FURNITURE OF TULA

The small-arms factory at Tula in central Russia, founded by Peter the Great, also produced steel furniture and ornaments from the early 18th century. Although few of the products of this period survive, there is a considerable quantity from the later 18th century, when steel furniture was made for Catherine the Great's palaces. Her own visit to Matthew Boulton's Birmingham factory in England probably influenced the style of much Russian cut-steel work, and it is possible that Birmingham craftsmen went to Russia and introduced Boulton's techniques.

Fireplaces, fenders, fire-irons, caskets and other small ornamental furnishings of burnished steel were decorated with Neo-Classical motifs in faceted beads and are strongly reminiscent of Adam designs. Of particular elegance are the folding X-frame chairs, some with backs and sides full of scrolling plant decoration and others with seats and backs formed by thin straps of metal. A development of the cut-steel technique was the encrusting of other metals – silver, pewter, brass and copper – on to the steel surface.

**NEO-CLASSICAL TEA CADDY;**
Tula steel work decoration.

Catherine's successor, Paul I (1796–1807).

### THE 19TH CENTURY

By the early 19th century, French influence was once more dominant, through the predilections of the francophile Tsar Alexander I (1801–25). He employed a Swiss artistic adviser, Thomas de Thomon (1754–1813), who designed furniture as well as carrying out architectural projects, and imported considerable quantities of French furniture for his palaces.

The two most important Russian designers of the early 19th century were Andrei Nikiforovich Voronkin (1760–1814), who had been trained in Paris and interpreted the furniture designs of Charles Percier and Pierre-François-Léonard Fontaine with a muscular exuberance unknown in France, and the Italian Carlo Rossi (1775–1849), whose work is an elegant distillation of the Empire style.

Most Russian craftsmen tended to produce furniture in a style deriving from both French and English models – a compromise between the work of Jacob Desmalter and that of Thomas Sheraton. This tendency to adopt the characteristics of European styles grew during the 19th century, and a great deal of mid-century Russian furniture is virtually indistinguishable from European examples. A more distinct identity was often conferred by the use of native woods, particularly Karelian birch, of light colour and interesting figuring (patterns).

Contrasting tones of wood were used with great effect on floors, which were usually inlaid in geometric patchworks of diamonds and squares. In the less grand houses these were often painted.

**CONSOLE TABLE AND PIER GLASS**
*Russian*
Mahogany and ormolu;
**c. 1810**

A tall, thin piece in the Neo-Classical style, the table-cum-pier glass shows strong French influence. Indeed, many pieces were made in France especially for the Russian market during this period.

THE PINE FORESTS OF SCANDINAVIA PROVIDED A RICH RESOURCE FOR
THE REGION'S FURNITURE-MAKERS. THEY PRODUCED A RANGE OF
GAILY-PAINTED PRODUCTS THAT MADE FOR COLOURFUL INTERIORS.

# SCANDINAVIA

Painted furniture – of birch, beech or ash as well as pine – was characteristic of Scandinavian houses (even those of the rich), almost all of which were themselves of timber. Even so, Sweden and Norway were as open as any other country to stylistic developments in Europe. The English demand for timber to reconstruct London after the Fire of 1666 brought both prosperity and English furniture design to Scandinavia in the late 17th century, and because English design was itself affected by Dutch, Scandinavian furniture of the period is distinctly Anglo-Dutch.

The high-backed, cane-seated or upholstered chair fashionable in late 17th-century England and the Netherlands was enthusiastically adopted in Scandinavia and persisted well into the 18th century. The general conservatism of

**BUREAU-CABINET**
*Danish*
**Painted wood; early 18th century**

Painted to simulate lacquerwork, this Scandinavian piece features chinoiserie scenes and figures on red marbled panels and blue borders.

Scandinavian chair-makers (traditionally separate from the more progressive cabinet-makers) ensured the lingering popularity of chair styles outmoded in other parts of Europe. The cabriole-legged, splat-backed chairs of the Queen Anne and early Georgian periods enjoyed an extended popularity in Scandinavia, where the chairs were fitted with turned stretchers long after these had been dispensed with in England.

English styles, as purveyed in many books of designs for gentlemen's furniture, considerably influenced bourgeois furniture in Scandinavia. The fall-front desk and the long-case clock were among the English forms that appealed to the Scandinavians and subsequently were made over a long period.

Because of its geographical closeness, Germany also strongly affected Scandinavian furniture types and styles. Many Scandinavian craftsmen learnt their trade in Germany, while German cabinet-makers often practised in Denmark, Norway or Sweden.

The Rococo in Scandinavia, at first confined to the court, tended to be interpreted in its Germanic form, especially in Denmark and Norway. Sweden was more francophile, and Paris-trained architects dominated the introduction of the style into the salons of Stockholm in the 1730s and 1740s. Enthusiasm for French art was not new. In the late 17th century both the old royal castles of Copenhagen and Stockholm had been replaced by grand palaces in the spirit of Versailles; and much of the furniture for them had been imported from France and the rest copied by Danish craftsmen from French models.

### NEO-CLASSICISM AND AFTER
French influence on Denmark became strong in the Neo-Classical period, largely through the appointment of the French sculptor Jacques-François Saly (1717–96) as director of the new Copenhagen Academy, where he raised Danish artistic standards. In Sweden, where Neo-

Classicism was adopted later than in Denmark, its interpretation included both French and English elements. Commodes followed French forms but were often veneered, English-style, in mahogany rather than in the decorative parquetry generally favoured in France. Mahogany was also used in solid construction, especially for splat-backed chairs of Hepplewhite and Sheraton derivation.

Georg Haupt (1741–84), the most important cabinet-maker working in Stockholm in the 1770s, had gained experience all over Europe and proved himself as capable of producing delicately crafted tables with a strong English flavour as of creating large-scale, ormolu-embellished masterpieces in the fully-fledged Louis XVI style. The Masreliez brothers, Louis Adrien (1748–1810) and Jean Baptiste Edouard (1753–1801), continued to adopt French styles for Swedish court furniture. But another major Swedish cabinet-maker working at the turn of the century, Gotlob Iwersson, was mostly inspired by English models.

Most imported furniture now came from Germany, and in the stylish and idiosyncratic simplicity of the ensuing Danish Empire style there are strong echoes not only of English Regency but of Biedermeier. Such classical elegance lingered on throughout Scandinavia until the second quarter of the 19th century but was then overtaken, first in Sweden and later in Denmark and Norway, by the eclecticism that pervaded the rest of Europe.

**CONSOLE TABLE**
*Swedish*
**Pine; c. 1815**

Both French and English influence can be seen in much Swedish furniture, like this dolphin-supported console table. Native pine, available in plentiful supplies, provided an ideal base for gilding. (*Right*)

**COMMODE**
*Georg Haupt*
Marquetry, marble and ormolu; 1780

This marble-topped Neo-Classical commode, with marquetry decoration and chiselled gilt-bronze mounts, was made by Georg Haupt, the versatile Swedish cabinet-maker. (*Left*)

## SCANDINAVIAN FURNITURE MAKERS

| | | | |
|---|---|---|---|
| **HAUPT, Georg** | 1741–1784 | Stockholm | Most important cabinet-maker in Stockholm in the 1770s. Versatility demonstrated in range of work, from delicately crafted tables to large-scale ormolu-embellished pieces in Louis XVI style. |
| **MASRELIEZ, Louis Adrien and Jean Baptiste Edouard** | 1748–1810 1753–1801 | Stockholm | Worked at the Swedish court. |

FURNITURE MAKERS IN THE NETHERLANDS MADE THE MOST OF MANY
OUTSIDE INFLUENCES THAT AFFECTED THEM, DISTILLING THEIR DESIGNS
INTO A CHARACTERISTICALLY MUSCULAR FORM.

# THE NETHERLANDS

The Dutch were supreme masters in the absorption of styles. Influences came from many quarters: France; Germany; the East, where the Dutch had had such trading success; Moorish southern Europe (as a result of the long period of Austro-Spanish domination of the Netherlands), discernible in the arabesque patterns and geometric motifs in Dutch furniture; and in particular, Britain, with whom an exchange of influences was strengthened when the Dutch William of Orange and the English Mary became joint monarchs in 1688.

### ANGLO-DUTCH FURNITURE

In the late 17th and early 18th centuries, when Dutch influence on English furniture was particularly strong, the Dutch in turn absorbed what they liked about English styles and types. The result was what has become known as the Anglo-Dutch style. Caning for chairs was a Dutch introduction that became equally popular in England, and the vogue for oriental lacquer and the development of japanning in imitation of it was also common to both countries.

Dutch cabinet-makers became leaders in the new craft of veneering, and by the end of the 17th century they had developed a specialized form of this, floral marquetry, using imported and native woods of many different and subtle shades. One of the art's first exponents – and one of its greatest – was Jan van Mekeren of Amsterdam (*fl. c.*1690–*c.*1735), much of whose work was exported.

The Dutch passion for porcelain led to the invention of the glass-fronted display cabinet, and corner cupboards, some with lacquered panels in the doors, were also used for displaying china collections. Both types were adopted in England. Another characteristic piece of Anglo-Dutch furniture was the bureau-bookcase, with a sloping fall front at the top of the bureau and above a bookcase with two doors and a double-arched pediment (moulded top). The piece was often japanned.

**DISPLAY CABINET**
*Dutch*
**Walnut; mid 18th century**

This piece features carved cresting in the Rococo style and decoratively scrolled glazing bars. The Dutch invented the glass-fronted showcase in response to the national passion for ceramics.

Dutch and English chairs also ran a parallel course; typical of the last quarter of the 17th century were carved frames in oak or walnut, with caned seats and backs. By the early 18th century, Dutch chairs had taken on the flowing lines of English examples, with cabriole legs, ball and claw feet and shaped backs with decorated splats, some of which had panels of floral marquetry. The burgomaster, or roundabout chair, was a type imported into the Netherlands from the East Indies during the late 17th or early 18th century. It had a round caned seat, a low back with carved splats and turned supports, and carved cabriole legs united by turned stretchers.

## DUTCH FURNITURE MAKERS

| | | | |
|---|---|---|---|
| **MAROT, Daniel** | c.1663–1752 | The Hague and London | Worked in France, Holland and England, and contributed to the Anglo-Dutch style. Produced state beds festooned with rich materials, and a new style of richly carved chair in walnut with elongated back. |
| **BREYTSPRAAK, Carel** | fl. c.1795–1810 | Amsterdam | Employed by Louis Napoleon in Amsterdam. Worked in the Neo-Classical style. |

Dutch examples, usually of walnut or oak, as well as Indian, were exported during the 18th century and were copied, usually in lighter form, by English chair-makers.

### BAROQUE AND ROCOCO

During the 17th and 18th centuries many craftsmen left the Netherlands to seek their fortunes in France or England, but at the same time just as many from abroad came to the Netherlands, often as a result of Protestant persecution in France. One such was Daniel Marot (1663–1752), who spent his formative years imbibing the courtly Baroque style in Paris, then successfully transposed it to the Netherlands. His furniture, from costly state beds festooned with rich materials to elaborately carved chairs set in rows around rooms, was distinctly sculptural. Marot's attachment to the court of William of Orange, both in the Netherlands and England, made him an important contributor to the Anglo-Dutch style, and his engraved designs for all kinds of furnishings were influential on both sides of the English Channel.

By the 1720s, Marot's heavy Baroque style was already being supplanted in the Netherlands by the lighter exuberance of the Rococo, and the influence of France was overtaking that of England. By the 1740s, bureau-cabinets were characteristically bombé in the lower stage, with curvaceous cornices and scrolled mouldings on door panels. Walnut, with its elaborate and irregular figuring, was the most favoured timber for veneered pieces, while mahogany, oak, elm and fruitwoods were used in the solid. The southern Netherlands were always the most influenced by France, as shown in a speciality of the Liège region: panelled oak cupboards decorated with lively carving of rococo scrolls, cartouches and asymmetrical tendrils.

Flowers, whether in the garden, in paintings, on china and textiles, or on furniture, had always been a great love of the Dutch, and floral mar-

**SIDE CHAIR**
*Dutch*
Walnut

In the Anglo-Dutch style, the chair has a vase-shaped splat, carved shell motifs on the top rail and knees of the front legs, and ball-and-claw feet. The floral marquetry is typically Dutch. (*Left*)

**COMMODE**
*Dutch*
Wood, marble and ormolu;
**18th century**

This French-style bombé commode features kingwood and tulipwood veneers on the sides and across the two-drawer front *sans traverse*. (*Below*)

quetry was one of the Netherlands' most striking bequests in furniture ornamentation. Bureaux, chests of drawers, cabinets, chairs and clock cases were all decorated with fabulous veneers of naturalistic flowers in vases, baskets, swags or bouquets. Such pieces show a distinctively Dutch combination of craftsmanship with serviceability, of solidity of form with exuberance of decoration.

### NEO-CLASSICISM

With the onset of Neo-Classicism veneered decoration became more restrained and symmetrical; flowers now appeared only in small

**CABINET-ON-STAND**
Walnut and rosewood; **late 17th century**

This piece is lavishly decorated with floral marquetry enclosed within oyster-veneered borders.

bouquets or sprays on inset lacquer panels. The fashion in the Netherlands for both French and English furniture continued in the second half of the 18th century, to the extent that Dutch cabinet-makers felt their livelihoods assailed by imports, particularly from France. In 1771 the protests of the Amsterdam Guild resulted in a ban on all foreign imports of furniture. The high standards of Dutch cabinet-making were maintained by the Amsterdam Joseph's Guild, which required that all furniture made there be branded.

During the last decades of the 18th century, when Dutch cabinet-makers were especially prosperous, a French-inspired version of Neo-Classicism prevailed. Rococo curves gave way to rectangular shapes and straight, tapered legs for chests, tables and chairs. Mahogany had by this time supplanted walnut for most furniture, but satinwood was also much used. The Dutch continued to make a speciality of marquetry in other exotic woods, often including *trompe l'oeil* architectural details such as fluting. Ormolu (gilt-bronze) mounts were used sparingly, but lacquer panels were sometimes incorporated into marquetry.

A typically Dutch item of this period was the *Opfluptafel*, a type of buffet commode with a two-door cupboard below, a lift-up top revealing shelves in the lid, and sometimes a basin set into the centre of the carcase. Side flaps provided additional serving space.

In the early 19th century the French Neo-Classical influence was reinforced by King Louis Napoleon, whose conversion of the town hall in Amsterdam into a royal palace in 1808 gave employment to Dutch craftsmen such as Carel Breytspraak (*fl. c.*1795–1810) and Joseph Cuel, who supplied stylish furniture in the more severe Empire style exhibited by the French furniture-designers Percier and Fontaine in their design book *Recueil de décorations intérieurs* (1801). This book was as influential in the Netherlands as elsewhere in Europe and did much to encourage the careful use of ormolu mounts as a contrast with the dark woods then favoured. All-over gilding of grandly carved furniture was also a feature of the later Empire style, which persisted for some time after Napoleon's downfall.

### BIEDERMEIER AND AFTER

Many Dutch people in the second quarter of the 19th century clearly preferred the restrained elegance of Biedermeier furniture,

for which lighter woods such as amboyna, ash and walnut were used as often as mahogany and fruitwoods and whose well-made, gently curving but essentially "Grecian" designs were eminently suited to the Dutch interior.

Before long, however, a demand for ostentatious ornament developed. New factories, such as those of the Horrix Brothers in The Hague and M. Roule in Antwerp, were able to supply it, and the Netherlands shared in a general European stylistic eclecticism. Dutch cabinet-makers once again made a speciality of floral marquetry, much of which was exported. In addition, plain old furniture was re-veneered with the Dutch flower-pieces of which the public all over Europe never seemed to tire.

**BUREAU-CABINET**
*Dutch*
**Walnut; mid 18th century**

This piece combines the strong proportions and exuberant marquetry of naturalistic flowers which have come to be associated with Dutch cabinet-making.

IN THIS ERA MANY INNOVATIVE DESIGNERS AND MAKERS MINGLED
RADICAL TECHNIQUES AND NOVEL MATERIALS TO CREATE A NEW
SYNTHESIS OF TRADITIONAL STYLES FOR THE AGE.

# BRITAIN AND EUROPE 1860–1920

The great mass of British and European furniture made during the period 1860–1920 is hardly distinguishable at first glance from pieces made over the preceding 300 years. Cabinet-makers usually imitated the various styles that had succeeded one another since the Renaissance. A second look, however, reveals such errors of proportion, debasement of materials and degradation of craftsmanship that it is impossible to confuse the imitation with the original. Some fine reproduction furniture was made, but the best pieces of the period are almost always original in their design and usually demonstrate a radical approach to technique and the types of wood used. They do, however, constitute only a small fraction of the furniture that was produced.

### BRITISH FURNITURE
The Gothic Revival furniture designed by A.W.N. Pugin (1812–52) began a movement in British furniture design towards simple construction and restrained ornament. At the

Medieval Court, a feature of the Great Exhibition of 1851 and the International Exhibition of 1862, such pieces were displayed by Pugin, John Pollard Seddon (1827–1906), Richard Norman Shaw (1831–1912) and Morris, Marshall, Faulkner & Co. Most of the work was decorated with painted ornament

**SIDE CHAIRS**
*E.W. Pugin*
**Oak; c. 1870**

The furniture designed by E.W. Pugin adhered to the principles of simplicity and clear construction that had earlier been preached by his father, the influential architect and designer A.W.N. Pugin. (*Above*)

**CABINET**
**Painted wood; c. 1861–2**

The cabinet is decorated with scenes from the life of St George painted by William Morris. The medievalism of the piece is typical of the furniture produced by Morris & Co during the 1860s. (*Left*)

incorporating scenes from medieval legends, with long strap hinges and with large lock-plates (plates protecting keyholes) and handles in chased iron or steel. The designers were trying to evoke, but not to imitate, the furniture of the Middle Ages, and they consciously avoided forms and decoration introduced during or since the Renaissance.

Much of the furniture produced by Morris, Marshall, Faulkner & Co. (or Morris & Co., as it was known from 1875) was designed by the architect Philip Webb (1831–1915), whose style was characterized by a subtle manipulation of volumes and a refined elaboration of structure. Gradually he liberated his work from the domination of the Neo-Gothic style and exploited a wide range of sources, including Japanese furniture forms.

**From Neo-Gothic to Queen Anne Revival**
The ethos of simple, well-made furniture in the Neo-Gothic or a vernacular style was widely disseminated by Charles Eastlake (1836–1906) in his book *Hints on Household Taste in Furniture, Upholstery and Other Details* (1868), illustrated with many of the author's own designs. Eastlake's book assisted the transition from Neo-Gothic to Queen Anne Revival, which became the style favoured by many architects and designers during the 1870s and 1880s. Some, such as Bruce Talbert (1838–81), E. W. Godwin (1833–86) and Charles Bevan, worked happily in both styles, the main point of their furniture being that it was plainly constructed and generally free of carving and

**CABINET**
*W. Gualbert Saunders*
Painted wood; **c. 1875**

The designer and craftsman W. Gualbert Saunders ran Saunders & Co, a firm established in 1865 by the architect William Burges, who had been associated with William Morris and his circle. The Gothic style of Saunders' furniture tends to be more archaic than that produced by Morris & Co. *(Right)*

**WASHSTAND**
*William Burges*
Painted and gilt wood;
*c.* 1880

Burges designed some of his most flamboyant furniture for his own Kensington house. By the time this washstand was made, its Neo-Gothic style had long fallen from favour. *(Above)*

veneers. The Japanesque furniture designed by Godwin and others shared these features. It was loosely based on the architectural forms of Japan as shown in the woodblock prints which were arriving in the West.

All these various styles contributed to Aesthetic Movement furniture, which was characterized by the extensive use of ebonized wood and was sometimes decorated with painted panels or ceramic tiles. Furniture designs by Christopher Dresser (1834–1904) included pieces in a wide variety of styles, including Greek, Egyptian, Gothic and Japanese.

The furniture that the architect Arthur Heygate Mackmurdo (1851–1942) designed for the Century Guild, founded in 1882, was derived from Queen Anne and other 18th-century styles. Two pieces, however, had a profound influence on subsequent furniture design and may be counted as important precursors of Art Nouveau. One was a side chair (one without arms) which was basically in early-18th-century style but whose fretwork back was decorated with a design of swirling submarine protozoa that looked forward to some French, Belgian and German furniture made towards the end of the century. The other influential piece was a desk by Mackmurdo, based on a Georgian orig-

## PRINCIPAL FURNITURE DESIGNERS 1860–1920

| | |
|---|---|
| **Charles Francis Annesley Voysey** | 1857–1941 |
| **Gustave Serrurier-Bovy** | 1858–1910 |
| **Louis Majorelle** | 1859–1926 |
| **Victor Horta** | 1861–1947 |
| **Josef Maria Olbrich** | 1867–1908 |
| **Hector Guimard** | 1867–1942 |
| **Koloman Moser** | 1868–1918 |
| **Charles Rennie Mackintosh** | 1868–1928 |
| **Josef Hoffmann** | 1870–1956 |
| **August Endell** | 1871–1925 |

inal but formed into uncompromisingly geometrical shapes and the ancestor of many similar pieces designed over the next three decades in England, Scotland, Austria and the United States.

Furniture designed by George Jack (1855–1932) and W. A. S. Benson for Morris & Co. during the late 1880s and 1890s was largely based on 18th-century forms, although Benson also created some pieces derived from country furniture. The Guild of Handicraft, founded in 1888 by Charles Robert Ashbee (1863–1942), produced furniture to his design. Loosely Queen Anne Revival, Ashbee's designs were often decorated with painted and gilt gesso.

Before setting up their own workshops in the Cotswolds, Ernest Gimson (1864–1919) and Sidney Barnsley (1865–1926) were both associated with Kenton & Co., an association of architects and craftsmen formed in 1890 to produce furniture of quality. Gimson's pieces were made up by skilled carpenters, but Barnsley constructed his own. The work of both is usually in a "farmhouse" style: massive, solidly built, with chamfered (bevelled-edge) stretchers (struts connecting legs) and supports and occasionally decorated with inlay or simple gouged ornament.

**Voysey and Baillie Scott** The designs of the architect C. F. A. Voysey (1857–1941) are among the most innovative in the entire history of English furniture. Characteristic features of his work include tall, narrow uprights, broad, flat cornices and large strap hinges with cut-out decoration. His furniture was oak, sometimes stained, and it was made by accomplished craftsmen, such as Arthur Simpson, who subsequently made furniture to his own designs in a style derived from Voysey's.

The furniture made by the Bedford firm of J. P. White to designs by M. H. Baillie Scott (1865–1945) was more elaborately decorated than Voysey's. Most pieces were inlaid with stylized flowers or birds. The forms, however, were quite simple. When some pieces designed by Baillie Scott for the Grand Ducal Palace at Darmstadt were made up by cabinet-makers at the Guild of Handicraft, Ashbee's own furniture became simpler; its decoration, too, was influenced by Baillie Scott's work.

**Mackintosh and his influence** The designs of the Scots architect Charles Rennie Mackintosh (1868–1928) show a virtuosity which is breathtaking, if sometimes self-indulgent. It is easy to

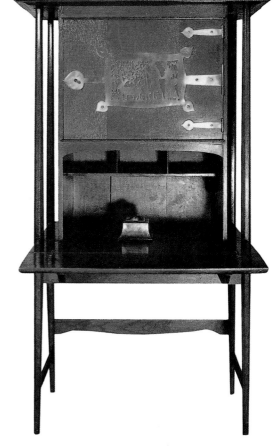

**WRITING DESK**
*C.F.A. Voysey*
**Oak; c. 1900**

The elaborate copper hinges hark back to the medieval influence of the 1860s and 1870s, but the general freedom from ornament and the simple lines proclaim Voysey's defiance of Victorian conventions. (*Right*)

**SIDE CHAIRS**
*C.F.A. Voysey*
**Oak; 1898**

The high backs, with their extended verticals, and the heart-shaped cut-outs in the splats, are typical of Voysey's furniture design. (*Below*)

understand why his furniture was not well received in England. Simplicity was sacrificed to sophistication, tradition was flouted and scant respect was shown for materials. The furniture was made from various woods, including oak, cypress, pine and mahogany, which were rarely left untreated; they were either French polished, stained, ebonized or painted.

Many of Mackintosh's designs were parodies of traditional types of furniture. For instance, his ladder-back chair has an exaggeratedly high back with its narrow uprights ridiculously close together. The designer George Walton (1867–1933), also based in Glasgow until 1898, when he moved to London, gave narrow, tapering legs to much of his furniture. One of his designs was an adaptation of a traditional, rush-seated chair that had arms curving forward from a narrow back with a narrow splat back pierced with a heart-shaped opening. This design was widely imitated both in Britain and on the Continent.

Around the turn of the century, several manufacturers produced furniture in a style often called "quaint" by contemporaries and loosely based on the work of Voysey, Mackintosh and other Arts and Crafts Movement designers. Liberty & Co. made stained oak furniture often decorated with repoussé (embossed by hammering from within) copper panels and fruitwood, metal and mother-of-pearl inlay. Another firm, Wylie & Lochhead of Glasgow, produced furniture in a style influenced by Mackintosh, although without his wilder idiosyncrasies. Like Liberty's furniture, it was often elaborately inlaid, and the wood was often stained unusual colours, such as grey or violet.

John Sollie Henry's firm in London made furniture in a similar style. Mahogany was generally used and Henry himself did much of the designing. However, he also commissioned designs from Voysey, Benson and Walton, and several of his pieces were designed by George Montague Ellwood. Other manufacturers producing similar furniture were the Bath Cabinet-makers Company (for which Ellwood designed) and the London firm of Shapland & Petter.

**Heal & Son** One furnishing company, Heal & Son of London, produced a wide range of furniture in the Cotswold style created by Gimson and Barnsley. It was designed by Ambrose Heal (1872–1959) and was featured in a catalogue of "Simple Furniture" issued by the firm in 1899. Oak was generally used, although chestnut or mahogany versions were also offered. The fur-

**SIDE CHAIR**
*Charles Rennie Mackintosh*
**Oak; c. 1900**

The form of the back splat, extended to a rail at the bottom of the legs, was a highly innovative treatment of a traditional design. (*Right*)

**WRITING CABINET**
*Charles Rennie Mackintosh*
**Oak and coloured glass; 1904**

The two views show the cabinet closed and opened up to serve as a writing desk. (*Below*)

**TABLE**
*Charles Rennie Mackintosh*
**Painted wood and coloured glass; c. 1905**

Inlays of glass, metal or mother-of-pearl were characteristic of the furniture designed in Glasgow. Often the wood was treated in some way. (*Below*)

**SIDE CHAIR**
*Omega Workshops*
Painted wood; **c. 1913**

It is not known exactly who designed this chair (sometimes called the Egyptian chair) but it was probably Roger Fry, the founder and director of the Omega Workshops. A variant has an extension to the back in the form of three-quarters of a ring, thus making the top rail into the Greek letter $\Omega$ (omega). The painted decoration is characteristic of Omega Workshop products, both in its painterly conception and in its amateurish execution. Roger Fry repudiated William Morris' insistence on good craftsmanship, maintaining that artistic expression was more important.

niture was more modest in scale and less rustic in style than Gimson's and Barnsley's, intended as it was for suburban homes.

**The Omega Workshops** In 1913 the painter Roger Fry (1866–1934) established the Omega Workshops in Fitzroy Square, London, close to Tottenham Court Road, where several leading furniture stores (including Heal's) had their premises. Omega furniture was designed by the painters Vanessa Bell, Duncan Grant, Wyndham Lewis and Fry himself and was made up in local workshops. It was painted or decorated in marquetry, in aggressively modern styles based on Fauvism.

FRENCH FURNITURE

"We all cribbed from Viollet-le-Duc," stated the architect and designer William Burges (1827–81), referring to the Neo-Gothic school of English designers. Eugène Viollet-le-Duc (1814–79) was a French architect, most of whose career was devoted to the restoration of Gothic buildings. He also designed furniture in a Gothic style for the châteaux of Pierrefonds and Roquetaillade – but his approach was archaeological and his furniture designs had neither strength nor originality. What impressed Burges and his friends were Viollet-le-Duc's books, particularly his *Dictionnaire du*

*Mobilier Français (Dictionary of French Furniture*, 1858–75), a comprehensive guide to the Gothic decorative arts.

Viollet-le-Duc had considerable influence on the work of the graphic artist Eugène Grasset, who designed some furniture for Charles Gillot, the owner of the press where most of Grasset's work was printed. The oak and walnut suite, made between 1879 and 1885, was decorated with low relief carving and elaborate iron fittings, but its most telling feature was the clearly indicated construction – stretchers, supports and brackets making a lively visual display.

In Paris, most cabinet-makers rested on their laurels, gained during the 18th century and the earlier part of the 19th. They continued to make furniture that was richly decorated with gilding, silvering, boulle-work (brass and tortoiseshell inlay) and metal mounts. Renaissance, Louis XV and Louis XVI styles were popular throughout the second half of the 19th century; pieces in the Renaissance style were often decorated with sculpted figures. In the extraordinary furniture made by the sculptor Rupert Carabin there was an element of parody in the carved female nude figures which, with their physical flaws and indecorous poses, were far from the idealized classical maidens and athletes usually associated with Renaissance decoration.

**Oriental influences** Another escape from the straitjacket of historical styles was achieved by the Paris cabinet-maker Gabriel Viardot. Since the 18th century there had been in France a taste for chinoiserie, and cabinet-makers such as Giroux, Sormani and Duvinage, contemporaries of Viardot, made pieces, usually of rosewood or ebony, designed and decorated in an oriental manner, with shelves turned up at the ends, curled feet and elaborate ornament of ivory, lacquer and enamels. Viardot's oriental creations, however, were original and fantastic, featuring complicated, asymmetrical arrangements of shelves, sculpted bronze dragons and lacquer panels. His sources included not only Chinese and Japanese forms and ornament but also the art of Vietnam, colonized by the French.

**Gallé and Art Nouveau** Emile Gallé (1846–1904), already renowned for his pottery and glassware, established furniture workshops at Nancy in 1884. His early pieces were in a variety of styles, including Japanese, rococo and Renaissance. Soon, however, he began to use natural forms, both for structural members of his furniture – table legs carved as dragonflies, chair backs shaped as blossoms – and for mar-

quetry decoration. When, in a further stylistic development, Gallé adopted curving supports and sinuous stretchers, he had effectively arrived at Art Nouveau. His furniture was generally made of oak or walnut.

Another Nancy cabinet-maker was Louis Majorelle (1859–1929), whose furniture during the 1890s was influenced by Gallé's work. Previously, his output had been predominantly rococo in style, and the lightness and elegance of

**TABLE**
*Emile Gallé*
**Walnut and fruitwood;**
*c.* **1900**

Gallé produced four- and three-legged versions of this table which was called *Libellule* (Dragonfly). Carving was one of the most typical features of French Art Nouveau furniture. Gallé particularly favoured motifs from nature, and his use here of an insect was probably inspired by Japanese art and decoration. (*Right*)

**ARMCHAIR**
*Louis Majorelle*
**Mahogany; c. 1900**

The Nancy cabinet-maker Louis Majorelle was influenced by the work of Emile Gallé, but Majorelle's version of Art Nouveau was more abstract, with an emphasis on long, sweeping curves and shallow carving. There is an elegance about Majorelle's furniture which reveals his roots in the 19th-century Rococo Revival. (*Left*)

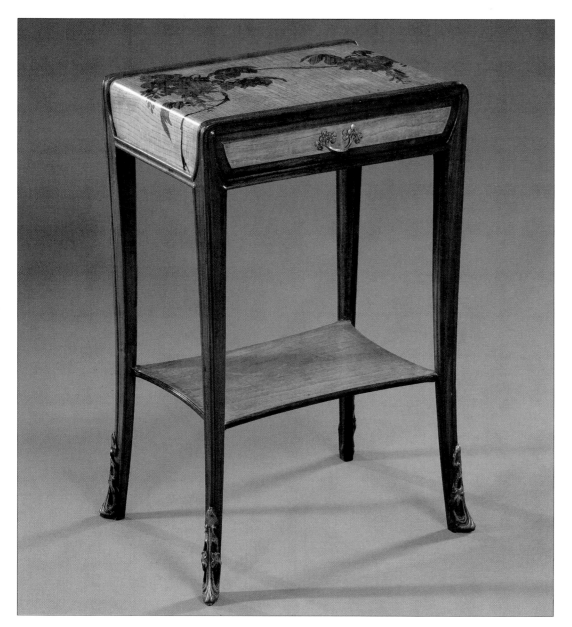

**SIDE TABLE**
*Louis Majorelle*
Walnut and fruitwood;
**c. 1900**

This example of Majorelle's work reveals his great respect for both the materials and the traditions of his craft; yet the table contrives to be unmistakably of its own era.

these Louis XV pieces persists in his Art Nouveau furniture. The gilt-bronze mounts which adorn his pieces also recall the work of the 18th-century *ébénistes* (cabinet-makers), although Majorelle's are moulded into botanical forms treated in the Art Nouveau manner. He most frequently used mahogany.

In 1900 Jacques Gruber (1870–1936), who had designed furniture for Majorelle, set up his own workshop to make furniture and stained glass. Some of the latter was incorporated in the doors of cabinets designed by Eugène Vallin (1856–1922).

Meanwhile, the Art Nouveau style had affected the furniture-makers of Paris. In 1895 Siegfried Bing (1838–1905) opened La Maison de l'Art Nouveau, where he sold furniture designed by Georges de Feure (1868–1943),

Eugène Gaillard (1862–1933) and Edward Colonna (1862–1948). De Feure and Colonna created furniture of great lightness and simplicity. Narrow, tapering chair and table legs have no stretchers, giving the furniture an airy, floating appearance, curves are gentle and carving is shallow and minimal. Some pieces were gilt, others were sparsely decorated with marquetry. The furniture was constructed of walnut or occasionally ash.

**Les Six** In 1897 a group of artists calling themselves Les Six held an exhibition in Paris which included furniture designed by the architect Charles Plumet and the brothers Pierre and Tony Selmersheim. Their work was Art Nouveau in style, often with a strong flavour of rococo in its sinuous lines and gilt metal fittings. Like the Nancy designers, Plumet and the

Selmersheims often alluded to natural forms in their work.

Another member of Les Six, the sculptor Alexandre Charpentier (1856–1909), designed furniture whose main effect was achieved by the treatment of the wood, its gilt-bronze reliefs and its colour: the wood was carved to give it a molten, sometimes almost liquid, appearance; the relief panels, handles and lock-plates represented female nudes; and the wood – usually hornbeam – was waxed to give it a yellow tint, somewhere between gold and honey.

Jean Dampt, another sculptor who belonged to the group, was a disciple of Ruskin and an admirer of the English Arts and Crafts Movement. His furniture is Art Nouveau, often with Neo-Gothic touches.

**Guimard** The Art Nouveau architect Hector Guimard (1867–1942), best known for designing the entrances to the Paris Métro stations,

**SIDE CHAIR**
*Eugène Gaillard*
Walnut; **c. 1900**

Gaillard advocated furniture forms inspired by nature but not in exact imitation of it. (*Right*)

**TABLE**
*Hector Guimard*
Waxed pearwood; **1904**

Guimard designed this table for the industrialist Léon Nozal. (*Below*)

also designed furniture. For the Castel Béranger, a block of flats that he built between 1894 and 1898, he created furniture which reflects his adherence to the principles of rational design taught by Viollet-le-Duc. Its construction, although visually flamboyant, is always justifiable in terms of strength and utility. The wave-like linear decoration carved in low relief is abstract but clearly inspired by natural forms. All traces of the Gothic that characterized Guimard's earliest furniture have disappeared.

While the Castel Béranger was being built, Guimard visited Brussels, and his furniture was influenced by the work of the architects and designers Henry Van de Velde (1863–1957) and Victor Horta (1861–1947) that he saw there. Guimard's chairs and sofas usually have seats and backs covered in leather incised with linear ornament. He furnished several of his subsequent buildings, including the Coilliot house in Lille, the Castel Henriette outside Paris, the Castel Val near Auvers-sur-Oise, his own house in Paris and a house for his friend Paul Mezzara, also in Paris. He used oak and pearwood, but particularly favoured eucalyptus.

**The reaction against Art Nouveau** Much of Guimard's furniture was made after the Paris Exhibition of 1900, which was dominated by the Art Nouveau style. Several of the leading Paris cabinet-makers showed elaborately carved pieces in the style, many decorated with extensive marquetry. The firms of Hugnet Frères, Perol Frères and Damon & Colin, among others, produced quantities of furniture in a debased version of Art Nouveau, so that, within a year or two of the 1900 exhibition, a reaction set in. Several designers started working in a much more restrained manner, drawing inspiration from 18th-century Neo-Classicism and French country furniture.

Paul Follot, formerly one of Eugène Grasset's pupils, exhibited at the 1909 Salon of the Société des Artistes-Décorateurs an interior furnished with pieces in a style of muted elegance reflecting the current taste for the Neo-Classical. Léon Jallot, once director of Siegfried Bing's workshops, designed furniture with strong vertical and horizontal accents. It was decorated with ornament which, although based on natural forms, was arranged in small areas of geometrical patterns.

From about 1910, the painter André Mare designed furniture in a style which owed something to traditional country pieces and some-

**COATSTAND**
*Gustave Serrurier-Bovy*
Metal; *c.* 1905

The Belgian designer Serrurier-Bovy started an extremely successful furniture-manufacturing business with his own retail outlets in Liège, Brussels, Paris, Nice and The Hague. This coatstand represents the geometrical style which he adopted towards the end of his career. (*Right*)

**CORNER CUPBOARD**
*Jacques-Émile Ruhlmann*
Rosewood, ivory and exotic woods; 1916

Ruhlmann's furniture signalled a radical departure from the Art Nouveau style. The exotic materials that he used, the luxuriousness of his furniture and the use of Neo-Classical motifs all look forward to the Art Deco style. (*Left*)

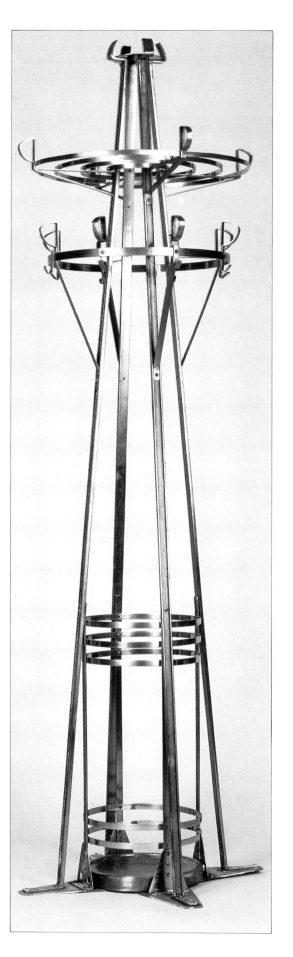

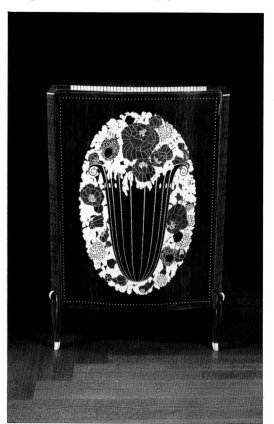

**BUFFET**
*Victor Horta*
**Wood; c. 1900**

The Belgian architect Victor Horta reveals his debt to Rococo forms in this piece he designed for his own house.

and scrolling curves of its ironwork, stained glass, woodwork and wall decoration. Some of the furniture designed by Horta for the Tassel house was, however, less innovative than the building itself. A buffet, for example, with glazed cupboards at each end surmounted by S-scroll pediments and carrying a pair of candelabra with several curling arms, would not have looked out of place in a rococo setting. On the other hand, the profusion of curved stretchers and supports under chairs and tables was pure Art Nouveau.

Horta's style moderated progressively through the 1890s, and by 1905 he had virtually abandoned the Art Nouveau style. His furniture is characterized by its abstract forms derived from nature and by its rather thin, spindly structural members. Horta created the idea of built-in furniture, which became such a typical feature of the Art Nouveau interior that the French writer Edmond Goncourt invented for it the sobriquet "Yachting Style"; a banquette, for example, would run along one wall, turn a corner and finish as a display case.

**Serrurier-Bovy** Horta had been influenced by his study of Viollet-le-Duc's writings, and another Belgian designer who came under the French architect's spell was Gustave Serrurier-Bovy (1858–1910). In 1884 he visited England and was deeply impressed by the theory and practice of William Morris, leader of the Arts and Crafts Movement. His earliest furniture was based on designs published in the London magazines *Cabinet Maker* and *British Architect*. The pieces that he showed in 1894 at the Salon de la Libre Esthétique, an exhibiting society formed by Belgian artists and designers, were still oriented towards the English Arts and Crafts style; but those he showed at the Salon the following year, although made of plain wood with iron mounts, acknowledged Continental Art Nouveau through the strongly curved elements in their design.

For the next decade Serrurier-Bovy's furniture reflected the dichotomy between his Morrisian delight in simple panel and plank construction and his enthusiasm for Belgian and French flamboyance. His furniture proved very popular, and he was soon running a large factory in Liège. In 1899 he opened a retail outlet in Paris called L'Art dans l'Habitation, and his furniture was seen at the 1900 Paris Exhibition in Le Pavillon Bleu. Like the English craftsmen he so much admired, Serrurier-Bovy generally

thing to Cubism. In 1912 he exhibited the Maison Cubiste, an interior complete with furniture and decoration in the style pioneered by Picasso and Braque.

The sensation of the 1913 Salon d'Automne was the furniture shown by the French cabinet-maker Jacques-Émile Ruhlmann (1879–1933). Constructed in exotic wood, such as amboyna, it was decorated with Neo-Classical motifs and geometrical patterns inlaid in ebony and ivory. These were a far cry from Art Nouveau.

## BELGIAN FURNITURE

The Belgian architect Victor Horta created a wild and flamboyant Art Nouveau for the house in Brussels he designed in 1892 for the engineer Émile Tassel: it was marked by the whiplash line

used oak for his furniture. Shortly before his death he started to design furniture that featured strong geometrical elements in both structure and decoration.

**Van de Velde** A third Belgian designer whose furniture is worthy of note was Henry Van de Velde. He started his career as a painter but in 1892 gave up painting and devoted himself to the applied arts. In 1895 he built himself a house, Bloemenwerf, in Uccle, near Brussels, for which he designed all the furniture himself. Like Serrurier-Bovy's, it incorporates features derived from both English Arts and Crafts practice and Horta's curvilinear style. It was made of oak, and some simply constructed sidechairs were rush-seated. But more elaborate pieces were decorated with carved ornament in a forceful Art Nouveau idiom.

Van de Velde had absorbed from the French Neo-Impressionist painters the notion of using lines to express psychological moods, and he attempted to impart emotional power to his abstract ornament. This intellectual approach seems to have appealed to the Germans: he designed office furniture for Julius Meier-Graefe, the German art critic who opened a shop in Paris selling modern furniture and decoration; in 1899 he designed pieces for the German firm of Löffler; and the following year

**SIDEBOARD**
*August Endell*
**Oak; c. 1900**

Endell based his designs on the psychological effects of line and proportion, believing that shape alone could induce feelings of serenity and satisfaction. His decorative motifs were derived from illustrations in scientific books dealing with primitive life-forms.

he moved to Berlin, after which his career belongs to the history of design in Germany.

### GERMAN FURNITURE
*Jugendstil* (Youth Style) was the German term for Art Nouveau. In Munich, during the 1890s, a number of architects, painters and sculptors, including Hermann Obrist (1863–1927), August Endell (1871–1921), Richard Riemerschmid (1868–1957), Bernhard Pankok (1872–1943) and Bruno Paul (1874–1954), turned their attention to the applied arts. In 1897 these five, among others, founded the Vereinigte Werkstätten für Kunst im Handwerk (United Workshops for Art in the Handicrafts). Obrist and Endell designed furniture in flowing, natural forms that were determined by a theory of interaction between physical appearances and psychological reactions. Obrist's furniture was made of oak, and Endell's of elm. Pankok's designs were also based on natural forms; he used oak, pearwood, walnut and spruce.

**Riemerschmid** Richard Riemerschmid's earliest experiments in furniture were some pieces he designed for his own apartment in 1895. They were in the Neo-Gothic style, made of stained and painted pine and decorated with elaborate wrought-iron hinges and foliate ornament carved in low relief. However,

Riemerschmid's style was to change, as a result of seeing in 1897 an exhibition at Dresden of Van de Velde's furniture, whose abstract Art Nouveau style had a considerable impact on all the Munich artists. The following year, Riemerschmid designed an oak side-chair, its back-rest carried on supports which descend in a sweeping curve to the feet of the front legs. A slightly altered version was soon being sold by Liberty's in London.

**CABINET**
*Otto Weinhold*
**Wood; c. 1900**

Elements of the English, German, French and Belgian versions of Art Nouveau can be detected in this cabinet.

Another Munich designer, Bruno Paul, also created furniture which was influenced by Van de Velde. Paul's work was characterized by elegant curved lines and was free of any ornament.

**The Dresden Workshops** One of the intentions underlying the work of the Munich artists was to create furniture cheap enough for a far larger public than could afford the hand-built furniture produced by the leading avant-garde designers of Paris, Nancy and Brussels. When selecting the forms their furniture would take, the Germans took into account the new woodworking machines being developed at the time. The leader of this tendency was Karl Schmidt, Riemerschmid's brother-in-law, who had trained as a cabinet-maker and in 1898 opened the Dresdner Werkstätten (Dresden Workshops). At an exhibition of industrial art held in Dresden in 1899–1900, Schmidt showed an apartment of two living rooms, bedroom and kitchen, inexpensively furnished with simple modern furniture. Five years later, the Dresdner Werkstätten produced a range of machine-made furniture designed by Riemerschmid.

**The German Workshops** In 1902 Adelbert Niemeyer, an artist, and Karl Bertsch, an upholsterer, founded a workshop in Munich for the manufacture of furniture and other items of interior decoration. In 1907 the workshop merged with the Dresdner Werkstätten and the two became known as the Deutsche Werkstätten (German Workshops); this should not be confused with the Deutscher Werkbund, an association of designers, craftsmen, manufacturers and retailers promoted by the German government and founded the same year. Niemeyer continued to design furniture for the Deutsche Werkstätten until his death. Other designers who occasionally worked for the Dresden concern were Baillie Scott and the Austrians Josef Hoffmann (1870–1956) and Koloman Moser (1868–1918).

**The Darmstadt designers** Baillie Scott's work was well known on the Continent, having been frequently illustrated in *The Studio* magazine. The illustrations had caught the eye of the Grand-Duke Ernst Ludwig of Hesse-Darmstadt, who in 1897 had had a drawing-room and a dining-room in his palace at Darmstadt furnished and decorated by Baillie Scott and Ashbee. He encouraged the establishment of an artists' colony in Darmstadt and gave some land for it. Seven artists were invited to join the colony and by 1900 their homes were being built. For his house, Peter Behrens

## CABINET AND CHAIR
*Josef Maria Olbrich*
**Wood; c. 1900**

Olbrich was an Austrian architect who started his career in Vienna and became one of the leading figures of the Secession. In 1899, however, he took up the offer of the Grand-Duke Ernst Ludwig of Hesse-Darmstadt to settle in an artists' colony at Matildenhohe on the outskirts of Darmstadt. The marquetry decoration on the cabinet doors shows the influence of the British Arts and Crafts designer M.H. Baillie Scott who in 1897 had furnished some of the rooms in the Grand-Duke's palace. (*Left*)

blend of organic shapes and geometrical ornament. And Hans Christiansen designed pieces in a geometrical style, decorated with inlaid patterns, marquetry or low-relief silver plaques.

**The Neo-Classical revival** Christiansen's furniture had a Neo-Classical character which became prevalent in German design during the years before the First World War. Two rooms displaying this were exhibited by the Deutscher Werkstätten at the 1910 Salon d'Automne in Paris and had a powerful impact on French design. They were the work of Niemeyer and Bertsch, who, with many other German designers, had responded to a governmental call for conformity to the principles of Classicism.

### AUSTRIAN FURNITURE

In Austria the Art Nouveau style was called *Secessionstil*, after the Vienna Secession which was formed in 1897: a group of architects, painters and sculptors seceded from the official artists' organization and held their own exhibitions in the Secessionhaus. One of the older Secessionists was the architect Otto Wagner (1841–1918), who designed some very plain furniture for his buildings. It was manufactured by the firm of Thonet Brothers, which had pioneered the technology of bentwood furniture.

Another Viennese architect, Adolf Loos (1870–1933), designed bentwood chairs manufactured by Thonet for the Café Museum. Loos had been impressed by the work of the English Arts and Crafts Movement and several pieces he

(1868–1940), a painter and architect who had been working in Munich during the 1890s, designed furniture which was close in style to the work of Van de Velde. Josef Maria Olbrich (1867–1908) from Vienna, another Darmstadt colonist, created furniture for his own and other artists' houses in a style which was a successful

## CHAIRS
*Koloman Moser*
Bentwood and brass;
**c. 1900**

The Viennese manufacturers Jakob & Joseph Kohn commissioned the Secession designer Moser to design several pieces of bentwood furniture. The upholstery on these chairs is covered with fabric in a contemporary pattern.

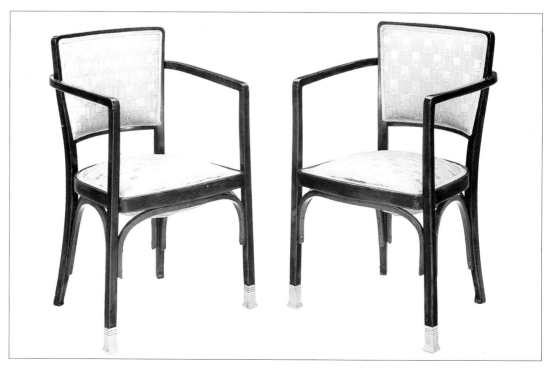

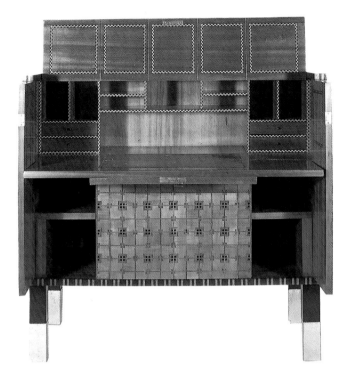

**DESK**
*Koloman Moser*
Elm, ivory, mother-of-pearl, ebony and jacaranda; **c. 1905**

Moser designed this luxurious desk as a special commission for a wealthy client. Its rigidly geometrical form and decoration are typical of the products of the Wiener Werkstätten. *(Left)*

**SIDECHAIR**
*Josef Urban*
Wood; **c. 1910**

Urban designed and furnished a number of apartments in Vienna before he was asked by the Wiener Werkstätten to decorate their New York branch. *(Right)*

designed were of simple, panelled construction. His work is marked by elegant proportions and a judicious disposition of simple reeding and metal fittings.

**The Vienna Workshops** Loos himself did not join the Secession and criticized its members for the ornament and deliberate artiness of the furniture they designed. Josef Hoffmann and Koloman Moser, two young architects who were the principal Secession designers, produced furniture which was at first in an organic style but later became severely rectangular. In 1903 Hoffmann and Moser founded the Wiener Werkstätten (Vienna Workshops), which produced a wide range of decorative objects, including furniture. Some of the pieces designed by Moser were richly decorated with marquetry or inlaid metals, while others were simply painted white.

Many of Hoffmann's furniture designs show the influence of Mackintosh, but he maintained a high level of personal inventiveness. Characteristics of his furniture are lattice-like chair backs and table aprons, and small spheres of wood for decoration at points of structural significance. Hoffmann's style gradually became more retrospective, using some Neo-Classical and Biedermeier (an informal 19th-century style) forms.

The same influence is evident in the furniture created by Otto Prutscher and Josef Urban (1872–1933), two other Wiener Werkstätten

designers. Prutscher also designed for Thonet. Other Viennese manufacturers that employed Wiener Werkstätten designers included Jakob & Josef Kohn (Hoffmann and Moser), Portois & Fix (Hoffmann), Franz Gloser (Hoffmann) and Richard Ludwig (Hoffmann and Prutscher).

ITALIAN FURNITURE

Italy made a unique contribution to the history of furniture through the work of the designer Carlo Bugatti (1855–1940). Bugatti started producing furniture in Milan during the 1880s, developing an idiosyncratic style partly based on the vogue for Moorish art. Elaborate geometrical patterns inlaid in ivory, metal and wood were complemented by the circular and rectangular forms of the furniture. Vellum painted with Arabian scenes was often used for the seats and

**SOFA**
*Ernesto Basile*
Wood; **c. 1900**

Basile's furniture is in a restrained version of Italian Art Nouveau. It was manufactured by the Palermo industrialist Vittorio Ducrot, and was widely praised when shown at the Turin international exhibition of 1902. *(Left)*

backs of chairs, decorative copper discs were laced to the framework with cord, and tassels were often hung from the extended uprights. In a bid to ride the wave of Art Nouveau, Bugatti presented at the Turin Exhibition of 1902 furniture sculpted into curving, organic forms, although still embellished with beaten copper and vellum.

**Italian Art Nouveau** Around 1900 the Italian architect Ernesto Basile created furniture in the Art Nouveau style, known as *stile Liberty* or *stile floreale* in Italy. The elegant forms of Basile's furniture are decorated with carved foliate ornament. The cabinet-makers Carlo Zen also produced Art Nouveau furniture. It is elaborately carved with floral decoration, and many pieces have a dual function.

## OTHER EUROPEAN FURNITURE

The Spanish architect Antoni Gaudí (1852–1926) created furniture for some of the buildings that he designed. He was influenced by Viollet-le-Duc, and much of his early work was in the Neo-Gothic style. Between 1885 and 1890 he built a palace in Barcelona for the Güell family for which he designed asymmetrical furniture in an organic style which prefigures Art Nouveau.

**Dutch furniture** The furniture produced in the Netherlands around the turn of the century was generally quite simple, although the work of K.P.C. de Bazel and J.L.M. Lauweriks was sometimes decorated with carved motifs derived from Egyptian or Assyrian art. Their pieces often have copper mounts. Theo

**DRAWING ROOM FURNITURE**
*Carlo Bugatti*
Wood, metal and vellum;
**c. 1900**

The Moorish style of this furniture was inspired by Italy's imperial ambitions in North Africa during the last quarter of the 19th century. Bugatti, father of the sports car designer, was an eccentric man who created a 30-stringed guitar, a seamless leather wallet and his own highly idiosyncratic clothes. (*Left*)

Nieuwenhuis C.A. Lion Cachet and G.W. Dijsselhof all designed furniture which was simply constructed.

A line of plain, functional furniture descends from the architect H.P. Berlage, through the work of Jacob van den Bosch, to the designer Gerrit Rietveld (1888–1965), who about 1918 created the well-known Red-Blue chair, composed of planks for seat and back and square-sectioned members for stretchers and supports.

**Scandinavian furniture** This reflected the contemporary Scandinavian interest in traditional folk culture. The furniture was simply constructed and often painted or carved with animal and floral motifs. In Sweden J.A.G. Acke and Carl Westman designed pieces which feature the curving, linear rhythms of Van de Velde's furniture, and Carl Bergsten's designs were influenced by the Wiener Werkstätten.

During the first two decades of this century the Norwegian Gabriel Kielland, the Dane Kaare Klint (1888–1954) and the Swede Carl Malmsten designed furniture marked by its elegance of line and high-quality materials. The furniture of the Finnish designers Louis Sparre and Eliel Saarinen (1873–1950), two pioneers of the international Modern Movement, reflects a preoccupation with construction and function.

**INTERIOR**
*Louis Sparre*
**Sketch design; c. 1903**

The Finnish designer Louis Sparre's furniture displays the clean lines and plain forms of the functionalist approach that has dominated Scandinavian style during the 20th century. In 1897 Sparre, who had trained in Paris as a painter, founded the Iris factory in Porvoo, which produced not only furniture but also textiles, metalwork and ceramics. However, the designs were too far ahead of their time, and, despite the international acclaim won by the factory during its short life, it had to be closed in 1902.

THE FURNITURE-MAKERS OF THE NEW WORLD COMBINED THEIR

EUROPEAN HERITAGE WITH A WILLINGNESS TO MAKE FRESH

INTERPRETATIONS OF TRADITIONAL DESIGNS. THIS DEVELOPED INTO A

UNIQUELY AMERICAN TRADITION.

# AMERICA

American furniture design is marked by its independence. Naturally, European styles, particularly British ones, did have some influence on American designers but they were outweighed by original ideas, brought about as much by new circumstances and materials as by native inventiveness.

### THE PILGRIM CENTURY TO 1715

For the first British settlers of the New World the pressing needs of sheltering and feeding their communities left little time for advanced craftsmanship in their furniture-making. Simplicity and sturdiness were the keywords, and most of the few chairs, benches and stools that survive from *c.*1650–70 are very basic. Among the few early pieces which did extend the skill of the artisan, chief were the oak or ash wainscot chair – so-called because of its high-panelled back, plain or carved – and more ornamented Carver and Brewster chairs. Named in honour of the first governor and premier elder of the Plymouth Colony, respectively, their high backs and arms were ranged with spindles.

The almost medieval character of these chairs was exceeded by that of the trestle tables, some of which were more than 2.4m (8ft) long. These large models had a removable top secured .with pegs and either a third trestle or removable vertical supports. Few of these anachronistic tables survive, since they were soon supplanted by the refectory-style table with an immovable top and supported by four turned legs connected by stretchers. Such full-sized pieces were echoed on a smaller scale in the common taproom or tavern table, made in oak, maple, pine, cherry, butternut and other fruitwoods. This was also popular for domestic use, when it often incorporated a decorated frame or skirt.

In the late 17th century, an even smaller piece appeared, the ancestor of many an occasional table to follow. This was the "stand", a plain rectangular or round top, set on four vertical or splayed legs, used for both hearthside and bedside. The gateleg table (one with framed legs that swing in to let down a drop leaf) was popular and also gave rise to a uniquely American version, the butterfly table, so-called from its butterfly-wing-like drop leaf supports. Both types of table are first found in maple, walnut or, less frequently, oak; leg and stretcher turnings become more elaborate towards the end of the century. The best examples have numerous

**CORNER CUPBOARD**
Blue-painted wood with glazed upper door and reeded columns; **early 18th century**

The lower doors have field panels and the original "H" hinges. Cupboards such as these, in the country Federalist mode, are much sought after.

legs, ingeniously arranged to aid both storage and use.

**Desks** In the days of early settlement the educated few wrote either at the single large table in the house or on a writing box that was also used to store writing materials. By about 1675 the writing stand, or desk-on-frame, had been introduced, but, although this continued to be made into the next century, it was soon supplanted in popularity by the fall-front desk.

**TRESTLE TABLE**
Wood; **mid to late 18th century**

The pine-board dining top and trestle supports are designed for easy storage. The table is a rugged example of a vital piece of early furniture.

## PRINCIPAL EARLY AMERICAN FURNITURE-MAKERS

| | | | |
|---|---|---|---|
| **DISBROWE, Nicholas** | 1612–83 | Hartford, Conn. | Specialist in elaborately carved oak chests. |
| **ALLIS, Captain John** | 1642–91 | Hadley, Mass. | Chest-maker. |
| **DENNIS, Thomas** | c. 1640–1706 | Ipswich, Conn. | Joiner and chest-maker. |
| **SAVERY, William** | fl. 1742–87 | Philadelphia, PA. | Wide-ranging cabinet-maker and chair-maker in country, "Queen Anne" and "Chippendale" mode, primarily in walnut. |
| **GODDARD, John** | fl. 1750–85 | Newport, RI. | Leading Rhode Island mahogany cabinet-maker; probable originator of blockfront styling who also favoured elaborate shell carving. Father of Stephen and Thomas. |
| **ELFE, Thomas** | fl. 1751–71 | Charleston, NC. | Leading southern exponent of "Chippendale"-style cabinet-making, particularly known for his fretwork; father of Thomas Elfe (1759–1825). |
| **RANDOLPH, Benjamin** | fl. 1762–92 | Philadelphia, PA. | Leading "Chippendale" cabinet-maker and chair-maker. |
| **AFFLECK, Thomas** | fl. 1763–95 | Philadelphia, PA. | Leading "Chippendale" cabinet-maker and chair-maker. |
| **GILLINGHAM, James** | fl. 1765–91 | Philadelphia, PA. | "Chippendale" cabinet-maker, particularly renowned for "Gothic" taste. |
| **TUFT, Thomas** | fl. 1765–93 | Philadelphia, PA. | "Chippendale" cabinet-maker, particularly respected for large case pieces. |
| **FOLWELL, John** | fl. 1770s | Philadelphia, PA. | Leading "Chippendale" cabinet-maker; known for his innovative designs. |
| **TOWNSEND, John** | fl. 1777–90s | Connecticut | Leading cabinet-maker in blockfront style; friend of John Goddard and scion of great family of furniture-makers. |
| **DUNLAP, Samuel II** | fl. 1780–1830 | New Hampshire | Leading member of New Hampshire family of cabinet-makers, known for maple case pieces with elegant scrolling and moulding. |
| **McINTIRE, Samuel** | fl. 1780–1811 | Salem, Mass. | Master carver of Sheraton-style furniture, case pieces and chairs. |

## STORAGE CHESTS

Among the most numerous surviving items of furnishing of the early colonial past are blanket chests (storage chests) of oak and/or pine, which doubled as seating. Usually about 63–76cm (25–30in) high and 1.2–1.5m (4–5ft) long, they commonly had bracket feet, a flat lid, a front divided into sunken panels and stylized floral carvings. There were four main types of chest. The Hartford, or "sunflower", chest attributed to Nicholas Disbrowe (1612–83), has a central panel carved with a sunflower and usually flanked by two tulip-and-leaf-scrolled panels and has two panelled drawers with applied spindles, bosses and turned knobs. Existing examples date from about 1660–80. Contemporary with the Hartford chest was the Ipswich (Connecticut), or (after its originator) "Dennis-style", chest, whose stiles (vertical members between sunken panels) and rails (horizontal members) carry ornate guilloches (interlacing bands or ribbons) and leaf designs.

The Hadley chest, attributed to Captain John Allis (1642–91), also had three panels, had up to three drawers and was painted black, brown, red or green. It lacks the applied spindles and bosses of the first two types but its carving is more flamboyant, consisting of a profusion of shallow-carved foliage. Hadley chests were popular from the late 1670s until the mid-18th century. The Guildford chest, another Connecticut piece, was atypical in that its decoration was painted.

**HADLEY-TYPE CHEST**
**WITH DRAWER**
Carved wood;
*c. 1680–1710*

**HIGHBOY**
Walnut and burl veneer;
*c. 1730–50*

This Massachusetts piece is a fine example of the evolving Queen Anne highboy. The six turned legs of the William and Mary period have become four cabriole legs, with the two turned apron knops marking their departure. The top has not yet developed the curved pediment favoured 20 years later.

During the William and Mary period in America, *c.*1695–1720, each desk of this type would be made of a variety of woods, consisting for example of a straight-grain maple top, curly (feathery-grain) maple sides, a burl (knot-patterned) maple front, walnut feet and string borders (thin inlaid lines), cherry pigeonholes and small drawers and pine interiors for the main drawers. In grander furniture marquetry made the most of the varying hues of available woods.

**Highboys and lowboys** By 1710 japanning had come into vogue. It was perhaps used to best effect in a new piece of furniture, the highboy, a chest of drawers with its upper, taller sections standing on a lower section with legs. In its first incarnation, during the William and Mary period, the highboy, usually of walnut, had six, or, rarely, four, spindle or ball-and-cone turned legs, connected by stretchers and terminating in ball feet.

The highboy was soon joined by the lowboy, the lower section of the taller piece given independence. Usually made of walnut or with a fine walnut veneer, often burled, both pieces were used in all rooms of the house.

**Beds** In the early settlements the "best" bed took pride of place, first in the parlour, later in the main upstairs room. Made of oak, maple or pine, it had hangings in crewel (a fine worsted yarn), brocade or, in poor families, homespun.

The late 17th century saw an innovation in the day-bed. Early examples were in the English Carolean style (1625–49): caning on the adjustable back and seat, and eight turned legs connected by ornate crested rails and ending in small ball feet. But it was not long before the rails gave way to simple turned stretchers and the legs were reduced in number to six and acquired Spanish (knuckle-like) feet.

### QUEEN ANNE STYLE

In the United States the term Queen Anne is generally used stylistically to describe pieces made roughly between 1715 and 1750. For Americans the graceful lines and elegant carving of this style were a revelation and fitted in well with the new colonial sense of expansion and prosperity. No longer did furniture have to proclaim its solidity. Hogarth's "line of beauty", the ogee, took precedence over the right angle; chair backs, seats and legs, the aprons (lower front edges) of chests and highboys, the edges of tables, all were designed to incorporate the wave-like bend.

The style of chair and table legs soon developed from simply curved to a fully-fledged cabriole (exaggeratedly double-curved). They ended in a pad or foot cleft into three, and the knee – and also the top rail of dining chairs – was often decorated with a scallop shell. Stretchers, carried over from the William and Mary period, were discarded.

Comfort was now an established factor in American chair design. The wing chair, with its tall back, face-level fire-protectors and rolled arms, was introduced. On this, as on other upholstered furniture, the turkeywork (fabrics made like Turkish carpets) and velvet of the 17th century were supplanted by silk, damask and wool. A small number of upholstered sofas in the Queen Anne style survive; more popular were all-wood settees and day-beds with bowed top rails.

An introduction of c.1725 was the American Windsor chair, an all-wood chair characterized by the use of turned spindles, socketed into the seat, for both back and legs. The colonial examples differed from their English relatives in the lack of a back splat (central upright) and the exaggerated angle at which the legs were set to the seat. This makes the American version lighter in feeling, a quality heightened in early examples by the larger number of thin spindles

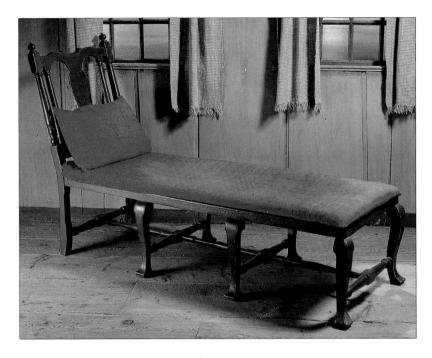

forming the back. Two styles were common: the bow back, with the top rail bent into a three-quarter hoop, and the comb back, with the top rail almost straight.

In tables, the popular gateleg gave way to the more elegant drop leaf, in which two of the four legs were movable, swinging in to let down the leaves of the round or oval top. Some of the best examples added an extra pair of legs, providing greater support when the leaves were down. Towards the end of the Queen Anne period, square and other rectangular drop-leaf-top

**DAYBED**
Mahogany; *c.* 1740–50

The eight legs on this transitional William & Mary/Queen Anne daybed have yet to reduce to six, while the bow back, with its flanking spindles, harks back to earlier influences. A multi-armed stretcher connects the legs. (*Above*)

**TRAY-TOP TABLE**
Cherrywood; *c.* 1760

This rectangular Queen Anne table is made of a typical American material, lending a special warmth to classical European lines. (*Left*)

tables were made. Ball-and-claw feet began to replace pad feet, as they also did on chairs. Gaming tables were introduced and small rectangular (later round) occasional tables were adapted for use in the serving of the newly fashionable tea.

### FEDERAL AND DIRECTOIRE STYLES

The American War of Independence (1775–83) brought an abrupt halt to the development of the decorative arts in the colonies. When the war was over, English design styles continued to be influential but the craftsmen of the triumphant new republic were eager to make of them something specifically American. As a result, the ideas of the three classical English designers, Robert Adam, George Hepplewhite and Thomas Sheraton, were largely amalgamated into a style commonly called Federal, which lasted roughly from 1790 to 1830. In furniture the rigid classicism of Adam played a minor role

– it was the more lyrical ideas of Hepplewhite and Sheraton that appealed to a nation looking to cast off its provincial reputation and assume the veneer of a man of the world. A key feature of the style was fine mahogany, inlaid with satinwood, maplewood and birch, with plain stringing a speciality of New York. More decorative patterns – shells, flowers, eagles – are found on pieces from Philadelphia, Baltimore, Salem and, to a lesser extent, Boston.

The period is also notable for the introduction of new pieces and the reinvention of old ones. The charming little sewing table, with its commodious pouch, made an appearance, as did the sideboard. The dining table assumed new dimensions with the adoption of French pedestal legs and the addition of supplementary leaves; later in the period, it was fitted with an accordion-type mechanism to enable easy extension. The day-bed reappeared as a Roman couch or *chaise-longue*, with high scroll back, and inward curled foot ends all carved, often gilded and richly upholstered. After surviving briefly into the Federal period, the taste for highboys and lowboys expired, and the cabriole leg gave way to the straight and narrow.

But the most important feature of the Federal period was the stylistic treatment of established pieces – chairs, occasional tables, bureau-bookcases, chests of drawers and bookcases. Shield- and oval-backed chairs – often with a carved central splat of plumes, wheat sheaves or urns, and with plain, tapering legs – displayed the Hepplewhite legacy; squarerbacked chairs with stronger lines and spade (tapering, square) feet showed the influence of Sheraton. A marriage of styles was apparent in larger pieces – sideboards, desks and bookcases, for example – where the serpentine curves of Hepplewhite were combined with the inlaid vignettes of Sheraton.

After 1810, the fine lines of the early Federal style gave way to the greater theatricality of the Directoire, based on the French style of the same name: pieces with sabre legs, animal-pawed feet, concavely arched chair backs and serpentine fronts, usually made in the currently popular rosewood or heavy mahogany.

The foremost exponent of the Directoire style was the Scottish-born Duncan Phyfe (1768–1854), who worked in New York. His elegant sofas, with their reeded legs, carved top rails and striped brocade, together with his lyre-backed chairs, monumental tables and X-shaped klismos stools, have a distinctive char-

**BROKEN-BONNET-FRONTED HIGHBOY**
Mahogany; **c. 1760**

The ball finials on apron and pediment are of brass, while the shell carving marks this late Queen Anne highboy as a fine New England piece.

acter. Only the French-born Charles-Honoré Lannuier (1779–1819), another New York furniture designer who worked in the massive classical mode, can vie with Phyfe in craftsmanship.

### SHAKER STYLE

The Shakers were a religious sect introduced into the United States in 1774 by Ann Lee, a dissident Quaker. The industry, self-sufficiency and communal spirit of the sect won many followers, despite the celibacy imposed on its members.

Every piece of furniture the Shakers made embodied their precepts. Respect for order decreed that drawers and standing cupboards provided the most effective storage space; drop leaves on tables and chests catered for the need for extra working space and the lack of standing room; nest boxes with fingered joins were for keeping bits and pieces until they were required; peg boards on the wall enabled chairs to be hung up when not in use.

The appearance of a piece was governed by its use. Once a design was achieved that was strong, easy to make and served its purpose well, it became the accepted prototype for that piece – bar a few regional differences in such features as chair finials and leg turnings – for all Shaker communities. The sexes were segregated in the community, and each had its own type of furniture. Chairs for the women were lighter and smaller than those for the men; women's tables were lower; and their chests of

**SOFA**
*Attributed to Duncan Phyfe*
**Mahogany and canework;**
**c. 1810**

Born in Scotland, Phyfe emigrated to New York in his early years. The cornucopia design on the crest and arms and the reeded klismos (X-shaped) legs are characteristic Phyfe embellishments, betraying his fascination with the style of ancient Rome. (*Above*)

**SHAKER ROCKING CHAIR**
**Cherrywood; c. 1840**

Acorn finials and mushroom handrests finish this extremities of this lovingly made chair. Shaker rockers are so cunningly constructed that it is virtually impossible to overturn the chair while in use. (*Right*)

drawers contained more compartments.

Fruitwoods and birch were the favoured woods; and the soft reddish colour of polished cherry, in particular, has become linked with the uncluttered lines of Shaker tradition.

Most Shaker pieces offered for sale today as antiques were made between 1815 and 1880 (the rest are high-quality reproductions of a somewhat later date).

**Highboys and secretaries** The artistic high point of the Queen Anne style was the highboy. The former six spindle or bell-and-cone legs became four cabriole legs and turned pendant knobs decorated the apron. The ogee suited the proportions of the piece well. In the 1730s the curve of the apron became more pronounced, and eventually even the flat top acquired a curved pediment. Except in Philadelphia, the earlier walnut gave way in popularity to mahogany.

Another tall piece to exploit the changes in cabinet-making was the secretary (bureau) bookcase. Made of walnut, maple or mahogany, it echoed the architectural lines of the Palladian architecture currently in vogue, particularly in the arched panelling of its doors and the details of its pilasters (flat-faced columns) and cornices (projecting crowns of the pilasters). A smaller relation of this large storage piece that first appeared at this time was the corner cupboard, either in simple pine or in walnut, with a carved shell top.

## CHIPPENDALE STYLE

Some elements of the work of the English furniture designer Thomas Chippendale (1718–79) had appeared in American pieces during the 1730s and 1740s, before he published his influential *The Gentleman and Cabinet-maker's Director* in 1754. But it was not until the 1760s that the full force of the work struck the fashion-conscious inhabitants of American cities and that Chippendale's Dutch-influenced rococo style, flavoured with elements of Gothic and Chinese, was embraced in its entirety. The finest Santo Domingo mahogany was used to embody it, and the dominance of walnut was never to return.

Philadelphia was the capital of furniture-making in the Chippendale style. Among its fine craftsmen were Thomas Affleck (*fl.* 1763–95), Benjamin Randolph (*fl.* 1762–92), John Folwell (*fl.* 1775), James Gillingham (*fl.* 1765–91), William Savery (*fl.* 1742–87) and Thomas Tuft (*fl.* 1765–93). The chairs, highboys and bureau-

### TEA TABLE
Mahogany; *c.* 1760

The "birdcage" mechanism under the top of this Chippendale-period table allows it to be tipped against the column for easy storage against a wall. Larger versions of this Philadelphia-made table were made as "breakfast" and occasionally gaming tables. (*Right*)

### DINING CHAIRS
Mahogany; *c.* 1790

The shield backs – with their carved openwork splats featuring corn husk and urn motifs – define them as "Hepplewhite style", though in American terms the lines between the influences of Hepplewhite and Sheraton are less distinct than in English pieces of the same period. (*Below*)

bookcases produced by these and other cabinet-makers were masterpieces of elegance, crisper in execution than their English counterparts, their curves less extravagant. And certain other features mark them out as uniquely American: the flame finials (decorative projections) which appear so frequently on pediments of secretaries and highboys, and the peanut carving enlivening the top rails and aprons of chairs.

New York, Boston and Salem followed the lead of Philadelphia, producing their own fine cabinet-makers, such as Thomas Burling (New York; *fl.* 1772–1800), Samuel Prince (New York; *fl.* 1760–78), John Cogswell (Boston; *fl.* 1769–1818) and Samuel McIntire (Salem; *fl.* 1757–1811), whose rendition of the monumen-

tal chest-on-chest places him among the best of the late practitioners of the Chippendale style. In the work of these craftsmen panelled doors continued to grace bureau-bookcases, even though glass-fronted versions had become more fashionable in Britain. In Boston an idiosyncratic version known as the kettle base, or *bombe*, appeared. The swollen base narrowed toward the top, giving a distinctly feminine feel to the piece.

However, despite the outstanding output of New York, Boston and Salem, it was the tiny colony of Rhode Island and neighbouring Connecticut that offered the more serious alternative to Philadelphia's dominance. The vigorous forms of the Queen Anne style were still alive there and were effortlessly integrated into the new style. Deceptively simple yet majestic

block-front desks, secretaries and chests of drawers made by such craftsmen as Benjamin Burham, John Goddard (*fl.* 1750s–85) and the Townsend family (*fl.* 1777–90s) have become as distinctively American in character as the highboy. It was on such large pieces that blocking (the projecting, squared, flat-carved facing particular to this region) was shown to its best advantage, often crowned with exquisite intaglio (incised) shells on the lower pediment or on the panelled doors.

**New interpretations** Chair-back settees and the new open-rolled arm (the arms curling outwards, away from the seat) wing chairs were made in small quantities. The tea table was now decidedly round, with its support elaborately carved, its tripod legs ending in claw-and-ball feet and its top rimmed with a pie-crust or shell

**BLOCK-FRONT BUREAU**
Mahogany; **c. 1760–70**

The vigorous lines of Queen Anne are still obvious in this elegant desk, probably from Rhode Island. The blocking on the front is characteristic of Rhode Island and Connecticut, and emphasizes the quality of the wood, as the undulating surface reflects the nuances of the light.

# THE PENNSYLVANIAN TRADITION

During the mid-18th century the Quaker and other non-conformist groups who had settled in Pennsylvania began to turn their prodigious energies toward idiomatic expression in furniture and decoration.

Among other national customs brought from Europe, came the tradition of the dower chest, given by parents and friends to the daughter of the family. Made to contain homespun linens, quilts, hangings and towels for a future marriage, the chests were painted to order in a background shade of soft blue – or less commonly, green, black or brown – and decorated with motifs from medieval myth and Christian legend. Symbols included unicorns (virginity), hearts (love), mermaids (sex), the tree of life (mortality) and flowers (fertility); doves (peace) and the pelican and fish (Christ). Several chests carry the owner's name or initials and the date it was made. From a stable of largely unknown artists, two of the most respected were Christian Selzer (1749–1831) and Heinrich Otto.

Other typical pieces included painted tables, chairs and beds, hanging wall cabinets, corner cupboards and pie safes with pierced tin panels. Their largest piece was the *schrank*, a heavy wardrobe of thick planks and medieval character, ornately painted or inlaid with the common mythological symbols or more temporal motifs, such as crowns and swastikas. Chests, schranks and cupboards were usually supported on ball or bracket feet. By the early 19th century such furniture had largely been assimilated into the wider American tradition.

**TWO-DOOR BLANKET CHEST**
*Johannes Rank*
Painted wood; 1789

---

pattern. A new birdcage-like mechanism enabled the top to fold flat against the support when the table was not in use.

Because of higher ceilings, bedposts were made ever taller, the most elegant being overtopped by a straight oblong wooden canopy with hangings of wool, crewelwork or linen. By the 1760s, the curtains at the foot of the bed were omitted and the exposed posts were ornamentally turned and fluted. Chippendale-style beds were produced in mahogany, cherry or maple, according to the area.

## VICTORIAN

The final years of the Federal period of 1790–1830 wound up in extravagances of Neo-Classicism, such as ostentatious carvings of acanthus leaves, pineapples and tassels. By the mid-1830s this was giving way to Gothic Revival: architectural motifs such as pointed arches, ogee (a concave curve giving way to a convex) mouldings and trefoils (three-lobed ornamentation) were used .

**CHAIR**
*Mexican*
Pine with chip carving;
**c. 1820**

The solid lines of the chair are lightened by its linear horizontal carving. Furniture of such simple construction and crude joints owed little to influences from more sophisticated regions. (*Left*)

**HITCHCOCK CHAIR**
Carved and painted wood;
**c. 1825–50**

This early piece demonstrates the factory's finest carving and hand-painting. The waterfall scene on the top rail is complemented by the back rest's sea motifs. (*Right*)

From the 1820s to the 1870s, Spool, or bobbin-turned, furniture could be found in ordinary homes all over the country; and from 1825 until 1852 the homely Hitchcock chair was popular. This was mass-produced in inexpensive birch or maple, either hand-painted or stencilled.

Mid-century saw a vogue for Rococo Revival in American furniture design, of which the most extreme expression were the productions of John Henry Belter in New York 1844–63: laminated rosewood or black walnut pieces elaborately carved on every available surface.

From the mid-1860s to the mid-1880s there was a new eclecticism in furniture design, and styles ranged from Louis XVI and Renaissance revivals to Oriental, including bamboo.

SPANISH SOUTH-WESTERN STYLE

In the 19th century the poorer ranchers and farmers of the south-western states of Arizona, New Mexico, Texas and California obtained their furnishings from peasant cabinet-makers and amateur carpenters. Using cheap yellow pine, together with mesquite, juniper and cottonwood, they produced copies of the fine Spanish pieces made by Mexican craftsmen.

**HALL BENCH**
*Gustav Stickley*
Oak; **c. 1910**

Stickley's workshop made much use of native hardwoods such as oak, the spartan lines of the design allowing the grain of the wood to "speak for itself". This bench is almost monkish, lending another dimension to the term "Mission furniture".

## PRINCIPAL LATER AMERICAN FURNITURE-MAKERS

| | | | |
|---|---|---|---|
| **PHYFE, Duncan** | *fl.* 1790–1847 | New York | The leading cabinet-maker in the Sheraton, Directory and Empire styles. |
| **LANNUIER, Charles Honoré** | *fl.* 1779–1819 | New York | Main competitor to Phyfe, particularly known for monumental pieces in Directory style. |
| **HITCHCOCK, Lambert** | *fl.* 1825–50s | Connecticut | Leading maker of painted furniture. Father of American mass-production and founder of Hitchcockville, Conn. |
| **BELTER, John** | *fl.* 1845–60 | New York | Maker of parlour and bedroom sets in heavy, laminated rosewood in Louis XV style. |
| **WRIGHT, Frank Lloyd** | 1869–1959 | Chicago, Ill. | Innovative architect and designer of furniture for his houses throughout the USA. |
| **ELMSLIE, George Grant** | 1871–1952 | Illinois and Midwest | Leading designer and maker, together with Maher (see below) of the Prairie School in Illinois and midwestern states. |
| **MAHER, George** | 1864–1926 | Illinois and Midwest | Partner with Elmslie in design group which led the Prairie School. Produced massive furniture in organic forms. |
| **HUBBARD, Elbert** | 1856–1915 | New York State | Founder of Roycroft School in upstate New York. Maker of plain hardwood pieces. |
| **STICKLEY, Gustav** | 1857–1942 | New York State | Originator of style known as "Mission furniture", largely oak, sometimes inlaid. |
| **GREENE, Charles Sumner** | 1868–1957 | Pasadena, Calif. | Originator of style known as "California Bungalow". Conceptualized entire contents of houses. |

Planks were hand-hewn, ornament was cursory and the finish rough. The main period of creativity was 1800–80.

Among the most sought-after of these southwestern pieces are pine chests with moulded and carved panels, or sometimes painted designs; the trasero, a kind of food safe with doors spindled or decorated with gesso (gilded plaster); chairs with tooled leather backs or sawtooth-carved horizontal back rails; and rustic tables. After 1840 traces of Empire and Gothic styles from the East can be detected, though they are expressed with beguiling naïvety in the better pieces.

ARTS AND CRAFTS STYLE

From about 1880 the ideas of the English Arts and Crafts Movement – that mechanization was dehumanizing and inferior to individual craftsmanship – took hold in the United States, where a reaction, led by the Chicago architect and furniture designer Frank Lloyd Wright (1869–1959), began against mass-production. In furniture-making major Chicago firms who brought the new aesthetic into the market place included the Tobey Furniture Company (*fl.* 1890s) and its subsidiary the Tobey & Christianson Cabinet Company (opened 1888). They often relieved their straight lines and plain surfaces with shallow relief-carving and suggestions of organic forms, such as stone and tree trunks.

The influence of many of the same Chicago-based architect-teachers who had instructed the young Wright can be detected in the pronouncements and work of Prairie School designers. George Grant Elmslie (1871–1952) and George Washington Maher (1864–1926), drew heavily on medieval and Renaissance traditions, using the scrolls, animal-head carving and deep arm- and back-rests of 16th-century Europe in combination with the sturdy woods and rugged individualism of the Midwest.

In 1898 Gustav Stickley (1857–1942) opened workrooms in Eastwood, outside Syracuse, New York, where he produced pieces in native hardwood, often oak, sometimes inlaid with pewter, iron or copper, or upholstered in leather or canvas. By 1915, however, he was bankrupt, mainly through his own uncompromising devotion to quality. New York state was also the home of a community of craftsmen headed by Elbert Hubbard (1856–1915) and working in Aurora. Christened the Roycrofters, they concentrated on the simplest pieces – oak

benches, tables, chairs and bookcases.

Together, the dark, austere work of the two New York groups is now referred to as Mission furniture; so-called because it was designed with "a mission to perform", it has also come to be associated with the mission architecture of California, where the pieces seem to belong.

In southern California the architect-designers Charles Sumner Greene (1868–1957) and Henry Mather Greene (1870–1954) created furniture to complement their grand Spanish-style mansions: pieces in rich woods, such as walnut, cedar and Honduras mahogany, inlaid with fruitwood and precious stones.

**FALL-FRONT DESK**
*Gustav Stickley*
Oak, other woods and pewter; **c.** 1904

The panelled fall is inlaid with stylized motifs in pewter and luxury woods. Fittings on other furniture items were often in copper, although Stickley never showed the extravagance of materials found in the work of the Greene brothers in California.

# ORIENTAL FURNITURE

Until the beginning of this century little was known in the West about Oriental furniture. Even today there is much confusion about its classification, dating and places of origin. Relatively uncharted and constantly attracting more interest, this is a field with considerable potential for the collector.

### CHINESE FURNITURE

Chinese furniture has popularly been considered the highest form of Oriental furniture.

**SCHOLAR'S CABINET**
*Chinese*
Huang hua-li and chi ch'i-mu
**1550–1650**

Square cabinets of this form with an enclosed display area at the top are extremely rare. This example, with its *paktong* (white brass) mounts, is of the finest quality, as exemplified by the carved decoration on the pierced doors and sides being different and by the extravagance of being finished on the back (even though this piece of furniture was obviously made to stand against a wall). Such details are indicative of furniture of the highest quality.

By the time of the Chinese civil war (1946–49) entire collections of furniture were leaving China to be eagerly absorbed by Western museums, largely in the United States. Ming (1368–1644) and Ch'ing (1644–1912) hardwood pieces were seen for the first time. This spawned major study and scholarship and the first published literature, which increased collectors' awareness and re-appraisal of such furniture.

Early Chinese furniture, up to the 16th century, was generally made of lacquered softwood, and consequently little remains. For a long time this furniture, perhaps because of its decorative appearance, was more highly prized, and thus better documented, than contemporary hardwood pieces.

In the West detailed knowledge of Chinese hardwood furniture has been limited to a few people who are able to assess the decoration and construction of individual pieces and assign a rough date to them, despite the fact that pieces were not dated or signed and there were no early inventories. Guidelines in this dating process have been miniature models found in early burial tombs and domestic scenes depicted in paintings.

Before the Chinese communists took power in 1949, the Nelson Atkins Museum in Kansas City assembled probably the most comprehensive collection of early Chinese hardwood furniture. In Britain, however, the Victoria and Albert Museum did not gain its first piece until 1969, and the significant addition of the Sir John Addis collection occurred as late as 1983. Other significant collections are possessed, in the United States, by the Museum of Art, Philadelphia, the Portland Museum, Oregon, and the Museum of Fine Arts, Boston, and, in Europe, by the Kunsindustrimuseet, Copenhagen, and the Musée Guimet, Paris.

During the Ming and Ch'ing dynasties the use of furniture was spreading from the imperial court, the upper classes and for ceremo-

nial uses to scholars and bureaucrats who needed functional as well as decorative pieces. The importation of Far Eastern hardwoods, such as Indian dalbergia rosewood, facilitated the manufacture of furniture strong enough to be packed and carried throughout China for use by travelling bureaucrats. While sturdy when assembled, much of the furniture was easily dismantled for carriage, there being no use of glue or nails. It was frequently used outdoors as well as indoors, and design features, such as the "floating" panel on large surfaces, allowed for wood expansion and contraction in varying climates to avoid splitting and warping.

There was an emphasis on symmetry in furniture design. Chairs were often displayed in pairs and generally conformed to one of three types: the horseshoe armchair with a rounded back, the yokeback chair with a single wide back splat (central upright) and flattened, shaped top, and the rose chair, a shorter-backed, more upright version of the yokeback chair. Certain items of furniture were designed to a standard specification; one example was the low *k'ang* table, used on a *k'ang* (brick platform) raised against a wall and often heated from underneath. Versatility was another consideration in furniture design – for example, a square table might be used not only for dining but for working or displaying objects. The practicality of materials was also regarded as important: camphor wood, for instance, was used in the

### PAIR OF YOKEBACK ARMCHAIRS
*Chinese*
Huang hua-li; **1550–1650**

Of the two standard types of yokeback armchair, this group with everted yoke– called *guanmaoyi* (official's hat armchair) – is the most elegant. These two are extremely well proportioned in the relationship of their slender, elegant members to the splat. (*Above*)

### RECTANGULAR K'ANG TABLE
*Chinese*
Huang hua-li; **1550–1650**

This is a fine example of a low table for use on a *k'ang*, or raised platform, which in a cold northern Chinese house took up about a third of the room. Such a table reflected a room's proportions, and was the centrepiece around which life was conducted on the *k'ang*. (*Below*)

### A FOLDING HORSESHOE ARMCHAIR
*Chinese*
Huang hua-li; **1550–1650**

Folding chairs appeared in China as early as the second century AD, when they were called *hu ch 'uang* or "barbarian" chairs. The metal reinforcements at the joints are both functional and decorative. (*Above*)

making of storage chests and cupboards to help protect against moths and other pests.

Another element of Chinese furniture-making that has helped to make dating difficult is an underlying continuity of basic structure. However, each period has been marked by its own characteristic differences in design and materials.

Experts generally recognize a classic period, ranging from the mid 16th to the mid 17th century – spanning the latter part of the Ming and the very beginning of the Ch'ing dynasties. This is marked by bold design, with relaxed, curving lines. Any carved decoration is detailed and finely drawn.

In the 18th and 19th centuries furniture lines tend to become stiffer and more upright, the decorations heavier and more perfunctory.

**Timbers** Another pointer to dating, and perhaps area of origin, lies in the types of wood employed. *Hua-li* timber, a tropical hardwood similar to rosewood, provided large planks of beautifully grained wood ranging in colour from pale yellow to deep orange. *Huang hua-li* was the most sought after. It appears to have become extinct in the early 18th century; however, smaller furniture pieces were often made up from timber recycled from earlier larger items. The very dark *tzu-tan* wood was equally prized and, being heavy and dense, lent itself to sharply carved decoration. These two timbers were generally used for important pieces, often contrasted with each other or inlaid with other

**A CANOPY BED**
Chinese
Huang hua-li; 1550–1650

Beds of this type are rare although not as rare as the "alcove" beds which are similar in construction but with a small antechamber. They are constructed both for easy dismantling and travel. The carving of the open fretwork "wave" pattern on this example is unusual and particularly fine. (*Above left*)

**TWO-TIER STAND**
Chinese
Hung-mu; late 19th century

With inset marble panels and of scrolling design, this stand would probably have been used to display objects or incense. There is a distinct change from the simpler forms of earlier designs. (*Above right*)

woods such as *hua-mu* (burl, or knotted, woods, used decoratively) or marble.

Everyday items were made from the feathery-grained *chi ch'i-mu* (chicken wing wood), dark-grained *j'ia jing-mu* and *hung-mu* (blackwood). Elm and camphor softwoods were used to make such furniture as low cupboards and storage chests and also often provided the back or shelves for *huang hua-li* cupboards, to give natural protection against insects.

Clay and lacquer would often be applied protectively to both softwoods and areas of exposed hardwoods, such as the underside of a table or top of a cupboard. Metal mounts were made of brass or paktong (a silver-coloured alloy of zinc, copper and nickel, resistant to tarnishing).

**Restored pieces** Largely for its simplicity and elegance, Chinese furniture is becoming extremely sought after. This has meant that the purveyors of good Ming and Ch'ing furniture are having to search deep into China to find their goods. Even then most of the pieces are in an extremely rough, frequently dismantled condition, calling for sympathetic restoration. But, then, restoration has long been a feature of Chinese furniture. In general, early repairs are the most acceptable, and in fact collectors virtually expect pieces which have gone through 300 years of wear and tear to show certain signs of renovation. Many pieces made from recycled *huang hua-li* are recognizable from a filled mortise (cavity in a furniture joint). The least prominent parts of a piece, such as chair foot-rests or the aprons (lower front edges) beneath them, were usually the most precariously attached and often needed to be replaced.

Most 16th- and 17th-century furniture designed for sitting or sleeping had soft straw-matting seats held in place by a string trellis. By the beginning of the 18th century, to avoid constant replacement of these seats, such furniture was being made with hard-matting seats or wooden ones.

One modification that is less acceptable (mainly in terms of spoiling its proportions but often also in reducing a piece's value) is the shortening of the legs of a side table to make a coffee table (for which the *k'ang* table is marginally too low). This can be seen either in the visible splicing of feet – an extra strip of wood added or in the re-carving of the mitred joint (where two 45-degree surfaces are fitted together to form a right angle) at the top of the

**A CHEST OF DRAWERS**
*Vietnamese (?)*
Various soft carcase woods covered with lacquer; **last quarter of 17th century**

In the past it was thought that such pieces were sent to the Far East to be lacquered, but there is no supportive evidence for this. The lacquer decoration on this piece closely resembles a group of documented lacquers in the Danish Royal collection which came from Vietnam. (*Above*)

**SQUARE COMPOUND CUPBOARD**
*Chinese*
Huang hua-li and hua-mu; **1550–1650**

This fine two-part cupboard is one of a pair, the other piece being in the Arthur Sackler collection in Washington, D.C. The two are believed to be the only pair with burlwood panels of shaped designs, in this case a double gourd, circle and square. (*Left*)

leg. Alterations to colour and surface finish can also reduce the worth of a piece – many have been irreparably exposed to water or ruined by recent staining or polishing.

**Chinese export furniture** This furniture was generally made to Western design and specification. Often lacquered and occasionally made of local hardwoods, the pieces conformed neither to Oriental standards of construction nor to the dimensions and craftsmanship of the European cabinet-makers whose work they were intended to imitate.

Single export items were constructed specifically to order from the West and transported by cargo-superintendents, who delivered this furniture for their own or for speculative purposes. From existing early-18th-century inventories it appears that there was not a large traffic in such furniture. For example, the Dutch records of the Honorable East India Company's Canton factory show only 33 pieces destined for export to seven people. Many of these early export pieces, originally ordered for rich European households or for those with trading connections, have now found their way into European museums, such as the Victoria and Albert in London and the Kunsindustrimuseet in Copenhagen.

OTHER ORIENTAL FURNITURE

Traditional Japanese and Korean houses did not allow much scope for furniture as we know it in the West. In Japanese dwellings most furniture was built-in, and only low tables and *tansu* (movable, stackable storage chests) existed. Today these *tansu* are most suitable for use in small apartments, because of their simple lines, often decorated with pierced and shaped ironwork, and because they combine optimum storage capacity with economic use of space. The low tables, although aesthetically poor imitations of the Chinese *k'ang* tables, are often more adaptable to Western use because, as people's feet went under rather than beside them (as in Chinese usage), they are normally higher than their Chinese counterparts.

**Korean furniture** Much more Korean than Japanese furniture is available to the collector today, indicating that there was a wider consumer market for it. Functionally, the two are

**KAIDAN TANSU**
*Japanese, Meiji period*
**Hinoki; late 19th century**

These were possibly used as staircases to sleeping or storage areas. With their front doors they provided capacious storage space. Most Japanese furniture was made from softwoods.
(*Right*)

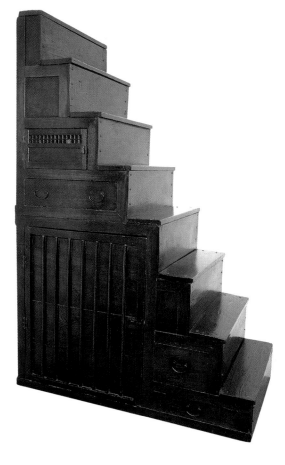

**BUREAU-BOOKCASE**
*English (export)*
**Hung-mu; c. 1750**

This is a fine example of a mid-Georgian pattern executed in Canton for the British market. The material and construction are essentially Chinese with moulded "floating" door panels, yet it is decorated in a European style with stop-fluted pilasters surmounted by Corinthian capitals.
(*Left*)

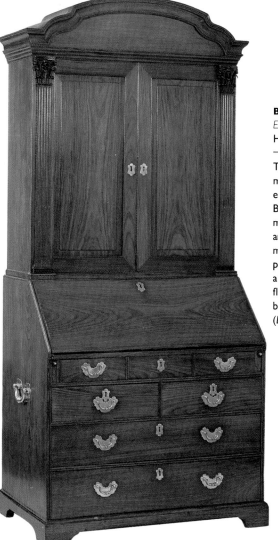

very similar, but Korean furniture has greater variation of form than Japanese and includes, for example, book-cases and shelf units of 20th-century European Modernist furniture type. Generally speaking, Korean pieces are inferior to Japanese. Metalwork is more restrained, construction more primitive and timbers of poorer quality. However, there are some Korean pieces of an extraordinary quality, surpassing all but the finest Chinese furniture (but generally more rustic in feeling).

**Other South-east Asian furniture** Thailand, Cambodia, Indonesia and the Philippines each produced its own, slightly adapted version of Chinese furniture. The Philippines produced fine examples of hybrid Dutch-Spanish colonial furniture, often made by Chinese craftsmen or in workshops run by Chinese entrepreneurs; Chinese techniques of construction were often adapted to baroque and rococo dining tables and cupboards.

The entire field of South-east Asian furniture with its hybridization of techniques and forms has been virtually ignored by Western furniture historians and provides a relatively uncharted and potentially rewarding area for the enterprising furniture collector.

## FURTHER READING

The following list of materials for further reading offers a broad range of literature. Both specialist and general works are included. While every effort has been made to give the date of the most recent edition, new ones may have been published since this book went to press.

Agius, Pauline
**British Furniture, 1880–1915**
London 1978

— and Stephen Jones (introduction)
**Ackermann's Regency Furniture & Interiors**
Marlborough 1984

Bazin, Germain
**Baroque and Rococo**
London 1964

Beard, G.
**Grinling Gibbons**
London 1989

— and Christopher Gilbert (eds.)
**Dictionary of English Furniture Makers 1660–1840**
Leeds 1986

Burr, Grace H.
**Hispanic Furniture**
New York 1964

Cathers, David M.
**Furniture of the American Arts and Crafts Movement**
New York 1981

Chinnery, Victor
**Oak Furniture – The British Tradition**
Woodbridge 1979

Collard, Frances
**Regency Furniture**
Woodbridge 1985

Comstock, Helen
**American Furniture**
New York 1962

Cooper, Jeremy
**Victorian and Edwardian Furniture and Interiors**
London 1987

Cornelius, Charles A.
**Early American Furniture**
New York 1926

Downs, Joseph
**American Furniture in the Henry Francis du Pont Winterthur Museum: Queen Anne and Chippendale Periods**
New York 1952

Dubrow, Eileen and Richard
**American Furniture of the 19th Century, 1840–1880**
New York 1983

Eames, Penelope
"Furniture in England, France and the Netherlands, 12th–15th Centuries", **Furniture History Society Journal**
Victoria and Albert Museum, London 1975

Edwards, Ralph
**The Shorter Dictionary of English Furniture**
London 1964

Eriksen, Svend
**Early Neoclassicism in France**
London 1974

Fairbanks, Jonathan L. and Robert F. Trent (eds.)
**New England Begins** (exhibition catalogue)
Boston 1982 (3 vols)

Flannagan, J. Michael
**American Furniture from the Kaufman Collection**
New York 1986

Furniture History Society
**Dictionary of English Furniture Makers**
Leeds 1986

**Furniture of Charles and Henry Greene: An Introductory Booklet**
Huntington Museum, San Marino, California 1987

**George Bullock Cabinet-Maker** (exhibition catalogue)
London 1988

Green, D.
**Grinling Gibbons: his work as carver and statuary**
London 1964

de Gröer, Léon
**Les Arts Décoratifs de 1790 à 1850**
Fribourg 1985

Hayward, Helena (ed.)
**World Furniture**
London 1990

Janneau, Guillaume
**Le Meuble Bourgeois en France**
Editions Garnier

Jervis, S. (ed)
**Printed Furniture Designs before 1650**
London 1974

Jourdain, Margaret
**English Decoration & Furniture of the Early Renaissance**
London 1924

Joy, Edward
**A Pictorial Dictionary of Nineteenth Century Furniture Design**
Woodbridge 1977

Ledoux-Lebard, Denise
**Les Ébénistes Parisiens (1795–1830)**
Paris 1951

MacGregor, A.
**The Late King's Goods**
London & Oxford 1989

Macquoid, Percy
**The Age of Walnut**
London 1905

Mercer, Eric
**Furniture 700–1700**
London 1969

Miller, Edgar G., Jr.
**Standard Book of American Antique Furniture**
New York 1950

Montgomery, Charles F.
**American Furniture: The Federal Period in the Henry Francis du Pont Winterthur Museum**
New York 1966

Morrazzoni, Giuseppe
**Il Mobilio Italiano**
Florence 1940

Nagel, Charles
**American Furniture**
New York 1949

Ormsbee, Thomas H.
**Field Guide to American Victorian Furniture**
Boston 1951

Payne, Christopher
**19th Century European Furniture**
London 1985

Schweiger, Werner J.
**Wiener Werkstätte: design in Vienna, 1903–1932**
New York 1984

Stalker, J. and G. Parker
**A Treatise of Japanning & Varnishing**
1688

Thornton, Peter
**Authentic Decor 1620–1920**

— **Seventeenth Century Interior Decoration in England, France & Holland**
London & New Haven 1978

Trent, Robert (ed.)
**Pilgrim Century Furniture**
New York 1980

Viaux, Jacqueline
**Le Meuble en France**
Paris 1962

Ward, Gerald W.R.
**American Case Furniture in the Mabel Brady Garvan and Other Collections at Yale University**
New Haven 1988

Wills, Geoffrey
**English Furniture 1550–1760**
London 1971

— **English Furniture 1760–1900**
London 1971

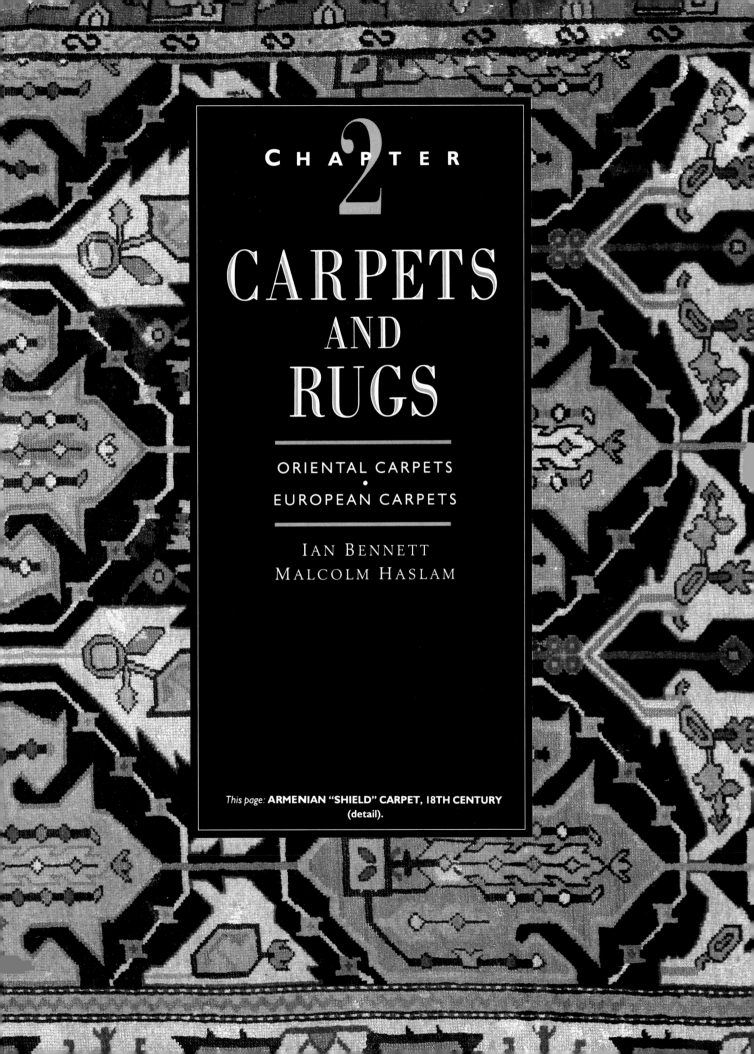

# CHAPTER 2

# CARPETS AND RUGS

## ORIENTAL CARPETS
·
## EUROPEAN CARPETS

IAN BENNETT
MALCOLM HASLAM

*This page:* **ARMENIAN "SHIELD" CARPET, 18TH CENTURY (detail).**

# CARPETS AND RUGS

BENEATH ONE'S FEET CAN LIE AN ANTIQUE TREASURE, A CARPET OR RUG OF EXOTIC DESIGN. THE FINE CRAFTSMANSHIP THAT HAS GONE INTO THESE WON THE ADMIRATION OF SUCH GREAT ARTISTS AS 14TH-CENTURY ITALIAN MASTERS OR THE 19TH-CENTURY GIANT GAUGUIN.

It can be presumed that the earliest "cloth" was woven for apparel and perhaps for cult purposes, as hangings bearing iconographic images in temples or sacred rooms; nevertheless, the weaving of both wall-hangings and floor coverings was probably not greatly separated in time. Symmetrically knotted pile weavings made entirely of flax and datable to the 16th-15th century BC have been found in Egypt, and the technical mastery demonstrated by these remarkably well-preserved arte-facts, probably bed covers but possibly intended for the floor, suggests that they do not represent anything new but are almost miraculous sur-vivors of an already widespread art form. By the 5th century BC, the date of the Pazyryk carpet found in the frozen tomb of a Scythian

**FLAT-WOVEN RUG**
*Italy*
Wool weft-faced
technique; **19th century**

The Abruzzi is the best-known Italian region for peasant weaving and a considerable number of rugs have survived. (*Above*)

**"ARABESQUE" OR "LOTTO" PATTERN RUG**
*Anatolia*
Wool pile on wool foundation; **17th century**

One of the most famous Ushak designs. This version of the pattern is called "Anatolian". (*Right*)

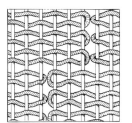

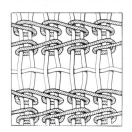

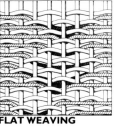

**FLAT WEAVING TECHNIQUES**

Top to bottom: slit tapestry or kelim weave; Soumak brocading with ground weave; weft-float brocading with ground weave. (*Above*)

**THE MOUNSEY RUG**
*Egypt*
Wool pile on wool
foundation; **early 16th
century**

Rugs in this distinctive
palette and design are
associated with the Mamluk
dynasty of Egypt (1250-
1517). However, such rugs
continued to be made long
after downfall at the hands
of the Ottoman Turks.
Thus in the early period of
Ottoman domination of
Egypt, rugs were made in
two distinct styles – the
older 'Mamluk' style and
the imported Ottoman
'court' style. This does
seem to be a fairly late
example of its type. Its
small size – 6ft 2in × 4ft 9in
(1.88 × 1.45m) – is typical
of the most numerous
group surviving of these
beautiful rugs. (*Above*)

prince in the Altai Mountains of Siberia, carpet weaving had already
achieved technical perfection. Indeed, in structural terms, there is no
difference between the Pazyryk and any symmetrically knotted rug
made during the last 500 years.

The word "weaving", however, covers a great diversity of production. Two of the most important weaving cultures – that of
pre-Conquest South and Central America in the West, and China in
the East – are not associated primarily with rugs, although China, in
the period between about AD 1400 and AD 1800, produced some of
the most outstanding masterpieces of Oriental rug weaving. That this
is only now beginning to be appreciated by researchers is probably
due to the fact that although Oriental, Chinese rugs fall outside the
Islamic focus that lends the study of Eastern carpets cohesion and
homogeneity.

The weaving of rugs is not exclusively an Oriental matter, of course,
and there is also a very long, splendid history of carpet production in
Europe. Not surprisingly, given the Moorish influence, the Iberian
Peninsula is one of the best-known European weaving areas, as are the
eastern European countries around the Balkans, which were under the
rule of the Ottoman Turks for many years. But England, France,
Germany, Scandinavia, Switzerland, Italy and Poland also have long
histories of rug and textile weaving – histories distinct from the well-
known 17th- and 18th-century carpets produced in the great commercial workshops of France and England. Despite the ubiquity of rug
weaving and its long history, there can be little doubt that, in the West,
its importance as an art form – and as far as the greatest surviving examples are concerned, they arguably constitute one of man's most glorious artistic achievements – has hardly been recognized.

In the 16th and 17th centuries, Oriental carpets were persistently
sought and greatly treasured by European rulers and aristocrats and, in
the 17th century, increasingly by the wealthy bourgeoisie. Yet from this
high point three centuries ago, the understanding and appreciation of
Oriental weaving have declined to the point where it now attracts a
comparatively small number of dedicated specialists. Both in critical
and commercial terms, Oriental carpet weaving is perhaps the least
understood of all great art forms.

**THE SEELEY
MEDALLION CARPET**
*Northwest Persia*
Wool pile on cotton
foundations;
**16th century**

This majestic carpet, now in
the Metropolitan Museum,
New York, is one of the
mysteries of Safavid
weaving. Stylistically, it
bears strong resemblance
to some of the small
medallion carpets
attributed to Tabriz, while
its main border pattern,
with roundels and indented
cartouches, is associated
primarily with the central
Persian city of Kashan.
Structurally, however, it
cannot be fitted easily into
any of these groups. (*Above*)

## ORIENTAL CARPET KNOTTING

These are the most common
types of Oriental carpet knotting.
The single warp knot is also found
on early loop-pile weavings
associated with Egypt.

1 Symmetric; Turkish or
Ghiordes knot. 2 Single
warp Spanish knot. 3
Asymmetric; Persian or
Sehna knot open to the left.
4 Asymmetric; Persian or
Sehna knot open to the
right. 5 Asymmetric 'jufti'
knot over four warps. 6
Symmetric 'jufti' knot over
four warps

THE SUMPTUOUS CARPETS OF THE ORIENT HAVE FOUND IMITATORS, BUT FEW TRUE RIVALS. THEIR GEOMETRIC, COLORFUL PATTERNS DELIGHT THE EYE AND FINISH THE DECORATION OF ANY WELL-APPOINTED ROOM.

# ORIENTAL CARPETS

There is much uncertainty regarding the early history of knotted pile, or pile weaving, the technique employed to make the finest Oriental carpets. In pile weaving, short lengths of yarn, usually wool but sometimes silk, are looped or knotted around warp threads, which are stretched vertically between the beams of an upright loom; the result is a "pile" that is perpendicular to the warp. Pile weaving generally is assumed to be an extension of plain weaving and tapestry weaving, and its use may have begun in the late Neolithic period, between the 9th and 7th millennia BC.

Among the earliest known examples of pile weaving using recognizable techniques are complete pieces made entirely of flax and knotted with the symmetrical ("Turkish" or "Ghiordes") knot; found in the Tomb of Ka in Egypt and datable to *c.*1500 BC, these are pre-served in the Museo Civico, Turin, and the Louvre, Paris. In 1947, a complete wool pile carpet in the same knotting technique was discovered preserved in the perma-ice that filled the tomb of a 5th-century BC Scythian prince in Pazyryk, Siberia. The sophistication of this object, probably of Persian origin and now in the Hermitage, Leningrad, suggests that by this time, pile knotting was already an ancient art.

## EARLY EGYPTIAN PILE CARPETS

After the Pazyryk carpet, the first substantial groups of carpets and large fragments to have survived are associated with Egypt. Such weavings, stylistically and structurally, fall into two distinct groups but in the main date from between the 6th and 9th centuries AD; one type, called the Antinoë group (after a fragment in the Metropolitan Museum, New York), has a wide

**THE PAZYRYK CARPET**
*Central Asian (Persian)*
Wool pile on wool foundations; **5th century BC**

This is the oldest surviving wool pile carpet and has 200 symmetric knots to the square inch. Discovered in 1947 in the burial chamber of a Scythian prince, it is now in the Hermitage, Leningrad. Considerable argument exists as to its place of manufacture. Its affinity with Assyrian stone "carpets" found at the palaces of Sennacharib (705–681 BC) and Assurbanipal (668–626 BC) suggests it may be a commercial product of the succeeding Achaemenian period.

range of colours and is constructed in the so-called asymmetric (or Sehna) loop; the second group has a geometric composition in the single-warp loop (or Coptic knot).

**The Antinoë Group** The Antinoë group consists of a number of complete rugs and fragments, most found by archaeological expeditions at sites at the southern tip of Lake Nasser. In ancient times, this represented the extremities of Upper Egypt, although the area in question, Nubia, ceased to be part of the Roman Empire under Diocletian at the end of the 3rd century AD.

All the examples of Nubian provenance are assumed to be Coptic work imported from Egypt, although the majority were found in 6th-century AD pre-Christian Nubian graves. Their Egyptian manufacture is based on their close relationship to the Antinoë fragment, said to have been found at the ancient site of that name just below Alexandria in Lower Egypt. The Antinoë rug is traditionally dated to the 5th century AD, but this may be a little early.

Two of the best preserved examples of the Antinoë group, now in the British Museum, London, were found before the Second World War at Buhen and Qasr Ibrim, respectively. An example similar to the second London rug is in the Helsinki National Museum, and a third belongs to the University of Chicago Oriental Institute. All these rugs are extremely colourful and several share a distinctive "arcade and tree" design in their main borders; indeed, in both colour and design, they are evocative of later Anatolian rugs. Like the beautiful patchwork of fragments from a rug of related type in the Keir Collection London, these rugs blend the influence of Roman mosaics with indigenous styles.

The Keir carpet, with its narrower colour range and linen foundations, might be later in date. However, it is more closely related structurally to the Antinoë group than the other well-known type of Coptic carpet, usually dated to the 7th and 8th centuries. This second group probably post-dates the Arab Conquest of Egypt in AD 641. Previously, the word "Copt" described the indigenous Egyptian population under Roman rule; following the Arab Conquest, it took on an ethno-religious meaning, referring to that part of the native population remaining Christian.

### EARLY ISLAMIC PILE CARPETS

Following this second group of Egyptian carpets, little of substance has survived from the "ancient" period. There are fragments of what are presumed to be Islamic rugs and one extraordinary complete example, the Franses Animal Carpet (now in the De Young Memorial Art Museum, San Francisco), tentatively dated to the 9th century and thought to have been found at Fustat, the old Islamic capital of Egypt (now a Cairo suburb). No large body of Egyptian carpets appears again, however, until the so-called Mamluk carpets of the 15th and 16th centuries.

All the Coptic carpets – indeed all Egyptian woollen textiles of the 1st millennium AD – have one distinctive characteristic relevant to an understanding and recognition of later Mamluk and Cairene Ottoman carpets now widely at-

**CARPET**
*Alcaraz, Spain*
**Wool pile on goat warps and wool wefts; 16th century**

The attribution of carpets with this distinctive "wreath medallion" design to 16th-century Alcaraz is based on contemporary Spanish documents describing carpets with "roundels" from Alcaraz. This example has the arms of the Order of Saint Dominic in its four corners.

tributed to Egypt. The wool from which they are woven is S-spun (ie, spun in a clockwise direction). This is a feature of Egyptian wool textiles and is thought to reflect the fact that flax (linen), the material from which most ancient textiles are made, lends itself more easily to S-spinning. Whether or not this is true, it is a fact that the rugs of no other major weaving culture, with a few exceptions (for instance, some 19th-century Tibetan pile weavings) have S-spun wool.

### TURKISH RUGS

The "modern" era of carpet weaving begins on somewhat shaky ground. Nevertheless, there are groups of Anatolian rugs, most likely dating from the 13th and 14th centuries, and also Spanish rugs made by the Moors attributed to the 14th century. Certain of the early Spanish rugs bear the coats of arms of the hereditary admirals of Spain and are thus known as "admiral" carpets. Others have designs related to Anatolian "small pattern Holbein" rugs, and there are distinct Spanish designs showing European influence, such as the "pomegranate lattice" and "wreath" rugs of the 15th and 16th centuries. Most Spanish carpet weaving is associated with the southern part of the country, in particular Alcaraz, Letur and Cuenca.

**Early Anatolian Rugs** Of the early Anatolian rugs, the most famous comprise two groups, one from the Alaeddin Mosque in Konya found in 1905 and the other discovered in 1929 in the Esrefoglü Mosque in Beyshehir. With one exception, all of these pieces are now in the Turk ve Islam Museum, Istanbul, or the Mevlana Museum, Konya; many are almost complete and, if their putative dates are accepted, give a good idea of what 13th-century "workshop carpets" looked like. The Alaeddin Mosque was completed in 1220 and the Esrefoglü Mosque in 1296; it has been assumed that the two respective groups of rugs are roughly contemporary with these dates. The majority of the rugs have tight, lattice-like designs in their fields and many of them border designs assumed to be stylizations, or abstractions, of Kufic script. They are symmetrically knotted and made entirely of Z-spun wool; technically, although not artistically, these rugs represent a decline from the standard achieved by the weaver of the Pazyryk rug nearly 2,000 years earlier.

**Tribal and Village Weaving** However, the history of Turkish weaving between the 12th and 17th centuries is very complex. Turkey is now, as it has been for centuries, dotted with thousands of tiny villages, all with their own small mosques. The practice of *vaqf* – pious donations – has always been an important part

of Turkish religious life, and it is for this reason that hundreds, possibly thousands, of very early rugs of types never exported to Europe have been preserved. These constitute what might be termed the tribal and village weaving orbit, as opposed to the court and commercial weaving milieu associated with western Turkey and in particular the Ushak region.

Turkey is unique among the great weaving cultures of the Near and Middle East, since no comparable body of tribal and village work has survived from Persia, the Caucasus, Central Asia or elsewhere which dates much before the late 18th century. Turkish weavings of this kind include both piled and flat-woven examples, the latter in the slit-tapestry technique called "kilim" in Turkey, *palas* in the Caucasus and *ghileem* in Iran. However, there is no unanimity of opinion about the dates of many of these rugs. In Turkey itself, there are considerable holdings of such rugs in the Turk ve Islam Museum and the Vakiflar Museum, both in Istanbul. In the West, perhaps the greatest collection of early Turkish kilims in existence is in the De Young Memorial Art Museum, San Francisco.

**Early Ottoman Weavings** These early and historically "difficult" weavings are in contrast to the best-known carpets of the early Ottoman period. Of these, the two most famous design types are usually referred to as "large pattern Holbeins" and "small pattern Holbeins" because of their appearance in that artist's work. The first type refers to rugs with large octagonal medallions in the centre, often flanked by smaller medallions to form a quincuxial arrangement. The small pattern Holbein has a more intricate arrangement of small octagons and lozenges alternating on the field.

The largest group of early Turkish "workshop" rugs are associated with the Ushak district. These fall into several design groups and have been given reference names such as "large medallion", "small medallion" (or "double niche"), "Lotto" (after the Italian painter), white ground "bird" rugs, white ground "Chintamani" (derived from a Chinese symbol) rugs, "star" and "lobed medallion". In general, these date from between the late 15th and early 17th centuries.

Also attributed to Ushak are the majority of rugs with various designs grouped under the generalized heading "Transylvanian", since a great many of them have been found in churches and collections in the part of Eastern Europe, once under Ottoman domination. Rugs of the

**RUG FRAGMENT**
*Probably Central Turkey*
Wool pile on wool foundation; **Ottoman period, 15th century**

The famous so-called "small pattern Holbein" design on this fragment appears in many European, especially Italian, paintings from the 15th century onwards. (*Above*)

**RUG**
*Ushak region, Western Turkey*
Wool pile on wool foundation; **Ottoman period, 16th century**

Another famous Anatolian workshop design is the "small medallion" or "double niche" motif seen on this rug. "Small medallion" Ushak rugs continued to be made into the 17th century. (*Left*)

Transylvanian family can be divided into several design groups, including the Lotto pattern, "triple column" prayer rugs, "Smyrna" rugs with their distinctive palette and floral patterns, and "medallion and wreath" rugs with "star and cartouche" borders. In the main, Transylvanian rugs probably date from the first half of the 17th century and many examples can be seen in European, and in particular Dutch, painting of this period.

### EASTERN MEDITERRANEAN RUGS

In 1517, the Ottomans conquered Egypt. Previously, Cairo had a thriving weaving industry producing rugs in what has become known as the Mamluk style, after the dynastic rulers whom the Ottomans overthrew. Mamluk-style

rugs continued to be woven long after the Turkish conquest, concomitantly with a newly introduced style of Ottoman "court" art. The latter resulted in the production of so-called Cairene Ottoman rugs, which have the full repertoire of Ottoman "court" motifs – tulips, carnations, curving *saz* leaves and so on. Designs were both secular and in the prayer-rug format, and some of the former can be extremely large.

There was once controversy as to whether these rugs were woven in Egypt or Turkey, especially as there is one group with silk foundations and another, more coarsely woven, with wool. However, since the wool used for these rugs is uniformly S-spun, an Egyptian characteristic, it is sensible to attribute all of them to Egypt. An example in the Pitti Palace, Florence (which entered the Medici collection in the early 17th century), is specifically described in contemporary inventories as a "Cairene carpet".

A continuing argument, however, rages over other groups of rugs with designs known as "Para-Mamluk" and "compartment" or "chessboard". In colour and details, both types, which are structurally identical, seem clearly within the Mamluk Egyptian orbit. However, their Z-spun wool probably rules out an Egyptian origin, while their asymmetrical knotting rules out a Turkish one. A widely accepted hypothesis is that they were woven in Damascus, which was once within the Mamluk and then Ottoman empires. The earliest Para-Mamluk rugs may date from the 15th century, with the compartment rug generally being dated to the late 16th and early 17th centuries.

### PERSIAN RUGS

Almost all surviving Persian rugs pre-dating AD 1800 are from the Safavid period, *c.*1500 to 1722. Recently, it has been suggested that a fragment in the Benaki Museum, Athens, is from the 15th-century Timurid period; this seems likely and if so represents the only extant Persian pile weaving from before the Safavid era. Less convincing is the suggestion that some of the so-called Tabriz medallion carpets are also Timurid, although the greatest of them may date from around 1500.

**Safavid Carpets** It is difficult to attribute Safavid Persian carpets to particular weaving centres. There are several key cities, ranging from Tabriz in the north-west to Herat in the far east, to which carpets have traditionally been ascribed. They include Kashan, Esfahan and Kerman, supposed sources of major groups of

**RUG**
*Syrian (?), possibly Damascus*
Wool pile on a wool foundation; **Ottoman period, early 17th century**

This rug, with its "compartment" or "chequerboard" design, is from one of two famous groups (the other the "proto-Mamluk") assigned to Damascus because it is difficult to attribute them to anywhere else! (*Above*)

**RUG**
*Cairo*
Wool pile on a wool foundation; **16th century**

In the "Cairene Ottoman" style, this rug is from a similar weaving tradition to the example above, but is distinguishable by its use of S-spun wool. (*Left*)

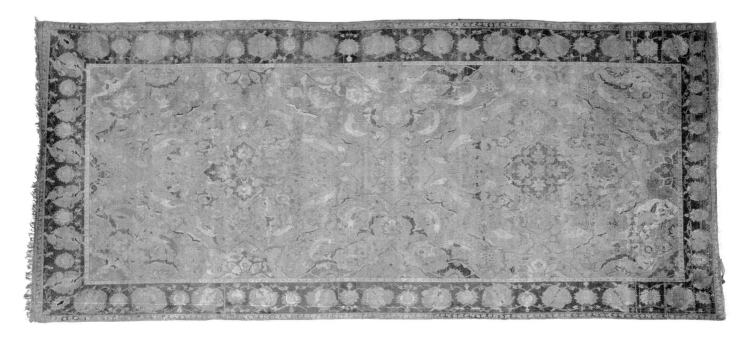

surviving carpets, as well as others such as Qazvin and Joshaqan, once weaving centres. The amount of documentary evidence linking individual or homogeneous groups of carpets with specific places or even specific periods is slight. Travellers to Persia frequently noted the appearance of carpets in individual towns and cities but such descriptions are never sufficiently detailed to allow a confident identification of a group or design type. It is clear, however, that weaving was widespread throughout 15th-, 16th- and 17th-century Persia and was carried on in many more places and in a far greater variety than the comparatively few surviving and identifiable groups allow for. However, the attribution of surviving groups – whose recognition has become increasingly due to an awareness of shared structures rather than shared designs – is not always easy or even possible. Some have been attributed to more than one place and several do not seem to fit easily into any well-established group and have not been satisfactorily attributed to a specific weaving centre.

**Significant Recorded Carpets** Only in two instances, perhaps, is a firm attribution on art-historical grounds justifiable, and only in another two is there sufficient structural information to allow slightly less firm attributions. In 1601, King Sigismund III of Poland commissioned an Armenian merchant named Muratowicz to visit Persia in order to acquire silk carpets and tapestries. In December 1602 Muratowicz presented a bill to the Polish court which included the cost of eight silk rugs. It is

assumed that among these was the pair of silk kilims with Sigismund's arms now in the *Residenz* Museum, Munich, as well as six other kilims in the same museum. Since it is reasonably certain when and where these pieces were acquired, it is also reasonable to attribute a substantial number of other contemporaneous and clearly related silk kilims to late 16th- or early 17th-century Kashan. The justification for dating some to the 16th century is the fact that one related example, in the Shosho-in shrine in Nara, Japan, belonged to the samurai Toyotomi Hideyoshi (d 1598).

However, at almost the same time, the Signory of Venice received the first of three recorded gifts of silk carpets from the Persian Shahs. The first arrived in 1603, the second in 1622 and the third in 1638. Five of the rugs, which are all of the type known as "Polonaise" ("Polish"), are still preserved in the Treasury of St Mark's. The rug from the first gift is very similar in design to another Polonaise given to the Shrine of Imam 'Ali at Al Najaf by Shah Abbas in the early 17th century. It is probable that ·these rugs were all made in the imperial workshops which Shah Abbas established in his new capital of Esfahan in the first five years of the 17th century.

**Other Design Groups** The attribution of these two specific groups to Kashan and Esfahan is generally accepted. This differs from other groups, such as the Tabriz medallion carpets, which are linked by shared designs, structures, wool and colours, and the carpets of the "vase" group attributed to Kerman, which have many

**"POLONAISE" CARPET**
*Isfahan, Central Persia*
Silk piled with metal brocading and mixed cotton and silk foundations; **second quarter 17th century**

More than 200 "Polonaise" rugs survive, of which only about 35 are of this size or greater. The majority of all "Polonaise" rugs have heavy cotton warps and mixed cotton and silk wefts and, for silk piled rugs, are comparatively coarse in knotting. However, some exist, most of them from the first decade or so of the 17th century, which have all-silk foundations and much finer knotting. Not all examples, regardless of their quality, have metal brocading and only two are known with pictorial images. One late "Polonaise" bears the Armenian signature "Yakob", Armenians having the monopoly of the silk trade under Shah Abbas.

### THE "EMPEROR" CARPET
*Central Persia, probably Kashan*
**Wool pile with metal brocading on silk foundations; Safavid period, late 16th century**

This carpet, one of a pair, is thought to have been among the carpets given to Emperor Leopold I of Austria (1658–1705) by Tsar Peter the Great. The inscription around the inner guard suggests that these rugs were royal Persian commissions. (*Right*)

### CARPET
*Heriz region, Persia*
**Wool pile on cotton foundations; Qajar period, second half 19th century**

This rug is one of a famous group of 19th-century Persian workshop carpets. Examples are sold under various names – Gorevan, Serapi, Bakshaish et al. – but they come from the same area. (*Below*)

different designs but are now generally considered homogeneous because of an easily recognizable shared structure.

Other "groups" which have been suggested include a substantial number of mostly 17th-century carpets with widely differing designs but a shared and distinctive structure to the province of Khorasan in eastern Persia; a number of carpets with wool pile, superb designs and colours, silk foundations and often metal brocading to Kashan, and a distinctive group of 17 small and four large silk rugs, the latter usually called "hunting" carpets, also to Kashan. The Kashan silks probably date from the second half of the 16th century.

**Problems in Dating** Chronology is another, although lesser, problem since the Safavid period lasted roughly for two centuries, during which most, if not all, of the carpets mentioned in connection with specific groups were made. Certain historically verifiable dates noted above give valuable clues as to what was going on when and (in a few instances) where. In addition, there are three dated 16th-century carpets, the earliest of which is the great wool hunting carpet in the Poldi Pezzoli Museum, Milan, which is signed by Ghyath ud-din Jami and dated 929 A. H. (AD 1522/3). The other two consist of the famous pair of "Ardabil" medallion carpets woven in wool on silk foundations, each of which bears the same long inscription and the signature of Maqsud of Kashan with the date 946 A. H. (AD 1539/40); these are now in the Victoria and Albert Museum, London, and the Los Angeles County Museum.

**Tribal Rugs** Safavid weaving was a part of court or workshop art. It was not until the 19th century that examples of Persian tribal art were made in this medium. Many of the famous Iranian weaving tribes and tribal confederations, however, are not of Persian stock; the Shahsavan, Qashqa'i, Afshars and so on are of Turkic, Arab or other ethnic origins. Only the Kurds and Lurs (of which the Bakhtiari are a distinct offshoot dating back at least to the 16th century) are considered native Persians, while the Khamseh, the other major tribal confederation in Fars, was an "artificial" political construct of the Qajar Shahs.

Numerous so-called tribal rugs have survived from between *c.*1850 and 1920. However, it is clear that many of these – in particular, several well-known groups of finely knotted Qashqa'i rugs – are not the products of a genuine tribal environment but were made in workshops

established by wealthy khans (tribal elders) for their own use and commercial reasons. This is true of the majority of so-called Bakhtiari rugs with cotton foundations, which were made in workshops set up and run by the Bakhtiari khans in the many towns and villages they owned in the Chahar Mahall valley west of Esfahan from the 1870s onwards.

Thus when the expression "tribal rug" is used in reference to a 19th- or early 20th-century Persian weaving, certain difficulties of definition should be remembered. Certainly, many of the utilitarian weavings, such as saddle-bags, which have survived are clearly definable as tribal, as are many of the coarse but often beautiful rugs with thick, shaggy piles known as *gabbeh*. These were made purely for domestic consumption and only recently have made any impact on Western collectors.

## INDIAN CARPETS

Little documentary evidence exists concerning Mughal Indian weaving of the 16th and 17th centuries. Surviving examples are few and generally fall into two distinct types. The first, perhaps the most unashamedly beautiful and luxurious demonstration of Eastern carpet weaving, is characterized by extraordinarily detailed and realistic depictions of flowers, wonderful colours and the use of the most luxurious of all materials for the pile, the soft, fine silky hair of the Kashmir goat called *pashmina*. They are also, perhaps, the only instances in the known history of carpet weaving where extreme

**RUG**
*Bakhtiari workshops, Chahar Mahall Valley, Persia*
Wool pile on cotton foundations; 1885–6

This rug represents an extensive group of 19th- and early 20th-century carpets woven in workshops established by the wealthy khans of the Bakhtiari tribal confederation in villages they owned west of Esfahan. (*Above*)

**CARPET**
*Indian, probably Lahore*
Wool pile on mixed wool and silk foundations; **Mughal period, second quarter 17th century**

One of the most beautiful of an extensive group of surviving carpets with rows of flowering shrubs on a red ground, this example was made for the Palace of the Maharajah of Jaipur at Amber. (*Left*)

brilliance of technique is combined with undoubted artistic greatness.

*Pashmina* rugs were probably woven in Kashmir in the early 17th century, possibly in the late 16th. Also from the 17th century come large numbers of more coarsely woven carpets with sheep's-wool piles. Many have red grounds and floral designs which seem influenced by the roughly contemporaneous red ground floral rugs of Persian Esfahan – although the Indian versions are clearly distinguishable by their colour and certain characteristic design elements.

There is also a large group of red ground carpets with rows of realistic flowers; these rugs are associated with the mid-17th-century site where most of them were found, the Palace of Amber near Jaipur, built by the Maharajah of Jaipur. These rugs vary considerably in quality, although the best do not approach early *pashmina* rugs in beauty. All of them, as well as various hunting and animal rugs, are usually attributed to workshops in Lahore, where some undoubtedly were made, although other cities such as Agra probably were also producing similar carpets during the same period. Towards the end of the Mughal era, in the late 17th and 18th centuries, there appeared another group of *pashmina* piled rugs, probably made in Hyderabad in the Deccan, known as "mille-fleurs" because of their dense floral patterns; a group of prayer rugs of this type has a large vase with a huge mixed bouquet, somewhat like a 16th-century Flemish flower painting.

### TURKOMAN WEAVINGS

The weavings of the Turkoman tribes of Central Asia have been at the forefront of research and collecting interest in the last two decades. In general, the work of the principal tribes of West Turkestan – including the Salor, Saryk, Yomut, Tekke, Chodor, Arabatchi and Ersari – have been well documented.

Turkoman weaving represents perhaps the purest surviving manifestation of an Eastern nomadic culture. Most examples have certain characteristics in common, principally the use of red in various shades as the predominant colour, and the arrangement of geometric medallions, called *güls*, as the most ubiquitous decorative motif. Russian scholars were of the view that these *güls* represented tribal emblems and each variation was at one point the exclusive property of individual tribes. They further argued that as one tribe was defeated and absorbed by another, so also were their *güls*, so

that eventually this exclusivity of representation was lost. This theory remains unproven and is the subject of considerable scepticism today.

**Types and Uses** Turkoman tribal weavings were made for use in the tent, both for decoration and warmth and for more utilitarian purposes. Weaving ability was rated very highly and, as in most Eastern weaving societies, was carried out mainly by women. Thus, great care was lavished upon even the smallest and appar-

**TURKOMAN MAIN CARPET**

*Salor tribe, Turkestan*

**Wool and silk pile on wool foundations; 19th century**

The main carpets of the Salor are among the most beautiful Turkoman tribal weavings. The repeated medallion in the field is a *gul*.

ently mundane objects, especially those made for a girl and her family as part of her dowry.

Each weaving had its own use and name. The main carpet was obviously the grandest, but there was also the *ensi*, used for covering the tent entrance, and the *kapunuk*, a weaving with two long narrow sides, hanging above the *ensi*. Turkoman weavers were also renowned for the quality and variety of their piled bags, the largest of which is called a *chuval*, the next size down a *torba* and the smallest a *mafrash*. Prayer rugs do not seem to have been used extensively by the Turkomans, although some beautiful examples were made by the Beshir Ersari.

Also of great importance were weavings that decorated animals, particularly the camel-flank hangings, which can be five- or seven-sided or,

in the case of the Salor, rectangular; these are called *asmalyk*. The *khalyk*, somewhat like a small *kapunuk*, was used to decorate the animal's breast.

## RUGS FROM THE CAUCASUS

The earliest group of rugs associated with workshops in the northern part of the huge province of Azerbaijan, north of the present Soviet border with Iran, are the so-called "dragon" rugs. Made in the 16th and 17th centuries, these have brilliant and barbaric designs and colours, with the dominant motif a repeated stylized dragon in a lattice. This design may derive from the animal and floral lattice carpets woven in Kerman, and changed in the 18th century into a purely floral composition known as the "blossom"

**TURKOMAN ASMALYK (CAMEL FLANK HANGING)**
*Yomut tribe, Turkestan*
Wool pile on wool foundations; **second half 19th century**

Many of the most beautiful Turkoman tribal weavings were made by a young girl as part of a suite of objects for her dowry. Weaving was almost exclusively carried out by women in tribal environments. *(Above)*

## CAUCASIAN CARPET
*Probably Shusha, Karabagh region, Azerbaijan*
**Wool pile on wool foundations; 18th century**

This rug is one of many probably made in workshops set up by rich local rulers. With the so-called "blossom" design, it marks a transition between earlier "dragon" rugs and village rugs of the 19th century. (*Right*)

## CAUCASIAN RUG
*Kazak region, southwest Caucasus*
**Wool pile on a wool foundation; second half 19th century**

One of the best-known and highly regarded design groups of later Caucasian weavings is the so-called "star design", of which this is a fine example. (*Below*)

design. The largest number of both dragon and blossom carpets are in Turkish museums, having been removed from mosques mainly in the central and eastern parts of the country. This fact, as well as the appearance of inscriptions in Armenian on some old examples, suggests that this people, whose involvement in weaving in Turkey, the Caucasus and Persia has never been thoroughly explored, may have been responsible for running the workshops where they were woven.

The blossom carpets, with their increasingly stylized motifs, lead naturally into the village and workshop rugs associated with 19th- and early 20th-century Caucasian weavers (which were imported into Europe and the United States in huge numbers). Individual areas – Kazak, Karabagh, Moghan, Genje, Shirvan, Talis and Daghestan – are associated, not always accurately, with individual designs, which even more inaccurately are connected to individual villages. These names – "Lori-Pambak", "Borchalu", "Fachralo" (all associated with Kazak) and others – have become entrenched in Western rug literature and, if treated with caution, form a useful verbal reference.

THE CARPET STYLES OF THE MIDDLE EAST ARRIVED WITH THE MOORS IN
SPAIN, AND LAID THE FOUNDATIONS FOR AN INDUSTRY THAT SPREAD
ACROSS EUROPE FROM THE MEDITERRANEAN TO THE BALTIC.

# EUROPEAN CARPETS

Although the circumstances in which carpet weaving has flourished in Europe have been many and varied, there have been comparatively few factors determining where and when manufacturing centres were established. Contact with the Near or Middle East has often been an important impetus, as has the ready availability of wool, the principal raw material. Sheep and goats are usually grazed on uplands, where a chilly climate precludes the cultivation of crops; communities were established which depended on wool not only for their livelihood but also for protection from the cold, with insulation often provided by rugs.

The socio-economic conditions which prevailed at royal courts or centres of trade have also favoured the introduction of carpet weaving. Courtiers and merchants enjoyed the prestige of owning luxury items such as carpets, and they usually had the means of maintaining a carpet-weaving industry. It was always important, too, that there be enough young women or children, whose fingers were small and flexible enough to tie knots or ply the needle. Another asset was an abundance of fast-flowing water, suitable for use in dyeing.

## SPANISH CARPETS

The first significant incursion of Islamic culture into Europe was the occupation of a large part of Spain by the Moors in the second decade of the 8th century AD. An administrative centre was established at Cordoba, and among the Moors settling there were men of culture and refinement who brought with them from Africa and the Middle East a taste for luxury and display. Their demand for carpets and rugs was eventually met by the establishment of a local industry. The towns of Alcaraz and Cuenca became the principal carpet-weaving centres, and carpets were also made at Almeria.

The Moors who made the earliest Spanish carpets were apparently of Egyptian origin. Among the Moors in Spain there were many Copts, Christian Egyptians, and they almost certainly introduced the single-warp knot, which was used exclusively until the 17th century. This knot, which became known as the Spanish knot, is tied around each alternate warp thread, and in the following row around the other alternate warp threads. Not many Spanish carpets known today date from earlier than the 15th century, by which time most weaving was done by Christian nuns.

The interaction between the Islamic and Christian cultures that was a significant feature of the manufacture of Spanish carpets is also reflected in the hybrid nature of their designs, particularly from the 14th century onwards.

**THE KALEBDJIAN CARPET**
*Spanish*
**Wool; 1450–1500**

Few of these carpets, decorated with a Gothic lattice pattern of pomegranates, have survived. This example, named after one of its owners, a carpet dealer in Paris during the late 19th century, was woven at Alcaraz or Letur in southern Spain. Like all Spanish carpets of this period, it is tied with the single-warp Spanish knot.

Typical Moorish motifs, imported from Middle Eastern carpet design, were stars and trees. Kufic script was sometimes incorporated in borders. During the 15th century many Gothic motifs were used, particularly heraldic arms and devices, and often combined with the Islamic elements. Geometrical designs, including the large and small Holbein patterns, are also found, probably the consequence of Anatolian carpets being imported into Spain. Persian potters, who in the 13th and 14th centuries executed the elaborate tiles covering the walls of the Alhambra Palace in Granada, introduced to Spanish carpet weavers motifs derived from Persian art, such as the endless knot design. The emblem of the city of Granada – which superseded Cordoba as the administrative capital of Moorish Spain – was the pomegranate, a fruit often decorating Spanish carpets. Examples from the 15th and 16th centuries feature motifs derived from Italian Renaissance art, such as floral wreaths and foliate scrolls.

In 1492 Ferdinand of Aragon conquered the Moorish province of Granada and ended the era of Muhammedan hegemony in southern Spain. Many Moorish craftsmen remained to meet the

**NEEDLEWORK EMBROIDERED CARPET**
*Portuguese*
**Wool; 17th century**

The design of this carpet, which was probably woven at Arraiolos, is based on several different types of Persian and Indian carpet, reflecting the extent of Portuguese trading links during this period. The predominating pale blue and yellow colours are typical of Arraiolos work, although the carpet is embroidered in a variant of the herringbone stitch usually found on these carpets. (*Right*)

**CARPET**
*Spanish*
**Wool pile on a wool foundation, "Lotto" pattern; late 16th century**

The distinctive colour of this carpet indicates that it was made in the major weaving town of Cuenca in southern Spain. Spanish versions of the Anatolian "arabesque" or "Lotto" pattern seem to have been made from a very early period, as in other European countries. (*Left*)

demand created by the Christian rulers and the style they created is called *mudéjar*. The Moors were expelled from Spain in 1609, after which time the quality of Spanish carpets began to decline. Increasing numbers of Turkish carpets were imported and Spanish weavers began to imitate their designs, colours and even technique; the Turkish knot was used for many of the carpets woven in Spain during the 17th and 18th centuries.

A carpet-weaving industry existed in the small fortified town of Arraiolos in Portugal from at least as early as the 16th century. The needlework carpets made there were decorated, generally in herringbone stitch, with designs from several different sources, including Turkish and Persian. Their palette is often that of Spanish carpets – red and green or pale blue and yellow in combination.

### THE ROYAL CARPET FACTORIES OF FRANCE

In France, a carpet-weaving industry was established at the time Spanish production was declining – the first quarter of the 17th century. Carpet weaving had existed in France for at least three centuries before that, but none of the results has survived. Following the Wars of

Religion which had badly disrupted the country, Henry IV was eager to establish new industries in France.

**Savonnerie** In 1608 Pierre Dupont was granted a licence to make carpets in a workshop attached to the palace of the Louvre in Paris. In 1623 he published a treatise claiming that he had mastered the Eastern technique of making pile carpets in silk and wool. Four years later he took on a partner, Simon Lourdet, and expanded his enterprise in premises on the outskirts of Paris. The building had been a soap factory, and by this name – Savonnerie – the carpets woven there came to be known.

Savonnerie carpets were woven to the highest technical standards, using the Turkish knot. But they were designed in purely Western styles derived from Renaissance decorative arts. They were woven by orphans from the nearby Hôpital Général, who were taken on between the ages of ten and twelve and served an apprenticeship of six years. With the accession of Louis XIV to the throne in 1661, the administration began to follow a policy of adding every possible magnificence to the royal court. Savonnerie carpets were much in demand over the next hundred years, for the Louvre and the Tuileries and later

**SAVONNERIE CARPET**
*French*
**Wool; mid 18th century**

The design of this carpet, probably made for the Palace of Versailles, includes typical rococo colours and motifs. (*Left*)

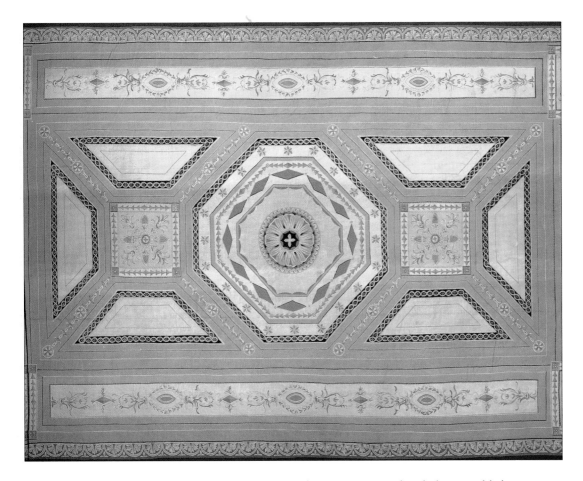

for the Palace of Versailles, completed in 1756. The French nobility toed the line and ordered Savonnerie carpets for their *hôtels* and *châteaux*.

Designs for Savonnerie carpets were supplied by Charles Le Brun (1619–90) and they often incorporated naturalistically rendered garlands of flowers with images of classical antiquity, such as acanthus scrolls and panels showing mythological scenes.

The Savonnerie workshops continued to produce carpets for French governments, up until the present era. The designs used have varied with the decorative style in fashion at the time. The pale colours and rococo motifs of Louis XV's reign gave way to the sombre earth hues and restrained geometry of the *style étrusque*, popular before the Revolution. A more pompous classicism characterized the designs provided by the architects Percier and Fontaine during the Empire period under Napoleon. In the 19th century a group of carpets were made to Neo-Gothic designs by Eugène Viollet-le-Duc.

**Aubusson** Another centre of carpet weaving in France was at Aubusson, some 320 km (about 200 miles) south of Paris. Tapestry weaving had existed in the locality for centuries, and in 1743 the government decided to establish a carpet factory there. Three years later the exclusive privilege of making carpets at Aubusson was granted to two Paris merchants, and since then the various workshops in the town have been privately run with sometimes more and sometimes less government supervision. Although a few Aubusson carpets were hand-knotted, the great majority have been flat-woven. Their designs tend to be less imposing than those of Savonnerie carpets, but no less sophisticated. A typical 19th-century Aubusson carpet is decorated with a design of intricate garlands or bunches of flowers rendered in minute detail with total realism.

THE HAND-KNOTTED CARPETS OF ENGLAND
Carpets were manufactured in England from the mid 15th century, but little is known about the workshops of the time. Nor is there much information about carpets woven at Barcheston and Norwich during the 16th century. Surviving 17th-century needlework carpets were worked by ladies of fashion assisted by their maids, and their designs followed the intertwined floral patterns used for contemporary embroidery.

**Wilton** In 1685 the Revocation of the Edict

**NEEDLEPOINT CARPET**
*French*
Wool (detail); 1795–9

This Aubusson carpet was woven during the Directoire period immediately preceding the rule of Napoleon. The geometric design and restrained ornament are characteristic of the *style étrusque* (Etruscan style) which had evolved in France as a reaction to the lavish scrolls and garlands of rococo decoration. The combination of terracotta and grey-blue was based, like the ornamental motifs, on the art of ancient Rome. *(Above left)*

of Nantes withdrew religious freedoms from the Protestants in France, and large numbers of Huguenots, including many weavers, sought refuge in England. By the end of the century carpet weaving had been established by French craftsmen at Wilton in an area of southern England renowned for its wool production and cloth weaving. In 1701 William III granted the Wilton factory a royal charter. Loop-pile carpets were woven, and the technique of cutting the loops was developed; the velvet-like pile which resulted came to be called Wilton.

**Fulham** In 1749 two dissatisfied master-weavers left the Savonnerie factory and came to London, where they enlisted the support of a Huguenot émigré, Peter Parisot (1697–1769), in setting up a carpet factory at Paddington, London. The enterprise was successful, and the factory was moved to larger premises in Fulham. Inspiration for the designs likewise came from the Savonnerie. In 1755 the Fulham factory was sold. However, the following year Parisot started another factory at Exeter (quickly sold to Claude Passavant), and it flourished for the rest of the century.

**Axminster** Thomas Whitty, a cloth weaver from Axminster, not far from Exeter, started making hand-knotted carpets in 1755, having acquired enough technical knowledge from surreptitious visits to the Fulham factory. He trained his daughters to tie the Turkish knot and within a year was producing carpets of great quality. The name Axminster eventually came to be used for all English hand-knotted carpets. Much of the output from Axminster was commissioned for houses built for the nobility and the wealthy, with designs often furnished by the patron's architect.

**Moorfields** Another factory making hand-

**DONEGAL CARPET**
Wool; c. 1900

This example was designed by the architect Charles Francis Annesley Voysey, whose patterns were used for wallpapers and textiles all over Europe and North America at the turn of the century. (*Above*)

**THE RADZIWILL-SARRE CARPET**
*Polish*
Wool; 1700–50

The name given to this carpet refers to the Radziwill family, whose coat of arms appears in the design, and to Friedrich Sarre, a German art

historian who once owned it. It is assumed to have been woven in the town of Brody, east of Lvov, which is situated today in the Russian Ukraine.

knotted carpets was opened in 1756 by Thomas Moore at Moorfields, London. In 1769 magnificent carpets were woven there to designs by Robert Adam and installed in Syon House, seat of the Duke of Northumberland.

**Arts and Crafts** The manufacture of carpets in England was progressively mechanized from *c.* 1800, and the fortunes of the workshops making the hand-knotted variety began to wane. In the last quarter of the 19th century, William Morris undertook the design and manufacture of hand-knotted carpets at Merton, south of London. Morris's designs were an amalgam of traditional English and Persian elements, and they inspired a revival of the craft of hand-knot-

ting. Similar enterprises were established throughout Europe, including Alexander Morton's factories in Donegal, Ireland, Ginzkey's at Maffersdorf, Bohemia, and workshops in Sweden. Leading architects and artists supplied designs in the Arts and Crafts, Art Nouveau and Viennese Secession styles.

### PEASANT RUGS

Peasant rugs have been woven in many parts of the Continent. In Spain, Alpujarra rugs were made in the valleys of the southern slopes of the Sierra Nevada, mountains between Granada and the Mediterranean. The rugs were coarse woven, with uncut loops, and many have a separately woven fringe on all four sides, suggesting they covered beds and tables, not the floor. Moorish elements in the designs imply that they were first made before the expulsion of the Moors in 1609. Motifs used to decorate the rugs include the tree of life, vases of flowers, birds, animals and the pomegranate.

The kilims made in Poland were usually decorated with geometrical patterns in bright colours. There were also floral designs, sometimes showing the influence of Aubusson carpets. Although most Polish carpets were woven in the context of peasant art, more sophisticated, hand-knotted carpets were made at workshops in Brody, established in the 17th century. The kilims and carpets of the western Ukraine were usually decorated with more or less elaborate floral designs, which also show strong French influence, while retaining a distinctive character of their own.

In Scandinavia various techniques of flat-weaving were employed to produce cushion and bed covers, but a type of pile rug (called a *rya*) was woven in Finland and Sweden using the Turkish knot. Designs often incorporated animals and flowers rendered in flat, diagrammatic shapes reminiscent of Near Eastern carpet patterns. Pairs of human figures often featured, probably referring to a marriage. In Finland the *rya* continued to be woven throughout the 19th century, often in purely abstract designs, but Swedish examples do not seem to have been made after *c.* 1800.

**THE STRADBROKE CARPET**
*English*
**Wool; c. 1790**

This Axminster carpet was woven for Sir John Rouse, later first Earl of Stradbroke, and was installed at Henham Hall, Essex, in c. 1795. (*Below*)

## FURTHER READING

The following list of materials for further reading offers a broad range of literature. Both specialist and general works are included. While every effort has been made to give the date of the most recent edition, new ones may have been published since this book went to press.

Bennett, Ian, (ed)
**Rugs and Carpets of the World**
London 1977

Bidder, Hans
**Carpets of East Turkestan**
London 1964

Dimand, M.S.
**Peasant and Nomad Rugs of Asia**
New York 1961

Edwards, A.C.
**The Persian Carpet**
(revised edition)
London 1975

Eiland, M.L.
**Oriental Rugs** (2nd edition)
New York 1976

Ellis, Charles Grant
**Early Caucasian Rugs**
Washington 1976

Emery, Irene
**The Primary Structure of Fabrics**
Washington 1965

Erdmann, Kurt, (trans. May Beattie and Hildegard Herzog)
**Seven Hundred Years of Oriental Carpets**
London 1970

Jacobs, Bertram
**Axminster Carpets**
Leigh-on-Sea, 1969

Jacobsen, Charles W.
**Oriental Rugs, a Complete Guide** (11th printing)
New York 1971

Jarry, M.
**Carpets of Aubusson**
Leigh-on Sea, 1969

Kendrick, A.F., and C.E.C. Tattersall
**Hand-woven Carpets**
New York 1973

Landreau, A.N., and W.R. Pickering
**From the Bosphorus to Samarkand: Flatwoven Rugs**
Washington 1969

Mankowski, T.
"Influences of Islamic Art in Poland" in **Ars Islamica** Vol. II, 1935

O'Bannon, George W.
**The Turkoman Carpet**
London 1975

Schlosser, I.
**The Book of Rugs, Oriental and European**
London 1963

Tattersall, C.E.C., and S. Reed
**British Carpets**
London 1966

Tiffany Studios
**Antique Chinese Rugs**
New York 1969

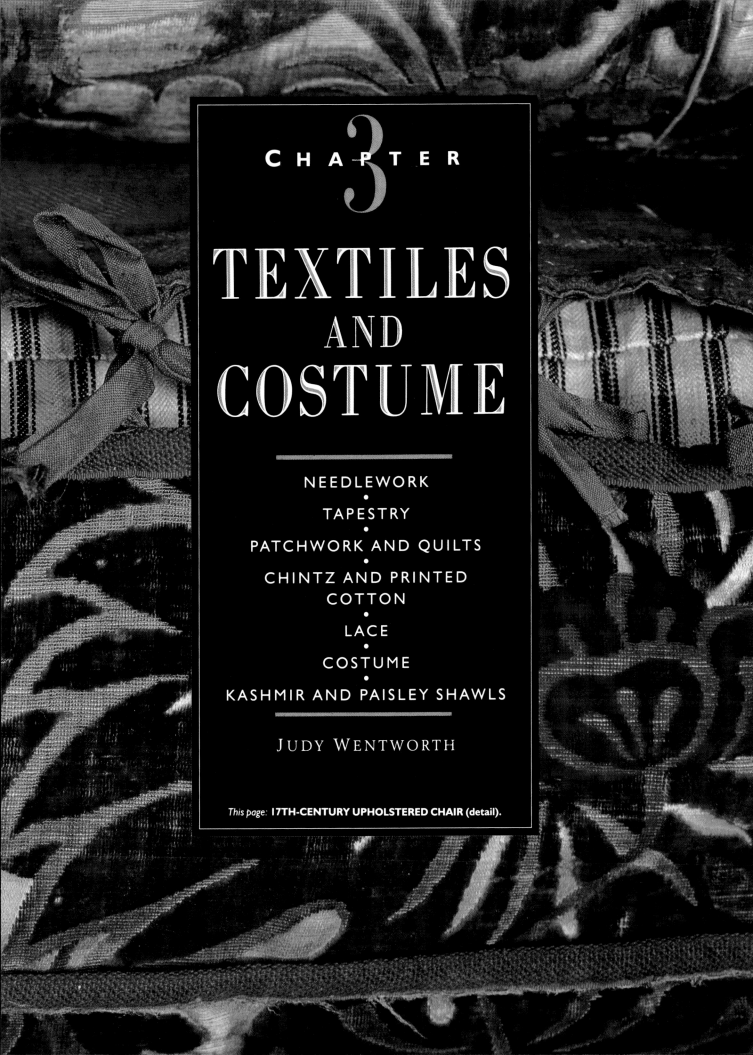

# CHAPTER 3

# TEXTILES
# AND
# COSTUME

NEEDLEWORK
·
TAPESTRY
·
PATCHWORK AND QUILTS
·
CHINTZ AND PRINTED
COTTON
·
LACE
·
COSTUME
·
KASHMIR AND PAISLEY SHAWLS

JUDY WENTWORTH

*This page:* **17TH-CENTURY UPHOLSTERED CHAIR (detail).**

# TEXTILES AND COSTUME

**T**HE FAMILIAR CATEGORY OF TEXTILES AND CLOTHING IS FULL OF
HANDIWORK DESERVING TO BE TREASURED. **T**HE FORTUNATE SURVIVAL OF
SOME OF THESE ITEMS MAINTAINS A LINK WITH THE DAILY LIFE OF THE PAST.

All of us use textiles. We sleep in them, sit on them, work in them
and wear them out. Most of us do not even think about them, but
clothing and the cloth from which it is made are part of the social
fabric of history.

Much needlework was made professionally, often by badly exploited cheap labour, but the amateur has always found satisfaction in the
creation of beautiful textiles and costume. Houses need furnishings
and people need clothes. Starting from this basic premise carpets, wall-
coverings, curtains, bed-hangings, upholstery and various accessories
have been created for centuries, to make the home functional and
agreeable to live in. Fashionable dress, with its requirement for what
was new or currently perceived as stylish, provides examples easily
dated by the rapid progression of change in the design of patterned
fabrics and the cut of the garments.

In the past textile manufacture was much more a part of ordinary
peoples' daily lives. In Europe by the 14th century textile production
had already spread from the town guilds to outworkers, middlemen
and merchants throughout the countryside. Many families and small-
holders owned looms with which to supplement their income weaving
wool and linen. The carding, spinning and warping was women's and
children's work, while the men wove. The great trade fairs and seasonal
cloth fairs enabled home grown products, both yarns and finished fabrics, to reach destinations all over the world, transported by carriers,
carters, and the ships of the maritime nations.

Cotton reached Europe by the early 17th century. Woven Chinese
silk, esteemed since pre-Christian days, with the secrets of its manufacture jealously guarded, was imported for centuries. Sericulture
came to the Romans, and thence the Mediterranean countries, in the
5th century AD. France was producing its own silk by the 15th century,
and Italy boasted power-driven silk mills by the early 17th century.

**OPEN ROBE**
*French* **1792**

By the 1790s dress was
becoming slimmer and
simpler. This fashion
plate shows a long-
sleeved open robe, or
dress worn with a
skirt-petticoat. The
skirt is long enough to
conceal the shoes.
Striped patterns with a
small repeat were
popular, in silk or
cotton. Tall hats added
to the impression of
height.

**CALICO PRINTING**
Engraving from Denis
Diderot's *Encyclopedie;*
**18th century**

Roller-printing enabled
cloth to be printed
more quickly than
laborious block
printing. (*Above top*)

**FURNISHING FABRIC**
*Alexander Morton and
Co.*
Silk and wool; **c. 1900**

This interesting pattern
shows peacocks and
heraldic beasts within a
leafy framework.
(*Above*)

King James I of England was keen to encourage silk production at home
and in the New World, and ordered extensive planting of mulberry
trees, the leaves providing fodder for silkworms. He shipped silkworms
to Virginia (USA) in 1607, attempting unsuccessfully to establish
American silk production.

In pioneering days in America, where supplies of ready-made goods
were scarce or non-existent, it was not unusual for women to clothe
and furnish their entire households from the raw materials they had
grown themselves. Cotton, wool and linen were grown, gathered or
bartered, then carded or combed, spun, woven and dyed at home.
Sheets and table-linen were woven and hemmed, and dress and furnishing fabrics were woven with basic patterns such as stripes and
checks. The Shakers, a millenarian American religious sect, wove fine
and subtle silks. Later luxury fabrics and many everyday cloths were
imported from Europe.

Today there are few of us who know how to collect and treat fibres,
spin them, and set up a loom to weave them. Two hundred years ago
many more people were involved in textiles, and today we can still
enjoy their work.

**TOILE DE JOUY**
*France* **c. 1796**

This rich cotton of
jewel-like colours
shows a less common
wood-block print, in
this case made for the
Provençal market in
France. It comes from
the "Bonnes Herbes"
range fashionable in the
1790s and later, in
which the background
is densely covered with
leaves on a black
ground.

THE NEEDLEWORK OF PAST TIMES PROVIDES NOT ONLY DECORATIVE
FABRICS OF AMAZING INTRICACY AND RICHNESS, BUT AN INSIGHT INTO A
SLOWER PACE OF LIFE THAT ALLOWED YEARS TO BE SPENT
ON A SIMPLE PIECE.

# NEEDLEWORK

Needle and thread have been in use for millennia, and their basic function has not changed – to join pieces of fabric, to add decoration or to repair. In recent centuries needlework was practised by every woman and many men, of high and low standing, from early childhood until old age. Every household required clothing and furnishings to be made, repaired and adapted, which was usually the province of the women and children of the house; bachelors, soldiers and sailors, too, were often adept with a needle. The advent of the sewing machine in the mid 19th century relieved the tedium of long hours spent sewing household linen and furnishings, but machines could never sew as finely as a skilled needleworker.

## CLOTHING

Professional embroidery was not confined to furnishings. In the 18th century much embroidered clothing was mass-produced – gentlemen's coats and waistcoats, dress materials and robings were embroidered in Lyon and sent both abroad and within France, to be cut to size and assembled by a tailor for individual clients. Embroidery was found more on gentlemen's clothing because women favoured brocaded dress silks, which had little need of further decoration. Velvets, satins, wool and linen coats, waistcoats, breeches and cloaks for men were often lavishly embroidered and sometimes quilted.

Silk, with its lustrous colours, was the most popular embroidery thread, but dyed wool was also used. Linen and cotton are mostly found in white-on-white embroidery. Sequins were fashionable at the end of the 18th century on waistcoats and, occasionally, women's dresses. Chenille embroidery – from the French for "caterpillar", so called because of the furry textured thread – was in use by the 1770s in North America and Britain and earlier in France. From the 1780s tambour work, in which chain stitch was speedily worked by means of a needle like a

**DETAIL OF
GENTLEMAN'S
WAISTCOAT**
*English*
Embroidered silk; *c.* 1730

Unusually, the embroidery has been worked on a damask patterned silk. Four different kinds of silver thread have been used, in addition to sequins and silver foil on the button (bottom right). The coloured silks are worked in simple split stitch, while couched thread outlines the stems and silver leaves. The silver threads are also couched, as they are too heavy to be pulled through the ground fabric.

fine crochet hook, was in vogue, worked in coloured silks on silk, for waistcoats and dress trim, and white-on-white cotton and coloured woollen embroidery for muslin dresses.

## EMBROIDERED FURNISHINGS

Sofas, chairs, stools and cushions were often upholstered with canvas work – embroidery in gros point (cross stitch) or petit point (half-cross stitch or tent stitch), or both. In early times all over Europe embroidered upholstery was worked with smaller versions of themes taken from the large woven tapestries in castles and large houses; this may be why embroidery on canvas is sometimes wrongly referred to as "tapestry", which is a woven textile, not embroidery. Biblical, mythological, hunting and courtly themes were popular, and floral design was ubiquitous. In France in the 1770s it was possible to buy prepared canvases for upholstering chairs and sofas which not only had the pattern drawn out but the difficult details already embroidered. Large areas were generally worked in cross stitch, finer details in tent stitch. This effective stitch, giving a dense surface completely hiding the canvas beneath, was also used in wool or silk for small accessories:

bell pulls, table-tops, purses, needlecases, slippers, belts and occasionally waistcoats.

Bed-hangings and curtains were important household goods from early times up to the end of the 18th century, offering protection from draughts and light, as well as privacy. State beds were dressed with rich hangings of velvets, silk damasks, appliqués and embroideries on silk, with lavish passementerie trim. In Europe embroidered silk and appliqué furnishings were customary, before printed cottons became popular in the late 18th and 19th centuries. In early 19th-century Europe, white rooms and bedhangings were fashionable, with chain-stitch or tambour embroidery; this fashion spread to North America, where sometimes candlewicking was used to make a tufted decoration.

Lyon, bastion of the French silk-weaving industry, had embroidery workshops within its silk-weaving factories employing over 6,000 workers toward the end of the 18th century. The Lyonnais firm of Desfarges delivered a spectacular set of embroidered white silk bedhangings to Marie Antoinette in 1787, which can be seen today at Versailles. Religious commissions for lavish silk embroideries were also sent to Lyon.

## CANVAS WORK
*English*
Silk and wool on linen;
**1730–50**

Floral embroidery was popular for upholstery; this piece would have enhanced a Georgian chair. Stout but loosely woven linen canvas was chosen for durability, closely embroidered with silk and wool in tent and cross stitches. (*Above*)

## DETAIL OF A VALANCE
*French*
**Late 16th century**

The mythical unicorn, favourite emblem of medieval artists, is worked in tent stitch against a background of trees and flowers, with birds and butterflies. His mane and tail are of floss silk in split stitch. (*Left*)

## CREWEL WORK

In Britain and North America woollen embroideries on a natural-coloured fustian (linen warp, cotton weft) ground, called crewel work, after the thin long-staple, double-stranded wool yarn used, were popular bed-hangings for domestic use. Such bed-hangings originated in the 17th century, and their bold Baroque designs, with vigorous leaves and blooms bursting from scrolling stems, influenced the patterns of the great chintz palampores, painted cotton bed-hangings designed in India for export to Europe. Both palampores and crewel-work bed sets often used a tree-of-life motif. By the 18th century smaller motifs reflected the prevailing taste, and the advent of the Rococo in Britain and the United States transformed crewel-work bed-hangings into light, scrolling, sometimes diagonally patterned textiles.

## STUMPWORK AND RAISED WORK

Raised work, with three-dimensional effects produced by padding the ground beneath the embroidery with string, cloth, leather, paper or carved wood, was produced in France and Italy from medieval times, largely for church vestments and formal court dress. In Britain stumpwork (as raised work was often known) was practised domestically in the 17th and 18th centuries for decoration on caskets, looking-glass frames and embroidered pictures. Much loved for their naïve charm, these pieces show royalty and courtly scenes in bright silks, with seed-pearl, coral, even mica embellishment.

## BEADWORK

In 17th-century Europe, beadwork was a popular decoration for trays, mirror frames, little bags or purses, and pictures. In Italy church altar frontals and other hangings were sometimes worked entirely of cylindrical-glass bugle beads. Venice, famous for many luxury goods, made and exported glass beads worldwide. In Britain domestic beadwork designs were similar to stumpwork. Some three-dimensional effects were achieved by threading the beads on wire and wrapping this around a metal framework to make swans, stags and flowers.

French ladies in the 18th and 19th centuries produced fine beadwork, called *sable* (French for sand) because the minute beads were likened to grains of sand. Scenes imitating paintings were made, with careful shading achieved by tiny, different coloured beads. Pouches, purses and bags were made of *sable* beads in the

**CREWEL WORK**
*English*
**c. 1700**

The vigorous and exuberant designs of this leafy woollen embroidery both influenced and were influenced by Indian chintz patterns. Crewel work was widely used for sets of bed-hangings. (*Right*)

**BERLIN WOOLWORK**
Silk on canvas; **c. 1840**

The canvas ground has been left open, representing a considerable saving of time. Cross stitch in graduated shades of silk was worked to the pattern printed on the canvas cloth. The fashionable flowers include auricula, hibiscus, passion-flower and morning glory. (*Below*)

17th century, and patch boxes of turned wood covered with panels of patterned beads, often with a motto, were made as love tokens or souvenirs. In the early 19th century, gentlemen's braces and babies' or young children's knitted clothing were sometimes decorated with beadwork. By the 1850s beadwork was enjoying great popularity. Victorian footstools, fire screens, glass-topped trays, tea cosies, slippers, smoker's caps and ecclesiastical hassocks and banners were all worked in many colours, sometimes highlighted with clear glass or metal beads.

The last great flowering of beadwork was on high fashion of the 1920s and 1930s. Dashing Art Deco designs were executed with multicoloured, metallic and clear-glass beads.

## BERLIN WOOLWORK

Following the late 18th-century vogue for embroidered pictures, squared paper printed with coloured patterns for canvas embroidery was sold in Berlin as early as 1804. By 1810 a print seller named Wittich began exporting these patterns, which quickly caught on in both Europe and North America, their popularity lasting for over 50 years. Their novelty lay in the ease with which a design could be embroidered on to the canvas by counting squares, rather than drawing the pattern. By the 1860s aniline dyes were available, and harsh purples, bright greens, loud oranges, yellows and pinks were prevalent. Many magazines and embroidery books published patterns (also sold by haberdashers and department stores) for cushions, fire screens, pictures, bell pulls, bags and slippers, and the more ambitious could work larger pieces such as carpets, table-carpets, upholstery and church furnishings.

Typical Berlin woolwork subjects were sentimental scenes from popular historical novels, biblical scenes, a pet dog or cat, birds and flowers. In Britain works of the animal painter Sir Edwin Landseer and copies of portraits of Queen Victoria and the royal family (often wearing tartan), were re-created. Cut-pile techniques gave a three-dimensional look to such embroideries as vases of flowers and baskets of fruit.

## SAMPLERS

Samplers began as a means of recording embroidery stitches and patterns. European samplers of the 16th century were collections of different designs worked at random, regardless of spacing

**SAMPLER**
*American*
**1774**

Eleven-year-old Hannah Taylor obviously took great pleasure in her sampler and included (at the top) her house and family, and perhaps herself in the green dress with its careful detail. Two alphabets, a verse from Psalm 90 and a verse on virtue are more typical, as children were instilled with piety from an early age.

or position. A fairly coarsely woven linen material was usually chosen, enabling threads to be easily counted so that each stitch could be meticulously spaced. Letters and numbers of interesting or complex design were also worked for future reference.

Seventeenth-century samplers were normally long and narrow, with examples of different patterns worked in rows across. Cutwork samplers and those showing stitches and patterns found in reticella needlelace were embroidered in white linen thread. Embroidery patterns for borders and spot motifs (emblems scattered across a plain ground) were worked in threads of coloured silks.

Samplers became broader and shorter during the 18th century, when pictorial designs, including houses, gardens, trees, flowers, potted plants and animals, began to appear. Couplets or verses extolling virtue or reminding the worker of the dangers of vanity or brevity of life were commonplace. The initials or name of the embroiderer, age and date of completion of the sampler were often included.

Darning samplers were beautifully made during the 18th century, showing various kinds of repairs in the worker's repertoire and using different coloured silk or linen threads. The darns are so fine as to be almost invisible. Towards the end of the century map samplers appeared. A printed map on silk was ready for completion by the child, who would learn geography while embroidering the coastlines, boundaries and town names. In the United States globe samplers were made; these were silk spheres embroidered with the map of the world, with lines of longitude and latitude couched on top.

The function of the sampler gradually altered. From being an *aide-mémoire* for an accomplished worker it developed into the slate upon which to teach a child letters and numbers. Children of well-to-do families would have many coloured wools or silks to use, but orphans or impoverished children in poorhouses would embroider samplers bearing religious texts, the alphabet and numbers in black wool, bereft of other decoration.

By the middle of the 19th century samplers had grown large and were embroidered with brightly coloured wools, probably influenced by Berlin woolwork. Cursive script appeared, as did ornate capital letters.

## MEN'S WORK

Embroidery was not the exclusive prerogative of girls, and it was quite normal to teach boys embroidery to learn their letters. Soldiers and sailors often turned to sewing to while away periods of inactivity. Samplers, embroidered woolwork, patchworks made of old uniform materials and fine petit-point accessories such as needlecases, hussifs (or portable "house-

**PICTURE WITH VERSE**
*American*
Embroidered; 1835

Children's clothing of the 1830s is worked in fine tent stitch against an earlier house. (*Above*)

**COPE**
*English*
Embroidered; c. 1485

Fine church vestments such as this are often unfaded as they were kept flat in coffers where light could not reach them. (*Below*)

wives", long narrow strips of fabric that roll up, concealing pockets for small tools), book and cushion covers, and upholstery were beautifully made by men on an amateur basis.

Nineteenth-century sailors made woolwork pictures of ships embroidered on canvas with large tent stitches, resembling lines drawn with coloured crayons. These represent mostly sailing ships, seen from the side, with rigorous attention paid to the rigging, sails and flags.

## PICTORIAL EMBROIDERY

This tradition possibly originated with ecclesiastical work, in which scenes from the lives of the saints would be designed for orphreys (the decorated central vertical bands of chasubles), front edges of copes and parts of altar frontals. In French, Spanish and Italian convents and professional workshops, many embroideries of a high order for church vestments and furnishings were made. Pictorial embroidery in coloured silks and gold and silver threads, sometimes with precious and semiprecious stones, would highlight the rich silk damasks, brocades and velvets chosen to bear them.

Eighteenth-century silkwork pictures were widely popular. Realistic subjects included bouquets of flowers, pastoral scenes and memorial pictures, with perhaps a mourning figure leaning on an urn, beneath a weeping willow tree. In Italy embroidered silk pictures were made for foreigners on the Grand Tour, showing religious scenes and views of famous buildings, places or paintings. Sometimes these were of laid work, in which a copy of a painting is made, and the areas of colours filled in with silk thread glued down in one continuous line, row upon row, often following the folds of clothing.

Embroidered pictures whose stitches mimic brushstrokes on canvas are known as needle-paintings. In the Rijksmuseum, Amsterdam, a needle-painting dated 1650 and signed by W. Haelwech is a realistic still life with tulips, jonquils and irises in a glass container standing on a table with fallen petals on the tablecloth. In France a Monsieur Rivet embroidered needle-paintings for Louis XV, specializing in portraits, and in England Mary Linwood (1756–1845) of Leicester was well known for her needle-paintings, in which she copied works by the Old Masters, taking care to imitate brush-strokes.

### ARTS AND CRAFTS EMBROIDERIES

William Morris (1834–96) was the chief exponent of the English Arts and Crafts Movement. His influence and output were vast and his belief in the dignity of work and craft led him to teach himself embroidery, tapestry weaving, carpet manufacture and textile printing, among other skills. His designs took their inspiration from various sources, including early Islamic textiles, Gothic art, Renaissance velvets and the English floral tradition. Morris and Company sold both designs printed on cloth ready for embroidery and designs which would be selected and completed to order by his workshops. Morris's daughter May (1862–1938), herself an embroidery designer, became manager of Morris's Merton Abbey workshops in 1885. J. H. Dearle, Morris's valued assistant and designer, designed much of the embroidery of this later period, as well as the tapestries for which Merton Abbey was famous.

Jessie R. Newbery (1864–1948) taught embroidery at the Glasgow School of Art from the late 1880s until 1910. Rejecting popular mass-produced (and badly designed) Victorian pictorial embroidery of sentimental subjects in vivid colours, Newbery favoured balanced designs, many of outline embroidery or appliqué, in cool, "painterly" colours. Like other Arts and Crafts adherents, she preferred natural, even humble, materials in harmonious colours, and held that everyday objects were worthy of good design and good lettering. The Glasgow School of Art had great influence on

**NECKERCHIEF (FICHU)**
*Possibly Austro-Hungarian*
Gold and silver lace;
**1740–60**

The edge of this pretty and expensive rococo accessory is decorated with rare gold lace, enhancing the gold and silver embroidered border. Most precious-metal lace was burned for its scrap content. In comparison with silk or linen lace, it was stiff and rigid. (*Above*)

**NEEDLE-PAINTING**
*Japanese*
Silk embroidery; **1860–80**

The extraordinarily realistic effects of feathers, grasses and maize or corncob have been achieved by the directional emphasis of painstaking embroidery in subtly graduated colours of fine thrown silk. The corvine has an almost tangible presence. (*Left*)

early 20th-century embroidery designs, such as those produced by groups such as the Wiener Werkstätte (Viennese Workshops), founded in 1903. They too opposed mass production in fashion and accessories.

STYLISTICALLY, TAPESTRIES CONFORM TO THE MAJOR ART MOVEMENTS –
GOTHIC, RENAISSANCE, BAROQUE – AND PROVIDED HIGH QUALITY
FURNISHINGS TO THE HOMES OF THE WEALTHY AND POWERFUL.

# TAPESTRY

Many different kinds of tapestry weaving have been practised worldwide. The most familiar type of tapestry is a large antique wall-hanging, woven in wool and portraying a biblical, mythological or sporting scene. Essentially tapestry is a weft-faced textile – woven, not embroidered, by hand – with each colour confined to only the area for which it is needed.

Designs for tapestries were often taken from classical themes, drawn by famous artists. A copy – the cartoon, or working drawing – was made to the same size as the finished work. Two kinds of looms were used, the high warp *(haute lisse)* and the low warp *(basse lisse)*. High-warp weaving was woven upright, producing an exact reproduction of the cartoon, whereas low-warp weaving was woven horizontally and produced a mirror image of the cartoon.

Probably the most famous tapestries in the world are the *Unicorn* sets, now in the Musée de Cluny, Paris, and The Cloisters, New York. For years the origin of these *Unicorn* tapestries was a mystery, but recent study attributes their manufacture to Brussels, *c.*1500.

### FLEMISH TAPESTRIES

The patronage of the court of Burgundy in the 15th century ensured success for the Flemish weavers of Arras, until the town was taken by Louis XI of Anjou in 1477. Typical Arras work showed orchards and gardens, or hunting scenes, and was filled with leaves and flowers.

**TAPESTRY**
*Aubusson*
**c. 1750**

This French tapestry is woven to a design by J. B. Oudry, who worked extensively with the Beauvais workshop. Oudry designed the famous set of the *Fables of La Fontaine* and many others, which were woven by both centres.

**VERDURE TAPESTRY PANEL**
*Oudenaarde*
**c. 1630**

On this Flemish panel the undemanding background of plants, leafy trees and distant fields is given importance by the deep border, which is filled with swags of fruit and vignettes containing vistas relating to the overall rural theme.

The weaving town of Tournai rose in importance as Arras declined, and its tapestries show in minute detail the ceremony, fashions, flowers and architecture of life in the contemporary court of Burgundy. Ypres, Bruges, Ghent and Oudenaarde were other centres for Flemish tapestry production. Brussels workshops became famous for high-quality work, and by the Renaissance many fine allegorical and biblical subjects were woven, as well as *millefleurs* and *verdure* (foliage). *The Acts of the Apostles*, the important set designed by Raphael for Pope Leo X, took four years to weave, and was copied by the Parisian Gobelins workshops and by the Mortlake workshops, near London, among others. Brussels tapestry weaving died out at the end of the 18th century.

### FRENCH TAPESTRIES
In the eighth century the Saracens invaded France, and some who remained after their army retreated brought with them the skills of tapestry weaving *(opus saracenicum)*. By the 10th century workshops were established in Saumur, Tours, Reims and Bellegarde. One of the most important early works is a set of seven panels showing 70 scenes from the *Apocalypse*, begun in 1376 for Louis of Anjou.

Louis XIV's Minister of Commerce, Colbert, recommended Gobelins be appointed *manufacture de la Couronne*, with a royal subsidy, in 1662. Under the direction of Charles Le Brun (1619–90) Gobelins flourished, weaving outstanding Baroque designs, such as *The Story of Diana*, designed by Toussaint, and *The Months*, after Lucas van Leyden. During the 18th century low-warp tapestries called *alentours* became fashionable, created by such painters as François Boucher. *Alentours* were upholstery panels for complete sets of chairs and sofas, which could be woven on the low-warp loom. These had a centrepiece of a framed pastoral scene or classical painting within a background imitating damask, adorned with cupids, swags and bouquets. Jean-Baptiste Huet (1745–1811), the famous designer at the cotton printworks at Jouy, also made fashionable rococo and chinoiserie patterns for Gobelins.

In 1684 Philippe Béhagle (d.1705) became manager of the tapestry workshop at Beauvais. Béhagle revitalized the declining workshops, producing about 20 different sets in 21 years. The designer Jean Bérain (1637–1711) worked for him, and they produced, among

others, the successful "Grotesques", using the oriental, marine and musical motifs for which Bérain is celebrated. In 1726 the designer Jean-Baptiste Oudry (1686–1755) was engaged, whose most famous Beauvais works were the much-reproduced *Fables of La Fontaine*. Boucher designed for Beauvais the famous "Italian" set, illustrating idyllic rustic life, and the "Chinese" set, a gift to the emperor of China from the king.

The products of Aubusson – *verdures*, hunting scenes and religious subjects – were derivative and not especially noteworthy until the mid 18th century, when there was great demand for

the decorative small upholstery at which the factory excelled. Oudry's Beauvais designs for La Fontaine's *Fables* were lent and used many times, and the standards of quality improved, bringing acclaim to these furnishings.

### ENGLISH TAPESTRIES
The earliest English tapestries extant are those made in the workshops of William Sheldon (d.1570) at Barcheston, Warwickshire, in the mid 16th century. Sheldon's speciality was maps of counties, woven with architectural and geographical features, with town names worked in roman capital letters. Pictorial pieces showing Flemish influence were also produced. The works fell into decline in the early 17th century with the ascendancy of the Mortlake workshops under royal patronage.

The Mortlake factory was founded in 1618 under the management of Sir Francis Crane (d.1636). The first tapestries made there, illustrating the story of Vulcan and Venus, were commissioned by the Prince of Wales, later Charles I. Probably the most famous Mortlake tapestries are *The Acts of the Apostles*.

Other tapestry workshops in England were established in Soho, where Paul Saunders (d.1770) wove fine pieces for many of the great houses, and at Fulham, where the factory of Pierre Parisot (1697–1769) wove fine, expensive screens and chair upholstery.

QUILTING HAS BEEN PRACTICED ALL OVER THE WORLD TO GIVE WARM
CLOTHING OR COVERINGS. PATCHWORK OFFERS A FLEXIBLE WAY OF
COMBINING DIFFERENT FABRICS INTO A HARMONIOUS WHOLE.

# PATCHWORK AND QUILTS

Patchworking, the piecing together of pieces of fabric to form a coherent whole, has been practised for centuries. Votive patchwork of silks dating from the sixth to the ninth century has been found in temples in India. A set of quilted bed hangings dated 1708 still exists in Levens Hall, in northern England: the pattern is made of late-17th-century Indian chintzes on a white pieced ground.

Quilting is the linking of two or more layers of fabric by stitching through all layers, with stitching visible on both top and under surfaces. Often wadding or stuffing – usually wool or cotton – is placed between, for extra warmth or to increase the effect of decorative surface patterns of light and shade made as the lines of stitches pull taut.

### AMERICAN PATCHWORK

The techniques of quilting and patchwork are usually combined in American pieced patchwork, typically composed of a small design unit that repeats over the whole surface of the cover, commonly with a contrasting edging and borders. Patchwork was an economical, quick method of making up covers, with the extra benefit of teaching simple needlecraft to children.

In the United States it was the custom to hold bees, social gatherings where the women of a community would meet to help each other with domestic work such as quilting. Each woman would contribute a patched piece or pieces towards the patchwork, or work on an area of the quilting.

### AMISH PATCHWORK QUILTS

The American Amish, a strict religious sect, are celebrated for their patchwork quilts, which they began to make at the end of the 19th century. The patchworks are in solid colours and abstract designs, with no printed patterns, and none of the flowers and plants, hearts and lovers' knots which are favourite motifs among

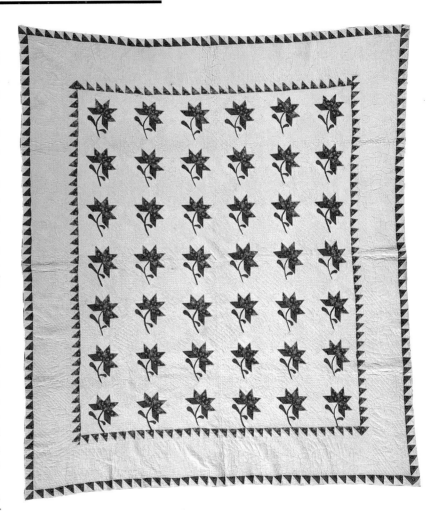

other quilters. This discipline, combined with a powerful colour scheme of dark greens, blues and purple, sometimes with red, orange or black, produced works of great visual impact.

### EARLY PATCHWORK

Not all early patchworks were quilted. A notable fashion in dress and furnishing at the end of the 17th century, continuing throughout the 18th, was applied work of chintz, a fine cotton brightly printed with natural dyes using mordants that rendered the colours fast to washing, something previously unachieved. These enormously popular fabrics, used in

**PIECED PATCHWORK**
*American*
Quilted cotton; **1860s**

On this beautifully made quilt each "Kansas Lily" is applied to a square set diagonally, and between each a flower has been quilted. The red and green sawtooth borders enclose a quilted scrolling feather pattern.

**COVER**

*English*

Cut chintz pieces applied to white cotton ground; **1815–20**

The central medallion of a basket of fruit was printed specially for this purpose. The pieces of chintz showing game birds were fashionable in Britain around 1815. The chintz borders were equally suitable for edging curtains. All these Regency-era cottons were block-printed. (*Right*)

**PATCHWORK COVER**

*English*

Cottons; **1780–1810**

Careful planning, good design and meticulous execution have resulted in an exceptionally fine bed cover. The sides of every individual hexagon measure only 2.5 cm (1 in) each. This kind of cover was seldom quilted, as the effect would spoil the sheen of the glazed cottons. The pattern, of hexagons separated by a single colour, is often called "Grandmother's Flower Garden". (*Below right*)

quantity for bed-hangings, wore out in parts, and some of the typical flowering branches and birds, butterflies and blossoms were salvaged and recycled. Motifs were carefully cut out, rearranged on a plain white cotton ground and stitched down to create a new design. This different kind of applied patchwork, called "broderie Perse", was immensely popular from the 1780s to the 1830s in England and North America.

## BRITISH PATCHWORK

Other than quilted work, broderie Perse and applied chintz covers, the most typical English patchwork of the first half of the 19th century was hexagonal pieced patchwork, generally lined but seldom quilted. The pieces of cotton were tacked to hexagonal paper templates, then painstakingly oversewn from the back so that the joined edges lay flat.

In Wales and the north of England there was a strong quilting tradition, using wholecloth or often broad strips of contrasting colour, highlighted by decorative stitched quilting patterns. Some patchworks combined applied work with pieced patchwork and quilting. Some British cotton printers designed medallions with commemorative or decorative themes especially for the centres of bedcovers, popular during the Regency period.

## FRENCH QUILTING

Provence has a fine tradition of quilted bed covers, called *boutis*. They are usually whole cloth quilts (one fabric) with superb quilting. Fine

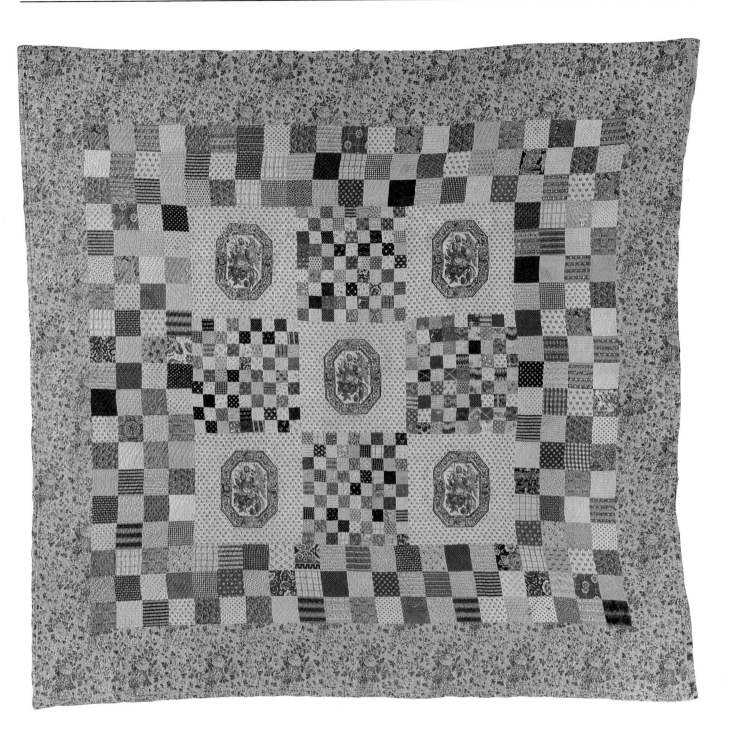

**COMMEMORATIVE PATCHWORK QUILT**

*Welsh*

**c. 1816–20**

The bold simple patchwork, boasting five medallions, is complemented by typically Welsh quilting of scrolls and circles. Each medallion bears the legend "Princess Charlotte of Wales married Prince Leopold of Saxe-Coburg May 12th 1816".

stuffed-work examples (in which the quilting pattern is first stitched through two layers and the filling or wadding is pushed in through small gaps made by teasing apart the warp and weft threads of the backing cloth) can be so tightly filled as to render the cover almost unbendable, and the design – perhaps including grapes, leaves and flowers – is thrown into high relief.

Provençal traditional costume also includes practical and beautiful quilted clothes such as waistcoats and skirts, often of block prints of small motifs in bright colours.

VICTORIAN SILK PATCHWORK

In the 1860s the advent of mass production in the silk industry and the recently invented bright aniline dyes meant that fashionable patchworks were no longer made of cotton. High Victorian taste enjoyed the dramatic effects that could be achieved with brilliantly coloured silks, satins and velvets.

"Crazy" patchwork, continuing to use many of the same kinds of fabrics, was popular in Britain and the United States from the 1880s.

CHINTZ CAPTURED EUROPEAN TASTE WHEN THE FIRST EXAMPLES
ARRIVED FROM INDIA IN THE 17TH CENTURY. THIS FASHIONABLE FABRIC
SET A STANDARD THAT EUROPEAN MANUFACTURERS STRIVED TO MATCH.

# CHINTZ AND PRINTED COTTON

When trade with the East opened up in the 16th and 17th centuries, exotic goods – including rich textiles – began to arrive in Europe, starting a fashion for all things with an Eastern flavour.

## CHINTZ

Chintz, a cotton with painted colourfast decoration, usually glazed, was originally made in India by a slow, painstaking method using mordants and resists. These are, respectively, chemicals to set the dye and substances to prevent dye colouring the areas to which they are applied. Chintz was extensively exported to the West in the 17th and 18th centuries for furnishings, including bed-hangings, wall-hangings, curtains, upholstery, barbers' cloths (to protect a man while he was being shaved), tablecloths and napkins.

Chintz was also wildly fashionable for clothing. Not only did women's dresses, jackets, shoes and the linings for clothes and hats come in chintz, but also men's caps for undress (informal wear in the house), waistcoats and banyans (loose undress coats).

## EUROPEAN COTTONS

Before the advent of chintz, European cottons were printed by wood-block with fugitive colours of uncertain fastness. The success in Europe of the bright, colourfast Indian cottons caused Western manufacturers to seek new ways of emulating them. Records indicate that calico (white cotton) was being printed in the Bouches-du-Rhône area of France in 1657 and 1661, and in Marseille after 1669. In 1676 a patent was granted to William Sherwin of West Ham, London, for block printing with mordants for madder-based colours. By 1700 printworks on the Thames and its tributaries were producing colourfast cottons in the madder palette of red, purple, brown and black.

In 1700, bowing to pressure from domestic silk weavers who were losing business to import-

**INFORMAL DRESS FOR INDOOR WEAR**
Indian chintz of hand-painted and resist-dyed cotton;
**c. 1785**

Imported Indian chintzes were highly fashionable during the 17th and 18th centuries for both formal and informal wear, as well as for furnishing. This dress has a pattern with a small repeat typical of the late 18th century. (*Left*)

**FURNISHING CHINTZ**
*British*
Block-printed glazed cotton; **c. 1810**

This pretty floral pattern typifies good quality block printing of the early 19th century. Each colour required its own set of carved wooden blocks. (*Below*)

ed fabrics, Parliament passed one of several acts banning the import of Indian calico and Persian silks for home consumption. Import for re-export was permitted, however, and smuggling was never eradicated. (Imported Indian chintzes and French-made imitations were also forbidden in France between 1686 and 1759, but were still legal in the Netherlands). British printers supplied demand by printing textiles in the Indian style. They could print on cotton for export only; for the home market they evaded prohibition by printing on fustian, a fabric of linen warp and cotton weft.

### BLOCK PRINTING

Block printing was executed with sets of wooden blocks, each no larger than could be lifted comfortably, about 30 x 20 cm (12 x 8 in). The background surface would be cut away, leaving the pattern element to be printed standing in relief. Both large background areas of solid colour and small blocks of detail could be print-

ed on the cloth. For a polychrome design, a separate set of blocks was necessary for each colour.

### COPPERPLATE PRINTING

Copperplate printing on cloth, first perfected by Francis Nixon in Ireland in about 1752, permitted the printing of fine lines and hatched detail. The lines to be printed were incised in the large metal plate, about a metre (1 yd) square, which was then applied with mordant. Then the surface of the plate was wiped clean, leaving the substance only in the incisions. The plate was pressed to the fabric, which would absorb the mordant in a mirror image of the pattern. When subsequently dyed, the mordant would fix the colour to the cloth, leaving the background, after several bleaching processes, clear. Extra colours were either "pencilled" in – fine detail added by brush – or added by block printing, which was better suited to areas of solid colour.

In 1761 and 1769 Robert Jones, a London

**FURNISHING COTTON**
*French*
**Block-printed and quilted; late 18th–early 19th century**

This handsome furnishing cotton was printed in Chervinges, near Villefranche-sur-Saône, by a factory known only by its initials, MFAJ. Such fabrics were used to dress beds and windows, to upholster furniture and to cover walls. In France cotton bed furnishings were often quilted, like this example.

**"PEACOCK IN THE RUINS"**

*Robert Jones, London*

Copperplate-printed cotton; **1761**

This famous design is the earliest dated copperplate print known, and it was extensively copied, with slight variations, in England and France. The printer's name and "Old Ford", his factory, were engraved on one of the slabs of fallen masonry. (Most factory marks are found at the end of the bolt of cloth and were frequently cut off before use.) The illustration shows only half of the design: the other copperplate showed classical ruins with a shepherdess and a young man.

immigrant Christophe Oberkampf (1738–1815) established his factory in Jouy-en-Josas outside Paris in 1760. A typical early block-printed cotton from Jouy, of 1764, was a robust wood-block pattern of bunches of flowers on a broadly striped background with an undulating line. The beautiful pastoral and figurative monochrome textiles for which Jouy became famous were printed by copperplate from the 1780s. The finest were designed by Jean-Baptiste Huet, whose first copperplate for Jouy was *Les Travaux de la Manufacture* of 1783, which shows all the processes in use at Jouy and includes portraits of Oberkampf, his young son and Huet.

Jouy produced a diverse range of textiles for both French and foreign consumption. In particular small floral patterns block-printed in vibrant colours were destined for Provence, where they were used for furnishing and traditional costume. Jouy printed goods of English design for English manufacturers from 1790 until 1793, when imports from France were prohibited following the outbreak of war.

Other printing centres in France developed, notably at Nantes, Rouen, Mulhouse, Orange and Bordeaux. Alsace-Lorraine and Switzerland also produced fine-quality printed cottons.

fabric printer, produced two copperplate printed furnishing fabrics of superlative quality. Exceptionally, they bear his name and the date. The 1761 monochrome print, much copied in France, has two large plate repeats, one of a peacock against some ancient ruins, the other of a shepherdess spinning and a young man playing pipes. The 1769 print, on fustian, is exceptional as it is polychrome, the blues, brown, red and yellows pencilled in. Also a double repeat, it shows ladies and gentlemen fishing, and a shooting party.

### IDENTIFICATION

The Calico Act was passed in 1774, stating that British manufacturers wishing to claim tax refunds on exported printed cottons were to weave three blue threads into the selvages of their goods, for identification. These provisions lasted until 1811 and are valuable to textile historians, as printed cottons bearing these blue threads undeniably date between 1774 and 1811, are British and were made for export.

### TOILE DE JOUY

In France, due to prohibition on its manufacture not lifted until 1759, copperplate printing was not perfected by the time the young German

### PATTERNS

The late 18th century favoured stripes and small repeats. In the cottons of the 1780s and 1790s, elegant dark grounds were preferred, densely strewn with sprigs of flowers. This dark ground was known as *fond ramoneur* ("chimney-sweep ground") in France, and as *nacht fond* ("night ground") in the Netherlands, where aubergine, burgundy, oxblood and dark browns also suited Dutch taste.

In Britain, from the 1790s to about 1825, printed panels for fire screens and the centres of appliqué or patchwork bed covers were made, both commemorative and purely decorative, usually based on medallions containing bunches of flowers. The pillar print, with variations of classical columns often entwined with flowers, was popular in furnishing cottons from the 1780s to *c.*1830. Exotic plants were in vogue from about 1812, combined with game birds.

Chinoiserie elements recur in textile patterns from the 17th to the late 19th century. English and French copperplate prints of the late 18th century have amusing designs incorporating the European vision of China, with pagodas, fanciful costume, kites and children. From

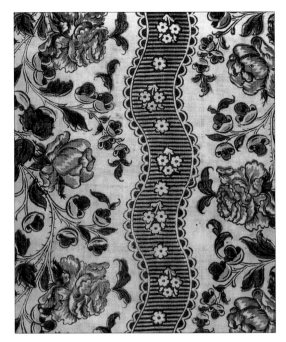

**TOILE DE JOUY**
Block-printed cotton; **1764**

This design is the earliest to bear the factory mark (*chef de piece*) of Jouy: *MANVFACTVRE C.P. OBERKAMPF ET COMPAGNIE A IOUY EN IOSAS. BON TEINT.* (*Far left*)

**LES PLAISIRS DE LA CAMPAGNE**
*Jouy*
Copperplate-printed cotton; **1785**

J. B. Huet designed this idyllic toile de Jouy, showing the clarity of this method of printing. (*Top left*)

**ROLLER-PRINTED COTTON
c. 1815**

The repeat of this pretty furnishing print, of unknown origin, indicates the circumference of the roller. (*Left*)

**"INDIENNE" OR PAISLEY SHAWL**
*Mulhouse*
Dyed cotton; **1820–40**

Complicated dyeing procedures were needed to make Turkey red, the vibrant background colour used in this small shawl or scarf. (*Below*)

around 1810 to 1830 polychrome chinoiserie block prints were made in England, often with the fashionable light tan "tea ground".

### ROLLER-PRINTING

Furnishing fabrics of the 19th century incorporated many dyeing and printing innovations. Stipple-engraving on metal rollers began in about 1815 and provided designers with a wider repertoire of patterns. Mulhouse in eastern France adopted this technique and the designer Georges Zipelius (1808–90) made a readily recognized range of roller-printed cottons, usually monochrome, stippled in fine detail with domestic or romantic scenes set on a floral ground, as well as a much-copied series incorporating birds and bowls of fruit.

The "Paisley" pattern, named *indienne* in France, never went out of fashion for long and was seen in European printed shawls, dress fabric and furnishing fabrics throughout most of the 19th century. Some of the most satisfactory prints were made on a warm "Turkey-red" ground. During the 1850s and 1860s in northern England, these cheerful, comforting materials, sometimes of brushed cotton, were made into strip quilts, down-filled petticoats and dressing gowns. They were also made in France and Russia.

False textures could be printed to imitate watered silks, lace, woven textiles and even patchwork. By mid century, the high point of "Victorian Chintz", full-blown flowers were a prominent feature.

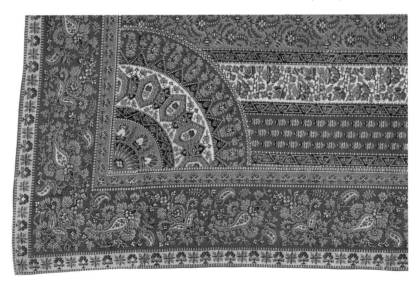

# JAPANESE TEXTILES

Japanese textile art is distinguished by its extensive technical expertise; its dyers, weavers and needleworkers achieved a rare understanding of their craft. Japan banned foreign travel and most contact with other countries from 1639 until the mid 19th century, and as a result a unique and identifiable style developed.

Tie-dyeing, a resist technique, reached the heights of sophistication in Japan in the 16th and 17th centuries, when *tsujigahana* was perfected. Robes and banners were tie-dyed and heightened with hand-painted decoration, gold or silver leaf, and sometimes embroidery. Other kinds of tie-dyeing *(kanoko)* included *shibori* (simple spots), produced by pulling the surface into a tiny peak which was then bound to protect the wrapped part from the dye. Highly complex patterns such as leafy bamboo canes in many colours were produced by tying off all areas not requiring the colour to be dyed and repeating the process with different tying for each additional colour.

Ikat, or *kasuri*, which is tie-dyeing combined with weaving, was practised in Japan, where it could take several years to make the piece of material required for a kimono – 9.15–11 m (30–35 ft) of 38–45 cm (15–18 in) width. Either warps or wefts could be patterned, or both, making double-*kasuri*. The pattern is set in the threads before weaving by stretching them out in exactly the order of weaving, dividing them into groups and binding off the parts not receiving the dye. After dyeing, the threads are unbound, leaving alternate coloured and uncoloured sections. The process is repeated, with different areas protected for each additional colour. When duly aligned and woven, the divisions between colours have a characteristically blurred edge. Silk *kasuri* was used for kimonos, while indigo cotton *kasuri* was made for working clothes and peasant wear. Summer clothing was made from vegetable fibres such as hemp, nettle and ramie, often combining *kasuri* with a gauze weave. *Kasuri* patterns ranged from tiny geometric repetitive motifs through bold abstracts, calligraphy and figurative designs.

Stencilling, another resist technique, was often used in conjunction with additional painting. Some stencils were so finely cut that they required the support of stretched hair, which held units in place but permitted dyes to pass. Effects could be either negative, in which a dye-resistant paste would be brushed through the stencil to leave that part uncoloured when the whole was dyed, or positive, in which the paint, mordant or dye would reproduce the design of the cut-out part of the stencil.

The Japanese were making *nikishi*, five- or seven-coloured brocades (textiles patterned by coloured threads other than the binding wefts) from the fifth century. These were used for *kesa*, Buddhist priests' rectangular patchworked robes, and *obi*, waist sashes worn with kimonos. From the eighth century onwards gold thread was incorporated.

Embroidery was used for screens, hangings, kimonos, *fukusa* (gift cloths) and for extra detail on stencilled cloth, paintings and scrolls. For Japanese ceremonial occasions, wrapped gold thread embroidery was often chosen, almost always couched ie, the threads laid flat on the surface and held down with loops of a fine silk thread worked from the back.

**Kimono**; Double Kasuri (ikat) in the characteristic brown of Oshima Island; **late 19th century**

**Fukusa (gift wrapper)**; Couched gold thread on silk satin; **mid 19th century**

**Indigo Ikats**; two 19th century pieces:
a) single ikat with red stripe
b) double ikat

THE FINE DETAIL OF HAND-MADE LACE AND LACE-WORK HAS ALWAYS
MADE IT ATTRACTIVE TO CONNOISSEURS OF DELICATE ORNAMENT UNTIL IT
BECAME POSSIBLE TO MANUFACTURE IT IN QUANTITY WITH MACHINES.

# LACE

Considerable passions and greed arose in the pursuit of lace from the end of the 16th century until the end of the 19th century, with enormous sums spent on a product intended purely for decoration. The extraordinary qualities of this many-faceted textile – its microscopic detail, its rich and varied textures, its breath-of-air lightness – defied reproduction until the 19th century.

### ORIGINS
Lace evolved among the European courts and nobility in the 16th century. By 1550 lace was made by ladies on an amateur basis, using pattern-books. Commercially lace was produced in Italy, mostly in convents, and in Flanders it was commissioned by merchants employing outworkers. Linen, made from the stems of the flax plant, was the fibre most often used, as it is supple, tough and pliable when damp. Coloured silk lace was also made, as was gold and silver lace for royalty and the aristocracy, but little has survived (the former because of decay, the latter because of the practice of unpicking (drizzling) and selling the precious metals for scrap value).

From the second half of the 16th century the separate techniques of needle and bobbin evolved and the commercial manufacture of lace developed in both Flanders and Italy.

### NEEDLE-LACE TECHNIQUE
Needle lace (or needlepoint) developed from the embroidery stitches and drawn-thread work techniques used on linen. When joining two pieces of linen edge to edge, for instance, a pattern could be created by leaving a space between the two and bridging this with decorative stitches. Cutwork was essentially a pattern created by cutting pieces from linen, leaving a pattern made by the holes. Reticella ("a little net") extended this technique to extraordinary lengths. Areas of the linen ground were removed, leaving a fine grid of carefully counted threads, usually in pairs. These were

**RETICELLA NEEDLE LACE**
*Italian*
**1600–20**

Superb skill, patience and eyesight were needed to produce the finest laces. The "rose-window" parts of this lace were built up with needle and thread from a skeletal framework of warp and weft threads left when the majority of the linen fabric was cut away. This border, 10 cm (4 in) deep, is edged with bobbin lace.

strengthened by binding them (stitching round them), generally with buttonhole stitch, and then a new pattern was built up by stitching bars across the spaces upon which devices such as rose windows and snowflakes were worked.

The geometric restraints of the linen grid were left behind in the early 17th century, with the development of freely formed needle laces such as *punto in aria* ("stitch in the air"), in which designs of delicate curving tracery were drawn on parchment, their outlines marked by a couched thread (held down at intervals) and the solid parts of the design slowly filled in with needleworked stitches. On completion the lace would be lifted away from the parchment.

### BOBBIN-LACE TECHNIQUE
Bobbin lace probably developed from the plaiting techniques used to make "laces" (cords, as in today's shoelaces), which served both utilitarian and decorative purposes. To prevent tangling, lengths of thread were wound on spools, or bobbins, which were then twisted around each other, in pre-arranged groups, forming a patterned fabric. Bobbin lace was made by pushing marker pins upright into the pricking (parchment pattern) laid on a cushion, and weaving

each bobbin, wound with its thread, back and forth across its neighbours.

### 17TH-CENTURY DEVELOPMENTS

The distinctive laces of the 17th century were Flemish, Milanese and Genoese bobbin lace; the Italian reticella, *punto in aria*, Venetian gros point and *point de neige* needle laces; and the French *point de France* needle lace. The spiky, dentate edges of 16th-century lace trim on ruffs and cuffs became the "Van Dyke" borders of the early 17th century; the long rounded scallops of the 1630s were smoothed into gently curving edges by the 1640s and became broad and flat by the 1650s.

**Italian Lace** *Punto in aria* flourished throughout the first half of the 17th century, and was extensively used for collars, cuffs, edging for fine linens, and church vestments and furnishings. After 1650 raised Italian needle laces came into fashion. Curves were graduated into three dimensions by working the stitches over pads built up from layers of thick thread. Gros point, its smaller version rose point and the rare *point d'ivoire* (so called because its deep relief resembles carved ivory) were baroque laces in fashion from *c.*1660 to 1680. By the end of the century scale was diminishing, as illustrated by *point de neige*, an incredibly fine raised needle lace with scatterings of picots (tiny loops or bristles) resembling snow crystals on the ground. Coraline, a Venetian flat needle lace with patterns like little coral branches, was also typical of the 1690s. The adaptable Flemish lace merchants, with their manufacturing tailored to the needs of their clients, were competent and copious suppliers of fashionable bobbin lace throughout the century.

**French Lace** *Point de France*, the first French lace of distinction, was made after 1675, by which date the efforts of Colbert, Minister of Commerce to Louis XIV, had taken root. So much money had been spent by the French on foreign lace that it had been decided to make French lace equal to the finest Flemish and Italian imports; to this end workers were cajoled from Flanders and Venice, and in 1665 a state factory was set up at Lonray, near Alençon. The wearing of foreign lace was forbidden. Typical patterns of *point de France* reveal the influence of the designer Jean Bérain (1637–1711), whose style was ideally suited to the fashions of the 1690s: figures beneath canopies, angels and trophies of arms against luxuriant scrolling grounds. An identifying feature of *point de*

**GROS POINT NEEDLE LACE**
*Venice*
**c. 1660**

This bold Baroque raised lace owes its three-dimensional quality to padded parts of the design. It was highly fashionable from *c.* 1650–80. The ground employs the same buttonhole stitches as Hollie point. (*Above*)

**NEEDLE LACE**
*Flemish*
**c. 1690**

This rare needle lace imitates the patterns of fashionable *point de France*. This detail measures 9 cm (3½ in) deep. (*Below*)

*France* is the ground mesh, which has tiny single picots on its buttonholed bars.

**English Lace** Lace-making was established in Buckinghamshire, Devonshire and other areas by the early 17th century. Some was made for export, and by 1640 Honiton "bone lace" (bobbin lace, named after the bone bobbins) was sent from Devon weekly for sale in London. Honiton lace is typically a floral bobbin lace, sometimes with a drochel (hexagonal mesh) ground.

Some English needle laces of the 17th century survive, rather solidly worked in buttonhole stitch, such as scalloped borders for handkerchiefs, and the falling bands that edged the neck when stiffened lace went out of fashion. Hollie point lace, made by the buttonhole-stitch technique, was a favourite device inserted into the centres of babies' bonnets and shoulder seams of shirts; it is a solid lace with geometric designs, often with a verse or date.

### 18TH-CENTURY DEVELOPMENTS

The laces of Flanders and France outshone those of Italy during the 18th century. The finest laces

of this period include the bobbin laces from Brussels, Mechlin, Valenciennes and Binche, and the needlepoints of Brussels, Argentan and Alençon. Each has distinctive characteristics, but dividing lines can easily blur. For instance, Alençon sent some of its lace to Brussels to have the mesh background made and put in, which produced a composite lace, the product of two different centres. Another misleading lace is *point d'Angleterre*, Brussels bobbin lace fashionable from the late 17th throughout the 18th century; it was called "English point" so that it could be imported into France without attracting the heavy taxes to which Flemish lace was subject. To add to the confusion, an English version of *point d'Angleterre* was made in Devonshire.

Lace design at the beginning of the 18th century comprised closely arranged pattern elements, but it became lighter in the Rococo period, when designs were distributed spaciously, revealing more background. The drochel or "vrai droschel" ground, a wonderfully light net originating in Brussels but also produced in

### HOLLIE POINT NEEDLE LACE
*English*
**c. 1800**

Hollie point was frequently used for babies' clothes, and this delightful piece, surrounded by whitework embroidery, was made for the centre of a tiny bonnet. Strips of hollie point were also inserted at the shoulder seams of shirts; it was never gathered or used as edging. (*Above*)

### TRIANGULAR SHAWL
*Brussels*
Bobbin appliqué; **c. 1800**

The gossamer-textured mesh ground ("drochel") was made from 2.5 cm (1 in) strips invisibly stitched together. The bobbin-made motifs were then glued or sewn to it. The threads used are incredibly fine. (*Left*)

England, had arrived by the 1760s. It was a bobbin-made hexagonal mesh worked with four threads and produced in strips, about 2.5 cm (1 in) wide, invisibly sewn together. The drochel ground was used extensively as the background for bobbin-made appliqué motifs, which were sewn or glued in place; occasionally needle lace was worked on it. It was suitable for large, filmy pieces of fashionable lace, such as aprons, fichus, veils, stoles and kerchiefs.

### 19TH-CENTURY DEVELOPMENTS

No great laces emerged in the 19th century, perhaps due in part to the advent of machine-made lace. The pretty Blonde bobbin lace made in northern France, named after the colour of the unbleached silk from which it was made, was the perfect accompaniment to the soft, light fashions of the early part of the century. It was also popular dyed black, when it was known as "black Blonde".

**Machine-made Lace** There had been many attempts to invent a lace-making machine ever since the stocking frame, producing a knitted mesh, had been invented in 1589. Patents for lace machines were taken out in England from 1758 onwards, but the most dramatic changes were caused by Heathcoat's machines, patented in 1808 and 1809. These made the first reliable "bobbinet", in widths up to 1.35 m (54 in). It cost a fraction of the price of hand-made net, looked authentic and was stronger than the drochel upon which it was modelled. It was eminently suited to the bobbin-made appliqué of Brussels and Devonshire, to the tambour embroidery of Coggeshall, England, and Limerick, Ireland, and to the muslin appliqué of Carrickmacross, Ireland. Quantities of shawls, veils and dress flounces were produced.

The Jacquard attachment, which revolutionized the textile industry, also made its mark on lace manufacture. By 1840 it was combined with the Pusher machine, which had been making honeycomb lace since 1812, and imitations of high quality bobbin-lace shawls and dress flounces were made in quantity.

By the end of the century machine-made lace had become so commonplace that people seeking to disguise their lace as inherited heirlooms would dip it in tea to make it look older. Firms dealing in antique lace struggled to survive, offering a repair and renewal service, and selling modern lace and reproductions. The swing against mass-produced goods of inferior manufacture inspired revivals of hand-made lace. In Italy the Aemilia Ars Society in Bologna, working along the principles of the English Arts and Crafts Movement, produced very fine copies of 17th-century needle and bobbin lace. The Burano Lace School, near Venice, made superb needle-lace copies of early pieces, and finely designed Art Nouveau lace was made at the Vienna Lace School.

**STOLE**
*Brussels*
Needlepoint appliqué;
**c. 1820**

The gauzy handmade drochel ground on this long, narrow stole is worked with needle lace, decorating the scalloped edges and the patterned ends. The piece measures 255 × 55 cm (8 ft 4 in × 1ft 10 in) overall. (*Above*)

**DETAIL OF LAPPET**
*Alençon*
Needle lace; **c. 1720**

Lappets were paired cap streamers fashionable from the late 17th century to the end of the 18th century. This detail shows the tip of a lappet measuring 55 × 8.5 cm (21 × 3¼ in) overall. The fine outlines are button-hole stitched around a horsehair for rigidity. (*Left*)

THROUGHOUT HISTORY, THE ATTENTION OF STATE, CHURCH AND
POPULAR GOSSIP HAS BEEN DRAWN TO CLOTHES. TECHNOLOGY AND
FASHION COMBINE TO MAKE DRESS STAND FOR MORE THAN
MERE BODY COVERING.

# COSTUME

Clothing might have begun as functional wear for warmth and protection, but it has long been inextricably involved with status. Initially, what was worn singled out the rich from the poor, the court and nobility from the middle classes, the gentry from the workers, the church from the laity and foreigners from one's fellow countrymen.

Sumptuary laws, permitting selected people the exclusive use of certain kinds of clothing, have been used by many countries but have generally failed in their purpose, ie, to keep the lower orders visibly below those above, to protect particular products from (often foreign) competition or to restrict excessive spending. But those in the vanguard of fashion have always laughed at restrictions. For instance, 18th-century laws were made in France and England forbidding the import and wear of Indian chintzes, at the behest of the silk weavers, who feared loss of trade. This did not stop Mme de Pompadour, Louis XV's mistress, from wearing chintz dresses, furnishing her château with it and giving presents of it to her friends.

WOMEN'S DRESS FROM 1750
An understanding of the fashionable silhouette is an indispensable means of dating costume. By the mid 18th century fashionable dress worn by the middle and upper classes in the West had assumed a basic structure which was to continue until the early 20th century.

The typical 18th-century dress was a robe – open at the front from neck to hem and generously décolleté – worn over a skirt called a petticoat, which was allowed to show, completing the dress. The gap at the breast was filled by a stomacher, an embroidered triangle pinned in place concealing the stays beneath. Elbowlength fitted sleeves were garnished with tiered sleeve ruffles (engageants), which could be made of lace, whitework or the dress material.

There were two principal styles: the English back, or robe à l'anglaise, and the sack back,

**FASHIONABLE DRESS OF THE 1780s**

The large beribboned hat and muff, the tiny high-heeled shoes and the skirt caught up Polonaise style with lining showing, are hallmarks of the 1780s.

robe à la française or Watteau, named after the French painter who portrayed so many of these beautiful dresses. The closely fitting English back was cut from curved panels, with a narrow central box pleat or pleats stitched down flat, following the spine, until they reached the skirt, where they broadened into the many widths of material of the skirt. The distinctive feature of the comfortable sack dress was the dramatic fall of material, at the back from neckline to hem, in two wide box pleats. The bodice fitted closely in front and was lined with linen that was slit and laced together under the pleats at the back for adjustment, obviating the need for stays. By about 1800 the stomacher was no longer in vogue and frocks, dresses with a back opening and one piece skirt, began to be made.

### FABRICS

The heavy brocaded European silks were wonderfully suited to these styles, as were painted Chinese silks and bright colourfast Indian chintzes. These, and oriental woven silks, were brought to Europe by the East India companies of the Dutch, Portuguese, British, Danish and French throughout the 17th and 18th centuries. Wonderful embroidered silks and muslins were made both in yardage and expressly for dresses.

As the Rococo movement developed during the mid 18th century dress became lighter, and by the 1790s stiff silks gave way to cottons and thin muslins. Open robes went out of fashion. Neo-Classical fashions dictated flat shoes and simpler hairstyles (often without wigs). By 1810 clinging dresses with high waistlines modelled loosely on ancient Greek and Roman styles, often with a train or trailing panels at the back were worn, with embroidery on hems, necks and sleeves.

White muslin from India was most fashionable, usually embroidered in white, sometimes imported with "thumbnail work" (metal embroidery) on panels for dresses, which were made up to fit. The embroidery patterns fashionable in the first 30 years of the 19th century echo Indian and Kashmiri shawl design; the "Paisley pine", a teardrop shape with curled tip, frequently appeared in whitework embroidery on dresses, and in lace stoles and bonnet veils.

Colours chosen for silk dresses of this period were often pastels, and pastel ribbons were often worn at the waist and neck of the ubiquitous white muslin dresses.

### FASHIONABLE SILHOUETTE

The waistline, which had risen with the turn of the century to just below the bust by 1810, had regained its natural position by 1825. Sleeves began to widen at the shoulder, reaching maximum width by 1830. They were supported by sleeve puffs constructed of whalebone hoops or down-filled pads.

Skirts also grew broader, and by the 1860s

**ROBE WITH ENGLISH BACK (À L'ANGLAISE)**
*c. 1780*

Stiff-figured silk brocades were ideally suited to the full-skirted dresses of the 18th century. The Spitalfields silk of this dress was woven originally in about 1745, but the dress was remade later in the 1780s. The flat pleating of the English back flows seamlessly into the skirt at the waist. (*Right*)

**PRINTED COTTON DRESS**
*c. 1800*

Neo-Classical fashions ousted full skirts and corseted waists. The waistline rose to just under the bust, and softly-draping muslins and cottons clung in folds to the more natural silhouette. Tiny, flat slippers with "winkle-picker" toes replaced high heels. (*Below*)

required crinolines to hold their shape. These were essential to maintain the proper silhouette and continued to be so until 1868, when the bustle came in. By then front fullness of skirts was being pulled tight across the stomach in drapes towards the back. This developed into an overskirt, which was caught up and bunched at the back, beneath which a slimmer, long skirt tapered to the waist. A bustle worn beneath gave the required bulge. The "cuirasse" bodice of the 1870s was longer at the front, hugging the figure. The introduction of the bustle rang the death knell for shawls; no longer would a woman wear a large shawl that hid the most glorious part of her dress.

### UNDERLYING STRUCTURE

The form of the torso was sculpted for centuries by a pair of stays, or corset – usually cut from stout linen or canvas cloth, sewn with heavy

LES JARDINS DU BAL MABILLE
(1855)

### DRESSES WORN WITH CRINOLINES, c. 1858

Skirts reached maximum width by 1860, due to the crinoline a light arrangement of wired hoops. (*Above*)

### TAPERED DRESSES 1878

In reaction to the excessive width of 1850s and 1860s, the newest silhouettes were slim and tapering. (*Below*)

### STYLES OF DRESS
### c. 1828

Flat pumps were still in vogue in the late 1820s, beneath the newly-filling skirts, tightly-corseted waists, and "imbecile" sleeves with The off-the-shoulder neckline of the late 1820s. (*Above*)

linen thread and braced by thin strips of whalebone. Stays were laced at back, front or both. By the 19th century there was normally easier front access with metal hooks, but back lacing continued. In Britain these were essentially undergarments, but in 18th-century France and Italy the rigid corset was often covered in sumptuous brocaded silk and worn as part of the dress.

In the 18th century skirts were supported by panniers, or hoops, but by the century's end slim light skirts rendered them obsolete. As skirts grew wider in the 1830s and 1840s multitudes of heavy petticoats were needed to support them. The lightweight crinoline enabled a wide skirt to be supported by a single underskirt. Originally "crinoline" meant a stiff fabric of horsehair and linen, but the word also came to be used for underskirts constructed with a series of concentric whalebone hoops suspended from the waistband by webbing.

Worth's approach to presentation and sales was as daring and innovative as his dresses were lavish and luxurious, and many couturiers subsequently emulated aspects of his originality. Maison Worth, established in Paris as Worth and Bobergh in 1857, dressed wealthy women irrespective of their breeding. Royalty, society ladies, opera singers, actresses and demimondaines, not only from France but from North and South America and all over Europe, flocked to his door. Worth commissioned luxurious patterned silks from Lyonnais weavers, more than doubling the amount of looms in use in Lyon in 1872, and used printed silks, Italian brocades, lace and velvets of all descriptions.

### DEVELOPMENTS INTO THE 20TH CENTURY

Paris continued to be the world capital of fashion. The Parisian designer Paul Poiret (1879–1944), who had spent two years with Maison Worth, created innovative dresses using beadwork patterns of Art Deco inspiration, fur trim, hobble skirts, Turkish trousers and tunics worn over skirts.

A host of international talents glittered in the firmament of early 20th-century Paris fashion. The Swiss Madeleine Vionnet (1876–1975) was celebrated for her masterly cut and seaming of fabric, the Spaniard Cristobal Balenciaga (1895–1972) for his exceptional understanding of sculptural form and colour. The crisp, simply tailored suits of jersey or tweed by the French Gabrielle "Coco" Chanel (1883–1971) were indispensable, while the British Captain Molyneux (1891–1974) designed elegant clothes with modern social life in mind. The Italian Elsa Schiaparelli (1896–1973) was renowned for her witty designs – principally knitwear, sportswear and buttons.

The fashions of the 20th century may be charted by the rise and fall of the skirt hem. Dresses had swept the floor or reached no higher than the ankle from the Middle Ages up to the 1920s: only the ankle had been allowed to show, legs were invisible. Skirts were ankle- to mid-calf-length from the 1910s to 1925, above the knee in the late 1920s. Skirts so short had never been seen before in fashionable women's dress, and were possibly the most startling break with tradition ever.

**BUSTLE-BACKED
DRESSES 1890s**

The pleats, frills and ruches of the front skirt panel were pulled backwards and were often tied in place with wide ribbons, emphasizing fashion's newest whim. The necessary silhouette was supported beneath with more wires, padding and whalebone. Tiny waists emphasised the hourglass shape. (*Above*)

The late 19th century saw women's figures moulded by corsetry into waists that were narrower from side to side than from front to back, with bosoms smoothed into a rounded silhouette. Bustles – made of wire, tape, horsehair or crinoline, with down or feathers for padding – ranged from a cascade of frills of woven horsehair and linen to crescent-shaped pads of gaily-printed, down-filled fabric.

The bust improver, forerunner of the brassiere, evolved in the 1890s. This was the first use of individual cups for the breasts. Cotton bust bodices, still often boned, began to replace the stays. Suspenders were first attached to the stays around 1900; for the sportswoman such stays were high cut over the hips, giving more freedom of movement.

### HAUTE COUTURE

The Englishman Charles Frederick Worth (1825–95) was one of the most significant figures in Parisian haute couture. The prolific

### DRESS REFORM

By the 1860s some women had begun to rebel against the restrictions of heavily boned corseting and the restrictive clothing of high fashion.

**CHANEL**

Casual elegance personified in Chanel's pleated skirt, hip-length cardigan and long strings of pearls. Chanel used textured fabrics with bold, often contrasting trim. (*Left*)

**EVENING ENSEMBLE CALLED "SORBET" BY PAUL POIRET, 1912**

This dress was worn with a tunic called a minaret, and a turban. Poiret introduced orientally inspired fashions around 1912. (*Above*)

**SILK VELVET DRESS BY LIBERTY'S, c. 1910**

This soft dress is in one of Liberty's favourite "natural" colours, a warm brown. Another typical Liberty feature is the smocking at neck and waist, which gathered the material in a decorative and functional way, echoed by the ruched sleeves. (*Above*)

In artistic circles the Aesthetic Movement grew from seeds sown by the Pre-Raphaelites, and nature and medieval dress were romanticized in a languid and sultry manner. Dresses of soft materials were distantly based on Grecian clothing, with flowing folds sometimes loosely tied at the waist, permitting freer movement. Fabrics, clothes and other needs of Aesthetic households were supplied by Liberty & Company, established in London in 1875. The textile department offered Indian cashmeres, Madras muslins, printed silks and "art" fabrics. By 1884 the firm had its own label for dresses and opened a branch in Paris in 1890, selling Aesthetic fashion.

There were other movements toward a healthier form of dress. In the early 1850s, the American Amelia Bloomer had devised a Turkish-influenced costume of ankle-length pantaloons worn with a full-skirted knee-length coat, which did away with heavy petticoats. The Free Dress League was actively campaigning for practical, healthy clothing in the United States from the 1870s. In 1883 the Rational Dress Society in London presented an exhibition of clothing that included dresses for boating, walking and tricycling, and efforts were made to popularize the divided skirt.

The luxuriant excesses of fashions at the end of the 19th century gave way to clothes of straighter cut by the 1910s. Newly emerging couture houses brought competition and marketing to new levels, but the First World War put an end to much of the gaiety and extravagance of *fin-de-siècle* life.

WHETHER GENUINE KASHMIR OR EUROPEAN IMITATION, THE SHAWL
BECAME THE INDISPENSABLE CLOTHING ACCESSORY ACROSS
WESTERN EUROPE DURING THE EARLY AND MID 19TH CENTURY.

# KASHMIR AND PAISLEY SHAWLS

The English word "shawl" comes from the 17th-century Persian *shal*. Under Mughal rule shawls were worn by men. During the 18th century they were sent back to the West by East India Company employees and by the British and French armies returning from war in India and Egypt. As demand for these luxury goods grew, they were sent by sea in bales to London to be sold at auction and travelled overland to other destinations by caravans.

### ORIGINS

The first shawls were woven in Kashmir, not from sheep's wool but from cashmere, the silky, creamy-white underfleece of the Himalayan mountain goat. At the end of the 18th century shawls were long rectangles (perhaps 140 x 335 cm – 4 ft 6 in x 11 in) with very narrow side borders woven with a coloured design, often scrolling flowers. The ends had deeper panels woven with repeating elements, usually called the "Paisley pine". Prized for their lightness, warmth, fresh colours and elegance, Kashmir shawls became increasingly fashionable and soon European manufacturers were trying to copy them.

### IDENTIFICATION AND TECHNIQUE

The design of European and Kashmir shawls was very similar; the basic differences were in the material and the weave. No fibre available to European weavers possessed the superior qualities of cashmere, so mixtures of silk and wool were used. Silk, with its long fibres, was stronger than wool and used for the warp threads, which take greater strain during weaving. However, during the 1830s French manufacturers perfected a finely spun wool strong enough for warps, enabling the production of all-wool shawls.

With a few rare exceptions, European shawls were woven on looms which, whether man- or machine-powered, sent the patterning weft threads across the shawl from one side (selvage)

to the other. When weaving many colours a large amount of surplus threads would be left "floating" at the back, when not needed in the pattern on the front of the shawl. In most cases these were clipped away, leaving tiny tufts of thread visible. Large mid-19th-century shawls could weigh as much as 2.83kg (100 oz) when taken from the loom; after clipping they would be reduced to 935 g (33 oz), making them much more manageable.

The patterned areas of Kashmir shawls were woven in a painstaking tapestry technique which requires each coloured thread, on its own little bobbin, to be moved by hand around the warps, the threads that run the length of the

**KASHMIR SHAWL**
Tapestry weave; **c. 1800**

Himalayan goat's fleece (*pashmina*) was used for the early Kashmir shawls, its natural creamy colour making a pleasing background to the harmonious vegetable dyes used for the tapestry-woven patterns. A shawl like this one, measuring 285 × 132 cm (9⅓ × 4⅓ ft) could take 18 months to make. (*Above*)

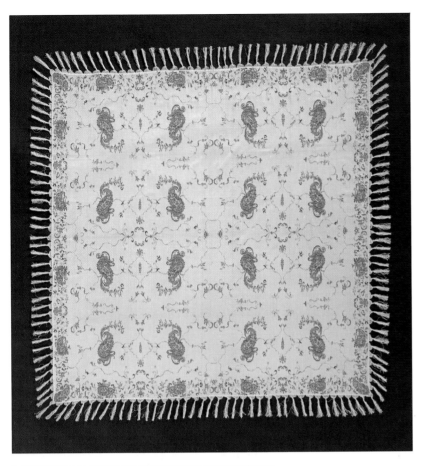

**SHAWL**

*Towler and Campin, Norwich*

Draw loom woven; 1847

Piracy of shawl design was so common that some firms registered their patterns at the Patents Office to try to prevent illicit copying. Sometimes this enables precise dating, although popular shawls would have been made continuously for several years. (*Above*)

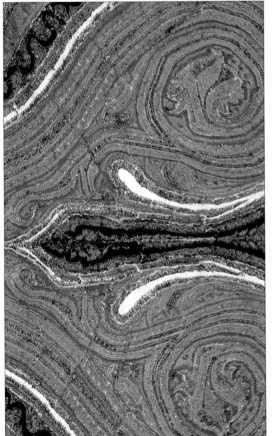

**REVERSE OF PIECED KASHMIR SHAWL**
**c. 1860**

The only cut ends visible on the back of a Kashmir shawl are those where two pieces have been sewn together. The tapestry technique is economical in thread but extravagant in weaver's time. (*Left*)

shawl. When viewed under magnification there are no cut ends visible on the back of a Kashmir shawl.

## BEGINNINGS

The first reference to British-made shawls occurred in 1784, when Edward Barrow of Norwich offered "imitations of Indian shawls" for sale. Shawls were being woven in Edinburgh by 1792, and their production continued until 1847, when manufacturers there were put out of business by the mass production of Paisley, west of Glasgow. Paisley weavers began making shawls in about 1808 and trade there was flourishing by 1812.

France was slower to take up the shawl fashion. Empress Josephine had some of her Kashmir shawls made up into dresses and cushions. And soon Paris and Lyon were producing a wide range of shawls, followed by provincial manufacturers in Rouen, Nîmes and elsewhere. Austrian-made shawls were woven in Vienna, on more than 4,000 looms in the 1830s.

## VARIATIONS AND EXPORTS

The difficulty of identifying the origin of European shawls is illustrated by the vast numbers of small manufacturers and outworkers used. In 1847/8, for instance, the order books of one Norwich firm show sales of 32,000 shawls, available in 26 different styles. In 1801 there were 16 shawl firms working in Norwich, so it would be reasonable to suppose that by 1847 that number would at least have doubled. Each manufacturer would have a different, though similar, product. Some shawl designs were patented to stop illicit copying during the 1840s and 1850s; Paisley was said to be able to have a design copied and on sale at a cheaper price within two weeks of its first appearance.

Shawls designed for export markets further confuse the issue of identification. Nîmes made shawls for the Dutch market, striped shawls for the Levant and others for North Africa; Norwich exported to South America; and Paisley sold to many markets, even India, where its products were treated with suspicion. In the early 19th century Russia produced fine "summer and winter" shawls, woven, like the Kashmirs, in tapestry twill, but in floral patterns less likely to be thought Indian. From 1820 to 1840 Austria wove shawls, sometimes silk squares with patterned borders sewn on by hand, similar to the products of Norwich and

Paisley. By the 1860s square shawls were being made in Massachusetts.

### INFLUENCES ON DESIGN

The Kashmir weavers had to adapt to survive. Initially the weavers did not want to alter their patterns, but by the 1850s European influence could be discerned in Kashmir shawls. There was also constant pressure to cut costs, so pieceworking evolved, whereby several men would each weave the component parts of a shawl, to be stitched together by an embroiderer. A shawl that would have taken one or two weavers up to three years to make could now be finished in a few months.

Another cost-cutting technique was embroidery. Some Kashmir shawls of the early 1830s have an embroidered, not woven, inner-corner decoration, which would have saved hours or days of a weaver's valuable time.

### PRINTED SHAWLS

In Europe printed shawls could achieve heights of sophistication. The Norwich firm of Towler and Campin produced high-quality block-printed shawls from the late 1840s throughout the 1850s. Fabrics used were light wool challis (gauze), sometimes with a woven overcheck of silk, and many grades and textures of silk gauze. Paisley produced block-printed shawls on wool of all grades. "Glasgow" shawls were cotton and silk mixtures, sometimes with a damask sub-pattern woven into the cloth bearing no relation to the printed pattern.

Lyons factories printed shawls on fine regular wool, usually in an orange palette and of an all over repeating pattern. Russian printed shawls can sometimes be identified by floral elements and, in the late 19th century, a range of aniline dyes including bright purple, pink, orange and green.

### STYLISTIC DEVELOPMENT

Early Kashmir design was the model for European shawls, which comprised a rectangle with a large plain central area having narrow patterned borders on the long sides, and deeper patterned ends.

Decoration began to grow, moving in from the edges and invading the field. By the 1850s only a small central area was left in plain colour, commonly black or white. Some manufacturers, mostly French, wove pseudo-calligraphic inscriptions into this. "Compartment" shawls, in which the central field was halved into two

colours, such as red and green or blue and white, were popular in the 1850s, as were rectangular or square "four seasons", with the field quartered into four different colours. By the 1860s all over repeat patterning was common and was always used for the double-sided "reversible" shawls made in Scotland and Norwich.

## DESIGNS

In the 1830s, particularly in France, attempts were made to introduce non-Indian designs, and there was a brief but unsuccessful vogue for Islamic patterns. The *style végétal*, with flowers forming the pine patterns, enjoyed a brief vogue from 1849 to 1851. Pivoting shawls *(à pivot)* appeared about this time and continued into the 1860s: these have large, sweeping patterns, in which one end, although identical to the other, repeats not in mirror image but only when turned through 180 degrees.

## END OF THE SHAWL TRADE

Despite efforts to continue promotion of shawls, by the 1870s the vogue was dying. Overproduction by mechanized means had cheapened the product and saturated the market; the Franco-Prussian War had impeded the French shawl trade, and the newly popular bustle dictated that the back of a woman's dress was a point to focus on, not hide. By the 1880s many shawls were converted into coats or capes.

**DETAIL OF PIVOTING SHAWL**
*Norwich*
**Silk and wool; c. 1850**

This spectacular shawl showed its magnificent swirling pattern to best advantage over the bell-shaped crinolines of the 1850s. *(Above)*

## FURTHER READING

The following list of materials for further reading offers a broad range of literature. Both specialist and general works are included. While every effort has been made to give the date of the most recent edition, new ones may have been published since this book went to press.

Arnold, J.
**A Handbook of Costume**
London 1973

Bradfield, N.
**Costume in Detail**
London 1968

Bridgeman & Drury
**Needlework, an Illustrated History**
New York and London 1978

Coleman, E.
**The Opulent Era**
Brooklyn 1989

Clabburn, P.
**The Needleworker's Dictionary**
London 1976

Earnshaw, P.
**Identification of Lace**
Aylesbury 1982

Geijer, A.
**A History of Textile Art**
London 1979

Hughes, T.
**English Domestic Needlework 1660–1860**
London 1960

Irwin, J.
**The Kashmir Shawl**
London 1973

Levey, S.M.
**Lace, a History**
London 1983

Lévi-Strauss, M.
**The Cashmere Shawl**
London 1987

Morris, B.
**Liberty Design**
London 1989

O'Connor & Granger-Taylor
**Colour and the Calico Printer**
Guildford 1983

Rothstein, N.
**Silk Designs of the 18th Century**
London 1990

Simeon, M.
**The History of Lace**
London 1979

Synge, L.
**Antique Needlework**
London 1989

Tozer and Levitt
**Fabric of Society**
Carno 1983

Victoria and Albert Museum
**English Printed Textiles**
London 1960

**— Four Hundred Years of Fashion**
London 1984

Weyhe, E.
**2000 Years of Silk Weaving**
New York 1944

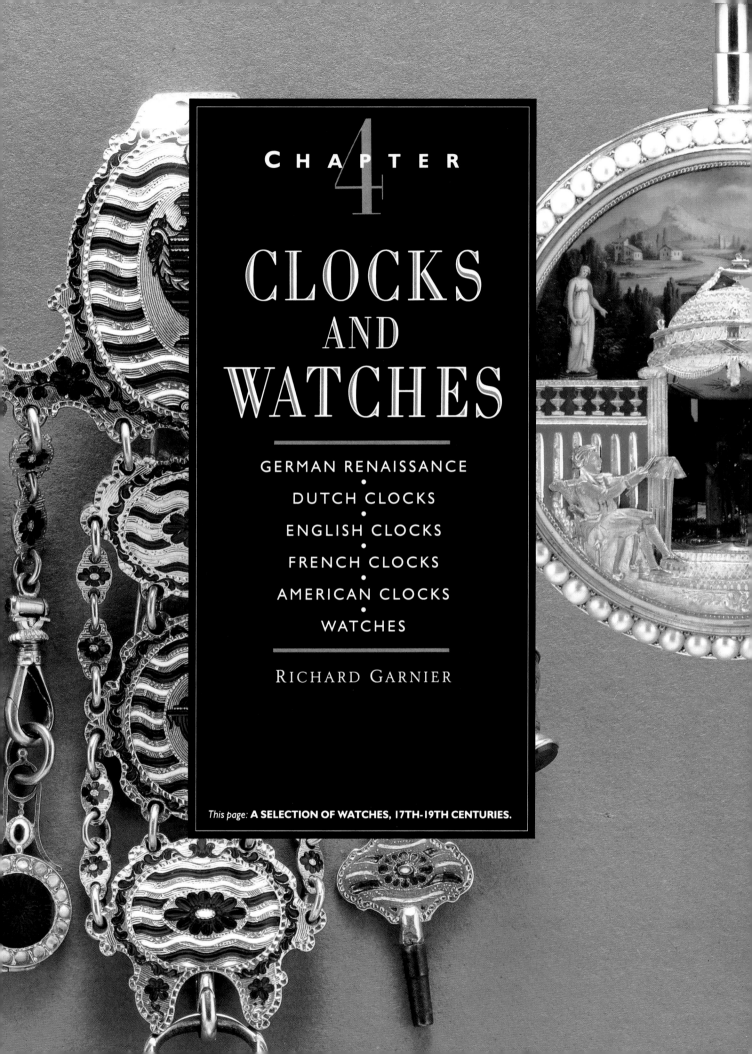

# CHAPTER 4

# CLOCKS
## AND
# WATCHES

GERMAN RENAISSANCE
•
DUTCH CLOCKS
•
ENGLISH CLOCKS
•
FRENCH CLOCKS
•
AMERICAN CLOCKS
•
WATCHES

RICHARD GARNIER

*This page:* **A SELECTION OF WATCHES, 17TH-19TH CENTURIES.**

# CLOCKS AND WATCHES

TELLING THE TIME WAS AN INEXACT ART UNTIL THE MECHANICAL

CLOCK WAS DEVELOPED. THE PROGRESSION OF TECHNICAL REFINEMENTS

WAS ACCOMPANIED BY A SUCCESSION OF STYLES IN ORNAMENT.

Mechanical clocks did not come into general use until *c*. 1350. They were first made in monasteries, to call the monks together for prayer in church and, once a day, for recitation of their rule in the chapter house. (This monastic origin explains the use of the term chapter for an individual hour on a clock-face; the chapter ring is the entire circle of hours.) By the mid 16th century most towns in Europe had a public clock in a tower, and from these early public clocks later developed town hall, church and country-house stable clocks, collectively known as turret clocks.

Domestic chamber clocks originated in the late 15th century. Initially comparatively bulky affairs, driven by weights, they ran for only 12 hours before needing rewinding and it was impracticable to move them. It was not until *c*. 1500 that it was found possible to make a mainspring suitable for powering a clock and thus satisfy the need for portable timepieces. The mainspring decreases in strength as it unwinds, and to compensate for this there was introduced the fusee, a spirally grooved truncated cone, on which is wound a cord attached to the spring.

### NORTHERN EUROPEAN DEVELOPMENTS

In Germany the stackfreed, a counterspring, was preferred to the fusee as being easier to make, but its operation was less effective and it fell out of favour in the early 17th century. Portable clocks were first made in quantity in southern Germany, principally in the cities of Augsburg and Nuremberg.

Table clocks are movable, spring-driven clocks for placing on furniture. The variation in design of 16th- and 17th-century German examples is extraordinary; most run for 30 hours before needing rewinding.

Before 1600 most clocks in England were either imported or made by foreign craftsmen in London. Spring-making was not as developed as in

**LANTERN CLOCK**
*Nicholas Coxeter, London*
**Brass; 17th century**

The dial has tulip engraving and there are dolphin-pattern frets below the bell.

**ENGLISH SELF-WINDING LEVER** *MONTRE A TACT*
*J.F. Cole, London*
Gold case, silver dial, gold and blued-steel hands; **1826**

This watch, which includes a perpetual calendar and indicates the phases of the moon, shows the influence of the French watch-maker A-L. Breguet. The maker, J.F. Cole, developer of the marine chronometer, may have trained with Breguet. Cole was the first to make carriage clocks in England.

Germany and the weight-driven chamber clock was more popular. A particularly English model of this was the lantern clock, so-called after its resemblance to the hand-carried medieval lantern.

True watches – as distinct from small clocks that could conceivably be slung on a chain round the neck – had been developed by the mid 16th century, also in southern Germany. The craft spread to France and, by 1600, to England. Cases were highly decorated with engraving, enamel and jewels, especially from 1580 to 1650.

The fragile nature of much watch decoration led to the pair-cased watch, one with a protective outer case of leather or metal. The outer case came to be decorated, particularly after late-17th-century improvements in the timekeeping of watches dictated that their movement should be housed in a simple dust-proof inner case. The decorated outer case was then sometimes given a protective third case.

### PENDULUMS AND BALANCE SPRINGS

In 1656 the pendulum was introduced to clocks by the Dutchman Christiaan Huygens (1629–95); and in *c.* 1675 the balance spring was introduced to watches. These two inventions dramatically improved the accuracy of time-keeping: from a loss or gain of a half to a quarter of an hour a day to one of no more than three minutes. As a result, minute hands became common and clocks were now made to run for eight days at a time. The anchor escapement, developed for pendulum clocks around 1670, along with the seconds-beating pendulum, further increased accuracy to a loss or gain of only a few seconds a week. This enabled clocks to be made to run for months, a few even a year.

From 1657 Salomon Coster of The Hague made pendulum clocks under Huygens' patent, creating a style known as the Hague clock. Ahasuerus Fromanteel, a clock-maker of Flemish extraction living in London, sent his son Johannes to Coster to learn the art, and on his return in 1658 Ahasuerus was able to advertise accurate clocks.

The years 1660–1720 were the classic age of English clock-making, when it became supreme in Europe. In this period the basic types – bracket clocks (spring-driven pendulum clocks, sometimes provided with wall brackets), longcase clocks (floor-standing clocks with weights and pendulum hanging down from the movement in a hood at the top) and pair-cased watches – were first developed and perfected, not least through the efforts of Joseph Knibb (1640–1711) and Thomas Tompion (1639–1713) and their pupils and associates.

In 1704 in England a patent was granted for a method of using jewels for pivot bearings, thus reducing friction and wear. This advance was par-

**LONGCASE CLOCK**
*John Chapman,*
**Mahogany-veneer;** *c.* **1790**

Birmingham-made painted dials, replaced brass dials outside London in the late 18th century.

## PRINCIPAL CLOCKMAKERS BEFORE 1720

| | | | |
|---|---|---|---|
| **BURGI, Jost** | 1552–1632 | Cassel and Prague | German Renaissance clocks and mechanical globes. |
| **KNIBB, Joseph** | *d.* 1711 | Oxford and London | Working *c.* 1670. Made bracket and longcase clocks. |
| **QUARE, Daniel** | 1649–1724 | London | Watches, bracket, longcase clocks. |
| **THURET, Isaac** | *d.* 1750 | Paris | Working in 1689. Watches and pendules religieuses. |
| **GRAHAM, George** | 1673–1751 | London | Watches, clocks and regulators |

**GERMAN STACKFREED CLOCK WATCH**
Gilt metal case, brass movement; **c. 1580**

The first pocket watches, of c. 1550, were circular, but between c. 1580 and c. 1660 most were oval or octagonal. The engraved silvered-brass dial and blued-steel hand of this watch are probably modern replacements approximately in the style of the originals.

ticularly significant for watchmaking and was confined to England for a considerable part of the century. The history of domestic clocks in 18th-century Britain is essentially one of changing fashions in cases and dials; movements developed into standard types.

In France a reaction set in against the *pendules religieuses* of Louis XIV's reign (1661–1715); French 18th-century mantel clocks showing a great deal of inventiveness and even whimsicality in their appearance and decoration.

In the first half of the 18th century French watchmaking was at a low ebb. Its revival was initially due to the Le Roy family. Julien Le Roy (1680––1759) was probably the first to use coiled steel gongs instead of bells for repeating. J. A. Lepine substituted individual bars or bridges for a top-plate to hold the wheels of a movement (a Lepine calibre). This and Le Roy's gongs enabled much thinner watches to be made. A-L. Breguet (1747–1823) then perfected the thin watch.

Besides making his own high-class watches, Breguet also imported Swiss ébauches (movements in the rough), then finished and cased them. Soon after 1800 Swiss makers began to challenge French supremacy in fashionable watches. Swiss success was founded on the mechanized manufacture of parts by home-based workers. The standardized parts were only assembled at the premises of the "watchmaker".

Clockmaking in America was a cottage industry until the 19th century, but then, in line with its other industries, first the production of clocks, then of watches, was mechanized. From the middle of the century the concept of interchangeable watch parts made by one company resulted in the mass-production of cheap and reliable watches. However,

# ABRAHAM-LOUIS BREGUET

Born in Switzerland in 1717, Breguet was living in Paris by 1762. He opened his own shop in 1775, but had to flee to Switzerland in 1793, during the French Revolution. Returning in 1795, he went on to be created *Chevalier de la Légion d'Honneur* and was elected in 1816 to the *Academie Royale des Sciences*.

Breguet first gained attention because of his *montres perpetuelles* (self-winding watches), which were wound by the oscillation of a pivoted weight. This was not Breguet's idea, but he perfected it. Breguet made the weight responsive to even the slightest movements of the watch. His *souscription* watches, so-called because they were paid for by the customer in advance, were of high quality but simplified as much as possible to keep down the cost. For instance, they had only one hand, but the dial was divided, so that it was easy to read the time to within three and a half minutes, which was perfectly adequate for every-day use.

Some of Breguet's other inventions included: the *tourbillon* which compensated

**BREGUET CARRIAGE CLOCK**
**with original case and certificate; 1823**

for the alteration in the going rate caused by the watch being held in different positions; and split-seconds hands for a stop-watch that can be run together but stopped individually.

Breguet's technical achievements and personal, elegantly functional styling make him the father of the modern watch. He died in 1823.

**BREGUET GOLD QUARTER-REPEATING CYLINDER WATCH 1802**

## PRINCIPAL CLOCKMAKERS AFTER 1720

| | | | |
|---|---|---|---|
| **LE ROY, Julien** | 1686–1759 | Paris | Watches, domestic and precision clocks. |
| **ELLICOTT, John** | 1706–72 | London | Watches, clocks and regulators. |
| **LEPINE, Jean-Antoine** | 1720–1814 | Paris | Watches, domestic and precision clocks. |
| **TERRY, Eli** | 1772–1852 | Massachusetts | Mass-produced domestic clocks. |
| **DENT, Edward J.** | 1790–1853 | London | In partnership of Arnold & Dent 1830–40. Watches, chronometers and the Westminster (Big Ben) clock. |

as methods of mechanical production advanced technically, the traditional Swiss division of skills told against the Americans. A single company could not hope to compete against the well-integrated but individually specialized Swiss workshops. In this way the 20th-century Swiss domination of the high-quality watch market was achieved.

In the 18th century, Dutch clockmakers, after their pioneering efforts in the mid 17th century, tended to steer a midway course between French exuberance and English stolidity. Some makers worked in a completely French style, but most Dutch spring clocks tended to have more severe cases and often housed imported English movements. Longcase clocks were the staple of Dutch urban clock makers, who again often imported English movements, combining them with more ornate dials and cases.

Soon after 1800, Breguet made the first carriage clocks. Previously, travelling timepieces looked like very large watches; they are known as coach watches. Following Breguet's lead, the manufacture of carriage clocks in France expanded rapidly from *c.* 1825–30 into a highly organized industry. At the same time, the French mantel clock industry went through a series of debased revivals and medleys of 18th-century styles. Carriage clocks were also made in England, but true English carriage clocks should not be confused with those bearing an English retailer's name but made in France. English carriage clocks were generally larger than French and of more individual workmanship, and they still used fusees.

**HALF-HOUR-STRIKING CARRIAGE CLOCK**
*Drocourt, Paris*
Gilt brass with Paris porcelain panels; **c. 1870**

The button plunger at the top of the case is for activating the "repeat" of the hour strike, a useful feature at night before the development of electric light. Porcelain panels, along with other clock mounts, including urns, were made by numerous factories in 19th-century Paris, working in the Sèvres style.

### THE LAST COLLECTABLE CLOCKS

Mantel clocks in England developed from bracket clocks. Meanwhile the English longcase clock died out from *c.* 1830, succumbing to competition from cheaper European and American mantel clocks, mass-produced from thin rolled brass and punched-out parts.

In the face of competing cheaper, less precise watches produced elsewhere, English manufacturers maintained a high standard during the late 19th century with the continued use of the fusee. There was even a late flowering of precision time-keepers in England at this date. Great numbers of marine and pocket chronometers were made, as well as complicated watches. Such English production continued until the First World War.

The French carriage-clock industry was also a casualty of the First World War. A slight revival occurred in the inter-war years with a range of expensive silver-gilt and enamel boudoir clocks (small, portable clocks for the bedside table or writing desk) and mystery clocks (of ornate form and with disguised movement) with cases constructed from semi-precious stones. These are the last quality clocks of interest to collectors. Some Art Deco household clocks of the 1920s and 1930s are also collectable.

VAST QUANTITIES OF CLOCKS IN A VARIETY OF TYPES WERE MADE IN
GERMANY DURING THE RENAISSANCE – WHEN THE COUNTRY BECAME
EUROPE'S FIRST LEADING CENTER FOR CLOCKMAKING.

# GERMAN RENAISSANCE

The first truly portable clocks were probably made in southern Germany in the early 16th century. Initially copied in countries further north, they ceased to be made there after the introduction of the pendulum and the spring balance in the second half of the 17th century, but in southern Germany production continued into the 18th century.

The earliest spring-driven clocks (*c.* 1520) were housed in gilt-metal canister cases with the dial at the upper end and a snap-on cover at the other to allow winding and regulation of the movement. One common type of clock that appeared in the 16th century was the horizontal dial table clock of square or hexagonal shape. Up to *c.* 1600 the bands of the case were often cast with Renaissance ornament, but from *c.* 1620 they were usually engraved. The bases of these clocks were hinged, carried the bell(s) and stood on feet.

### THE PEAK OF GERMAN WATCHMAKING

From these horizontal dial clocks developed the numerous square or hexagonal table clocks of *c.* 1650–1730 made throughout Germany, and also in Bohemia (Prague) and Poland. Before *c.* 1680 these had only one hand, but thereafter, with the advent of the spring-balance, minute hands became common.

At their most complex (when they are known as "masterpiece" clocks), tabernacle clocks represent the peak of German Renaissance clockmaking. The case carried dials on each vertical face and was surmounted by balustraded galleries and finials (spire-line ornaments). Some tabernacle clocks are capable of showing hours and quarter hours, length of day and night throughout the year, a calendar of saints' days, and much else besides.

Fantasy (or form) clocks were made for ostentatious display. They were of extravagant form (for example, with an animal holding up the dial) and of expensive material (some were gem-studded).

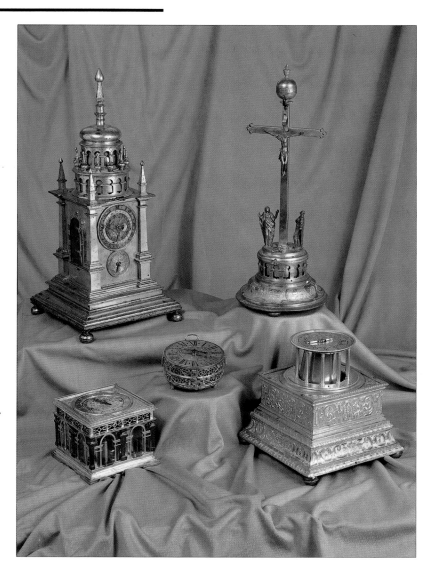

**GROUP OF GERMANIC TABLE CLOCKS**
Gilt-metal; **late 16th and early 17th centuries**

The common types shown here are the tabernacle clock (top left), crucifix clock (top right), square table clock (Flemish – bottom left) and travelling coach watch cum table clock (centre). An aid to dating is that the skirted foot of the cases are universally concave before 1590. By 1610 they were all of ogee profile.

EVEN THOUGH ENGLISH INFLUENCES WERE STRONG ON DUTCH CLOCKMAKERS, THE LATTER PRESERVED AN INDEPENDENCE OF STYLE THAT MAKES FOR A DELIGHTFUL RANGE OF TIMEPIECES.

# DUTCH CLOCKS

Hague clocks, made during the third quarter of the 17th century, are now rare. These clocks were hung from the wall by loops at the back of the case or could stand on a piece of furniture. They had an ebony-veneered box case with glazed side panels and front door, and a velvet-covered dial with an applied brass chapter ring. The maker's signature is normally on a plaque hanging below the chapter ring; on examples that come up for sale the plate is often missing or is sometimes not genuine.

Spring-driven clocks of the 18th century were closely based on French or English types, but often had the additional feature of music played every three hours.

### LONGCASE CLOCKS

Longcase clocks were the normal stock-in-trade of Dutch urban clock-makers from 1680. Early examples (1680–1720) had cases of panelled ebony, walnut or kingwood with a straight frieze and erect ornamentation at the top. Dials were commonly velvet covered, and the hands were elaborately pierced. Clocks of the transitional period (1720–35) show English influences, especially in the dial. The plinth often has a concave spreading foot moulding and stands on pear-shaped feet.

Longcase clocks in the Rococo and Empire styles (1735–1820) have a burr-walnut-veneered case; a bombé (bulging at the base) plinth on paw feet; a shaped trunk door; a hood with a double caddy top, surmounted by carved giltwood figures of Atlas flanked by angels blowing trumpets; and a dial which has a moon-phase indicator above the chapter ring (which encloses calendar indications) and on its lower half is commonly painted with a landscape or maritime scene.

### OTHER TYPES OF CLOCK

Stoel clocks (Friesland clocks) were made in the 18th century. They are 30-hour, weight-driven clocks with a rectangular painted dial and side doors and stand on a canopied wall bracket. In the 19th century they were replaced by Staart clocks, whose movement and arched dial were housed in a hooded wall bracket.

**STOEL (FRIESLAND) CLOCK**
**Second half 18th century**

This clock has a brass and steel movement, painted dial, painted, cast-lead frets on the dial, and cresting. (*Left*)

**STAART CLOCK**
**Mid 19th century**

Housed in a maddered oak case, the clock has a painted iron dial and carved giltwood figure finials. (*Right*)

**LONGCASE CLOCK**
*Jan van der Swelling*
Inlaid walnut veneer case, with silvered-brass and painted dial; **c. 1770**

This clock, made in Leyden, exhibits a characteristic shape with bombé plinth and figure finials of Atlas flanked by trumpeting heralds. (*Above*)

ENGLISH CLOCKMAKERS WERE THE EUROPEAN LEADERS DURING THE
18TH AND EARLY 19TH CENTURIES. THE ERA IS CHARACTERIZED BY
RELIABLE MECHANISMS AND HANDSOME, ORNAMENTALLY
RESTRAINED CASES.

# ENGLISH CLOCKS

The introduction of the pendulum clock to England in 1658 heralded radical changes in English clock-making. Two new clock types were developed: bracket and longcase. Their two characteristic features were plates to hold the trains of wheels and wholly wooden cases.

Most bracket clocks were made to stand on pieces of furniture (chimney-pieces with mantel shelves were not made until *c.* 1760). Floor-standing longcase clocks were screwed to the wall through the backboard of the case, since they were notably top-heavy when the weights were fully wound up to just under the movement in the hood at the top of the case.

ARCHITECTURAL PERIOD (1665–75)
In English clock-making the period 1665–75 is known as the architectural period: cases of bracket and longcase clocks – in oak veneered with ebony or ebonized pearwood – have a correctly classical form, with corner columns and a full entablature (frieze and cornice) topped by a pediment. Bases and capitals of columns are cast and chased in gilt-metal, as are other mounts, such as finials. As some cases are quite bulky to turn round – to regulate the pendulum – they swivel on turntable bases.

Longcase clock cases have an architectural hood that is pushed up to allow key winding through the dial. The hood rests on a convex "throat" moulding above a narrower trunk with raised panels on the sides and the long door. Trunk doors are hinged directly from the case sides with no intermediate front frame (see convex period). The clock's base is a plain plinth on bun feet. By 1673 walnut or olivewood

## BRACKET CLOCKS

Wooden clock cases were an innovation introduced around 1658 at the same time as the pendulum in England. The first cases were strictly architectural. This fashion had ceased by around 1673, when the cushion-moulded basket or caddy top case was in vogue, to be followed by the styles shown here.

1 Basket or caddy (1670-1725)

2 Repoussé basket top (1690-1725)

3 Inverted bell top (1720-70)

4 Bell top (1760-1810)

5 Balloon (1780-1820)

6 Arched top (1765-1830)

7 Lancet (1810-60)

8 Chamfer top (1815-40)

# LANTERN CLOCKS (1620–1800)

So-called because they resembled portable medieval lanterns, lantern clocks were a peculiarly English variant of earlier and bulkier German and Dutch chamber clocks. They were fitted with a single hand and a weight-driven movement, but many were altered in the later 19th century to incorporate a minute hand and an eight-day spring-driven movement of bracket clock type. These converted clocks were drilled with two winding holes, often awkwardly piercing the decorative engraving in the central area of the dial. Where this engraving is in a band around a central reserve there would originally have been an alarm-setting disc.

London lantern clocks fall into three main periods:

**1620–40** No clock from this period survives complete or unaltered. The running duration was 12 hours.

**1640–60** Again, there are few complete clocks from this period, especially from the Civil War years 1642–9. The running duration was still 12 hours. The practice of

tulip engraving first appeared during this period (see main text).

**1660–1700** Makers of lantern clocks in this period benefited greatly from two inventions by the Dutchman Christian Huygens: the pendulum, which gave accuracy, and endless rope drive, which increased running duration to 30 hours. Dials were engraved with tulip or other flower forms.

Lantern clocks continued to be made in country towns throughout the 18th century as a comparatively economical alternative to a longcase or bracket clock.

**STANDARD LANTERN CLOCK WITH ALARM;** Brass; c. 1685

This typical late lantern clock is fitted with an alarm rather than an hour-striking mechanism, a device that had fallen out of favour by 1700. (*Far left*)

**"WINGED LANTERN CLOCK" WITH PENDULUM AND ALARM** Brass; c. 1685

A central swinging pendulum in the shape of an anchor is incorporated into this clock, which, like that shown left, has an alarm. (*Left*)

veneer had become alternatives to ebony and ebonized pearwood.

Dials of bracket clocks, slightly smaller than those of longcases, consist of a narrow chapter ring mounted on a metal plate that initially had an overall matt surface except for a 1.6 mm (¼ in) border. Very soon the spandrels (dial corners) are usually mounted with winged-cherub-head castings but are sometimes engraved with vegetable motifs. For a short period around 1670 the dial centre is sometimes engraved with flowers, especially tulips. Striking is controlled by a numbered count-wheel (a wheel with graduated cut-outs on its perimeter, to count out an increased number of blows at each hour up to 12) positioned high up on the backplate.

Longcase clocks are signed by the maker at the base of the dial, bracket clocks sometimes there but always on the backplate.

### CONVEX PERIOD (1675–c. 1700)

During this period (so-called because throat mouldings on cases remain convex) cases are no longer strictly architectural. However, longcase clocks retain the angle columns (now sometimes spiral) and frieze and cornice of the earlier period. Rising hoods were phased out by 1690, after which the hood pulls off forwards for access to the movement. It also has a door to the dial for weekly winding and for hand setting. Many hoods have a cushion moulded "caddy" (dome) at the top, but others are flat-topped. The trunk now invariably has plain, flat, veneered sides and a front frame from which the door is hung.

Longcase clocks are taller, bracket clocks smaller than in the architectural period. The frame of bracket clock cases is closer to the movement and soon becomes a rectangular box with a spreading base moulding reflecting that of the cornice. The top is either a cushion moulded "caddy" under a central handle or a cast gilt-metal dome repoussé (hammered from the reverse side) with fruit and putti among acanthus scrolls.

Most bracket clocks are veneered in ebony or ebonized pearwood, but a few in burr walnut, olivewood or kingwood; marquetry is very occasionally found. On longcase clocks ebony or

**30-HOUR LONGCASE CLOCK**
*Donisthorne, Birmingham*
**Oak case, brass and silvered-brass dial; c. 1760**

*(Above)*

**LONGCASE CLOCK**
*Benjamin Heeley*
**Black-japanned case on pine carcass, brass and silvered brass dial; c. 1735**

*(Left)*

**GEORGE III BRACKET CLOCK**
*Andrew Dickie, Edinburgh*
**Ebonized pearwood case. brass and silvered brass dial; late 18th century.**

*(Below)*

ebonized pearwood veneer increasingly gives way to burr walnut. The parquetry decoration of the architectural period is now replaced by floral marquetry. This was first confined to reserves (areas within a decorative frame) on the trunk door and plinth but by 1680 fills both. By 1690 it covers the whole front face of the case, often within borders of seaweed marquetry (fine patterns resembling seaweed).

In the 19th century many plain burr walnut cases were "improved" with marquetry in order to make them more valuable. This is now sometimes difficult to distinguish from genuinely period marquetry.

**Dials and backplates** Longcase dials are 25.5 cm (10 in) square from 1675 to 1690, 28 cm (11 in) square from 1690 to 1700 and 30.5 cm (12 in) square after 1700. Chapter rings are wider, the 5-minute numerals are now engraved outside the minute ring and half-hour markers between the chapters become larger and more florid. Signatures of makers, except those of the very best, are often on the chapter ring. The very best signed the dialplate itself.

Bracket clock dials are commonly 12.5–15 cm (5–6 in) wide. By 1695 they are sometimes rectangular with the signature in a band at the top.

Engraving of stylized tulips is found on the backplate *c.* 1675. By *c.* 1680 these cover the entire plate and surround the signature in a symmetrical design. About five years later the tulips become buds, and by *c.* 1690 engraving is of acanthus foliage, sometimes with birds or putti.

CONCAVE PERIOD (*c.*1700–20)
Bracket clocks of this period (in which longcase throat mouldings are concave) are similar to those of the previous period. However, from *c.*1710 they sometimes have inverted bell tops instead of caddy tops. Cases are usually of ebony or ebonized.

Longcase clocks become even taller than before. Plinths stand on a plain kickboard skirting rather than bun feet. Burr walnut is the most common veneer. Marquetry becomes less floral and more sinuously arabesque in character, but from 1710 it is gradually replaced by japanning (imitation lacquer).

**Dials and backplates** Bracket clock dials are now sometimes signed in an oval disc mounted in the matted centre. Longcase dials commonly have an engraved wheat-ear border and either cherub-and-scroll or crown-and-crossed-sceptre spandrels. Engraving on bracket clock backplates incorporates fewer birds and putti within the scrolling foliage.

### ENGLISH CLOCKS (1720–1830)

The decorative history of clocks in the early Georgian period lags some 25 years behind that of furniture. Mahogany was used extensively in furniture-making from the 1730s, but not until *c.* 1750 for clock cases. The influence of "upholders", finally brought clocks into step with furniture. Until then walnut continued as the principal wood, with straight-grain, or "red", walnut being preferred from *c.* 1735.

At the start of the period marquetry had been replaced by japanning. Black was the most common ground colour for japanning, but today examples in scarlet, yellow, bright blue and green are the most popular and therefore the most expensive to buy.

### BRACKET CLOCKS

Ebony or ebonized cases are as common as any up to 1800. Walnut, then mahogany, were the other main woods used, although there are a few

**MANTEL CLOCK**
*Charles Frodsham & Co*
Rosewood veneer; **c. 1860**

*(Above)*

**LONGCASE CLOCK**
*John Wise*
Burr walnut veneer;
**c. 1685**

Decorated with floral marquetry, this clock has "barley-sugar" twists typical of the furniture of the period. *(Right)*

## THOMAS TOMPION

Tompion (1638–1713) was born in Bedfordshire, and was in London by 1671. In 1674 he met the eminent scientist Robert Hooke, through whom he came to the notice of Charles II. Tompion went on to hold an unrivalled position in English horology, partly thanks to his royal commissions.

After initial years of experimentation, Tompion established a style and started to produce timepieces in batches. The parts for a particular clock or watch had to be identified before assembly, and so from *c.* 1680 he started to use serial numbers. There were separate series for clocks (bracket, longcase and lantern), for timepiece watches and for repeating watches. He had numbered about 4000 timepiece watches and 580 clocks by the time he died, and the serial numbers were continued by his nephew and successor, George Graham (1673–1751).

Tompion's clocks and watches are characterized by a consistently high standard of design and finish. The standards he set raised English clockmaking to the position of prominence it held into the 19th century.

**HOUR-STRIKING BRACKET CLOCK NO. 270 WITH PULL QUARTER-REPEAT**
*Thomas Tompion, London*
Ebony-veneered case, gilt and silvered-brass dial, brass movement; **c. 1700**

This was Tompion's standard pattern of bracket clock, made in three set sizes.

**ACT OF PARLIAMENT CLOCK**
*Thomas Bentley, Darlington*
Black-japanned decoration on pine, with applied hand-coloured print to the trunk door; **c. 1780**

Act of Parliament clocks commonly do not strike the hour. This clock exhibits an early example of a circular dial. The elegant tear-drop-shaped trunk is unusual. (*Left*)

overall; in the provinces, from *c.* 1785, they were often made of a lightly fired off-white painted metal plate in imitation of pure white, true enamel dials that had been current in London from *c.* 1765. Painted dials became very common in the Regency period, both in the provinces and in London.

Engraving on backplates, predominantly rococo, was particularly fine during this period. This engraving exceeded that found on domestic silver both in frequency and in the number of engravers employed in its decoration.

### LONGCASE CLOCKS

Longcase clock cases were simpler and cleaner in line in London than in the provinces. From *c.* 1730 the arched dial was followed by an arched trunk door. Gothic details, such as cluster angle columns (several columns attached to each other on the angle of the case) and pointed case doors, were introduced. Many Regency clocks had circular dials; otherwise, dials evolved in the same way as those of bracket clocks.

In London longcase clocks ceased to be made by *c.* 1820, in the provinces from *c.* 1830.

### OTHER TYPES OF CLOCK

Act of Parliament (or tavern) clocks were made for public places, such as taverns and law courts, and also for servants' halls. It is often claimed that they originated in response to an Act of 1797 that imposed a tax on clocks and watches (with the result that most people could not afford them and had to rely on public clocks), but in fact, they were first made *c.* 1720. They were characterized by a large dial and a trunk extending down below. The maker's name was displayed prominently in large copperplate script. From *c.* 1720 to 1780 cases were japanned and had gilt chinoiserie decoration, and dials were shaped. After that, until *c.* 1830, cases were generally mahogany and dials circular and often painted white.

Cartel clocks (hanging wall clocks) were made for a short period – 1755–75. They were of carved giltwood; in an English version of French Rococo, and had a silvered and engraved dial, with a false-pendulum aperture above a copperplate script signature of the maker.

Wall dials, which developed *c.* 1770, were a smaller alternative to Act of Parliament clocks but with a silvered dial of the same type as a cartel clock and a turned mahogany bezel (rim) to the glass covering the dial.

**WALL DIAL TIMEPIECE**
*Le Grave, London*
Engraved silvered-brass dial, brass rim, turned mahogany case; **c. 1790**

Earlier wall dials had a false pendulum aperture below the figure XII on the dial. Later wall dials, especially Victorian and Edwardian ones, had white-painted iron dials. (*Above*)

satinwood ones at the end of the 18th century. After 1800 mahogany was almost exclusively used. In design, bracket clock cases continued to have an inverted bell top until *c.* 1760, when the ogee curves are reversed into the "bell" top. This design remained in fashion until *c.* 1810, but at the same time other shapes were developed: balloon (*c.* 1780), arched (*c.* 1770), lancet (*c.* 1810) and chamfer, (also *c.* 1810). The development of flat-top cases *c.* 1830 heralded the mantel clock of the next period.

Bracket clock dials became arched instead of square from *c.* 1720; after *c.* 1760 some were circular. Dials commonly had a false pendulum bobbing from side to side below the XII, in a matted centre, and a plain, square date-of-the-month aperture above the VI. From *c.* 1730 chapter rings lost half-hour markings, and from *c.* 1730 lost their inner quarter-hour ring. From *c.* 1750 spandrels evolved from a late Baroque mask-and-scroll pattern to Rococo leaf-like scrolls. From *c.* 1770 dials were often silvered

THE HISTORY OF CLOCKS IN FRANCE IS BOUND UP COMPLETELY WITH THAT OF FURNITURE AND THE DECORATIVE ARTS, WITH AS MUCH INTEREST IN THE BEAUTY OF THE CASE AS IN THE ACCURACY OF THE MOVEMENT.

# FRENCH CLOCKS

In France the *ébenistes* (cabinet-makers) dictated the appearance of clocks for much of the 18th century. The Louis XIV style (until 1715) was heavy, with rich ormolu (gilt-bronze) decoration on a tortoiseshell ground. The Régence style (1715–23) was less imposing and cases had a more flowing outline, with sides indented before curving out again at the base. The Louis XV style (1723–74) was marked by fantasy but by the time of Louis XVI (1774–92) a Neo-Classical reaction had set in. This reached full expression during the Empire period (1804–15) and after 1815 continued into the reigns of Louis XVIII (1815–24) and Charles X (1824–30).

## TYPES OF CLOCK

***Pendules religieuses*** These clocks, a development of Hague clocks, had a rectangular movement suspended on the back of a velvet-covered dial with an applied brass chapter ring. Unlike their Dutch models, *pendules religieuses* commonly had a case of brass- or pewter-inlaid tortoiseshell with ormolu mounts.

## CARRIAGE CLOCKS

Carriage clock movements were made in standard sizes which were fitted in cases of varying degrees of elaboration. The corniche is the most frequently used case and can house a timepiece up to a full *grande sonnerie* movement with calendar and alarm. However, such complicated movements are often found in the more elaborate case styles shown here.

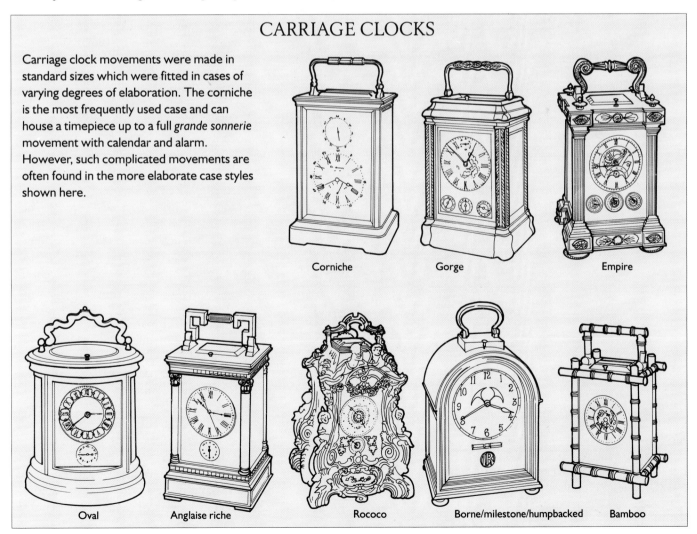

Corniche    Gorge    Empire

Oval    Anglaise riche    Rococo    Borne/milestone/humpbacked    Bamboo

**Bracket clocks** Such clocks, made from 1710 to 1760, had a case of sinuous outline, rococo angle mounts forming open-work foliage at the hips, shoulders and top.

**Cartel clocks** These wall clocks, which developed at the end of the Régence, often combined chinoiserie figures with flowing leaf-like scrolls and rocaille (shell and rock motifs) executed in ormolu or porcelain.

**Longcase clocks** These are less common than other French clocks. Louis XIV and Régence types took the form of a *pendule religieuse* or transitional bracket clock standing on a separate pedestal. Neo-Classical longcase clocks were rectilinear, their ormolu ornament was architectural and their cases commonly had a long, glazed door revealing a gridiron pendulum (made of alternate steel and brass rods) with a large bob (weight) at the base. Many of these precision clocks were capable of running for a month or more.

**Mantel clocks** These were first developed under Louis XV and are by far the most common type of French antique clock. Until *c.* 1780

## SWISS CLOCKS IN THE 18TH CENTURY

Swiss bracket clocks were similar in shape to French examples but not in decoration; instead of boulle marquetry, they were of plain red tortoiseshell or *vernis martin* (18th-century French imitation-Japanese lacquer), showing sprays of flowers on a coloured or gilt ground. The bronze mounts in Swiss clocks were cast with a hollow back surface; the enamel dials were commonly serpentine (with a double-curved cross-section) and had a sunken centre. Movements were often linked to a separate musical movement in the lower half of the clock case.

The Neuchâtel clock, which was produced throughout the 19th century in Switzerland, was a debased form of rococo bracket clock of serpentine outline with a gilt-bordered wooden case.

**MUSICAL BRACKET CLOCK,** *c.* 1770

**LOUIS XV MANTEL CLOCK**
*Anaiom, Paris*
Ormolu, bronze and porcelain; **c. 1760**

**LOUIS XV MANTEL CLOCK**
*Lepautre, Paris*
Ormolu, marble base; **c. 1780**

they were designed to be placed on pieces of furniture rather than mantels. Most have a circular enamel dial and the movement housed in a drum canister. The drum is either the central feature or incidental to a composition focusing on a modelled figure or figures. In some popular Louis XV models the clock is borne on the back of an animal and surmounted by a chinoiserie figure under a parasol.

**Carriage clocks** The first true carriage clock was made by A-L. Breguet in 1796. Previous travelling clocks had been in the form of large watches or of rectangular-cased clocks with a watch escapement (the clockwork part controlling the force of the spring). Breguet placed the escapement on a platform above the plates of the movement and provided a sturdy case with glazed panels. Other makers simplified the clock and made it suitable for mass-production, which lasted from 1830 until 1915. Cases and movements of carriage clocks are made in set grades of quality and any one grade of movement can be housed in various types of case.

The most sought-after types have a *grande sonnerie* movement (striking both hour and quarter hour at each quarter hour), with alarm and calendar, and are in an engraved, enamelled or enamel- or porcelain-panelled case. The better makers include Jacot, Margaine, Drocourt, Le Roy, Lamaille and Japy.

IMMIGRANT CLOCKMAKERS TO THE COLONIES AND LATER TO THE NEWLY INDEPENDENT UNITED STATES BROUGHT THEIR SKILLS, AND ESTABLISHED AN AMERICAN INDUSTRY THAT BLENDED THE VARIED STYLES OF THE "OLD WORLD"

# AMERICAN CLOCKS

In the 18th and early 19th centuries, a few fine longcase clocks were made in centres such as Boston. They were either related in style to those of the English provinces or had wooden movements made in the German Black Forest tradition. A popular clock at the start of the 19th century was the wag-on-the-wall, a 30-hour, weight-driven wooden clock with a pendulum swinging in front of the dial.

The banjo clock was invented by Simon Willard (1753–c. 1845) in 1802. It had a circular dial above a tapered trunk and box-shaped base. Banjo clocks did not usually strike the hour. Other makers developed the banjo clock into the lyre clock, which had curved sides and applied carving, and the girandole clock, which had a circular base.

### SHELF CLOCKS

The first shelf clocks were made by Simon Willard and his brother Aaron (1757–1844). Known as Massachusetts shelf clocks, they were about 1.2 m (4 ft) high and constructed with a wider base section like a chest-on-chest.

In 1816 Eli Terry (1772–1852) patented a small rectangular shelf clock about 75 cm (2 ft 6 in) high. The dial was at first painted on the glass door but soon it was fitted between the door and the movement. The half-seconds-beating pendulum was hung originally to the right, after 1823 in the centre. The movement was driven by weights in the sides of the case, their lines running over pulleys at the top.

The finest shelf clocks are of pillar-and-scroll design (introduced by Terry in 1817): slender, turned pillars flank the case, which has a wavy apron (lower front edge) and a swan-neck pediment (moulding on top) with brass urn finials (spire-like ornaments).

The shelf clock was an inexpensive timepiece and was exported to Europe in large numbers. Later developments included the "bronze and looking-glass clock" (with thick half-columns on the door beside the dial and with bronze mounts) and the ogee (or OG) clock (rectangular, with an ogee-moulded door). Other clocks produced by makers such as Chauncey Jerome, had gabled doors flanked by spire finials.

**AMERICAN BANJO CLOCK**
*Anonymous*
**Giltwood case with inset reverse-painted glass panels; c. 1815**

*(Below)*

**AMERICAN PILLAR-AND-SCROLL SHELF CLOCK**
*Eli Terry, Connecticut*
**Mahogany-veneered, brass finials, white-painted wooden dial, reverse-painted glass panel; c. 1820**

Eli Terry's shelf clocks were inexpensive, elegant, and popular. *(Above)*

**GERMAN BLACK FOREST WALL CLOCKS**
**Wooden movements, painted wooden dials; first half of the 19th century**

*(Left)*

# 19TH-CENTURY CLOCKS

The 19th century saw a series of revivals of previous styles, including the Rococo, Régence, Baroque, Renaissance, Neo-Classical and Gothic. These revivals were never quite true to the original and often incorporated elements of other styles. From mid-century clocks were mass-produced in the USA and Germany, batch-produced in France but still individually made in England.

**Mantel clocks** These (known as clock sets when they have a flanking pair of candelabra) were mainly of French make, in cast-ormolu cases and often with porcelain mounts, such as urns and inset panels. The candelabra stems often take the form of ormolu putti or porcelain urns. Porcelain ornamentation was painted in the Sèvres style with sprays of flowers against a blue, pink, yellow or green ground. Dials were always circular, in enamel and protected by glass; hands were ormolu, pierced and engraved.

Late in the century Belgian black marble was increasingly used. The movements of marble clocks were comparatively cheap but reliable, and many are still in excellent condition. Their plinth-shaped cases often have coloured-marble insets or incised decoration. The most valuable have a calendar dial below the standard dial.

**Four-glass clocks** In France these clocks, which were like giant carriage clocks, had brass-framed glazed cases and circular movements and dials; before 1860 striking was on a bell, thereafter on a coiled steel gong. In England their cases were normally wooden and their dials large, rectangular and of white enamel, gilt or silvered metal.

**Mystery clocks** were so made that the connection between hands and movement was hidden. They took several forms. In one with a transparent dial the hand was carried round by a rotating inner sheet of glass, held between two fixed sheets. In another, a turtle figurine floating in a basin of water was carried round past the chapters by the pull of a magnet on a rotating arm below. And in another the clock dial was at the base of a pendulum swung from the outstretched hand of an imperceptibly oscillating female figure, the clock hands being driven by the motion

**FRENCH MYSTERY CLOCKS**
Glass dials, ormolu and patinated-brass cases, wood bases; **c. 1845** (*Above, left and right*)

**FRENCH NOVELTY CLOCK**
Ormolu and marble; **c. 1880** (*Above, centre*)

**ART DECO MYSTERY CLOCK**
*Cartier, Paris*
Gold, enamel, diamonds, rock crystal and other hardstones; c. 1925 (*Below*)

**ENGLISH SKELETON CLOCK**
*Anonymous, England*
Brass and silvered brass; **c. 1860**

of the pendulum.

**Skeleton clocks** These clocks had their plates pierced to reveal the wheels of the movement. First made in late 18th-century France, they were produced only in small numbers until the mid 19th century, when they became popular in England. There the plates were elaborated in shape to represent the façades of buildings, especially cathedrals. Many skeleton clocks were simply non-striking timepieces or struck merely one blow at each hour rather than the number of the hour. Better clocks had a full hour strike and many of the cathedral clocks had quarter-hour chimes.

**Industrial clocks** These are so-called because they were automata (clocks with a moving figure or other object) modelled on pieces of industrial machinery, such as steam engines and windmills, or on other prosaic items, such as a kitchen hearth. The eight-day movement for the time dial of these clocks was separate from the 12-hour movement for the automaton.

**Vienna regulators,** made mainly in Germany after having originated in early-19th-century Vienna, were wall clocks with a woodrod pendulum. The Viennese clocks

were individually and superbly made, having high-quality movements and simple cases with narrow-wood-framed glazed panels. From mid-century German types were characterized by heavy, turned-wood cases with bulbous finials at the top and pendants (suspended ornaments) at the base. On later examples dials had a recessed centre and some cases showed an Art Nouveau influence.

**English wall dials** were a development from those of the Georgian period. There were two basic types. In the simpler dial clock the movement and pendulum were contained in a box completely covered by the dial; in the drop dial clock the box extended downwards below the dial to take a longer pendulum, visible through a glass aperture. Dials were painted on iron. The rim holding the glass in front of the dial was commonly turned in brass and hinged from the ma hogany dial surround, itself often brass-inlaid.

**Cuckoo clocks** had originated in the Black Forest, southern Germany, c. 1730, but production greatly increased c. 1840. They were not made in Switzerland until this century.

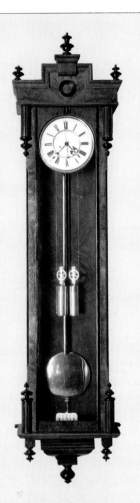

### STEAM-HAMMER INDUSTRIAL CLOCK
*Anonymous, France*
Gilt and patinated brass, marble; **c. 1900**

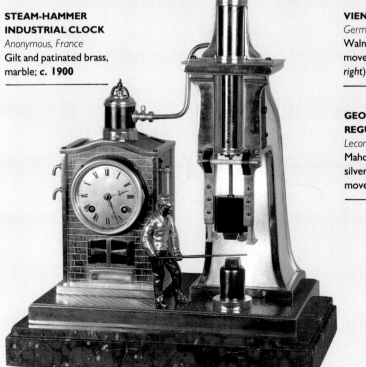

### VIENNA REGULATOR
*Germany*
Walnut case, brass movement; **c. 1880** (*Above right*)

### GEORGE IV LONGCASE REGULATOR
*Lecomber, Liverpool*
Mahogany-veneered, silvered-brass dial, brass movement; **c. 1830** (*Right*)

THE POCKET TIMEPIECE HAS LASTING APPEAL BOTH FOR THE GREAT SKILL
INVOLVED IN ITS MANUFACTURE AND ITS EXTREME CONVENIENCE AND
UTILITY FOR TELLING THE TIME.

# WATCHES

By 1600 the centre of watchmaking had shifted from southern Germany to France, where it was concentrated in Paris, Blois and Lyon; but during the first half of the 17th century it was Geneva and London that were showing signs of developing into the great centres of watchmaking.

Early watches were poor timekeepers and were made mainly as expensive items of jewellery. Cases were in gilt-metal, silver, silver-gilt or gold and were set with rock crystal, studded with gems or enamelled.

Enamelling at the beginning of the 17th century was confined to the use of opaque and translucent enamels in reserves (areas within a decorative frame) or on separate parts of the case. But *c.* 1630 the Toutin family of Blois perfected the technique of painting in colours on a white enamel ground, and this led to a school of Blois enamellers which specialized in exquisite floral and religious work. The cases are typically circular but of oval cross-section, a form known as bassine. The interior of the case and cover is also enamelled; this is known as the counterenamel.

Most plain metal watches from the early 17th century are oval, with vertical sides and slightly bowed covers. The exterior of the watch, and sometimes the inner surfaces of the covers, is commonly engraved with mythological or allegorical subjects within scrolling Renaissance foliage. Dials are of metal and have a narrow chapter ring applied to a similarly engraved plate, with little locating lugs on the plate extending into the rim of the case. The single hour-hands, made of blued steel or brass, are sturdy, shaped and faceted.

Form watches, which originated shortly before 1600, were modelled on various subjects, including books, flowers, birds and skulls. Puritan watches were very plain English watches and reflect a reaction to the highly decorated watches made by French immigrant makers in early 17th century London but

of the same form. Their oval cases with the bowed covers characteristic of the period are of plain undecorated silver or gilt-brass.

BALANCE-SPRING WATCHES: 1675–1735
In *c.* 1675 the balance spring was introduced to watches, which as a result became much more accurate timepieces and for the first time incorporated a minute-hand and minute divisions on the dial.

Most early French and Swiss balance-spring watches are known as *oignon* watches, from their onion shape, and have cases of plain brass, gilt-brass or silver. The plain brass ones are commonly covered with leather, fixed by gold or silver stud pins in a decorative pattern or monogram. Gilt-brass or silver cases are usually engraved with symmetrical designs within scrolling acanthus foliage. Some of the earliest enamel dials are featured on *oignon* watches.

English pair-case watches were developed about the same time as *oignon* watches. The decorated outer case might be engraved in the French style, embossed or covered with leather or tortoiseshell. Early dials were made of *champlevé* metal with hollowed-out areas between the hour and minute chapters which are left raised and polished. However, in the mid-

**FRENCH SKULL FORM WATCH**
*Robert Hubert, Rouen*
Silver case, brass movement; **c. 1620**

*(Above)*

**GERMAN OCTAGONAL STACKFREED WATCH**
Rock crystal, gilt metal and blued steel, brass movement; **c. 1615**

*(Right)*

**ENGLISH PURITAN WATCH**
*Edward East, London*
Silver case, brass movement; **c. 1635**

The plain Puritan watch is in sharp contrast to the baroque ornament of its French contemporaries.
*(Above)*

**REPOUSSÉ PAIR-CASE WATCH**

*J. Welldon, London*

**Gold cases, champlevé gold dial, brass movement; 1731**

(Above)

**PAIR-CASE WATCH**

*Richard Peckover, London*

**Repoussé Gold case, brass movement; 1734** (*Far left*)

**REPOUSSÉ PAIR-CASE WATCH**

*Jacob Mayr, Germany*

**Repoussé gold case, brass movement; c. 1745** (*Left*)

**PAIR-CASE CYLINDER WATCH AND CHÂTELAINE**

*James Tregent, London*

**Gold and enamel; c. 1790**

(Above right)

18th century and later many dials on earlier watches were changed to enamel ones which are more legible.

By 1720 more and more English watch-makers were using serial numbers, displayed beside the signature on the backplate and also sometimes on the inner case. From *c.* 1690 English watches often incorporated quarter-repeating: on depressing the pendant, the last hour and quarter hour is sounded.

The most notable makers of enamel watches were the Huaud family of Geneva (active *c.* 1670–1724). Bright blue, garnet red and yellow-orange predominate in their enamels, whose subjects are taken from engravings after early-17th-century painters. The enameller's signature is on the band of the case between landscape vignettes: the counterenamelled interior is also of a landscape.

### THE ROCOCO: 1730–70

During this period (and until the late 19th century) watches were often worn as prominent pieces of jewellery. The English pair-case watch was the most respected type of watch in Europe. Most of these watches had undecorated silver or gilt-brass cases. Dials of white enamel were introduced, at first following the layout of *champlevé* dials of the previous period, but later becoming simpler. The inner cases of repeating watches were engraved and pierced round the band to let out the sound; otherwise, decoration was confined to the outer case.

From *c.* 1715 there was an increasing vogue for repoussé decoration (embossed by hammering from within). Today the highlights of

repoussé cases have often been rubbed or worn through. The best preserved are those with an additional protective case.

**French watches** These were commonly single-cased, with dials of white enamel and the half-hour marks and the hands often studded with diamond or paste brilliants. Enamel was popular on cases, subjects being taken from Watteau, Boucher and Fragonard and commonly framed with rococo scrolls, sometimes stone-set. Decoration in four-colour gold was popular, especially from *c.* 1765.

**Dutch forgeries** Some continental watch-makers tried to enhance the salability of their watches by giving them spurious London signatures. The movements were Swiss and the watches were assembled in Holland. The same invented names were used over and over again, including "Tarts" and "Neveren", and the cases had false English hallmarks.

### THE NEO-CLASSICAL STYLE: 1770–1870

In England repoussé decoration was now replaced in popularity by enamel. A central oval panel with a Neo-Classical cameo-style scene in grisaille (grey tints) or *camieux* was typically surrounded by bands of translucent guilloché (the ground engraved with overlapping circles) enamel and opaque enamel. From *c.* 1790 completely guilloché backs in translucent red, blue, green or mauve enamel within simulated-half-pearl borders were common. Many pair cased watches for the poorer classes have a rural or arcadian scene painted on the underside of a horn veneer to the case. Dials were often of plain white enamel, and from 1800 they bore hour chapters only. Watches for the Turkish market were produced in large numbers either with repoussé or enamelled cases.

**Swiss watches** Swiss watches for the European market commonly had fine cases of

Genevan enamel. The enamelled back was contained within a frame that became narrower and narrower and was set with real or enamelled half-pearls. The panel itself was either of plain guilloché enamel or a miniature Neo-Classical painting. Much use is made of gold and silver foil *paillons* within the enamelling to heighten the design.

**Fantasy watches** were another Swiss speciality. Form watches were revived; their gold cases were decorated in a mixture of guilloché and opaque enamel and were set with pearls. Some of these form watches incorporate automata or musical movements of great ingenuity and complexity or are set in opera glasses, model pistols, bird cages or snuff boxes. The most common automation is on a quarter-repeating, jacquemart watch, which incorporates a pair of automaton figures striking a pretend bell in time

**AUTOMATON WATCH**
*Jean Carrisol, Geneva*
Gold, enamel and pearls;
**c. 1810**

Dancing couples appear in the domed portal while the harpist "plays". (*Above left*)

**FRENCH *MONTRE A TACT***
*Hilaire Bassereau, Paris*
Gold, enamel, diamonds and pearls; **c. 1820**

The time is read either by rotating the diamond-set arrow or conventionally on the reverse face. (*Above*)

**PAIR-CASE POCKET CHRONOMETER**
*William Ilbery, London*
Gold and enamel case, brass movement; 1813 (*Above*)

**WATCH CASE AND WATCHES**

From left to right: protecting case of repoussé pair-case watch, underpainted horn, *c.* 1800: pair-case watch by Thomas Parker (Dublin), silver, *c.* 1745: English duplex watch, gold, 1847. (*Right*)

to the quarter repeat that is actually sounded on gongs coiled round the movement.

**French watches** In the decoration of these the themes of idealized love and offerings to love now predominated. The watches of A-L. Breguet were typified by sobriety and functional elegance. The dials are white enamel, silver or gold, the thin, sharp hands end in a hollow ring and the cases are especially flat. His style rapidly spread through followers, indeed many imitations have spurious Breguet signatures.

### 1830–1935

Watches were flat and thin with the covers curving into the band. Some, even thinner, in imitation of Breguet continued to be made until the mid 19th century. The output of Genevan enamellers was increased, but of more variable quality than before. Continental dials were of plain white enamel or engine-turned silver or gilt-metal.

In England the pair-case watch was replaced *c.* 1830 by a single-case type in gold or silver. Mid-century saw the development of the hunter case with a hinged cover over the dial to prevent breakage of the glass. A half-hunter case had a chapter ring engraved or enamelled on the cover around a small aperture which enabled the

### ENGLISH HUNTER-CASE STOPWATCH
*Charles Frodsham, London*
Gold case; **1904**

This precision stopwatch is an example of the finest English craftsmanship from shortly before the demise of English watch-making. The two split-second chronograph hands are for timing two competing runners, such as horses. A tour-billon (revolving mechanism), rotating every six minutes, equalizes the different rates of the spring unwinding caused by the watch being held in different positions. (*Right*)

hands to be read. American mass-produced watches were mainly of either hunter cased or open-faced type in imitation of English watches. Keyless winding via the crown button, introduced in Swiss watches 1850–60, was not adopted in England until the 1880s.

Swiss watches were generally of inferior quality until after the First World War, when a high standard of mechanization enabled them to capture the quality market.

Decorative standards, which had declined in the second half of the 19th century, underwent a partial revival with the Art Nouveau style (1890–1910) and later Art Deco (1920–30).

## FURTHER READING

The following list of materials for further reading offers a broad range of literature. Both specialist and general works are included. While every effort has been made to give the date of the most recent edition, new ones may have been published since this book went to press.

Allix, C. and P. Bonnert
**Carriage Clocks**
Woodbridge 1974

Baillie, G.H. (Vol 1) and B. Loomes (Vol 2)
**Watchmakers and Clockmakers of the World**
London 1929

Britten, F.J.
**Old Clocks and Watches and their Makers**
London 1932

Clutton, C., and G. Daniels
**Watches**
London 1968

Cuss, T.A. Camerer
**The Camerer Cuss Book of Antique Watches**
Woodbridge 1967

Daniels, G.
**The Art of Breguet**
London 1974

Dawson, P.G., C.B. Drover and D.W. Parker
**Early English Clocks**
Woodbridge 1982

Edwardes, E.
**The Grandfather Clock**
Altrincham 1949

Jagger, C.
**The Artistry of the English Watch**
Newton Abbot 1988

Lee, R.A.
**The Knibb Family, Clockmakers**
Byfleet 1964

Lloyd, H.A.
**Collectors' Dictionary of Clocks**
London 1964

— **Some outstanding Clocks over 700 years, 1250–1950**
Woodbridge 1981

Loomes, B.
**The Early Clockmakers of Great Britain**
London 1981

Robinson, T.O.
**The Longcase Clock**
(revised edition)
Woodbridge 1985

Symonds, R.W.
**Thomas Tompion**
London 1951

Tardy, Henri Lengellé
**La Pendule Francaise**
Paris 1948

White, G.
**English Lantern Clocks**
Woodbridge 1989

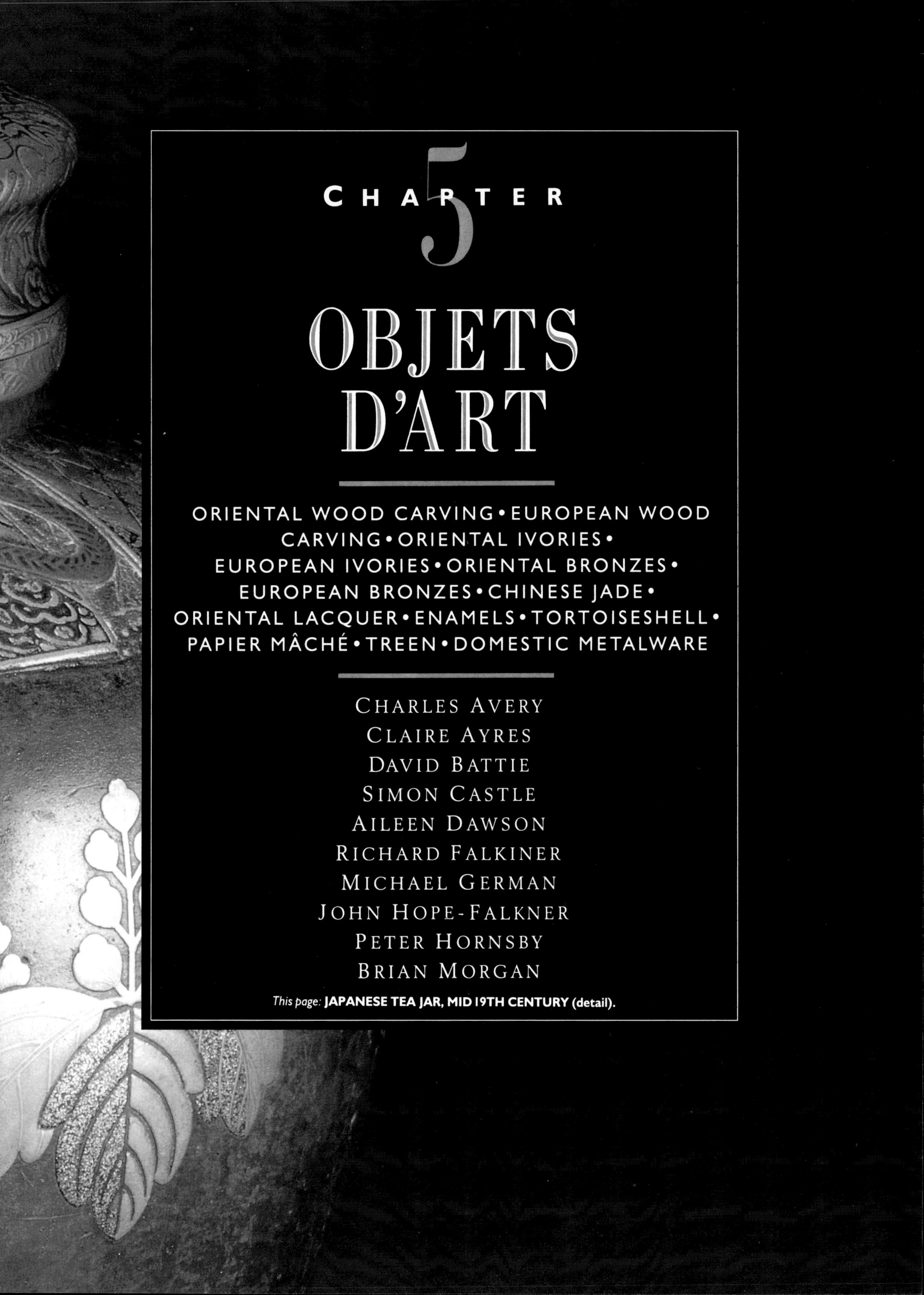

# OBJETS
# D'ART

ORIENTAL WOOD CARVING • EUROPEAN WOOD
CARVING • ORIENTAL IVORIES •
EUROPEAN IVORIES • ORIENTAL BRONZES •
EUROPEAN BRONZES • CHINESE JADE •
ORIENTAL LACQUER • ENAMELS • TORTOISESHELL •
PAPIER MÂCHÉ • TREEN • DOMESTIC METALWARE

CHARLES AVERY
CLAIRE AYRES
DAVID BATTIE
SIMON CASTLE
AILEEN DAWSON
RICHARD FALKINER
MICHAEL GERMAN
JOHN HOPE-FALKNER
PETER HORNSBY
BRIAN MORGAN

*This page:* **JAPANESE TEA JAR, MID 19TH CENTURY (detail).**

# OBJETS D'ART

THE ORIGINAL ANTIQUES WERE THE HANDSOME SCULPTURES AND
CERAMICS SURVIVING FROM THE WORLD OF ANCIENT EGYPT, GREECE AND
ROME. THEIR TRUE DESCENDANTS ARE THE OBJETS D'ART, A CATEGORY
THAT ENCOMPASSES A VAST REALM OF BEAUTIFUL THINGS.

**STANDING FEMALE
FIGURE**
*Chinese*
Wood; 17th century

This chapter is devoted to those small antiques that do not necessarily have a practical function, but are beautiful pieces in their own right. Such a broad definition can easily be expanded to cover just about everything this book has placed into separate chapters. Some watches, for example, are nicer to look at than to tell the time with. The owner of a watch, however, can at least pretend he or she is using the timepiece purposefully; the owner of a bronze statuette lacks similar grounds for excusing his or her aesthetic luxury – except as a paperweight perhaps.

This broad definition encompassing such a diversity of material by its nature creates a problem. The potentially vast amount of information that the student of objets d'art needs to learn has to be handled by some further subdivision. All kinds of antiques are classified within their own field, and objets d'art have to be treated in the same way.

Nowhere in the field of antique collecting is the question of classification more fraught than in the realm of objets d'art. To take one example, a small ivory panel of the 14th century could be classed under the broad heading of "Ivory". But then it might jostle uncomfortably with the Lewis chesspieces and Japanese netsuke. Classing it with other European ivories would simplify matters a little by placing it within a specific artistic tradition. However, this mingles sacred objects such as a bishop's crozier with the profane depictions that might appear on the panel. The intent behind the production of such objets is in a very different light. Perhaps a different subdivision, dividing religous and secular objects, might help. But much religious carving is in another material, wood.

The argumentative can indulge their passion to their heart's content in this field, but at some point a line has to be drawn. Objets d'art have to be placed in some categories, even if only on a temporary basis. What follows in this section of the book covers most types of objets d'art, and

**SUZURIBAKO**
*Japanese*
Gold lacquer; **19th century**

Both the inside and outside of this writing case are decorated with landscape scenes.

gives a lead as to where to find out more information.

In some areas the information is scattered, and the precise identification of a piece is hard to establish. But in others the study and categorization has been well organized, in some cases since the Renaissance; information is readily available.

On the broadest basis, objets d'art fell into two categories. There are pieces that were created to satisfy the needs of connoisseurs of fine art, whether medieval churchmen furnishing a cathedral or a Chinese prince seeking jade for display. There are also domestic pieces, usually handmade, that either fashion or machine manufacture for a mass market have made exotic examples of practically lost handiwork skills.

In both cases a variety of different materials have been used. In some instances, such as ivories or tortoiseshell, environmental concerns have made it unlikely that in future many objets d'art will be made in these categories. In others, such as bronzes, the expense of the material itself has made it unfamiliar in the modern world. A third group cover those materials most people have handled at some point in their lives. Those who remember their papier mâché projects from school will see just what a skilled command of the material can achieve.

To explore the rich range of objets d'art is a little like venturing into the mansion of some connoisseur of the Victorian era. The collection may be eclectic. Each room holds some new surprise, an odd juxtaposition of unexpectedly related pieces. It is always interesting, always stimulating and – just occasionally – astonishing.

**CIGARETTE CASE**
*Alexander Tillander, St Petersburg*
Gold and enamel; **1893**

An engraving of the double-headed eagle of the Romanov tsars of Russia is visible through the enamel. The case has a match compartment, a tinder cord attachment, and is set with a cabochon sapphire thumbpiece.

BOTH THE CHINESE AND THE JAPANESE PRODUCED SOME EXCELLENT
EXAMPLES OF WOOD CARVING, ESPECIALLY IN A VERY SMALL SCALE THAT
MAKES THE DETAILED WORK ALMOST INCREDIBLE.

# ORIENTAL WOOD CARVING

The arrival of Buddhism from India, and its establishment as a state religion in the 4th century AD, was instrumental in the development of Chinese sculpture. Initially, stone, bronze and clay were the predominant media, but around the 6th century wood sculpture began to come into prominence. Wood had obvious advantages: it was easier to carve than stone and more convenient to transport.

Perhaps strangely to Westerners, in China sculpture was not held in anything like the esteem with which painting was regarded, so few practitioners of the art were recorded. This was not, however, the case in Japan, where there are many major Buddhist works by known and revered sculptors.

Subjects were first carved from a block of solid wood, then embellished with gesso, (a plaster base, usually moulded), lacquer, gilt and/or paint. Eventually, carvings of solid wood were replaced by those of sectionalized wood, whose pieces were joined. The sculptor would then render the fine details, often using the wood grain to emphasize the contours of the subject. Of the variety of finishes that oriental wood carvers used, gilding has the most appeal to modern Western eyes.

### RELIGIOUS CARVINGS

Buddhism is essentially an iconographic religion, and rival religions, such as Shintoism and Taoism, also employed images, though to a lesser extent. The sculpture of these images was for long a vigorous art in the Far East, but later changes came about. For example, in China, as the Ming Dynasty (1368–1643) progressed, the original vitality of wood sculpture diminished, and in Japan, when the more meditative aspects of Zen Buddhism became popular in the 14th century, smaller images were produced, probably more for domestic than for temple use.

The high point of religious wood carving in China was from the 6th to the 14th century; in Japan from the 8th to the 15th. The carvings of

**STANDING WOOD FIGURE OF A MALE DEITY**
*Japanese*
**Wood with traces of old pigment; 11th–12th century**

The robust yet serene quality of this Heian period Jizo Bosatsu is a good example of early Japanese religious carving. Such was the reverence for early work that damaged parts would be meticulously replaced, such as in this example, whose hands and feet are later additions. (*Right*)

**NETSUKE: LOVERS**
*Japanese*
**Wood and polychrome details; late 19th century**

An unusual and sensitive group, this *netsuke* employs different woods for the clothes, faces and hands. Deliberately rubbed to suggest age, it is a charming example of the miniature carvings used as toggles to secure objects to the *obi*. (*Below*)

these periods were usually of Buddha in his many manifestations and of his acolytes, such as the female deity Kuan Yin (Kannon in Japan). Representations ranged from sublime, meditative Buddha figures that induced inner peace to ferocious Japanese temple guardians that instilled terror.

Some very fine pieces of smaller wood sculpture were created in China during the Ming Dynasty. And the 18th and 19th centuries saw some skilful and imaginative larger Chinese work, such as the usually gilded and lacquered carvings that can still be seen over the doorways of temples and theatres.

### JAPANESE CARVINGS

It was in Japan that the finest examples of miniature sculpture were perfected, during the 18th and 19th centuries, in the form of *netsuke* (toggles). These small carvings, often only a few centimetres tall, were used to secure small

**OKIMONO: RATS**
*Masamitsu*
**Wood and ebony; 19th century**

This group of rats climbing over bean pods is a good example of the *netsuke* carver turning his hand to larger works. (*Below left*)

**SEATED DEITY**
*Chinese*
**Wood and gesso; Ming Dynasty (1368–1643)**

This is an early Chinese depiction of a Buddhistic figure seated on a raised throne. (*Below right*)

hanging objects to the *obi* (kimono sash). They were made from many materials, of which the most important were wood and ivory.

*Netsuke* depicted a wide variety of subjects, including scenes from everyday life and animals, which are perhaps the most endearing to the Westerner and whose vigorous rendering on such a small scale is an outstanding example of the wood-carver's art.

In addition to *netsuke*, Japanese carvers experimented with such diverse objects as masks, screens, boxes and miniature shrines. Those created for the home market tended to be of finer quality than those for the burgeoning export market of the 19th century. However, there were some notable exceptions. Some *okimono* (standing things) – table ornaments that could be described as larger versions of *netsuke* and more revered in the West than in Japan – were visually stunning and of fine craftsmanship.

SOME OF THE MOST STRIKING SCULPTURES IN EUROPEAN ART HAVE BEEN
PRODUCED BY WOOD-CARVERS. THE SMALLER PIECES CAN REVEAL AN
EXQUISITE MASTERY OVER THE MATERIAL.

# EUROPEAN WOOD CARVING

Wood has played a part in the making of works of art from ancient times. It was used to create luxury objects in Egypt from the earliest dynasties in the fourth millennium BC, and because of the dry climate much of this work has survived (there are, however, forgeries on the market). Reference is also made in the Bible (*Exodus* 35, 33) to "carving of wood, to make any manner of cunning work" (written, according to modern scholarship, between the 9th and 5th centuries BC).

### DATING TECHNIQUES
The authentication of wood-carving of all periods is fraught with problems. However, there are tests that can help establish the age of a piece. One is dendrochronology, the comparative study of annual growth rings in trees, which has found characteristic patterns, going back thousands of years, in the trees of many given areas. From the style of a wood-carving, its area of origin is often known, and if there is doubt about its age, it may be possible to take a cross-section of its wood and compare the pattern of rings in this with the standard pattern for wood of that area and age. In this way, if the age of the wood is less than that of the claimed date of the carving, then a fake has been revealed. This test is used particularly to date paintings on wood panels, but it

**DEATH OF THE VIRGIN**
*South German*
Polychrome limewood;
**early 16th century**

Figure groups were popularly used as an integral part of church decoration. The fine grain and softness of the wood enabled carver's to achieve fine definition. In carvings of this type, the paint, which deteriorates with age, is often replaced at different periods. (*Left*)

can sometimes also be used on carvings without damage to them.

Another important dating technique is the Carbon-12 test: because wood is an organic material, the molecular structure of its carbon changes with age, and an examination of this can demonstrate the age of the wood.

While providing a date for a given piece of wood, neither test can of course show when it was actually carved. If a carving is painted, analysis of the paint may reveal the period when it was made, but in this case it has to be taken into account that the painting may postdate the carving. Another factor to be borne in mind is that even if the date of a carving has been authenticated by tests, certain parts of it – those subject to breaking off, such as hands and even heads – may be replacements supplied at a later date.

## ATTRIBUTION

During the 19th century, and to a lesser extent in the 18th, there was widespread copying of Gothic wood sculpture, sometimes openly as part of the Romantic Revival but sometimes with deceitful intent. For this

**ST ANNE AND THE VIRGIN AND CHILD**
*Circle of Veit Stross, German*
**c. 1500**

St Anne was the mother of the Virgin Mary and is represented here in a traditional pose. This piece is carved in flat relief rather than in the round. (*Left*)

**ADAM**
*German*
**16th century**

Figures such as this were used to help train artists. (*Above*)

**THE ANNUNCIATION**
*Tyrolean*
**Early 16th century**

The extensive use of gilding is typical of the Tyrol and north Germany on works of this type and period. The subjects are mostly religious. (*Left*)

**MINERVA**
*Netherlandish, the circle of Gabrielle Grupello*
**Late 17th century**

The close grain and hardness of fruitwood enabled the carver to achieve great detail. By the 17th century in northern Europe, the prevailing styles were leaving their Gothic heritage behind and adhering to the more Mannerist ideals employed by goldsmiths and engravers. This sculpture clearly owes much to silversmiths' work of the period. The subjects were also becoming increasingly secular. (*Right*)

reason, it is essential that would-be collectors obtain good advice before buying.

Another area that calls for great caution on the part of the inexperienced collector is that of Renaissance wood figures used as props in artist's studios for the teaching of apprentices. Intended as guides to perfection of form, they tended to be archaic in style, which can make period attribution difficult. These figures have often suffered damage.

The identification of small wood sculptures, particularly those of Germany and the Netherlands, can be made easier by reference to contemporary or later prints and engravings. In the case of the work of the German artist Albrecht Dürer (1471–1528), for example, imitations of his engraved and woodcut work were made in his lifetime, many bearing his distinctive monogram. Whether they were made with intent to deceive we do not know. With the advent of a demand for antique carvings in the 19th century, copies of Dürer carvings were in turn copied. Telling them all apart requires considerable expertise.

## TYPES OF WOOD

The smallest wooden sculptures, such as miniature figures and gaming pieces, tended to be carved from box because, like holly, it is very fine-grained and hard and is therefore suitable for the carving of fine detail. Such small pieces, which tended to have secular or mythological subjects, were used to decorate the German *Kunstkammer* (curio cabinets) that were so fashionable in the 17th century.

The expansion of maritime trade in the 17th century led to many exotic hardwoods finding their way to the studies of European artists. For large-scale work, trees with sizeable branches had to be used. Before the depletion of Britain's oak forests in the 18th century, brought about by the building requirements of the navy, oak was the common wood used for furniture, panelling and the fittings of churches and great houses. It is a very hard wood, and consequently carvings from it have a heavy look and lack fine detail. In Italy, Spain and Portugal, walnut, with its pleasant markings, was in more general use. It was often enhanced by inlay in, for instance, box or bone (which was sometimes stained green). For panelling and furnishing, German wood-workers were particularly fond of lime, a soft but close-grained wood, which could be carved in great detail and in high relief. However, it was the Dutch-born English carver Grinling Gibbons (1648–1721) who realized the full possibilities of lime with his magnificently ornate, detailed and realistic carvings of flowers, animals and other natural forms.

Used more for furniture than carving, the most prized wood of the 18th century was mahogany. There are extant a few carved pieces in this wood dating from the beginning of the 17th century. Yew is very close-grained and hard and was used for the same kind of work as box was. In addition to all these woods, over the past two centuries many that were rare before then have become available to carvers.

A detailed knowledge of timber, such as, for example, the world distribution of tree species, can be beneficial to the collector of wood-carvings. For example, a European piece made from a species of tree known to be limited to Australia cannot be authentic if the carving is in the style of a period before the beginning of the 19th century, because no Australian timber found its way to Europe before then.

**THE VIRGIN AND ST JOHN**
*Attributed to Joseph Matthias Götz, Austrian*
**Polychrome and giltwood; 18th century**

The flowing garments of this pair of figures are typical of the Rococo style at its height in the 18th century. Their almost windblown image is a far cry from the Gothic style. The poses still owe something to long obsolete Gothic ideals, but this is now scarcely discernable. Yet these statues represent a late flowering of a continuous tradition of religious carving. To judge from their size, this pair would have adorned a crucifix in a private chapel.

# ORIENTAL IVORIES

The translucence, hardness and subtle colour shades of ivory have tested the carver's virtuosity since prehistoric times, and the craft has been revered in the Far East for centuries.

## CHINESE IVORY

The indigenous elephants of China had been hunted to extinction by the 6th century BC, and thus ivory had to be imported. This was no problem: China's extensive trade network ensured that the material reached the country's centres of culture.

From AD 1000 Chinese traders were resident in the Philippine Islands, the hub of sea-borne Far Eastern trade. Ships plied between these islands and China, Japan, India, Arabia and various European countries (including Spain, which traded Mexican silver for Chinese goods). The obvious influences of India on China – most notably Buddhism – and of Arabia – as is evident from Muslim inscriptions on bronzes, buildings and sculpture – suggests that Indian and African ivory reached China via this Far Eastern trade network.

Ivory from the elephant tusk was considered the most valuable, but the material also came from the walrus, hippopotamus, narwhal (tusked whale) and even, in fossilized form, the mammoth and Siberian mastodon. Ivory carvers also worked in bone and horn.

Ivory was employed for inlaid decoration and to make a vast range of objects, from the deity statuettes produced in the Ming Dynasty (1368–1643) to the wide variety of pieces created from the mid 17th century to the close of the 19th century. Towards the end, these latter were often produced for export and might most kindly be described as being notable more for their complexity than for their artistic quality.

Carved ivory objects most likely to be familiar to the Westerner are fans, patterned and perforated concentric spheres, dice, combs, snuff bottles and models of junks, pagodas and temples. One of the most notable objects was that

**STANDING FIGURE OF A MALE IMMORTAL**
*Chinese*
Ivory with traces of pigment; **Ming Dynasty (1368–1643)**

The Eight Immortals were born at different times, and the first is thought to have originated in the Chow Dynasty (1027–221 BC). These legendary figures, who achieved immortality through their understanding of Nature, represent all the conditions of life: the male and female, poverty and wealth, youth and age, the learned and the uneducated. They were adopted by the Chinese cult of "The Way"–Taoism.

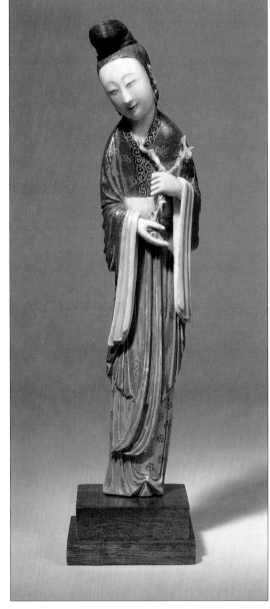

given to Napoleon's wife Josephine, depicting temples, pagodas, bridges and figures in a formal Chinese garden; the piece, now in the Victoria and Albert Museum, London, is 104 cm (3 ft 5 in) high and 84 cm (2 ft 9 in) wide.

Carvings for the home market included calligraphy-brush holders, arm and wrist rests, chopsticks, mouthpieces for opium pipes and cricket cages. Among carved figures were small models of recumbent nude females, used by female medical patients to indicate to male doctors – who were not allowed to examine them – where they felt pain. Even back-scratchers were carved, though for some reason they were usually made from walrus ivory.

Chess pieces were of carved ivory. Once thought to have emerged around the 6th cent-

**PICNIC BASKET**
*Chinese*
Ivory; **late 18th century**

In this intricately carved and pierced piece, technique has taken over from aesthetics. (*Above left*)

**STANDING FIGURE OF A FEMALE IMMORTAL**
*Chinese*
Ivory with polychrome; **late 18th century**

The vivid colouring suggests the flamboyant decoration that was to come in the 19th century. (*Above right*)

ury, chess is now believed to have reached China much earlier, during the 3rd century.

PALACE FACTORIES

The last flowering of Chinese ivory carving was during the reign of the Emperor K'ang Hsi (1662–1722). In 1680 this enlightened monarch established a number of factories within the precincts of his Peking palace. Skilled craftsmen from all parts of the empire were gathered to create a wide variety of items, including ivory carvings. These ateliers were active for over a century but were gradually closed down during the reign of Ch'ien-lung (1736–95).

**Mass production** Canton was the main centre for mass-produced ivory. The scrupulous

# NETSUKE

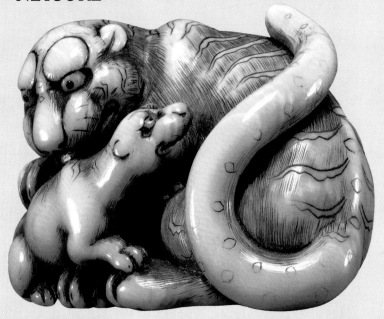

Netsuke were made of a wide range of materials, including ceramics, metal, lacquer, horn, wood and ivory. The forms in which *netsuke* were produced were various. They could be figurative, *manju* (bun-shaped), with variations such as a small shallow bowl with decorated metal lid or very deeply undercut and carved; or of exaggerated length, sometimes modelled as a bean pod or catfish. Religion inspired depictions of Rakhan (disciples of the Buddha), Daruma (the founder of the Zen sect of Buddhism) and the popular female deity Kannon. And from mythology came a legion of demons, ancient heroes undertaking valorous deeds and fabulous beasts, of which the best-known is the dragon.

*Netsuke* subjects from nature included flowers, insects, reptiles and wild and domestic animals. It is the carvings of everyday figures, however, which provide

**VARIOUS NETSUKE**
Ivory; 18th century
(*Above* and *below*)

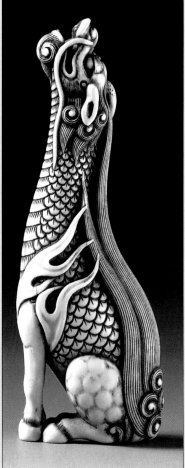

the most fascinating insights into the life of "Old Japan": actors putting on their masks, children playing with animals and geisha girls arranging their hair.

**Dating *netsuke*** Subject-matter was once used as an approximate guide to the age of *netsuke*. It is true that, very roughly speaking, simple pieces were more common in earlier times, that more elaborate animal signs of the zodiac, legendary figures and foreigners were popular in the 18th century, and that everyday subjects, such as birds, animals, flowers and vegetables, were common in the 19th century. However, there are so many exceptions to these guidelines that they should be treated with great caution.

*Netsuke*, in one form or another, have been in existence for hundreds of years. They were first referred to as an individual branch of the decorative arts in the late 1690s, and the first mention of *netsuke* carvers by name appeared in a woodblock book of 1781. In the 19th century, merchants became so wealthy that they, and not the militaristic *samurai*, dictated artistic tastes, and it was around this time that *netsuke* began to be signed as a matter of course rather than an exception. *Netsuke* craftsmen of the late 18th century included Masanao, Yoshimasa and Okamoto of the Kyoto School and, of the 19th century, Garaku, Kaigyokusai and Masaka of the Osaka School.

representationalism and high technical finish of this 19th-century mass-produced ivory leaves nothing to the imagination, unlike earlier works.

### JAPANESE IVORY

With the demise of monumental temple sculpture in the late Muromachi (1392–1573) and Momoyama (1573–1615) periods, Japanese craftsmen displayed their skill in the creation of smaller, everyday items, in particular *netsuke* (toggles). *Netsuke* were used to secure *sagemono* (hanging things) – *inrō* (small medicine or seal boxes) *tonkotsu* (tobacco pouches) and *yatate* (writing implements) – to the *obi* (kimono sash).

### THE END OF ISOLATIONISM

Japan's self-isolation from the rest of the world, begun in the 17th century, ended in 1853, when a US naval squadron under Commodore Perry arrived. The overthrow of the ruling military dynasty in 1868 was followed by the restoration of the emperor, modernization and an assimilation of Western influences. The *netsuke* carver turned his talents to producing items that would sell to the increasing number of overseas visitors. These items, known as *okimono* (standing things), were larger versions of the *netsuke*, used as table ornaments. There was no sacrifice of quality in the carving of some, but many were of indifferent quality and heralded a gradual and general degeneration in Japanese ivory carving.

In modern times the ivory export ban of the late 1980s has virtually dealt a death blow to ivory carving.

**PUZZLE BALL**
*Chinese*
**Ivory; early 19th century**

Supported on a tall stem with figures on the base and finial, this is a good example of the complexity of late Chinese ivory carving. (*Right*)

**OKIMONO: HAWK**
*Signed "Maruki"*
Ivory, bronze and wood; **late 19th century**

*Netsuke* carvers and followers turned their hand to purely ornamental items, such as the *okimono* (standing thing). This fine carving depicts an ivory hawk with bronze legs standing on a wood base; the latter was probably found rather than carved. (*Below*)

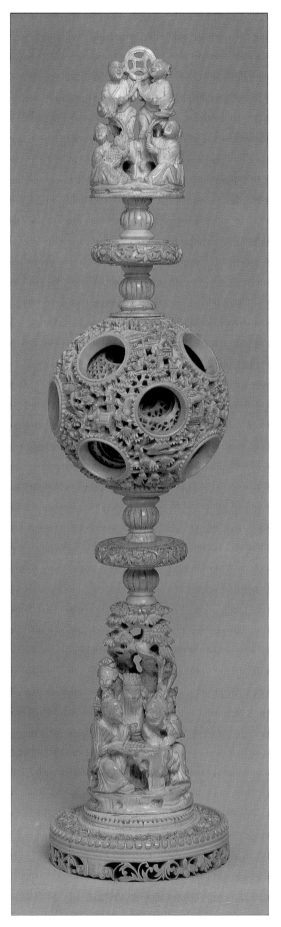

THE INGENUITY OF CARVERS HAS PRODUCED SOME FINE WORK IN IVORY,
WITH OBJECTS RANGING FROM SACRED ALTARPIECES TO THE PROFANE
GROTESQUES MADE FOR THE COURTS OF 17TH-CENTURY PRINCES.

# EUROPEAN IVORIES

**MR FRANCIS
SAMBROOKE**
*David le Marchand*
**1704**

The sitter (b. 1662)
belonged to a family of City
merchants who traded with
Turkey, but was himself a
lawyer. His luxuriant wig
and waxy-looking drapery
are characteristic of Le
Marchand's technique of
ivory carving: here he used
the whole of a tusk to
create a powerfully
modelled portrait bust in
the round, a full 19 cm (7½
in) high. Often initialling his
work "D.L.M.", the artist
was a Huguenot immigrant,
who spent most of his
career in London,
portraying royalty (Louis
XIV, Queen Anne and King
George I), nobility (the
Duke of Marlborough) and
literary and scientific
notables (Pope, Pepys and
Sir Isaac Newton). He also
depicted fellow Huguenot
businessmen and artists.

Ivory is a material with a fine, even grain,
which lends itself readily to carving and
whose surface may be polished to an appealing
gloss. Viking and Anglo-Saxon (and, until our
own time, Eskimo) craftsmen used *morse*
(walrus) ivory. Indian and African elephant
ivory, a rare commodity, was initially imported
to Europe overland along the spice and silk
routes then, from the late 16th century, by ship.

From the solid tip of the tusk can be carved
figures completely in the round; from the
circumference of the lower, hollow part of the
tusk, quite large, roughly rectangular plaques;
and from the remaining slivers miniatures.
Ivories often show traces of the tusk curvature
at their edges or of the browner lining around
the nerve cavity. Together with the just visible
grain, these are good signs by which to check
that pieces are authentic ivory rather than
silanes or bone (the latter has minute pores).

Surviving ivories from the earliest European
civilizations, such as Egypt and Greece, are rare.

From the early Christian era ivory took its place
alongside other precious materials for use in
church services: bishops' croziers, holy-water
buckets, ceremonial combs and other liturgical
items are still preserved in many of Europe's
cathedral treasuries.

## MEDIEVAL IVORIES
In the 14th and 15th centuries the diptych
(a folding, two-leaved miniature ivory altarpiece) was used by pilgrims. The holy imagery
was carved on the inside, within an architecturally ornamented border, and the outside was
left plain. The leaves were hinged together with
iron wire threaded through holes in the borders;
and so, on panels that have become separated,
one should find either traces of the holes, often
discoloured by rust-marks, or repairs at the
relevant places. A small panel without such
features is automatically suspect, for during the
19th century, in Paris, Dieppe and Erbach in
Germany, many fake medieval ivory diptych
panels were produced that today are sometimes
hard for even an expert to distinguish.

As well as diptychs (and triptychs), sizeable
ivory statuettes, especially of the Virgin and
Child, were carved in the Middle Ages and set
into separately carved Gothic shrines. Nearly all
medieval ivories had relief backgrounds and
touches of gilding and bold colour on garments.

## 17TH-CENTURY REVIVAL
During the Renaissance ivory was less popular as
a medium for carving, but it re-emerged in the
17th century. Dieppe now became a great
centre for ivory work, producing secular, as well
as religious statuettes, portrait-medallions and
utilitarian objects such as snuff-boxes.

In the 17th century the voluptuous Baroque
figures of Rubens were reproduced in ivory all
over Flanders and Germany by skilled carvers.
Popular in southern Germany were carved ivory
sleeves for fitting around silver beer-tankards.

The heyday of the ivory portrait-medallion

was at the turn of the 17th century in Dieppe. Jean Mançel (active 1681–1717) was the pioneer, followed by the more sophisticated Jean Cavalier (d 1699) and by David le Marchand (1674–1726), a Huguenot *émigré* to Britain who produced deeply carved relief portraits as well as busts, statuettes and groups.

### MODERN IVORIES

From the early 19th century, ivory, becoming readily available and therefore less expensive, has been used in successive stylistic movements: its pure, whitish gleam appealed to both Neo-Classical and Art Nouveau taste. For much of the 19th century it was used for historical-revival pieces, which appealed to the bourgeois taste of the day.

In the 20th century ivory has been especially favoured in France, Germany, Central Europe and the USA, between the World Wars, and, was much used for decorative figurines to ornament the mantelpiece .

**TANKARD WITH BACCHIC SCENES AND A LADY IN 18TH-CENTURY COSTUME**
*French school*
**19th century**

These two ivories are typical of the bourgeois taste for historical revival themes, which was quite out of touch with the Industrial Revolution and contemporary art. (*Above*)

**STATUETTE OF THE VIRGIN AND CHILD**
*French school*
**Last quarter of 13th century**

The curving and conical form of this Gothic group is dictated by the natural shape of an elephant's tusk. (*Right*)

WHILE IN CHINA BRONZE WORKS WERE HELD IN HIGH ESTEEM FROM
ANCIENT TIMES, IN JAPAN THE BEST QUALITY WORKMANSHIP APPEARED IN
THE 19TH CENTURY, IN RESPONSE TO EUROPEAN INTEREST.

# ORIENTAL BRONZES

The Chinese Bronze Age spanned *c.*1500 BC to *c.* AD 200. Surviving examples of Chinese bronzes are among the most outstanding objects from the ancient world; they include utilitarian wares, particularly weapons and chariot fitments, and ritual vessels buried with the dead, an indication of the esteem in which bronze was held.

### CHINESE SHANG VESSELS
It was during the Shang period (18th/16th century–1028 BC) that the best Chinese bronze wares – wine and food vessels – were made. The earliest recorded descriptions of them occur in books of the Han dynasty (206 BC–AD 23),

**GU**
**Shang dynasty**

This archaic Chinese bronze wine vessel is 29cm (11½ in) high. (*Below left*)

**TOKYO BRONZE GROUP**
*Signed Teidagawa Sho-o*
**c. 1900**

This large and appealing Japanese subject is 57 cm (24 in) high. (*Below right*)

which ascribe functions to each type of vessel, but there is no guarantee that these later attributions were correct. By the Song dynasty (960–1279) these ancient bronzes were being collected and venerated.

Most Shang vessels were probably cast using the *cire-perdue* (lost-wax) process (in which the wax original is destroyed in the casting process). Other examples were cast using direct moulds. Some are plain, relying for effect on their massive proportions, but most have complex ornamentation, mainly in the form of highly abstract leaf-like motifs, animal or human *taotie* (masks) and, in particular, tight scrollwork. The linear decoration is generally deeply carved.

Handles are more decorative than functional, except for overhead swing handles on *yu*, a baluster-shaped, covered food vessel. Masks are so abstract that many are barely recognizable, with their large bulging eyes, scroll noses and outlines that wander off into complex scrolls.

Some vessels have vestigial handles in the form of rabbit or deer heads. The most frequently encountered forms are the *jue* (a wine

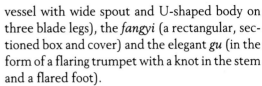

**KAKUHINBA OTEIROKU**
*Miya-o*
Bronze with gilt details;
**c. 1900**

This figure of a Japanese warrior is 67 cm (28 in) high.

vessel with wide spout and U-shaped body on three blade legs), the *fangyi* (a rectangular, sectioned box and cover) and the elegant *gu* (in the form of a flaring trumpet with a knot in the stem and a flared foot).

Some of the vessels bear inscriptions or pictograms – mostly in untranslatable archaic script – recording family names, makers and the form of the vessels. More rarely they indicate that the piece was a royal gift.

### OTHER CHINESE BRONZES

The other main category of early bronzes was the mirror. This was thin and circular and had no handle, but there was usually a central pierced suspension boss on one side, surrounded by cast dragons, scrollwork or other motifs. The reverse was highly polished.

Through centuries or even millennia of burial, many early bronzes have acquired a rich patina in tones of green, silvery grey and coppery red; the value to the collector lies in the depth and subtlety of the patina.

During the Ming dynasty (1368–1644) and later, bronze was used mainly for incense burners or charcoal room-warmers. The former were often of depressed circular form and had two small loop handles and three stub feet. Most, though they bear the six-character reign mark of the Emperor Xuante (1426–35), were made in the 19th century.

### JAPANESE BRONZES

The Japanese did not have a bronze age equivalent to that of China. Indeed, bronze was not a highly regarded metal, except for the making of Buddhist statues. Iron had more appeal, and the Japanese achievement in sword blades was unsurpassed. Bronze did, however, appear in fittings for the sword hilt and on the scabbard, usually inlaid with gold, silver or other metals.

Bronze in Japan was at its best during the 19th century under European influence. After the opening up of Japan to the West in 1853, the country soon began to produce works of art for Western consumption, including bronze vases, some very large for international exhibitions. These are true *tours de force*, cast with foliage, dragons, animals and figures. Later, at the end of the century, under the influence of the Tokyo School of Art, bronze-sculptors cast superb animals and human figures, often with gilt decoration and with a fine red-brown patina. The best-known of these artists is Miyao, noted for his gold and silver inlay work.

SMALL BRONZES PROVIDED A MEANS FOR SOME OF EUROPE'S MOST
NOTED ARTISTS AND SCULPTORS TO CREATE BEAUTIFUL OBJECTS
OF LIGHTNESS AND GRACE TO ENHANCE THE HOMES OF THEIR PATRONS.

# EUROPEAN BRONZES

Bronze is an alloy of copper and tin, in a ratio of approximately 9:1; but these proportions vary with date and place, and deliberate admixtures of zinc, lead or silver also occur. The higher the copper content, the softer the alloy is and the easier to work.

The simplest technique of casting is to make from a model a pair of hollow moulds of fine sand, held in two boxes. These are tightly joined, leaving only a funnel for the molten metal to be poured in. After cooling, the boxes are separated and the solid object in alloy is removed, the funnel (now of solid metal) is sawn off and the surface is cleaned.

More useful for fine art work, and probably developed in Europe by goldsmiths in the late Middle Ages, was the process known as *cire-perdue* (lost-wax). This enables an artist to model figures with greater undercutting, and with a more ambitious projection of limbs into space. The sculptor makes a model in fireclay and coats it with a "skin" of wax as thick as the wall of bronze is to be. Into the soft wax he models every detail he wants in the metal casting.

At this point the model was often handed over to specialist foundrymen to replace the wax skin with a bronze one. Then the sculptor himself again became involved, since the raw casting needs after-working, or chasing, to create the texture that is so aesthetically important. This involves incising details with a chisel, or varying the way the metal reflects light by hammering, punching, filing or polishing. The choice of techniques was often particular to an artist, and so enables his work to be identified almost as surely as if it were signed.

After chasing, the metal has a bright, natural colour, which, if left alone, will naturally oxidize like a penny. To preserve the golden colour, a clear lacquer may be applied. The surface may also be gilded, or treated with acid to give various colours – for example, sulphuric acid gives green. At times – for example, in Padua during the Renaissance – a rich, black varnish

was applied to darken the surface. This tends to rub off on the high points, and the exposed metal then gains a natural chestnut colour, all of which gives the classic "Old Master" patina.

In general, earlier bronzes were heavily cast, in a coppery alloy, and were unique. Later bronzes had thinner, lighter walls, and an alloy with more zinc (akin to brass) was used. This permitted virtual mass-production and has led to the world market being flooded with many identical artefacts.

THE RENAISSANCE

The early years of the Italian Renaissance (*c.* 1420–30) saw the reappearance of bronze statuettes, a type of sculpture that had barely existed during the Middle Ages. They may have been produced at first as fakes to supplement the number of genuine antiquities then being excavated and collected. Free-standing statuettes gradually emerged from quasi-architectural contexts, such as niches on shrines, to become objects of art in their own right. They represented in miniature things dear to their Renaissance owners, such as famous antiquities, patron saints and favourite animals.

Copies or variants of surviving antiquities were the nucleus from which the statuette evolved during the first century of its existence. The earliest datable examples were made in Florence by Donatello (1386–1466) and his partners and reflect the interest of his patrons in mythology. However, the most imposing example · is a rendering by the architect-sculptor Filarete of the monumental gilt-bronze equestrian statue of Marcus Aurelius in Rome.

**The influence of Donatello** In each city where Donatello worked he founded a tradition of sculpture in bronze: in Rome he was followed by Filarete; in Florence by Verrocchio (1435–88), Pollaiuolo (1431–98) and Bertoldo (1420–91), all of whom tended to produce statuettes of muscular male figures; in Siena by Vecchietta (1412–80) and Francesco di Giorgio

**APOLLO BELVEDERE**
*Antico*
Bronze, partly gilded, silver eyes, initialled; **1490s**

This is a miniature copy of an actual ancient marble statue in Rome, and is very rare in being signed by its maker. (*Right*)

**HERCULES RESTING**
*Antonio Pollaiuolo*
Bronze; **1460-70**

This statuette, now in the Bode-Museum, Berlin, is characteristic of the early Renaissance interest in classical heroes, and in showing the muscular nude body. (*Right*)

(1439–1501/2); and in Padua by a team of skilled assistants, some of whom, such as Bellano (1435–96), became famous in their own right.

The most gifted exponent of the bronze statuette (arguably of all time) was Andrea Riccio (*c.* 1460–1532), who recreated in Padua a whole world of classical nymphs, satyrs, handsome nude shepherd boys, animals, monsters, weirdly shaped lamps, grotesque masks and erotica.

The third great Paduan sculptor in bronze was Severo da Ravenna (active 1496–1525),

**KNEELING SATYR**
*Severo da Ravenna*
**Bronze; c. 1500**

Mythological monsters were popular as supports for inkstands, but the functional parts were cast separately. (*Above*)

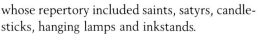

**FLYING MERCURY**
*Giambologna*
Bronze; *c.* 1570-80

This brilliant statuette was given by the Medici as a diplomatic gift to the Habsburgs, and is now in the Kunsthistorisches Museum, Vienna. Its outflung limbs exploit the tensile strength of bronze. (*Below*)

whose repertory included saints, satyrs, candlesticks, hanging lamps and inkstands.

In Mantua, at the court of the Gonzaga, Antico (1460–1528) used the technique of buffing his nude figures to a high polish, darkening them, then ornamenting them with partial gilding and sometimes even inlaying their eyes with pure silver.

## MANNERISM IN ITALY

During the High Renaissance less attention was paid to the production of statuettes, owing to the obsession of the greatest sculptor of the day, Michelangelo (1475–1564), with marble carving. Upon his departure from Florence in 1534,

artists again turned to the statuette as a medium for self-expression.

Around 1540 Bandinelli (1488–1560) made a series of bronze statuettes based on ancient Roman statues; and Cellini (1500–1571), a goldsmith by training, also produced statuettes. A classic series of eight statuettes was commissioned around 1570 to fill niches in the Palazzo della Signoria, Florence: the various nude gods and goddesses show the varying styles and capabilities of the eight sculptors, among them Giambologna (1529–1608), who produced an extremely Mannerist Apollo.

**Giambologna and Susini** Giambologna combined Michelangelo's skill in composition with a mastery of modelling for casting. His earlier statuettes are unique, or cast in only a few examples, but he later delegated production to Antonio Susini (active *c.* 1580–1624). The repertory of Giambologna/Susini extended beyond the traditional confines of mythological characters, to include animals and elegant genre figures, such as *The Bagpiper* and *The Shepherd.* The models were cast and recast for over half a century in the Florentine workshops of Antonio Susini's nephew Gianfrancesco (*c.*1575–*c.*1653) and by Giambologna's successors as court-sculptor to the Medici Pietro and Ferdinando Tocca.

**Sansovino and Vittoria** With the arrival in Venice of Jacopo Sansovino in 1527, a veritable flowering of bronze sculpture occurred there: reliefs, statuettes and portrait-busts poured from the foundries, involving a host of craftsmen, of whom the greatest was Alessandro Vittoria (1525–1608). Vittoria managed to amalgamate Sansovino's suavity of modelling with the pent-up energy of Michelangelo.

## RENAISSANCE IN NORTHERN EUROPE

Bronzes, being portable, served to spread a direct knowledge of the Renaissance from Italy all over Europe. The French in particular would have come across them when they invaded Lombardy *c.* 1500, and Francis I subsequently employed the Italians Cellini and Primaticcio to cast bronzes for his new palace at Fontainebleau. Native sculptors began to employ bronze for monuments and also created statuettes as a by-product; among them were Ponce Jacquiot (*c.* 1515–72) and Prieur (1536–1611). A great tradition was thus founded in France, and it has continued until this century.

In southern Germany, especially in Nuremberg, bronze statuettes to adorn table-fountains

**VENUS AND CUPID**
*Tiziano Aspetti*
Bronze; late 16th century

Bronze groups such as this come in pairs and were used as finials on large andirons. This example has been detached from its ornamental base. (*Right*)

**VENUS DRYING HER FOOT**
Barthelemy Prieur
Bronze; **c. 1600**

Prieur was a French contemporary of Giambologna. He produced many statuettes like this, of attractive female nudes doing their toilettes.

**SAPPHO**
*James Pradier*
**Silvered bronze, cast by
Victor Paillard; 1848**

*(Top left)*

**LA DANSE**
*Jean-Baptiste Carpeaux*
**Bronze; after 1869**

Carpeaux modelled this
group for the façade of the
Paris Opéra. *(Top centre)*

**THE JEWISH GIRL OF
ALGIERS**
*C.-H.-J. Cordier*
**Bronze, partly gilded and
enamelled, with amethyst
and onyx; dated 1863.**

The exotic subject and
mixture of materials are
typical of French sculpture
of the time. *(Above)*

and inkwells were manufactured by Peter Visscher the Younger (1487–1528). In Augsburg and Munich, about 1600, a distinct school of bronze-sculptors emerged. Several had worked in Florence with Giambologna: Adriaen de Vries (1545–1626); Gerhard (*c.* 1550–1620) and Reichle (*c.* 1570–1642). De Vries became court sculptor in Prague to the Emperor Rudolf II.

### THE BAROQUE IN ROME AND FLORENCE
An interesting innovation of the Baroque period in Rome was that statuettes were often cast from sculptors' working models. There are examples from the studios of Gianlorenzo Bernini (1598–1680), Alessandro Algardi (1595–1654) and their associates. In Florence the tradition of producing independent small bronzes was deliberately revived in the 1680s by the Medici family. Foggini (1652–1725) and Soldani (1656–1740) produced figures in violent motion or in languid, swooning poses which

after casting were built up into dramatic compositions, with landscape settings, and given ornamented bases and stands.

### 17TH- AND 18TH-CENTURY FRANCE
The outstanding 17th-century French sculptor of bronze statuettes was Michel Anguier (1612–86). In 1652 he modelled a series of six classical gods and goddesses, which were much reproduced at various scales.

In the 1660s and 1670s a team of sculptors and founders was established to furnish Versailles with statuary, mostly to the designs of Charles Le Brun. Almost all of these were reproduced on a domestic scale, with exquisitely wrought detail. Individual statuettes – some with genre subjects – abounded. The Versailles school used a reddish alloy with a high copper content, enhanced by a translucent reddish or golden lacquer.

During the Neo-Classical and Empire periods French bronzes were technically superb, in both casting and chasing as, for example, in the vast output of Thomire (1751–1843), whose impassive figures were incorporated into chandeliers, tripod stands and clocks.

## THE 19TH CENTURY

After the Napoleonic Wars and the emergence of the Romantic Movement, French sculptors supplied models with popular appeal to the entrepreneurs running bronze-foundries on an industrialized basis, such as Barbedienne. Medieval, Renaissance and ethnic figures became popular, and the surface of the statuette was often gilded, enamelled or otherwise coloured. This helped to disguise the substitution of spelter (cheaper base-metal alloys) for bronze. Genuine articles were stamped *"vrai bronze"*. Even so, most of the great sculptors avoided such excesses of bad taste.

David d'Angers (1788–1856) and François Rude (1784–1855) were the two French pioneers of Romantic sculpture, and many of their compositions were popularized by reductions in bronze: the latter's *Neapolitan Fisherboy* (1831) became one of the icons of the movement. Dalou (1838–1902) won many commissions for public monuments, and his statuettes are mostly by-products of them; most appealing are his studies of peasants and labourers.

## THE ANIMALIERS

One manifestation of Romanticism was the depiction of animals, preferably in dramatic confrontations. Beginning in the 1830s, Antoine-Louis Barye (1796–1875), earliest and greatest of all the *animaliers*, produced a series of spirited studies of exotic beasts in combat, which brilliantly translated fur, feathers and hide into bronze. P. J. Mêne (1810–79) preferred domestic or hunting animals; Moigniez excelled in depicting birds.

In the 20th century, this popular field has attracted two major exponents, the Italian Rembrandt Bugatti (1884–1916), whose animals have wittily abstract forms, and the American Herbert Haseltine (1877–1962), even more abstract.

## THE LATE 19TH AND EARLY 20TH CENTURIES

In England there was no tradition of bronze sculpture until, in the Victorian era, a deliberate attempt was made by the Art Union of London to foster it. The finest result was *Queen Victoria on Horseback* by Thomas Thornycroft (1853), a reduction of a monumental statue.

Between about 1870 and 1920, there flourished the New Sculpture school, parallel with the Continental Art Nouveau movement. Alfred Gilbert (1854–1934), its most celebrated exponent, produced bronze male nudes, such as *Perseus Arming* and *Comedy and Tragedy*. In the same vein were *Teucer* by Hamo Thornycroft (1850–1925) and *Athlete Wrestling with a Python* by Lord Leighton (1830–96).

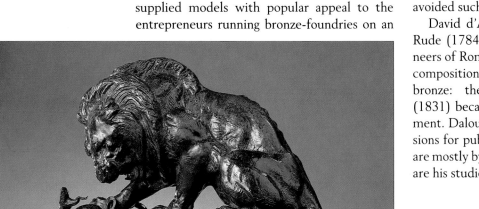

**LION AND SERPENT**
*Antoine-Louis Barye*
**Bronze; c. 1840-50**

One of the sculptor's earliest compositions, this epitomizes the enthusiasm of his period for the romance of savage beasts in conflict. (*Above*)

**ICARUS**
*Alfred Gilbert*
**Bronze; after 1884**

The subject was a tragic figure of Greek mythology, son of Daedalus, who made him wax wings. Icarus flew too near the sun, his wings melted and he was killed. The style of Gilbert recalls the sensuous representations of male nudes by Donatello and Cellini. (*Right*)

THE CRAFTSMEN WHO WORKED JADE WERE SHAPING SOME OF THE
HARDEST MINERALS ON EARTH. THEIR EXQUISITE PRODUCTS ARE A
TESTAMENT TO DELICATE SKILLS AND HARD WORK.

# CHINESE JADE

The term jade is used to describe two mineralogically distinct stones: nephrite (silicate of calcium and magnesium) and jadeite (silicate of aluminium and sodium). In the long history of Chinese art, nephrite, slightly softer than jadeite, is the more important. It was used in China from the fourth millennium BC and accounts for more than 90 per cent of all known jade. Jadeite, on the other hand, seems to have been introduced into China no earlier than the 18th century.

At its most recognizable, nephrite is a pale, translucent green, usually with cloudy areas within, but it can range in colour from almost white to spinach green, brown or black. Sometimes the translucent green includes a more opaque green, creating a marble-like stone. The colour of jadeite is, at its best, a brilliant emerald green, sometimes suffused with an almost amethystine purple. Rust brown can sometimes be seen on jadeite objects, where a section of the outer surface of the pebble from which it has been cut has been retained for emphatic contrast.

## JADE-WORKING

Jade is an extremely hard mineral. The amateur's test for ascertaining its genuineness is to use a penknife on it: unlike serpentine, bowenite and other softer stones, it cannot be scratched. Because it is so hard, it cannot be carved and has to be ground into the desired shape. In Neolithic times a quartz-containing limestone was used for grinding; later corundum, a mineral second in hardness only to the diamond, was used.

In the fourth millennium BC the Chinese used jade to make implements, masks and other objects. Some of these were decorated with elegantly incised designs of consummate artistry. Over the centuries the ancient techniques of working jade improved through the development of such abilities as drilling straight-sided holes. The history of ancient jades is a study in itself, in which the dating of objects can be

corroborated by archaeological evidence.

**Decorative forms** From very early times designs depicting birds were common. But most decorative motifs were based upon knowledge of animal life.

Even though some decorative patterns became increasingly complex, the means of effecting them became increasingly simple. Thus, whereas in Shang art of the 12th century BC the outlines of forms are indicated by a raised thread produced by carving a line on either side, by the 8th century outlining has been simplified to the use of a groove of which one side is less vertical, more inclined than the other. Again, the surfaces of jade in the period of the Warring States (480–211 BC) are for the most part profusely covered with a complicated arrangement of elaborate comma shapes, but by the Han period (206 BC–AD 220) these have been simplified to rows of smooth protuberances.

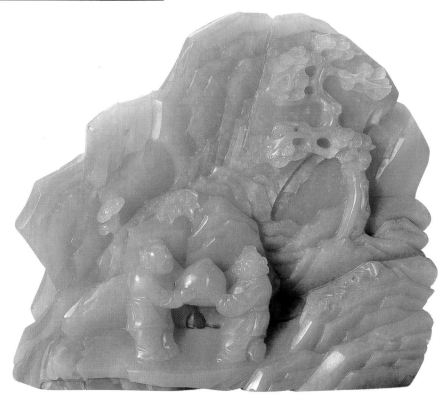

**BOULDER CARVED TO
REPRESENT A
MOUNTAIN
Late 17th or 18th
century**

The mountainous landscape includes two boys holding a vast peach symbolizing "happiness". In the background there is a gnarled pine tree, one of the "three winter friends" and a magic *lingzhi* fungus, emblem of longevity. The white flecks of the nephrite have been skilfully used to suggest mist and cloud. The other side represents rocks and the brown "crust" of the stone has been left for added effect.

**CUP**
**Song/Yuan period,**
**before 1320**

The cup is formed as a peach, the handle as its branches, with a long-tailed bird. The Song period was the first in which plants became a principal feature of decoration. (*Right*)

**COILED DRAGON**
**Late Shang Dynasty,**
**c. 12th century** BC

In this circular pendant the dragon is biting its own tail.

The seemingly raised lines are equivalent to those on ritual bronzes cast into clay moulds. (*Above*)

**APPLIQUE**
**Neolithic, 3rd**
**millennium** BC

This humanoid representation must be among the earliest from the period of China's prehistory. (*Left*)

**MYTHICAL BEAST**
**Six Dynasties, 3rd–7th century**

Fierce beasts carved in the round were subjects of great appeal at the same time as the arrival of Indian sculpture in China. (*Above*)

**TRIBUTE BEARER**
**Tang/Song period, 7th–11th century**

This fellow is a foreigner, with his big nose and curly hair. He brings a boulder as tribute. Such a stone would presumably have been jade from its source on the Silk Road, along which there was a flow of culture and merchandise during the Tang Dynasty. (*Above*)

In the last two millennia of Chinese jade carving, naturalistic forms vie with archaistic yearnings after the past. Animals, both real and mythical, are depicted humorously, especially during the foreign influenced Tang period. In the Song period (AD 960–1279) flora join fauna as decorative motifs. The problem for the antiquary or collector trying to date individual pieces of antique jade is that decorative subject matter is no guide to period, since, despite the introduction of new themes from time to time, the old are never discarded.

**Historical times** The principal source of jade in historical times seems to have been Sinkiang (Chinese Turkestan). Nephrite was found in forms of various sizes, ranging from boulders to rounded pebbles, and these determined to a great extent the subject of the jade work. For example, a boulder could be used to represent a mountain and lightly worked to include small figures, whereas a pebble was more suitable for representing, say, a small animal.

From the 17th century the availability of jade seems to have increased enormously with improved methods of recovering it from deposits. Many jades of the Qing (Manchu) period (1644–1911) are extremely large, allowing full play to that dynasty's preference for complex designs on a single plane. Subjects, such as small animals, buffaloes with waterweeds and groups of boys, continue to be well worked, but the execution is perfunctory.

The skills of the ancient Chinese craftsmen persist into modern times, and, with the availability of sophisticated modern grinding and polishing techniques, outstanding jades to rival those of the past are produced. Even the most perspicacious expert can find it difficult to demonstrate that they are not the antiquities they seem to be.

THE CONSIDERABLE VERSATILITY OF LACQUER ALLOWS FREE REIN TO THE
ARTIST'S CREATIVITY, ENABLING THROUGH DILIGENCE AND PATIENCE THE
MAKING OF SOME EXTRAORDINARILY INVENTIVE PIECES.

# ORIENTAL LACQUER

Lacquer is the sap from the tree *Rhus verni-cifera*. When applied to objects it forms a hard, tough, lustrous varnish, and, used as a decorative pigment, it is perhaps the closest the Orient gets to Western oil painting.

The method of extracting lacquer sap from a tree is similar to that of tapping rubber: an incision is made in the trunk and a cup collects the sap. This is white but turns black on contact with air and has to be purified and strained before use.

There are various lacquering techniques, but all are basically similar. A coating of lacquer is applied to every surface of the object to be treated, which is usually of wood. Left to dry, it is then ground smooth, another layer of lacquer is applied and smoothed, and so on, until the coating is many layers thick – a lengthy and arduous process. This would explain why good lacquer work was expensive and thus the prerogative of the rich.

The reason lacquer has always been sought-after is that it is so durable. Lacquer utensils

**INRŌ**
*Japanese*
Gold lacquer ground; **late 19th century**

This example of late Japanese lacquer work, richly embellished with frogs, demons and flora, is in the flamboyant style known as Shibayama. An *inrō* is a sectionalized medicine box hung from the sash. (*Above*)

**SUZURIBAKO**
*Japanese*
Gold lacquer; **early 19th century**

The *suzuribako* is the writing box containing the essential implements for the revered art of calligraphy, including a brush and inkstone. This example, richly decorated in a variety of techniques, depicts a Chinese-style landscape. (*Left*)

were much used because of their resistance to acids, alkalis, most solvents, heat and damp. It is said that the material accompanied the Chinese from cradle to grave: they were fed with lacquer spoons from lacquer vessels and buried in a lacquer coffin.

The early history of lacquer is hidden in the mists of time, but it is thought to have been first used as far back as 2000 BC. One of the oldest examples on public display is the winged pedestal cup attributed to the late Chou Period in China (5th-4th century BC), in the Freer Gallery of Art, Washington.

## CHINESE LACQUER

Early Chinese craftsmen generally produced bold shapes and decoration, but from the Ming Dynasty (1368–1643) onwards decoration became more ornate. It is from this period that the Chinese produced their famous carved red lacquer, probably the most familiar Chinese lacquer in the West, especially the boxes and plates. Ming lacquer is considered to be the finest that China produced – though some superb pieces were produced later.

The Emperor Ch'ien-lung (1736–95) is reputed to have been particularly fond of lacquer; one of the multitude of objects he commissioned was a magnificent throne, now in the Victoria and Albert Museum, London.

## JAPANESE LACQUER

Brilliant though some Chinese lacquer work was, it was the Japanese who perfected the art. Thought to have come to Japan from 6th-century China, probably through Korean craftsmen, lacquer was initially used by the Japanese for religious sculpture.

It was the perfection of the *maki-e* (sprinkled picture) technique that initiated a truly distinctive Japanese lacquering style. The essence of *maki-e* was that the design was sprinkled in gold or silver dust on a coat of wet lacquer brushed on to a previously applied and dried ground of

**PAVILION BOX**
*Chinese*
Red lacquer and gilt bronze;
**18th century**

A fine example of the red
lacquer technique
perfected by the Chinese,
this piece possibly depicted
one of the court pavilions
and would have been made
as an important gift for a
high-ranking nobleman.
(*Right*)

**TEA JAR**
*Japanese*
Pewter, gold and red
lacquer; **mid 19th
century**

This is a rare example of
pewter decorated with
various lacquer techniques.
The "floral" emblems are
Japanese *mons*, or crests. It
is in the form of a lidded jar
that would normally be
made of ceramic. (*Below*)

lacquer. This decorated layer was then ground
smooth. The process was repeated many times,
one decorated layer after another being built up
until the desired effect was achieved: a speckled
appearance called *nashiji*. Small pieces of furniture, sword scabbards and boxes were made
with this method.

It was during the Edo period (1615–1868),
when Japan was isolated from the West, that
lacquer artistry reached its zenith. Such masters
as Kōrin (1661–1716) and Ritsuo (1663–1747)
were encouraged to exercise their imagination,
and they and their followers produced extraordinary *inrō* (medicine boxes) *suzuribako*
(writing cases) and *kogo* (incense containers).

As was the case with most Far Eastern art,
Western influences in the late 19th century led
to decadence in lacquer work. But some of even
the most outrageously flamboyant lacquer
wares could not conceal the exquisite artistry
developed over the centuries. Late-19th-
century visitors to the newly opened-up Japan
were fascinated by its arts and crafts, and many
of the fine American and European lacquer collections were created around that time.

ONE OF THE OLDEST AND MOST ENDURINGLY POPULAR OF DECORATIVE

TECHNIQUES IS THE DELICATE ART OF ENAMELWORK, WHICH

CHARACTERISTICALLY PRODUCES PIECES WITH A RICH BLEND OF COLORS.

# ENAMELS

Enamelling (fixing powdered glass, coloured by means of a metal oxide, to metal) has been used as decoration since prehistoric times. One of the earliest techniques used was cloisonné, in which compartments are formed by soldering thin metal strips, usually of gold or copper, on to the metal object, filling these with glass paste and firing at 750–800°C to fuse the enamel to the metal. Cloisonné was popular in late-19th- and early-20th-century Japan.

The *champlevé* technique, familiar to the Celts and Romans, involves putting the powdered glass into hollowed-out depressions on the surface of the piece, then firing it. Medieval German and French reliquaries and liturgical objects were often decorated with *champlevé*.

In *basse-taille* (low-relief) enamelling, which originated in medieval times, translucent enamels are fired over a low-relief design engraved into the metal. From the mid 18th century the technique was used to decorate costly gold snuffboxes, bonbonnières (sweet boxes), étuis (cases for small articles) and watch-cases, mostly of French or Swiss workmanship. *Basse-taille* was also used to great effect by the Russian jewellers and goldsmiths Fabergé in the late 19th and early 20th centuries.

*Émail en ronde bosse* (encrusted enamelling) was another medieval technique and was used on Renaissance jewellery all over Europe. In *plique à jour*, also introduced in medieval times, the metal backing is removed from cloisonné work to leave a transparent enamel plaque. It was used extensively in late-19th-century Europe for bowls, spoons and dishes, and for jewellery, particularly by French makers such as René Lalique (1860–1945).

## PAINTED ENAMEL

The most common enamelling technique in 18th- and 19th-century Europe was painted enamel, originally developed in the 15th century. Fine painted enamel dishes, ewers and plaques were made in Limoges in the 16th and

**SNUFF-BOX**
*Michel-Robert Hallé (or Hallet), Paris*
**Gold, chased and enamelled; 1750**

Luxurious snuff-boxes such as this, with its decoration of *basse taille* enamel for the foliage and trellis and painted enamel for the flowers, were often intended as presentation pieces.

17th centuries. These enamels, commonly depicting mythological and biblical subjects and the seasons, often reveal a subtle use of grisaille (greyish tints) and flesh tones. The reverse surface of dishes and plaques was coated with a colourless enamel to prevent distortion in firing.

Painted enamels probably spread to England from France in the late 17th century. In the mid 18th century the technique, together with printing on enamel, was developed in London, Birmingham, South Staffordshire and Liverpool. Between 1745 and 1770 there were at least 25 enamellers working in London, and many miniaturists also worked in enamel. Finely painted flowers on a white ground, similar to those found on contemporary Chelsea porcelain "toys" (such as scent-bottles and étuis), are often attributed to London. Birmingham specialized in larger containers, such as tea caddies, caskets and knife boxes. In the

**CASKET**
*Birmingham, England*
Enamel on copper, painted;
mounts of engraved gilt
metal; **c. 1755**

The scene is based on a
painting by Antoine
Watteau of a gallant
subject, "Pour garder
l'honneur d'une belle, c'est
trop peu de Pierrot pour
faire une sentinelle" ("To
guard the honour of a
beautiful young woman,
Pierrot is too poor a
sentinel"), engraved by
Cochin the Younger. (*Left*)

**BOX AND SPOON**
*Fabergé, Moscow*
Gold, enamel; **c. 1910**

The spoon is typically
Russian in form, and the
filigree work with *en plein*
enamelling in a
characteristic palette was in
widespread use in Eastern
Europe. The painted
enamel scene on each
depicts a medieval boyar
(nobleman). (*Below left*)

**PLAQUES**
*Battersea, London*
Enamel on copper, painted;
mounts of engraved gilt
metal; **c. 1753-6** (*Below*)

Birmingham suburbs of Bilston and Wednesbury
many small boxes with charming inscriptions,
card trays, thimbles and other small-scale enamelled items were produced between *c.* 1760 and
1840. In Liverpool theatrical and political
subjects were printed in deep brown or black on
plaques by John Sadler and/or Guy Green from
1749 until 1790.

### ENAMELLING IN MODERN TIMES

Watch-case enamelling was carried out on a
grand scale in Geneva throughout the 18th century and at least up to 1850. Filigree enamel, a
variant of cloisonné in which the enamel is held
between beaded or twisted wires, was popular
in Eastern Europe and Russia in the 19th century. Painted enamels decorated the large jugs
and caskets made in Austria in the second half
of the century. Old techniques were revived in
the late 19th and early 20th centuries, and
enamels continue to fascinate contemporary
artists and craftsmen.

TORTOISESHELL, WITH ITS RICH HUES AND DISTINCTIVE TRANSLUCENT

QUALITY, HAS ALWAYS OFFERED AN ATTRACTIVE MEDIUM FOR CRAFTSMEN,

WHO GUARD CAREFULLY THE SECRETS OF THEIR TECHNIQUES.

# TORTOISESHELL

Tortoiseshell is in fact made from the shells of turtles – normally from the Hawksbill marine turtle found either off the coast of Brazil or in the Seychelles in the Indian Ocean. The plates on the back are mottled in amber, dark brown and red; those on the belly are blond or yellow and, especially in Japan and Spain, traditionally used for fashioning women's combs, because they stand out decoratively against brunette hair. Its pleasant touch and attractive lustre have made it a much sought after treasure of the sea for thousands of years. The Romans imported it from the East and tortoiseshell has been used for inlay work on furniture and small decorative articles ever since.

For the craftsmen it is a most rewarding material to work in. Individual "flakes" or plates of the shell can be selected for colour. With the application of heat through boiling in brine it becomes malleable and individual scraps of shell can even be welded together to almost any desired shape by nipping the joint wrapped in wet linen rags with red-hot iron pincers.

**BOOK COVER**
Tortoiseshell and silver;
**early 18th century**

Only about 6 cm (2½ in) square, this example of piqué work has flowers and foliage inlaid in tortoiseshell with silver mounts. (*Right*)

**SEWING BOX**
Tortoiseshell veneering with pewter stringing and ivory outline; **1800-30**

The hinged chamfered lid has a central glazed inset with a locket of hair that is complemented by the blond tortoiseshell. (*Below*)

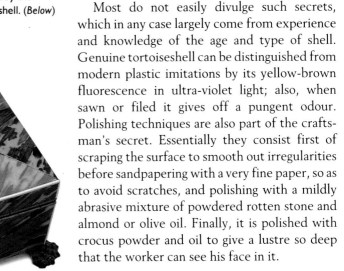

Most do not easily divulge such secrets, which in any case largely come from experience and knowledge of the age and type of shell. Genuine tortoiseshell can be distinguished from modern plastic imitations by its yellow-brown fluorescence in ultra-violet light; also, when sawn or filed it gives off a pungent odour. Polishing techniques are also part of the craftsman's secret. Essentially they consist first of scraping the surface to smooth out irregularities before sandpapering with a very fine paper, so as to avoid scratches, and polishing with a mildly abrasive mixture of powdered rotten stone and almond or olive oil. Finally, it is polished with crocus powder and oil to give a lustre so deep that the worker can see his face in it.

### BOULLE WORK
A single plate of shell can be split or sawn into several veneers and used to inlay furniture. The technique for inlaying tortoiseshell with brass and other metals applied to furniture decoration

**STATIONERY CASKET**
*J.C. Vickery, London*
**Boulle work; 19th century**

This handsome box, measuring 23 × 16 cm (9 × 6½ in), shows the revival for the fashion of boulle work in the Victorian period. (*Left*)

**TOBACCO RASP**
Tortoiseshell and silver; **late 17th–early 18th century**

This piece features silver-mounted piqué-work birds, masks and a cartouche engraved "Souvenir". It is 12 cm (5 in) in length. (*Below*)

originated in Italy in the 16th century. By the 17th century it is found in Germany and in the Low Countries, and in the 17th and 18th centuries in France and England.

The technique was most highly developed by André-Charles Boulle (1642–1732), who was appointed master *ébéniste* to Louis XIV in 1672 and made much of the furniture for Versailles. Boulle work was fashionable in England during the 18th century and was a popular style of decoration on longcase clocks.

From the 1820s onwards tortoiseshell received a revival in popularity and with automation of the cutting process Victorian reproduction of the Boulle style came back into vogue for a range of decorative articles.

The tortoiseshell barrette or hair slide came into fashion in the late 1870s to hold the fashionable "Catogon" plait or braid of hair in place at the nape of the neck. This gave way to more flamboyant hair decoration with high Spanish-style combs that became popular after the

first production of the opera *Carmen* in 1875. Victorian combs were invariably tortoiseshell.

Tortoiseshell was used especially as an elaborate and very attractive decoration for bracket clocks with the shell plates either applied in natural colour or, less commonly, stained. Victorian reproduction boulle veneering also appeared on writing stands, correspondence bases and other bureau accompaniments.

Tortoiseshell was even more extensively used for objects such as snuff boxes or toilet articles, often with piqué ornament (a form of inlay) in the form of piqué pose (fine gold or silver strips) or piqué points (points with tortoiseshell and ivory forming the design). Piqué decoration applied to a tortoiseshell base was popular for the outer cases of English watches in the late 17th century.

Tortoiseshell had a long lasting vogue for the backs of mirrors, brushes and combs and imitation tortoiseshell continued to be very popular for dressing table items well into the 1930s.

THE SURPRISING VERSATILITY OF PAPIER MACHE IS BORNE OUT BY THE
VARIETY OF OBJECTS – FROM TRAYS AND DISHES TO LARGER ITEMS SUCH
AS STOOLS, TABLES AND FIRE SCREENS – MADE FROM THIS MATERIAL.

# PAPIER MÂCHÉ

The art of making decorated articles from paper pulp is known by the French words "papier mâché", which literally translated mean mashed paper, but the technique's origins are oriental rather than French. Although introduced into England by French immigrants in the 1600s, paper-making originated in China, where the technique of moulding the pulp into small boxes and containers subsequently japanned or lacquered and decorated in typically oriental fashion was well known.

The only detailed information concerning the making of papier mâché is from English texts. The famous scientist Robert Boyle (1627–91) had noted that in Japan people had a method of making bowls, plates and other vessels from paper and sometimes sawdust, and in 1732, with the help of Boyle's notes, J. Peel developed a method of mashing and boiling brown paper into a pulp and mixing with gum so that it could be pressed and moulded. From the 1750s English production was mainly the work of a few individuals making small quantities of pulp products such as gilded wall brackets, sconces and ornamental mirrors.

Descriptions of similar techniques being used in other countries are scanty or nonexistent. The Duke of Brunswick, Karl I (1735–86) introduced English techniques to Germany, and set up a factory managed by George Sigmund Stobwasser (b.1740) in 1763. A list of goods dated 1780 shows there were nearly 1,300 objects produced – not only snuff boxes, but tables, chests and plates. Stobwasser's signature began appearing on his snuff boxes in 1800.

## NEW METHODS
In 1772 Henry Clay of Birmingham patented the method of producing heat resistant paper board that was capable of being handled like wood and stove dried without fear of warping. Panels were made from laminated sheets of unsized paper glued on a metal core or mould. Flow line production involved women and girls

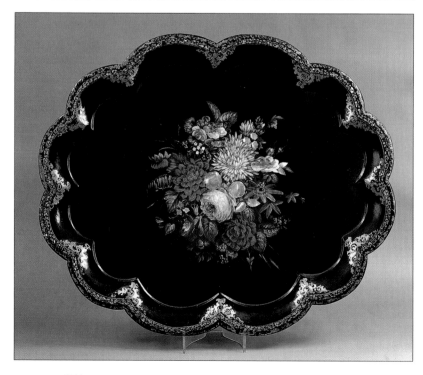

## SNUFF BOX
### c. 1800

The 8.8-cm (3½-in) diameter lid is painted with a portrait of a bearded Turk. (*Right top*)

## TRAY
### early 19th century

This late Regency example, 78 cm (31 in) wide, features fashionable oriental decoration. It is stamped "CLAY KING ST., COVT. GARDEN". (*Left top*)

## SNUFF BOX
### early 19th century

This interesting box is inscribed "Les Adieux de Fontainebleau" and shows Napoleon, beneath the Tricolour, taking leave of his officers in the courtyard. It is 8 cm (3¼ in) in diameter and is inscribed "Stobwasser's Fabrik in Braunschweig". (*Right bottom*)

## TRAY
### Papier mâché, gilding and mother-of-pearl; 19th century

The lobed outline has been heightened with gilding and inlaid in mother-of-pearl with a typical mid-Victorian spray of flowers. (*Left bottom*)

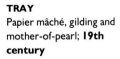

seated at tables cutting paper to size and passing it on for pasting where each sheet was carefully smoothed by pressing it with a trowel-like tool to remove air bubbles. The edges were then trimmed and the panel soaked in linseed oil to make it waterproof before drying at a temperature of around 38°C. The panel then was planed and smoothed. Colouring followed and the panel received repeated stovings to fix the layers of opaque japan varnish that were finished by hand polishing.

Little more than trays and panels were made until 1816 when Clay's successors Jennens & Bettridge produced an endless variety of small wares and in 1825 patented a method of inlaying mother-of-pearl. In 1846 they patented a further technique for applying steam to soften the panels and make them pliable enough to mould to virtually any shape.

During the 1830s the English method of producing papier mâché was used in Russia. The Lukutin family at Fedoskino, near Moscow, were the most successful producers of papier mâché. They produced boxes, chests and trays marked with a double eagle within an oval.

In the 1830s Richard Brindley developed a method of shaping wet sheets of pulp between dies in a cheaper process capable of turning out ornamental architectural mouldings and building up stools, fire screens, table desks and work tables. The distinctive curves of the chairs and footstools were made possible by the lack of grain, which enabled the material to be shaped at angles impossible to achieve in wood.

A number of examples of such furniture appeared at the Great Exhibition of 1851. This was the high period of popularity for papier mâché, when techniques were developed for painting it to imitate malachite, blue john, coloured marbles and agates that are very difficult to tell from the original.

### GLITTERING FINISH

Finishing papier mâché was an art form in its own right. Glittering finely ground metallic powders or bronzes were used from 1815 onwards and went well with oriental motifs such as temples, trees and pagodas, which were very much in vogue from 1825 onwards. A method of bronzing known as the Wolverhampton style, which contrasted sun and shadow in attractive Gothic atmospheric scenes of sunlight streaming through pillared church interiors, appeared about 1855 and continued through until about 1860 with aluminium and silvery moonlight cloud edgings.

Oil painting, particularly of landscapes with sporting and coaching scenes, is common on trays dated from the 1780s until the 1820s, when these tend to give way to colourful flowers with backgrounds of bamboo, palms, grasses and butterflies. Floral decoration went through various fashions from early conventional designs to the more flamboyant styles of the 1830s against black japanned backgrounds.

By 1850 flower painting had become very vivid and set against backgrounds of white, yellow and green. Peacocks and sea shells were specialities of Frederick Norman. Gilding appeared very early in the century and remained fashionable for allegorical and oriental scenes.

Genuine landscape paintings on papier mâché panels can be of fine quality and were originally intended for interior decoration. By the 1860s, however, decoration had become vulgar and overdone.

MANY ITEMS USED IN THE HOME OR THE WORKPLACE – TODAY MADE OF
PLASTIC, CARDBOARD, OR METAL – MIGHT IN PAST TIMES HAVE BEEN MADE
OF WOOD. THEY MAKE A COSY CATEGORY OF ANTIQUES.

# TREEN

A medieval term meaning "made from the tree", treen denotes any small domestic object, such as a goblet, made from wood. The key word in this definition is "small". To qualify for the description treen, items need to be of a size that can easily be transferred from place to place. Domestic items are the most common form of treen.

Britain was the major producer of treen, and most of the items available to the collec-

**COUNTRY COLLECTION**
Fruitwood, sycamore, walnut and beech; **late 18th to mid 19th century**

This assortment includes three butter moulds and a rare butter scoop with an amusing hand handle.

tor today are British, dating from the period 1650–1900; anything earlier is extremely rare.

### A RURAL SOCIETY
Seventeenth-century British culture was insular. Large numbers of people never strayed from the village of their birth. Families would eat off circular wooden plates for generation after generation. Even though they may have heard of pewter, it would never cross their minds to

**WASSAIL BOWL**
Lignum-vitae; **c. 1680**

Such bowls – this one is initialled "DF" – are highly regarded. The rarest bowls also have a cover, spice pot and dipper cups. (*Left*)

**COTTON REEL STAND**
Mahogany, boxwood, ebony and ivory; **c. 1820**

Special features are the three tiers, which revolve, and the ivory decoration. (*Right*)

change from cheap, readily available utensils to new, more expensive ones. What new ideas were assimilated were brought to rural areas by itinerant labourers and gypsies. Industry was in its infancy – it would be another 200 years before its influence was felt throughout the land and cottage industries thrived. What country people needed, they made themselves. And what material was more available and extensive than wood?

Seventeenth-century treen consisted of a wide and assorted range of objects, including the thimble, spinning wheel, dipper cup, used to dip into a wassail bowl, candlestick and miniature domestic fire engine (a box on wheels with a pump). The woods used might be soft or hard and the objects plain or decorated. Vast numbers have been catalogued in museums, but there exists an even larger number of unrecorded items made by unknown loving hands with care and precision.

The very earliest treen pieces discovered today are generally religious. One such is the mazer (a shallow ceremonial cup), made of bird's-eye maple and with a silver rim, used in monasteries and the wealthier parish churches. Inventories and wills date mazers to the 14th – 17th centuries.

Every large estate and country house would have had a wassail bowl (used for hot spiced ale). These bowls – also known as lamb's wool bowls, because of the froth on top of their contents – were at the height of their popularity in the mid 17th century, when large numbers were made; few exist today, however. Most other early items found today were also associated with drinking: this was an important social activity, and the type of vessel the host offered his guest reflected his social standing. All the woods used, such as lignum-vitae, were of the finest quality. The giving of drinking vessels was popular, and decorative wooden goblets were highly prized. Whether the gift was a loving-cup (one passed round at the end of a feast for all to

drink from) or a royal standing cup, it was preserved with care.

For collecting purposes, treen breaks down into three main types of item: formal, country and decorative.

### FORMAL TREEN

Formal and decorative treen is best described as for "upstairs use", as opposed to the "downstairs use" of country treen. A well-appointed middle-class Georgian house of the late 18th to early

**COLLECTION OF SMOKING AND SNUFF ACCESSORIES**
Various woods and brass;
**first half of 19th century**

During the 18th and 19th centuries smoking was extremely popular, and its accessories were of a wide variety of designs and materials, including treen. The figure at left is called "The Bürger" and dates from c. 1840. The rarest of the figure tobacco jars, it is hinged at the waist, lined and used for storing tobacco. The tall clay-pipe stand (now holding modern pipes) is Dutch, and its mahogany base is lined with brass. An elegant piece of smoking "furniture" from c. 1820, the stand would have been found in the home. The lignum-vitae covered jar on the right, c. 1820, is a snuff container that would have been used in a shop. The finial unplugs, allowing a little snuff to be poured on to a tray, and the main cover breaks two thirds of the way up the body of the jar. The pipe case lying at the front of the group is simple and elegantly made in mahogany, with a brass hinge on the bowl cover; it dates from c. 1820.

19th century would have had a considerable amount of treen, as an imaginary walk from room to room will show. In the book-lined study are several turned mahogany candlesticks, and on the large desk stands an impressive rosewood double inkstand with a matching rosewood-veneer blotting pad. Alongside are a pounce pot (for sprinkling ink-absorbent powder), scrivener's knife (for cutting pen nibs), paper knife and quill holder, all of wood. Beside the chair in front of the fire is a smoker's wooden compendium consisting of tobacco jar, snuff pot, pipe stand, match strike and tobacco stopper. On the mantlepiece stand a pair of wooden spill vases and a collection of engine-turned (made with the help of machinery) decorative items. A folding set of library steps rests against the bookshelves. On the table lies a gallery glass, a large rosewood-framed magnifying glass with an elegantly turned long handle, for studying the paintings on the wall. Next to the glass is a simple telescopic bookstand for supporting the catalogue of the room's books. The warmth and colour of the woods used blend with those of their surroundings.

The dining room is again lit by candlelight, but this time the wooden sticks are taller and more impressive, with bronze finials. On the sideboard stands a pair of mahogany, string-inlaid knife boxes and Chippendale gallery mahogany oval tray and bottle coasters (small

trays). On the dining table is an extremely rare set of sycamore roundels (decorative plates) – one side of each is plain wood, off which to eat; on the reverse is inscribed a song, and at the end of the meal the guests will each sing a verse (hence the term roundelay). At each end of the table is a collection of spice pots with covers and delicately turned mahogany open table salts (cellars), and in the centre of the table is a revolving mahogany tray for sweet dishes. (If it were 200 years earlier there would

### SEWING ACCESSORIES
Walnut, boxwood and ivory; **19th century**

### SEWING ACCESSORIES
Walnut, boxwood and ivory; **19th century**

The tall item is a rare Regency sewing urn, while the boxwood cup is a mould for a purse and the central spiral is for threads and ribbons. At right is a walnut sewing box of c. 1840. (*Below*)

### CANDLESTICKS
Various woods, bronze and brass; **18th and 19th century**

The rarest of this group is the tripod-foot mahogany pair with bronze sconces at left, c. 1775. At front centre is a Georgian mahogany pair with bronze thistle sconces and in front of these is a pair with walnut twist carved base and brass sconces, c. 1860. The tallest sticks are walnut with a thick twist and wood sconces (c. 1860), while the short cannon-barrel sticks, from c. 1840, are of rosewood. (*Left*)

be trenchers (early plates), goblets of lignum-vitae and there would be a far more robust look to all the accessories.)

The withdrawing room is filled with wooden treasures collected on the owner's travels. Sitting in the hearth is an elegantly carved pair of walnut bellows; by the chairs nearest the fire are delicately decorated hand-held, individual fire screens and on a side table stands an impressive burr-walnut tea-caddy. (Containers of all descriptions – lap desks, paint boxes, sewing boxes, vanity boxes – were a passion of 18th-and 19th-century householders.) In one corner is a sewing chair, surrounded by wooden sewing accessories – bobbins and lace wheels, sheaths for knitting needles and reel stands. A fragile-looking French walnut spinning wheel with ivory finials stands to one side, more for decoration than serious use. On the other side of the room is the games table with a corner cupboard

## DOMESTIC LEATHER

From the earliest times leather has been used for garments, purses, saddles, scabbards and book covers. In the domestic sphere water "bougets" (containers for carrying water), bottles, jacks, buckets and tankards were made from leather.

Leather was prepared and worked by many different trades. In London the "bottellers" were operating as a guild in the 14th century but by the 16th century the Cordwainers were also making leather bottles. Throughout Britain and Europe, the wide availability of hides meant that leather was worked in most local communities. Leather goods were sold at local markets and fairs. In Britain during the 17th century Northampton and Walsall developed as major centres of leather working.

Two types of leather bottles or black jacks predominated from the 16th to the 18th centuries. The first, a barrel-like container, was known as a "bottell", the other was a baluster-shaped measure known as a "Jack".

All such vessels were shaped over a wooden form, on which the leather was softened with steam. Sides and bases were cut into shape and together with any seams

were sewn up with thread. They were then sealed with pitch and blackened on the outside; hence the term "black jack". Tankards with silver mounts also occur but unless the silver is hall-marked, the mounts may not be original.

**LIDDED BALUSTER-SHAPE "BLACK JACK"**
*English*
**17th century**

**KITCHEN ACCESSORIES**
Various woods; **17th to 19th century**

The mortar and pestle here, of elm and fruitwood, date from c. 1760. Corkscrews came in a wide range of styles; this c. 1860 example is of fruitwood, as is the late 17th-century spice grinder in the centre. The two boxwood spice towers, c. 1850, comprise 5-cm (2-in) boxes that screw on to each other. Towers can be found with three to six sections, and they should have their original contents labels. On the right is a c. 1820 wine funnel of yew wood, with a fine patina. In front is a large, decorative lemon squeeze with a silver-plated hinge and sieve; it dates from c. 1880. (*Above*)

full of intricately carved wooden games – chess, a horse racing game, a card sheaf containing a pack of cards, roulette wheels, shove-halfpenny boards, indoor skittles, a zogroscope designed to look at specially prepared prints, a bilboquet (an early game of catching a ball on a stick) and many other amusements.

### COUNTRY TREEN
Going downstairs to the kitchen and work-rooms, we find country treen: grinders, crushers, stirrers, receptacles and other utensils. The design and type of wood chosen for each piece have evolved over the centuries to best fit the job for which it is intended. The woods are not as rich as those found upstairs, but their colour and grain, especially after years of hard wear, are still decorative.

The large kitchen area has a central pine table, where pastry-making is in progress – sycamore bowls of flour, rolling pins, boards and measures stand ready. For the finishing touches, there is an array of fruitwood pastry markers and pie and gingerbread moulds. The wall shelves are packed with mortars, graters, coffee mills and spice towers (a unit of five cylindrical sections each containing a separate kind of spice) made from lignum-vitae, elm and box-wood. A chopping table is covered with wooden cutters (a wooden handle on a blade) and slices (a board with attached wire) for bread, cheese and vegetables. There are wooden squeezers for fruit and nippers for sugar.

In the scullery, dirty plates are stacked ready for washing in a pair of mahogany plate buckets;

standing in a corner are scrubbing boards and washing dollies (a tool for stirring washing); hanging from the walls are salt boxes, spoon racks and candle boxes. On the larder floor, next to the grain bins and dry-store jars, are two strange boxes with sliding doors, weights and pulleys and a piece of cheese at one end – crude but effective mousetraps. By the wine-cellar door stands a display of turned wooden wine funnels and corkscrews.

### WOODS USED
The woods used were chosen very carefully to suit the finished article's use. The wood turner

**ASSORTED PIECES**
Various woods;
**19th century**

From left to right are: three boxwood medicine-bottle holders; an ash string barrel; a cider costrel; two Scandinavian chipped carved boxes. Also pictured are a pillbox, three willow butt bowling balls, a Welsh love spoon and a beech ladle. (*Above*)

**GOBLETS**
Various woods; **early 18th to early 19th century**

At far left and right are rare, early 19th-century burr walnut goblets of classic design; they were made more for decoration than use and represent the glory of wood, with its simple, natural beauty. The oak goblet in the middle copies an earlier style. The smaller goblets are of coquille nut and have decorative fret metal handles and feet; the pair dates from *c.* 1720. (*Left*)

### TOBACCO JARS
Carved wood; **c. 1860**

Both the night watchman and the drinking monk hinge at the right to reveal lined tobacco jars. (*Left*)

### ASSORTED PIECES
Various woods;
**19th century**

In the group are a pair of hard wood bottles and a pair of rosewood rose vases; an olive wood travelling candlestick; a burr walnut and two lacquered tea caddies; a fruitwood wool winder; and a gavel and spice pot of mahogany. (*Below*)

would base his decision on the wood's grain, its density, its oil-retention and other qualities. For the treen collector, lignum-vitae will always have a special appeal. This wood was first brought into Britain in the 16th century: cargo boats returning from the West Indies were usually relatively empty and needed ballast, and it was discovered that lignum was ideal for the purpose – retaining a large percentage of its oil, it was extremely dense and heavy. If the turner had the patience and strength to work through lignum, the end result was breathtaking. It consisted of a basic dark grain shot with vivid yellow or green flashes.

The woods used for treen changed over the years, according to fashion. During the Queen Anne period (1702–14) walnut was the most popular wood; for most of the rest of the century it was mahogany and oak; at the turn of the century rosewood was the favourite; then, as the Victorian reign and the British Empire

flourished, every kind of wood was used: padauk from Burma, snakewood from South America, redwoods from North America, hardwoods from Africa, softwoods from the East. But by the end of this era, hand-turned wood had become a less desirable medium for small artefacts – early plastics were beginning to flood the market and the age of mass-manufacture was well under way.

### OTHER PRODUCERS OF TREEN

Other countries produced treen – though to a lesser extent than Britain – particularly those in the northern hemisphere, with a ready supply of timber. Sweden and Norway had a unique style of treen that used a lot of birch. Many pieces are finely chip-carved or painted. Dutch treen was very similar in style to that of Britain. Germany (in particular the dense Black Forest region) and Switzerland both made a considerable amount of treen, most of it highly decorated with intricate carvings and often extremely ingenious –

**DINING-ROOM TABLE ITEMS**
Various woods;
19th century

The items include three pairs of turned open salt cellars in mahogany and rosewood, as well as, at centre right, a lignum-vitae salt with engine-turned decoration. Above and below this is a pair of coquille nut salt and pepper pots. At centre right in the back is a carved wine-bottle coaster, and at centre back is an olive wood caster. At left is an oak spice pot and in front are a carved dog nutcracker and a burr walnut coaster.

for example, carved figures that opened to reveal a lead-lined tobacco jar, and nut crackers carved with animal heads and grotesque human heads. France and Italy, although renowned for their carving, made very little treen; their domestic items were mainly pottery. Treen from southern Europe was usually made of olive. A particular Italian speciality was Sorrento-ware – objects, for example, boxes, fans, and picture frames, decorated with inlay of brightly coloured wood. During the 19th century olive wood souvenirs from the Holy Land also began to be collected. One of the more common items was a travelling candlestick known as the "Brighton bun".

Treen was taken to North America by immigrants and there took the form of folk art. Most of the production was country treen; formal treen was imported from Europe.

Apart from wood, two other materials were occasionally used for treen – coconut and coquilla nut (from the Brazilian piassava palm).

# WALKING STICKS

For the collector of walking sticks – or canes, as they are sometimes also known – there are two main periods of interest. One is the 17th and 18th centuries, when a walking stick denoted wealth and importance. The other period is the 19th and early 20th centuries, when carrying a cane was more a matter of fashion; by the late 19th century more than 30 firms were listed in the London area alone as manufacturers of walking sticks, parasols and similar items.

### MATERIALS USED

The two constituents of the walking stick are the handle and the shaft. The former was always the show-piece of the stick: ivory, gold, silver and porcelain were the chief materials used in earlier times. In the 19th century a much greater variety of materials was used, including tortoiseshell, carved woods, enamels, ivory and steel.

Certain rules applied to the shaft. A Malacca cane, with a light brown, strong shaft made from the stem of a climbing palm, was considered most suitable for day use; a hardwood shaft, usually ebonized, was the chosen type for evening use and special occasions. In addition, the country dweller often had sticks carved from other types of wood. The average well-to-do citizen would probably have had at least a dozen sticks in all. Many women carried a light delicate cane as an accessory.

### CHANGING STYLES

The earliest sticks that collectors are likely to find today are the so-called Piques, fashionable in the second half of the 17th century and the early 18th. They had an ivory handle inset with a pattern of silver studs that often incorporated the owner's initials and date of manufacture.

The walking stick often incorporated another function. For example, swordsticks were in use from the 17th century, and in the emerging scientific age of the early 19th century adaptations of such useful items as telescopes, musical instruments, watches,

**PIQUE**
Ivory and silver; *c. 1690*
(*Below far left*)

**MALACCA CANE**
*c. 1770* (*Below left*)

**VICTORIAN CANES**
(*Below left to right*)
Ivory dog head with silver collar; *c. 1870*
Drinking cane; *c. 1880*
Lady's cane; *c. 1860*
Crook handle; *c. 1899*

**TELESCOPE HANDLE CANE**
Compass inside; *c. 1860*
(*Below right*)

**9mm GUN CANE**
Covered with Malacca; *c. 1880*
(*Below far right*)

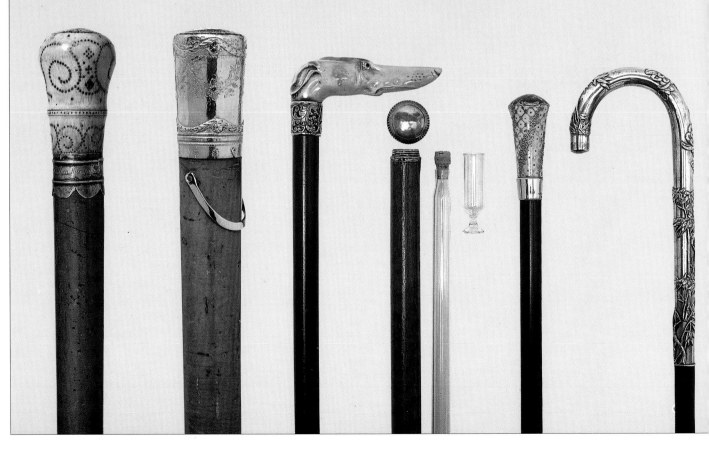

snuff-boxes, microscopes and pistols were all designed to fit into the average cane (Illus. 3).

From about the 1840s the fashion for sticks from the Near and Far East resulted in the import of many Turkish, Indian, Chinese and Japanese handles, which were then usually fitted by the stick-maker to a shaft of the customer's choice. In both Europe and America the decorative handle became more elaborate.

Europe remained the leader of fashion and by the end of the 19th century was producing an enormous variety of canes (Illus. 4). In America the cane was no longer a symbol of class. A Sears Roebuck catalogue of 1897 advertises a "gold-handled" (actually gilt) evening cane for $4.45.

### PARASOLS AND UMBRELLAS

Parasols have been used to provide protection from the sun since antiquity, but it was not until the 18th century that they became an object of high fashion. The French court created the vogue for carrying parasols at most times and this led to their wider practical use in the next century. The popular

folding carriage parasol was delicate and often beautifully made, with elaborate silk, lace and cotton covers. Unfortunately, it tended to deteriorate badly with age.

The umbrella as we know it today started to become prevalent during the early 19th century. As with canes, many variations and improvements were designed, notably the steel frame of Henry Holland in 1840 and that of Samuel Fox (still in use today).

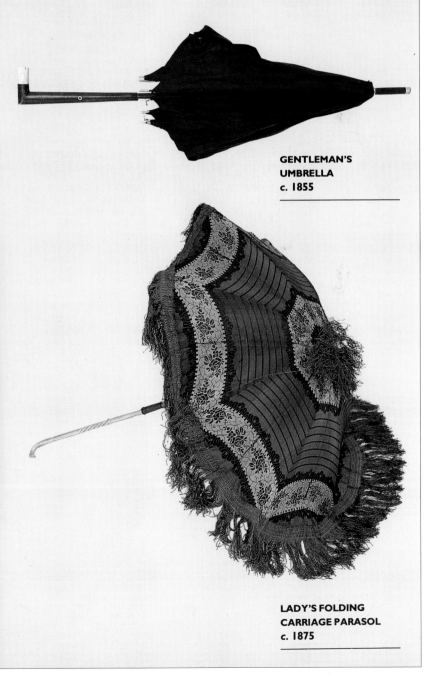

**GENTLEMAN'S UMBRELLA c. 1855**

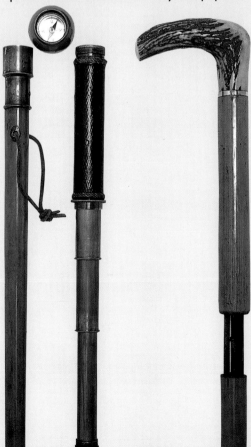

**LADY'S FOLDING CARRIAGE PARASOL c. 1875**

**A** VARIETY OF COMMON HOUSEHOLD OBJECTS – POTS, KETTLES, LADLES,

CANDLESTICKS – MADE IN PART OR ENTIRELY FROM DIFFERENT KINDS OF

METAL PROVIDE A VIVID TESTAMENT TO THE HOMES OF DAYS GONE BY.

# DOMESTIC METALWARE

Over the centuries a wide range of non-precious metals has been used to fashion vessels and utensils for domestic use. The principal materials discussed here are copper, brass, bronze, paktong, pewter, tin and iron.

### COPPER

Copper is difficult to cast but easy to hammer into shape and consequently it was generally used in sheet form. After an item had been shaped by craftsmen it was, if necessary, seamed to make it watertight.

Throughout the Middle Ages the main domestic use of copper was for hearthware – most commonly for cettles (large vats for boiling water) and wort pans (used in brewing). Copper became increasingly popular in the 18th century, when it was used for cooking utensils and other kitchen tools.

Although factory methods were adopted in the 19th century, most copper items were made by individual craftsmen in small workshops, and these would have been found in every town where there was a local demand.

Until the 17th century all copper used in Britain was imported from Europe. In the USA copper was mined and smelted in limited quantities in the 18th century and some copper and brass wares were made.

### BRASS

Brass, an alloy of copper and zinc, was used in homes from the 15th century. The lack of mineral zinc (not discovered until the late 18th century) meant that calamine (zinc carbonate) powder had to be employed in brass manufacture – a lengthy, wasteful and costly process. Until the 1770s copper would not absorb more than 30 per cent of calamine, and most items made before then have a low zinc content.

Brass has the advantage over copper that it is easily cast and harder and thus lends itself to more elaborate shapes. Until the 19th century it was cast in sand or clay moulds, but from then

**SKILLET**
**Lead-bronze; 17th century**

These would be used for cooking over an open fire. The handle is plain but many examples were inscribed. (*Right*)

**ALMS DISH**
*Nuremberg*
**Copper alloy; c. 1500**

This design is known as the "Seated Lady". Bowls of this form were used at table for cleaning the hands between courses. (*Below*)

on some was made in iron moulds. The first widespread use of brass in the home was for candlesticks, but by the 18th century a great variety of objects was being made for daily use. Some were initially silvered.

The major centres of brass production included Augsburg, Nuremberg, Dinant, the Low Countries, and later Sweden and Britain.

## MORTAR AND PESTLE
*Edward Neale (mortar)*
**Brass; c. 1660**

Small mortars such as this were used for grinding herbs and spices. Meat, fish or grains were ground in larger examples.

By the 1780s mineral zinc had become available, and as a result the production of brass expanded greatly. Bristol was the first main centre of activity in Britain, but by the 1850s Birmingham had become the leading producer of domestic brass in the world.

### BRONZE

Bronze, an alloy of copper and tin, has many excellent properties. It is easily cast, is hard and will withstand higher temperatures than brass. It was used for many domestic objects, mainly cooking utensils for the open hearth. Most common before 1750 were cooking pots and skillets (long-handled pans), but candlesticks and mortars (vessels in which substances were pounded) were also popular.

Bronze was cast in sand or clay moulds. Production was centred on the same areas that made domestic brass. The choice of brass or bronze by the manufacturer was partly dictated by the availability of calamine or tin and partly by the function of the object.

In Britain bronze was made in London by members of the Founders Company and else-

where by individual craftsmen, but after 1700 its scale of production was far more limited than that of brass. This was mainly because the discovery of mineral zinc and of effective iron-casting techniques made both brass and iron cheaper than bronze.

### PAKTONG

Initially an alloy of copper and nickel used in China, paktong, which has a silvery look, was imported both in the form of a limited range of completed objects and later, in greater quantities, as an alloy to be worked up in Europe. The proportions vary, but it is a copper-based alloy with zinc and nickel added.

Paktong was used for decorative objects, such as candlesticks, grates and fire irons, and most items were constructed in current silver styles. The use of paktong continued into the 19th century but was relatively unimportant after 1800.

### PEWTER

Throughout Europe the word for pewter is the same as that for tin, and it is only the English who coined a separate name for this alloy of tin and other elements. Pure tin is brittle and difficult to cast, but with the addition of other

**CANDLESTICK**
Brass; c. 1740

Most brass candlesticks followed the styles set by silver examples. (*Above*)

**COOKING POT**
Lead-bronze; 16th century

The join where the two halves of the outer mould came together is seen clearly. The decorated feet became plainer in the 17th century. Some pots were very large and were often used to supply hot water. Smaller versions were employed to make sauces. (*Above*)

metals, most commonly lead, copper or antimony, or any combination of these, it becomes easy to work and more robust.

Roman pewter had as much as 60 per cent lead in it, but from medieval times nearly all the craft guilds, which controlled pewter production in Britain and Europe, adopted similar standards for top-grade pewter, based on a high percentage of tin (over 90 per cent), with strict limits on lead and other metals. Copper was widely used as a constituent of pewter until about 1720 but seldom amounted to more than 10 per cent. Antimony was employed in France in the 16th century but not in Britain until almost 1700; it seldom accounted for more than 5 per cent of any pewter alloy.

Pewter was usually cast in iron or bronze moulds and then hammered to give it additional hardness. The alloy cannot be used near heat because of its low melting point but it was employed in the home for serving food and drink, lighting equipment and many other functions. The most commonly made objects were dishes, chargers, plates and saucers, but candlesticks were also popular until the 18th century.

In the 19th century pewter for domestic use faced heavy competition from pottery, brass and silver plate, but it continued to be used in taverns, and many tankards and mugs survive.

In the 1770s Britannia metal was developed. This is a hard, lead-free pewter, differing from

**CHARLES I FLAGON**
*"EG"*
**Pewter; c. 1625**

Most flagons were used in the Communion Service.
*(Right)*

**GROUP OF PEWTER OBJECTS**
**17th century**

The tankard with a flat lid is decorated with wriggle work. The candlestick, from the reign of Charles II, has an octagonal base with a low drip tray. The style of the Scottish pint pot belly measure originally evolved in the Netherlands. The small bowl and swirled stem of the capstan salt are typical of the 1690s. *(Left)*

pewter in its method of production rather than its composition. Sheets of the metal were bent round a wooden master held in a chuck and spun on a lathe. Many 19th-century Britannia metal tea and coffee pots still exist.

Pewter was nearly as common in homes of the 17th and 18th centuries as plastic is today. Most pewter-making was carried on by individual craftsmen; Britannia metal was made in the larger factory units that emerged in the 19th century.

### IRON

From the earliest times iron was worked by tens of thousands of individual blacksmiths, who heated, forged and beat it into a variety of

**COFFEEPOT**
Toleware; **early 18th century**

Not everyone could afford domestic wares in silver and porcelain, so sheet-tin articles, like this one from Massachusetts, with asphaltum varnish and bright hand-painted or stencilled decoration, provided a homely alternative. Toleware centres included Connecticut, Vermont, Pennsylvania, New York and Massachusetts. (*Below*)

**SPOONS**
Pewter; **18th century**

The spoon with the anchor and initials "GH" is from Greenwich Hospital. The portrait spoon is of George III and Queen Caroline. (*Below*)

weapons, tools and domestic items such as ladles, flesh hooks, knives and skimmers. Iron was, however, hard to cast, due to the presence in it of excess carbon and other impurities, and it was not until the invention of the coke-smelting process by Abraham Darby in the early 18th century that iron could be cast effectively and cheaply. Thereafter, throughout the 18th and 19th centuries, cast iron was used widely. The most commonly surviving items today are rounded pots, mortars, grates and stoves.

### TIN

Although brittle and hard to work, pure tin was used to make domestic objects. In the late 18th and the 19th centuries it was especially popular in the USA.

In the 18th century tin was also used in the form of tinplate (thin sheets of tin applied to a very thin iron base), and articles made in this were known as tinware. They were often painted and varnished to resemble Toleware (enamelled or lacquered ironware). The principal centres of tinware production were Pontypool and Usk in Wales, Germany and, in the 19th century, the USA, especially New England.

## FURTHER READING

The following list of materials for further reading offers a broad range of literature. Both specialist and general works are included. While every effort has been made to give the date of the most recent edition, new ones may have been published since this book went to press.

Davey, Neil K.
**Netsuke: A Comprehensive Study Based on the M.T. Hindson Collection**
London 1982

Devoe, S.S.
**The Art of the Tinsmith**
Exton, Pennsylvania, 1981

Gentle, R., and R. Field
**English Domestic Brass, 1684–1810**
London 1964

Hornsby, P.R.G.
**Collecting Antique Copper & Brass**
Ashbourne 1989

**– Pewter of the Western World**
Exton, Pennsylvania, 1983

Jahss, Melvin and Betty
**Ivory and Other Miniature Forms of Japanese Art**
London

John, W.D., and K. Coombes
**Paktong**
Newport 1970

Kauffman, H.
**American Copper and Brass**
New York 1979

Lion-Goldschmidt, Daisy, Jean-Claude Moreau-Gobard, R. Soame Jenyns and William Watson
**Chinese Arts: The Minor Arts**
Fribourg and London 1966

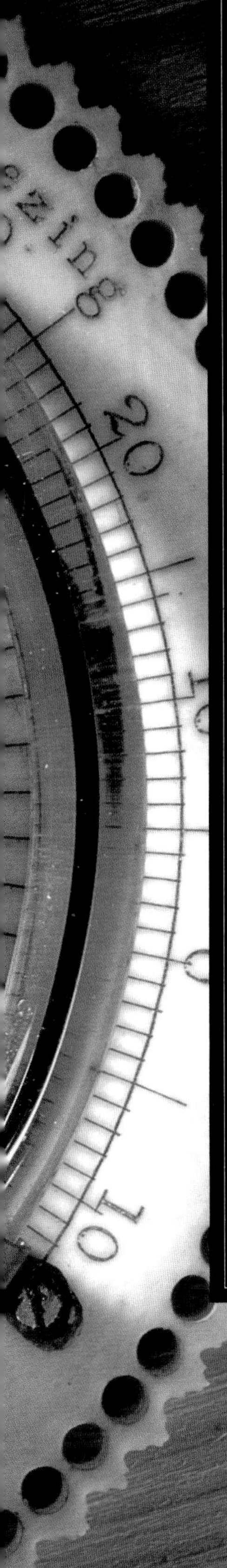

CHAPTER 6

# SCIENTIFIC INSTRUMENTS

NAVIGATIONAL INSTRUMENTS
•
GLOBES
•
BAROMETERS AND METEOROLOGY
•
SUNDIALS
•
MEDICAL INSTRUMENTS
•
OPTICAL INSTRUMENTS
•
SURVEYING INSTRUMENTS
•
"PHILOSOPHICAL" INSTRUMENTS
•
WEIGHING AND MEASURING
MACHINES

ARTHUR MIDDLETON

This page: **COMBINATION COMPASS AND CURVED MERCURY THERMOMETER, c. 1840.**

# SCIENTIFIC INSTRUMENTS

THE DELICATE INSTRUMENTS SCIENTISTS HAVE USED THROUGH HISTORY ARE BY THEIR NATURE THE PRODUCTS OF SKILLFUL MANUFACTURE AND ARE OFTEN MASTERPIECES OF FINE CRAFTSMANSHIP IN THEIR OWN RIGHT.

The earliest scientists were the high priests of the Babylonian and Assyrian empires, who studied the night sky 3,000 years ago. They noted the movement of the sun, moon, planets and stars, all of which they worshipped; and observed, for example, that Venus returns to the same point in the night sky every eight years but that Mercury takes 46 years to do so. They also worked out a calendar year of 365 days.

Towards the end of the 4th century BC Alexander the Great founded Alexandria on the southern shore of the Mediterranean and close to the Nile delta. The city became the ancient world's greatest centre of learning: the Great Library alone may have housed over half a million volumes. In 240 BC its librarian Eratosthenes calculated that the circumference of the earth was 25,000 miles, shown to be surprisingly accurate when the British astronomer Sir William Herschel (1738–1822), measured the circumference as 24,860 miles.

**TELLARIUM OR ORRERY**
*Parkes and Hadley,*
*Birmingham*
**Late 19th century**

The top plate is of cast iron and the mechanism is moved by hand; the moon orbits the earth, which in turn rotates around the sun, represented by a candle in the centre. (*Left*)

**THERMOMETERS**
**19th century**

At left is an intricately carved and turned ivory pillar, with scales in Fahrenheit and Reamur, and at right is a *pietre dure* obelisk inlaid with coloured stone, probably made in Florence. (*Above*)

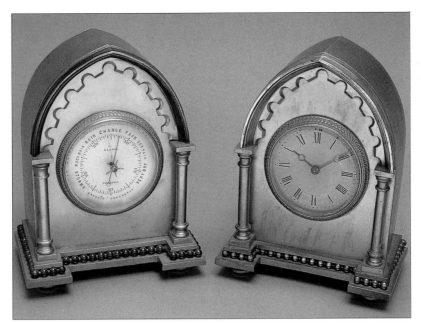

**CLOCK AND
BAROMETER DESK SET**
Gilt brass; **late 19th
century**

The two are fashioned in
the Gothic Revival manner
and their silvered dials are
signed "Slade, Tourquay".
Almost certainly Mr Slade
was not their maker but,
rather, a local optician and
retailer.

In the 2nd century AD the Alexandrian astronomer Claudius
Ptolemy (*c.* AD 100–70)proposed that the sun circled the earth. Only
1300 years later, during the Renaissance, did scientific enquiry re-start
in earnest partly prompted by the desire of navigators to find out what
was on the other side of the world and partly by the translation of
Ptolemy from Greek into Latin, the common language of most scholars. His work was published in Rome in 1496 and inspired Copernicus
in Poland and Galileo in Italy.

The foundations of modern scientific thought were laid in the hundred years from the late 15th century. The work of Copernicus was
substantiated by Johannes Kepler (1571–1630), who went on to
produce his law of "Planetary Motion". The 17th century saw
great advances in exploring the earth's crust; and the blank globe, since
the time of Ptolemy only showing the Mediterranean, began to fill up
rapidly. During the 18th century, scientists were called as such for the
first time.

By the mid-19th century the tools of discovery had been greatly
improved. For example, telescopes were by now so far advanced that
in 1846 the German astronomer Johann Galle (1812–1910) was able
to discover the planet Neptune, approximately 4,350 million km
(2,700 million miles) from the Earth.

There is a relatively small number of well-informed people who collect early scientific instruments. They appreciate the fine craftsmanship and materials – mahogany, brass, silver or gold, or a combination
of these. The 18th century yields the finest items, and instruments
from that period are still available, although in ever-fewer numbers and
at ever-increasing prices.

Scientific instruments have always been undervalued in comparison
with good-quality pictures or furniture. For example, a rare pocket
sundial by an eminent 17th-century maker can be had for a fraction of
the price of a second-rate Van Gogh. Some collectors concentrate on
one particular field, which might be, say, the first letter scales, early
electrical apparatus, medical instruments with ebony or ivory handles
or even early X-ray machines.

**SUNSHINE RECORDER**
*English*
*c.* **1920**

Behind the glass sphere is
placed a strip of
photographically sensitive
paper, and the sun's rays
burn a thin line along this
(but only, of course, when
the sun is shining). The
instrument retailed in Italy.

**O**N THE EMPTY SURFACE OF THE OCEAN THERE ARE NO SIGNPOSTS. **T**HE
DEVELOPMENT OF PROPER NAVIGATIONAL INSTRUMENTS OPENED THE
WAY FOR THE EUROPEAN EXPLORATIONS OF THE 18TH CENTURY.

# NAVIGATIONAL INSTRUMENTS

On their sea journeys the navigators of the ancient European and Middle-Eastern world were guided solely by the stars. Then, during the 11th century AD, Arabian sailors, who had long ranged over the Indian Ocean, came across some Chinese who carried with them a navigational instrument – a compass. The Chinese had used a lodestone (a piece of magnetic iron oxide) to find north from as early as the 1st century AD. Their first primitive compass was simply a sliver of soft iron magnetized by a lodestone and floating on a straw in a bowl of water. (Many collectors of maritime antiques include a lodestone in their collection.)

The use of the compass spread rapidly through Arabic North Africa and Western Europe during the 11th and 12th centuries. The compass was gradually refined, taking the form of a magnetized needle pivoted on a pin, later glued under a circular direction-marked card, which then revolved. Sixteenth-century French sailors introduced the gimbal, a self-aligning contrivance of rings and pivots which kept the compass horizontal, whatever the ship's movement. Larger steering compasses were mounted in a teak housing, known as the binnacle, which was set at a convenient height for the helmsman. According to the size or importance of a vessel, or even the vanity of its owner, the binnacle might be carved, sometimes elaborately, in the

**POCKET COMPASSES**
**Brass; 19th century**

The example at top left is by Watkins and Hill of Charing Cross. The compass at top right has an enamel dial, while the one at bottom left has a printed paper dial and blued steel needle. At bottom centre is a pocket sundial with printed paper card, gnomon and convex glass. Their average diameter is 6cm (2¾ in).

It is rigged for electric illumination at night, and has movable iron balls on each side to counteract the effect of the ship's ironwork. So reliable that mariners nicknamed them "Faithful Freddy", they were small (46 cm/18 in high) and intended only for inshore craft or fishing vessels. (*Right*)

**COMPASS**
Brass; c. 1835–40

The printed paper compass card is a good-quality steel engraving. These were used by ship's boats when rowing ashore (Charles Darwin used something similar when exploring inland from the *Beagle*. (*Above*)

form of a matelot, for example, or of a trio of sporting dolphins holding up the compass on their tails. With the advent of iron-clad ships in the 19th century, the effect of the ship's ironwork on the magnetic needle had to be counteracted: an iron ball was mounted on each side of the binnacle.

INSTRUMENTS FOR SHOWING LATITUDE

The first instrument to determine the altitude (angle of elevation above the horizon) of heavenly bodies was an Arabian device, the astrolabe (see page 283). From the 11th century onwards, mariners used small astrolabes to determine the altitude of the midday sun and so discover their latitude (distance north or south of the Equator). The 16th-century Portuguese explorer Magellan took 24 astrolabes with him on the first voyage around the world, and every ship of the Spanish Armada possessed several – yet only 66 authenticated examples survive today in museums or collections. Many are dated between 1600 and 1640.

The astrolabe was succeeded by the cross staff, a wooden device serving the same purpose; but it suffered from the same disadvantage as its forerunner – to use it meant looking directly at the sun, both difficult and dangerous in the tropics. The next development was the back-staff, which, as its name implies, the observer used facing away from the sun; the angle of the sun's elevation was given by the shadows cast by two movable vanes on an outer circle of degrees. Considerable numbers of back-staffs were made in the 17th and 18th centuries and they are still found now. Nearly all are made of the wood lignum vitae and have a scale engraved on boxwood, but there are rare examples made of solid ivory or pear-wood.

By 1750 James Hadley in England and the Baradelle brothers in France had both produced an improved version of the back-staff – the quadrant. With this triangular instrument the observer could look directly at the sun, while sets of filters cut out the harmful glare. The instrument has retained this basic shape over the years: the main change came at the end of the 18th century, when they were made in brass rather than the original models of mahogany or ebony, since brass was less likely to warp in the tropics.

In the 18th century the invention of the dividing-engine enabled finely divided lines to be inscribed on instrument scales. The scale material best suited to receiving such fine inscription was silver or gold; the frame then needed to be made of brass, since it was impracticable to inlay a metal scale into a wooden instrument. However, some old sextants are found with ivory scales inlaid into brass, unsatisfactory though they must have been, and others with ebony frames were included in makers' catalogues until the mid-19th century, since they were still popular with old-fashioned ship's captains.

INSTRUMENTS FOR SHOWING LONGITUDE
Longitude is the distance east or west of the prime meridian, a line running from one pole to the other and passing through Greenwich, London. It is ascertained at sea by comparing local time on the ship, determined by the posi-

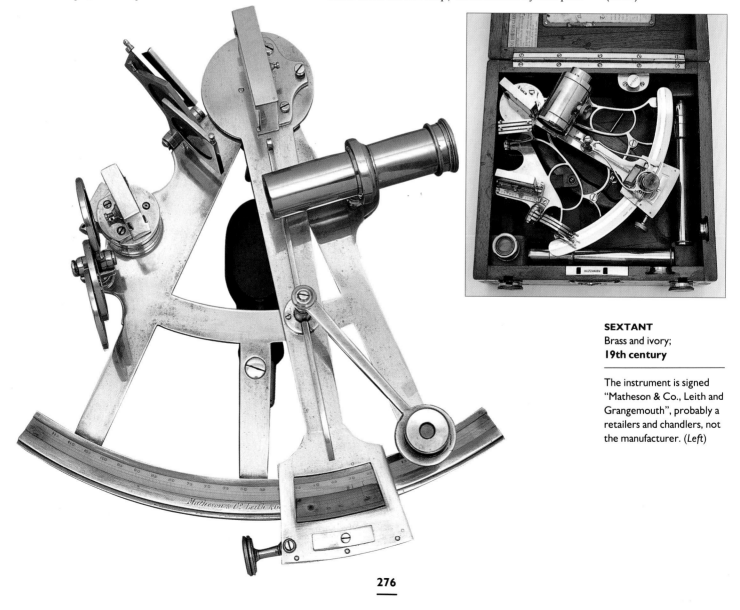

**SEXTANT**
*Heath & Co., New Eltham*
**Brass; late 19th century**

The sextant was sold by T.L. Ainsley of South Shields, complete with all accessories, in a fitted brass-bound mahogany box. (*Below*)

**SEXTANT**
Brass and ivory;
**19th century**

The instrument is signed "Matheson & Co., Leith and Grangemouth", probably a retailers and chandlers, not the manufacturer. (*Left*)

**8-DAY MARINE CHRONOMETER**
*Signed "Barwise, London"*
Mahogany and silvered metal; **late 19th century**

The two smaller dials show the seconds, and when to rewind it. Better-quality chronometers had 8-day movements, but normally they ran for 56 hours. *(Above)*

**HALF-HOUR SAND GLASS**
Turned oak and pine case; **c. 1820**

The sand glass was retailed by "W. Lowe, Optician and Spectacle Maker, 182 Upper St., Islington". *(Above right)*

tion of the sun, with Greenwich Time on a clock, accurately set at the port of departure. However, a ship's movements and temperature changes made it impossible for timepieces to remain accurate at sea. Then in 1759 the British clock maker John Harrison (1693–1776) perfected the chronometer, which maintained correct time in all conditions.

The chronometer had a balance spring mechanism resistant to temperature changes. The movement was encased in a brass bowl slung between a pair of gimbals. The square outer box was usually of mahogany, coromandel or rosewood, with brass trim at the corners. The main dial had gold hands and two smaller dials, one at 12 o'clock and the other at 6 – one dial showed seconds and the other when the mechanism needed rewinding. The mechanism usually ran for 56 hours, or sometimes eight days.

OTHER NAVIGATIONAL INSTRUMENTS
Measuring a ship's speed through water was for centuries a primitive process. Originally a lump

of wood was thrown overboard at the bow and timed as it passed the stern. In later centuries a weighted float tied to a rope was used. The time the rope took to run-out was measured by a sand-glass in a wooden or brass frame. The late 18th century saw the introduction of the "mechanical" log, which rotated in the water, its revolutions being counted on a dial mounted on the stern. Later models had a built-in rev counter, and by the late 19th century these were named "Neptune", "Trident" or "Harpoon" logs. They are found today in maritime auction sales, as are ship's sand-glasses.

Plotting a course on the sea-chart needed a pair of dividers, usually of brass with iron tips. "Single-handed" dividers had a bulbous top end. Parallel rulers were ebony with brass hinges, and some had a 180-degree scale marked round three sides; otherwise a circular brass or silver protractor with a 360-degree scale was used. The station pointer was a brass protractor with two long movable arms, used for course plotting or hydrography.

THE FAMILIAR SHAPE OF THE GLOBE – THE BEST WAY TO LOOK AT MAPS OF
THE PLANET – BECAME COMMON ONLY IN THE 17TH CENTURY, WITH THE
DEVELOPMENT OF COMMERCIAL GLOBE-MAKING.

# GLOBES

Alexandria declined rapidly in the period following the fall of the Roman Empire, but after the death of Muhammad in AD 632 the old Greek knowledge became the foundation on which Islamic geography, astronomy and philosophy was built. Islamic globe-makers made celestial globes of silver, copper or brass and engraved on them the Greek outlines of the constellations.

### TERRESTRIAL GLOBES

The Greek mathematician and philosopher Pythagoras had suggested that the Earth was a sphere as far back as the 6th century BC, and by the 3rd century BC, the astronomer and geographer Eratosthenes had made a surprisingly accurate measurement of its circumference. It is known that the Greeks made terrestrial and celestial globes and many centuries later the Emperor Charlemagne (c.742–814) had a small silver globe of the Earth (lost to posterity). However, there is little evidence of other globes being made in the Middle Ages. In 1492 Martin Behaim of Nuremberg, having returned home from a voyage down the West Coast of Africa,

was invited by the city council to construct a globe to show the latest discoveries. It is still in existence in Nuremberg, the oldest surviving globe of the world, 51cm (20 in) in diameter, and made of plaster overlaying wooden hoops. The exterior was covered with strips of vellum and the details painted on by Georg Glockenthon. The makers were just too early to record on their globe the West Indies, discovered by Columbus on his momentous voyage of 1492: the furthest western reaches of the Atlantic are still empty and decorated with sailing-ships and fantastical sea-monsters.

The earliest English globe, dated 1592, is at Petworth House, Sussex. It clearly shows the track of Sir Francis Drake's circumnavigation of the globe (1577–80), but the newly established colony of Virginia was not clearly marked and neither particularly was its latitude, in order to conceal its location from the Spaniards.

**Dutch globes** In 1492 Ferdinand and Isabella expelled the remaining Moors from Spain, and later ejected the Jews. Suddenly a large company of intellectuals – professors, teachers, physicians, scientific instrument makers and map- and globe-makers among them – were obliged to flee. Many moved north to the Low Countries, and there the globe-makers established the greatest European centre for their craft for the next 300 years. Among Dutch globe-makers of the next century was the mathematician-astronomer Gemma Frisius, who in 1536 made a terrestrial globe, 37cm in diameter. A pair of globes by Frisius are known to have existed in the small town of Zerbst, about 75 km (47 miles) north-west of Leipzig, but they were destroyed in 1945. The Flemish instrument-maker Gerardus Mercator (1512–94), later to become famous for his maps, was a pupil of Frisius and soon produced his own globes – first a terrestrial one in 1541, then a celestial one 10 years later.

Dutch globes were sold all over Europe. In 1607 two Dutch makers, Hendrik van Langren

**SMALL DESK GLOBE**
*English*
**1850s**

This is signed in the cartouche: "Malby's terrestrial globe compiled from the latest and most authentic sources including all the recent geographical discoveries ... London 1854".

(1573–1640) and his brother-in-law Jacob Reyersz, agreed to make jointly 300 pairs of small globes (one of each pair terrestrial, the other celestial). This was a huge output for the time, despite the introduction of printing, which speeded up production: printed paper gores (triangular panels) were run off the press, trimmed with a knife and pasted on to the surface of the waiting sphere. The earliest European globes were turned wooden spheres, but as they increased in size these became too heavy, and also were likely to warp or crack in extremes of temperature. They were replaced by hollow balls using the lath-and-plaster technique and covered with printed details. A wooden rod formed the axis between north and south poles and projected from both ends: this provided the means for the globe to be mounted in a brass ring, which revolved in a wooden cradle, enabling the whole of the globe's surface to be examined. Of the 600 globes produced by van Langren and Reyersz, only one pair (separated) survives: the celestial is at Frankfurt in Germany, the terrestrial at Besançon in France.

Willem Janszoon Blaeu (1571–1638) was another important Dutch globe-maker. In 1602 he offered a pair to the Admiralty in Zeeland "...for the promotion of Navigation and the Prosperity of these Lands...". But globes were in fact of doubtful value to mariners. The Dutch East India Company decreed that each of their vessels should carry a pair on board, but most of their captains preferred to use a flat chart instead. At least that could be rolled up and stowed away in anticipation of rough weather. Globes in fact became more of a reference for men of learning, or even a fashionable decorative item for a gentleman's country residence, than a piece of equipment vital for the merchant seaman. A chart recently compiled of the present distribution of early globes around Europe shows some concentrations in the Netherlands and the United Kingdom, with a scattering in France and Spain. However, the chart also showed a significant quantity located in Central Europe – Austria, Bavaria, Bohemia, Saxony and Silesia – land-locked countries with no seafaring history but noted in the past for their learning and scholarship.

**The changing face of globes** By the end of the 17th century, globes showed the outlines of the principal continents, but the details of their interiors, the coastlines of northern Russia and Canada, and the precise outlines of Australia

and New Zealand had to wait another 100 years to be completed. The British and Dutch East India Companies sent trading fleets eastwards to India, Java, Sumatra, the Philippines and China, and these parts were reasonably well defined on globes, but traffic westwards developed more slowly.

The great voyages of discovery in the Pacific Basin took place in the 18th century, and globes of that time, and even up to the 1840s, show the routes as dotted lines which criss-cross the whole area, marked, for example, "...Capt Cook's outward, in search of a North-West passage, 1778" or "Capt Vancouver's track, April 1792". Groups of islands shown on the larger globes often had snippets of information printed next to them – for example, "Lord Auckland Islands, discovered 1806, Not Inhabited" or "Maria Lajara, discovered by the Ship *Hercules* 1781, Well Inhabited".

The 18th century also saw the rise in popularity of something peculiarly English – the pocket globe. The first examples were made by Joseph Moxon in the 1690s and were no more than 7–10 cm (3–4 in) in diameter and contained in a black fish-skin-covered case, hinged to open out into two hollow halves. Inside each was pasted a map of the known heavens. A later pocket terrestrial globe, "A New Globe of the Earth by R. Cushee 1731", shows only part of Australia (called "New Holland") and represents California as an island. The north coast of Canada and Alaska is blank except for the words "Unknown Parts". Twenty years later, on a "New Globe by Nathaniel Hill 1754", most of these omissions have been

## PAIR OF GLOBES
*Smith of London*
**Mahogany stands; c. 1870**

The terrestrial includes "the latest discoveries in Australia, Africa and the Arctic regions, also the directions of the ocean currents". The celestial shows star magnitudes and positions "according to Mayer, Hershel and Bradley". Each has a diameter of 30 cm (12 in). (*Above*)

## TWO POCKET GLOBES
**Fish-skin cases; 18th century**

The top globe, by Cary, is dated 1791 and has a table of latitudes and longitudes inside its lid; the bottom example is by Nathaniel Hill and dated 1754. Both are 7.5 cm (3 in) in diameter. (*Left*)

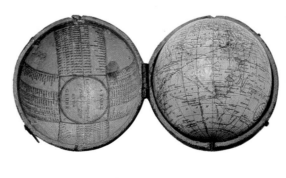

corrected and California is an isthmus. The craze for pocket globes died out by the 1840s.

Nineteenth-century globes are still fascinating for what they do not show. The last continent to be explored by Europeans was Africa. Cape Town had been established in the 18th century and the slave ports in the West carried on their trade at that time, but only in the 19th century did proper exploration inland begin – first along the River Niger and then the Nile. On globes of the 1840s and 1850s one or more of Africa's great lakes are marked, but often in the wrong place and sometimes wildly out of shape. Globes in the early 1850s show the Nile ending in a line of dots until, by 1865, Lake Victoria Nyanza was added.

Globes from the late 19th century up to the outbreak of the First World War in 1914 show the result of the "Grab for Africa", as the great powers seized large tracts of the continent. France controlled the northern territories facing

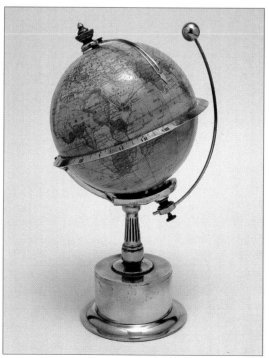

**TABLE GLOBES**
J. Lebeque, Paris
**late 19th century**

The terrestrial shows ocean currents and shipping lanes, the celestial the principal constellations (but not pictorially) and the Milky Way. (*Above*)

**GLOBE CLOCK**

Patented in 1906, the clock is designed to show the time in any part of the world. The moon orbits the earth and the clock mechanism is concealed in the base. (*Left*)

her across the Mediterranean, Britain gained Egypt, Sudan and large swathes of central and southern Africa, Germany took Tanganyika and parts of the east, and Spain and Portugal smaller territories in the south-west. The opening of the Suez Canal in 1869 provided an important and quick route to India and the Far East. In recognition of this fact, many late 19th-century globes showed shipping lanes crossing the Mediterranean and continuing south through the Red Sea.

### CELESTIAL GLOBES

Of the celestial globes known (from their writings and those of others) to have been made by the ancient Greeks only one that can be attributed with any certainty to that period has survived. This is the Atlante Farnese, a marble sphere resting on the shoulders of Atlas, now in the Uffizi Museum, Florence.

Ptolemy's system of the universe, dating from the 2nd century AD, described 48 constel-

lations. Until 1515, in representations these groups of stars were always shown in a bald fashion, as collections of positional dots, each surrounded by a boundary line. Then the German engraver Albrecht Dürer published his first two star charts, which depicted the constellations as hand-coloured pictorial images. Dürer's figures formed the basis for all the celestial maps and globes which followed over the next 400 years. They are attractive to look at, especially on 17th- and 18th-century globes, and helped to popularize study of the night sky.

The first systematic study of the night sky in the southern hemisphere did not take place until the mid-18th century, when the French priest and astronomer Abbé Nicolas Louis de Lacaille spent two years there and charted the positions of 10,000 new stars. Lacaille decided to name his new constellations after artistic and scientific tools and his proposals were quickly adopted. From the 1760s celestial globes showed a new variety of constellations around

**DETAIL OF A CARY CELESTIAL GLOBE 1818**

The star positions on this 38 cm (15 in) globe are calculated to 1820. Shown are the pictorial constellations: at the top Lynx and Leo Minor, with part of the Great Bear (Ursa Major); in the centre, from left to right, Gemini, Cancer and Leo Major, with part of Hydra and Sextans below them. At the top right is part of the meridian ring and at the bottom is part of the horizon ring showing September, October and November.

**CELESTIAL GLOBE**
*Gemma Frisius*
**16th century**

The southern hemisphere is relatively uncharted. Many of its constellations would not be identified and named for another two hundred years.

the South Pole (an area hitherto blank on globes). The names were Latinized but most people could understand their meaning: Octans (the octant), Fornax Chemica (the chemical furnace), and Machina Electrica. This presented globe-makers of the day with a literally heaven-sent opportunity to advertise their own wares by making and selling globes with constellations depicting their products. For example, George Adams of London lost no time in showing the constellation Antila Pneumatica as his new vacuum pump.

As with scientific instruments, celestial globes of the 18th century are more attractive than any others. By the late 19th century globes had become more functional but less pleasing to the eye. As the century ended, celestial globes reverted to their original style of showing constellations simply as groups of dots, each with a boundary around it.

# ASTROLABES AND ORRERIES

An original astrolabe, a medieval instrument used to determine the altitude of celestial bodies, and thus the hour, is rarely found today. It consists of a flat brass plate 7–30 cm (3–12 in) across, engraved with a map of the constellations, the star names most commonly being in Arabic, Persian or Indian script. The rarest astrolabes are European, with Latin names. On the front is the rete, or star-pointer, under which are plates engraved with different maps for different latitudes. Astrolabes are expensive to buy, and the purchaser must beware of copies.

The orrery is a mechanical scale model of the solar system, invented in the early 18th century by the English instrument-maker George Graham (d.1751). John Rowley made one in 1712 for his patron, Charles Boyle, the 4th Earl of Orrery, who gave his name to the instrument. The orrery shows the move-

ment of the planets around the sun. The few models seen in sale rooms today are all basically of the same design. A brass drum about 25 cm (10 in) across, supported on a brass column with three curved feet, contains gear-work and has an ivory handle on one side. When the handle is turned, horizontal arms extending from the centre of the drum and each with a model of a planet at the end, revolve at different speeds around the sun in the centre. The innermost planet, Mercury, has the shortest arm, and the outermost the longest. In models built after 1781, the outermost is Uranus, discovered in that year; in models before that it is Saturn. Neptune, further out than Uranus, was discovered in 1846, but to show it would have meant an arm of excessive length and for this reason it is usually omitted from orreries made at the time.

**PLANISPHERE**
*French*
Brass and cast iron;
**mid 19th century**
*(Below)*

**MECHANICAL ORRERY**
*George Phillip and Son,*
*London*
**late 19th century**
*(Right)*

**TELLARIUM**
*John Shaw, Lancashire*
**c. 1868** *(Below)*

"WHAT'S THE WEATHER GOING TO BE?" IS A COMMON QUESTION, AND ONE THAT SCIENTISTS, STARTING IN THE 17TH CENTURY, BEGAN TO ANSWER USING A NEW SET OF MEASURING INSTRUMENTS.

# BAROMETERS AND METEOROLOGY

In 1641 the Italian scientist Galileo Galilei (1564–1642) invited Evangelista Torricelli (1608–47), to work with him. Three months later Galileo died, but the younger man discovered some notes in the Master's papers concerning earlier experiments in the measurement of atmospheric pressure (and thus weather changes) and decided to continue the research. The experiments involved filling a long, thin tube with water, inverting it and putting the open end in a bucket of water. It was discovered that although the level of the water at the top of the tube dropped, leaving a small vacuum at the top of the tube, it did not drop by much, because of the effect of atmospheric pressure on the surface of the water already in the bucket. A column of water up to 9 m (30 ft) can be supported in this way. Torricelli discovered that if you use mercury instead of water in the tube and "cistern", the maximum height of the column is only about 75 cm (30 in). Torricelli went on to construct a tube in which the level of mercury moved up and down as atmospheric pressure varied. He had made the first barometer. But curiously, he failed to take the final, obvious step of adding a scale to the top of the tube, to measure the movement of the mercury, and it was not until after Torricelli's death that this was done, by the celebrated French philosopher and scientist René Descartes (1596–1650).

### MERCURY BAROMETERS

The Irish scientist Robert Boyle (1627–91) was responsible for introducing the mercury barometer into England, in the form of a standard mercury column with a visible vacuum at the top. Robert Hooke (1635–1703), his young employee, improved this "stick" type by producing the "wheel" or "banjo" barometer. This had a U-bend at the bottom of the tube and it was there that the movement in the mercury level took place. A float on the top of the mercury was connected by a thread round a pulley-wheel to a counterweight, and when there was a change in

the mercury level the counterweight moved a pointer round a dial. The dial could be anything up to 45 cm (18 in) in diameter (usually nearer 30 cm–12 in), and clearly recorded even minor changes in mercury level, and thus atmospheric pressure. Although Hooke was subsequently appointed chief experimenter to the newly formed Royal Society, his barometer was slow to find public favour. It was expensive, the thread kept jamming in the pulley-wheel and the simple stick barometer was, though less precise, much easier to read.

The first barometers, of both types, were on sale in London shops between 1680 and 1690. Most surviving barometers from the William

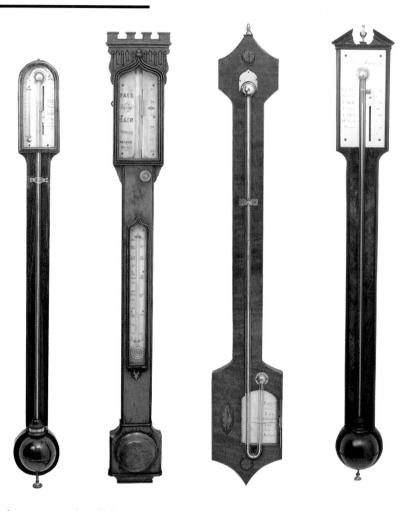

**BAROMETERS**

From the left: a coromandel-wood round top stick barometer, c. 1840; a Victorian Gothic oak stick with castellated top and bone scale, c. 1880; a rare inverted mahogany stick with the silvered brass scale on the short arm and stringing and paterae to the case, c. 1810; and a mahogany stick by Dollond, c. 1780.

and Mary period (1688–1702) and the Queen Anne period (1702–14) are either solid or veneered walnut. Both clock- and instrument-makers found a slowly increasing market for barometers and surviving trade cards show them hanging on showroom walls. Between 1700 and 1710 Daniel Quare produced an elegantly slim pillar instrument, with an ivory body and four short legs to stand on a table. Examples of these are now very rare.

For the next two hundred years the wheel and stick types were sold side by side. There was not much variation in the design of the cases, because, as the instrument's makers' realized, it had to have room for a 75 cm (30 in) column of

mercury. Eighteenth-century French makers used Hooke's mechanism in elaborately carved, oval or circular gilt-wood cases, to get away from the wheel or stick shape. The dials were numbered and drawn on paper in ink, by hand, and the maker (or retailer) added his own name and often "Selon du Torricelli".

Another variation was made in Britain by Samuel Morland, who realized that mercury would expand or contract whether the tube was vertical or not. He bent it through an angle of about 75 degrees, and for every inch the mercury rose up a straight tube it rose 30 cm (12 in) along his bent one. Such barometers are called "sign-post", or less commonly "angle-tube",

**MERCURY WHEEL BAROMETER**
Negretti & Co., English
*c. 1800* (*Above far left*)

---

**MERCURY WHEEL BAROMETER**
*c. 1840* (*Above centre*)

---

**MERCURY WHEEL BAROMETER**
*c. 1795*

---

The dial is engraved "Bapt. Ronkelli". (*Above*)

barometers. In the 18th century some were fitted around two sides of a mirror, with a thermometer on another side.

Precisely when the first mercury barometer was taken to sea is unknown, but it was not long before a pillar version was, like compasses and chronometers, mounted in gimbals (self-aligning contrivances of rings and pivots) for use by mariners. Gimbals were necessary to prevent the movement of the ship in a storm thrusting the mercury to the top of the tube and bursting it. It was Hooke who suggested that a narrowing, or waist, in the tube just above the cistern would also help reduce such violent movements. Officially, the first marine barometer of Hooke's type was produced by Edward Nairne (1726-1806) and taken by Captain Phipps on a Polar Expedition in 1773, but it is probable that such instruments were used before then. They had a wooden body, and at the top a small door (inside which was a thermometer) that enclosed the scales. Some of the mid-19th-century examples had a body with a pleasing carved "rope-twist" and a brass cistern. Later that century models were made with the entire tube of brass and with a sliding scale-marker operated by a rack and pinion mechanism (a small cog wheel engaging with a toothed bar).

The Italians, having invented the instrument, found that their best market was Britain. Several hundred craftsmen made their way and settled there in the 19th century, and a roll of makers in London's Clerkenwell (the centre of the trade) for 1860 reads like the Milan telephone directory.

**Measuring height** It was not long before scientists realized that the instrument could be taken up mountains to measure decreasing air pressure, and thus height. In the 18th century a ratio between pressure and height was worked out: every rise of 9m (30ft) in height produces a fall of what is now termed 1.9 millibars. Most early experiments were carried out by French or Swiss physicists in the Alps, and by the end of the 18th century they had produced a proper mountain barometer with an extended scale, which was capable of giving a reading at the top of Mont Blanc.

The French found yet another use for the barometer. After the first balloon flight, over Paris in 1783, balloon journeys took place all over France, and barometers were carried in them as altimeters. In 1865 the English meteorologist James Glaisher (1809–1903) made his record-breaking balloon ascent to 10,000 m

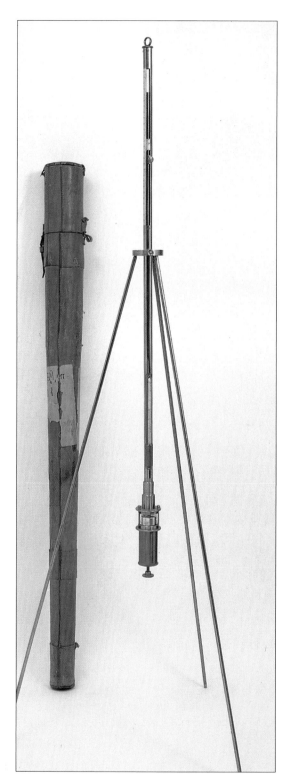

**MOUNTAIN BAROMETER AND CASE**
*French*

The instrument bears a faded label for the "Inspecteur des Travaux Publiques". (*Above*)

**MARINE BAROMETER**
*c. 1890*

A gimbal arm and visible glass tank at the bottom are featured. The scales read in inches or centimetres. (*Right*)

(33,000 ft). When he had scraped the frost from the glass of his barometer, he saw that it read 28 cm (11 in), but observers on the ground refused to believe him until other instruments on board confirmed his claim. Normal ballooning barometers were made to read up to 4,500 m (15,000 ft), the accepted maximum for scientific study, while most pleasure trips took place well below 3,000 m (10,000 ft).

When the English naturalist Charles Darwin made his expedition to South America in the 1830s, his ship the *Beagle* was commanded by Lieutenant Fitzroy, who eventually became an admiral and was appointed meteorological officer to the Board of Trade. Fitzroy produced a barometer, bearing his name, which has a printed paper scale and, on each side of the tube, "Remarks" on how to forecast the weather; predictions on the left side are based on rising pressure, those on the right on falling pressure. The Fitzroy barometer is commonly seen today, often in an oak frame with the top carved in the Victorian Gothic manner.

## ANEROID BAROMETERS

Since nobody wished to carry a 3ft tube of mercury on a journey, travellers sought a more portable barometer. In 1698 the German philosopher and scientist Gottfried von Leibnitz

(1646–1716) extracted some of the air from a pair of bellows and re-sealed them to create a partial vacuum. As the atmospheric pressure outside the bellows varied, it caused them to contract or expand slightly, and this movement was measured by a pointer moving round a dial. This was the first aneroid barometer ("aneroid" simply means "dispensing with liquid"). Its basic principle was sound and the apparatus was reduced in size to fit into a coat pocket, but no successful prototype was made until the end of the 18th century when Nicolas Conté, a professor at the French Ballooning School at Meudon, took up Leibnitz's invention because he was exasperated with the wild oscillations of mercury barometers during flights. Conté constructed the first working aneroid barometer but found that it was very susceptible to changes in temperature, and it too was never produced in commercial quantities.

In the mid 19th century Lucien Vidie invited Antoine Redier to make the prototype of a commercial aneroid barometer, to be manufactured by Breguet. This was patented by Vidie, in France in 1845 and five years later in England, where it was tested by being taken up to the dome of St Paul's Cathedral and by train round the Scottish Highlands. In all locations readings corresponded with those

**ANEROID BAROMETER**
*English*
**Brass and walnut; c. 1890**

Intended for desk, table or mantelpiece, the barometer has a silvered face and is graduated from 71–78 cm (28–31 in). Below this are twin thermometers, alcohol for Centigrade (left) and mercury for Fahrenheit (right). This type of instrument, with its visible movement, was popular as people could almost see how it worked: the aneroid is the circular corrugated chamber at the back, whose relatively small movement (caused by changes in the atmospheric pressure) was magnified by the linkage to turn the hand. The additional pointer compares the reading from the previous day.

of the mercury barometer to well within acceptable variations.

The idea of using an enclosed, partially evacuated chamber had also occurred to the French scientist Eugène Bourdon (1804–84). Bourdon manufactured a "turret" barometer, with a two-and-a-half-turn spiral tube 37 cm (15 in) high. He supplied one of these to the town hall of the 1st Arrondissement in Paris, where it can still be seen. Bourdon's instruments are considered by many barometer collectors to be more elegant than Vidie's disc-like design. Even so, many general antique dealers fail to make such aesthetic distinctions, and the price for a Bourdon aneroid barometer is often no more than the going rate for other types.

Pocket aneroid barometers took many forms. Some were tiny – no more than 2 cm (³/₄ in) in diameter – set in a gold case. Others were 2.5–7.5 cm (1–3 in) across, in a silver case. Larger versions in a brass case, up to 20 cm (8 in) across, were made to be hung in a hallway or a ship's cabin, or else sat in a carved oak or mahogany stand on a desk or writing table.

**Barographs** In the 19th century a few mercury barometers were made that provided a continuous recording of changing air pressures on a graph. However, these barographs, as such instruments are called, proved complicated and expensive to make and were, anyway, unreliable. The introduction of the aneroid barometer made the construction of a barograph much easier and in 1866 a successful one was made by

Breguet of Paris. The changes in pressure are registered by a stylus and a pen nib, which makes a record on graph paper moved along by a clockwork-driven drum. The mechanism is contained in an oak- or mahogany-framed glass case with a drawer in the base for charts. Most modern versions are still fundamentally the same, since the design is hard to improve on. Some types, however, have a circular dial. The thermobarograph has an extra nib which records the temperature.

OTHER METEOROLOGICAL INSTRUMENTS
The hygrometer, a small device for measuring humidity in the air, was invented by the Swiss Baron Horace Benedict de Saussure in 1783. The first examples, made for him by Pixii of Paris, used human hair, which lengthens in

**BOURDON-TYPE BAROMETER c. 1875**

The evacuated chamber is the circular disc towards the centre. The design won the gold medal at the Paris Exposition of 1849 and again in London in 1851. Thereafter the original inventor Vidie sued Bourdon for infringement of copyright.

**FOUR POCKET BAROMETERS mid to late 19th century**

The example at top left is brass cased, its dial graduated from 45–78 cm (18–31 in) and from zero to 4,500 m (15,000 ft). The barometer at top right is silver cased and was made in London, 1886–7, its dial is graduated from 53–78 cm (21–31 in) only to 3,000 m (10,000 ft). The smaller-sized example at bottom left is marked "C.W.Dixey, Optician to the Queen, 3 New Bond St", and it is in an engine-turned silver case.

### BAROGRAPH
*Short & Mason, London*
**1900**

The case is mahogany, with bevelled-glass sides and top, and the corners are decorative pillars. A drawer in the base holds previous as well as new charts. The stack of aneroids is in the centre of the mechanism and controls the pen's movement on the drum. (*Left*)

### COMBINATION COMPASS AND CURVED MERCURY THERMOMETER
*c. 1840*

Mounted on a circular ivory base, the compass has an enamel dial. (*Below*)

humid conditions. A later version used a thin strip of whalebone. The hygrometer aroused little interest until the mid-19th century, when it was used to ensure a constant laboratory humidity for repeated experiments. In 1875 one thoughtful maker produced a pocket model for travellers, especially those obliged to spend the night at a dubious inn. "It will tell," said the catalogue, "whether the beds be damp or not."

The cup anemometer (wind gauge), which consists of cups that rotate on a vertical shaft, arose as a direct result of 16th-century observations of windmill sails rotating on a hill top, but it was not produced commercially until Dr Robinson made a model in 1846. From this came the air-meter, which was issued to inspectors appointed by the Factory Act of 1846 to ensure there was sufficient ventilation in mines and factories.

The sunshine recorder, introduced by English scientist Sir George Stokes (1819–1903) in 1880, consisted of a glass sphere, mounted in a semi-circular brass holder. The sphere focused the sun's rays to burn a thin line along a photographically sensitive strip of paper marked with hours.

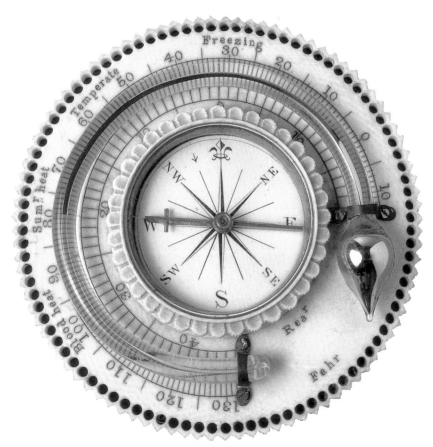

BEFORE CLOCKS BECAME WIDESPREAD, THE ONLY MEANS OF TELLING THE
TIME WAS BY SUNDIAL. A FASCINATING VARIETY OF SOPHISTICATED
DEVICES WERE DEVELOPED.

# SUNDIALS

**290**
**RING DIAL**
*English*
**Brass; late 17th century**

The two rings are hinged,
and the instrument folds
flat to fit into a pocket.
When the dial is held up,
the sun shines through the
pin hole in the centre strut
on to the hour ring.

The ancient Egyptians used sundials to tell the hour outdoors and notched candles and sand-glasses for the same purpose indoors. The length of an hour was not standardized until the 14th century, when churches were built with towers that contained clocks. The first European mechanical clocks, which appeared in the 13th century, were crude and notoriously unreliable, but could be checked by readings from the sun: to do this most churches had a vertical sundial mounted on one wall. By the 16th century clock-making had improved, but instead of making the sundial redundant this had

the opposite effect – more dials were needed. In addition, some of the early watches were supplied in small cases with the watch on one side and a dial on the other.

The eventual demise of the sundial took place in the 1830s, when the new invention of the electric telegraph was able to transmit the correct time anywhere and the sundial was therefore no longer required as a check on faulty clocks. It then became relegated to a garden ornament.

HORIZONTAL DIALS
The earliest horizontal sundials were round or square and engraved on sandstone or slate, later brass. From the centre protruded an upright rod, the gnomon, which cast the sun's moving shadow. The angle of the gnomon to the face of the dial was critical and conformed to the latitude of the place where it was used. Many dials have this latitude engraved on them.

The cannon dial, or noon gun, is a refined version of the horizontal dial. A small brass cannon on the dial has above its touch-hole an adjustable lens, which at noon concentrates the sun's rays on gunpowder in the hole, setting off the charge. It was an early-19th-century invention – by Chevalier of Paris – which soon caught the imagination of landowners, who had such cannon dials mounted in the courtyards of their châteaux; when the gun sounded across the fields and vineyards, the workers knew it was time for lunch.

MINIATURE AND PORTABLE DIALS
Since cheaper watches in the 17th and 18th centuries were inaccurate, merchants and travellers carried small pocket-sized dials. Provided the sun was shining, they could obtain a quick, if approximate, time of day. The simplest and most popular of these miniature dials, the diptych, consisted of two panels of wood or ivory that opened out like a book. The gnomon was a piece of string that stretched tight when the two

**291**
**NOON GUN**
*French*
Marble and brass

The lens can be adjusted to suit the time of year. The gnomon is aligned for the 47th parallel. The instrument would have been mounted on a marble pedestal.

panels were at right angles to each other. A small compass let into the base allowed the instrument to be orientated north and south, and on the panels were printed papers with vertical and horizontal scales. Many diptychs were produced in the Augsburg and Nuremberg regions of Germany in the 18th and early 19th centuries.

Better-quality ivory diptych dials had their information punch-stamped on to the panels. Every available space was used to give the latitudes of important cities, together with wind-roses (rosette-like diagrams of wind strengths and frequencies) and a scale for the Julian or Gregorian calendar. These diptychs were made both in southern Germany and in Dieppe.

A more elegant type of diptych dial was introduced by Michael Butterfield, an Englishman who lived and worked in Paris from about 1685 to 1725. Usually of silver, sometimes of brass, and in a shagreen-covered case with green silk-velvet lining, it has an elongated octagonal shape and a small, hinged gnomon that can be slightly raised or lowered.

The compass dial is even more common than the Butterfield dial, having been made in many

parts of Europe. It is a small, circular brass case with a printed-paper compass-rose (a rosette-like diagram of compass directions) glued in the base. Made from the 17th to the end of the 19th century, the compass dial could be used only in the latitude it was specifically made for, since the gnomon is not adjustable.

For general use, travellers took with them the equinoctial or universal dial, which was made all over Europe from about 1700 to the 1880s. It was also called an "inclining" dial, because the hour-scale is hinged and can be adjusted appropriately along the latitude scale, both folding flat when not in use.

Ring dials, which fold flat but open out for use, made from the 17th to the mid-19th century, are of much simpler construction but the larger ones are surprisingly accurate. They are mostly of brass, occasionally of silver, and the standard of the engraving varies enormously. The best 18th-century examples are mounted vertically.

Other types of dial include the pillar (or shepherd's) dial, various kinds of polyhedral dial (these vary greatly in size) and the scaphoid dial.

THE MYSTERIES OF THE HEAVENS, THE PROPERTIES OF LIGHT, AND THE SMALL-SCALE WORLD OF SINGLE-CELLED CREATURES WERE REVEALED WITH THE HELP OF OPTICAL INSTRUMENTS.

# OPTICAL INSTRUMENTS

Glass-making dates from very early times. Certainly the Greeks, then the Romans, made mirrors and burning-glasses, and the Romans made quantities of domestic glassware. The natural step from glass-making to lens-making was due to the need for spectacles. They were first produced in England by the Franciscan friar and scholar Roger Bacon (*c.*1214–94), but there is evidence that they were also made in Italy and China at the same time.

TELESCOPES

The first "modern" optical instrument was the telescope, introduced in the early 17th century and first offered to the public at the Frankfurt

**REFRACTING TELESCOPE**
Brass; **mid 19th century**

Meant for a desk or table, the telescope has a clamp at the top of the stand which enables the instrument to be carried around or taken on board ship without the stand. (*Top*)

**REFLECTING TELESCOPE ON TABLE TRIPOD**
*French*
**c. 1825**

Engraved on the instrument is "Haring, Opticien du Roi de Wurtemburg, Palais Royal, No 63 a Paris". (*Left*)

Fair of 1608. A year later an example had found its way to Galileo, who then made an improved version. This was the refracting telescope; all early telescopes were of this type and consisted of tubes of vellum, the outer one frequently decorated with gold tooling, and discs of turned horn to hold the lenses. They were sought after by military commanders and astronomers. In 1663 the Scot James Gregory (1638–75) put forward the idea for a reflecting telescope, in which light is collected and focused by a mirror and diverted to the eyepiece by another mirror, thus avoiding the colour distortions produced by lenses. Gregory failed to find a lens-maker capable of grinding the mirrors finely enough, but five years later the English mathematician and physicist Sir Isaac Newton (1642–1727) overcame the problem and built the first reflecting telescope.

By the late 18th century telescope tubes were being made of mahogany, then brass. Elegant stands were added, for desks or library tables, and taller ones for the floor. Larger examples had two wooden handles which operated slow-motion gearing, especially useful for following a ship at sea or a star at night.

There was a continuing problem of poor-quality lenses in refracting telescopes. Ship's telescopes worked well enough by day but at night they failed to show the colour of different signalling lanterns. Remove one of the lenses and the image was clearer (though inverted), but such an instrument was awkward to use by day. As a result, many ships carried several telescopes, some marked "night glaff", (i.e. glass) others "day glaff". However, from about 1760 the English optician John Dollond (1706–61) began producing telescopes with achromatic lenses (which reduced colour distortion). Many other makers copied these and a flurry of legal action followed until the patent expired. There are many surviving early 19th-century tele-

scopes engraved "Day or Night". The long and cumbersome mahogany tube was replaced with a shorter, extending one made up of two or three smaller brass tubes. By the 1850s this extending telescope was covered with canvas, leather, knotted string or plaited horsehair as a protection against knocks.

### BINOCULARS AND OPERA GLASSES

In the early 17th century the Italians, as well as making monocular telescopes, developed a binocular version, consisting of two parallel tubes. Since it was difficult to focus, and the lenses were still unsatisfactory, the idea lay dormant until the 19th century. Miniature binoculars were then introduced, intended not for serious use but rather as amusing gifts. They had a short focal length and were ideal for viewing the stage of a theatre from a box. These opera glasses, as they came to be known, were made in combinations of ivory, gilt-brass, shagreen,

**FOUR HAND-HELD TELESCOPES**
Brass; 19th century

From top to bottom: 3-draw, leather-covered end, 34 cm (13½ in) long; 3- draw, mahogany case, 38 cm (15 in); 6-draw, leather- covered end, 42 cm (16½ in); 7-draw engraved "James Miller, 1855". (*Above*)

**NATURALIST'S FLEA-GLASS c. 1850**

This pocket microscope screws into the outer container for field excursions. Specimens could be put in the glass container and observed. (*Below*)

silver and enamel.

The French reintroduced binoculars and started manufacturing them commercially from the 1830s. They were made of brass with leather trim, and had a central focusing knob operated by finger and thumb. The twin-tube system remained until the German firms of Zeiss and Leitz introduced prismatic binoculars in the 1880s, which allowed a longer focal length – and strength – to be compacted into a shorter instrument.

### MICROSCOPES

Since, from the 17th century onwards, lenses were made for almost any focal length, the microscope was a natural development of the refracting telescope – it was merely a very close-focusing version of that instrument. The most common type, the compound microscope, with two lenses, was invented by the Dutchman Zacharias Janssen in 1590. Galileo helped develop the earliest models, which were made from vellum, pasteboard, horn and wood. By 1660 the microscope had been used to observe that blood circulated in frogs and fishes, which seemed to confirm the idea of William Harvey (1578–1657) the English physician that the same thing happened in humans.

In the 17th century Britain became the major centre of microscope manufacture. In 1665 the English physicist Robert Hooke (1635–1703) published his *Micrographia*, which described the latest microscope, how to use it and what could be observed with it. The English manufacturer John Marshall (1663–1725) produced a large microscope, 50cm (20in) high, made of the wood lignum vitae, brass and gold-tooled leather and adjustable by a ball-joint at the base. The light was reflected up the instrument by a mirror, and between this and the first lens was the stage, which held an ivory slide and the object to be examined.

In the early 18th century the English manufacturers Matthew Loft and Edmund Culpeper made alternative fixed upright models, still wood, with some brass, shagreen and gold-tooled leather. The Culpeper type was still being produced in the early 19th century. During the 18th century another English maker produced for George III a splendidly ornate silver model, now in the Science Museum, London. Other English manufacturers of the time included John Cuff (1708–72), Benjamin Martin (1705–82) and Jesse Ramsden, (1735–1800), who all made their instruments in

brass. Attractive-looking though these were, they had one drawback: the line between mirror, stage and lenses was still vertical, so that the observer had constantly to stand up to use the instrument. Then, at the end of the 18th century, two English makers, William and Samuel Jones (1763–1831 and 1784–1838) reintroduced the ball-joint at the base of the microscope, allowing it to be tilted to a convenient working angle and the user to sit. This version was called "Jones Most Improv'd Model", and was made into the 1830s.

While these large instruments sat on the desks of 18th-century scientists (now being called such for the first time), there was an obvious demand for smaller, more portable models. The first was produced by the Dutchman Anthony van Leeuwenhoek (1632–1723) in the late 17th century and had just a single lens. In the 18th century simple single-lens pocket microscopes were popular with naturalists, who took them into the countryside with a selection of different lenses. A more satisfactory arrange-

**CULPEPER-TYPE MICROSCOPE**
*English*
**Brass, with mahogany case; late 18th century**

Focusing is by draw tube, which was common in the earlier models: 19th-century examples had a rack-and-pinion mechanism. The accessories include five consecutively numbered objectives and three ivory slides, a live box and a pair of small tweezers for holding an insect under the lens. The last models were made in the 1830s.

JONES-MOST-
IMPROVED-TYPE
MICROSCOPE
*Signed "Dollond, London"*
**c. 1810**

The machine folds flat to fit
into its case, which also
holds accessories. (*Far left*)

FOLDING BINOCULAR
MICROSCOPE
*Swift & Son, London*
**Brass; c. 1880**
(*Left*)

MICROSCOPE
*Watson & Sons, London*
**Brass; 19th century**
(*Below*)

ment was introduced by the English manufacturers John and William Cary (1754–1835 and 1759–1825) in the early 19th century: a microscope whose parts came in a small box and could be assembled to screw on to the lid.

Early microscopes suffered from the same problems of colour and image distortion as early telescopes. It was not until 1830 that the English wine merchant and optical experimenter Joseph Jackson Lister (1786–1869) adapted Dollond's telescope lenses to the smaller instrument. Notable English microscope-makers of the 1840s were Hugh Powell (1799–1883) Peter Lealand and Andrew Ross, (1798–1859), who made the first binocular microscope by incorporating above the first lens a small prism that split the image of the object being viewed.

On the Continent equally high-quality instruments were made during the 19th century. In Paris the firms of Chevalier (père et fils) and Nachet were notable, and in Germany the huge enterprise of Carl Zeiss of Jena got under way from 1875. By 1900 there were nine makers in Britain, seven in Germany, four in France but only three in the United States.

### OTHER OPTICAL INSTRUMENTS

Sir Isaac Newton was the first to show that ordinary (white) sunlight, when passed through a prism, separated into the colours of the spectrum. To conduct their own experiments into the nature of light, amateur scientists of the 18th and 19th centuries could buy mirrors in sets of three: one concave, one flat, one convex.

## KALEIDOSCOPE
### 19th century

The stand enabled the kaleidoscope to tilt down to the light of the oil lamp and thus be used in the evening. Other versions comprised a simple tube held up to the light and looked through like a telescope. (*Right*)

## PRAXINOSCOPE

Images were placed in the drum and reflected by the mirrors. Advanced models had drums rotated by a handle, a pulley and two cogs. (*Above*)

## ZOETROPE
*English or French*
### c. 1850

The tin drum is spun around by hand, and with the eye some 20 cm (8 in) away from the slits apparent movement is seen. In the bottom of the drum were placed strips of paper images. (*Above right*)

The 19th century saw the development of highly specialized instruments for investigating the properties of light. Among them were the polarimeter, for measuring the polarization of light; the spectroscope, for splitting up white light into its constituent colours; and the goniometer, for measuring angles between crystal faces and thus correctly identifying gems.

### OPTICAL TOYS

Most optical toys were developed in the 18th or 19th centuries, but some date from much earlier. For example, the anamorphoscope (derived from the Greek "to form anew") was popular from the 16th century. This was a small vertical cylindrical mirror which when carefully positioned on a distorted drawing on a card would rectify it, making its subject recognizable.

In 1818 David Brewster registered the patent of a Kaleidoscope (from the Greek "beautiful form"), in which small coloured pieces at the bottom of a viewing tube are seen in triplicate, through the incorporation of two mirrors set at an angle of 60 degrees to each other.

In 1825 the English physician Dr John Paris (1785–1856) produced a toy called the thaumatrope based on his medical knowledge that the human brain retains the image of an object for about $1/30$ second (known as persistence of vision). The toy consists simply of a small cardboard disc, with a subject painted on each side – scarcely a scientific instrument.

The mid-19th century saw the production of two toys based on persistence of vision. One was the zoetrope, an invention of W. G. Horner of Bristol. This was a tin drum with thin viewing slots cut at intervals around it. Inside the drum was a wide strip of paper on which were drawn the successive stages of a movement performed by a person or animal. When the drum was spun, the movements – for example, of a child throwing up a ball – were seen, as the result of persistence of vision, as one continuous movement.

The second device, the praxinoscope, patented by the Frenchman Émile Reynaud in 1877, was simply an improvement on the zoetrope. In the centre of the drum was another, this one stationary and with small mirrors fixed round it. The viewer revolved the outer drum and looked into the nearest mirror which gave a reflection of the apparent movement. Advanced models incorporated an oil-lamp so that the apparatus could be used to entertain family or friends in the evenings.

**The magic lantern** Another optical toy, invented in the 18th century, was the magic lantern: a light source – at first a candle or an oil-lamp, later acetylene or electricity – projected a picture on a glass slide through a lens on to a blank wall or screen. Depending on the power of the light source and the size of the lens, the image could be quite small or could fill a large screen in a lecture theatre. Ingenious efforts were made to simulate movement on the screen. Large wooden-framed slides were made which had moving parts; by turning a handle the operator could make these revolve while the rest of the slide remained still. (This was especially useful for demonstrating the revolution of the planets around the sun.) Some advanced models used several lenses simultaneously, fading out one slide, dissolving in the next. The most common surviving slides are one showing the text of the Lord's Prayer and another depicting a black-robed, scowling Queen Victoria.

WHILE OFTEN FINELY CRAFTED, THE SIMPLE AND OFTEN BRUTAL
LOOKING MEDICAL INSTRUMENTS OF THE PAST GIVE A VIVID INSIGHT
INTO THE LIMITATIONS OF MEDICAL SCIENCE UNTIL THE PRESENT CENTURY.

# MEDICAL INSTRUMENTS

By Roman times medical practice had been divided into two groups: physicians, who diagnosed illness and prescribed a cure, and surgeons, who carried it out. Roman surgical instruments – thin bronze scalpels and probes – were discovered at Pompeii when excavations began there in 1763. Later many more were made during the 19th century mostly for the benefit of English milords doing the Grand Tour.

Medical knowledge advanced little between Classical times and the Renaissance, and instruments were only of the most basic kinds.

For chest and stomach wounds there was little to be done except remove foreign bodies, bind the wounds up and hope for the best. Surgeons on the battlefield would make a wounded soldier eat a clove of garlic, and then sniff to see if the intestines had been punctured.

In the 16th century the French army physician Ambroise Paré (*c.*1510–90) attempted to codify medicine and surgery and published a textbook on the subject, with wood-block engravings, in 1580. By the time the English edition came out in 1620, using the same blocks, woodworm had infested them and the pictures are dotted with little blank spaces. The instruments shown remained almost unchanged until the late 18th century. Sets of these were

**CHEST OF SURGICAL INSTRUMENTS**
**19th century**

Included are amputation knives, large and small saws, scalpels, catheters, and dental and trepanning instruments. Note there are no gynaecological instruments so the case was probably supplied for men only, i.e., for a naval or military surgeon. Most of the handles are of carved ebony and were outdated by 1875, when instruments had to be sterilized before use and wooden handles were replaced by metal ones.

became an indispensable diagnostic instrument, and the only change made to it was to give it more of a trumpet shape. It was not until 1856 that the now-familiar binaural model was produced by Dr George Cammanon of New York.

### ANAESTHESIA AND ANTISEPSIS

Experiments with anaesthetics took place in the early 19th century. In Britain the chemist Sir Humphry Davy obtained relief from the pain of an infected tooth by inhaling nitrous oxide (laughing gas), and in the United States in 1842 Dr Crawford Long gave ether to a patient. Four years later the first operation under a general anaesthetic was undertaken by Dr W. T. G. Morton (1819–68) at Massachusetts General Hospital. Morton's apparatus is now in the Smithsonian Institution, Washington DC. In London the new technique using chloroform was first used later the same year. It revolutionized surgery and was given royal approval when one of Queen Victoria's children was born with the help of chloroform.

Ether was reintroduced. Dr Snow simply slung a bag full of it over his shoulder and made the rounds of his hospital, administering whiffs where needed. In 1906 the French physician Dr D'Ombredanne introduced ether equipment consisting of a brass globular container, a copper face mask, a stop-cock and a face bag to show the patient's rate of breathing. Its popularity became so lasting that it was still being used as late as 1982, by the Argentine Army Medical Service during the Falklands War.

In the 1860s the English surgeon Joseph Lister (1827–1912) became the first man to introduce antisepsis into surgery. He used a carbolic acid spray to destroy germs and so reduce the risk of infection, which had killed so many previous surgical patients. Later he also introduced asepsis (the creation of a sterile environment), which included boiling all instruments before use. This last measure, once it had been accepted by the medical fraternity, had a profound effect on the construction of surgical instruments: the old ivory or ebony handles, chequered like a gun-stock (to stop a hand slipping), gave way to metal, which could be more thoroughly and easily sterilized. The transition was completed by 1890. Even so, eight years later one London maker still possessed instruments it had had in stock since the end of the Crimean War in 1856, and in an attempt to unload them in 1899 sent them to the British army in South Africa.

**DR D'OMBREDANNE'S**
**ETHER APPARATUS**
**First produced 1906**

The waxed paper bag indicated how the patient was breathing. Inside the globe were cotton wads to soak up the ether. (*Top*)

**GRIGG'S "PATENT**
**CONICAL ELECTRICAL**
**MACHINE"**
*G.R. Francis, Cheltenham*
**c. 1878**

A branch of Victorian quack medicine believed that an electrical current passed through the body could cure aches and pains. The mahogany case contains copper windings with a movable soft-iron core. (*Above*)

usually carried in fitted brass-bound wooden cases, especially by naval or military surgeons, but many country doctors simply wrapped them up in a leather wallet and stuffed this into an overcoat pocket.

If leeches were used they arrived at the bedside in small pewter containers, having been kept at the local chemist's in larger porcelain jars with pierced lids (leeches live in water but breathe air). These jars were attractively decorated and normally came in labelled sets of four – Leeches, Bears Grease, Tamarinds and Honey, each being a particular approved remedy.

In 1816 the Breton doctor René Laennec (1781–1826) introduced the stethoscope, for listening to sounds made by the heart or lungs. The first model was nothing more than a turned fruitwood cylinder with a hole bored down the centre for applying to one ear, but its use was published in Britain in 1820 and in the *New England Journal of Medicine* in 1822. Soon it

TAKING THE MEASURE OF LAND WAS BASED ON ROUGH-AND-READY
SYSTEMS UNTIL THE 16TH CENTURY, WHEN NEW INSTRUMENTS WERE
DEVELOPED THAT ENABLED ACCURATE SURVEYS TO BE MADE.

# SURVEYING INSTRUMENTS

The Greek scholar Hero of Alexandria wrote a treatise on surveying as early as the 1st century AD, but land-surveying as a profession did not arise until the late 16th century. An astrolabe adapted to measure angles for land use, with a compass in the centre, was first made by Galterius Arsenius and published by the cartographer Gemma Frisius in 1529.

In 1585, the work of English mathematician Leonard Digges (1510–58) "...briefely shewing the exact meafuring, and speedie reckoning of all manner of land, squares, timber, stone, steeples, pillars, globes etc." was published. Digges is best remembered for mounting part of one astrolabe on another, so that it could measure both vertical and horizontal angles at once. This instrument was eventually called the theodolite. The first theodolites were made in England by Humphrey Cole in 1574. In Prague Erasmus Habermel also began making the instruments in 1600. With modifications the theodolite remained the staple tool of surveyors

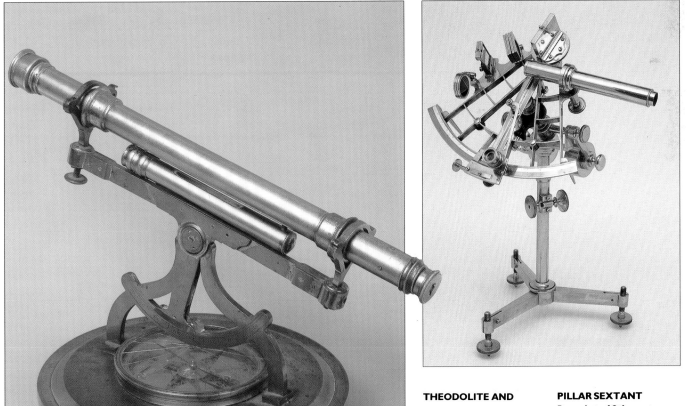

**THEODOLITE AND COMPASS**
*Benjamin Cole*
Brass and silver; *c.* 1800

Scales for measuring both horizontal and vertical angles equip this theodolite. (*Left*)

**PILLAR SEXTANT**
Brass; **late 19th century**

The sextant itself could be used at sea, and the whole ensemble for surveying on land. The column is adjustable for height and the base has three levelling screws. (*Above*)

until the introduction of measurements by laser in the late 1970s. In the late 18th century silver scales replaced those of other materials on theodolites, for greater accuracy.

The instrument long used for measuring distances was the waywiser, or perambulator, which was pushed like a wheelbarrow. A brass dial told off the distances in feet, yards, chains, furlongs and miles. For more precise measurement the surveyor's chain was introduced by the Englishman Edmund Gunter, Professor of Astronomy at Gresham College, Oxford, 1619–26. It was exactly 66 ft (22 m) long and had 100 links, with a brass tag on every tenth link. With this instrument land area could be measured accurately for the first time. Chains were used until 1905.

### THE SPIRIT LEVEL
In 1666 the French constructor J. M. Thevenot introduced a way of determining a perfectly horizontal surface when he invented the spirit level, a water-filled glass tube containing an air bubble. The tube is placed on the surface, which is shown to be horizontal only if the bubble moves to the exact centre. The spirit level was quickly adopted in England, where, however, the imported skills of Italian glass-makers were needed to blow the thin glass tubes. As well as being used by masons and carpenters, spirit levels were mounted on surveying instruments.

The spirit level gave rise in 1875 to two small instruments for determining the height of buildings. One, designed by the British army engineer Captain Abney (1843–1920), with a fixed scale and an open sight (one without a telescope), and the other manufactured by Casella. Both have a compass and an inclinometer.

Mining required specialized surveying instruments. Special compasses, or miners' dials, were developed, with folding sights and two brass hooks to hang them between two pit-props.

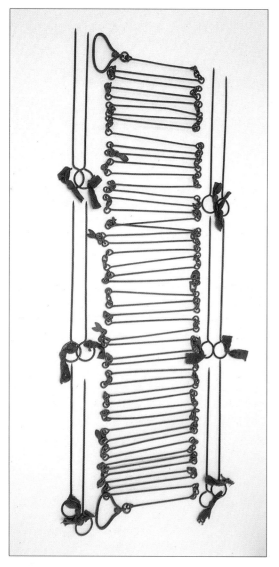

**POCKET SURVEYING INSTRUMENT**
*John Browning, London*
**c. 1880**

This complex little instrument incorporates a compass on one side and on the other an inclinometer. Through the middle runs a telescope that can focus on near or far objects. It was an improvement on Abney's level of 1875, although not as accurate as the theodolite. (*Below*)

**SACCARIMETER**
*Duboscq of Paris*
**Brass and cast iron; c. 1870**

This is an adaption of the polarimeter, which measures the optical activity of a solution. (*Left*)

**SURVEYOR'S CHAIN**
**Iron and brass; 19th century**

There is a brass tag every 10 links. The 12 spikes with red felt tabs are for pegging it to the ground. (*Far left*)

# DRAWING INSTRUMENTS

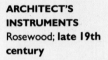

**CASE OF ARCHITECT'S INSTRUMENTS**
*James Search, London*
Tortoiseshell, steel and brass, with three ivory rulers; **late 18th century**

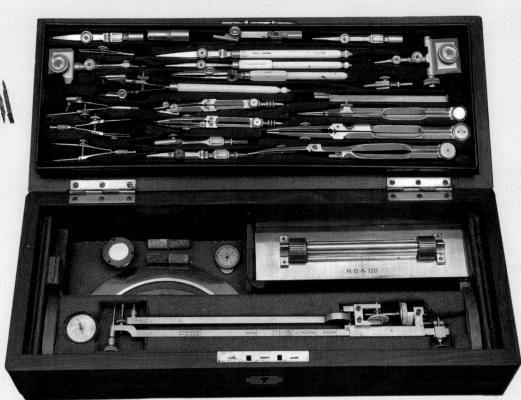

**ARCHITECT'S INSTRUMENTS**
Rosewood; **late 19th century**

Included are various sizes of dividers and compasses, a protractor, parallel ruler and planimeter. Some of the pens have ivory handles, but nearly all the other instruments by this time are nickel-plated. (*Above right*)

**MARINER'S PROTRACTOR**
*Robert Bancks, London (worked 1791–1827)*

The two arms fold outwards. Its wooden case is also circular. (*Above*)

The "proportional" compass, invented by the Swiss Jost Bürgi (1552–1632), was, despite its name, actually a pair of dividers whose two arms could be adjusted by means of a central joint; it was used to scale sets of plans up or down. The pantograph, a jointed framework of parallel pairs of rods, introduced for general use in the 18th century, did the same job of copying on a different scale but much faster. The eidograph was a 19th-century improvement on the pantograph. The planimeter, invented by the Swiss Jacob Amsler in the mid-19th century, could provide the measure of any area on a map or plan simply by tracing round its outline. The chartometer was (and is) a small device with a wheel and a scale for measuring the length of roads, rivers, railways or boundaries. The ellipsograph, designed by the English civil engineer John Farey (1791–1851) in the early 19th century, enabled perfect ellipses to be drawn.

For centuries surveyors, architects, engineers and draughtsmen have needed small instruments to draw scale plans. The first were the set-square, T-square and parallel rulers and dividers, which were by the 16th century supplied in a fitted box. A high-quality set of brass and iron instruments was supplied in a gold-tooled leather case. The more commonly available 18th-century sets typically have an upright case with a flip-top lid (not unlike that of a pack of cigarettes), covered with black fish-skin or mottled green and white shagreen. The instruments inside slide into small holes or compartments cut into a wooden block. The three ivory rulers should all have the same maker's name on them – otherwise they are replacements. (It is better to have an original set than an assemblage of instruments from different periods.) Early-19th-century sets are still available, and these may include a set of watercolour paint blocks and brushes.

ELECTRICAL MACHINES, VACUUM PUMPS, GLASS OR COPPER RETORTS –
THE INSTRUMENTS USED BY EARLY SCIENTISTS MAKE UP AN UNUSUAL
CATEGORY OF ANTIQUES.

# "PHILOSOPHICAL" INSTRUMENTS

Since early scientists were regarded as philosophers the instruments they used were called "philosophical". For hundreds of years, until the demarcation of the sciences in the mid-19th century, this general term was used to describe all apparatus used to investigate natural phenomena, as opposed to instruments for what were termed the exact sciences, such as mathematics, astronomy and surveying. Makers' trade labels from the 1750s advertised "Optical, Mathematical and Philosophical Instruments".

The 17th and 18th centuries saw the start of public scientific lectures and demonstrations. In England this was chiefly due to the founding in 1660 of the Royal Society for the Improvement of Natural Knowledge, under the patronage of Charles II. Later it was called simply the Royal Society, and many leading scientists of the day were members.

### MECHANICAL INSTRUMENTS

In his *Principia Mathematica* (1686–7), Sir Isaac Newton set out the three fundamental Laws of Motion, concerning the behaviour of bodies when acted on by external forces. Applying Newton's principles, the English scientist George Atwood produced in 1780 the Fall Machine, which combined a pillar 2.1 m (7 ft) high, a scale and a clock mechanism with pendulum to show the rate of acceleration of a falling body. Other Atwood apparatus demonstrated the Moments of Forces and the effect of gravity. A popular toy of the time, still seen, is the equilibrist, a carved ivory or wooden figure balancing on top of a column. Its long arms have weights at the end which lower the centre of gravity to below the point of balance, so that no matter how much the body wobbles or rotates, it seldom falls off. Other items showed the principles of levers, wedges and pulleys and how a block and tackle can be used to raise a heavy load with minimum effort by the operator.

In the 19th century the French physicist Jean Foucault (1819–68) rediscovered the gyroscope, (known as a children's toy beforehand), whose rotating flywheel maintains a stable axis independent of surrounding movement.

### HYDROSTATIC AND HYDRODYNAMIC INSTRUMENTS

Hydrostatics and hydrodynamics are the studies of the equilibrium of, and the pressures exerted by, fluids at rest and in motion respectively. Ancient Greek hydrostatic and hydrodynamic devices included a series of interconnecting glass jars of different shapes and sizes, in all of which, when they were filled with water, the water level settled at the same height; a metal column with a line of holes up it showed that the

**EXPERIMENTAL GYROSCOPE**
Brass; mid 19th century

The gyroscope was another invention by the Frenchman Jean Bernard Leon Faucault, who also used the pendulum to demonstrate the rotation of the earth. This instrument can do the same thing, but it also developed into a toy. As with a compass needle the spin is maintained in a fixed direction. It remained a demonstration apparatus or educational toy until the mid-1920s, when German scientists realized its first practical use could be in the inertial guidance system of a rocket they were designing.

**SET OF LEYDEN JARS**
*French*
Brass and glass; oak case;
**early 19th century**

The bottles, used to store
static electricity, are
connected by a "spider" to
a central contact point.
(*Above*)

**DIP CIRCLE**
*Signed on base: Robinson, 38
Devonshire St, Portland Place,
London*
**Brass; early 19th century**

The instrument has a blued
steel needle resting on a
double fulcrum; the circular
scale is silver and engraved
in four quadrants with two
movable magnifiers to read
it. The magnetic needle of a
dip circle moves in a

vertical plane in contrast to
the horizontal movement
of a compass and measures
the earth's magnetic field.
(The maker of this
example, Thomas Charles
Robinson, was an optician,
mathematician and
philosophical instrument-
maker who worked
between 1821 and 1835).
(*Right*)

# CALCULATING INSTRUMENTS

The abacus, a counting-frame with wires
along which beads are moved, was used by
the Greeks and Romans and is still employed
by street traders in some parts of the world.
No further progress with calculating aids was
made until the Scottish mathematician John
Napier (1550–1617) invented logarithms in
the early 17th century. This led to the invention in 1621 of the slide rule by the English
mathematician William Oughtred. This was
usually made of boxwood and had the numbers stamped on it. In the 19th century Fuller
invented a cylindrical version, no more than
30 cm (12 in) long but with the capability of a

slide rule 9 m (30 ft) long. It is not hard to
find nowadays and is relatively inexpensive.

In 1645 the French philosopher and
mathematician Blaise Pascal (1623–62)
invented the first mechanical calculating
machine, which could add and subtract by
means of a system of gear wheels. By 1888 it
had been improved to multiply and divide as
well. Another Frenchman, Thomas de
Colmar, produced his arithmometer in 1820.
As with other similar machines, the numbers
in the calculation were first set in a line of
small windows, then an ivory handle at the
side was turned to provide the result.

**ELECTRIC MOTOR**
*English*
**late 19th century**

This was used to
demonstrate the motive
power of electricity.

**ELECTRO-STATIC FRICTION GENERATOR OF THE RAMSDEN PATTERN**
Brass, glass and walnut;
**early 19th century**

force of a jet depends on the head of water; and a siphon glass, showed how liquid can be drawn off by atmospheric pressure. Later, in the 17th century a double pump with two cylinders and two handles showed how a continuous stream could be produced; large versions were used by firemen until the 1850s and the introduction of the steam fire-pump.

The specific-gravity balance gave the mass of small objects in water. It became popular when gold guineas began to be counterfeited in the late 18th century: a false coin which weighed the same as a genuine one in air would not pass the test when weighed in water.

Wines and spirits imported into England were subject to a tax related to their alcoholic strength. In 1826 a scientific determinant of this became available when the optician and instrument-maker Robert Brettell Bate invented the hydrometer, with which the specific gravity of a liquid could be tested by means of a float and attached weights. These were supplied together with a thermometer and sliding rule, in a fitted mahogany box. Home brewers still use hydrom-

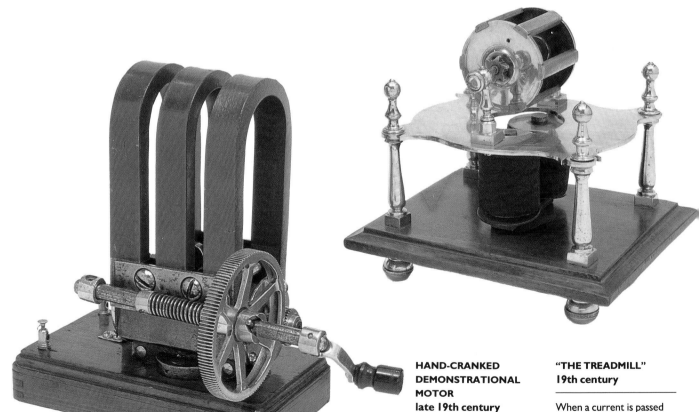

**HAND-CRANKED DEMONSTRATIONAL MOTOR**
**late 19th century**

The windings rotate between the poles of three vertically mounted magnets. (*Left*)

**"THE TREADMILL"**
**19th century**

When a current is passed through its windings a magnetic field is created that attracts the iron base of the cage, making it revolve. (*Above*)

eters, and collectors seek out early examples, notably silver ones made in continental Europe.

Most of the experiments described here became much more important in the late 19th century when hydraulics, the use of liquids as motive power, began to be used in industry.

### PNEUMATIC INSTRUMENTS

Pneumatics is the science of the properties of air and other gases. The chief experimental device was the vacuum pump. The first British air-pump was made by the Irish philosopher Robert Boyle (1627–91) and described in 1660. By the start of the 18th century Francis Hauksbee's model was generally adopted first in Britain, then on the Continent. This had an elegant design not unlike that of the microscope being made by Edmund Culpeper at the same time, and both instruments were shown as constellations on celestial globes after 1765.

Public demonstrations of the workings of the vacuum pump fascinated viewers. For example, the sound of a ringing bell in the pump would diminish as the vacuum increased; and a guinea and a feather would float down together when released simultaneously under a bell jar, in which a pump was creating a vacuum.

Nineteenth-century vacuum pumps are seen regularly at specialist auctions. Seventeenth-century ones often have wooden frames; early to mid-19th-century ones (often French) are entirely of brass. Collectors should ensure that the glass dome over a vacuum pump is the heavy duty sort and not lightweight, fit only for a stuffed owl or an ormolu mantel clock.

### ELECTRICITY-GENERATING INSTRUMENTS

A piece of amber rubbed on the sleeve had long been known to produce a static electric charge that attracted small objects, but the discovery of a method of increasing this force had to wait until 1709, when Francis Hauksbee, following the construction of his vacuum pump, made the first electrostatic friction generator, a revolving glass globe that came into contact with a pad of sheepskin or leather. By 1780 it had been improved by Edward Nairne, John Cuthbertson and Jesse Ramsden, and eventually in 1880 James Wimshurst produced the most efficient model with two counter-rotating glass discs. As opposed to current electricity, which provides power for industry and home, static electricity has little use. Until the end of the 19th century, however, one version was used by doctors to give what they believed to be beneficial small

shocks to certain patients. These machines, contained in a compact mahogany box, are still easily found today; they can still give the user an unpleasant jolt.

### CHEMICAL INSTRUMENTS

Until the mid-19th century chemists were generally regarded as apothecaries and suppliers of medicines and leeches, and in addition a distinction was made between organic chemistry, concerned with carbon compounds and therefore with living things, and inorganic, concerned with all the other elements. However, as the 19th century progressed there developed an increasing interest in the properties of individual chemicals and the scientific laws governing their interaction.

Chemical instruments had remained the same for centuries. Retorts, or alembics, used for distillation, were of copper or glass, and pestles and mortars were of bronze, stone, glass or lignum vitae (a dense hardwood). As proper scientific experiments got underway in the mid-19th century, slender glass pipes, burettes (tubes for measuring liquids) and pipettes (tubes for measuring and transferring) were introduced in response to the need for greater precision. It was also realized that old methods of weighing were not exact enough for chemistry, and, to take one example, balances began to be made with glass pans, so that there would no longer be the risk of a reaction between a substance and the metal pan it was in, upsetting the measurement. The German chemist Ludwig Oertling (1818–93), who worked in London, made the best chemical balances of the late 19th century. They were enclosed in glass cases, in order to prevent interference from draughts or foreign bodies.

In 1855 the German chemist Robert Bunsen (1811–99) invented the gas burner named after him. This produced an instant source of high-temperature but easily controllable heat for laboratory work.

**CHEMIST'S PESTLE AND MORTAR**
Turned lignum-vitae;
**18th century**

This wood is impervious to water and indeed sinks in it, one of only two woods to do so. Traditionally, it was said that magicians' wands were made of the same material.

THE COMPLICATED PATCHWORK OF TRADITIONAL SYSTEMS OF WEIGHTS
ENSURED THAT MACHINES FOR MEASURING THESE ARE AMONG THE
OLDEST EXAMPLES OF ALL SCIENTIFIC INSTRUMENTS.

# WEIGHING AND MEASURING MACHINES

Accurate weights and measures have been needed since the time that man first started trading. The two most common types of balance, made all over Europe, were the equal-arm type, where the pivotal point is in the centre and the object to be weighed is placed in one scale and counterbalancing weights in the other; and the Roman, steelyard or unequal-arm type, in which the short arm takes the thing weighed and a single weight is moved along the long, graduated arm. Both types are still in common use, but the Roman balance has the advantage of not having any small weights that can get lost.

Most countries had their own gold coinage by the Middle Ages – for example, Spain its pistoles, Italy its sequins. When a merchant from one country accepted payment in the coins of another it was advisable to do so by weight and not at a numerical exchange rate, since it was not

unknown for coins to be clipped or "sweated" (removing parts of the metal by friction). For this reason small portable balances were common. Notable examples were produced in the Netherlands and southern Germany in the 17th and 18th centuries, and examples with an interesting trade label and a complete set of weights are much sought after.

In 1775, the English scale maker Anthony Wilkinson produced a slim folding balance to be carried in a gentleman's waistcoat pocket. The outer case was mahogany, but rare examples are found with brass, ivory or tortoiseshell cases. A French version from the same period has a cursor and a table in the lid listing all the gold coins then circulating in Europe.

The introduction of the penny post in England by Rowland Hill in 1840 meant that for the first time letters were sent by weight and

**LETTER SCALE**
*Stamped: "G.T. Ratcliff, Maker"*
**Brass and mahogany; late 19th century**

---

Unusually, the scale includes a full set of square weights (the little ones are often missing). It is constructed using the French inventor Robertval's design, so that the two pans remain parallel to the table as they tilt. The rest of the mechanism is hidden in the base.

**BANKER'S SCALE**
*Stamped: "J. Hare, Maker Brighton"*
**Brass; 1880s**

The steel knife edges rest on agate pivot points. This would have been used for weighing bags of coins – even gold sovereigns. The pedal in the front operates the erection mechanism which raises the pans off the table once they have been loaded with coins and weights.

**EQUAL-ARM LETTER BALANCE ON AN OVAL BASE**

The pans are Wedgwood plaques. (*Top left*)

**"KNEELING BOY" LETTER SCALE**

*Stamped: H.B. Wright, No 130, London, Decr 20 1839"*

**SET OF COUNTY STANDARD WEIGHTS**

*Stamped: "County of Ayr 1859"*

not according to distance. "The first four ounces for One Penny" was the rule, and the penny black postage stamp became famous. Scale manufacturers produced a wonderful variety of small scales to weigh letters.

Since the time of Henry VII, at the end of the 15th century, the standard capacity measure for ale, wine or corn had been established as the Winchester (named after the ancient capital of Saxon England), which was subdivided into bushels, half-bushels, quarts and gills. Traditionally, farmers harvested their grain by the bushel, a measure by volume, but sold by weight. In 1824 the chondrometer, or corn bal-

ance, a small scale which converted one to the other, was introduced.

For hundreds of years, trading standards officials checked traders in the towns and shires to see that they were offering fair measure or weight. In the 19th century each county kept standard sets of heavy bronze measures, the larger ones with two handles on each side. Some were also made for overseas and were engraved with relevant information – for example, "Colony of Grenada 1834". Standard sets of weights were also made. They were usually of brass, spherical or bell-shaped, and supplied in sets from 56lb to ¼oz.

# PHOTOGRAPHY

The camera obscura had been known for centuries. A small hole in the wall of an otherwise enclosed chamber projects an

Milanese mathematician Girolamo Cordano first fitted a lens to the aperture, to improve the brightness of the image, in 1550; a few years later the Venetian Daniele Barbaro (1528–70) introduced a diaphragm in order to improve the definition of the image produced by a simple convex lens. The camera obscura was well-known in China and Europe of the Middle Ages, and was especially useful for observing eclipses of the sun. In 1800 Thomas Wedgwood, of the famous pottery family, experimented with this principle and exposed paper coated with silver nitrate to sunlight; he came close to inventing photography, but died early at the age of 34.

Research continued in France. Joseph Nicephore Niepce (1765–1833), in retirement in the countryside, coated pewter plates with bitumen and produced the first photograph, of the roof-tops of the family home, in 1827. He was joined by Louis Daguerre (1787–1851) three years later and by 1839 the Daguerreotype was launched. By 1841 thousands of studios had opened in Paris and London, putting a great many portrait artists out of work.

Niepce died in 1833 and Daguerre in 1851, but in England William Henry Fox Talbot (1800–77) started his own experiments and by

1835, having fitted a lens to his camera obscura, succeeded in fixing an image to a paper plate. He was granted a patent in 1841 and called it a "Calotype", from the Greek "beautiful". His process had one enormous advantage: from one "negative" any number of "positives" or prints could be made.

The first photographic cameras were two simple wooden boxes, the smaller, with the lens, sliding in and out of the larger. At the back of the larger box, opposite the lens, was the sensitized plate on which the image would be fixed. The cases were walnut, beech or later mahogany, with brass trim and fittings. By 1844 the back and front of the camera were in two separate parts united with a leather concertina between them. The two halves were moved in and out by a rack-and-pinion mechanism which had the effect of focusing the image.

**ROSS WET-PLATE CAMERA WITH ACCESSORIES** c. 1860

## FURTHER READING

The following list of materials for further reading offers a broad range of literature. Both specialist and general works are included. While every effort has been made to give the date of the most recent edition, new ones may have been published since this book went to press.

Banfield, Edwin
**Barometers** (3 vols)
Trowbridge, Wiltshire

Bennett, J.A.
**The Divided Circle**
Oxford 1987

Bennion, Elisabeth
**Antique Medical Instruments**
London 1979

**The Billings Microscope Collection** (museum catalogue)
Washington D.C.

Burnett, J.E., and A.D. Morrison-Low
**"Vulgar and Mechanick": The Scientific Instrument Trade in Ireland, 1650–1921**
Edinburgh 1989

Crawforth, M.A.
**Weighing Coins**
London 1979

Gouk, Dr P.
**The Ivory Sundials of Nuremburg 1500–1700**
Cambridge 1988

Daumas, Maurice
**Scientific Instruments of the 18th and 19th Centuries**
New York 1972

Hambly, Myra
**Drawing Instruments**
London 1989

Randier, Jean
**Marine Navigation Instruments**
London 1980

Turner, Anthony
**Early Scientific Instruments: Europe, 1400–1800**
London 1987

Turner, Gerard L'Estrange
**Nineteenth Century Scientific Instruments**
London 1983

**— Essays on the History of the Microscope**
Oxford 1980

**— The Great Age of the Microscope**

Wynter, Harriet, and Anthony Turner
**Scientific Instruments**
London 1975

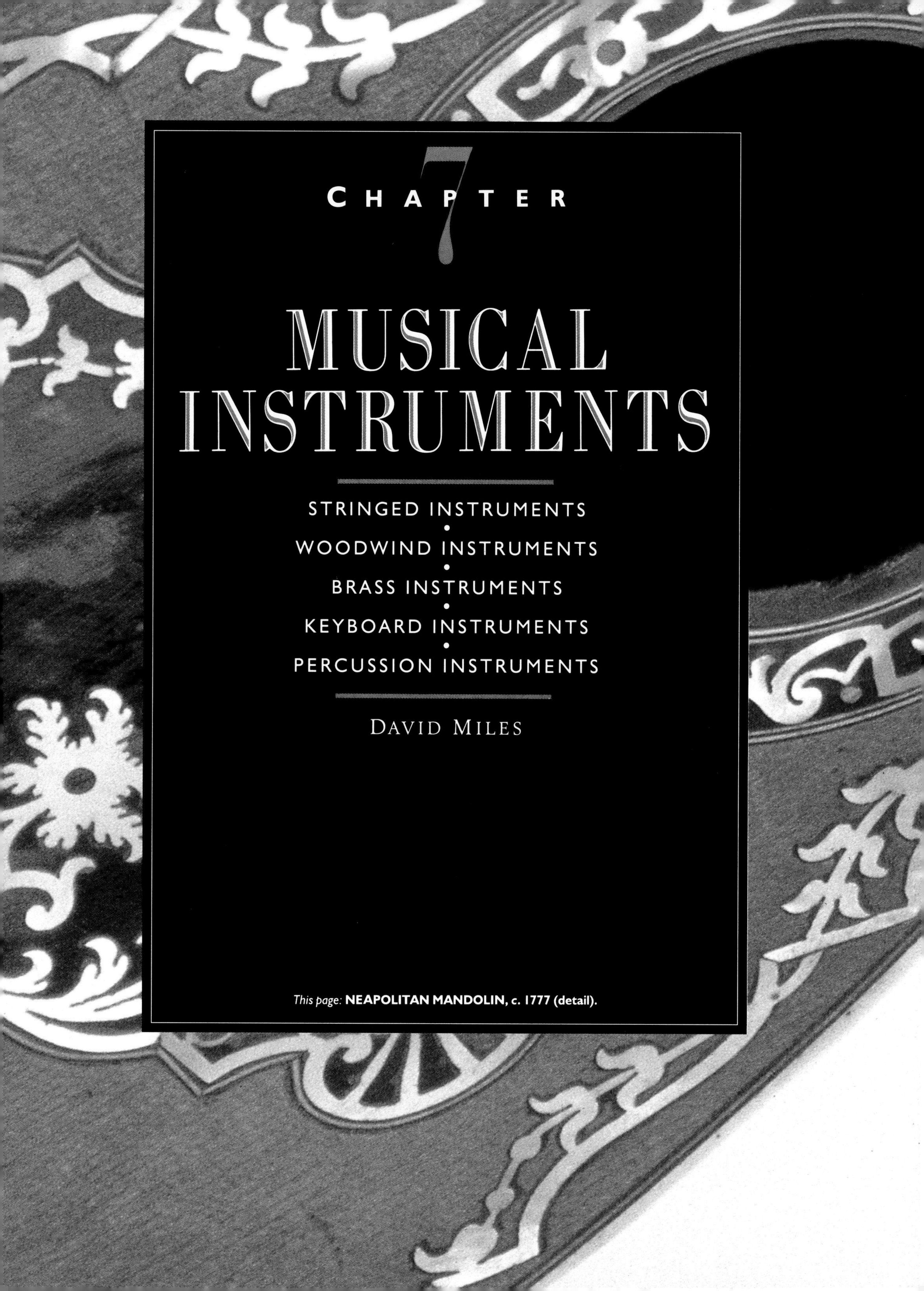

# CHAPTER 7

# MUSICAL INSTRUMENTS

STRINGED INSTRUMENTS
·
WOODWIND INSTRUMENTS
·
BRASS INSTRUMENTS
·
KEYBOARD INSTRUMENTS
·
PERCUSSION INSTRUMENTS

DAVID MILES

*This page:* **NEAPOLITAN MANDOLIN, c. 1777 (detail).**

# MUSICAL INSTRUMENTS

THE GRADUAL DEVELOPMENT OF THE SOPHISTICATED ENSEMBLE OF
INSTRUMENTS RECORDS CONTRIBUTIONS FROM THE
CHANGING TASTES OF SUCCESSIVE AGES.

**CITTERN**
*John Preston*
**c. 1770**

This cittern, or English
guitar, is a good example of
its period, with pine belly,
ink purfling, a metal rose,
and striped maple sides and
back. The tortoiseshell
fingerboard is tuned by
watch-key tuning.

While most European musical instruments can be easily recognized
in today's modern orchestra, their origin and development may
be traced back to Greek and Roman times.

With the fall of the Roman Empire causing political conflict and
chaos, the only source of harmony in the West was found in the teach-
ings of the early Christian missionaries. However, because the Church
forbade the use of musical instruments in worship, few instruments
have survived from that period until the 12th century.

It was not until the 13th century that several stringed instruments
were mentioned in early texts: the dulcimer, psalteries, rebec and
trumpet marine. The rebec, related to the two-stringed Arabian instrument called the rabab, also appeared in the West at this time, and was
played with a short, arch-shaped bow. The dulcimer and psalteries
were primitive zithers.

So far as the development of woodwinds is concerned, two types of
flute appeared at this time: the transverse flute and the upright flute,
later known as the recorder. The principal reed instrument was the
shawm, which was called the chalumeau in France. The bagpipe, too,
can be dated from this period, and it has remained in use, with some
modification, until the present day.

Even up to the 13th century, the Roman Empire influenced military
musical instruments, especially horns: these were mainly of animal
horn and followed the Roman pattern of being played in the fashion of
a military fanfare. The oliphant, made, as its name suggests, of elephant
tusk, was used as a grand ceremonial horn.

Keyboard instruments were first mentioned at the beginning of the
15th century, when the harpsichord and clavichord were introduced.
Virginals and spinets might also have been known. The hurdy-gurdy
was first referred to in manuscripts dating from the 12th century; this
was mainly a folk instrument played by minstrels and street musicians.

Percussion instruments consisted of small cymbals and kettledrums, known as nakers. Tambourines were introduced, and at this time were long, narrow drums struck with sticks.

### RENAISSANCE PERIOD

During this time, a distinction was made between various families of musical instruments. As the range of one instrument's register was perceived to be restricted, the development of another to encompass a wider range became inevitable, thus making possible an overall family of instruments comprising treble through descant, alto, tenor, baritone, bass and contrabass.

The most widely known stringed instruments of the Renaissance were the lute, originally an Arabic instrument introduced to Spain by the Moors and thence to the rest of Europe, the guitar, also of Spanish origin, and the bowed fiddle, originally a medieval minstrel's instrument, which later developed into the family of viols. At the height of the Renaissance the viols, or viole da gamba as they were known in Italy, encompassed a complete range of instruments from treble to bass. The small bowed fiddle was not entirely superseded by the viols, but was transformed into the viola da braccia, itself the forerunner of the modern violin and cello.

The woodwind section was evolving in a similar way: various sizes of recorder were used, from treble to contrabass, and offshoots of the recorder such as the tabor pipe and flageolet coexisted with them. Transverse flutes could also encompass higher and lower registers. Later in the 16th century ranges of reed instruments were developing, the most important of which was the double-reeded section of crumhorn, racket, shawm, curtal, fagott, pommer and dulcian. The fagott, or bassoon, later developed into its own family to give an extended register.

During the Renaissance brass wind instruments, while not necessarily made of brass until later, were forming an independent instrumental section for the first time. Most widely used was the cornett, which was made of horn or wood with finger holes along one side. The serpent appeared toward the end of the 16th century and, as its name suggests, was shaped like a snake with finger holes along the body of the instrument. The sackbut, or trombone as it was later known, first appeared in the early 16th century and became widely recognized under the influence of the brass manufacturers at Nuremberg.

Keyboard instruments developed by increasing the number of strings. In the case of the harpsichord, several strings would be attached to each key. The organ improved with the addition of a second keyboard, together with a mixture of stops to give a variety of sounds.

In the percussion section, the kettledrum, or timpani as it was later called, was a large, bowl-shaped instrument originally introduced by the Arabs to Europe in the 15th century. The xylophone and a variety of handbells also were being played at this time.

### BAROQUE PERIOD

From the mid 17th century, with the decline of the Renaissance and the emergence of the Baroque period, instruments were gradually transforming to cope with the more demanding and flexible music that had begun to develop.

The lute continued to be played during the 17th century and in addition showed some variations from the original instrument as may be

**CHITARRONE**
*Michielle Horton, Padua*
**c. 1610**

This instrument shows stringing for six double courses plus six single bass courses. On the belly is a good example of a fine triple fretwork rose.

**KEY BUGLE**
*Stamped on the bell garland
"McFARLANE'S IMPROVED
MANIFACTURED BY I.
KOHLER LONDON"* **1835**

This instrument is made in
silver with a silver-gilt
garland and has ten keys.

seen by the advent of the theorbo and the chitarrone, which may be
recognized by their extended necks. The guitar became firmly established, and the mandolin appeared at the beginning of the 18th century.
Although the viol was well established throughout most of Europe, the
violin was becoming more popular towards the middle of the 18th
century, especially in Italy.

Up to the 17th century most woodwind instruments were
restricted, since the notes produced did not exceed the number of finger holes and the style of monody required a much wider range of register and dynamics. Many instruments became obsolete, but some
developed into the established instruments of the orchestra, such as
the transverse flute, oboe and bassoon. At the beginning of the 18th
century, the French chalumeau was modified and transformed into a
single-reed instrument – the clarinet – which was able to produce a
greater range of register.

Although trombones and trumpets remained relatively unchanged
up to the 18th century, it is at this time that the French hunting horn
developed into the orchestral French horn.

The further development of keyboard instruments first may be seen
in the harpsichord, which evolved into either a continuo or a melodic
solo instrument. This resulted in harpsichords with double or even

treble keyboards, which allowed greater emphasis of timbre and dynamics. Keyboards were also extended to permit better expression of the range of music in the late 18th century. At the same time the clavichord had also been transformed from a fretted to an unfretted instrument with the addition of an extended keyboard to five octaves. The organ improved with the addition of stops, voicing strings and vocals. Pedal boards were also introduced.

### CLASSICAL PERIOD

With the advent of the classical period in the late 18th century and Romanticism in the 19th century, there was a necessity for musicians to achieve a much better tonal quality and dynamic sound. This coincided with the ability of instrument makers to improve their manufacturing techniques, which helped musicians to become more technically proficient, giving the desired tonal and dynamic effects.

Stringed instruments were broadly divided into two sections, bowed and plucked strings. With the introduction of the viola, cello and double bass to complete the violin family, the orchestral string section was formed. In the early 19th century the harp underwent development with the introduction of seven pedals, which had the ability to raise notes in each octave by a semitone. Although the guitar and mandolin were widely used in their respective countries of origin, Spain and Italy, it was the cittern, or English guitar, which predominated in England during the late 18th and early 19th centuries. There were also some hybrid plucked instruments such as the harp lute, dital harp and lyra guitar, which developed in Europe from the late 18th century but fell out of use during the mid 19th century.

As with stringed instruments, the woodwind benefited from improved instrumental manufacture. While players at the height of the Classical period were able to produce chromatic notes with the aid of cross fingering, the addition of mechanical keys to the body of the instrument helped to produce an easier chromatic scale. Over the Classical and Romantic periods, additions were made to the woodwind sections of flute, oboe, bassoon and clarinet by extending each family of instrument to give greater range. In the middle of the 19th century there appeared a new single-reed instrument in France. This was the saxophone, which became most popular in French army bands and later spread to England and North America. A double-reeded instrument appeared at about the same time: this was the sarrusophone.

Brass wind instruments remained relatively unchanged until the end of the 18th century with the introduction of keys to the trumpet, these, however, were superseded in the mid 19th century by the invention of the valve mechanism. This gave the trumpet much more versatility and brilliance. At the same time the serpent was replaced by the ophicleide, a large metal keyed instrument used as a bass in the brass range. The ophicleide was in turn replaced in the latter part of the 19th century by the tuba, which had much better intonation because of valve mechanism. Horns also benefited from the application of valves to give better intonation and chromatic flexibility.

Although the harpsichord developed with some modification until the end of the 18th century, it was the piano that established itself as the major keyboard instrument. Pianos developed from the early square, upright instruments to the cast-iron framed models of the mid 19th century. They became the most widely used of all instruments because of their tonal versatility and overall register.

**BASSET HORN**
*I. Miraz, Udine*
**c. 1830**

This basset horn in "F" has fourteen square brass keys and is made of stained boxwood with ivory mounts. There are three joints with a 120-degree bend in the middle joint. The globular bell is set at right angles to the lower joint. This model has a transitional shape between the earlier "box"-formed lower joint and metal bell and the later straight model.

**SERPENT**
*Haye, London*
**c. 1825**

This example has three keys and is made of wood with leather binding and brass mounts, bell rim and crook. The instrument is typical of serpents used in military bands.

THE VARIETY OF STRINGED INSTRUMENTS GIVE SOME IDEA OF THEIR
IMPORTANCE TO MAKING MUSIC – AN IMPORTANCE IN PART OWED TO
THE GREAT RANGE OF SOUNDS THEY ARE ABLE TO REPRODUCE.

# STRINGED INSTRUMENTS

While it is desirable to collect stringed instruments that have little or no restoration and are in perfect working order, the probability of finding such a treasure is unlikely. Therefore it is necessary to make a judgement on the degree of repair that has been carried out on the instrument. The most common causes of damage are expansion, which creates body cracks, and twisting or raising of the neck, due to string tension. Ornately carved roses may be badly damaged or totally missing from the belly, and although this may not affect the playing ability of the instrument it should be considered when collecting. As an aid to collecting, some stringed instruments are labelled by the maker. These labels are stuck inside the body of the instrument and can be read through the F-holes of bowed instruments and the sound hole of plucked instruments. Occasionally a maker's stamp can be seen at the base of the neck.

### VIOLA-DA-GAMBA

The family of viola-da-gamba ("leg viola" in Italian) is so called because the instruments were all held between the legs while being played. They were developed in Italy in the 16th century but soon spread throughout Europe, where they continued to be played until the late 18th century. The family consists of trebles, tenors and basses, although for each size there could exist dimensional variations that suited each player best for their consort ideas. The approximate size for body length of instrument is: treble, 35–40 cm (14–16 in); tenor, 42–53 cm (17–21 in); lyra viol, 54–60 cm (21–24 in); divisional viol, 62–67 cm (25–27 in); bass, 68–71 cm (27–29 in). While the usual number of strings for most viols is six, it is not uncommon to find five at various periods of development and, for the bass viol, five, six or seven.

### VIOLIN

Violins were members of the viola-da-braccia family and were known to have been played in

Italy in the mid 16th century. The family comprised tenor and bass violin, corresponding later to the viola and violoncello, as well as the instrument known simply as the violin, the treble instrument of the family.

The shape of the violin remained relatively unchanged until about 1800, when certain modifications were made to the bridge, neck, bassbar and fingerboard of the instrument to assist players with the demands of more modern music and a higher playing pitch.

The viola, which is the next larger member of the violin family, is tuned a fifth of an octave lower than the violin and is therefore deeper in pitch. The comparative length of body between violin and viola is: violin, 33–36 cm (13–15 in); viola, 40–47 cm (16–19 in).

The violoncello had originally been intended for the bass part of the violin orchestra, but in the early 18th century developed into a solo instrument. Violoncellos previous to 1700 were large instruments, but after this date they

**VIOLA-DA-GAMBA**
*Joachim Tielke*
Labelled "in Hamburg/an 1685"

The back shows a decorated carved relief of an oval medallion of acanthus leaves and flowers surrounding a female figure; she holds a bow and arrow and is seated on a chariot drawn by stags. The pegbox is surmounted by a carved head. (*Left*)

**POCHETTE**
*Labelled by the maker:*
*"Bonci/Sebastiano/anno/1770/ in/Castiglione/Fiorentius"*

This pochette has a maple body with a neck and head comprising one piece. (*Below*)

## MAKERS OF BOWED STRINGED INSTRUMENTS

| | | | |
|---|---|---|---|
| **AMATI, Andrea** | 1511–80 | Cremona | Violin |
| **AMATI, Antonio** | b c. 1540 | Cremona | Violin |
| **ROSE, John** | *fl.* second half 16th century | London | Viola-da-gamba |
| **DA SALO, Gasparo** | 1540–1609 | Brescia | Viola-da-gamba, violin |
| **AMATI, Hieronymus Girolamo** | 1561–1630 | Cremona | Violin |
| **MAGGINI, Giovanni Paolo** | 1580–1632 | Brescia | Violin |
| **AMATI, Nicolo** | 1596–1684 | Cremona | Violin |
| **STAINER, Jacob** | 1617–83 | Absam (Tyrol) | Violin |
| **TIELKE, Joachim** | 1641–1719 | Hamburg | Viola-da-gamba |
| **STRADIVARI, Antonio** | 1644–1737 | Cremona | Violin |
| **NORMAN, Barak** | 1670–1740 | London | Viola-da-gamba |
| **GUARNERI, Giuseppe** | 1698–1744 | Cremona | Violin |
| **LE JEUNE, François** | 1753–89 | Paris | Viola-da-gamba |

**VIOLIN**

*Antonio Stradivarius*
Labelled "Antonio Stradivarius Cremonensis/ faciebat Anon 1706"

This violin, known as the Ex-Tipolini, is alleged to have been the property of Franz Liszt, who gave it to the Marchese Scipione Tadolini, a sculptor.

gradually became smaller, with a body length of about 75 cm (30 in).

Although violins, violas and cellos have four strings, those on double basses vary from three to six. The size of double basses also varies, from the giant 17th-century Italian bass to the small chamber basses of the 18th century. The average orchestral bass, however, has a body length of about 120 cm (48 in).

The pochette, or dancing master's violin, was made from the mid 16th century to the end of the 18th century, and was used as an accompaniment for dance instructors giving private tuition. These instruments are small, tube-like violins built from either a single hollowed-out piece of wood or from separate ribs glued together. They were also made in the shape of miniature violins, but with extended necks.

### BOWS

The earliest bows were generally convex in shape with a tapered point, but with the need for more dynamic sound at the end of the 18th century, they gradually became longer and concave in shape with a swelling towards the tip. The "frog" is the name given to that part of the bow held by the player; it was made of ivory or ebony, and sometimes inlaid with mother-of-pearl or silver. The pre-eminent makers who perfected the shape of the bow at the end of the

18th century were John Dodd in England and François Tourte in France.

### LUTE, THEORBO AND CHITARRONE

Although the lute was an important instrument by the 15th century, it was replaced at the end of the 17th century by the theorbo, the chitarrone and other lesser variants. The classic pear shape of the lute is achieved by means of very thin ribs formed around the flat "belly" of the instrument; the upper ends of the ribs are attached to a broad neck, upon which a fretted fingerboard rests, and the head of the instrument that carries the tuning pegs is mounted at an angle of 90 degrees to the neck and fingerboard, resulting in a very distinctive outline. The strings are tied to a bridge, which is glued to the belly of the instrument, pass over a sound hole, which may have a beautifully carved insert known as a "rose" and travel over the fingerboard to terminate at the tuning pegs. The standard lute is strung to give six courses, which allow for either single or double stringing.

The theorbo was developed to provide longer bass strings. It has a longer neck than the lute, and a divided pegbox to give from six to eight essential courses on one, and six or seven extra bass courses on the other.

The chitarrone is a larger version of the theorbo. The courses are divided between a pegboard mounted lower down the neck of the instrument and one at the head. The usual stringing is of six double courses plus eight single bass courses.

### GUITAR

The guitar had its origins in Spain and was played throughout Europe by the 18th century. At this time the size of the guitar, which had a vaulted back, intricately carved rose, richly inlaid fingerboard and finely shaped head, was somewhat smaller than later instruments. By 1800 the shape of the guitar, which had been narrow and deep, became wider and shallower, with curved sides. The carved rose had disappeared to give an open sound hole, and the string courses changed from four or five to six. The fingerboard was lengthened, and the head was altered to accommodate machine pegs.

### CITTERN

Citterns developed throughout Europe from the 16th century. It was not until the middle of the 18th century, however, that a more specific form appeared, namely, the English guitar, with

**HARP-LUTE**
*Buchinger, London*
**c. 1810**

Painted and gilded, this instrument is in fine condition and comes in its original gold-stamped red leather, covered-wood case. The instrument's five sympathetic strings can clearly be seen. (*Above*)

**GUITAR**
*Louis Panormo, London*
**c. 1840**

Panormo was the only maker of guitars in the Spanish style working in London at this time. This example has ribs and back of rosewood, and a pine belly with purfling around the edge of the soundhole. The head is of sycamore with brass machine heads. (*Left*)

**LUTE**
*Mahler*
**c. 1740**

This six-course lute has a sycamore body and an ebony fingerboard. The typical pear shape of the lute remained relatively unchanged from the 16th century until the late 18th century. (*Above*)

its flat back, rounded pear-shaped outline and metal fretted fingerboard extending over the body toward the curved rose. The metal stringing, which usually has six double courses, passes from the lower end of the body over the bridge towards either a pegbox or a machine head, which allows strings to be inserted at the top of the head and then tightened by means of a watch key for tuning.

### LYRE GUITAR AND HARP LUTE

These instruments date from the late 18th century until about 1840 and are hybrid developments of the guitar, lyre and lute.

The lyre guitar is essentially a six-stringed guitar that stands on a flat base. It comprises a central fretted fingerboard flanked by two extended arms in the manner of a lyre, joined at the head by a crossbar. There may be either a single central sound hole or two smaller sound holes at each side of the stringing.

The harp lute is distinguished by a decorative pillar, in the manner of a harp, which extends from the body of the instrument and is joined to a parallel fingerboard by a curved arm. The instrument is strung along the full length of the curved arm to below a carved rose, the strings terminating at a wide bridge that may be diagonal or straight.

### MANDOLIN

By the late 18th century in Italy, the small lute, or mandora, had developed into the mandolin, the best-known models being the Neapolitan and Milanese. These round-backed instruments had four double courses, tuned like a violin with tortoiseshell mounts on the belly and ornate inlay on the fingerboard. The earlier Milanese mandolins had gut strings and were played with the fingers, whereas the Neapolitan mandolins had wire strings and were played with a plectrum.

### ZITHER AND DULCIMER

Early examples of zithers and dulcimers from the 17th and 18th century are known, but the Southern German and Austrian instruments of the 19th century are more common.

Zithers have a flat-backed soundboard, strung with up to 35 metal strings that are tuned by means of "wrest pins", somewhat in the manner of a piano. The instrument, however, is plucked and also has a fretted fingerboard.

The dulcimer is commonly used as a folk instrument, especially in Romania and Greece.

**MANDOLIN**
*Antonio Vinaccia, Naples*
**c. 1777**

This fine four course mandolin by the most famous Neapolitan mandolin maker has a ribbed pear-shaped back with mother-of-pearl inlay, and tortoiseshell inlay on the belly and fingerboard. *(Left)*

**ZITHER**
*Engleder, Monaco*
**c. 1740**

This form of zither has thirty strings, of which four run over frets. The head shows a typical "wave-shape" design for this style of instrument. *(Below)*

It differs from the zither in that there are no frets. The strings are stretched across a flat sound box and, unlike the zither, which is plucked, the dulcimer is played with a pair of sticks or beaters.

## BANJO

The earliest reference to the banjo appears to date from the beginning of the 19th century, when it developed in North America. It was brought to England in the middle of that century by the Christy Minstrels. The banjo is made up of a wooden hoop over which is stretched a vellum belly, held in place by either metal tacks or tension screws. A long neck extends from the tuning head down through the hoop to beneath the vellum. Unfretted banjos were more common in the early 19th century, and it was not until the plectrum style of playing was introduced later that fretted fingerboards and metal strings became usual.

## HURDY-GURDY

From the 12th century the hurdy-gurdy was known in many parts of Europe as a folk instrument. In France this instrument was refined somewhat in the 18th century by making the shape either rounded, like a lute back, or flat, like a guitar back. The strings are sounded by turning a wheel mounted on an axle that is placed inside the body of the instrument. As the wheel is turned by a handle next to the sound box, the strings are stopped by an arrangement of keys mounted in a key box above the body. At the other end of the body from the turning han-

**DULCIMER**
*Italian*
**c. 1700**

This early dulcimer has a black and gilt painted pine belly with two gilt fretted roses. Its base and legs are carved and gilt. *(Above)*

**HARP**
*James Hanley*
**c. 1840**

This English double action pedal harp is gilded with a painted soundboard in the Neo-Classical style. *(Right)*

**HURDY GURDY**
*Stamped "Varquain", Paris*
**c. 1750**

This example is decorated in ebony and ivory. *(Below)*

dle is the pegbox for six strings, three passing either side of the key box. By the late 18th century, the heads were usually ornately carved into a scroll or even male or female heads.

## HARP

The harp had been known from medieval times and developed in the Renaissance, when the demands of newer music required change. This was achieved by the invention of the double harp, or arpa doppia, which had a row of chromatic strings alongside the diatonic ones. By the middle of the 17th century, a triple harp

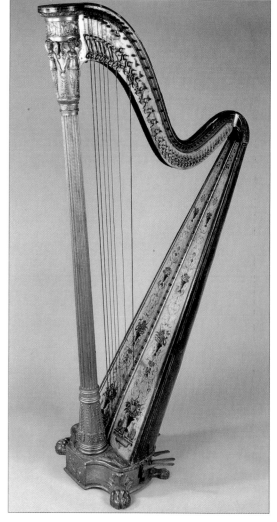

was invented, giving two outer rows of diatonic and an inner row of chromatic strings. This became a popular soloist's instrument in England by the end of the 17th century, but it was adopted more enthusiastically in Wales and developed into the traditional Welsh harp of the 18th and 19th centuries.

In Bavaria and the Tyrol, meanwhile, experiments were being conducted on a single strung harp. This instrument was tuned by means of hooks fixed to the neck and turned manually to raise the pitch by a semitone. This system was unsatisfactory during the playing of fast passages, because it was only with great difficulty that strings could be raised or lowered in pitch without interrupting the flow of music. This problem was resolved by the introduction of pedals in the early 18th century: seven pedals were situated in a semicircle around the base of the sound box and connected to the string mechanism by a series of levers inside the pillar of the instrument. By depressing each pedal the strings could be raised by a semitone. Later an extra row of pedals was introduced, which enabled the strings to be raised a further semitone.

By the late 18th century the decoration of the harp's pillar with carvings of Greek motifs, together with fine gilding, led to its being referred to as the Grecian harp. Later, in the mid 19th century, the harp acquired a further treble string and two bass strings, so becoming slightly larger. The manner of decoration also changed, with carvings of angels and arches giving this model the name Gothic harp.

Early Irish harps were just over 60 cm (24 in) long, but in the 18th century they developed into larger instruments with 30–50 strings made of brass. These instruments were played mainly by folk musicians until the decline of traditional playing in the late 18th century. Attempts were made to revive the tradition by introducing a portable gut-strung harp fitted with the hook mechanism (by John Egan of Dublin in 1819), and it is in this form that players have continued the tradition of Irish folk music.

## MAKERS OF PLUCKED STRINGED INSTRUMENTS

| | | | | | | | |
|---|---|---|---|---|---|---|---|
| **MALER, Laux** | d. 1552 | Bologna | Lute, theorbo, chitarrone | **BATTAGLIA** | c.1770 | Milan | Zither, dulcimer |
| **DUIFFOPRUGCAR, Gaspar** | 1514–71 | Lyon | Lute, theorbo, chitarrone | **LUPOT** | c.1780 | Orleans | Lyre guitar, harp lute |
| **HARTUNG, Michael** | fl. second half 16th century | Padua | Lute, theorbo, chitarrone | **PRESBLER, Francisco** | c.1780 | Milan | Mandolin |
| **TIEFFENBRUCKER, Wendelin** | 1552–1611 | Padua | Lute, theorbo, chitarrone | **COUSINEAU, Georges** | 1733–c.1800 | Paris | Harp |
| **SELLAS, Matteo** | c.1630 | Venice | Lute, theorbo, chitarrone | **LIGHT, Edward** | c.1747–1832 | London | Lyre guitar, harp lute |
| **VOBOAM, René** | c.1640 | Paris | Guitar | **ERARD, Sébastien** | 1752–1831 | Paris | Harp |
| **STRADIVARI, Antonio** | 1644–1737 | Cremona | Guitar | **NADERMANN, Henri** | c.1780–1835 | Paris | Harp |
| **HOCHBRUCKER, Jakob** | b.c.1673 | Donauwörth (Bavaria) | Harp | **PANORMO, Louis** | d. c.1850 | London | Guitar |
| **LOUVET, Pierre** | 1711–84 | Paris | Hurdy-gurdy | **PAGE, Josef** | c.1800 | Cadiz | Guitar |
| **HINTZ, Frederick** | c.1760 | London | Cittern | **COLSON** | c.1840 | Mirecourt | Hurdy-gurdy |
| **ZUMPE, Johannes** | c.1760 | London | Cittern | **TIEFENBRUNNER, Georg** | c.1850 | Munich | Zither, dulcimer |
| **PRESTON, John** | c.1770 | London | Cittern | **TORRES, Antonio** | c.1860 | Almeria | Guitar |
| **VINACCIA, Antonio** | c.1770 | Naples | Mandolin | **ERARD, Pierre** | c.1860 | Paris | Harp |

F ROM THE HUMBLE RECORDER TO THAT 19TH-CENTURY NOVELTY THE
SAXOPHONE, WOODWIND INSTRUMENTS HAVE BEEN A POPULAR
ACCOMPANIMENT TO STRINGS AND VOICES IN ALL KINDS OF MUSIC.

# WOODWIND INSTRUMENTS

Woodwinds, like string instruments, suffer from expansion cracks and because of this the joints of an instrument may have been repaired or replaced. As with the string section, this does not affect the playing ability of the instrument but it should be considered when collecting. Prior to the introduction of mechanical keywork, makers usually stamped their name or trademark on each separate joint. After mechanization, maker's marks were usually seen stamped on the upper joint. Another point to consider is the age of a replacement part: as wood ages a patina develops with handling, and therefore a joint that is replaced at a much later date can be recognized, by its having a different colour and possibly no maker's mark.

### RECORDER

The recorder came to prominence during the 16th century as a consort instrument. It was constructed of a tube with a narrow wind passage or mouthpiece at the head of the instrument, with seven finger holes along the front of the tube and a thumb hole at the back. The earlier recorders of the Renaissance were built as one piece and were therefore unable to be tuned, resulting in a range of sizes to blend with the different playing pitches of the other consort instruments. The typical range and size of early recorders was: descant, 32 cm (13 in); treble, 42 cm (17 in); tenor, 63 cm (25 in); bass, 93 cm (37 in).

While the one-piece cylindrical bore of the body gave a mellow tone that blended with other instruments of the consort of the Renaissance, a better form of recorder was later required – one that was capable of giving a more dynamic performance for the solos and small ensembles of the newer music of the Baroque. During the mid 17th century a three-jointed recorder was invented by a wind instrument player and maker in Paris called Jean Hotteterre. This three-section recorder was divided into a mouthpiece in the head joint, a

tapering middle joint with six finger holes and a foot joint with one finger hole. The head joint could be extended to adjust the tuning and the foot joint could be turned to give the most comfortable position for the player's index finger, although a key might have been fitted to close or open the seventh hole.

As with earlier recorders, the full family range was used in Baroque music, although in the 18th century the most important was the treble, for which much solo music was written. Because of their popularity, many fine examples of ornately carved treble recorders can be seen that date from this period.

From the mid 18th century onwards the recorder fell into decline. It was superseded by

**A SELECTION OF RECORDERS**

From left to right: Treble recorder, Johann Benedikt Gahn, Nuremberg, boxwood, c. 1700; Recorder in "A", Hartley, England, stained boxwood, c. 1750; Sopranino Recorder, J. Mason, London, boxwood, c. 1755; Picco pipe, stamped "Improved/London", cocuswood, c. 1860; Flute d'Accord, stamped "Jame/a Paris", boxwood with silver bands, c. 1780; Pitch pipe, stamped "Liddle/85 Devonshire St./Queens Sque/London", cocuswood, with brass and ivory mounts, c. 1860.

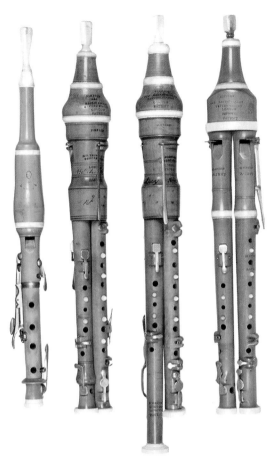

From left to right: French
flageolet, Gautrot, Paris,
boxwood with ivory bands
and five brass keys, c. 1860;
Pair of double flageolets,
stamped "Simpson/266
Regent Street/Oxford
Street/London/Patent",
boxwood, with ivory bands
and silver keys, c. 1830;
Double flageolet, stamped
"Simpson/266 Regent
Street/Oxford Street/
London/Improved/Patent",
boxwood, with ivory bands
and ten silver keys, c. 1835.

the transverse flute, which was better able to
cope with the more expressive music of the
Classical era.

### FLAGEOLET

Flageolets can be traced to medieval times, but
were more common in France from the 17th to
19th centuries. This instrument was a one-piece
pipe that had four finger holes and two thumb
holes and was played by blowing through a small
bone or ivory mouthpiece attached to the head.
Early flageolets were used to imitate bird calls,
but later they developed into larger instruments
used for playing dance music.

The flageolet was further advanced in
England at the beginning of the 19th century
with the invention of the double and triple flageolet. The single flageolet comprised a single
tapered body with six finger holes, whereas the
double flageolet consisted of two pipes that
were inserted into the head joint and could be
played either together or independently by
means of a "cut-off" key mounted in the head
joint. The third tube of the triple flageolet was
used as a drone accompaniment for the other
two pipes, and it incorporated a tuning plunger
and extra keys for giving bass notes.

## MAKERS OF UNREEDED WOODWIND INSTRUMENTS

| | | | | | | | | |
|---|---|---|---|---|---|---|---|---|
| **HOTTETERRE, Jean** | c.1648–1732 | Paris | Recorder, flute | | **GRENSER, Heinrich** | 1764–1813 | Dresden | Flute |
| **DENNER, Johann Christoph** | 1655–1707 | Nuremberg | Recorder | | **BAINBRIDGE, William** | d. c.1831 | London | Flageolet |
| **ROTTENBURGH, Jean** | 1672–1765 | Brussels | Recorder | | **LAURENT, Claude** | 1790–1857 | Paris | Flute |
| **BRESSAN, Peter** | fl. 1685–1731 | London | Recorder, flute | | **BOEHM, Theodore** | 1794–1881 | Munich | Flute |
| **STANESBY, Thomas** | c.1668–1734 | London | Recorder, flute | | **KEY, Thomas** | c.1810 | London | Serpent |
| **STANESBY, Thomas Jr** | 1692–1754 | London | Recorder, flute | | **PIFFAULT** | c.1810 | Paris | Serpent |
| **QUANTZ, Joachim** | 1697–1773 | Potsdam | Flute | | **PROWSE, Thomas** | 1816–56 | London | Flute |
| **GEDNEY, Caleb** | c.1769 | London | Flute | | **BUFFET, Auguste** | 1820–80 | Paris | Flute |
| **GRENSER, August** | 1720–1807 | Dresden | Flute | | **SIMPSON, John** | 1826–69 | London | Flageolet |
| **LOT, Thomas** | fl. 1740–85 | Paris | Flute | | **RUDALL, George and ROSE, John Mitchell** | fl.1821–71 | London | Flute |
| **POTTER, Richard** | 1726–1806 | London | Flute | | | | | |
| **FLORIO, Pietro** | c.1730–95 | London | Flute | | **FORVEILLE** | c.1830 | Paris | Serpent |
| **POTTER, William Henry** | 1760–1848 | London | Flute | | **HASTRICK** | c.1850 | London | Flageolet |
| **FRICHOT, Louis A.** | 1760–1825 | London and Paris | Serpent | | **LOT, Louis** | d.1890 | Paris | Flute |

## FLUTE

The early flutes of the Baroque era were built in three sections: a cylindrical head joint that contained an adjustable cork stopper for tuning, a middle conical joint and a foot joint that was fitted with a key for the closed E-flat finger hole. By the middle of the 18th century, the middle joint of the flute was subdivided into an upper and lower section. An extra three to six interchangeable upper parts were made of varying lengths for tuning to the required pitch. Further adjustments of tuning were also made with the introduction of a slide at the base of the foot joint that could be extended. During the 18th century the one-key flute was played extensively, and it was not until the latter part of the 1700s that extra keys were added to the body of the instrument.

By about 1800 the modern concert flute of the time had acquired eight keys. It was usually made of boxwood or ebony, with ivory or brass mounts between each joint and over the head and foot joints. This style of flute, referred to as the eight-keyed flute, continued to be played during the 19th century, with variations such as an eight-keyed glass flute by Claude Laurent of Paris and a flute with enlarged finger holes to give greater volume by T. Prowse of London.

During the 19th century a great deal of experimentation was carried out on the flute due to the introduction of mechanization. The most successful model was made by a flautist and engineer working in Munich, Theobald Boehm (1794–1881), who devised for each finger hole an arrangement of ring keys, which were connected to rods along the body of the flute. Because of the combination of more accurate tuning and fingering, the playing of a chromatic scale became much easier. The later development of the cylindrical Boehm-system flute in the mid 19th century differed very little from the modern orchestral flute of today.

## OBOE AND COR ANGLAIS

In the late 17th century experiments were conducted, mostly in Paris, to replace the shawm with a more modern double-reeded instrument. The oboe was the result: the narrowness of bore, smaller finger holes and narrower reed gave a much more refined sound. The oboe was made in three joints with finger holes. The upper two conical-shaped joints fitted into a bell-shaped lower joint. The third and fourth finger holes were doubled to give better tuning for their respective notes, and the lower

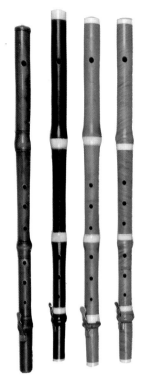

**18TH CENTURY FLUTES**

From left to right: by John Just Schuchart, London; by Cahusac, London; by Lépoule, France; stamped "Martin/Metzler/ Carlsruhe".

**OBOES**

From left to right: by W. Milhouse, London, c. 1815; English, c. 1760; by Goulding, London, c. 1820.

C and E-flat finger holes had keys fitted. During the second half of the 18th century, especially in England, a straight top joint to the oboe was found, but this was soon replaced by the introduction (from France and Germany) of a top joint with an onion-shaped finial. This was to become the classic shape throughout Europe until the mid 19th century.

Towards the end of the 18th century additional keys were fitted to the oboe, and in the early 19th century in France the oboe underwent more radical change by becoming simpler in outline, with a narrower bore. With the introduction of a much better key mechanism, the oboe was able to develop into a very sophisticated instrument. By the end of the 19th century a mechanical system known as the "Conservatoire" model was being widely used, and this in turn became the basis for the modern oboe of today.

The cor anglais, first seen in the mid 18th century, was curved in shape with a flared bell. As this instrument developed in the 19th century, its body changed from curved to straight, with a bulbous bell. Eventually it developed in the same way as the oboe to become the tenor voice in the orchestra to the oboe's treble.

## BASSOON

The bassoon seems to date from the latter part of the 17th century, when it replaced the 16th-century instrument called the curtal. Built in four sections – the wing, butt, long joint and top joint (called the bell) – it is assembled by inserting the wing and the long joint into their respective sockets in the butt and sliding the bell over the upper end of the long joint. The wing has a socket large enough to receive a brass "crook", which in turn holds an interchangeable double-reeded mouthpiece. The height of the bassoon in the 18th century was 122–127 cm (48–51 in), and it was commonly made of maple or pearwood. The standard instrument for most of the 18th century had four keys, but eventually two more were added, resulting in the more common six-keyed bassoon.

In early 19th-century France, further key additions were made and a better mechanism introduced, which led to this particular model being copied later in England. The bassoon was also redesigned in Germany, the end product being a much improved instrument that later became known as the Heckel-system bassoon.

Various sizes of bassoon were made from the 18th century onward: the tenoroon was a small

**BASSOONS**

From left to right: English, stained maple with six brass keys, c. 1780; by G. Astor, London, stained maple with ten brass keys, c. 1800. (*Above*)

**CLARINETS**

From left to right: clarinet in "C", Whitaker & Co., London, boxwood with ivory bands and six brass keys, c. 1821; clarinet in "C", Astor & Co., London, boxwood with ivory bands and eight brass keys, c. 1810; clarinet in "E-flat", stamped "Noe Freres/a Paris", boxwood with five brass keys, c. 1820; clarinet in "G", stamped "Widmann/Freiburg", boxwood with horn bands and five brass keys, c. 1840; clarinet in "A", stamped "F. Muss/Wien", stained fruitwood with ten brass keys, c. 1850. (*Right*)

instrument pitched a fourth above the standard bassoon already described, and a contrabassoon was built to play an octave lower. The latter instrument had a body length of about 166 cm (66 in) and playing it was assisted by means of an extended butt, which meant it could be played in the same way as a standard four-keyed bassoon. Later models of the contrabassoon were modified in France, but a more modern version was developed in Germany in the late 19th century.

### CLARINET AND BASSET HORN

The clarinet seems to have derived from the 17th-century French instrument called the chalumeau, which was a cylindrical pipe with seven finger holes, a thumb hole and a single reed tied to the mouthpiece. The drawback of this instrument was that the range only covered one-and-a-half octaves. At the beginning of the 18th century the instrument maker J. C. Denner developed and introduced the clarinet to France and later to England. This early clarinet was recognized by two cylindrical joints leading to a flared bell with a cane reed tied to the mouthpiece. Usually made of boxwood, it was fitted with two keys and had an overall body length of about 48 cm (19 in).

From the middle of the 18th century the clarinet developed into a five-keyed instrument that could have up to six joints: the mouthpiece;

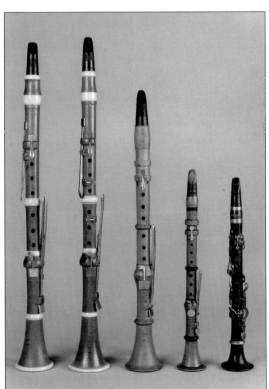

a short joint, or "barrel"; an upper left-hand joint; a lower right-hand joint; a fifth joint for index-finger hole and keys; and the bell, which had become more elongated in shape. Toward the end of the century a sixth key was added. It was in this form that the clarinet enjoyed considerable popularity until the beginning of the 19th century, so much so that additional clarinets were made not only in standard concert pitch but also in B-flat and E-flat.

During the first half of the 19th century, examples of eight-, twelve- and thirteen-keyed clarinets appeared throughout Europe, but it was not until the development of the "Boehm-system" method of keywork later in the century that the clarinet was transformed into an instrument of superior technical ability.

Alto clarinets pitched in E-flat and bass clarinets pitched an octave below the standard concert pitch C clarinet were developed in the early 19th century. The earlier bass clarinets had been modelled on the shape of a bassoon but later were designed with a straight body and turned-up metal bell.

The basset horn was invented in Germany around the middle of the 18th century and is similar in pitch to the alto clarinet. Its original shape was curved, but later the upper and lower joints formed an obtuse angle. The lower end of the lower joint fitted into a "box" from which a metal bell extended. Later on a straight model was developed in which the bell was either metal or wood. This instrument was used mainly in German wind bands during the 19th century.

### SAXOPHONE AND SURRASOPHONE

Of the newer forms of single-reed instruments that appeared in the 19th century, the most popular was the saxophone. This was because the metal-bodied instrument had a large bore capable of producing a greater dynamic sound than other instruments of the woodwind section. The tube was of brass with large wind holes totally covered by the key action. The inventor of the saxophone was Adolphe Sax, who developed the instrument during the mid 19th century in Brussels and then moved to Paris. The range of saxophones comprised soprano in B-flat, alto in E-flat, C melody, tenor in B-flat and baritone in E-flat. Some rare sopranino saxophones also were made.

In the 1860s the saxophone was taken up by the French Army band and later in the century was introduced into other parts of the world, notably North America, where it became one of the most popular wind instruments.

At about the same time Adolphe Sax was developing the saxophone, a French bandmaster called Surras introduced a double-reeded brass-tubed instrument called the Surrasophone, which was roughly bassoon-shaped and similar in range to the saxophone. Its success was relatively short-lived, however, probably because of the ineffectiveness of the notes in the higher register of the instrument, which were too dull and faint for the military marching band.

### SERPENT

The serpent is related to the curved cornett of the 16th and 17th centuries, but is pitched about an octave lower than the tenor cornett. It seems to have developed in France during the 17th century and was brought to England in the latter part of that century. The instrument consists of a serpent-shaped wooden body with a conical bore. Covered with leather, it displays six finger holes and is played by blowing through a hemispherical mouthpiece made of ivory or horn, which is attached to a brass crook that fits into a socket at the upper end of the body.

The serpent of the early 18th century was usually keyless and used as a church instrument, but towards the end of the century a four-keyed instrument was produced. These were played until the mid 19th century, when they became obsolete.

Other forms of serpent with narrower bores were produced in the early 19th century. The bass horn, for instance, had two parallel tubes connected at the base by a U-shaped tube of equal bore. Another example is the serpent Forveille, which has the lower part of the wooden body covered in leather attached to an upper part made of brass tubing. These fell into decline toward the end of the 19th century.

**SAXOPHONES**

*Adolphe Sax*

All these brass saxophones were made in Paris and stamped with the A.S PARIS monogram. They are from left to right: soprano saxophone in "B-flat", 1859; alto saxophone in "E-flat", 1859; tenor saxophone in "B-flat", 1868; baritone saxophone in "E-flat", 1862.

## MAKERS OF REEDED WOODWIND INSTRUMENTS

| | | | |
|---|---|---|---|
| **DENNER, Jacob** | 1681–1735 | Nuremberg | Bassoon |
| **PRUDENT, Thiessiet** | c.1770 | Paris | Clarinet, basset horn |
| **MAYRHAFER, A.** | c.1770 | Passau | Basset horn |
| **GRENSER, Augustin** | 1720–1807 | Dresden | Bassoon |
| **PORTHEUX, Dominique** | c.1780 | Paris | Clarinet, basset horn |
| **GRUNDMANN, Jakob** | 1729–1800 | Dresden | Oboe, cor anglais, clarinet, basset horn |
| **CAHUSAC, Thomas (the Elder)** | d.1798 | London | Clarinet, basset horn |
| **BAUMANN** | c.1800 | Paris | Clarinet, basset horn |
| **TRIEBERT, Guillaume** | 1770–1848 | Paris | Oboe, cor anglais |
| **MILLHOUSE, William** | 1763–1836 | Newark | Clarinet, basset and London horn |
| **GRENSER, Heinrich** | 1764–1813 | Dresden | Oboe, cor anglais, clarinet basset horn |
| **CAHUSAC, Thomas (the Younger)** | fl.1781–1814 | | Clarinet, basset horn |
| **TUERLINCKX, Corneille Jean Joseph** | 1783–1855 | Mechlin | Clarinet, basset horn |
| **SAVARY, Jean-Nicolas** | 1786–1853 | Paris | Bassoon |
| **ALMENRAEDER, Carl** | 1786–1843 | Mainz | Bassoon |
| **BROD, Henri** | 1799–1839 | Paris | Oboe, cor anglais |
| **HECKEL, Johann Adam** | 1812–77 | Wiesbaden | Bassoon |
| **SAX, Adolphe** | 1814–94 | Paris | Saxophone, |
| **GAUTROT, P. L.** | c.1855 | Paris | Surrasophone |

THE BRASS SECTION WAS A COMPARATIVELY LATE DEVELOPER. ONLY WITH
THE ADVENT OF SUPERIOR METAL-WORKING TECHNOLOGY COULD THEY
BECOME THE FLEXIBLE INSTRUMENTS WE HEAR TODAY.

# BRASS INSTRUMENTS

The biggest problem collectors of brass instruments have to deal with is the fact that metal perishes and thus the pieces are easily dented. Most brass prior to the early 18th century has had some restoration, and instruments of a later period may show repair patches on the bell or along the tubing to reinforce the seams. As with woodwinds, makers can be identified by a stamp on the flared part of the bell or sometimes by an engraved name on the garland.

### HORNS

Not until the late 17th century did curved, metal instruments first appear. They were either semicircular or tightly looped, and were used either as hunting horns or military horns. It was the introduction of the French hunting horn in the late 17th century that established the shape of the later orchestral horn. This instrument was constructed in a wide circle or in one or more coils, with a flared bell at the lower end and a mouthpiece socket at the other.

Horns were made in various pitches because only a harmonic series of notes could be played on any given instrument. By adding to the number of loops, the pitch could become lower. This was achieved by increasing the length of tubing. When "crooks" were introduced in the early 18th century, the French horn became more of an orchestral instrument. This orchestral horn was constructed with a removable crook incorporated into the total windway of the instrument. By replacing the crook with others of varying length, the pitch of the horn could be raised or lowered.

The playing method known as "hand-stopping" was introduced in the middle of the 18th century. In this method the right hand was placed inside the bell and by restricting the wind passage in various ways the harmonics could be flattened or sharpened, thus adding semitones to the natural harmonic series.

The method of playing the French horn remained relatively unchanged until the intro-

**HORN**
*Stamped "FAIT PAR REIDLOCKER SEUL ELEVE ET SUCCESSEUR DE FEU CORMERY/RUE PORTE FOIN NO 8 A PARIS"* **c. 1790**

This natural orchestral horn of brass has a tuning shank, coupler, set of crooks and mouthpiece. It is in its original case.

duction in the mid 19th century of valve mechanism, in which the windways of the tube were controlled by piston or rotary valves that enabled players to perform chromatic scales with more flexibility and intonation.

### TRUMPET AND BUGLE

Up to the end of the 18th century trumpets were used as ceremonial instruments, either straight or S-shaped prior to the 17th century but later a single looped brass or silver tube. This latter form of trumpet, subsequently known as

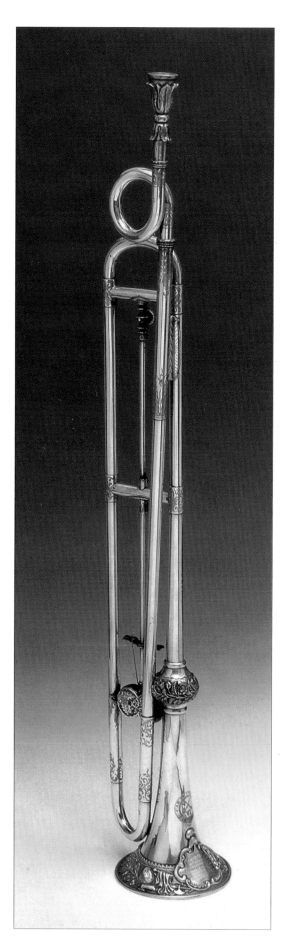

**TRUMPET**
*Robinson, Russell & Co.*
*Dublin*
**c. 1840**

The trumpet is of embossed and engraved silver, and bears the Dublin hallmark for 1840. It was the subject of a military presentation of the period.

the natural trumpet, had a flared bell with an extra rim fitted to the lower section called a "garland", which was sometimes embellished with ornamentation. As the trumpet became a more frequent feature of military bands and orchestras during the 18th century, the requirement for pitch variation became a desirable feature. In order to lower the pitch, it was necessary to extend the overall length of tubing: this was achieved by inserting different lengths of tubing as appropriate into the mouthpiece end of the loop.

At the end of the 18th century a keyed trumpet was introduced. This had four to six windholes cut into the body of the trumpet that were covered by closed brass keys. When played these keys could be opened to alter the harmonics by specific musical intervals. Although the keyed trumpet continued to be made until 1840, it was the keyed bugle that was prevalent in bands at the beginning of the 19th century. The keyed bugle was adapted from the single coil copper bugle and was pitched in either C or B-flat. The earlier models had four keys but later two more were added. While these keyed bugles were widely used on the Continent, they became more important in England and North America, where they were played until the mid 19th century.

As with horns, it was the introduction of valve mechanism in the mid 19th century that revolutionized the trumpet. By replacing the keys with piston valves, more accurate intonation was achieved.

### TROMBONE

The earliest known trombones were the so-called sackbuts made in the 16th century by the brass instrument makers of Nuremberg, who established the basic shape and method of playing for the next 400 years. The trombone is basically an elongated S-shaped instrument played by extending the slide to a given position for the required note. The longer the slide is extended the longer the windway becomes, thereby producing a lower-pitched note. By the 18th century the tubing towards the bell end of the instrument became more conical, with the bell changing from the early funnel shape to a more distinct flare.

In the early 19th century the principal sizes of trombone were established, giving alto in E-flat, tenor in B-flat and bass in E-flat. Some treble instruments pitched an octave above the tenor were also made, but these were not com-

# MAKERS OF BRASS INSTRUMENTS

| | | | |
|---|---|---|---|
| **CHRETIEN** | 1643–1715 | Paris | Horns |
| **HASS, Johann Wilhelm** | 1649–1723 | Nuremberg | Horns, trumpet, bugle, trombone |
| **EHE, Johann Leonhard** | 1669–1743 | Nuremberg | Trumpet, bugle, trombone |
| **WINKLING, Nicholas** | c.1740 | London | Horns |
| **RAOUX** | c.1770 | Paris | Horns |
| **STOLZEL, Heinrich** | 1772–1844 | Berlin | Trumpet, bugle |
| **SHAW, William** | c.1780 | London | Trumpet, bugle |
| **KRUSPE, Franz Carl** | 1808–85 | Erfurt | Horns |
| **HALLIDAY, Joseph** | c.1810 | Dublin | Trumpet, bugle |
| **HALARY, Jean** | c.1820 | Paris | Trumpet, bugle, trombone ophicleide |
| **PERINET, François-Etienne** | c.1830 | Paris | Trumpet, bugle |
| **PACE, Charles** | c.1840 | London | Trumpet, bugle |
| **SCHUSTER** | c.1850 | Markneukirchen | Trumpet, bugle |

**TROMBONE**
*Jorg Neuschal, Nuremberg*
**c. 1557**

The tubing of this tenor sackbut trombone is of brass with the flat stays showing traces of the original fish-scale engraved decoration. This instrument is the second oldest sackbut known to exist. It is also the only instrument by any member of the Neuschal family of brass instrument makers that is known to have survived. (*Above*)

**OPHICLEIDE**
*French*
**c. 1860**

This is a typical example of a brass nine-key ophicleide in B-flat. It was used both as an orchestral and military instrument throughout Europe in the 19th century. (*Right*)

mon. With the invention of valve mechanism the replacement of the slide by valves was adopted by some European marching bands, which have continued to use the trombone in this form until today.

### OPHICLEIDE

The ophicleide is a development of the bass-keyed bugle and was invented by Halary in the early 19th century. It is basically a bassoon-shaped instrument made of brass, with eight to twelve keys mounted on "pillars" attached to the body that cover the open windholes. A brass crook is fitted into a socket at the upper end of the brass tube. A mouthpiece is inserted into this crook.

The ophicleide was usually pitched in B-flat, although some alto instruments in E-flat were made. This remained a relatively successful band instrument throughout Europe and was still being played up until the beginning of the 20th century.

AS THE CENTERPIECE OF SO MUCH MUSIC, KEYBOARD INSTRUMENTS
PRODUCE A MAGNIFICENT VARIETY OF SOUNDS THAT ALMOST CERTAINLY
ENSURES THEIR PLACE AS THE ROYALTY OF MUSICAL INSTRUMENTS.

# KEYBOARD INSTRUMENTS

Keyboard instruments suffer mainly from cracked soundboards, probably caused by excess string tension. Many early instruments have been restored, mainly by replacing the original mechanism with modern parts in order that the keyboard can be played satisfactorily. Wherever possible, the original case should always house the restored mechanism. Most of the early makers had their inscriptions incorporated into an ornamental panel above the keyboard that in later years was simplified to a nameplate.

### HARPSICHORD

The harpsichord was found in Italy in the early 16th century and later spread to the Low Countries, where instrument making was centred in Antwerp. In the early 17th century France became the centre for the later development of the instrument. The demand for harpsichords in England was met by imported instruments from the Italian or Flemish makers, and it was not until the early 18th century that harpsichords were made in England.

Harpsichords have varied considerably over the years, ranging from single keyboard instruments with one string for each key to two keyboard instruments with several strings for each key controlled by hand stops and pedals. The mechanism consists of a small piece of wood called a "jack", the base of which rests on the far end of the key. The head of the jack holds a plectrum, and when the player's finger depresses the key, the leverage causes the jack to rise to the string, which is plucked by the plectrum.

During the 16th century the single keyboard instrument with a four-octave range was adequate for the music being played at the time, but as it became necessary to use the harpsichord as a continuo instrument to accompany vocalists, a double keyboard was used, with each keyboard tuned to a different pitch. By the mid 17th century the harpsichord was modified so that both keyboards were tuned to the same

**DOUBLE MANUAL HARPSICHORD**
*Jacob Kirkman, London*
**1761**

The case is veneered with finely figured burr walnut banded and crossbanded with walnut and boxwood. The interior has marquetry of scrolling foliage, figures and a trophy of instruments. The soundboard is decorated with a gilt rose and the instrument stands on a base with walnut cabriole legs carved with acanthus.

pitch and could be sounded separately or together for greater volume; the keyboard was also extended to give a range of five octaves.

The early harpsichords of the European school were set into cases that were highly decorated with paintings or other ornamentation and rested on finely carved stands. The English harpsichords made during the 18th century were usually set in fine walnut-veneer cases with brass fittings and were rested on either oak or mahogany stands.

### VIRGINAL

The virginal has the same origins as the harpsichord but differs in shape. Whereas the harp-

*Signed on jack rail "Joseph Mondini Fecit in Firenze 1631"*

This virginal is made of cypress wood and decorated with ivory dots. The interior of the lid is beautifully painted with exotic birds and a reserve panel depicting Apollo pursuing Daphne. This instrument was shown at the Fishmongers Hall Exhibition in London in 1904.

board. The instrument was either rested on a table or perhaps a stand.

## SPINET

The spinet is similar to the harpsichord, in that the string is plucked, and to the virginal, in that there is one key for each string. The spinet derived from early Italian instruments and was probably introduced in the mid 17th century; it was played until about 1800. The instrument may be recognized by its wing-shaped soundboard, in which the strings run at an angle from the keyboard. It is usually contained in a walnut case attached to the lid by fine brass hinges, and rests on a stand of oak or mahogany.

## CLAVICHORD

A type of clavichord can be traced to medieval times, but the instrument is better recognized in its 15th-century form, which had ten strings and a chromatic keyboard. The clavichord is a rectangular instrument with strings running parallel to the keyboard. The mechanism is simple: a brass blade, or "tangent", is set up at the far end of each key. When the key is depressed the brass tangent is levered up to strike the string and remains in contact with

sichord is characterized by a wing-shaped soundboard somewhat similar to a horizontal harp, the virginal is contained in a rectangular case with strings placed at an angle to the keyboard. Although the strings are plucked in the same manner as the harpsichord, the virginal is a much simpler instrument, having one key for each string and a range of four octaves (and in later models four-and-a-half octaves).

Virginals were normally elaborately decorated, especially on the inside of the lid, with fine inlay on the panels that surrounded the key-

## MAKERS OF KEYBOARD INSTRUMENTS

| RUCKERS, Hans | c.1550–98 | Antwerp | Organ |
|---|---|---|---|
| RUCKERS, Jan | 1578–1643 | Antwerp | Organ |
| RUCKERS, Andries | 1579–1645 | Antwerp | Organ |
| HITCHCOCK, Thomas | c.1700 | London | Organ |
| CRISTOFORI, Bartolomeo | 1655–1731 | Florence | Organ |
| SILBERMANN, Gottfried | 1683–1753 | Saxony | Organ |
| HASSE, Johann Adolf | c.1699–1783 | Hamburg | Organ |
| BROADWOOD, John and SHUDI, Birkat | fl. 1702–73 | London | Organ |
| KIRCKMAN, Jacob | 1710–92 | London | Organ |
| TASKIN, Pascal | 1723–93 | Paris | Organ |
| STEIN, Johann Andreas | 1728–92 | Vienna | Organ |
| BLANCHET, François II | 1729–66 | Paris | Organ |
| ZUMPE, Johannes | c.1770 | London | Organ |
| SOUTHWELL, William | 1756–1842 | Dublin | Organ |
| FIELD, John | 1782–1837 | London | Organ |

it until the key is released, thus sustaining the sound. The essential difference between the clavichord and the previously mentioned keyboard instruments is that the keys of the clavichord are struck, not plucked, as is the case with the others.

As the clavichord developed in the 16th and 17th centuries, the number of strings increased to fourteen pairs, with a range of four octaves. In this form it was used by musicians throughout Europe. By the 18th century the clavichord had developed into an unfretted instrument with a separate pair of strings for each key, together with a wider range of five octaves. The clavichord was played in this form until the beginning of the 19th century.

### PIANO

The piano was originally a harpsichord whose strings were struck with a hammer rather than plucked with a plectrum. The pianos of the early 18th century had a very heavy action with little control over tone production, but toward the end of the century pianos were introduced with light hammers that enabled the struck string to produce a sustained tone of greater clarity.

During the mid 18th century a smaller instrument known as the square piano was introduced, which was designed as a replacement for the spinet. Although this instrument was first invented in Germany, it gained widespread popularity in England and may be recognized by its rectangular case, which is usually rested on a wooden stand.

From 1800 onwards the development of the piano was designed to cope with increasing string tension, which in turn caused increased pressure on the soundboard. Because of this problem the metal-framed piano was developed in the early 19th century, and it was perfected by the Steinway model, which has lasted until the present day.

While the grand pianoforte shape successfully evolved from the harpsichord shape, it was the modification of the square piano that gave rise to the upright piano. In the late 18th century examples could be seen of the soundboard set in a vertical position at right angles to the keyboard. This set the pattern for pianos to be developed into the upright models of today.

### ORGAN

While the organ had its origins in Greek and Roman times, it was the late 15th-century church organ that gave rise to subsequent devel-

**CLAVICHORD**
*Joannes Adolph Hass*
**1763**

This five-octave keyboard has ivory naturals faced with ebony arcading and ebony accidentals. The case is of pine and painted in simulated tortoiseshell with brass ribbon hinges. The facia-board is veneered with kingwood and the interior of the lid is decorated in gilt with chinoiserie on a red lacquer ground. *(Above)*

**GRAND PIANO**
*Anton Marcus Thim, Vienna*
**c. 1810-15**

The case is veneered in exotic woods and the edging panels, nameboard and keyboard cheeks are decorated in fine brush and penwork. The legs and lyre are carved in ebonized and gilded wood. *(Left)*

opments. The great schools of organ building were centred in the Netherlands and Italy up until the early 17th century. The French school of organ building developed in the late 17th and early 18th centuries.

The main difference between the French and Dutch or German organs was the construction of the pedal-board. In the French organ, wooden strips were connected to the pedals from the manual keys in order to sound some of the deeper-pitched pipes. The pedal-board

operated about 10 keys, which in later models contained as many as 32 keys. However, this system did not adapt well to the playing of rapid passages of music.

The German-style pedal-board had closer-spaced, longer keys. This allowed additional voices to be sounded, with the higher-pitched voices being played on the manual keyboard. The Dutch and German organ also offered a greater variety of stops than the more restricted French instrument.

Although organs had been widely used in continental Europe, it was not until the early 18th century that the instrument developed in England, where it then consisted of only a pedal-board with no more than a few notes. In the mid 19th century further development was to be seen with the introduction of the "Romantic" organ. This instrument contained numerous devices for simplifying the action and served as a basis for the modern organ.

### SQUARE PIANO
*Nameboard inscribed*
*"Fredericus Beck Londini Fecit 1786/10 Broad Street, Soho"*

This five-octave square piano has a mahogany case with boxwood stringing on a beech stand. (*Above*)

### ORGAN
*Attributed to Samuel Green, London*
**c. 1790**

This chamber organ has a mahogany case with gilt false pipes in the doors and seven stops. (*Left*)

## PIANOLA

Towards the end of the 19th century mechanical instruments became more widely used, especially with the introduction of a mechanism using pneumatic pressure. Pedals were fitted externally to the keyboard instrument enabling air to be pumped to the internal component. Initially, this component consisted of a perforated paper roll which was inserted behind the keyboard of an ordinary upright piano. By means of pneumatic action air was passed through the holes in the perforated paper roll causing small hammers to strike the corresponding note on the keyboard.

**PIANOLA; LATE 19TH CENTURY**

PERHAPS THE OLDEST OF MUSICAL INSTRUMENTS KNOWN TO HUMANS,
THE STEADY BEAT OF THE PERCUSSION SECTION MARKS TIME FOR THE
REST OF THE BAND IN SO MANY MUSICAL COMPOSITIONS.

# PERCUSSION INSTRUMENTS

Although drumskins can be easily damaged, they can just as easily be replaced. The biggest problem is the loss of decoration and paintwork around the body of military drums, which hampers identification.

The most important early drums in Europe were kettledrums, which in the 15th century were used in pairs by cavalry regiments and by the early 18th century accompanied trumpets in ceremonial orchestral works (by this time they were known as timpani). These large, bowl-shaped drums were either fixed with iron leg supports or rested on iron stands, and were 60–80 cm (24–32 in) in diameter with T-shaped tension screws around the perimeter of the instrument for tuning. Timpanis have since remained relatively unchanged, except for some variation in size and certain modifications to the tuning mechanism.

The side drum, which developed from the early Renaissance tabor, was played frequently with the fife in military bands. At the beginning

**BASS DRUM**
*English*
**c. 1800**

This bass drum is constructed of wood and covered with canvas painted with the royal coat of arms of George III. It is a regimental drum of the British Army. (*Left*)

**TIMPANI**
*German*
**c. 1740**

The pair of copper-bowled timpani have original metal stands with elaborate tension screws. (*Below*)

of the 18th century the cylindrical hoop of the drum was made of wood but later brass was also used. During the 19th century these drums were more commonly used in marching bands and would be played using either sticks or soft beaters.

The bass drum has been known from the late 18th century and was played in military bands. It was suspended across the chest of the player and struck on either side with beaters. The early models have a hoop length of about 70 cm (28 in) and a diameter of 80 cm (32 in), but early 19th-century models became bulkier, with a hoop length of 53 cm (21 in) and a diameter of 76 cm (30 in). Later in the 19th century single-skinned orchestral bass drums were made with tuning tension screws.

### XYLOPHONE AND GLOCKENSPIEL

Of the solid percussion instruments, the xylophone and glockenspiel are the best known; both date from the 18th century. The glockenspiel is made of strips of wood, metal or glass arranged in the manner of a keyboard and struck with beaters. The xylophone is made of tuned blocks of wood, also arranged in keyboard style and played with sticks or hammers.

**XYLOPHONE**
*Basson, London*
**c. 1900**

The instrument is a good example of a four-octave xylophone on stand. (*Above*)

**GLOCKENSPIEL**
*German,*
**c. 1900**

This two-octave example has wooden blocks. (*Left*)

## MAKERS OF PERCUSSION INSTRUMENTS

| **KEY, Thomas** | c.1810 | London | Drums |
|---|---|---|---|
| **WARD, Cornelius** | 1805–70 | Liverpool and London | Drums |

### FURTHER READING

The following list of materials for further reading offers a broad range of literature. Both specialist and general works are included. While every effort has been made to give the date of the most recent edition, new ones may have been published since this book went to press.

Baines, Anthony
***Musical Instruments Through the Ages***
London 1973

— *Woodwind Instruments and Their History*
London 1977

—*Brass Instruments, Their History and Development*
London 1978

Bellow, Alexander
**The Illustrated History of the Guitar**
New York 1970

Blades, James
**Percussion Instruments and Their History**
London 1984

Day, C.R.
**Descriptive Catalogue of the Musical Instruments in the Royal Military Exhibition of 1890**
London 1891

Galpin, Canon Francis W.
**A Textbook of European Musical Instruments**
London 1937

Harding, Rosamond
**The Pianoforte, Its History Traced to the Great Exhibition of 1851**
Cambridge 1933

Hayes, Gerald R.
**The Viols and Other Bowed Instruments**
London 1930

Hollis, Helen Rice
**The Piano**
London 1975

James, Philip
**Early Keyboard Instruments**
London 1930

Langwill, Lyndesay G.
**An Index of Musical Wind Instrument Makers**
Edinburgh 1977

Remnant, Mary
**Musical Instruments of the West**
London 1981

Rensch, Roslyn
**The Harp**
London 1969

Russell, Raymond
**The Harpsichord and Clavichord**
London 1973

Sumner, William Leslie
**The Pianoforte**
London 1966

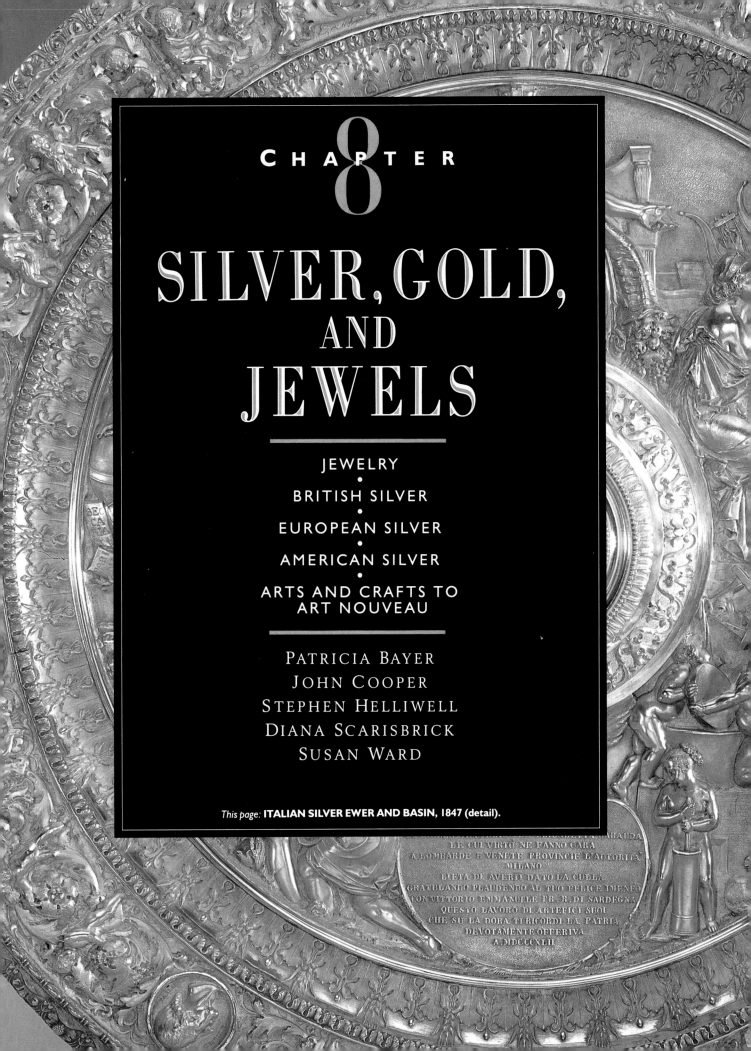

# CHAPTER 8

# SILVER, GOLD, AND JEWELS

JEWELRY
·
BRITISH SILVER
·
EUROPEAN SILVER
·
AMERICAN SILVER
·
ARTS AND CRAFTS TO
ART NOUVEAU

PATRICIA BAYER
JOHN COOPER
STEPHEN HELLIWELL
DIANA SCARISBRICK
SUSAN WARD

*This page:* **ITALIAN SILVER EWER AND BASIN, 1847 (detail).**

# SILVER, GOLD, AND JEWELS

AS WELL AS POSSESSING A LARGE MONETARY VALUE, OBJECTS MADE FROM PRECIOUS METALS AND GEMS HAVE SUPPLIED THE MEANS OF EXHIBITING A VERY HIGH STANDARD OF CRAFTSMANSHIP.

Gold, silver and jewels retain a special hold on the imagination: even those indifferent to fine paintings, furniture, porcelain or glass will, when confronted with spectacular objects fashioned from precious metals and gems, usually be suitably impressed.

Over the centuries men have gone to extraordinary lengths to obtain gold, silver and precious stones. In the Gold Fever of mid-19th-century America, for example, men abandoned their families, homes and jobs and risked danger and enormous hardship to stake their claims on a small patch of what they hoped was gold-bearing ground. This desire to find precious metals and gems probably goes beyond the mere accumulation of wealth and includes a sense of their more mystical and symbolic value. They were revered by our early ancestors and were used to make objects of great religious significance. Later they were enjoyed by the rich and powerful, becoming status symbols to impress less wealthy, weaker rivals. Today, of course, gold and jewels are also re-garded as symbols of love, and the choosing of a diamond engagement ring is an important ritual in Western society. In addition, jewellery can have the added value of association: when, for example, that of a for-mer screen goddess is auctioned, the saleroom sees an excitement often far greater than the worth of the pieces deserves.

One of the most fascinating aspects of precious metals and stones is the fact that items of great beauty can be created from ordinary-looking raw materials. Gold and silver ore is smelted to extract the valuable contents, which can then be worked in many different ways: the metals can be beaten and stretched or cast into any shape imagin-able and can be decorated with any of a vast range of techniques. Indeed, it sometimes seems as if the only limits to the use of gold or silver in *objets d'art* are those of the creative powers of the craftsman. Brilliant, lustrous gems are created from dull lumps of rock by the revelatory skills of the cutter and polisher.

Deposits of gold and silver ore and precious stones are comparatively

**17TH-CENTURY CUP**
*Maker's initials P.H.;*
*German*
Silver-gilt, coral, nautilus
shell; **c. 1630**

This splendid piece was made purely for display. Continental silver of this period is most rare; so much was destroyed in Europe's many wars.

# SEALS

For many millennia seals have been used to denote ownership, ensure privacy in correspondence, ratify a treaty or guarantee authenticity. Even today aristocrats and religious leaders wear seals in the form of rings, and countless others offer their "seals of approval" – whether in paper, wax or even verbal form. Signet rings, with their alphabetic or heraldic devices, are a latter-day version of seal rings.

The first seals – possibly descended from amulet beads whose tradition stretched back to Palaeolithic times – were used as early as the 7th millennium BC; examples have been excavated in Syria and southern Turkey. They were made of baked clay or stone, the latter the primary material for all seals, although any substance robust enough to withstand repeated pressing into clay or wax has been used in their manufacture. Early seals at first bore cross-hatched lines, but soon animal and human motifs appeared; generally, they were pierced in order to be threaded on a thong and then, presumably, worn around the neck for safekeeping. Later they were worn on the wrist. It was not until thousands of years later that the finger-ring seal came about.

Designs on seals have also varied,

**STAMP SEAL AND CYLINDER SEAL**
Steatite and Haematite;
**4th and early 2nd millennium BC**

---

(Below left)

**ITALIAN RENAISSANCE CAMEO**
Agate; **16th century**

---

(Below right, top)

**INTAGLIO SEAL AND IMPRESSION**
*Roman*
Glass; **1st/2nd century AD**

---

(Below right, bottom)

according to culture, religion and the preferred iconography of a time and place, essentially mirroring the fine-art style of a period. Seals from ancient Greece and Rome can be considered an important manifestation of classical sculpture, for instance, and indeed some extant examples have helped provide valuable information to archaeologists regarding now-lost monumental works of art. Early Islamic seals were epigraphic in nature, evincing the ban on images of that faith; their motifs reflected prevailing calligraphic styles. The Chinese employed epigraphic seals as well, placing them on textiles and paper.

During the Renaissance private individuals began to use seals in Europe, mostly for trading and legal purposes and largely in heraldic form. In the 18th century a fob seal became an important decorative item and status symbol, particularly in England, and it was worn outside the clothing on a chain which, along with its precious-metal setting, would echo popular styles in jewellery. The Victorian era witnessed the decline of the seal in terms of its true function, although it retained a decorative significance, with seal-inspired baubles made in great quantities and worn by fashionable ladies.

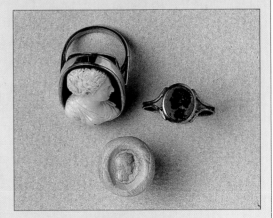

**ALEXANDER THE GREAT PORTRAIT SEAL WITH COIN**
Sapphire seal and silver coin; **4/3rd century BC**

---

(Right)

**GENTLEMAN'S HERALDIC SIGNET RING**
*England*
Gold; **20th century**

---

(Left)

**LIDDED EWER**
*Adam van Vianen, Utrecht*
Silver-gilt, embossed and
partly chased; **1614**

The van Vianen family
produced consistently fine
work, moulding, casting and
chasing the metal to create
a wonderfully flowing and
tactile effect. Silver is
extremely ductile, and the
skilled craftsman can create
any shape he wishes, the
only limitation being that of
his imagination.

scarce, and their mining often involved considerable danger. Moreover, in the days before accurate geological surveys and aerial photography they were extremely difficult to locate. Indeed, in the past the majority were found totally by accident. As a result, their value was enhanced by their rarity. Once again, this ensured that only the rich could afford to buy such treasures. It also meant that only the most skilled craftsmen were given the opportunity to work with them. Consequently the workmanship was generally of the highest quality until the mid-19th century. At this time ever-increasing amounts of gold, silver and jewels were imported into Europe as better mining techniques were developed, and consequently workmanship suffered to some extent, as the middle classes could only afford cheaper, mass-produced copies of fine pieces. Fortunately, there remained a nucleus of skilled metal-workers and gem-cutters, who carried on working in a tradition that has survived to the present day.

Sadly, the intrinsic value of gold and silver objects led to the destruction of many over the centuries. Some were melted down to finance wars, or were looted and then broken up. Others were employed to provide the raw materials for new, more fashionable pieces or were melted down to offset the cost of producing the new pieces. This was standard practice throughout Europe, as wealthy owners simply did not value the possessions of their forebears. Fortunately, today we are more enlightened – although in recent times heavy Victorian jewellery has been broken up so that the stones can be inserted into modern pieces. And in 1980 a great many silver pieces were also lost when the Hunt brothers, Texan oil tycoons, tried to corner the market by buying up all stocks of silver.

This chapter explores the fields of *objets d'art* made from precious metals and stones in both Europe and America and traces the history of their design from the Renaissance to the early part of this century. No country enjoyed a particularly national style: fashions spread across both political and geographical borders quite quickly, when one considers how little-travelled most people were. Of course, the wealthy, the very people who could afford items made from gold, silver and jewels, did enjoy the luxury of travel, and many British noblemen spent months on the Continent, broadening their outlook as they completed the Grand Tour. Inevitably, they came home with new ideas and tastes, among them a fashion for classical decoration inspired by visits to the ruins of Pompeii and Herculaneum.

In the decorative arts France was undoubtedly the most influential of all European countries in the 17th and early 18th centuries. The French court enjoyed enormous wealth and power, and its ambassadors travelled with vast quantities of gold and silver plate, designed primar-

**SCENT BOTTLES**
*English*
**19th century**

These are typical of the
output of the Birmingham
'toymakers', although the
example in fitted case
(*centre left*) was actually
made by Sampson Mordan,
a London maker better-
known for manufacturing
pencils. The mounted
seashell (*left*) is very
rare. (*Left and right*)

# FILIGREE

Filigree is a type of decoration in which fine threads of silver or gold wire, sometimes twisted and plaited, are used to form delicate and intricate designs. (In Roman times bronze was also used.)

The oldest type of filigree consisted of soldering the wire on to a backing of sheet metal. This technique remained popular in the Carolingian (768–c. 900) and Romanesque (c. 1000–c. 1200) periods, particularly for jewellery-making, and to a lesser extent for book covers, reliquaries and other ecclesiastical items, which often incorporated precious stones, enamels, ivories or cameos. The later type of filigree was "openwork", in which the wire was used on its own, a technique popular in European jewellery until the 15th century.

From the late 17th century onwards groups of filigree craftsmen worked in the Netherlands, Germany and Scandinavia, making small decorative objects such as caskets, handles for spoons and forks and miniature pieces of furniture.

In 1814 the Italian Fortunato Pio Castellani opened up a small business in Rome, producing Etruscan-style filigree jewellery.

**SUITE OF NECKLACE AND TWO BRACELETS**
Silver filigree; **mid 19th century**

This became so popular that it was imitated by French and English jewellers. Filigree jewellery still remains popular in Portugal, Italy and Norway, where it survives partly because of the tourist trade.

ily to impress their host nations. The French fashion for luxury and display became particularly prevalent in Britain when Charles II returned from his exile in France. The youthful monarch had spent much of his formative years as a guest of the French court and so, inevitably, he and his retainers introduced objects heavily decorated in the Baroque style. After almost 20 years of simple, even plain, taste favoured by the Puritans during The Commonwealth, Britain was more than ready for a return to luxury, and the extravagant Baroque style spread rapidly, eventually reaching all levels of society.

The second wave of French artistic influence occurred in the late 17th century, when many Huguenot craftsmen left France, travelling throughout Europe and to America to spread their styles and knowledge. Their work soon became popular, and the local workers in precious metals and gems had to adapt quickly, producing wares in the French taste in an attempt to compete.

Although early gold and silver objects and jewellery are, understandably, very costly today, one can still find large quantities of later pieces at more affordable prices. Indeed, many antique items are less expensive than their modern counterparts, with the added bonus that they will certainly prove to be a more sound investment. Gold and silver items will never be cheap, unless badly-made or damaged, but the patient and selective collector can still buy well, amassing a whole range of objects both useful and decorative, without spending a fortune.

THROUGH THE AGES THE JEWELER HAS USED THE BRILLIANCE AND
SPLENDOR OF PRECIOUS AND SEMI-PRECIOUS STONES AND METALS TO
CREATE EXQUISITE SYMBOLS OF WEALTH AND STATUS.

# JEWELRY

Jewels have always been an essential part of the image of royalty, setting them apart from the multitude. In the Renaissance, especially, talented goldsmiths fashioned exquisite jewels for titled and otherwise privileged patrons.

### THE RENAISSANCE
Both Henry VIII and Francis I spent fortunes on the jewellery paraded at the Field of the Cloth of Gold in 1520, and again in 1532 when the English and French monarchs met in Calais. It was the same throughout Europe: from Lisbon to Vienna, each princely house assembled a treasury of jewels to symbolize dynastic glory.

Patronage from this stratum of society raised jewellery to the level of a fine art. Great artists such as Hans Holbein and Giulio Romano in Italy were required to design jewels as well as paint in fresco and oil. Craftsmen of the calibre of Benvenuto Cellini (1502–72) brought the traditional techniques of enamelling, chasing and casting to a peak of perfection. Although the only authenticated work by Cellini to survive is

**THE GRESLEY JEWEL**
Gold, pearls and enamel;
**c. 1580**

On one side of this jewel, made in the highly sculptural Renaissance style, Nicholas Hilliard's miniature of Sir Thomas Gresley is set in a locket with cover. On the other side, the fine cameo of a Negress is framed by cornucopias and boys firing Love's arrows upwards. (Above)

**CEREMONIAL COLLAR**
*Hans Reimer*
Gold, diamonds, emeralds, rubies and pearls; **c. 1560**

The collar was made for Duke Albrecht V of Bavaria after a design by Hans Meilich. Each link of fine scrolls, set with precious stones and pearls, is a jewel in itself. (Left)

not in fact a jewel but a bejewelled object – the famous salt cellar now in the Kunsthistorisches Museum in Vienna – it does epitomize his strong sculptural style.

Under Cellini's influence jewels were composed of figures modelled in the round, bright with enamels and hung with milky white pearls; instead of dominating the composition, the gems provide no more than decorative accents. These jewels not only express Christian doctrine and personal sentiments – as indeed they did in the Middle Ages – but reflect the influence of antiquity, illustrating themes from classical art, mythology and history.

### THE ART OF THE CAMEO
The ancient Roman art of cameo cutting and engraving intaglios in hardstones (such as onyx and sardonyx) for jewellery was also revived. Trained in the centres of Rome, Florence and Milan, cameo cutters went north of the Alps and set up workshops in Prague, Paris and London. They brought the repertory of classical motifs up to date by adding to it episodes from the Bible, images of Christ, the Virgin and saints,

and portraits of illustrious contemporaries. The standard was high and the gems engraved by great masters such as Alessandro Cesati compare with those of Imperial Rome.

### JEWELS FOR THE HEAD

In his *Autobiography*, Cellini described how in 1524 it was the fashion for gentlemen to pin little gold medallions bearing the device of their choice to the upturned brim of the hat. He made such ornaments, and described how difficult it was to model the miniature figures in the round and then to enamel them in different colours. A few have survived and some can be seen in portraits: they usually illustrate a scene from the Bible or mythology.

Women threaded strings of pearls through the hair or might place a jewelled ornament in the centre high above the brow. From mid-century jewelled bands of gems alternating with pairs of pearls, known as upper and lower biliments, were wound around the back and front of the head. In their turn they were succeeded by the fashion for bodkins (long, ornamental hairpins) with jewelled tops and by aigrettes (tall brooches placed on the side of a piled-up coiffure). For most of this period ears were covered by hair or a hood, so earrings generally were not worn. The few shown in portraits and

**HAT BADGE**
Gold and enamel; c. 1540

The Annunciation is enacted in a garden by a trellis on this French badge. The archangel Gabriel and the Virgin Mary are shown with golden hair, naturalistically enamelled faces, hands and limbs, and bright red, blue and green clothing. The scene is like a tableau from a play condensed into medallion form, framed in cable wire. The four loops for sewing the jewel to the hat stand out at the sides.

recorded in inventories are pear pearls, which hung from gold rings, bell-shaped pendants and bunches of gold grapes affixed to bowknots.

### CHIVALRY AND RELIGION

Close-fitting tailored bodices with low necklines were set off by jewelled collars, chains and necklaces. Women might wear round white pearls strung into chokers high at the throat or in long ropes falling down below the waist. Necklaces were composed of elaborately wrought links of enamelled gold set with gems in high collets (metal bands encircling and securing stones) and alternating with pearl clusters. Each link was a jewel in itself, demanding skills of a high order.

Similarly challenging was the making of chains: they came in intricate designs in lengths varying from the neat collar to the long rope wound around the neck so many times that the wearer seemed imprisoned by the burden of so much gold. As a mark of rank Henry VIII wore a great gold collar across his broad shoulders; the one depicted by Hans Holbein in the portrait in the National Gallery of Early Art, Rome, is set with huge rose red spinels and pearls in floral and leafy mounts.

The pendant, which hung from the chain, necklace or collar or might be pinned to a ribbon on the sleeve, was also an expression of cultural or spiritual interests. As the symbol of Christian faith the cross was worn by many devout men and women; it might be encrusted with gems and hung with pearls, and bear additional symbols such as the Instruments of the Passion – the crown of thorns, ladder, nails and so on. Other religious jewels comprised the monogram of Christ, "IHS". Gemstones were set "a jour" (not closed at the back) so the magical properties accredited to them might pass directly to the wearer. Sometimes these powers were reinforced by incantations inscribed on the jewel.

Goldsmiths employed a vast range of secular motifs – allegories, flora and fauna – and symbols such as the hunting horn, evoking the favourite princely pastime, and the ship, a rebus for happiness. Some preferred pendants composed of their own initial: Henry VIII ordered jewelled Hs for himself, Bs for Anne Boleyn.

### BRACELETS, BELTS AND RINGS

Some bracelets were bands of goldsmith's work set with gems and pearls, while others comprised chains of gold links with clasps enamelled with ciphers, heraldic crests and, for a bride,

hands holding a crowned heart.

Trim waists were emphasized by sumptuous belts. Cellini fashioned one as a wedding present, ornamented with putti, masks and trails of acanthus leaves. Others were chains of agate "nuts", which opened up to show tableaux of biblical or mythological scenes. From them hung the aids to comfort and convenience transformed by Renaissance taste into jewels – sickle-shaped toothpicks, pomanders to sweeten the air, prayer books, fans and mirrors.

More rings were worn than any other jewel. Designs emphasize three component parts, the hoop, its architectural or sculptural shoulders and the high bezel (setting for a central stone) set with a gem supported by the shoulders. After 1540 this setting is given independent enamelled ornament. Signets, which were essential for business, have coats of arms engraved on gold or crystal, the colours on foil below. There are gimmel (from the Latin *gemellus*, or

"twin") rings with double hoops and bezels symbolic of the indissolubility of marriage. Some contain surprises: a ring once in the collection of Queen Elizabeth I and bearing her initial E set with diamonds, opens up like a locket to reveal enamelled portraits of the monarch herself and her mother, Anne Boleyn, both bejewelled.

POST-RENAISSANCE AND BAROQUE
By 1600 a change of style was evident as jewels became more a statement of wealth conveyed by quantities of stones rather than the artistic expression of intellectual concepts. The French took the lead in design, which they have maintained ever since.

The emphasis on stones rather than settings was made possible by the increased supply resulting from the enterprise of merchants such as the East India Company. Great progress was made in faceting the diamond. Early in the cen-

**POMANDER**
*German (?)*
Gold, pearls and enamel;
*c.* 1600

The style of the green, blue and white cloisonné enamels compares with that on the dress jewels made for two Austrian princesses and which survive in the Museum für angewandte Kunst in Vienna. The pomander, filled with aromatic substances to sweeten the air, would have hung from a long chain at the girdle. It was made for the Countess of Devonshire, who left it to her daughter, Anne, Countess of Exeter, whose descendants still own it.

**PRANCING HORSE**

*Spanish*

Gold, rubies, emeralds,
pearls and enamel;
**c. 1580**

This enamelled gold
pendant, part of the
collection of the Countess
of Devonshire, originally
featured a figure of Cupid
astride the jewelled saddle.
Illustrating the victory of
Love, the image imitated
the triumphs of such heroes
of antiquity as Alexander
the Great. Both back and
front are enamelled and
jewelled to the same high
standard. The pendant
might have been worn on a
chain at the neck or pinned
to the sleeve.

tury the rose cut with multiple facets came into
general use, and from the 1660s the brilliant cut
was adopted. Pearls were so much in demand
that their price tripled in the first 60 years of the
century: there was a flourishing trade in imitations
made in Venice and Paris. To avoid any
yellow reflections, diamonds were now set
in silver, except in Spain, where gold was still
preferred.

Enamel was relegated to the backs and
sides of densely gem-encrusted ornaments, but
remained the main means of decoration for
watch cases and miniatures. A new technique
developed in Paris and Blois made it possible to
paint these surfaces in a range of colours imitating
the canvases of the great Baroque masters in
miniature. The pattern-books, most of them
French, show a passion for flowers in design, followed
by classical influences.

Women entwined pearls in their hair and
kept the chignon in place with long bodkins
topped with jewelled insects, ships, shepherd's
crooks and flowers. By the end of the 17th century
as coiffures grew higher, aigrettes of large
sprays laden with pearls were stuck in at the side

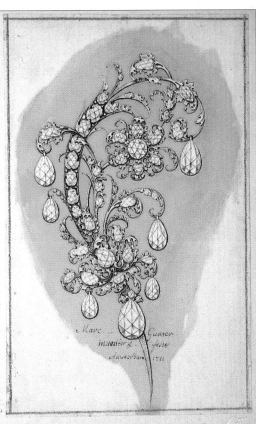

**DESIGN FOR AN
AIGRETTE**

*Marcus Gunter*
**1711**

Born in Leicester, Marcus
Gunter earned his living
designing jewels for rich
European patrons. This
flower was for a client in
Amsterdam, the centre of
the diamond trade. Studded
with rose-cut diamonds and
hung with *briolettes*, it
would have been worn at
the side of the head with
court dress. The piece
illustrates the passion for
diamonds which, in contrast
to the wrought-gold
sculptural ornaments of the
Renaissance, dominated
baroque jewellery. By this
date silver, not gold, was
used for settings.

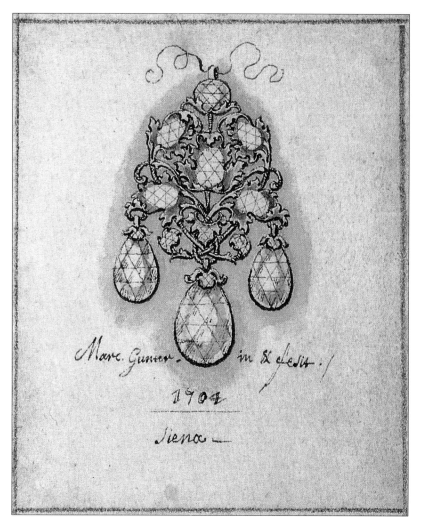

Marc. Gunter · in & fecit · /

1704

Siena —

**DESIGN FOR AN EARRING**

*Marcus Gunter*

**1704**

Itinerant jeweller Gunter designed and executed this rose-cut diamond earring in Siena. Because of its three *briolettes*, this type of earring is called a girandole, after a type of three-branched candlestick. Originating in the late 17th century, the girandole has been in fashion ever since. The acanthus-leaf motif is typical of the period and occurs not only in jewellery but also in silverware.

of the head. Men's hats were encircled by jewelled bands, chains and strings of pearls around the crown. Loops kept turned-up brims in place.

PEARLS AND DIAMONDS

In spite of the immense popularity of pear pearls in the ears, there was still a demand for gems set in gold and silver. The elegant girandole, often consisting of top, bow-shaped centre and three (or more) pendent drops, was the favourite alternative to pearls. Simpler styles were composed of a single pendant hanging from a button-like cluster set with foiled stones. Men tended to prefer a single earring of significant size, such as the pearl Charles I wore to his execution.

Large round white pearls were threaded into necklaces tied at the back with ribbons. The new brilliance of the cut diamond challenged the pearl and by the early 18th century the diamond necklace had become the grandest status symbol, with rose-cut stones in heavy silver mounts (enamelled behind) linked into several rows falling like festoons. Men, too, wore chains: they

were the standard reward for diplomatic and official service.

A large jewel in the middle of a low neckline was *de rigueur* for fashionable ladies in the first half of the century. Like crosses, these jewels were often pinned to a ribbon tied into a bow, but from the mid century the bow itself was executed in metal and stones. By the end of the century the settings were embellished with acanthus leaves. Oblong-shaped jewelled Brandenburgs, adapted from the frogging on the jackets of Prussian soldiers and made into sets of graduated size pinned from neckline to waist, were a fashion originating in Versailles and adopted internationally. Floral themes remained popular for brooches throughout the period. In France jewellers tried to represent the leaves and petals naturalistically using coloured stones as well as diamonds, and by perching butterflies and birds on the stems.

RELIGION, DEATH AND POLITICS

Crosses were worn in every country by Protestants and Catholics alike. Reliquaries and rosaries continued in use in continental Europe, while in England there was increasing interest in *memento mori* jewels. These rings, lockets and bracelet slides (worn on velvet bands passing through twin loops at the back) bearing the symbols of death – skulls, crossbones, coffins, skeletons, hourglasses, an angel sounding the last trumpet – usually contain locks of hair identified by gold-wire monograms.

Increasingly it was realized that brooches, buttons, sleeve clasps, earrings, necklace, aigrette and buckles matching in design and material were more elegant than a miscellany of ornaments, however magnificent individually. The jewels on the funeral effigy of Frances Stewart, Duchess of Richmond (d 1702), which were copied from her diamonds and are still in Westminster Abbey where she is buried, illustrate the style of these early parures.

Two innovations in men's jewellery appeared in England during the early 1660s. The sleeve button, forerunner of the cuff link, was made to fasten the cuff at the wrist, replacing ribbons, and the shoe buckle was introduced.

ROCOCO AND NEO-CLASSICAL

The high standards prevailing in all branches of the decorative arts were also applied to the jewellery of the 18th century, which reached a level of elegance rarely equalled since. Inspired by discriminating patrons, of whom Louis XV's mistress Madame de Pompadour was the most influential, the Parisian makers set the standard for the rest of the world. In Germany and in England the Huguenot craftsmen who had fled from France in 1685 attracted the richest and most aristocratic clientele, and French jewellers also were appointed to the courts of St Petersburg, Madrid and Copenhagen.

Taking stylistic elements at first from the Rococo style and then from Neo-Classicism, jewellers maximized the beauty of coloured stones and diamonds revealed through improved faceting and foiling. The supply of stones from India was supplemented by imports from Brazil, where diamonds were discovered in the 1720s. Designs from the previous century – aigrettes, butterflies and other insects for the hair, bowknots on the bodice and girandole earrings – were reinterpreted in a lighter mood. Acanthus foliage went out of favour, as did black enamel. In their place lighter outlines and scrolls came, as well as a sense of asymmetry in

**PENDANT/BROOCH**
Gold, peridot, diamonds
and enamel; **c. 1640**

This jewel could be worn either pendent on a ribbon passed through the loops at the back or as a brooch sewn to the centre of the neckline. The peridot was a favourite stone of the time, but the old-fashioned table-cut diamonds must have come from an earlier piece. The flowers on a white ground on the enamelled back represent the period's enthusiasm for botany, which ultimately led to the foundation of the great gardens of Europe. (*Left*)

**FLORAL SUITE**
*Spanish (?)*
Gold, silver, diamonds,
emeralds and rubies; **1760**

The matching set of necklace and earrings is in the *giardinetti*, or floral, style typical of the mid-18th century. The earrings are a lighter and brighter interpretation of the baroque girandole. The flowers and leaves in the necklace have been linked into garlands joined to a velvet ribbon. The emerald leaves and the ruby and diamond petals demonstrate a high standard of stone setting rarely equalled since. (*Below*)

**CHATELAINE**
*English*
Gold, diamonds and
enamel; *c. 1770*

The chatelaine was hooked
over the girdle so that the
miniature case, or watch,
with key, seals and trinkets
hung down from it, as seen
here. The severe but
elegant navette-shaped
plaques are in the Neo-
Classical style, in fashion
from the 1770s. The rose-
diamond stars and royal
cipher ("GR", for George
III) stand out well against
the rich, dark blue
enamelled ground, which
was a speciality of London
jewellers. The chatelaine,
miniature case and
matching watch (not
shown) was a gift from
George III to the
Viscountess Harcourt, wife
of the Master of the Horse,
great friends of the royal
couple. The piece is still in
the collection of the
Harcourt family.

jewels combining the two. Since the backs were
no longer enamelled and silver tarnished clothes
and skin, from the 1760s gilt was applied.

Enamels of superb quality appear on the surfaces of watch cases, chatelaines, miniatures and
bracelet clasps, some reproducing in miniature
canvases by famous artists. As an additional
refinement after 1750, machine-engraved surfaces – "engine turned" – broke up the surface
into patterns that when covered with enamel
glistened like moiré silk. From the 1760s a
beautiful royal blue enamel was used to outline
the borders of settings, and as a ground for
diamond-set motifs and ciphers on rings
and bracelet clasps.

### SENTIMENTAL AND MEMORIAL

Sentimental jewellery – brooches, rings, lockets, bracelet clasps – was much worn by day.
Most contained miniatures or curls of hair identified by ciphers and framed in small round
pearls, or borders of blue enamel; some are
inscribed with loving mottoes, nearly always in
French. From the 1770s the fichu at the neck
was pinned with an oval, octagonal or navette-
shaped brooch ornamented with a love motif.

The memorial jewellery that was of such significance in the previous period continued to
appeal. The hair of the dead was plaited or
woven into mesh-like patterns and worked into
landscapes, weeping willows and funerary urns.
Those in mourning wore these emblems with
suites of jet and black enamel.

At cards, the theatre, masquerades and balls,
powdered heads sparkled with naturalistic
sprigs of flowers, insects, such as moths, flies
and butterflies and birds pecking at berries or
bearing olive branches. In the last decades of the
century stars and feathers were placed in high
coiffures topped by nodding ostrich plumes.
The brims of the wide hats worn by women
might be pinned with trophies of love, garden-
ing, war and the arts; men preferred plainer
loops and buttons.

### DECORATIVE TRIMMING

The grandest evening necklaces were composed
of diamonds linked into graduated rows, if large
enough, or if small then worked into clusters or
intricate garlands of flowers and ribbons. The
large loop that often hung down from the front
of the neck was called an *esclavage*. Lines of
stones strung into tassels or hanging in festoons
reflected the fashion for designs inspired by the
decorative trimming, or *passementerie*, on up-

holstery or curtains of the 1770s and 1780s.

Pearls played a most important role: strung into single rows, twisted into torsades, mixed with diamonds into broad chokers or in elaborate compositions of bows and festoons tied at the back with coloured ribbons. These arrangements of stones might be mounted on flat velvet ribbons, which showed off the design to its advantage.

Magnificent brooches called stomachers occupied the area between a woman's neckline and waist. They were designed as huge floral bouquets, as bowknots echoing patterned silks and in "V"-shaped compositions combining

**AIGRETTE**
**c. 1726**

The jewelled tuft of peacock feathers was worn in the hair, pinned to a panache of plumes by the Duchess of Wharton, lady-in-waiting to the Queen of Spain. Feathers, like flowers and ribbons, are recurring motifs in 18th-century jewels. This is a particularly attractive example, in large part due to the contrast of the blue and white stones.

both flowers and ribbonwork. Smaller models were made up into sets of graduated sizes. The suites of buckles, loops, tassels and buttons flashed more light and warm colour from sleeves, shoulders and wide skirts.

### SECOND BEST

Even the richest had jewels of less expensive cornelian, moss agate, amethyst, aquamarine and garnet foiled to simulate the glow of rose red rubies. Pinchbeck and similar alloys provided cheap substitutes for gold. Paste – white, coloured and opaline – was perfected and set into decorative necklaces, aigrettes, bracelets and earrings, as well as useful buttons and buckles for shoes, garters and belts. *Coq-de-perle*, from the shell of a snail found in the West Indies, was widely used as an alternative to pearls, framed in marcasite for glitter.

Although women were the prime concern – and customers – of the 18th-century jeweller, men of fashion were highly conscious of their rank and appearance. Only the privileged few adorned their court dress with the insignia of the Orders of Chivalry, but every gentleman owned a sword with an enamelled and jewelled hilt, carried a fine watch with a seal suspended from it and sported a miniature on a chain at his neck and precious rings on his fingers. Cravats were pinned with sparkling brooches, cuffs were attached with sleeve buttons and shoes were buckled with cut steel or paste. Buttons might be set with gems or paste, as well as enamelled with motifs indicative of sporting, cultural and political interests. From the 1770s, as style took a plainer, more conservative turn, men's buttons grew larger – and became a target for satire.

### EMPIRE AND ROMANTIC PERIOD

With the outbreak of the Revolution in France in 1789 came the opportunity for London jewellers to shine. The lead came from Rundell, Bridge and Rundell, whose shop was one of the finest sights in London (and indeed was promised by Napoleon to one of his generals should the invasion of England succeed). This illustrious firm enjoyed the patronage of the royal family, and in particular that of the Prince Regent, the future George IV, who spent prodigious sums on jewellery.

Recognizing the political importance of pomp and display, Napoleon commissioned the court painter Jacques Louis David to devise an art form that expressed the theme of imperial grandeur. The jewels made under David's guid-

ance for the coronation of 1804 set the pattern for court jewellery for the rest of the 19th century. This "Empire" style was in tune with the prevalent tastes and symbols of the Napoleonic age. The rich parures – tiaras, combs, earrings, necklaces, belts and pairs of bracelets – set with diamonds, pearls, coloured stones and cameos in motifs derived from classical art, were adopted by the leaders of society everywhere in Europe.

The passion for rich display continued after Napoleon's defeat at Waterloo, although with the return of the Bourbons in France Napoleonic bees and classical motifs were superseded by the royalist lily and naturalistic flowers, leaves and feathers.

Supplementing the supply of diamonds and precious coloured stones were imports from Brazil, including amethysts, peridots, topazes, chrysoprases and chrysoberyls. Turquoises were at the peak of popularity: in fact, the Marchioness of Londonderry, England's celebrated heiress, was so attached to her turquoise rings that she was buried in them. The mounts for these large stones were substantial in appearance but wrought from filigree and stamped by machine into designs of shells, scrolls and plants. There were striking contrasts of colour – garnets and yellow gold, pink topazes and brilliants, turquoises and pearls – these often in combination with deep royal blue, bright green and turquoise enamels. This mixture of bright coloured stones, rich enamel and yellow gold evoking the jewels of the Renaissance was called "à l'antique".

### ROMANTICISM AND SENTIMENT

Nostalgia for the past, fostered by the immensely popular historical novels of Sir Walter Scott, influenced jewellery in other ways. The influential magazine, *The World of Fashion*, declared in 1839 that "the forms of our bijoux are now entirely borrowed from the Middle Ages". Such jewels were not exact replicas of the few authentic pieces which had survived, but rather hybrids created from elements derived from the architecture, sculpture, textiles, manuscripts and painting of both the Middle Ages and Renaissance.

The leading master in France was François-Désiré Froment-Meurice (1802–55) whose friend, the poet Victor Hugo, called him the Benvenuto Cellini of Romanticism. He revived the figurative style associated with Cellini but in a highly individual way, using oxidized silver

**MATCHING BRACELET AND PENDANT**
*French*
Gold, diamonds and garnets; **c. 1835**

The bracelet was the favourite jewel of the Romantic period, worn in groups from wrist to elbow. The pendant was worn pinned to the bodice. (*Above*)

**MUFF CHAIN**
*English*
Gold; **c. 1830**

The burnished gold scrolls contrast with the matt centres. The chain divides into a choker and bracelet. (*Right*)

**BRACELET**
*English*
Gold, pearls, aquamarine, rubies and enamel; **c. 1840**

The large aquamarine centrepiece is guarded by knights in armour standing in Gothic-style niches; there are military trophies above and below. The allusion to chivalry is in tune with the historical spirit of Sir Walter Scott's novels, then at the peak of popular success. (*Right*)

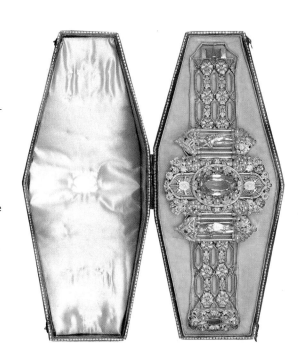

**PANSY**
*English*
Amethyst, topaz, chrysoprase and diamond; **1810**

The pansy was made for the Countess of Listowel, whose name is inscribed on the back. (*Left*)

**SHELL CAMEO**
*Italian*

The cameo, cut in Rome, is a portrait of Isabella, wife of the 4th Marquess of Exeter, who is shown veiled like an empress. (*Below*)

rather than gold and presenting his themes like scenes from a play.

The religious revival encouraged by Romanticism was also expressed in devotional jewellery: long chains with crosses, rosaries and Books of Hours with enamelled covers that hung from the chatelaine hooked over the belt. The Gothic Revival architect A.W.N. Pugin (1818–52) designed a suite on this theme for his wife Jane to wear with her wedding dress. The gold and *champlevé*-enamel headband drew its inspiration from those worn by the singing angels in the 15th-century altarpiece painted by Jan van Eyck for Ghent Cathedral, and was inscribed with a declaration of faith: *CHRISTI CRUX EST MEA LUX* ("the cross of Christ is my light").

Sentiment continued to inspire a large category of jewels commemorating friendship, love and marriage. Hair continued to be worn, woven into necklaces, bracelets and chains, enclosed in lockets and combined with miniatures, often of the eye alone. In the same category are jewels with the emblem of eternity, a snake with its tail in its mouth; the ivy, a symbol of fidelity; the pansy, for thought, and the forget-me-not. Loving messages were spelt out by the stones themselves: "REGARD" being conveyed by a *R*uby, *E*merald, *G*arnet, *A*methyst, *R*uby and *D*iamond. Mourning was scrupulously observed and the jewels worn with black clothes bore appropriate symbols: butterflies, snakes, torches, crosses, forget-me-nots, rose buds, celestial crowns, ciphers and inscriptions such as "MEMORIA AETERNA".

### LOCAL SPECIALITIES

Those travelling abroad brought home souvenirs of their adventures. There was iron jewellery from the foundries of Berlin, ivory lockets and rings from Dieppe and Switzerland, and from Geneva, enamels representing young women in the peasant costumes of the various Swiss cantons. The principal towns of Italy had their specialities: Venice was noted for glass beads and gold chains, Genoa for silver filigree. Coral was carved into cameos in Leghorn (Livorno) and Naples, bacchantes and cherubs being the preferred motifs.

In Rome cameo cutting still flourished, reproducing the masterpieces of ancient and modern sculpture. Also from Rome came mosaic jewellery, derived from the ancient technique used for floors and walls. The most popular motif was adapted from a mosaic in the

## MOSAIC SUITE
*Italian*
**Gold and glass; c. 1820**

The matching necklace, comb and earrings are made of glass in the technique brought to perfection in Rome at this time. With the exception of the spaniel depicted on the largest segment of the necklace, the motifs of birds and butterflies derive from frescoes found in the ruins of Pompeii, seen by most visitors to Rome. Other such mosaic designs could be topographical or represent picturesque peasant life.

## IRON JEWELLERY
*Berlin*
**c. 1830**

The necklace, pendent earrings and bracelet, made in the iron foundries of Berlin, combine Neo-Classical honeysuckle and acanthus with Gothic motifs. These jewels were worn with mourning dress as an alternative to jet and black enamel.

Capitoline Museum, which shows doves drinking from a golden bowl. For more Romantic tastes there were views of the landscape outside Rome enlivened by idyllic scenes of peasant life.

There was no need to cross the Channel for regional jewellery: from Ireland came bog oak carved into harps and shamrocks, from Derbyshire hardstones inlaid into bouquets of flowers for brooches and from Scotland cairngorms (amber- or brown-hued citrines).

Notwithstanding the great concentration on jewellery for women, jewellers still supplied various ornaments to the dandy. His jewels included watch chains, jewelled studs, buttons, cuff links, lockets, dangling seals and perhaps most individual of all, stick pins for his cravat.

WHILE MANY FINE PIECES HAVE BEEN MELTED DOWN FOR THEIR
INHERENT VALUE, THOSE THAT HAVE SURVIVED PROVIDE
A REVEALING GLIMPSE OF FASHIONABLE TRENDS OVER
THREE HUNDRED YEARS.

# BRITISH SILVER

The development of styles in British silver can be seen broadly as an evolution of contrast, following the influences of varying cultures. Continental designs affected British fashions, the well-travelled rich introducing new shapes and styles of decoration gradually accepted by the rest of society. Changes of style occurred quite regularly in London-made silver, the fashionable going from one extreme to another as if rejecting completely the tastes of their forebears. Of course, things were not this simple. Old-fashioned clients would prefer to stick to the tried and tested styles of their youth,

or might commission pieces to match their existing silver. Moreover, new designs could take many years to spread from London to the more conservative market in the provinces. In the 19th century old designs were consciously copied, sometimes with some adaptation to contemporary tastes but often with great accuracy. Thus, one can see that design can be used only as a guide to dating silver, the hallmarks providing proof, as explained below.

Many looked upon the family silver as a source of ready money. Pieces could be melted down to make currency or pawned when times

## OLD SHEFFIELD AND ELECTROPLATE

One of the most successful methods of covering base-metal objects with a silver "skin" was discovered by Thomas Boulsover (1704–88) of Sheffield around 1743. He found that if a thin layer of silver was fused on to an ingot of copper, the two metals could be rolled as one, each expanding at the same rate under pressure. Thus sheets of silver fused on to copper could be manufactured, which were then cut up to make objects. At first the copper was plated on only one side, but by the mid 1760s both sides of the ingot could be plated.

Boulsover only made small pieces such as snuffboxes and livery buttons, but other Sheffield and Birmingham metalworkers quickly exploited his discovery. By mid-century a vast range of goods appeared, particularly large pieces such as tureens and trays. Much Old Sheffield plate is unmarked, and can only be dated by comparison with hallmarked silver pieces.

Plating base metal by electrolysis was first used commercially in the mid 19th century by cousins George Richards Elkington (1800–65) and Henry Elkington (c. 1810–52)

**VICTORIAN CRUET**
Electroplated; c. 1880

The Victorians loved naturalistic, novelty pieces, usually modelled with great realism. Although some were made in silver, the majority were produced in plate, to cater for a new and important middle-class market.

of Birmingham. In this process, the thin deposit of silver covered up solder and, in many cases, shoddy workmanship. Victorian and later electroplate is often marked with makers' initials. Items designed by Dr Christopher Dresser (1834–1904) and marked with a facsimile of his signature are in particular demand due to their stylishly simple forms.

# PROOF OF PURITY

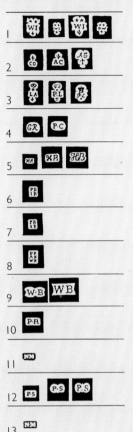

1. David Willaume (1658-1741)
2. Augustine Courtauld (1685-1751)
3. Paul de Lamerie (1688-1751)
4. Paul Crespin (1694-1770)
5. Hester Bateman (1709-94)
6. Peter Bateman (1740-1825) Jonathan Bateman (1747-91)
7. Peter Bateman (1740-1825) Ann Bateman (c. 1750-1815)
8. Peter Bateman (1740-1825) Ann Bateman (c. 1750-1815) William Bateman (1774-1850)
9. William Bateman (1774-1850)
10. Philip Rundell (1743-1827)
11. Nathaniel Mills (1746-1840)
12. Paul Storr (1771-1844)
13. Nathaniel Mills II (1811-1873)

British silver is usually marked with a series of punches, showing date of manufacture, the assay office where tested and marked, the maker and the silver standard. The latter was set at 925 parts of silver per thousand parts of metal in 1238, although the stamp indicating the presence of sterling silver – a leopard's head, sometimes wearing a crown – was not introduced until 1300. From 1363 each maker had to put his mark on his wares. Symbols were used for this purpose at first, but by the mid 18th century the first two initials of the silversmith's surname were usually employed. By about 1720 the initials of his Christian name and surname were generally used, as today. In 1463 the annual date letter was introduced, the letters running for 20 or so years until the start of a new letter style. Today date letters run alphabetically, but in the past they were sometimes more haphazard. A fourth mark, the lion passant, appeared from 1543.

A new, higher standard of silver was introduced in 1697: Britannia standard consisted of 958 parts of silver per thousand parts of metal. The old sterling standard marks were replaced by marks depicting Britannia and a lion's head in profile. But silversmiths and their customers complained that the new alloy was too soft, so in 1720 the old standard was readopted.

In 1784 the government decided to tax silver at six pence per ounce, introducing a new mark, the head of the reigning monarch in profile, to indicate payment of this duty. The mark was used until 1890, when British silversmiths successfully petitioned Parliament to remove the tax. Monarch's head stamps have since been used only on an irregular basis.

Throughout the 19th century much silver was reshaped or covered with later decoration, thus conforming with current styles while retaining their antique hallmarks. This vandalism is regrettable, but one can still usually sell such pieces quite legally. However, it is against the law to sell pieces whose original function has changed. Any added silver must also be assayed and marked.

Fakes have been in circulation for centuries; likewise, hallmarks have long been forged. Hallmarks are often faked by taking a casting of a genuine item; small granulations left by the sand commonly used in the casting process are generally the giveaway. Pieces reproduced by the lost-wax method of casting are more difficult to detect.

Some forgers have made their own punches, which can be very convincing. Comparison with genuine marks usually reveals slight differences.

Perfectly genuine marks were sometimes removed from legitimately assayed and marked small pieces, then cut out and soldered into place on large pieces. This practice eliminated payment of substantial duty on the silver used. Modern forgers also transpose hallmarks, removing stamps from damaged or inexpensive pieces and soldering them on fakes.

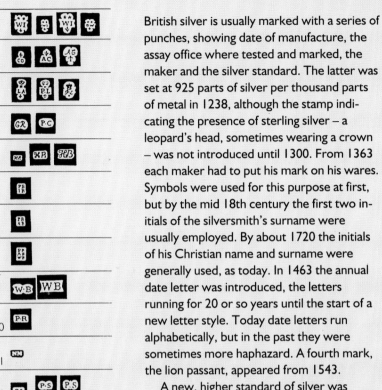

**London** 1716, Britannia standard

1736, Sterling standard

1756, Sterling standard

1776, Sterling standard

1796, Sterling standard

1816, Sterling standard

1836, Sterling standard

1856, Sterling standard

**Birmingham** 1773, Sterling standard

1849, Sterling standard

**Sheffield** 1824, Sterling standard

1844, Sterling standard

**Edinburgh** 1780, Sterling standard

1806, Sterling standard

were hard. Fortunately, Britain has enjoyed a relatively stable history, so a fair number of 17th-century pieces have survived. Continental silver from this period is scarcer, due to the number of European wars, when silver was collected and converted into bullion to pay the troops. Unfortunately, the appreciation of antique silver in Britain is a relatively new phenomenon, dating largely from the mid 19th century. Before this old silver was regularly melted down to provide the raw material for the manufacture of up-to-date pieces. The records of 18th-century silversmiths show, time and again, the receipt of many ounces of "old plate" scrapped to provide bullion, its value offset against new accounts.

### THE COMMONWEALTH

The Commonwealth (1642–60) saw the destruction of huge amounts of family silver, which was melted down by both Royalists and Cromwellians to finance the English Civil War. Moreover, the Puritans despised ostentatious displays of wealth and disapproved of depictions of Christ. Thus much church plate was destroyed, while many "apostle" spoons were defaced, their offending figure finials cut off and melted down. The few objects made in silver during this period were small and purely functional; decoration was minimal, usually restrained to simple vertical flutes. These were a necessary strengthening device, as the silversmiths were very economical with the metal, using thin sheet silver to create simple, practical pieces. Survivors in this style are now very scarce, due to their inherent fragile nature.

### THE BAROQUE

In France and the Netherlands the restrained Baroque style had been popular since the early 17th century. This gradually became more exaggerated, and by the 1650s their wares were covered in complex naturalistic scrolls, shells, birds and putti. When Charles II returned from his exile in France he introduced this style to Britain, along with a taste for sumptuous luxury and display. Vast pieces and services were produced, including splendid toilet sets with boxes, bottles, brushes and mirrors. The new, frivolous style spread throughout Britain, influencing even the design of everyday objects. The shape of cutlery changed to accommodate baroque chasing, while pieces of simple outline were often flat-chased with charmingly naïve chinoiserie scenes.

### "QUEEN ANNE"

The Restoration of the monarchy created, to some extent, a new aristocracy, as many minor noblemen were rewarded for their loyalty to Charles II. Eager to exploit their new wealth and status, they were avid buyers of silver. As a result, by the end of the 17th century the Exchequer was suffering from a serious shortage of bullion silver to manufacture coinage. Moreover, the practice of clipping the edges of coins was widespread, and so Britannia standard silver was introduced. This was too soft for the creation of elaborately decorated wares, and the French fashion for simple lines took hold. This so-called "Queen Anne" style, made throughout the first quarter of the 18th century, was characterized by plain surfaces alternating with flutes or facets. Powerful decoration in keeping with the sturdy outlines was popular, and cut-card work (soldering foliate patterns cut from flat silver sheets to a vessel), horizontal and vertical straps, and gadrooned rims (rims

**COMMONWEALTH WINE CUP**
*London*
**1650**

This tiny, fragile piece is a rare survivor from a short and troubled period. Only 6 cm (2½ in) high, it presumably escaped the melting pot as it weighs only two ounces. Notice the broad vertical flutes, chased into the thin metal to add strength. Purely functional, the cup has a simple but elegant shape.

decorated with reeding) added strength and interest, with engraving restricted to armorials. This style has been reproduced since the late 19th century, often in Britannia standard silver, so one must be wary of pieces with worn marks, as the date letters and maker's initials may have been deliberately defaced in an attempt to deceive.

## THE HUGUENOT INFLUENCE

In 1598 the Protestants of France, the Huguenots, had been given religious freedom by the Edict of Nantes, granted by Henry IV. However, in 1685, Louis XIV revoked the Edict. This led to a huge emigration from France, many wealthy and influential Protestants fleeing to America, the Netherlands and Britain. Some emigrant craftsmen were

**CHARLES II TOILET SERVICE**
*London*
**Mostly 1675 and 1676**

Although used in some wealthy households, such sets were made mainly to impress honoured guests. (*Above left*)

**GEORGE II FLUTED DISH**
*Paul de Lamerie, London*
**1746**

Simple and functional, this piece is more typical of de Lamerie's earlier works. (*Above*)

**QUEEN ANNE CHOCOLATE POTS**
**18th century**

The pot on the left was made by Seth Lofthouse in London (1712); that on the right by Joseph Walker in Dublin (1706).

involved in the precious metal trades, and their arrival in Britain greatly influenced fashions in the silve. industry.

Among the Huguenot craftsmen were Augustine Courtauld (1685–1751), Paul Crespin (1694–1770), David Willaume (1658–1741) and Paul de Lamerie (1688–1751), the latter the most celebrated of British silversmiths. Apprenticed to a fellow country-man, Pierre Platel (1664?–1719) in 1703, de Lamerie was made free in 1712 when he registered his first mark, "LA", a star and a large crown above, a fleur-de-lis beneath. De Lamerie settled in Soho, London, where he manufactured both splendid, immensely valuable pieces and more humble domestic objects. All were well-made using heavy gauge silver, and some of the more spectacular wares were finely engraved with armorials, probably by the young William Hogarth (1697–1764).

De Lamerie's early wares were in the plain "Queen Anne" style with flat surfaces, ideal for engraving, alternating with broad curved flutes and sharp angles. By the 1740s he became one of the chief exponents of the Rococo, producing masterpieces of exuberant casting and chasing.

## THE ROCOCO

By the 1730s many silver buyers were tired of the old, plain fashion and demanded more decoration and fanciful new shapes. The Rococo, an asymmetrical style incorporating shells, flowers and scrolling foliage, already popular in France, was now adopted by British craftsmen as they tried to compete with their Huguenot rivals.

**TWO GEORGE II TEA CADDIES WITH SUGAR BOX**
*Thomas Heming, London*
**1752**

Chinoiserie decoration was popular in the mid 18th century. Here Chinese figures are enhanced by arabesques. (*Above*)

**TWO GEORGE II COFFEEPOTS**
*George Wickes and Paul de Lamerie, London*
**1742**

Both examples are superbly chased with Rococo decoration. Wickes was highly skilled, but he does not carry the same kudos today as de Lamerie.

The British work was less exuberant than that of its Continental counterparts, combining restraint and strength with delicacy and balance. Chinoiserie decoration was peculiarly British, and many tea pieces were smothered with exotic scenes and plants. Although the best pieces were often cast and of great weight and quality, the fashion for the Rococo was widespread, with many smaller items, such as

**GEORGE III
CANDLESTICKS**
*John Schofield, London*
**Silver-gilt; 1791**

This fine quality set is restrained and surprisingly sturdy. Much Neo-Classical silver is light and flimsy, as it was constructed from machine-rolled metal, thus saving money in order to compete with Old Sheffield Plate. Candlesticks were all too often shoddily made, with inset iron rods to add strength, and pitch or plaster-filled bases, to ensure stability.

delightful baskets hand-pierced with flowers, leaves and birds, manufactured for the middle classes.

## NEO-CLASSICISM

A complete contrast to the frivolous and unrestrained Rococo, Neo-Classicism came into favour in the 1760s. Its popularity spread as the wealthy travelled on the Continent, exploring newly excavated classical ruins. Architect-designer Robert Adam (1728–92) was very influential, his drawings copied and adapted by silver and porcelain manufacturers, who produced countless vase-shaped objects decorated with laurel swags, ram's masks and hooves, paterae (type of low relief ornament), bows and beading. Candlesticks were normally of column form, with Corinthian or Doric capitals. Growing competition from Old Sheffield plate forced silversmiths to produce many cheaper wares, these manufactured from flimsy sheet metal machine-rolled to a uniform gauge. By the 1780s bright-cut engraving, executed with a special tool that created facets to sparkle in the

## THE BATEMAN DYNASTY

Hester Bateman (1709–94) is Britain's best-known woman silversmith. Her work, stamped with "HB" in script, is highly collectable, though primarily of poor-quality, standard design, manufactured from thinly machine-rolled metal enlivened with minimal bright-cut decoration.

Hester inherited the firm from her husband, John (1707?–60), who apparently specialized in making watch and jewellery chains. Upon John's death, Hester took over and even expanded the business, with the help of her two sons, John and Peter. John (1730–78) died prematurely, so Peter (1740–1825) and his brother Jonathan (1747–91) took over the firm. Their joint mark, "PB" over "IB", registered in 1790, is extremely rare, as Jonathan died a few months after the punch was entered at Goldsmiths Hall. His widow Ann (1750?–1815) joined forces with her brother-in-law, her youngest son William (1774–1850) becoming a partner in 1800. By 1815 William was head of the firm, and he manufactured silver until his death.

The Bateman family worked from the late

Rococo period, through Neo-Classicism, into early Victorian naturalism. Large, impressive Bateman pieces survive, but their speciality was inexpensive, simple, domestic silver for the middle class.

**GEORGE III SERVICE**
*Peter and Ann Bateman, London*
**1796, 1798, 1799**

light, had become fashionable. This technique was used by silversmiths to attract potential customers, as it was impossible to engrave Old Sheffield plate without exposing the copper beneath.

### THE REGENCY PERIOD

By about 1810 customers were tiring of coldly elegant and insubstantial silver, demanding massive and more flamboyant pieces. Although classicism persisted during the first quarter of the 19th century it became much heavier in style, awash with vine swags, bacchanalian friezes and Egyptianesque motifs, often cast and then applied to a plain but substantial body. Silver bullion from North and Central America was now plentiful and inexpensive, so financially the silversmiths were unrestrained. They let their imaginations wander freely, providing their clients with well-made, monumental objects. Towards the end of the period taste began to deteriorate. Silver became increasingly overdecorated, and elegance was often sacrificed for sheer bulk.

### THE VICTORIAN ERA

In the 19th century large companies, often employing hundreds of workers, manufactured

**GEORGE III EPERGNE**
*Thomas Pitts, London*
**1773**

This piece represents Neo-Classicism at its most dynamic. Although one can see many typical elements – laurel swags, urn medallions, beading and shells – the maker has combined them to create a lively and exuberant *tour de force*.

## PAIR OF GEORGE III WINE COOLERS AND STANDS

*Benjamin Smith, London*
Silver-gilt; **1807**

These are particularly fine examples weighing in at a massive 348 ounces. Their shape is typical of the late Neo-Classical period, the "campana" form used for goblets and even tureens. Huge numbers of similar-shaped coolers were made in both silver and Old Sheffield Plate, but the majority were of inferior quality. These have cast mounts and handles, and even the armorials are cast in solid silver, rather than engraved.

# PAUL STORR

The most celebrated Regency period silversmith was Paul Storr (1771–1844). After being apprenticed to a Swedish-born silversmith, Andrew Fogelberg, for six years, Storr joined forces with William Frisbee. Their partnership lasted only three years, and Storr was soon established in his own right as a major silversmith, creating his first important piece, a gold font commissioned by the Duke of Portland, in 1797. His fame spread, and in 1799 he was commissioned to make the "Battle of the Nile Cup" for presentation to Admiral Lord Nelson.

Around 1803 Storr was approached by silversmith Philip Rundell (1743–1827) to work with him; he had already persuaded sculptor John Flaxman (1755–1826) to join him as a designer. Storr turned him down, although he did work for Rundell from about 1806, still retaining his own mark for independent work. He resigned from the company upon realizing he was being exploited, joining forces with John Mortimer in 1822 and setting up in business in New Bond Street. Storr retired in 1839, dying five years later in comparative poverty.

Paul Storr's work was invariably of the highest quality, with even the most insignificant pieces well-designed and executed in heavy gauge silver.

**Inkstand** by Paul Storr, 1803

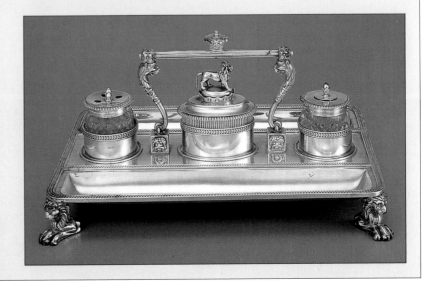

# FLATWARE

Flatware, or cutlery, from the mid 18th century onwards is readily available to collectors. Earlier flatware, often with cast finials formed as apostles or balusters, can be very expensive, clear marks attracting great interest. A number of 17th-century spoons are extant: these were popular christening presents and many still bear the initials of the child and his godparent. Forks are much rarer, however, as they generally were not introduced into British society until the mid 17th century.

The Restoration of the monarchy in 1660 saw the introduction of French styles of flatware. Forks came into widespread use, their old-fashioned cast finials replaced with flattened handles. These were ideal for displaying chased or stamped decoration, and also enabled flatware to be produced more cheaply, since each piece could be made from one sheet of silver. Sets of matching pieces could also be manufactured quite easily, although it is now quite difficult to find sets still together. One drawback of assembling a set of flatware is that many pieces will be engraved with the initials or crests of the original owners, showing at a glance that the set is composite.

Period knives are difficult to find, as most had handles made from thin sheet silver with a pitch core. When immersed in hot water the core would expand, splitting the metal. Ivory-handled knives with steel blades, popular in the 19th century, are now often badly corroded, many handles cracked or discoloured.

**Selection of spoons
19th to 17th century**

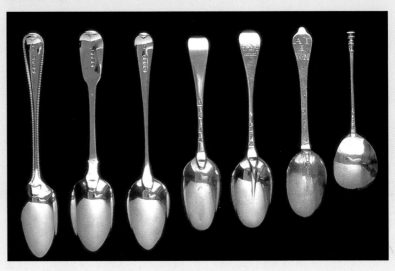

masses of inexpensive silver wares. Quality inevitably suffered, and much was now mass-produced with machine-rolling and stamping. Of course, some silversmiths continued to use traditional methods, largely because of the tastes of their wealthy, discerning clients. Reproductions of earlier fashions were popular, while the late 19th century saw the arrival of Art Nouveau from the Continent, the designs of that exuberant, curvilinear style often toned down to appeal to the masses. Perhaps the main Victorian style was naturalism, in which plant, animal and human forms were exploited, creating a host of objects, small and large, appealing and grotesque.

**VICTORIAN TEA
SERVICE**
*Edward Farrell, London*
**1839**

Farrell fully exploited the Victorian taste for the naturalistic, manufacturing a number of pieces smothered in cast and chased designs, often incorporating scenes of drunken peasants in the manner of the Dutch artist Teniers.

**VICTORIAN VASE**
*Paul Storr, London*
**1838**

A monumental piece 83 cm (33 in) high, weighing 264 ounces, this was made one year before Storr's retirement. *(Above)*

## "THE TOYSHOP OF EUROPE"

Birmingham has been an important centre for the manufacture of silver and jewellery since the early 18th century, specializing in making trinkets such as "Seals, Tweezer and Tooth Pick Boxes, Smelling Bottles and Fillegree Work, Watch Chains, Stay Hooks, Sugar Knippers etc." *(Sketchley's Birmingham Directory,* 1767). Huge amounts of such inexpensive "toys" were made, and on this basis Birmingham, along with Sheffield, appealed to the government for their own assay offices, which they were granted in 1773. For its hallmark symbol Sheffield chose a crown, Birmingham an anchor (apparently after a London pub, The Crown and Anchor, the place where the two cities' delegates met).

Birmingham had long suffered an unfair reputation for producing shoddy pieces, doubtless instigated by the London makers'

jealousy of the city's success. Indeed, the adjective "brummagem" became synonymous with showy, mass-produced wares of poor quality, although in reality the small pieces such as snuffboxes, card cases and vinaigrettes produced in Birmingham were difficult to fault. Made primarily to appeal to the middle-class market, they were often produced from thin sheet silver with the minimum of simple engraved or engine-turned decoration. The majority were beautifully constructed, with well-concealed joins and firm hinges.

A popular Birmingham specimen was the "castle top" box made in the mid 19th century. Inset with views of famous buildings or sporting subjects, the best examples of such boxes are cast in high relief, the second grade are die-stamped and then finished with hand chasing.

**VICTORIAN PILGRIM BOTTLES**
*Messrs Carrington, London*
**1893**

These excellent reproductions of mid-17th-century originals are of superb quality, weighing 339 ounces. Although the prototypes were used as wine flasks, these copies were designed for display. Their value is enhanced by the later inscriptions, recording that they were presented to Prince Alexander of Teck as wedding gifts in 1904, one given by his brother-in-law, George, Prince of Wales, the other by fellow officers of the 7th (Queen's Own) Hussars.

**W**ITH THE GREATER AVAILABILITY OF SILVER, AND THE INCREASED
PATRONAGE THAT OCCURRED BETWEEN THE 17TH AND 19TH CENTURIES
ON THE CONTINENT, SILVERWARE ATTAINED NEW HEIGHTS OF QUALITY.

# EUROPEAN SILVER

From the 17th century onwards, Continental silver underwent a revolution in scale and function. During the Baroque period the metal was given a new role: to furnish the interior. Deriving from Italian *pièces de parade*, such as outsized ewers and basins, silver furniture – including wine fountains and coolers, mirror frames, tables and jardinières – became popular throughout Europe, principally due to the patronage of Louis XIV and the subsidized extravagance of the Gobelins factory. Secular versions of the giant Spanish *custodia* (portable tabernacles) of the Renaissance period emerged in the form of thrones, chandeliers and over-sized stands and vases, most later melted down to convert into coin.

In the 18th century, when the production of silver furniture declined as the fashion for ormolu increased, vast *surtouts de table*, incorporating centrepieces, candelabra, soup and ragout tureens, and other vessels, replaced the toilet set in the repertoire of most continental silversmiths. Tea, coffee and chocolate, introductions of the mid 17th century, came into their own with the evolution of the Rococo style, and complex *equipages* for these drinks included kettles and urns on stands, trays, canisters, milk jugs and basins. At the end of the century, Neo-Classicism straightened out the curves and regularized the shapes of silver in most European centres.

The 19th century began with the Empire style emanating from a revitalized imperial France. In spite of experiencing an almost continuous state of war, since 1792, European silversmiths and designers imitated French shapes and decoration. In part they drew their inspiration from the pattern-books by Charles Percier (1764–1838) and Pierre-François–Léonard Fontaine (1762–1853), rather as their Neo-Classical predecessors had been influenced by the designs of Piranesi and Robert Adam. Gilding enjoyed a strong revival, suitably complementing the Greek and Egyptian

grandeur that imperial taste evoked. In Austria and Germany, Biedermeier, an adapted and more simple style emerged. In the rest of Europe, a romantic yearning towards the Gothic and the Rococo, rather as an antidote to the prevalent grand taste, ushered in a long period of historicism.

Technological advances greatly added to the virtuosity of design and availability of product, especially with the new achievements in electroplating. Following Napoleonic examples,

**TOILET MIRROR**
*French*
Silver-gilt; embossed and chased; 1660

This mirror, from a dispersed toilet set, bears rings for suspension as well as a hinged support. The repoussé work (or embossing) is typical of the "floral-foliate" style of the middle of the 17th century. Made as a wedding present for James, Duke of York, (later James II) and Anne Hyde in 1660. (*Right*)

**EWER AND BASIN**
*North Italian*
Silver-gilt; embossed and chased; *c.* 1610

A typical *pièce de parade* intended mainly for display. (*Right*)

**EWER AND BASIN**
*Christian van Vianen, Utrecht*
Silver, embossed and
chased; 1632

Two pieces in the fleshy
Auricular style introduced
by the van Vianen
workshop.

large ceremonial plate took the form of triumphal shields, plateaux or mirrored table centres, while urns and vases were designed as sporting trophies and sculptural testimonial edifices. The timely influences of the British Arts and Crafts Movement and of naturalistic Japanese design relieved a succession of Rococo and classical revivals regularly fuelled by international exhibitions.

ENGRAVING AND EMBOSSING

By its nature Mannerist and Baroque silver demanded from the silversmith a considerable fluidity of technique. Although overall engraved decoration continued in vogue well into the 17th century, the tendency in most centres was towards thinner gauge silver, which was better suited to embossing, or repoussé work, and finishing by the chaser. One major exception to this rule was the innovative output of the Dutch van Vianen family, particularly Adam and his son Christian, who mastered the art of

## PRINCIPAL EUROPEAN SILVERSMITHS

| JAMNITZER, Wenzel | 1508–85 | Nuremberg | Leading Mannerist goldsmith, based in Nuremberg. |
|---|---|---|---|
| VAN VIANEN, Adam | 1565–c.1627 | Utrecht | A founder of transitional Mannerist-Baroque Auricular style. |
| VAN VIANEN, Paul | 1570–c.1613 | Utrecht and Prague | Brother of Adam. Most accomplished of the Auricular goldsmiths. |
| LUTMA, Johannes (Jan) | c.1587–1669 | Amsterdam | Influenced by the Van Vianens. Leading Amsterdam goldsmith of Baroque period. |
| VAN VIANEN, Christian | c.1609–67 | Utrecht and London | Son and pupil of Adam. Worked in England. |
| DA FORLI, Giovanni Giardini | fl. 1675–1722 | Rome | Roman goldsmith of the late Baroque. |
| THELOTT, Johann Andreas | 1655–1734 | Augsburg | Celebrated embosser of Baroque period. |
| GERMAIN, Thomas | 1673–1748 | France | Rococo goldsmith who trained in Rome. |
| MEISSONIER, Juste-Aurèle | 1693–1750 | Paris | Noted for introducing rococo forms into designs for silver and interiors. |
| AUGUSTE, Robert-Joseph | 1723–1805 | France | Goldsmith. Worked for Louis XVI, Catherine the Great and Portuguese court. |
| ODIOT, Jean-Baptiste-Claude | 1763–1850 | France | A rival of Biennais with a reputation as an innovator. |
| BIENNAIS, Martin Guillaume | 1764–1843 | Paris | Principal goldsmith to Napoleon. |

tions at the palace of Versailles. Jean Le Pautre (1618–82) furnished hundreds of designs described either as *à la romaine* or *à la moderne*, in which an austere figure style was combined with rigid acanthus ornament or spiralling *rinceaux* and grotesques. A more fundamental change was the increase in heavy gauge metal to which ornament was applied, having been cast separately, and later chased. This transition took place during the 1670s and 1680s in the major centres of Paris and certain provincial cities. The technique of cut-card work, an overlay of fretted silver applied to the body of the host vessel, also evolved into heavy pre-cast straps of sculptural proportions during the same phase. These techniques were adopted by silversmiths in neighbouring countries, largely through the migration of Huguenot craftsmen which took place both before and after the Revocation of the Edict of Nantes in 1685.

In non-Protestant Europe, French designs were copied, but often without abandoning the thinner gauge "sheet" silver mode of assembly. Table candlesticks, made by casting the base and stem in three sections in the French style, could weigh two to three times more than the equivalent sheet-silver objects. Where the gauge of silver used precluded embossing, flat-chasing was one of the normal methods of decoration, apart from applied ornament. Engraving was used but was more susceptible to wear; armorials, ciphers and inscriptions being better suited to this technique.

embossing, leaving the surface unchased and only polished in much of their output.

The scientific approach to the study of botany yielded an output of engraved illustrations contemporary with the flowering of the Dutch still-life school, which was influential in the decorative arts, especially from the second quarter of the 17th century until *c*.1700. In silver, engraved decoration of a naturalistic and spirited character was popular in northern Europe. German, Dutch, Italian and Spanish tankards, cups, salvers, beakers and other vessels were often embossed in high relief with scrolling foliage, animals and flowers, as well as figurative compositions. The gauge of most large-scale objects, including furniture, was often alarmingly thin, in order to economize on weight and cost. Embossing, however, served to strengthen the metal itself through constant hammering and regular annealing.

The long reign of Louis XIV (1643–1715) inaugurated a new sophistication in metalwork design and techniques. Within France the spirited, naturalistic Baroque style underwent a classicizing purge, which gradually spread to neighbouring countries. The sources of this new emphasis were largely architectural and derived from the king's architects and designers, notably those concerned with the building and decora-

**SALVER ON TRUMPET FOOT**
*Paul Beuren, London*
Silver, embossed and chased on matted field;
**1683**

High relief embossing of fruit, flowers and figure subjects, or animals and birds – such as on this salver from London – enjoyed a peak of popularity in silver and other forms of decoration from *c*. 1650 to the 1680s.

## CASTING

Casting silver handles of figurative asymmetrical form, as well as ornate finials and even entire objects of heavy and complex form, was usually done by means of the *cire-perdue*, or "lost wax", method. Spouts, handles and candlestick stems, taking the example of French silver from *c*.1675 onwards, were cast in sand in two halves subsequently soldered together along a seam. The expense of using a greater weight of silver than was traditionally employed enhanced the additional finishing processes.

Another innovation, for which the Italians and French were largely responsible – especially later during the time of the French Régence (1715–23) – was double-struck flatware. Crude handles and the reverses of spoon bowls had been struck in the earlier Baroque styles, usually in low relief, but the heavier gauge fashion of the later 17th century demanded similar modifications in the size and decoration of spoons, ladles, forks and other accessories. These resulted in the die-stamping of stems and bowls with a variety of escutcheon-shaped motifs, which in the past had only been engraved. Stems became round in section and assumed a cursive profile.

The Rococo period witnessed a renaissance of embossing and chasing, with casting and heavy gauge work remaining the favoured techniques for larger or high-quality work. The enlivenment of the metal into scrollwork and cursive fluting emphasized the metal's malleability and ductility. Neo-Classicism did not at first deter high-relief embossing and cast-work – especially in France, which took the design lead. In Germany, however, close links with the porcelain industry from the 1720s had ensured a parallel development from the Régence through the Neo-Classical period, with modellers adapting their skills to both art forms.

### INDUSTRIALIZED METHODS

The industrialization of many crafts during the latter half of the 18th century – mainly through the adoption of steam power in factories – encouraged technical revolutions in silver and its new partner, Sheffield plate, introduced in

**PAIR OF PERFUME BURNERS**
*Attributed to Giambattista Boucheron*
Silver-gilt; **c. 1780**

These burners, showing strong Louis XVI influences, are of heavy cast construction, with billing doves as finials to the openwork covers. (*Right*)

**SOUP TUREEN**
*Stamped J Bte Cde Odiot*
Silver-gilt; **1819**

A superb example of the Empire style from the Branicki Service, utilizing casting by the lost-wax method. (*Below*)

England. The stamping of ornament and openwork formerly achieved by hand could now be done with a fly-press, saving many hours work. Mills driven by steam engines could roll ingots into sheet of unprecedented evenness and to a much thinner gauge. Neo-Classicism, which coincided with the relatively barren French design period immediately following the Revolution, exploited plainer surfaces and lighter weights, using engraved decoration or embossing to compensate. Sheffield plate was widely exported and influential. Only when France emerged from the Directoire and Consulat with Napoleon as emperor did its designers again influence taste and techniques throughout the Continent. This happened largely through conquest and occupation, but also through the assertiveness of the "Empire" style.

Technically, the Empire style brought a return to a robust, heavy gauged form of classicism, derived in part from Louis XVI shapes but relying on plain surfaces to which cast and often stamped motifs were applied. In tune with the heroic pace of the period, gilding and severe Greek and Egyptian allusions occurred in most larger-scale silver, a fashion which spread widely, notably to Regency Britain.

For some decades following the fall of Napoleon, the severity of French taste was retained in such places as Germany, Austria and Italy. The styles and techniques of past periods first began to appear in c.1810, mainly in Britain and as an antidote to Greek severity, rococo and then 17th-century silver providing the spur. On the Continent, this taste for antiquarian styles emerged in the 1820s and 1830s, and became the dominant fashion by the

time of the 1851 Great Exhibition in London, where the work of overseas silversmiths was first seen *en masse*.

## ELECTROPLATING

The reproductive techniques of electroforming or electrotyping, derived from the galvanic process of electroplating (which began to oust Sheffield plate from the 1840s) made a considerable impact. This new plating process extended the range of cheaper but still sophisticated wares to the public – at about a third of the price of the equivalents in silver. The more monumental output of the craft developed into a major industry, especially in Paris, Berlin, Vienna and other centres. Sculptors, enamellers, chasers and engravers, as well as specialist craftsmen engaged in die-stamping, damascening and etching, often combined resources in single outsized testimonial centre-pieces and other elaborate table ornaments. So great was the necessity to allude to exotic styles and to outdo one's rivals that surfaces were rarely left plain.

## FRANCE

France suffered extensively from the mass meltings of plate occurring during its political disturbances. The little plate to survive the late Mannerist era is by no means a representative guide to the prodigious and sumptuous court commissions made under Henry IV and Louis XIII. It can be presumed, however, that the "international Mannerist style", incorporating Italianate and Germanic elements, must have been a dominant factor. Only on the occasion of the majority of Louis XIV in 1661 and the subsequent foundation of the Gobelins factory did a clearly national style emerge, one that came to rival the dominance of Italy. Louis XIV demanded a classical grandeur compatible with the artistic pretensions of Versailles, under the direction of Charles Le Brun (1619–90) and an army of decorative artists, whose engravings were influential throughout Europe.

Pattern-books such as Nicolas Cochin's *Livre nouveau de fleurs très-util pour l'art d'orfèvrerie* had appeared as early as 1645 and helped establish an effuse floral-foliate style of embossing and chasing, often open-worked. French workmanship began an ascendancy that predominated for nearly two centuries, and was reflected in the silver of neighbouring countries. Toilet services made in this style began to be manufactured by the mid-17th century, utilizing a

**PAIR OF TOILET BOXES**
*Hubert Horion-Dore, Mons*
Silver, embossed and chased; 1678–9

Showing the finest quality decoration of the naturalistic Baroque of Northern Europe before the more formal classical Baroque began to dominate. (*Right*)

**SOUP TUREEN, COVER AND STAND**
*H. Adnet and P-F. Bonnestrenne, Paris*
Silver; 1734–40

Almost entirely cast and chased, this tureen and its pair, a tour de force of French rococo design and craftsmanship were made under the supervision of Juste-Aurèle Meissonnier, a pioneer of Rococo. (*Below*)

formal acanthus design known as "Roman" or "French leaf". By the 1680s, the gauge used for silver was increased and sheet silver was replaced with cast handles, finials and applied ornament. A new style of greater classical austerity complemented this process. Unfortunately for the craft, in 1689 Louis XIV sent all his large furnishing plate to be melted for coin, and restrictions thereafter were imposed on the size and weight of silver and gold objects. The craft declined, but emphasis increased

upon smaller-scale ornament, cast and chased as well as engraved. The designs of Jean Bérain (1640–1711), freely adapting the lightweight Mannerist motifs of Jacques Androuet DuCerceau of the 1550s and 1560s, came into their own under these circumstances. Bérain was followed by Daniel Marot (1663–1752), who in 1685 brought the style to the Netherlands, and subsequently to England.

**Rococo** Silversmiths such as Nicolas Delaunay (*fl.* 1672–1705), Claude Ballin (*fl.* 1672–1709) and Alexis Loir (1640–1713) projected the Bérain style into the 1700s. Fine strapwork and areas of diaper ornament, together with roundels containing profile busts, shells and paterae (small circular ornaments), decorated many objects of this period, such as soup and ragout tureens, introduced in the last years of Louis XIV's reign. After this, Bérain's informality began to flow and deviate from the vertical axis, with handles becoming more sinuous. In the later 1720s, after the Régence period, the Rococo style was born. Nature assumed the prime role in form and decoration, prompted by Italian design and the paintings and decorations of Jean-Antoine Watteau (1684–1721). The pioneering designer of the period was Juste-Aurèle Meissonnier (1693–1750), and the leading goldsmith was Thomas Germain (1673–1748).

**Neo-Classicism** When reports of the excavation of Pompeii which began in 1748, first reached Paris, they almost immediately engendered a reaction against Rococo. By the 1760s, the Rococo smith François-Thomas Germain, son of Thomas, was succeeded at the French court by Jacques Roettiers (1707–84), a Neo-

Classicist who was himself succeeded as *Orfèvre du Roi* by his son, Jacques-Nicolas (*c.*1745– after 1777). Their work is characterized by an almost baroque use of classical shapes and ornament. Another great family of silversmiths during this period were the Augustes, Robert-Joseph (*c.*1723–1805) and his son, Henry (active *c.*1785–1809). A more purely geometrical series of shapes was favoured by the mid-1770s, becoming more austere by the mid-1780s, somewhat in tune with the Neo-Classical epics of the painter Jacques-Louis David (1748–1825).

**Empire** The two major French goldsmiths to emerge during the periods of the Directoire, Consulat and Empire were Martin-Guillaume Biennais (active *c.*1798–1843) and Jean-Baptiste-Claude Odiot (1763–1850). The latter

eign rivals. In the 1870s and 1880s, French silver showed oriental influences, particularly Japanese, together with further surges of the Rococo, Renaissance and classical.

### THE NETHERLANDS

After gaining independence from Spain in the late 16th century, the northern Netherlands experienced a period of increasing prosperity and artistic creativity, confirmed by the Peace of Westphalia in 1648. As in France and Germany, many Dutch artistic centres boasted strong guilds of goldsmiths, with Utrecht and Amsterdam prominent in the Baroque period.

**Auricular Style** The van Vianen family, Adam (1565–1627), his brother Paul (c. 1570–1613/4), who also worked for Emperor Rudolph II in Prague, and Adam's son, Christian (c. 1609–67), evolved a fleshy Mannerist style of both form and ornament based upon 16th-century Italian engravings.

acquired most of Henry Auguste's models in 1809, ensuring the continuity of the earlier style. All three goldsmiths favoured gilding and designs contrasting formal figurative elements with largely plain surfaces relieved with stamped or cast and applied ornament. The *Receuil de Décoration*, published periodically from 1801 onwards by the architect-decorators Percier and Fontaine, together with the still fashionable designs of Piranesi and the 1802 work of Dominique Vivant-Denon, *Voyage dans la Basse et la Haute Egypte* (evoking the archaeological discoveries and acquisitions of Napoleon's Egyptian campaign) all played their part in inspiring the "Empire" style.

On the Bourbon restoration in 1815 and until the 1830s, the Empire style continued to dominate French taste. As elsewhere in Europe, literary romanticism, coupled with nostalgia for the 18th century and the Ancien Régime, then kindled a variety of revivals, that of the Rococo being prominent. Exposure of important examples of "antiquarian" plate at French national exhibitions ensured the popularity of the *style troubadour* (a medievalist romanticism) throughout the fine and decorative arts well into the later 19th century. Electroplating and electroforming had as great an impact in France as in England, and became categories at the international exhibitions. Prominent exhibitors included Charles and later Paul Christofle, and François-Désiré Froment-Meurice, whose work was technically far superior to that of their for-

**SOUP TUREEN, COVER AND STAND**
*Jacques-Nicolas Roettiers, Paris*
Silver, cast and chased;
**1770**

This is one of the 22 tureens from the Orloff Service. (*Above*)

**TWO-HANDLED VASE**
*Paul Christophle and Henri Bouilhet, Paris*
Silver, parcel-gilt; **c. 1865**

Originally a pigeon-shooting-contest prize cup, this was presented by Napoleon III in 1867, and also exhibited in the Paris Exposition Universelle of that year. Typical of the High Art techniques of the mid 19th century in which electroforming frequently supplanted traditional embossing and chasing techniques.

Called variously "Auricular" (after the ear's shape) and "Cartilaginous", the mainly marine designs used bear little or no chasing, relying upon rounded sculptural embossing instead. The Amsterdam goldsmiths, principally Johannes (or Jan) Lutma (1587–1669) and Thomas Bogaert (1597–1657), adapted the style, but they were also influential in the floral-foliate manner, which was naturalistic until *c.* 1675 and then came under more formal French influence, relying upon the straight rather than scrolling acanthus. As elsewhere in northern Europe, the engraver enjoyed great popularity as a silver decorator throughout the 17th century.

**Foreign Influences** With the arrival of Huguenot designers and silversmiths at the Dutch court, in particular Daniel Marot, figurative and strap ornament of Bérainesque type became popular. Also, through William III of Orange, there was a current of influences from London. However, the Dutch did not favour the heavier gauges of the French and English, and the later Rococo period shows a greater lightweight "flow" in design. Pierced-work and geometrical shapes typified the Neo-Classical Dutch style, while under French domination (from the 1790s to 1815) plainer compromises with the French Empire were usual. Silversmiths then became attracted to the antiquarian revivals of the rest of northern Europe.

## ITALY

Mannerism deriving from the art of Rome, Florence, Venice and Genoa continued to influence form and decoration in Italy until the mid 17th century. The strong architectural and sculptural forces behind 16th-century design in the applied arts, epitomized by followers of Michelangelo and Cellini, softened into the Baroque, with less staccato and more cursive results. Venice, whose prominence in the visual arts reached a peak in the redecoration of the Doge's Palace in the 1580s, began to lose its dominance to the rival city of Genoa around the turn of the century. Very little secular plate survived later meltings, but a number of *pièces de parade*, largely ewers and basins, testify to the fine craftsmanship continuing earlier tradition. Genoese silver showed strong Flemish influence, not surprising, since both Rubens and Van Dyck enjoyed patronage there.

During the later Baroque and Rococo periods, papal commissions ensured both scale and grandeur and a commensurate thin gauge of

**PAIR OF WALL SCONCES**
*Adam van Vianen, Utrecht*
Silver; **1622**

An embossed and openworked design exploits the reflective properties of silver and the sculptural skills of the silversmith simultaneously. Made at the height of the Auricular period anticipating the Dutch Baroque. (*Right*)

**BEAKER**
*Antoni Magnus, Deventer*
Silver; **c. 1664**

This is an outstanding example of the engraver's skill used for all-over decoration. This type of tall beaker is mainly found in the Netherlands and Germany during the later 16th and 17th centuries. The subject matter consists of satirical figures after Abraham Bosse and Jacques Callot, with several grotesque masques. (*Right*)

frequently shows strong Italian characteristics.

In some centres, the floral-foliate style maintained strong influence until the 1750s. However, Italian and French Rococo designs and decoration, albeit in restrained form, were gradually adopted, and a fertile Louis XVI style flourished from *c*. 1780 to 1830. In the mid to late 19th century, conservatism and revivalism combined in national styles deriving from both Gothic and Moorish sources. Also incorporated were the traditional technique of filigree and orthodox foreign influences.

Portugal's maritime position provided that country with greater international trading relations than Spain. Considerable English and French cross-currents are evident in Portuguese

silver employed for altar plate, candelabra and other fixtures. An exceptional goldsmith, who continued Bernini's sculptural, theatrical style, was Giovanni Giardini (1646–*c*. 1722) of Forli.

A centre to gain prominence at this time was Turin, capital of Savoy, whence it could be said the "Rococo" style of Venice fuelled that of France. Here influence from France gained in the 18th century, although much Italian silver follows a more "international Rococo style". In the south, Naples and Catania gained reputations for supplying Roman Catholic churches over much of the world, mainly in a mixed Baroque-Rococo style. During the Neo-Classical period in Rome and Turin, Luigi Valadier and Giovanni Battista Boucheron produced sculptural inventions of Piranesi-like severity.

The Napoleonic era influenced Italian taste. In Rome, Pietro Belli (1780–1828) was among several leading silversmiths to produce Empire-style designs from around 1815 to 1830. Later, historicism came to prominence through international and national exhibitions. An embosser and chaser who also practised damascening (gold or silver inlay), Vicenza-born Antonio Cortelazzo had some influence in England and elsewhere.

## SPAIN AND PORTUGAL

Well into the 17th century, Spanish silver continued to be dominated by the austere Herrera style, whose origins lay in the architectural massiveness of the Escorial Palace designed by Juan de Herrera (*c*. 1530–97) for Philip II. Little secular plate remains, but recently colonial pieces that reflect rare Spanish types have been found on wrecks. More church plate has survived and

**TWO COFFEE POTS**
*Genoa*
Silver, embossed and part-chased; *c*. 1760

The spiralling fluting is typical of baluster coffee and chocolate pots in much of mid 18th-century Europe. (*Above*)

**SOUP TUREEN AND STAND**
*Naples*
Silver; 1770

The free and lively use of rococo ornament on porcelain inspired silversmiths' attempts to achieve similar effects. The

fashion for the Neo-Classical was sweeping Europe at this time, stimulated by the rediscovery of Pompeii and Herculaneum. These tureens offer evidence that Naples could still produce pure rococo silverware. (*Below*)

decorative arts, including silver, particularly in the 18th century.

## GERMANY

At the onset of the 17th century, Augsburg had succeeded Nuremberg as the major centre of German goldsmithing. This resulted from the conservatism of Dürer's native city, its inward-looking government and its "closed" guild system, as opposed to Augsburg's more cosmopolitan nature. Renaissance and later Italian fashions were more accessible in Augsburg; likewise, the Reformation did not affect that city's role in providing plate, almost on a mass-production scale, to both church and laity, whereas largely Protestant Nuremberg suffered.

The Thirty Years War (1618–48) caused a serious decline in both population and output of most German goldsmithing centres. Generally, the more exquisite silver elements of the previous century gave way to thinner gauge ebullience, floridity and spectacle. Exporting became the main goal, the fairs at Leipzig and Frankfurt-am-Main the principal market places. Rich embossed wares, influenced by French and

**TAZZA ON PEDESTAL FOOT**
*Martin Rodriguez, Valladolid*
Silver-gilt and enamel;
**c. 1650**

An enamelled boss surrounded by pricked scrollwork decorates this shallow bowl. (*Above*)

**BEAKER**
*Christoph Jamnitzer, Nuremberg*
Silver-gilt; **c. 1600**

The quatrefoil shape of the bowl and foot is a vestige of a 17th-century Gothic revival. (*Below*)

**EWER**
*Spanish*
Silver gilt and blue enamel;
**c. 1640**

This vessel is typical of the Herrera style of the reign of Philip II. (*Right*)

Dutch engravings alike, were widely produced by such masters as Johann Andreas Thelot (d. 1734). After 1700, Bérain's designs brought about more formal discipline, although the thicker gauge of French silver, with its highly chased surfaces and cast handles and finials, was far superior. From the 1640s to the 1680s, Auricular-style handles, borders and mouldings also influenced German silver, particularly at centres like Hamburg. High-relief friezes, embossed into tankards, typical German and northern European vessels, were also popular.

Along with the major cities such as Hamburg and Munich, Dresden and Leipzig also grew in importance in the early 18th century. The Elector of Saxony employed Johann Melchior Dinglinger (1664–1731), principally responsible for the bejewelled treasures of Dresden's Green Vaults (the elector's collection of fine jewels, gold and silver), and Johann Jacob Irminger (*fl.* 1682–*c.* 1722), who designed many of the earlier Meissen porcelain forms. French Régence shapes and ornaments also enjoyed popularity, especially in the south. The new forms required for soup, tea and coffee were of serpentine bombé form.

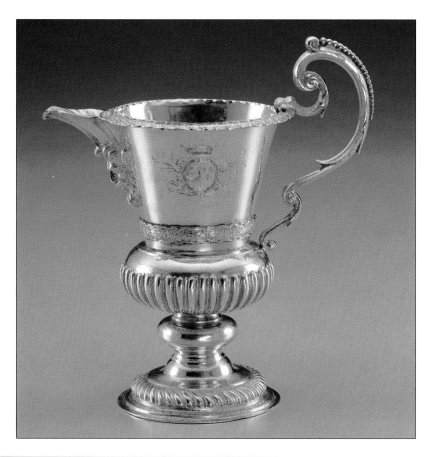

### EWER
*Ludwig Spitta, Brunswick*
**Silver; 1704**

This lively baroque vessel is embossed with half fluting to the baluster bowl, complete with flanged rim and applied band to the waist. (*Above*)

### TRAVELLING SERVICE
*Augsburg*
**Silver-gilt; 1729–33**

This is an example of the smaller *couvert* style of service built around the *écuelle*, a vessel of typical *Régence* style. (*Left*).

In the later Rococo period, German silver frequently followed the lightweight excesses of porcelain design, for instance, in table centres consisting of arbours and trellises, or extensive toilet sets including flower, fruit and vegetable allusions. The Rococo slowly declined in most of Germany, succumbing to classical revivalism.

The French invasions determined new shapes and decoration according to the Empire taste in the early 19th century. As in Austria, this style continued.in simplified form, particularly in furniture and silver, almost to the 1840s – under the name Biedermeier. English silver enjoyed popularity and was influential largely in northern Germany, particularly Hamburg. By midcentury, historicism began to dominate silver.

RUSSIA

The centre of the goldsmiths' craft in 17th-century Russia was Moscow, where the Kremlin Armouries contained the workshops. Only after the foundation of St Petersburg by Peter the Great in 1703 was there any attempt to emulate Western European tastes. Many German silversmiths were drawn to the Russian court, where they established their own guild system. Moscow and Novgorod on the whole remained conservative in their output, with traditional shapes such as the *kovsh* and *bratina* (kinds of drinking vessels) continuing to be made, decorated with niello (black metal alloy), filigree and enamel. The Russian Orthodox Church exercised a considerable restraint upon novelty of any sort, so its gold and silver commissions (eg, icon frames) repeated forms which had been unchanged for several centuries. Sometimes baroque or rococo elements would intrude, but mostly at a much later date. The Russian patron liked German Renaissance and even Gothic shapes; many of these were emulated until as late as the mid 19th century.

With the "enlightened" despotism of the tsars from the mid to late 18th century, more discriminating tastes became apparent. The quantity of Western art treasures coming into the country served to upgrade taste to more contemporary standards. Catherine the Great's most auspicious commission went to France: the influential Orloff Service of the 1770s, a triumph of the baroque-Louis XVI taste.

In spite of a retrograde period at the end of the 18th century, Western influences prevailed during and after the Napoleonic invasion, especially after the addition of Finland to the Russian Empire in 1815. Many Finnish crafts-

men settled in St Petersburg, and a thriving centre in Warsaw also served Russian tastes for the next hundred years. An immigrant jeweller of Huguenot origin, Gustav Fabergé, settled and set up shop in St Petersburg in 1842. His son, Peter Carl Fabergé (1846–1920), took over the family firm in 1870, transforming it into a multi-branched business with an imperial appointment at home and extensive patronage and acclaim abroad.

**SOUP TUREEN**
*Peffenhauser* (?), Augsburg
Silver; **c. 1730**

All-over flat chasing decorates this fine example of the use of a Meissen porcelain tureen shape. The applied cast plaques of Spring and Autumn are in the French *Régence* style.

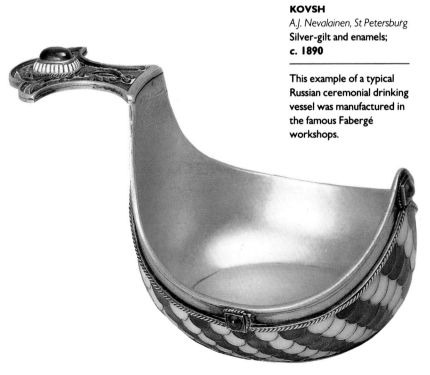

**KOVSH**
*A.J. Nevalainen, St Petersburg*
Silver-gilt and enamels;
**c. 1890**

This example of a typical Russian ceremonial drinking vessel was manufactured in the famous Fabergé workshops.

ALTHOUGH WORKING WITHIN THE EUROPEAN TRADITIONS AND
FASHIONS OF THEIR CRAFT, AMERICAN SILVERSMITHS DEVELOPED THEIR
OWN INDIVIDUALISTIC APPROACH.

# AMERICAN SILVER

In the 17th century, the working of silver was controlled by the Goldsmith's Company in London, and master craftsmen for both precious metals were termed "goldsmiths". Many of the wealthier settlers brought family silver with them, so much of the goldsmith's early custom centred on melting down unfashionable pieces to create new ones, or simply rendering them into local currency, since controls on minting were notoriously lax. The few pre-17th-century pieces that have been authenticated or attributed to American craftsmen include beakers, caudle cups and porringers, and tankards.

## EARLY DAYS

The first goldsmith to have established a clientele was John Mansfield of Charlestown, Massachusetts, known to be in business in 1634. The craftsmen whose dated and archived pieces claim to be among the first in the tradition of American silversmithing were John Hull (1624–83) and Robert Sanderson (1608–93). Hull trained and gained his articles in Massachusetts; he was Master of the Massachusetts Mint by the age of 28, and co-owner of his own business with the London-trained Sanderson soon after. Only one piece of Hull-marked silver survives, but some 40 bearing the double mark of Hull and Sanderson, and a few only Sanderson's (after Hull's death), are extant. The importance of Hull and Sanderson to American silver rests not only in their own product, but also in the fact that they trained many of the next generation's talented craftsmen, including Jeremiah Dummer (1645–1718), America's first native-born goldsmith; Timothy Dwight (1654-91), of whose work only two elegant pieces remain; and John Coney (1655–1722), acknowledged as the finest early silversmith.

## MARKS ON AMERICAN SILVER

Unlike English silver, American silver was never subjected to a universal rating system. The only city to establish an assay office was Baltimore, from 1814 to 1830, where the mark for high-percentage silver was the town mark – a liberty head – and a date letter. Otherwise, it was left to makers to devise their own assurances of quality and identifying marks. The former could take the form of "pseudo marks": a cartouche in the shape of a star, eagle's head, or other approximation of the British lion.

In the mid 1800s the maker's first initial and last name began to appear, as did a stamp indicating quality – such as "standard", "C" or "coin" (hand-hammered), "quality" or "premium" – on the back of spoons or along the rim or foot of tableware. After 1868 this quality stamp became standardized to "sterling", denoting 925/1000 parts silver.

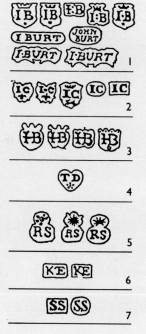

1 John Burt (1691-1745)
2 John Coney (1655-1722)
3 H. Boelen (1684-1755)
4 T. Dwight (1645-1691)
5 R. Sanderson (1608-93)
6 K. Ten Eyck (1678-1753)
7 S. Soumain (1685-1750)
8 Paul Revere (1735-1818)
9 Samuel Kirk and
   John Smith (1815)
10 Wm. Gale (1824-1850)
   with "pseudo marks"
11 Tiffany & Co (1875-91)
12 Tiffany & Co
   (1891-1902)
13 Baltimore Assay mark
   (1815)
14 Sterling quality and date
   mark used by Dominick
   & Haff (1872-1928)

# PRINCIPAL EARLY AMERICAN SILVER-MAKERS

| | | | |
|---|---|---|---|
| **MANSFIELD, John** | 1601–74 | Boston | First recorded American silversmith, c.1634 in Boston. |
| **SANDERSON, Robert** | 1608–93 | Boston | Settled in Boston in 1640. Partnership with John Hull, 1652. Tankards, beakers and ecclesiastical silver. |
| **HULL, John** | 1624–83 | Boston | Settled in Boston 1635. Mint Master, 1652. |
| **LE ROUX, Bartholomew** | 1663–1713 | New York | Huguenot who settled in New York. His son, Charles (1689–1745), grandson, Bartholomew II (1717–63) carried on the business. |
| **DUMMER, Jeremiah** | 1645–1718 | Boston | Tankards, porringers and candlesticks. |
| **DWIGHT, Timothy** | 1654–91 | Boston | Known for chinoiserie. |
| **VAN DER BURGH, Cornelius** | 1653–99 | New York | First native New York master. |
| **KIP, Jesse** | 1660–1722 | New York | Active in New York 1682–1710, making tankards and bowls particularly. |
| **CONEY, John** | 1655–1722 | Boston | One of the greatest colonial makers, known for engraving. |
| **EDWARDS, John** | 1670–1746 | New England | London-trained maker who worked in New England, followed by sons Thomas and Samuel. |
| **WINSLOW, Edward** | 1669–1750 | Boston | Outstanding Boston maker notable for ornate rococo pieces. |
| **KIERSTEDE, Cornelius** | 1675–1757 | New York and New Haven, Conn. | Maker of Dutch-influenced tankards, punch bowls. |
| **SYNGE, family** | | Philadelphia | Philip (1676–1739) settled from Dublin. Son Philip (1703–89) became renowned smith. |
| **RICHARDSON, Francis** | 1681–1729 | Philadelphia | First American-born silversmith to work in the city. His son Joseph (1711–84) and grandsons Joseph II (1752–1831) and Nathaniel (1754–1827) also worked there. |
| **BOELEN, Henderick** | 1684–1755 | New York | Tankards. |
| **VAN DYCK, Pieter** | 1684–1750 | | Queen Anne-style silversmith in heavy Dutch manner. |
| **SOUMAIN, Simeon** | 1685–1750 | New York | London-trained and Dutch-influenced. |
| **GHISELIN, Cesar** | d. 1733 | Philadelphia and Indianapolis | French silversmith. |

Unlike the restrained, elegant handiwork of London-influenced Massachusetts, the silver of New York reflected its Dutch roots, lightened by the French tradition of its refugee Huguenot craftsmen. New York porringers possess fancifully pierced handles, while those of Boston show less openwork; New York tankards are larger and heavier, ebulliently engraved and embossed, while those of Massachusetts demonstrate an unmistakable English reticence. Early New York makers included Jesse Kip (1660–1722), Ahasuerus Hendricks (fl. 1675–80), Gerrit Boelen (c.1654–1729), Keonraet Ten Eyck, Cornelius Kierstede

(1675–1757), Peter Van Dyck (1684–1750) and, most celebrated of all, the first native New York master, Cornelius Van der Burgh (1653–99). Less is known of the Huguenot masters, but two notable artisans were Bartholemew LeRoux (1663–1713) and Simeon Soumaine (1685–1750).

In the late 17th century, silver workers became established in Pennsylvania, producing tankards and spoons that reflected the influence of New York and Massachusetts, respectively. Its founding lights did not stay long, however; Cesar Ghiselin, Philadelphia's first goldsmith, re-established himself in Annapolis to become

Maryland's first silversmith, while Johannis Nys opened Delaware's first shop.

### FROM QUEEN ANNE TO ROCOCO

The popular tankard was a partial index of the changes occurring in design. In Boston, the clean, pure lines and chased decoration of 1690 to 1720 began to give way to the pear-shape, domed lid and finials of the Queen Anne style. In New York, however, the flat lid was retained and set with a coin, while the traditional scroll handle might be made even more elaborate with the addition of embossing and a corkscrew thumbpiece. But the triumphal progression of "the line of beauty" was more determined than this dichotomy would imply, and generally New York and Boston silver between 1720 and 1745 began to demonstrate more similarities than ever before.

The new style was particularly suited to two new pieces that emerged during this period. Following their introduction in England, tea- and coffeepots appeared in the colonies in the first quarter of the 18th century. The rounded shape aided the infusion and brewing of the beverages, at the same time reflecting their luxury status. The "line of beauty" erupted into a full-blown "C" with the characteristic "apple" or "bullet" shape of Boston and Philadelphia pots, while the elongated "pear" of New York was more reticent. But the distinctions were often blurred, with makers from both traditions assaying the other form. The pear shape established the greater staying power, transmuting into the Rococo "Chippendale" style – with "double-bellied" body, low-moulded pedestal foot, finial-topped lid and ebonized "C"-scroll handle – popular from 1750 to 1790.

### REFLECTIONS OF AFFLUENCE

The Rococo vogue may have found a perfect medium for expression in tea- and coffeepots, but its confident curves and stylized acanthus leaves, reeding and pineapple finials enlivened other pieces that complemented the lifestyle of the merchant class, who first became aggravated with the restrictions of British rule and taxation and whose household ornaments and tableware reflected their burgeoning affluence and political independence. The lavishness inherent in Rococo decoration was present in centrepieces, monteiths (a large silver bowl) and tureens executed by Myer Myers (1723–95) and Daniel Christian Fueter (*fl.* 1754–76) of New York; Daniel Henchman (1730–75), Paul Revere, Jr (1734–1818) and Benjamin Burt (1729–1805) of Boston; and Philip Synge, Jr (1703–89), Philip Hulbeart (*fl.* 1750–64), Joseph Richardson (1711–84) and Richard Humphreys (*fl.* 1771–96) of Philadelphia. Pierced scrolls, shell and other motifs derived from nature were grafted on to

## PRINCIPAL LATER AMERICAN SILVER-MAKERS

| | | | |
|---|---|---|---|
| **HURD, Jacob** | 1702–58 | Boston | Smith of high reputation. Son Nathaniel (1729–77) carried on business. |
| **REVERE, Paul Sr and Jr** | 1702–54 1734–1818 | Boston | Revere Sr was Huguenot maker who settled in Boston and changed name in 1722. His son, probably the best-known American silversmith. |
| **BANCKER, Adrian** | 1703–72 | New York | Cutlery and tankards. |
| **MYERS, Myer** | 1723–95 | New York | Equally famous for his classical and rococo work. |
| **HENCHMAN, Daniel** | 1730–75 | Boston | Elegantly classical coffee pots and table pieces. |
| **FORBES, William** | 1751–1840 | New York | Smith of Neo-Classical pieces. |
| **HULBEART, Philip** | *fl.* 1750–64 | Philadelphia | Maker in Rococo style. |
| **FUETER, Daniel Christian** | *fl.* 1754–76 | New York | Influential in the shift to English Rococo from Dutch style. |
| **HUMPHREYS, Richard** | *fl.* 1771–96 | Philadelphia | Responsible for famous pieces for Continental Congress and George Washington. |
| **BAYLEY, Simon** | *fl.* 1789–96 | New York | Neo-Classical smith. |
| **SCHANK, Gerrit** | *fl.* 1791–93 | New York | Neo-Classical silversmith. |
| **HIMMEL, Adolphe** | *fl.* 1851–65 | New Orleans | Elaborate centrepieces and tableware. |
| **KUCHLER, Christopher** | *fl.* 1852–9 | New Orleans | Pieces in Victorian baroque. |

**TEAPOT**
*Jacob Hurd*
Silver and wood; **dated 1758**

Jacob Hurd (1702–58) was the founder of a prominent silvermaking family in colonial America. The globular teapot has the characteristic "apple" or "bullet" shape beloved of mid-18th-century Boston. The "C"-curve handle originally would have been ebonized.

# PAUL REVERE, JR (1734–1818)

The greatest American silver maker was Paul Revere, Jr, better known to the average American as a patriot, the hero-subject of Longfellow's "Midnight Ride", who carried the message of British aggression from Massachusetts' Mystic River to Concord, igniting the initial conflict of the American Revolution. His contribution to the nation's decorative arts, while hardly as dramatic, is also of inestimable value.

The son of Apollos Rivoire – a French Huguenot silversmith who immigrated to Boston in 1715, was apprenticed to the great John Coney and anglicized his name to Paul Revere – Paul was apprenticed to his father and at first undertook much subcontracted work for other well-respected Boston silversmiths, including Samuel Minott (1732–1803), John Coburn (1725–1803) and Nathaniel Hurd (1729–77), son of Jacob Hurd, a respected contemporary of Coney. Like many of his contemporaries Revere practised dentistry, and put his talent as an engraver and caricaturist to use in the patriot cause. But by 1759 he was making plate for the Old South Church, Boston, and in 1768 he crafted the most celebrated piece of

American silver, the "Sons of Liberty Bowl", now in the Museum of Fine Arts, Boston.

After Independence, Revere resumed his place at the forefront of American silver, producing elegant and refined canns (mugs), bowls, sauceboats, pitchers and teapots in the Neo-Classical style.

**PORRINGER, Paul Revere, Jr., 1760–90.**

**CANN**
Engraved silver; **1750**

The typical American lidless mug, known as a "cann", was a fashionable drinking vessel of mid-18th-century New England, largely replacing the tankard which, by 1780, had all but disappeared from the craftsman's repertoire. These Boston canns are engraved with contemporary initials "BSC" and, below, the name "Collins".

the sinuous curves of Queen Anne silver. With a growing population came new silver centres, including Salem, Massachusetts; Lancaster, Pennsylvania; Newport, Rhode Island, and Baltimore and Annapolis, Maryland.

### FEDERAL AND EMPIRE SILVER

With the resumption of normal trade after the War of Independence, the preoccupation with Rococo gave way in the 1790s to a preference for the Neo-Classical motifs embodied in the Federal style. Its main decorative embellishments were reeding, fluting and gadrooning, and it found happy expression in the tea- and coffee services that first came into fashion in the 1790s. In Boston it partnered bright-cut, straight-sided or fluted oval teapots with helmet-shaped sugars and creamers; in Philadelphia pierced galleries (a band of open-work decoration around the opening) and beading supplanted the engraving. The succession of the opulent Empire style in the 1820s and 1830s saw spouts grow more curving, the pot's body become rounder, and moulding and chasing – of both flowers and animals – more extravagant.

The capital of silvermaking shifted to New York during the Federal period. Among the notable New York silver craftsmen were partners Daniel van Voorhis and Gerrit Schank (*fl.* 1791–93), Simon Bayley (*fl.* 1789–96) and William Forbes (1751–1840). Philadelphia boasted Joseph Richardson, Jr (1752–1831),

and John and James Black; while Boston could rely on the equally long-lived Revere and Benjamin Hurd (1739–81).

### MID- TO LATE-VICTORIAN STYLING

The highly chased silver of the Empire period melted quite comfortably into the florid exuberance of High Victorian style. New Orleans became a centre of Southern silvermaking, with the establishment of the firm of Hyde & Goodrich in 1829. Making some silverware of their own, they acted primarily as agents for German-born Adolphe Himmel (*fl.* 1851–65) and Christopher Kuchler (*fl.* 1852–9), as well as for other silversmiths. The work of the New Orleans school was both airy and ornate, delighting in beading, latticework and gadrooning.

Gothic and Italianate influences held sway in the silver centres from the late 1850s to the early 1870s, becoming most extravagant in the heavy, cathedral-like edifice of the castor set or the tilting pitcher/wine stands. Silverplate examples by Reed & Barton of Taunton, Massachusetts, were commended by the Philadelphia Centennial Exhibition of 1876 for being as attractive as their solid sterling equivalents. Other contemporary companies producing popular ornamental tableware included Ball, Black & Company (Ball, Tompkins & Black until 1851) and Wood & Hughes, both of New York; and Shreve Brothers of San Francisco. As well,

### EMPIRE SAUCEBOATS
*Anthony Rasch*
Silver; 1808–19

The Empire fascination with Roman animalistic ornament is amply demonstrated by this pair of ferocious yet elegant sauceboats. The snake handles, ram's-head spouts and griffin feet are both realistically and finely delineated, while the pedestal foot and elongated lines of the bowls lighten what, in less capable hands, could have been an overpowering exercise in the silversmith's art.

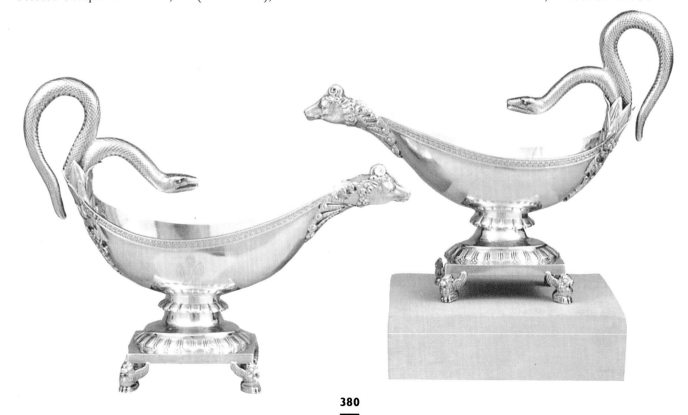

America's two greatest silver companies came into their own.

### THE ORIGINS OF ART SILVER

In 1831, Gorham & Company was founded by Jabez Gorham in Providence, Rhode Island. Initial growth was careful and slow, but with the takeover of John Gorham in 1847, a major expansion programme was put into effect. It was an auspicious moment, since it coincided with the discovery of gold and silver in the West and an unprecedented economic boom.

By 1861 Gorham had opened an additional office in New York, and gained national prominence by designing several pieces bought for Mary Todd Lincoln at the White House. By 1878, two more outlets were acquired, in San Francisco and Chicago. Its rise was matched by that of New York's Tiffany & Company. Founded in 1834, Tiffany began its silver manufacture in earnest in the late 1860s.

In the 1870s, Tiffany and Gorham began to break free from European influence, looking to the East for inspiration. Tiffany's change of heart was directed by their new president and chief designer, Edward C. Moore, a keen orientalist and collector. The Centennial Exhibition helped his case, since its display of Japanese decorative arts received widespread attention and launched a Japanese craze lasting through the 1890s.

The appeal of mixed metalwork, after the fashion of Japanese metalware, tempted both Tiffany and Gorham to experiment with several creative combinations, including silver set with gold, copper and brass appliqué and copper with silver chasing. Tiffany was awarded a gold medal at the Paris Exhibition of 1878, and from that point its designs went from sheer opulence to occasional unredeemed vulgarity. The shift from oriental-style designs to the fluidity of Art Nouveau was gradual but inexorable. The style's trademark undulating lines embraced caskets, bowls and vases. Languorous silver caryatids supported clocks, lamps and iridescent glass bowls; whole cutlery sets carried naturalistic motifs.

In addition to Tiffany and Gorham, other companies producing oriental/Art Nouveau silverwork were Black, Starr & Frost (reorganized from Ball, Black & Company in 1876), the Whiting Manufacturing Company, and Dominick & Haff. The Art Nouveau style was at its peak from the mid-1890s to the second decade of the 20th century.

**VASE AND HUNTING KNIFE**
*Gorham & Company*
Silver; **late 19th century**

Both these extravagant articles – the embossed vase and the knife and scabbard of Ottoman design – bear trademark Gorham birds, the peacock and crane.

**COFFEEPOT, CREAMER AND SUGAR BOWL**
*Tiffany and Company*
Copper ground with applied silver decoration and mounts; **late 19th century**

Bamboo and bullrushes were favourite floral motifs of both Tiffany's and Gorham's Japanese-inspired tableware of the 1880s and 1890s.

THE SINUOUS SHAPES AND STRIKING USE OF ENAMELS AND
SEMI-PRECIOUS STONES GIVE A DISTINCTIVE CHARACTER TO THE
JEWELRY AND METALWORK OF THE LATE 19TH AND EARLY
20TH CENTURIES.

# ARTS AND CRAFTS TO ART NOUVEAU

The mid 19th century witnessed the beginning of an age of individuality and innovation in terms of jewellery and precious metalwork. Many designers and craftsmen, seeking new sources of inspiration, looked back to earlier times and outward to exotic cultures. Adapting past or foreign styles to machine-age methods of production and to novel materials, they created exciting new *objets d'art*.

### BRITAIN

From the 1860s to the early 1900s the Arts and Crafts Movement, whose principal exponents were John Ruskin (1819–1900) and William Morris (1834–96), inspired craftsmen to produce silver (and sometimes gold) jewellery and beautiful objects often enhanced with coloured enamel and semi-precious stones. True Arts and Crafts pieces were hand-crafted, but the term Arts and Crafts is often applied to any period piece exhibiting a motif or material related to the style, such as Celtic-style interlacing and coloured enamels.

Many of the finest precious-metal pieces were made under the auspices of crafts guilds. Best known was the Guild of Handicraft, which Charles Robert Ashbee (1863–1942) set up in London in 1888. Ashbee's designs were in part inspired by the Celtic Revival and continental Art Nouveau, but he also used motifs of his own device. His silver and gilt-metal objects included covered cups, salvers and ceremonial spoons. His jewellery – decorated with peacocks, blossoms, even galleons – comprised necklaces, cloak clasps, brooches and buttons enhanced with blue and green enamel or semi-precious stones.

Connected at one time or another to the Bromsgrove Guild of Applied Art (founded *c*1890) were Joseph Hodel, whose silver buckles, brooches and pendants were in foliate and fruit form and dotted with semi-precious stones, and Arthur Gaskin (1862–1928), whose jewellery contained cabochon (domed,

**BOWL ON STAND**
*C. R. Ashbee, Guild of Handicraft*
**Silver and chrysoprase; late 19th century**

This elegant bowl, awash with organic motifs, has an openwork stem resting on a base with ball feet. Besides precious-metal objects and jewels, the Guild created furniture and printed matter.

unfaceted) stones, rope borders, silver or gold filigree wires and clusters of silver beads and tendrils. From 1899 Gaskin worked with his wife, Georgina Cave France (1868–1934).

The sophisticated designs of Henry Wilson (1864–1934) and John Paul Cooper (1869–1933) showed a knowledge of Byzantine and medieval goldsmithing. Alexander Fisher (1864–1936) was renowned for his handcrafted enamel work, often comprising layers of enamel on a foil ground. Among those he influenced were Phoebe Traquair (1852–1936), his daughter Kate Fisher, the

Gaskins and Nelson (1859–1942) and Edith Dawson (active 1900–14). After their marriage the Dawsons set up a workshop, out of which came lovely objects in *champlevé* (enamelling on copper or bronze), *cloisonné* (enamelling on metal, in compartments separated by metal wire) and other types of enamelling. Another noted couple were Harold (1872–1945) and Phoebe Stabler (d 1955), who designed enamels and jewellery.

**Liberty** A great deal of British silver and jewellery was marketed by Arthur Lasenby Liberty (1843–1917), whose London emporium offered a wide range of metalwork, both precious and nonprecious. Liberty took advantage of the Celtic Revival sweeping Britain, giving its silver and pewter lines the fashionably Celtic names of, respectively, "Cymric" and "Tudric". Liberty's designers at the time were anonymous, but they included some of Britain's foremost talents, among them Bernard Cuzner (1877–1956), Arthur Gaskin and Rex Silver (1879–1965). Most closely identified with Liberty silver was Archibald Knox (1864–1933), who created some 400 designs and whose speciality was Celtic ornament. Another notable Liberty designer was Scottish-born Jessie M. King (1875–1949), whose designs – for example, buckles enamelled with stylized roses and birds – owed much to the Glasgow School.

**Scottish Art Nouveau** This movement – whose foremost exponents were the Glasgow Four, Charles Rennie Mackintosh (1868–1928), his wife, Margaret Macdonald (1864–1933), her sister Frances (1873–1921) and Frances' husband, James Herbert MacNair (1868–1955) – bore some resemblance to Arts and Crafts, but its repertory of motifs was very much its own and more in the spirit of Secession Vienna (Austrian Art Nouveau). Among the silver and jewellery designs of the Glasgow Four were stylized birds, leaves, blossoms and hearts and Mackintosh's handsome elongated silver cutlery.

FRANCE

The jewellery of René Lalique (1860–1945) was among the most original, finely crafted Art Nouveau creations. Lalique abhorred the ornate, historicizing, diamond-dominated jewellery in fashion in France. Instead he sought to create jewels that were fresh and vibrant. From 1895 until the 1910s – when he turned to glass design – Lalique produced rings, brooches,

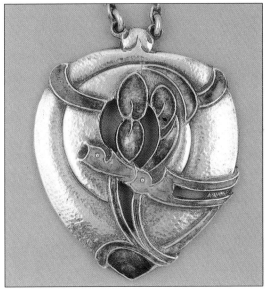

**NECKLACE**
*Archibald Knox, for Liberty & Co.*
**Gold and opal; early 20th century**

Knox, an exponent of the Celtic Revival, began working for Liberty in 1899. This elegant necklace, comprising elements of interlaced gold set with opal "mosaics", is characteristic of the designer, who was much influenced by the *entrelac*-dominated Celtic art of his native Isle of Man. (*Above*)

**PENDANT**
*Jessie M. King, for Liberty & Co.*
**Enamelled silver; c. 1902**

In addition to creating Liberty jewels, whose designs were largely influenced by Charles Rennie Mackintosh and the Glasgow School, Scottish-born King was a noted book illustrator. (*Above*)

**TEAPOT**
*Christopher Dresser*
**Silver and wood; 1881**

Although few in number, metal objects by the versatile Dr Dresser (1834–1904) were noted for both their simplicity and their proto-modernity. This teapot features a jaunty side handle that is both aesthetically pleasing and practical. (*Right*)

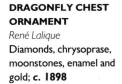

**DRAGONFLY CHEST ORNAMENT**
*René Lalique*
Diamonds, chrysoprase, moonstones, enamel and gold; **c. 1898**

*Plique-à-jour* enamel wings feature on this part-human/part-insect, 27 cm (11 in) long jewel created by Lalique.

buckles, tiaras, watch cases and other jewels in not only precious stones but, more commonly, horn, ivory, pearl, jade, turquoise and even aluminium and steel. His subjects ranged from naturalistic flowers to fantastic hybrid insect-women.

Other notable French Art Nouveau jewellery designers include Georges Fouquet (1862–1957), who sometimes worked with the Moravian-born artist, Alphonse Mucha (1860–1939); the brothers Paul (1851–1915) and Henri Vever (1854–1942), who ran Maison Vever; Lucien Gaillard who favoured unusual materials, notably horn and ivory; Eugène Feuillâtre (1870–1916), celebrated for his delicate *plique-à-jour* enamels (transparent plaques sometimes known as stained glass enamel); and the German-born Edward Colonna (1862–1948), whose curvilinear, usually asymmetrical creations in silver and gold were decorated with stone or enamel.

### BELGIUM

Two names stand out in precious-metal design in Belgium: Henry Van de Velde (1863–1957) and Philippe Wolfers (1858–1929). The first, who was influenced by British Arts and Crafts design, created simple curvilinear or recti-linear jewellery, usually of silver and semi-precious stones. Wolfers, whose family firm was jeweller to the Belgian Crown, made pieces akin to those of Lalique. He favoured themes from nature, primarily flowers and insects, but also depicted female heads and nudes. As well as metal, he often used ivory.

### SCANDINAVIA

The leading Scandinavian silversmith for several decades was the Dane, Georg Jensen (1866–1953), who opened his Copenhagen atelier in 1904. His early pendants, brooches, combs, buckles and bracelets, embellished with semi-precious stones, were in an elegant, curvilinear mode that approached the stylization of Art Deco. Later he created large silver pieces, such as coffee pots and candelabra; the vessels were mainly fluted and decorated with his trademark clusters of silver beads.

Other Danish silversmiths included Morgens Ballin (1871–1914), whose simple, organic style influenced Jensen; Harald Slott-Möller, whose ornate pieces had subjects as diverse as long-haired nudes and sailing ships; and Thorvald Bindesböll (1846–1908), who produced curved and scrolled jewellery.

In Norway the firm of David Andersen, founded in 1876, produced handsome silver lamps, tea services, vases and other objects. Much of the firm's delicate *plique-à-jour* en-amel was created by Gustav Gaudernack (1865–1914). The Viking-inspired "dragon style" dominated Andersen's early work; softer Art Nouveau lines appeared *c*1900.

### AUSTRIA

Precious-metal design in early-20th-century Austria was dominated by the Wiener Werkstätte (Vienna Workshops), a co-operative of painters, architects and designers set up in Vienna in 1903 by Josef Hoffmann (1870–1956) and Koloman Moser

(1868–1918). These two – along with Carl Otto Czeschka (1878–1960), Joseph Maria Olbrich (1867–1908), Dagobert Peche (1887–1923), Otto Prutscher (1880–1949) and others – designed jewellery and precious- and base-metal objects, sometimes subtly curvilinear, sometimes boldly rectilinear. A typical design, made in silver and white-painted sheet metal, comprised a grid of squares in endless geometric configurations.

Less austere were the hammered, matt and gleaming silver vessels, usually by Hoffmann, on which touches of ivory or semi-precious stone often appeared: they could be gently curving, fluted all over or robustly geometric. The rococo exuberance of Peche revealed itself on several silver pieces; Czeschka's jewels and objects were marked by their stylized leaf, blossom, scroll and bead motifs; Moser's designs tended towards strict geometry.

## GERMANY

*Jugendstil* (German Art Nouveau) held sway over late-19th- and early-20th-century German precious-metal and jewellery design. In Munich Peter Behrens (1868–1940), Bernhard Pankok (1872–1943), Richard Riemerschmid (1868–1957) and Fritz Schmoll von Eisenwerth (1888–1963) helped set up in 1897 workshops where they and others designed metalwork in curvilinear mode that could be light, delicate and Gallic-looking, or bold, square and more Austrian in appearance. Two years later Peter Behrens also helped to establish an art colony in Darmstadt, whose

members – including Patriz Huber (1878–1902), Joseph Maria Olbrich and Ernst Riegel (1871–1939) – showed an aesthetic affinity to the Vienna and Glasgow movements. Theodor Fahrner (1868–1928), a prolific jewellery-maker with a factory in Pforzheim, used many Darmstadt artists' designs.

### OTHER EUROPEAN COUNTRIES

In France, around 1907–10, Italian-born Carlo Bugatti (1856–1950) created outstanding silver objects, made by the Parisian Adrien A. Hébrard. They combined various subjects, materials and techniques in an unusual manner. For example, one tea and coffee service comprised a long tray with a bizarre animal head at each end, both terminating in long ivory tusks, and a coffee pot, teapot, cream jug and sugar bowl in the shape of boar-like animal heads, also with ivory tusks.

Working mainly from St Petersburg, master-jeweller Peter Carl Fabergé (1846–1920) included Art Nouveau pieces in his glittering work, including gold cigarette-cases with flower and leaf mounts and silver mounts for glass made by New York jeweller Tiffany and German glassmaker Loetz.

### UNITED STATES

American jewellery and precious-metalwork were influenced by the British Arts and Crafts Movement, Continental Art Nouveau, Japanese design, native American art and other styles.

At the luxury end of the market two firms were dominant. Tiffany & Company, the New York jeweller, silver manufacturer and retailer, was established in 1837. It produced outstanding silver in Japanese, Indian and Moorish styles and, from the 1880s, in Art Nouveau style. From 1902, under Louis Comfort Tiffany (1848–1933), the premier exponent of American Art Nouveau, the company created, in addition to its conventional lines, specialized "art jewellery", most of which combined gold and enamel with stones, sometimes in Byzantine or medieval style.

Gorham Manufacturing Company founded in 1831, in Providence, Rhode Island, was Tiffany's chief rival in silverware, and also produced electroplated silver. Its fine-quality silver included, in the 1880s, Japanese-style wares and, later, hand-crafted pieces in the Gallic Art Nouveau and Arts and Crafts styles. All were marketed as "Martelé" (hammered) silver.

Other American firms producing Art

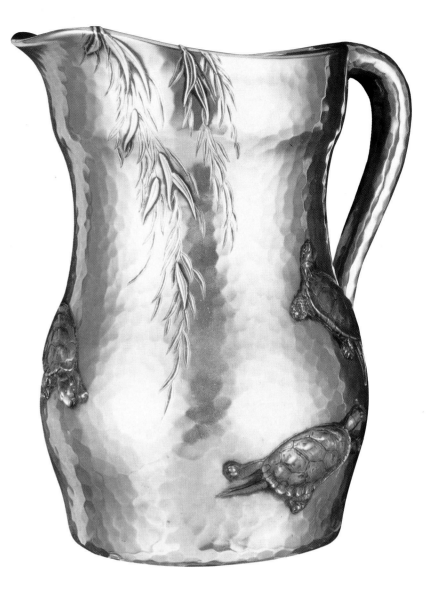

**JUG AND BOWL**
*Tiffany & Company*
Silver, silver-gilt and copper; **late 19th century**

The applied turtles on these two hammered pieces are typical of Tiffany's Japanese-style wares, which featured natural motifs and a combination of metals. Such pieces were part of the "Japanese craze" that swept through the United States in the latter third of the 19th century, following the opening up of Japan to the West by Commodore Matthew C. Perry in 1853.

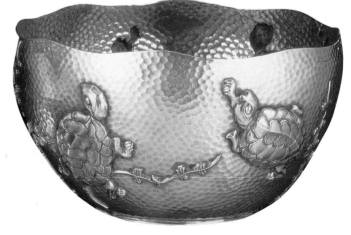

Nouveau silver included Unger Brothers, Newark; Bailey, Banks & Biddle, Philadelphia; William B. Kerr & Co., Newark; Lebolt & Co., Chicago; Shreve & Co., San Francisco; and Reed & Barton, Taunton, Massachusetts.

Many individuals hand-crafted silver and jewellery from *c*1890 to 1915, one of the most notable being the Bostonian Elizabeth E. Copeland, who produced enamelled silver in simple, even primitive forms.

**Chicago** In Chicago several associations devoted to English Arts and Crafts ideals were formed at the turn of the century. Working in the city from *c.* 1893 to 1917, Robert Riddle Jarvie (1865–1940) exhibited silver and copper bowls, candlesticks, trophies and other items, in Native American, rectilinear and other designs. Other Chicago silversmiths included Frances Macbeth Glessner (1848–1932), and Clara Barck Welles (1868–1965), who in 1900 started up the Kalo Shops, in Park Ridge, Illinois. These produced hammered silver vessels often decorated with ornate monograms.

Working on the West Coast was Clemens Friedell (1872–1963), whose hand-wrought silver included both naturalistic depictions of flowers and classic repoussé (hammered from within) work.

# FURTHER READING

The following list of materials for further reading offers a broad range of literature. Both specialist and general works are included. While every effort has been made to give the date of the most recent edition, new ones may have been published since this book went to press.

Avery, C.L.
**Early American Silver**
New York 1920

Barsali, Isa Belli (translated by Margaret Crosland)
**Medieval Goldsmiths' Work**
London 1969

Becker, Vivienne
**Art Nouveau Jewelry**
London 1985

— **Antique and Twentieth Century Jewellery**
Colchester 1987

— **Fabulous Fakes, The History of Fantasy and Fashion Jewellery**
London 1988

Blair, Claude
**The History of Silver**
London 1987

Bradbury, Frederick
**History of Old Sheffield Plate**
1983

Brunner, Herbert
**Altes Tafelsilber**
Munich 1964

Carpenter, Charles H., Jr.
**Gorham Silver, 1831–1981**
1982

Clayton, Michael
**Christies Pictorial History of English and American Silver**
London 1985

Culme, John
**The Directory of Gold and Silversmiths, Jewellers and Allied Trades 1838–1914**
London 1988

— **Nineteenth Century Silver**
London 1977

Curran, Mona
**A Treasury of Jewels and Gems**
New York 1962

Dubin, Lois
**The History of Beads**
London 1987

Glanville, Philippa
**Silver in England**
London 1987

Grimwade, Arthur G.
**London Goldsmiths 1797–1837, Their Marks and Their Lives**
London 1982

Helliwell, Stephen
**Collecting Small Silverware**
London 1988

Hernmarck, Carl
**The Art of the European Silversmith** (2 vols)
London 1977

Hinks, Peter
**Jewellery**
London 1969

Honour, Hugh
**Goldsmiths and Silversmiths**
London 1971

Jackson, Sir C.J.
**English Goldsmiths and their Marks**
Dover 1964

— **An Illustrated History of English Plate**
London 1969

Jones, Kenneth Crisp (ed.)
**The Silversmiths of Birmingham and their Marks, 1750–1980**
1981

McClinton, Katharine Morrison
**Collecting American 19th Century Silver**
1968

Mourey, Gabriel, Aymer Vallance, et al.
**Art Nouveau Jewellery and Fans** (reprint)
New York 1973

Mulvagh, Jane
**Costume Jewellery in Vogue**
London 1988

Newman, Harold and Joan Robertson
**An Illustrated Dictionary of Silverware**
London 1987

Oman, Charles
**English Domestic Silver**
London 1967

Pickford, Ian (ed)
**Jackson's Silver and Gold Marks** (3rd Edition, revised)
Woodridge 1989

— **Silver flatware**
Woodridge 1983

Rainwater, Dorothy
**Encyclopedia of American Silver Manufacturers**
West Chester, Pennsylvania, 1986

— and H. Ivan
**American Silverplate**
1988

Rogers, Francis, and Alice Beard
**5000 Years of Gems and Jewelry**
New York 1947

Scarisbrick, Diana, Jack Ogden, Ronald Lightblown, Peter Hinks, Patricia Bayer, Vivienne Becker and Helen Craven
**Jewellery Makers, Motifs, History, Techniques**
London 1989

Schroder, Timothy
**The National Trust Book of Silver**
1988

Schwartz, Marvin D.
**Collector's Guide to American Silver**
1975

Taylor, Gerald
**Silver, An Illustrated Introduction**
London 1956

— **Continental Gold and Silver**
London 1967

Ward, Anne, John Cherry, Charlotte Gere and Barbara Cartlidge
**The Ring: From Antiquity to the Twentieth Century**
London 1981

Zucker, Benjamin
**Gems and Jewels, A Connoisseur's Guide**
London 1984

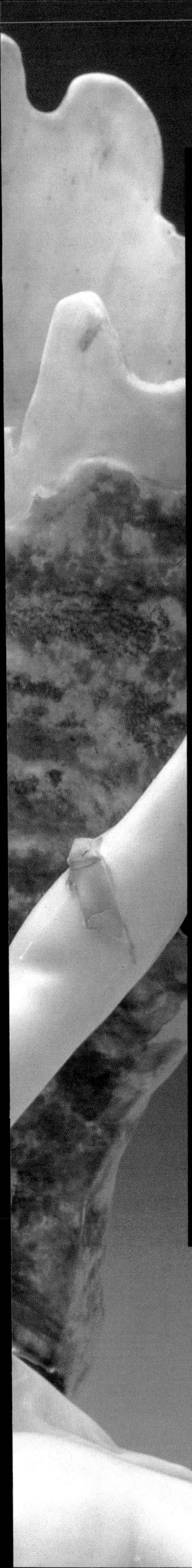

# CHAPTER 9

# CERAMICS

CERAMICS OF THE ANCIENT WORLD •
CHINESE CERAMICS • JAPANESE CERAMICS •
CERAMICS OF THE ISLAMIC WORLD •
EUROPEAN POTTERY • EUROPEAN PORCELAIN •
BRITISH CERAMICS TO 1820 •
EUROPEAN CERAMICS 1820–1920 •
AMERICAN CERAMICS • FAKES, FORGERIES, AND
REPRODUCTIONS

DAVID BATTIE
SEBASTIAN KUHN
GORDON LANG
LORI LANG
MARK NEWSTEAD
FELICITY NICHOLSON
LARS THARP
SUSAN WARD
PETER WILLIAMS

*This page:* **HÖCHST PORCELAIN AMYNTHAS AND SYLVIA GROUP, c. 1770 (detail).**

# CERAMICS

THE SURVIVING PRODUCTS OF POTTERS FROM THROUGHOUT HISTORY
HAVE AN IMMEDIACY THAT IS UNMATCHED BY MOST OTHER CATEGORIES
OF ANTIQUES. THE PIECES THAT HAVE SURVIVED IN GOOD CONDITION TO
OUR DAY SHOW ALMOST EXACTLY WHAT THE MAKER ACHIEVED WHEN IT
WAS JUST OUT OF THE KILN.

**SAMARRAWARE BOWL**
*Northern Mesopotamia*
**5000-4500 BC**

All primitive societies make earthenware of similar appearance and the black decoration is often based on the same geometric and natural symbols. Pottery skills first achieved results other than purely basic in Mesopotamia.

Ceramics were the first entirely man-made objects produced by primitive societies. Because the basic materials – unrefined clay and water – and the basic techniques remained unchanged for millennia, all ancient ceramics are similar in appearance.

Coiling was the simplest technique for building a pot: a sausage of clay was rolled by hand, then wound round a roughly circular base. The resultant pot varied in form according to whether it was intended to be used for carrying water, storing grain or cooking. When the pots had dried a brushwood fire was built over them to produce a low-fired terracotta; but their fragility resulted in high wastage. It is the survival of so many of these terracotta shards that has given us our understanding of most early civilizations.

A revolution in potting technique came with the introduction of the potter's wheel, probably in Egypt *c.* 1500 BC. Clay was placed at the centre of a disc, this was revolved by the potter's hand or foot, and the walls of the pot were drawn up by hand into the desired form. The wheel, which produced thinner pots than those obtained from coiling, demanded more refined clay and better control over firing, which resulted in permanent kilns.

Low-fired clays are not naturally watertight but can be made so by glazing (applying a layer of glassy material). Early glazes were made from a range of naturally occurring materials including the original clay mixed with lead, borax, tin or soda and glass or ground flints. To produce salt-glazed stoneware, salt was thrown into the kiln when the temperature was about 1000°C. The salt formed a thin glassy coating.

The major revolution in ceramics occurred in China during the 7th century AD with the discovery of kaolin (china clay). Mixed with petuntse (china stone) and fired at about 1300°C, it produces a hard, white, translucent body with a musical ring when struck: hard-paste, or true, porcelain.

**CHINESE COPPER-RED DISH**
*Late Yuan*

A fine dish with a barbed rim, the shape is based on a Middle-Eastern metal original and made for export to Persia or elsewhere in the Islamic world.

**GOMBROON BOWL**
*Persian*
**Early 18th century**

These thinly potted and finely pierced vessels in which the glassy glaze fills in the holes forming "windows" are very sophisticated.

Early pieces of porcelain were decorated with incising or moulding, but later the techniques of underglaze decoration in iron, copper or cobalt used on other ceramics were applied to porcelain. By the early 14th century underglaze copper-red and cobalt-blue, the only two colours able to withstand high-firing temperatures, were being made. In the 15th century overglaze enamels were developed. On hard-paste porcelain they stand proud of the glaze.

Occasional examples of Chinese porcelain appeared in Europe in the 13th century. Admiring these but not knowing how they were made, Europeans attempted to imitate genuine, hard-paste porcelain by producing an artificial, soft-paste material. The first experiments in this were undertaken in Italy under the Medici in the late 16th century, but the attempts were unsuccessful and Europe had to be content with Eastern imports until the French revived the art of making soft-paste porcelain in the late 17th century.

In Europe intense competition to discover true porcelain was finally won by the German Johann Böttger at Meissen, near Dresden, in 1708. Knowledge that kaolin was the secret ingredient spread rapidly throughout Europe. In England few factories made true porcelain; most produced artificial pastes containing various ingredients, such as soapstone, bone ash or glass.

Earthenwares were not supplanted by porcelain. They were generally cheaper to produce and, until Josiah Wedgwood brought them to new heights in the second half of the 18th century with his jasper ware (fine white decorated stoneware), basaltes (unglazed black stoneware) and refined creamware, they were mostly made for the lower classes. Potters often tried translating the porcelain figures of Chelsea and Meissen into pottery; the results often have considerable charm.

**RUBY LUSTRE DISH**
*William de Morgan*
**c. 1885**

William de Morgan's pottery harked back to both Islamic and Hispano-Moresque originals but were in no sense copies. Many of de Morgan's pieces, particularly dishes of the later periods, are bought-in blanks.

A WINDOW ON THE WORLD OF ANCIENT GREECE IS PROVIDED BY ITS CERAMIC ART. THE SCENES PAINTED ON THIS POTTERY DEFTLY DEPICT ALMOST ALL ASPECTS OF ANCIENT DAILY LIFE.

# CERAMICS OF THE ANCIENT WORLD

Pottery vessels were manufactured extensively throughout the ancient Greek, Hellenistic and Roman worlds. They have survived chiefly in tombs where they were buried with their owners. These vessels were primarily utilitarian, being used for household purposes, in funerary rites and as prizes filled with oil at athletic contests in Athens. They were fashioned by potters but in many cases, particularly from the Geometric period (*c.* 9th–8th century BC) onwards, were painted by a different hand. Some of the potters can be identified where there are signatures, and many of the

**KYLIX**
*Euphronios*
Red-figure ware; **c. 520 BC**

The mythological scene depicted is drawn from Homer's *Iliad*. Euphronios is one of the most famous of all Greek vase painters. He worked between 520-500 BC, shortly after the introduction of the red-figured technique. (*Above*)

**AMPHORA**
Geometric Ware; **8th century BC**

This large jar is decorated on the neck with a group of female mourners, and on the body with a "lying in state". This theme is often encountered in Geometric art. The amphora was a storage jar chiefly for wine or oil. (*Left*)

great Greek vase-painters of the 6th and 5th centuries BC, such as Exekias, the Amasis Painter, the Sosias Painter, Euphronios and the Berlin Painter, can also be identified by their individual styles.

Crete was the chief centre of manufacture during the Neolithic and Minoan periods (*c.* 6000–1050 BC). The pots made here and elsewhere in the Greek world at this time were of simple hand-made form and were rarely painted. Then, with the advent of the potter's wheel in Crete in about 2000 BC (it was known earlier elsewhere), they became more sophisticated. They began to be painted in polychrome and by the Late Minoan period (*c.* 1550–1050 BC) a large repertoire of designs based mainly on natural forms and marine life had developed. The end of the Minoan civilization coincided with the Mycenaean (*c.* 1450–*c.* 1150 BC) on mainland Greece, and the pottery of the two was closely related.

During the Geometric period in Greek art the human figure, only rarely seen on pottery vases before, began, together with animals and birds, to play a prominent role. Highly stylized and painted in brown or black silhouette, the subjects included funerary processions, the lying in state of the dead, battle scenes and processions of horsemen and chariots. The decorative motifs included the multiple zigzag, lozenge, diagonal, dots and horizontal and vertical bands.

Corinth became the most important trading centre of Greece in the 7th century BC and exported vast quantities of small, fine-quality vases, mostly unguent containers, all over the Greek world. Their decoration was much influenced by motifs found on objects imported from the Near East at this time: the vases are encircled by friezes of exotic birds and animals, sphinxes, sirens, padded dancers, warriors, riders and chariot races. These were painted in black or dark brown against the natural pale colour of the clay. Details were incised and the decoration enriched with added red and white paint.

It was, however, in Attica (the area around Athens), in the 6th and 5th centuries BC, that Greek vase-painting became one of the greatest arts of the ancient world. The technique used in the 6th century BC is known as "black-figure": the figures are silhouetted in black paint against a light background with incised and red-and-white-painted details. Late in the same century

**HYDRIA**
Black-figure ware; **c. 520-500 BC**

---

The scene depicts the departure of Herakles for Mount Olympus accompanied by Athena and other attendant figures. There is a combat scene on the shoulder, and animals and a siren below. (*Left*)

**ARYBALLOI AND PYXIDES**
*Corinthian*
**625-500 BC**

---

These six small vessels measure between 3⅛-4¾ in (80-120 mm). They are decorated with various motifs. There are four round-bodied *aryballoi* used for unguents or oils. The other two vessels are known as *pyxides* – small round cosmetic boxes. (*Above*)

the "red-figure" technique emerged: the figures were drawn in outline on a light ground, with the inner details marked with a brush instead of an incised tool, and the background was filled in with black paint. The most common subjects included scenes from daily life, the symposium or banquet scene, marriage, courtship, athletics, warriors in combat and stories from Greek mythology and religion.

In the 4th century BC, the Greek colonies of southern Italy produced great quantities of vases based on Attic prototypes. The Hellenistic and Roman periods saw the decline of the painted vase; the emphasis was placed more on relief decoration.

THE CHINESE BEGAN MAKING EARTHENWARE AROUND THE START OF THE
5TH MILLENNIUM BC. BUT THEIR MOST RENOWNED PRODUCTS ARE IN
THE REFINED AND VARIED PORCELAIN WARES.

# CHINESE CERAMICS

The Chinese have been making fine pottery since the Neolithic period (*c.* 5000–*c.* 2000 BC). Some of the earliest wares are coiled vessels fired in low-temperature kilns and decorated with a minimal repeated pattern of indentations. Other pieces are remarkably sophisticated; their carefully burnished sides are painted in black and purple and have lively geometric patterns or sharply defined profiles, achieved by turning on the wheel.

High-fired (heated to a very hot temperature) wares appeared during the Shang dynasty (*c.* 1525–*c.* 1027 BC), together with fine white-bodied pottery. Shang pottery is finely moulded, with complex bronze-type ornament. The final contribution of the Shang potter was glaze, to make wares watertight.

It is likely that early pottery fulfilled two roles, the utilitarian and the ritualistic. Wares of the latter type, superficially more impressive, are often more poorly made than the unassuming, useful pottery.

### LEAD-GLAZED WARES

During the Han dynasty (206 BC–AD 220) brilliant, thickly-applied lead glazes were introduced and transformed the appearance of pottery. The glazes were either yellow ochre (unadulterated lead) or green (lead and copper). Almost all extant lead-glazed wares are *mingqi* (tomb furniture); pottery dishes and jars made as substitutes for costly bronze ritual vessels; earthenware models of farms, farmyards, cattle pens, grain silos and domestic animals; and, of a more elaborate nature, gate-houses, watch-towers, Taoist mountains, and wild animals, such as the rhinoceros.

Following the Han dynasty the use of lead glaze declined and was not revived until the second half of the 6th century. During the Tang dynasty (618–906) polychrome and *sancai* (three-colour) lead glazes were employed to great effect. White, ochre, green and blue were splashed or sponged on to fine white-bodied

**JAR**
Stoneware; **Eastern Zhou**

Many of the forms and decoration on wares from China's early historical periods reflect those found on contemporary bronzes. Generous bulbous forms and the use of repeated impressed patterns are characteristic of this period.

earthenware funerary figures and other items, which attest to the skill of the northern Chinese potters of this period. Certain types of lead-glazed ware, slightly simpler than the tomb wares, appear to have been exported.

Excavations at kiln sites near Loyang and Anyang in northern China have revealed the presence of both *sancai* and fine white wares. The earliest polychrome glazed wares have been excavated from a tomb of the late 7th century.

### PORCELLANEOUS WARES

Parallel with the development of white-bodied *sancai* in northern China was that of porcellaneous stoneware, the immediate ancestor of true porcelain. These translucent white wares were considered fine enough to be given as tribute to the emperor. The designs of some of the early wares were based on silver vessels, many of Western Asian form, but many more were undecorated and probably made for the domestic utilitarian market or for export. Ninth-century white wares of simple form have been found in the Persian Gulf and at Samarra in Iraq, indicating a widespread export trade.

### SONG DYNASTY WARES

During the Song dynasty (980–1278) Chinese potters produced the classic wares of Ding, Jun, Ru and Guan. The first three were made in northern China during the Northern Song dynasty (980–1127).

Ding ware has a fine white body, with a faint orange hue on some specimens. Thinly potted, it has a creamy or ivory-coloured glaze, which tends to dribble or run in darker greenish or brownish streaks. Bowls or dishes are the commonest wares, usually fired upside down, the mouth rim left unglazed but the foot ring and base entirely covered in glaze. As the rim was bare and probably vulnerable to chipping, it was bound in a neat copper-alloy band or in silver. The very rare hollow wares, such as vases or bottles, were fired upright.

Ding porcelain is decorated by carving or moulding. Carving is invariably executed with confident, fluent strokes, gouging deep channels

**TOMB FIGURE**
**Tang dynasty**

Coloured lead glaze covers this finely modelled, life-like animal. Although earlier, isolated examples of such glazing exist, the technique only entered general use in the 8th century. (*Above*)

**DING WARE DISH**
*Hopei*
Porcelain; **Northern Song dynasty**

This thinly potted dish is characteristic of early 12th-century Ding ware. Its carinated form – the flat centre and widely flared but straight sides – is common. The lotus design has been carved over the whole surface, ignoring any restrictions imposed by the contours of the dish. The lotus is perhaps the most popular decoration for these wares, although birds and fish are also found. (*Left*)

## CHINESE PERIODS

| | | | | | |
|---|---|---|---|---|---|
| **NEOLITHIC** | c. 6500–1700 BC | **EASTERN HAN** | 24–220 | **FIVE DYNASTIES** | 907–960 |
| **SHANG** | c. 1700–1027 BC | **THREE KINGDOMS** | 221–280 | **NORTHERN SONG** | 960–1126 |
| **WESTERN ZHOU** | 1027–771 BC | **SIX DYNASTIES** | 265–589 | **SOUTHERN SONG** | 1127–1279 |
| **EASTERN ZHOU** | 771–221 BC | **NORTHERN DYNASTIES** | 386–581 | **JIN** | 1115–1234 |
| **QIN** | 221–207 BC | **SUI** | 581–618 | **YUAN** | 1279–1368 |
| **WESTERN HAN** | 206 BC–AD 9 | **TANG** | 618–906 | **MING** | 1368–1644 |
| **XIN** | AD 9–24 | **LIAO** | 907–1125 | **QING** | 1644–1911 |

which when filled with glaze subtly emphasize the design. Moulding allows a much more complex or crowded design, because the stoneware mould could be incised with great precision. With this method of decoration, dishes or bowls could be mass-produced. Moulded Ding wares are not always artistically successful – they are often too "busy" and lack the nice contrast between design and space of carved wares.

**Jun stoneware** This is a grey-bodied stoneware usually dressed in an iron-brown slip (clay and water) under an opalescent lavender-blue glaze, occasionally with purple splashes, or very rarely with a plain yellowish-green glaze. Sometimes the opaque and

**RU WARE BOWL**
Stoneware; **early 12th century**

Ru is pre-eminent among the "five classic wares" (Ru, Ding, Jun, Guan, and Ge) of the Song and Yuan dynasties. Ru ware is extremely rare, and has been extolled for its beauty and subtlety by scholars and connoisseurs alike. (*Right*)

cloudy surface has isolated "pin-holes" or "worm-tracks" (shallow irregular veins in the glaze). Jun wares generally have no surface decoration, apart from the occasional splashing. Shapes include shallow saucer dishes, bulb bowls and jardinières.

**Ru wares** Similar to, and perhaps evolved from Jun wares are the imperial Ru wares of the Northern Song dynasty. Composed of a fine buff or pinkish-yellow stoneware, Ru has a smooth, dense bluish-green glaze. Apart from shallow moulded designs on some dishes, most Ru wares are undecorated. The forms are beautiful in their severe simplicity and include oval brush-washers, narcissus bowls and bladder-shaped bottles with tall, elegant necks and lipped rims. The glaze on dishes covers the entire surface except for a small spot where it was supported by a tiny spur known as a "sesame seed".

Ru wares were made for only a few years at the beginning of the 12th century, production ceasing with the departure of the Northern Song court in 1127.

**JUN WARE DISH**
*Northern China*
Stoneware; **Song dynasty**

Jun ware is noted for its classic forms, often derived from lacquer objects or archaic bronzes. The greyish body appears to be partly or wholly covered in an iron-brown wash (usually evident on the base or foot) before the thick glaze is applied. (*Left*)

### YUE WARES

The relatively high-fired wares (1200°C) known variously as proto-Yue, pre-Yue or early green wares first appeared in the old Kingdom of Yue during the Eastern Han dynasty (24-220). They are composed of a greyish-white stoneware and have a thin, translucent glaze varying from olive green to a brownish-green. The unglazed areas are often reddish, on account of the presence of iron. The foot ring on many specimens of Yue is splayed and the base is concave.

Early Yue wares show the influence of the southern Neolithic culture, in their impressed decoration, and also the influence of bronze technology, in their forms.

The early bronze-shaped vessels that copy the shapes of bronze counterparts were decorated with various motifs, including a fine trellis pattern, a comet tail, a bean sprout, simple circlets and a rope twist. Probably in the late Han or early Six dynasties (220-589) Yue ware ceased to be merely functional or funerary and became considered worthy to grace the scholar's table, as lamps, water pots and other utensils. These were often in the form of stylized rams, lions, bears, toads and other animals. Other notable wares included "chicken-head" ewers and bronze-shaped vessels decorated with rouletted motifs or incised naturalistic ones. Occasionally wares were splashed with blobs of iron.

Very little is known of Yue ware between the Six dynasties (220-589) and the late Tang. There are a number of pieces from tombs that can be dated with which we can again pick up the story. The wares of the late Tang are somewhat organic in form – bladder-like or oviform. Short rudimentary spouts projecting from the shoulder of vessels barely upset their contours; handles are usually grooved and form a slender, elegant bridge between the shoulder and the flared mouth.

In the 9th and 10th centuries forms remained squat but each section was clearly defined by grooves or sharp angles. Spouts became longer and handles more exaggerated. Sides were often panelled with fine raised ribs, and carved or incised with vegetal themes. Banks of overlapping leaves encased the lower half. Some wares were decorated with incised work called cat-scratch, which developed into a delicate technique whose designs included ribbon and scrollwork, birds and flower subjects.

In the early years of the Song dynasty (980-1278), pieces from the Yue kilns were presented as tribute to the emperor. They were also widely exported to India and the Middle and Near East.

### CELADON WARES

Celadon is a relatively modern term for green-glazed stoneware made in both northern and southern China. The name is probably derived

**BOX AND COVER**
*Yueyao*
**Late Tang**

The top of this vessel is moulded in relief with a duck in flight enclosed by lotus flowers and stems.

**BOX AND COVER**
*Yaozhou*
Carved peony scroll decoration; **Northern Song dynasty**

Like contemporary Ding ware porcelain, Northern celadon was either carved or, from the early 12th century, moulded. The translucent and bubbled olive-green glaze is thinly applied allowing the off-white stoneware body to show through on edges and on the raised parts of the design. Unglazed areas such as the foot-ring tend to burn a brownish rust colour which is very similar in appearance to Jun ware, another northern stoneware.

from the character Céladon, who wore green ribbon, in the stage version of the French writer Honoré D'Urfé's popular 17th-century romance *L'Astrée*.

The northern variety of celadon was made in present-day Shaanxi province from about the 10th to the 13th century. It can be plain, carved or moulded. Carved wares, produced during the 11th and early 12th centuries, are generally considered the best. Moulded wares, of later date, tend to have overcrowded, monotonous designs, usually floral but also based on fish and birds. The Yaozhou body is composed of a greyish-white paste that turned a brownish honey colour on exposed areas during firing.

## SOUTHERN CELADON

Southern celadon, more refined than northern, was produced for the Southern Song court in Linan (later Hangzhou), in Zhejiang province, between 1127 and 1278. Guan ware is a dark-bodied porcellaneous stoneware with an extremely thick bluish- or greenish-grey glaze, usually with a soft iron-brown or blackish crackle (deliberate hairline fractures). Bowls, cups, bottles and censers are undecorated, the ware relying entirely on form and glaze. Bowls and dishes are often flower-like in form, bottles

**VASE**
*Longquan*
**Southern Song dynasty**

The form of this vase is that of an archaic ritual jade vessel, a *cong*. The broad crackle was contrived by the potter and alludes to the appearance of more ancient ceramics. A number of other ancient forms appears at this time, especially bronze ritual objects of the Zhou dynasty. (*Right*)

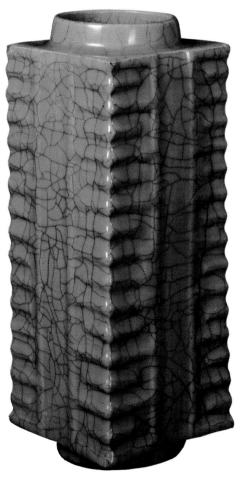

and jars globular or oviform.

Longquan celadon, manufactured in southern Zhejiang from the 10th century, is frequently confused with Guan ware, as the form, and sometimes the glaze, is very similar. Longquan celadon has a white porcellaneous body, which oxidizes to a bright red due to the presence of iron in the clay. The white body can be seen more clearly where the glaze is thin, as on a raised rib or ridge. The thick, cloudy glaze on the best Longquan is a bluish-green, except on Yuan and early Ming (1280-1465) pieces, when it is a much warmer yellowish-green.

Most surviving Longquan pieces are dishes and bowls, but bottles, vases, censers and funerary urns exist. The earliest pieces were often boldly carved with scrolling foliage and stiff leaves, but by the 12th century, apart from lotus petals carved on the outside surfaces of bowls and vases, decoration was absent.

Around the end of the Song dynasty and the beginning of the Yuan, Longquan wares became larger and more complex, with greater emphasis on relief or moulded decoration. Panels of birds and animals were enclosed within borders or zones of dense scrolling foliage. On some pieces the relief decoration was left on the biscuit (unglazed portions) which fired to a bright orange in the kiln.

The Chinese economy depended for part of

**CELADON JAR**
*Longquan*
**Yuan dynasty**

The generous, full-bodied form, massively potted, with complex, crowded decorative styles gives Yuan wares a more baroque feel than their southern Song predecessors. The vessel's shape seems irrelevant to the decorative arrangements. Whatever the form of the vessel, the bands of stiff leaves, scrolling foliage or any other motifs sweep laterally across the surface breaking it up. The reddish oxidization on unglazed areas is due to the presence of iron in the body of Longquan wares. (*Below*)

**QINGBAI VASE**
*Kiangsi*
**Porcelain; 11th–12th century**

A fine example of early *yingging* (misty blue) porcelain, the potter draws on floral or vegetal forms for his inspiration. The glaze has gathered and deepened in intensity in the crevices. (*Left*)

its revenue on the export of ceramics, and Longquan celadon has been found in burial sites in the Philippines and Indonesia and as far westwards as Turkey and Egypt. Some of the earliest recorded ceramics in late medieval Europe are probably Longquan celadon.

In the 15th century Longquan entered a long period of decline, culminating in the clumsily potted, poorly decorated and watery-glazed wares of the late Ming dynasty (1522-1644).

### QINGBAI WARES

The southern counterpart to the Ding wares of northern China, Qingbai was manufactured at a large number of sites in Fujian, Guangdong and Jiangxi provinces from the Song dynasty until well into the Ming. It is a fine white-bodied porcelain with a translucent greenish or bluish glaze.

Qingbai was made in enormous quantities and not only supplied to the domestic market but also exported to South-East Asia, India, the Middle East and Africa. Qingbai apparently datable to the 12th century has been excavated at Fustat (Old Cairo), and it is perhaps from here that the odd piece reached Europe in the form of a gift from a rich merchant or potentate.

Chinese porcelain was rare and highly prized in medieval Europe. The very few pieces recorded are invariably fitted with sumptuous gold or silver-gilt mounts inset with precious stones. Perhaps the most celebrated example is the Gaignières-Fonthill Qingbai vase, presented by Louis the Great of Hungary to Charles III of Durazzo in Italy in 1381.

Different Qingbai forms include dishes, bowls, covered boxes, incense burners, bottles, vases and funerary urns. They were decorated by carving or combing or, from the later Song

squared scroll (very similar to the Greek key pattern), wave pattern and several types of scrolling foliage such as peony, chrysanthemum and lotus. The human figure is extremely rare on Yuan porcelain. Dishes are often seemingly more crowded than the hollow wares but rarely employ more than three or four registers.

The major centres of underglaze-decorated porcelain were at Jingdezhen in Jiangxi province, southern China. The decoration frequently gives an impression of fullness and complexity; there is order but the eye is a little confused. Lotus panels in blue on white, perhaps enclosing Buddhist motifs and symbolic vegetation usually encircle the base or the underside of a dish. Another common border pattern consists of rather lively waves. This wave motif continues into the 15th century,

### WINE JAR
Porcelain; **Yuan dynasty**

---

The combination of underglaze copper red and cobalt blue is of the greatest rarity. (*Left*)

### BLUE AND WHITE DISH
Porcelain; **Yuan dynasty**

---

The central medallion of lotus petals enclosing Buddhist emblems is often seen on 14th-century porcelain. (*Below*)

period, by moulding or applied decoration. Subjects are mainly floral, with the odd bird or animal. Vases and other hollow vessels are often lobed, giving a vegetable- or gourd-like effect. Vases and bottles of the Yuan dynasty sometimes have both carved and applied decoration on the same piece, the design being effected with apparent indifference to its contours. Bowls and dishes were fired upside down on the mouth rim, leaving a narrow unglazed margin.

### UNDERGLAZE-DECORATED PORCELAIN
The earliest underglaze-painted porcelains, which date from the mid 14th century, generally follow the forms and the carved, moulded or applied patterns of contemporaneous ceramics such as Qingbai or Longquan celadon. During the Yuan dynasty (1279-1368) the emphasis was on decoration using bold, crowded and not always coherent designs. Many hollow vessels of the period have, in addition to their main theme (usually an animal or vegetable subject), up to nine bands of ornament: cloud collar (a pendant leaf motif resembling the playing-card club), classic scroll, lotus panels,

when, however, it loses its vigour, becoming conventional and stiff. A barbed or bracket shaped rim is the rule until the early 15th century.

At the beginning of the Ming dynasty the shortage of cobalt required for blue pigment necessitated the extensive use of copper red as a substitute. The potters of Jingdezhen were rarely successful in achieving a good colour, the usual result being a dull greyish- or mushroom-pink. The painting is slightly more controlled than before. Popular minor decorative elements of the Yuan and early Ming included a frieze of classical scrolling on the foot, and about the narrowest part of the neck a double-celled squared scroll. Jingdezhen wares of the period are covered in a waxy-looking viscous bluish or greenish glaze that gathers and runs in streaks, and where it is thin it has a slightly yellowish appearance.

YONGLE, XUANDE AND CHENGHUA PORCELAIN
The porcelains of the 15th-century reigns of Yongle (1403-23), Xuande (1425-36) and Chenghua (1465-87) are among the very finest Chinese ceramics, ranking alongside the five classic wares of the Song dynasty.

Early 15th-century blue-and-white is painted in a greyish cobalt blue containing accidental darker flecks, an effect known as "heaped and piled", which characterizes almost all the porcelain of the period. The potters of the Qing dynasty tried to fake this fault, but the results looked too mechanically contrived.

Whereas the main theme on 14th-century porcelain occupies a relatively narrow zone, sandwiched between many bands of minor decorative orders, on 15th-century ware it is pre-eminent and the ancillary themes are simply there to support the main subject and emphasize the changing contours of the vessel. Scrolling vegetation, birds and animals, and very rarely human subjects, continue to form the decorative motifs.

The range of 15th-century hollow vessels includes moon flasks (of flattened-disc shape), gourd-shaped flasks, pear-shaped bottles with tall trumpet necks, *guan*, lotus bowls and plain-rimmed dishes with sunken centres.

From the early 15th century porcelain was inscribed with six-character (or, rarely, four-character) reign marks and wares with the solid imperial yellow glaze appeared, as did those with bright overglaze iron-red enamelling.

Chenghua is the most refined of all Ming porcelain. Whether blue-and-white or poly-chrome, the decoration seems languid when

**BALUSTER VASE**
Porcelain; c. 1403–24

The underglaze blue of this time is often greyish in tone and looks a little blurred under the thick bubbled glaze. Yet the defects in the pigment are diminished by the control and vitality of the brushwork. (*Left*)

**BLUE AND WHITE DISH**
Porcelain; **early 15th century**

The wavy or barbed rim continues a 14th-century tradition, but the position and balance of the design is essentially early 15th century. The symmetry of the blue decoration and white porcelain is almost perfect. (*Below*)

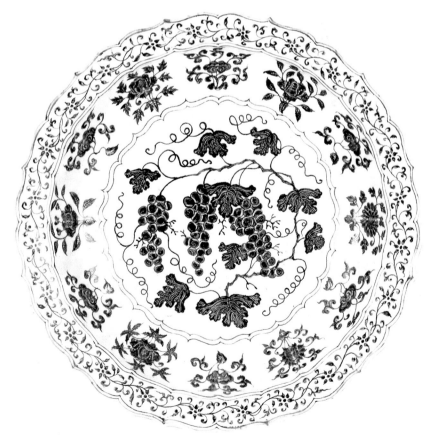

compared with early-15th-century wares. Furthermore, there is less variety of vegetation and considerable stylization, especially in leaves and flowerheads. Epitomizing the reign of Chenghua are the celebrated "palace bowls" and exquisite *doucai* (contrasting-colour) porcelains. The former are finely potted and delicately painted with undulant rather than scrolling foliage; the flowers are in a distinctive soft, greyish cobalt blue with little or no black flecking. *Doucai* porcelains are invariably small, painted in a combination of underglaze blue outlining and overglaze yellow, iron-red, manganese-brown, green and black enamels.

### ZHENGDE PORCELAIN
Porcelains of the Zhengde period (1506-21) include two noteworthy blue-and-white groups. The first is wares – usually saucer dishes, leys jars (large wine jars) and bowls – painted with dragons enmeshed in scrolled lotus with spiky blooms and small curling leaves. The second group has Arabic or Persian inscriptions surrounded by weed-like vegetation. Most of this ware was intended for the scholar's table – brush rests, pen boxes, lamp holders. The thick glaze is generally bluish or greenish.

### JIAJING PORCELAIN
The establishment of a large export trade in the early 16th century was partly responsible for a general decline in the quality of Chinese porcelain. However, some fine wares were produced. For example, the imperial wares of Jiajing (1522-66) are handsome and vigorous, if lacking 15th-century finesse and subtlety. Leading figures of the Daoist religion are popular subjects, together with the crane, the rose-deer, the

### BLUE AND WHITE "PALACE BOWL"
Porcelain; *c.* 1465–87

Compared with the dramatic and powerful porcelains from the early 15th century, those of the reign of Chenghua (1465–87) have a more refined appeal. The "soft-focus" look of the early 15th century is replaced with a sharper image, owing to the thinner glaze. (*Above*)

### JAR
Porcelain; *c.* 1465–87

The design is painted in the delicate, if somewhat languid, manner of the day using underglaze blue as an outline, completing it in overglaze yellow, iron red, manganese purple and green. (*Right*)

pine tree and *lingzhi* fungus, all associated with Daoism. These themes remained part of the potter's vocabulary until the end of the Ming dynasty.

Non-Daoist figure subjects, such as children playing and gatherings of dignitaries and scholars were also used on Jiajing wares. The perennial dragon had now become a centipede-like, almost humorous creature. Polychrome decoration was generally exuberant. In the 16th century blue was employed not only as an outline but as a wash. Jiajing porcelain had an off-white body, a glassy bluish glaze and a brilliant purplish-blue underglaze, which tended to run and obscure the design.

Some export pieces had European, especially Iberian, motifs. A few are inscribed in Portuguese. Much was of poor quality.

### KRAAK PORCELAIN
The reigns of Longqing (1567-72) and Wanli (1573-1619) continued the traditions established during that of Jiajing. By the 1570s a new type of porcelain appeared, one decorated with repeated, usually rectilinear, panels, each enclosing a motif. It is called *kraak* ware, a Dutch name, presumably coined because the Portuguese vessels which carried these wares were known as carracks. The porcelain cargoes of two were sold by auction in the Netherlands, and among the buyers who paid very high prices were Henry IV of France and James I of England. Overnight a fashion was created for the hitherto exclusive ware. The recently-formed Dutch East India Company quickly realized the commercial potential of *kraak* porcelain and began large-scale shipments of it abroad.

### "TRANSITIONAL" PORCELAIN
Gradually the Dutch encroached upon the Portuguese trading monopoly in the Far East and

**BLUE AND WHITE BOWL**
Porcelain; **early 15th century**

A surprising number of early Ming wares, such as this one, show the influence of the Islamic world in terms of forms being borrowed from metal or glass, although inscriptions are extremely rare.
(*Above*)

**PEN BOX AND COVER**
Porcelain; *c.* 1573–1620

Boxes of various forms – circular, hexagonal, or oblong – were relatively popular in the 16th and early 17th centuries. The style combining underglaze cobalt blue and overglaze enamels, such as on this example, is known as *wucai*.
(*Right*)

## KRAAKSPORSELEIN DISH
Porcelain; *c.* 1600–50

The arrangement of the border into segments or compartments is typical of most late Ming export ware. Especially common are the beribboned leaves and the sunflower-type flowers. (*Left*)

## "SLEEVE" VASE
*Jingdezhen*
Porcelain; *c.* 1640

The shape of this vase is known as "rollwagon". (*Below far left*)

## BLUE AND WHITE VASE
Porcelain; *c.* 1662–1722

A subtle incurve towards the base has altered the simple profile of the earlier rollwagon vases. (*Below centre*)

## BALUSTER VASE
Porcelain; *c.* 1662–1722

The painting of a landscape and mountain is in the style of the Kangxi period (1662–1722). (*Below*)

established a network of fortified trading posts throughout the area. After 1624 the Dutch began shipping back from China a new and highly refined type of porcelain. Heavily potted and finely painted, these "Transitional" wares (made at the end of the Ming dynasty and the beginning of the Qing) were shipped to the West.

"Transitional" porcelain is invariably hollow ware, whereas *kraak* could be either flat or hollow. A number of new shapes appeared, some based on European metal, glass or stoneware originals. They included cylindrical brush pots; rollwagons (tall cylindrical vases with a waisted neck), oviform jars with short drum-shaped covers, beaker vases, mustard pots and cylindrical tankards. Quite a number were painted with figure subjects taken from printed romances or legendary tales; many of these paintings are informal and naturalistic, the scene taking place in a mist-wrapped hilltop garden with banana plantains and pine trees. A feature of these narrative scenes is the use of small sickle-shaped strokes to convey the idea of grass.

**BALUSTER VASE**
Porcelain; **Late 17th century (?)**

The "famille-verte" (green family) palette has been used for the decoration of this vase. (*Right*)

**MOON FLASK**
Porcelain; *c.* 1723–35

The "famille-rose" (pink family) palette, developed in the reign of Kangxi (1662–1722), supplanted the bold and vivacious "famille-verte" (green family) colour scheme. (*Below*)

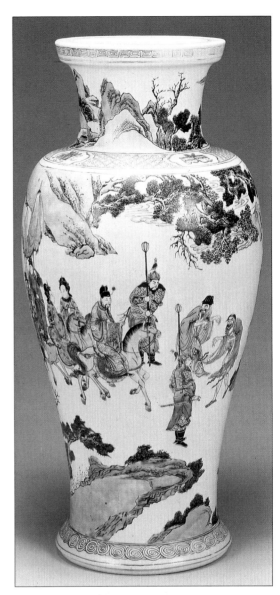

PORCELAIN FOR THE JAPANESE MARKET
Chinese potters also catered for the Japanese market. These wares are divided into two categories: Shonzui and Ko-sometsuke. Shonzui wares are more refined and are decorated in a controlled, somewhat academic way, with extensive use of diaper (repeated diamonds or squares) patterns. Ko-sometsuke porcelain, by contrast, is casually, sometimes carelessly, potted and is sketchily painted with figures of ascetics or Daoist immortals or with lakeland landscapes that are spare but alluring. Most of these wares are decorated in underglaze blue, but a few are heightened in overglaze enamels.

*FAMILLE VERTE* AND *FAMILLE ROSE*
During the early years of the Qing dynasty (1644-1912) civil unrest interrupted porcelain production and it was not until about 1680 that

**BOTTLE VASE**
Porcelain; **early 18th century** (*Above*)

**PUNCHBOWL**
Porcelain; **c. 1800**

The view shows London's Ironmongers' Company Hall. (*Below*)

the export trade was restored. In the meantime the newly-established porcelain industry in Japan, encouraged by the Dutch East India Company, made up the shortfall in supply. At first the Dutch wanted Chinese-style blue-and-white, but later the native "brocaded" Imari porcelain and beautiful, more reticent, Kakiemon-type wares became extremely popular and thereby presented the Chinese with a challenge. This was answered with the brilliant *famille verte* (green family) porcelain, developed during the reign of the emperor Kangxi (1662-1722). The almost pure white body of this is enamelled in iron-red, purple-blue and yellow with flowers, birds, mythical beasts, figure subjects or precious objects and has a thin, glassy green enamel overglaze. During the Kangxi period much *famille verte* was decorated with petal- or leaf-shaped reserves, often enclosing various themes.

Towards the end of the Kangxi period *famille rose* (pink family) was introduced. This had an entirely new palette, the colours being rendered pastel by mixing in white and dominated by pink. This lighter, somewhat frivolous colour scheme was put to good effect on new designs that were much smaller in scale and intimate.

QING PORCELAIN

The early Qing dynasty was a period of both innovation and revivalism: as well as a range of entirely new monochrome glazes and decorative techniques, there was a re-introduction of old, long-forgotten types of porcelain.

The new monochrome glazes included peach-bloom, a copper-derived pinkish tone suffused with patches of moss green; *clair-de-lune*, a pale greyish-lavender-blue; iron-rust, a lustrous, speckled bronze; tea-dust, a matt, deep olive green; robin's egg, a purple-flecked turquoise; and many others. Among the retrospective porcelains were copies of the classic wares of the Song, Yuan and Ming dynasties; the early-15th-century copper-red or blue-and-white ware; and the delicate *doucai* porcelains of Chenghua's reign.

After the departure of Tang Ying, the great director of the kilns at Jingdezhen, there was a steady decline in standards: over-elaboration in design and less attention to refinement and detail. (Even so, some fine porcelains were produced in the late 18th century and throughout the 19th). Many wares were traditional – of similar form and decoration to those of the earlier Qing – but tend to lack life.

In the export market, too, competition from European porcelain factories and the Staffordshire potteries brought about a lowering of quality. Canton-style porcelains are overcrowded with repetitive scenes of mandarin figures in compartments on indigestible green and pink floral grounds.

THE JAPANESE CERAMIC TRADITION WITH ITS SPECIAL BLEND OF
ASCETICISM AND TECHNICAL MASTERY HAS PROVIDED INSPIRATION NOT
ONLY FOR THE POTTERY OF OTHER EASTERN CULTURES BUT ALSO FOR
MODERN EUROPEAN STUDIO CERAMICS.

# JAPANESE CERAMICS

The field of Japanese ceramics is vast, covering approximately 8,000 years of prehistory and history. Early wares, though idiosyncratic, often reveal techniques and traditions imported mainly from China and Korea. The later arrival of Buddhism and its fusion with indigenous Shinto created a quite distinct set of values, encouraging the appreciation of spontaneity rather than the pursuit of perfect symmetry. This was further accentuated by the introduction of the tea ceremony by Buddhist monks in the 12th century with its emphasis on things humble and close to nature. These values even survived into the wares exported to the West in the 17th and early 18th centuries and, after a period of decline, resurfaced in the late 19th century.

### EARLY WARES

Early pottery vessels produced in Japan were made by a coiling and beating process. A favoured method of decoration on the typical urn forms of the Jomon culture – the Japanese Neolithic (c. 4,500 BC–3rd century BC) – was, as in Europe, the use of corded and woven material impressed into the still supple clay. Such ornament may wholly cover the pot, giving a ribbed effect, or it may be applied more selectively, in spirals and counter-spirals with space between them. It is often contained within applied, raised borders, especially about the rim. The clay is generally coarse and lumpy, contrasting with the refinement of the decoration,

## JAPANESE PERIODS

| JOMON | Until c. 200 BC |
|---|---|
| YAYOI | c. 200 BC–c. AD 250 |
| TUMULUS (Kofun) | c. AD 250–c. 552 |
| ASUKA | 552–710 |
| NARA | 710–794 |
| HEIAN | 794–1185 |
| KAMAKURA | 1185–1392 |
| MUROMACHI | 1392–1568 |
| MOMOYAMA | 1568–1615 |
| EDO | 1615–1868 |
| MEIJI | 1868–1912 |

**POTTERY JAR**
*Middle Jomon period,*
**c. 3000–2000 BC**

In common with prehistoric pottery the world over, patterns on Jomon wares suggest woven forerunners.

and the pottery is unglazed. By the latest period jars were often painted in red.

Of all early ceramic cultures the world over, Jomon (cord pattern) ware is probably the most complex and accomplished.

Yayoi ware, named after the first site at which archaeologists found examples, spans the 3rd century BC to the 3rd century AD, a period roughly overlapping the Han Dynasty in China. Vessels were now being produced on a potter's wheel. Typical shapes include narrow-necked bottles, bag-shaped vessels and vases reminiscent of Chinese green-glazed pottery imitations of metalwork. Unlike their Chinese contemporaries, Japanese potters at this time still did not produce glazed ceramics. Geometric patterns increase but display a horizontal zoning, perhaps encouraged by the use of the wheel for decoration after throwing.

In the Tumulus period (5th–7th century) typical keyhole-shaped burial mounds were often furnished with ceramic "headstones". Originally mere cylinders arranged in a circle on top of the mound, they were later surmounted by portraits both animal and human, known as Haniwa pottery. Typical figures stand 0.6–0.9 m (2–3 ft) high, are hollow and have simplified features and pierced eyes and mouth.

Few prehistoric wares come on to the open market. Occasionally Haniwa pieces appear but inevitably are always to some degree restored.

### KOREAN POTTERS

The Tumulus period also saw the emergence in Japan of home-produced glazed wares: arriving from nearby Korea, a new wave of potters started to produce grey stoneware covered or splashed in a celadon (grey-green) glaze, known as Sue ware. Typical of the type are round-bellied vessels with a splayed foot pierced to allow the vessel to be heated over fire.

Later, during the Nara period (710–784), the influences of the Chinese T'ang Dynasty (618–906) reached a climax: broad-bellied forms continued, but alongside Sue and Shirashi (high-quality ash-glazed wares based on Chinese celadon and porcelain) wares appeared a lead glaze stained by the addition of a limited number of metallic oxides, colours inspired by the *sancai* (three-colour) palette from China. The effect was often heightened by applying wax to the clay as a resist; the body retained its underlying straw colour and was invaded at the edges by rivulets of colour.

During the Nara period, with the support

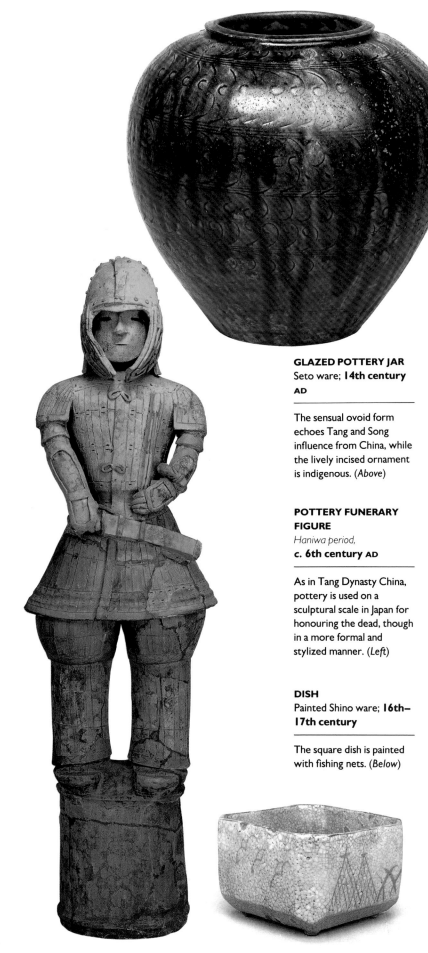

**GLAZED POTTERY JAR**
Seto ware; **14th century AD**

The sensual ovoid form echoes Tang and Song influence from China, while the lively incised ornament is indigenous. (*Above*)

**POTTERY FUNERARY FIGURE**
*Haniwa period,*
**c. 6th century AD**

As in Tang Dynasty China, pottery is used on a sculptural scale in Japan for honouring the dead, though in a more formal and stylized manner. (*Left*)

**DISH**
Painted Shino ware; **16th–17th century**

The square dish is painted with fishing nets. (*Below*)

of the court, Buddhism became the dominant religion and became also the single most significant element in shaping the character of Japanese arts and crafts thereafter.

**Divergence from Chinese influence** From the middle of the ensuing Heian period (AD 794–1185) – so-named after the capital to which Nara was moved – Chinese influence waned. What followed was the native germination and growth of the seeds of outside influences sown up until this point. The Sue and Shirashi traditions continued with Yakishimeto ware, starting in the late 12th century. Seto became the foremost producer of high-quality wares – typically, bottle-shapes and jars stamped or incised with flower motifs and covered in brown glazes.

Seto, Bizen (fine brown unglazed stoneware), Echizen, Tamba, Tokoname and Shigaraku and Iga constitute the "Six Old Kilns" believed to have started at various times between the later Heian and the Muromachi (1338–1568) periods. When it is remembered that each of these groups may be represented by hundreds of kilns, many with sub-groups, it will be seen how vast the field is and how difficult classification and chronology become.

### SPIRITUALITY AND CERAMICS

In general, the ceramic traditions of Japan until the early 17th century present a fundamental divergence from the studied perfection of Chinese monochrome glazes of the Song Dynasty (960–1279). Vases are thrown with an informal abandon and glazed (if at all) with a spontaneous flourish. Whereas post-Tang Chinese ceramics evolve towards greater technical refinement and symmetry of form, Japanese wares seem to hark back to the spontaneity of Jomon times. The reasons are to be found in the ideological background of Japanese society. Native Shinto beliefs had fused with imported Buddhism to produce a powerful blend of nature worship and other-worldly spirituality. In a unique way, the Japanese potter's art is an encapsulation in clay and glaze of these fundamental philosophies.

**Tea Wares** To the Western mind the cultivation of spontaneity may seem a contradiction in terms. Certainly it is inconceivable that a post-Renaissance European society could have produced the asymmetric tea bowls and vases associated with the Japanese tea ceremony. Nor could such "imperfect" objects have been treated with such respect that, once cracked or even broken, they would be painstakingly reassembled using costly gold lacquer. Such inanimate objects were even given an individual proper name. The Japanese believed that the potter became the almost passive vessel through which forces inherited through generations, were uncontrollably and fleetingly poured.

Into such a society came the *Cha-no-yu* (hot water for tea), or tea ceremony, which has played a central role in Japanese culture from the 16th century onwards. Tea masters, fully versed in all aspects of tea preparation, supervised the choice of utensils, their presentation

**TEA BOWL**
Low-fired Raku ware with black glaze; **17th century**

At their best Shino, Oribe and Raku wares appear to be natural phenomena, discovered rather than made: a geometric design is partially overrun in an act of bravura by a totally unrelated glaze, or maybe a painted design is modest and stylized, occupying very little of the surface area. Such pieces have had a powerful effect on European studio potters of the 20th century.

**DISH**
Oribe ware with green glaze; **Late 16th century**

Colliding entirely different designs remains a favourite Japanese technique. (*Left*)

and the selection of a suitable painting and spray of flowers. The appeal of such a ritual to Japanese society was reflected in the ceramics manufactured for it.

### BLACK GLAZING

Both Shino and Oribe stonewares supposedly take their names from two of the earliest tea masters, Shino Soshin (*fl* late 15th century) and Furuta Oribe (1544–1615). These, as indeed most tea wares, came out of Mino province, where the Seto tradition continued. Bowls were often *temmoku* (black-glazed) – from Tien Mu in China, the area associated with the original black-glazed tea wares – in order to show off the frothy tea once it had been whisked to an opaque vivid green colour. Raku ware, introduced by Chojiro (1516–*c*.1592) in the Momoyama period (1568–1614), was a low-fired, coarse-grained pottery covered in a clear glaze, usually black but also red or yellow. Brocade-inspired geometric patterns playfully contradicted the surface shape. For the first time the use of brushwork on pottery became important; simple and spontaneous, such calligraphic decoration was appropriate to the humble yet sophisticated ritual. Most famous of the Raku potters is probably Hon' Ami Koetsu (1558–1637).

Calligraphic decoration can also be seen on Karatsu stonewares. These were made at dragon kilns (communicating fire chambers rising on a gradient) founded by Korean immigrants in the mid 16th century.

The Momoyama period drew to a close as Japan invaded Korea. This campaign brought yet another influx of Korean potters into Japan, as prisoners or refugees, familiar with a material hitherto unknown in Japan, porcelain. Settling in Kyushu, like so many other waves of Koreans before them, the new arrivals found a workable porcelain clay, though admittedly not one so refined as the Chinese. The earliest Japanese porcelain appears to have been manufactured at the Karatsu kilns around 1620.

### EXPORT WARES

Porcelain arrived in Japan at the height of the popularity of the tea ceremony, a custom which was now to stimulate native kilns to a higher degree of innovation.

The earliest Japanese porcelain wares, made largely for the domestic market, are called shoki-Imari (early Imari) and were made by a number of kilns in the Arita area. In addition to the manufacture of *kosometsuke* (straightforward blue-and-white), celadon pieces were made – many at the Maruo kiln – and also wares with a brown iron-rust wash, often used in combination with decoration done in cobalt blue underglaze. Although by this time the Chinese had been producing their own blue-and-white for almost 300 years, it appears that their Tianqi period wares (1621–27), made at about the same time as Arita wares, were influenced by the informal style of the infant Japanese industry; it has to be said, however, that many were obviously intended for export to Japan.

**Arita wares** In 1641 the Dutch East India Company succeeded in its schemes to usurp the monopoly of European-Japanese trade, which until then had been held by the Portuguese. Under the Portuguese, significant quantities of Chinese porcelain, but little of the new and comparatively inferior Japanese porcelain, had been imported into Europe. The Dutch trade mission was established on Deshima Island, in Nagasaki harbour. Soon, the disruption caused to Chinese kilns by the collapse of the Ming Dynasty in 1644 gave a further boost to the

**ARITA DISH**
Porcelain painted in underglaze blue; **late 17th century**

The pattern of pomegranates and persimmon is also found on Chinese export ware of the period, minus the "VOC" monogram (which stands for "Vereenigde Oostindische Compagnie", the Dutch East India Company). At a time when the Chinese export porcelain industry had been re-established it is sometimes difficult to decide where the original idea for some export wares originated: China, Japan or even Europe.

# CHINESE AND EARLY JAPANESE PORCELAIN

An Arita *kraak*-style dish compared to a Chinese original demonstrates the very clear differences between Chinese and Japanese porcelain at this time. The Chinese piece is usually lighter in weight; both foot and rim are sharp and are crisp to the touch, the glaze breaking on the rim edge. The rim edge is cut with foliations. There may be sand adhering to the underside of the foot, where chatter-marks (the radiating grooves left by the tool used in cutting the foot well) may also be seen.

By contrast, the Japanese piece looks and feels much more like satin, less brittle to the touch. The rim is left uncut, as well as being rounded on the edge with no fritting (breaking of the glaze during firing); the underside of the foot often has tell-tale marks which show that the piece was supported on small stilts in the firing. Furthermore, the cobalt blue usually appears deeper in colour than on the Chinese piece. This can be the result of iron impurities that occasionally produce a yellowish-brown stain. The blue is often so saturated that it becomes black and rises to the surface of the covering glaze. The glaze itself, filled with millions of microscopic bubbles in suspension (clearly visible under a magnifying glass), scatters light, rendering the outlines of the design indistinct.

**ARITA DISH**
Porcelain painted in underglaze blue; **late 17th-early 18th century**

Decorated with landscape medallion and border panels, this dish is a breathtaking *tour-de-force* of painting. The distance between the wet plains of the foreground and the far mountains seems to contain an infinity of space, emphasized by the mists in between. The style is akin to Kangxi period painting, while the border panels (possibly by a different hand) are executed in a more conservative, almost European manner of some fifty years earlier.

young Japanese porcelain industry: Dutch orders previously sent to Jingdezhen in China were switched to Japan. So large were these orders that Arita kilns were forced to restructure and merge.

The term Arita is currently used in the West to denote those pieces from the Arita area painted solely in underglaze blue. Blue-and-white, which resembled the Chinese porcelain so popular in Europe, naturally made up the greatest volume of the trade. And not surprisingly, the Dutch placed orders for repeats of the recognizable Chinese blue-and-white patterns previously imported. Among these were Arita versions of the Chinese *kraak* style: dishes with a central star-shaped panel containing a landscape with birds or animals, all framed by radiating panels filled with repeated flower motifs against a ground of blue scales.

**Enamelling** Enamels appear to have been in use on Japanese porcelain before the export trade got under way. However, it was largely thanks to the foreign trade that there was a flowering of the technique in the second half of the 17th century. Among enamelled work were copies of Chinese *kraak* designs. The enamels used differed from the Chinese *famille verte* palette of the same period (translucent green glaze over yellow, purplish-blue and iron red) the Japanese used a superior cobalt blue but seem to have had trouble obtaining a suitable yellow, which was little used by them until later in the century.

Already there seems to have been a division between potters and decorators: although some kilns had their own enamelling workshops attached, there were also independent enamellers who bought undecorated or only partially decorated pieces and painted them. For this reason, it is difficult to attribute wares to a particular pottery on grounds of painting style alone.

## STYLES

**"Kakiemon"** – taken from the name of a family of distinguished potters some of whose work is decorated in a palette of turquoise, blue, iron red, yellow, black and gilding – has assumed a

## PAIR OF ARITA EAGLES
### Late 17th century

Such figures were highly
fashionable among
European nobility. In 1731
Meissen made copies for
Augustus the Strong's
"Japanese Palace". (*Right*)

## "KRAAK"-STYLE ARITA DISH
### Late 17th century

Painted in overglaze
"Kakiemon" enamels, this
dish follows the design of an
earlier Chinese "Kraak"
dish painted in underglaze
blue. (*Below*)

## KAKIEMON JARS AND COVERS
Painted in enamels; **late 17th century**

On all three pieces the
figures clearly follow a
European idea of the
Orient. (*Right*)

**IMARI VASES**
Painted in underglaze-blue, enamels and gilding; **late 17th–early 18th century**

Garnitures such as this one, comprising five vases, often embellished European chimney-pieces or surmounted furniture with suitable ledges. (*Above*)

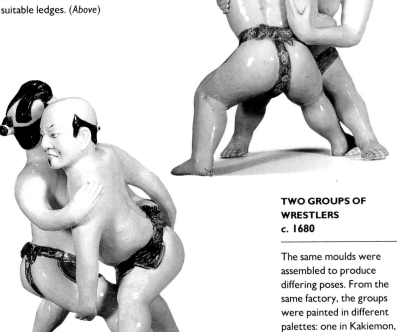

**TWO GROUPS OF WRESTLERS**
*c. 1680*

The same moulds were assembled to produce differing poses. From the same factory, the groups were painted in different palettes: one in Kakiemon, the other in Imari colours. (*Above and left*)

generic meaning, being used to encompass all pieces decorated in the above colours, whether exclusively by the kiln associated with the family, by other kilns or by outside decorators.

The discovery at a kiln at Nangawara of shapes known in Europe to carry only Kakiemon colouring has identified it as the Kakiemon site. Furthermore, shards of the famous *negoshide* (milky-white) body, a refined porcelain material and glaze associated with Kakiemon pieces, were plentiful at the site. However, the material recovered also included bowls and dishes of the standard Arita body carefully painted in underglaze blue and often "dressed" with a brown iron oxide rim.

**Imari** More plentiful than Kakiemon are Imari wares, named after the nearby port through which both were exported. Essentially, this category is again defined by a palette: underglaze blue, iron red and gilding. Other enamel colours are sometimes included, notably black, green, yellow and aubergine. A lustrous pink wash probably derived from gold is also seen. This colour scheme sometimes appears on pieces demonstrably from the same moulds as others bearing Kakiemon colours: the two were undoubtedly produced at the same time and decorated (perhaps by an outside enameller) in two different styles.

**Kutani** The characteristic Imari colours are thought to have evolved from an earlier style dating from the second half of the 17th century, though not exported to Europe at the

**KUTANI DISH**
Enamelled; **probably late 17th century**

The dish is a visual paradox: at first sight perhaps abstract and asymmetric, the circular form disguises a more complex yet balanced construction. Repeated zigzag patterns on the leaves of each fan deliberately suspend the mind between abstraction and reality. Such visual wit is peculiarly Japanese – half-revealed or overlapped objects and brocades abound into even the late Imari period. By the late 19th century, however, the technique generally suffered from overcrowding.

time. The pieces of this latter group are painted in a distinctive palette incorporating green, dark iron red, smoky yellow and aubergine. The category was once attributed to the Kutani kilns of Honshu – and therefore called *Ko*-Kutani (old Kutani) – but has been re-ascribed to the Arita group. The wares of a second Kutani group have a much heavier appearance: the entire top surface of its typical saucer-shaped dishes is filled with smoky green, yellow, aubergine and black enamel. The green is often predominant, hence the name *Ao*-Kutani (green Kutani). But how many, if any, of this second group can be dated to the 17th century is as yet unclear; most appear to be 19th-century and related to the later red-and-gold Kutani wares of Kaga.

**Nabeshima** As the export trade was reaching its peak in the early 18th century (but only to dwindle to nothing by mid-century), another Arita group, this time manufactured for the lords of Hizen, intended as tribute for the Shogun, came to the fore: Nabeshima.

Whereas Imari and Kakiemon porcelains sometimes contained underglaze blue as a solid "wash" in the design or as a border decoration, on the finest Nabeshima ware the Chinese *doucai* (contrasting colour) technique was employed – that is, the use of underglaze blue to outline the design (and perhaps also as a "wash"), with the design being filled in with clear enamels. Typical shapes were saucer-form dishes upon larger than usual tapering feet decorated with a comb (vertical parallel lines) bor-

der. The designs are among the most sophisticated and artistically satisfying ever produced in Japan.

The best Nabeshima wares are generally dated to the first half of the 18th century. The style continued into the 19th century, when pieces can often be faulted on stiffness of design or poor draughtsmanship.

### THE LARGER MARKET

In the hundred or so years between the beginning of Japan's isolationism, around 1750, to its opening itself up once more to Western influences in the 1860s, Arita, Imari and other wares apparently continued to be produced but seemingly without much innovation. It is probably later in this Edo (1614–1868) period that Hirado porcelain at Mikawachi – established perhaps as early as the mid 17th century – reached the height of its production. This porcelain is a highly refined, glassy white ware, occasionally painted in underglaze blue with typical "jumping boys" designs.

**Revival of exports** The Meiji period (1868–1912) saw a programme of modernizing reforms and Japan began to be represented at the great international exhibitions. Once again, from the mid-19th century, oriental culture began to exert a profound influence upon the West. Accordingly, great quantities of Imari ware, of widely varying quality, were produced in Japan for export to the West. The ware was geared to supply a European bourgeois market much larger than the former predominantly aristocratic and mercantile one of pre-revolutionary, pre-industrial Europe. The most mass-produced pieces show the use of stencil printing in underglaze blue, a technique inferior to the transfer printing on much earlier porcelain and on English earthenware from the 1760s onwards.

**Makuzu Kozan and Fukagawa** By the year 1900 some porcelain, for both export and domestic consumption, again reached a technical brilliance. At the heart of the eclectic styles of Makuzu Kozan porcelain lay a return to the finest underglaze-blue porcelain painting of the late 17th century, coupled with a new experimentation with additional underglaze pigments and with forms.

The Fukagawa factory also skilfully used a range of underglaze colours, often combined with moulded or applied decoration. In 1909, its own production having been assisted by German porcelain experts, the Fukagawa

**NABESHIMA (ARITA) DISH**
Painted in underglaze blue and enamels; **late 17th–early 18th century**

The technique of painting on porcelain with underglaze pigments (in this case cobalt blue) followed by overglaze enamels allows a design to assume a three-dimensional effect. Even though the descending layers of enamel, glaze, cobalt and the underlying porcelain surface all occur within no more than 1 to 2 millimetres, this is sufficient for the light from each surface to reflect in a different way. On restrained Nabeshima wares such as this, painted with a field of buckwheat, the effect can be masterly, conveying a convincing spectrum of textures in an open "canvas".

**NABESHIMA (ARITA) DISH**
**Late 17th–early 18th century** (underside of dish above)

The gold lacquer repairs such pieces received when broken is evidence of the esteem in which they were held by their owners.

**VASE**
*Makuzu Kozan*
Porcelain; **c. 1900**

The vase is a masterpiece of three-dimensional realism: not only is the throwing of Makuzu Kozan's vases often a *tour-de-force*, but it is usually matched by the skill of painting in the round.

factory took over the Hirado works.

**Kutani** The predominantly iron-red-and-gold Kutani wares imported by Europeans and Americans in the last quarter of the 19th century were mostly produced at the Kaga kilns on Honshu. The body of Kutani wares varies from a thick almost earthenware clay at one extreme to an "eggshell" porcelain at the other, with several intermediate grades. This suggests that there must have been various decorating workshops outside Kaga producing wares in the Kutani style.

## MASS PRODUCTION

From the large quantity of eggshell Kutani porcelain tea services possessed by humble households, it is obvious that these wares became a staple European commodity up to the

1920s. Occasionally, the painting (usually in tones of grey heightened in pink, yellow and other enamels) is of a high standard, but usually it is not.

**Noritake** In the late 19th and early 20th century the Noritake Porcelain Company mass-produced eggshell and other wares in a purely European style, often classically shaped vases painted with alpine landscapes or even with sunset Egyptian scenes. The palette is very often similar to that of the Royal Worcester Factory.

**Satsuma** Just as prolifically produced was the well-known Satsuma earthenware. The term Satsuma has been extended from its strictly correct meaning of ceramics from the Satsuma area to incorporate those from kilns at Kyoto, Bizen and elsewhere. The common denominator is the material: a slightly yellow earthenware of a chalky consistency, covered in an ivory-coloured clear glaze that exhibits a controlled, very fine crazing (deliberately induced network of cracks). Decoration is executed in enamels ranging from raised to a very thin wash, often heightened or outlined in gilding. Painting on the highly mass-produced wares is often large and sketchy. On the fine pieces painting shows a miniaturist perfection typical of so many applied arts in Meiji Japan. The finest decoration is probably that done by Yabu Meizan (*c.* 1900). The often fine products by Kinkozan (*c.* 1900) have a wider range of quality, being aimed at different markets. Panels are often reserved in a cobalt-blue ground, which sets off a meticulously executed silver and gold design.

Some authorities believe that Satsuma production began as far back as the 17th century, but more evidence is needed before this claim can be substantiated. All that can be said for certain is that it is likely that a group of Satsuma earthenware – the Thick Blue Enamel group whose enamels include a vibrant blue alongside raised gilding – pre-dates the known late-19th-century export ware. A somewhat battered Satsuma vessel sold by Sothebys in 1990 was marked with the date equivalent to 1806, so it is reasonable to date Thick Blue Enamel back to at least the early 19th century.

There was a gradual lowering of quality in Satsuma ware as the 20th century progressed: high-quality gilding gave way to a more silvery mirror gilding; matt black came to the fore; outlines were executed in a cake-icing technique in a variety of colours; transfer printing of heads replaced free-hand painting; and by the 1920s a garish orange entered the palette.

**VASES**
*Yabu Meizan and Tawara
Koseki workshops*
Earthenware; **c. 1900**

At their best, straw-
coloured "Satsuma" wares
demonstrate a miniaturist
perfection.

**LANDSCAPE VASE**
*Makuzu Kozan*
**c. 1900**

Breathtaking panorama on
a three-dimensional surface;
distant Fujiyama is optically
further for the eye than the
nearby forest, placed on the
wide belly of the vase. The
fine control of underglaze
blue in geometric layers
echoes Arita wares of the
late 17th century.

THE ISLAMIC WORLD DERIVED MOST OF ITS CERAMIC STYLES AND FASHIONS THROUGH CONTACT WITH CHINA EITHER THROUGH WAR OR FROM TRADERS AND MERCHANTS TRAVELING THE "SILK ROUTE."

# CERAMICS OF THE ISLAMIC WORLD

Trade with China from the 7th to the 9th century was probably the most influential factor in the development of early Islamic pottery. Another was probably the unsuccessful Chinese invasion of Transoxiana in about 750, which resulted in Chinese prisoners showing their potting techniques to the native craftsmen. From this time Islamic pottery began to develop its characteristic qualities.

Unglazed wares in the buff or pink clay available to Islamic potters lacked refinement, and by the 9th century potters in Mesopotamia, part of the Islamic world, were dressing the body in a white slip (a mixture of clay and water) or covering it in a tin glaze (white glaze of tin oxide).

Probably at about the same time lustre decoration (a thin metallic film) was introduced; this technique was transmitted throughout the Islamic world until it reached southern Spain in the 14th century. Lustre wares from Malaga, and later from Valencia, were exported throughout Europe and were partly responsible

**DISH**
*Mesopotamia*
**9th century**

An early example of Islamic pottery, this utilizes a lead glaze that traces its ancestry back to Roman times in the eastern Mediterranean, especially to Egypt. It was probably introduced to Mesopotamia by Egyptian potters. Typical of this early group is the design moulded in shallow relief with "punched" decoration perhaps simulating metalwork. There are traces of lustre, a tech innovation, almost certainly adapted from glass technology.

for raising pottery to an art form.

The finest early Islamic wares were those from Nishapur and Samarkand in Persia. These were painted in brown, green, yellow and pink under a transparent glaze. Decoration was mainly geometric, with concentric bands or zones of hatching or stippling. Other types of decoration included split palmettes (stylized palm leaves), animals and, rarely, human figures. Some pieces were decorated in garbled Kufic script in brownish-black on a creamy slip ground. Most of the early extant wares are dishes and bowls strongly influenced by Tang pottery. The forms of many – high-shouldered jars with flat bases and domed covers – also show Chinese influence.

By the 10th or 11th century, Islamic potters had developed a finer, whiter body that combined clay with silica. This allowed moulded and pierced decoration, often in Chinese motifs, to be introduced. In addition, new glazes, of turquoise and rich purplish-cobalt, were used.

In Kashan, in Persia, lustre ware decoration became extremely complex after the 13th century: human figures enmeshed in calligraphy, arabesques, interlacing bands and tight foliate scrolls. In Syria, at the same time, potters combined copper-lustre and cobalt glazes, decorating pottery with foliate motifs on stippled grounds. Also produced during the Seljuk period were the famous Minai wares, painted blood red, manganese and black, and usually highed with gilding.

**SLIPWARE BOWL**
*Eastern Persia*
**10th century** (*Above*)

**EARTHENWARE EWER**
*Syria*
**14th century** (*Above*)

**MINAI WARE BOWL**
*Persia*
**12th century** (*Below*)

Alongside the complicated pierced and carved forms of the Seljuk period, covered in monochrome blue or green glazes, are wares painted in underglaze blue and lustre, models of animals and humans depicted in everyday activities, with lustre or turquoise glazes, and tiles with a shallow-relief frieze of animals or human figures.

In Persia, during the Ilkhanid (Mongol) period of the 13th and 14th centuries, the complex Lajvardina wares appeared, with designs perhaps inspired by damascene (gold- or silver-inlaid) metalwork or in the manner of contemporary Chinese wares – for example, bowls or dishes decorated with two or four fish. In the 16th and 17th centuries, during the Safavid period, Kerman and Meshed wares were strongly influenced by late Ming export porcelain designs. Meshed wares were often painted with underglaze blue and black outlines that gave a crisp look to the design. Another "borrowing" was the incised or shallow-carved foliate decoration usually confined to borders. This was based on the subtle so-called "secret" decoration found on Chinese "Transitional" period porcelains. Blue-and-white was by far the most popular ware, but Persian potters also employed sage green and blood red, in combination with copper-lustre glazes.

## TURKISH CERAMICS

Turkish wares, which present considerable problems in dating because of a dearth of documentary or archaeological material, were among the most accomplished of early Islamic ceramics. Tiles, as wall covering in places of worship and in tombs, formed by far the greatest part of ceramic production, especially at Iznik. Other wares were apparently considered a sideline, even though decorated wares were exported not only throughout the rest of Asia Minor but also to Russia, northern Europe and Italy. (This pottery was obviously held in some regard, since copies of it were made in Italy, particularly at Padua in the late 16th century.)

**Iznik wares** The two main areas of Turkish ceramic production were Iznik and Kutahya. Iznik not only specialized in tile manufacture but also produced a wide range of other wares, including mosque lamps; large-footed bowls and basins; jugs and tankards with bulbous bodies and wide, straight necks; elegant, pear-shaped flasks and bottles with tall, slender necks knopped (swollen) at the mid-point; pen boxes; candlesticks of Venetian metal forms; cylindri-

cal tankards based on European or Balkan stitched-leather forms, onion-shaped hanging ornaments; deep dishes with barbed rims in the Chinese manner; plain bowls; saucer dishes; and flat, circular trays based on Turkish metalware.

The earliest wares, datable to c.1530, or earlier, and including the so-called Golden Horn wares, are painted in underglaze cobalt blue, sometimes with details in a runny turquoise, with scrolled foliage that resembles concentric or spiralling strings of beads. Other early designs include the extensive use of leaf-shaped reserves, zones of solid cobalt, and many foreign elements, such as highly stylized lotus flowers, scrolled Chinese-style foliage, endless knot motifs and squared scroll that resembles the Greek key (a right-angled, maze-like motif) but again probably borrowed from the Chinese.

**LUSTREWARE CAT FIGURE**
*Persia*
**12th/13th century**

Animal or human figures are rare in Islamic pottery. However, during this period a considerable number were made. (*Left*)

**LAJVARDINA BOWL**
*Persia*
**Early 14th century**

Lajvardina was among the most sumptuous wares in Persia. It is so-called because the ground was a dark blue of lapis lazuli (lajvard). Decoration is extremely intricate, based on stylized foliage or natural themes. The blue ground is painted in red, white or gold. (*Above*)

By the mid-16th century the range of colours included manganese, olive green, black and a brilliant tomato-red derived from earth saturated in iron (this pigment stands proud of the surface and is easily detectable by touch). Decorative themes from this period are largely floral, with large blooms and leaves occupying most of the available surface. The most popular plants were tulips, carnations, roses, hyacinths and heavy hydrangea-type flowers, which were probably intended to be pomegranates; and bold, saw-edged leaves were also much used. A favourite border theme, particularly on dishes with barbed rims, is the whorl pattern, a debased form of the wave pattern commonly found on 14th- and early-15th-century Chinese blue-and-white porcelain.

In the late 16th century Iznik wares were very lively, decorated with solid turquoise grounds and with panels or reserves of repeated overlapping scale. As well as the continuing repertoire of flowers, strange animals appear,

**IZNIK JUG**
*Turkey*
**16th century**

The stiff and undulating foliage is probably inspired by Chinese pottery. (*Above*)

**IZNIK BOTTLE VASE**
*Turkey*
**16th century**

The shape follows a contemporary metal form, copied in the Ming period by Chinese potters. (*Left*)

almost certainly derived from the phoenix, hare, deer and kylin (a fabulous beast) of late Ming export ware flooding out of China.

Iznik pottery is composed of a granular white body that over the years often turns brown where unprotected by glaze. This glaze, which can vary from cold white to a greenish or bluish colour, is irregularly applied and sometimes gives a streaked effect.

**Kutahya ware** These are similar to Iznik pottery but generally have a clumsier, somewhat primitive look. Almost the entire production was of tableware – jugs, ewers, flasks, mortars and dishes, many based on Ottoman metalwork forms or on European pottery.

LOOKING BACK FROM THE VANTAGE POINT OF 1820 OVER EIGHT CENTURIES OF DEVELOPMENT IN CERAMICS TECHNIQUES, THE IMPRESSIVE INGENUITY AND ADAPTABILITY OF EUROPEAN POTTERS IS STRIKING.

# EUROPEAN POTTERY

The process of producing a transparent glaze by adding lead oxide to the clay before firing had been known in Europe during Roman times. In Italy, functional wares were sometimes made non-porous by the application of a coloured lead glaze. By about 1000 Byzantine and Islamic influences became apparent with the appearance of Sgraffito decoration – that is, incising a design in a coating of slip (clay and water) to reveal the colour of the body underneath. During the Renaissance this technique was widespread. Bold abstract leaf motifs were a feature of the 15th century, becoming more representational and sketchy during the 16th.

In France, glazed tiles were being produced by the 12th century, and the technique was fairly widespread by the 14th. During the 16th century production of lead-glazed earthenware was at its height and high-quality wares were produced. Bernard Palissy (*c.*1510–*c.*1590) made extraordinary wares with a variety of mar-

**SCHNELLE**
*Siegburg*
Stoneware and pewter;
**dated 1572**

*Schnelle* were typically decorated with vertical relief bands consisting of sections stamped from separate moulds. This example depicts King David, Joshua, Hector of Troy, and scenes from the Creation story. (*Right*)

**OVAL DISH**
*School of Palissy*
Moulded lead-glazed earthenware; **17th century**

Casts of animals and foliage taken from life were used to achieve this naturalistic decoration. (*Below*)

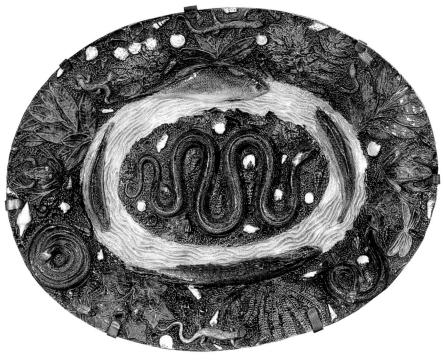

bled, coloured glazes and relief modelling of figures, foliage and small animals.

In northern Europe lead glaze was used from 900, particularly on stove tiles.

### STONEWARE

Stoneware was developed towards the end of the 14th century in Germany. It is much harder than earthenware, consisting of high-fired ground-up rock and a clay impervious to liquids. Although it does not need a glaze, it was sometimes covered in a salt glaze (produced by putting common salt in the kiln).

Some of the earliest stoneware was manufactured at Siegburg and is marked by elegant form and distinctive, light-coloured body. Siegburg's *Jakobakanne*, dating from the early 15th century, are slender jugs with a decoration of horizontal lines. By the following century they had developed into *Schnelle*, tall, elegant, pewter-covered tankards.

Cologne was an important centre of production during the 16th century, and is noted for the *Bartmannskrug* (bellarmine – a bulbous jug decorated with a bearded face). Late in the century, distinctive wares were produced at Raeren, notably somewhat cumbersome jugs with narrow feet and necks. Migrants from Siegburg to the Westerwald produced stoneware from around 1590, initially using Siegburg and Raeren moulds, though with a distinctive blue glaze. Good-quality blue stoneware was also produced from the early 16th century at Beauvais in France.

### TIN-GLAZED EARTHENWARE

Tin-glazed earthenware (earthenware with an opaque, white glaze, produced by adding tin oxide to it) dates from the 8th century, when the methods of manufacture were passed from China to the Islamic world. By the early 13th century it was being produced at Malaga in southern Spain.

The early Hispano-Moorish phase of Spanish tin-glazed earthenware has schematic or geometric decoration based on Islamic sources. During the 14th century Valencia became an important centre of production, and designs began to incorporate European Romanesque and Gothic styles. These wares were widely exported including, via Majorca (hence the term Maiolica), to Italy, where they stimulated large-scale local production. The second phase of Spanish tin-glazed earthenware, beginning during the second half of the 16th century, ironi-

**JUG (BARTMANNSKRUG)**
*Cologne*
Glazed stoneware and pewter; **early 16th century**

The bellarmine, or *Bartmannskrug*, was covered in salt glazes in shades of brown. The bearded-mask decoration probably derives from Roman pottery. (*Right*)

**JUG (BAUERNTANZKRUG)**
*Raeren*
Glazed stoneware and pewter; **dated 1597**

The *Bauerntanzkrug* derives its name from the frieze decoration of dancing peasants. (*Above*)

**JUG**
*Raeren*
Glazed stoneware and pewter; **dated 1606**

This armorial jug has the arms of the Reichsadler of Habsburg flanked by those of six of the seven electors: Pfalz, Sachsen, Brandenburg, Trier, Cologne and Mainz. (*Right*)

cally reflects the influence of Italian maiolica in its figurative, colourful, lively style.

**Italy** The earliest Italian tin-glazed earthenware dates from the 11th or 12th century and is boldly decorated in a primitive style. The early 15th century saw a period of decorative innovation, principally in Tuscany, though, in general, decoration remained subordinate to shape. Typical of this period are the two-handled drug jars with stylized oak-leaf decoration produced in Florence.

The late 15th century saw a number of innovations in Italy, such as a warmer palette and the mixing of colours, and the appearance of the *albarello* – cylindrical drug jar with a waist. Renaissance influence becomes apparent around the turn of the century, with the use of architectural backgrounds and classical, religious and historical scenes. These narrative depictions are known as the *istoriato* style, and were pioneered early in the 16th century at Faenza (hence the term faience). The *istoriato* style reached its peak around 1530 in the sumptuously painted wares of Nicola da Urbino and Francesco Xanto Avelli. The latter not only elaborately signed his works but often included

### DRUG JAR
*Florence*
Tin-glazed earthenware;
**c. 1440**

The jar's form is Italian, but its decoration of stylized oak leaves derives from the Hispano-Moresque tradition. At this early stage, decoration remained subordinate to an object's shape. (*Right*)

### BROAD-RIMMED BOWL
*Urbino*
Tin-glazed earthenware;
**c. 1520**

This is a fine example of the *istoriato* (narrative) style by Nicola da Urbino. Its subject is a woman, representing calumny, accusing an innocent prisoner. By the early 16th century decoration dominated form. (*Below*)

a fragment of text that also indicated the source for the decoration.

By the mid 16th century the *istoriato* style began to decline. The extent of colour and decoration were both limited, silver shapes were introduced and a thicker, whiter glaze was used. This new style (*compendiario*) was pioneered at Faenza around 1540, and was much imitated throughout Europe. The best examples of a pictorial style until the late 18th century come from the factory at Castelli. Its wares have a greyish palette, and heavy scrollwork and putti.

**Delftware** Italian immigrants first settled in the Netherlands in 1508 and within a few years they had begun producing tin-glazed earthenware in Antwerp. The two principal factories produced tiles and wares decorated in Italianate style. Their techniques spread to other Dutch towns, including Delft in 1584, and as far afield as England.

At the beginning of the 17th century two ships arrived in Amsterdam laden with cargoes of Chinese blue-and-white porcelain. Thereafter, in northern Europe, delftware becomes synonymous with blue-and-white earthenware. The first half of the century saw fairly close imitation of Chinese porcelain, continuing production of tiles and some remaining Italian influence, particularly in Haarlem and Rotterdam.

The greatest period of production at Delft was between about 1660 and 1730. One of its most important factories was the Greek 'A' factory, whose earliest wares, from 1675, are decorated with a deep, pure blue that closely resembles that of their Chinese originals. Towards the end of the century, designs became more elaborate, and European shapes started to appear. Under the management of Adrian

Kocks, production included large elaborate vases and cisterns, copies of Chinese Kangxi (1662–1722) wares and landscape plaques after Dutch engravings. An important technique characteristic of delftware is "trekking" – the outlining of designs in manganese underneath the glaze to heighten detail.

The Roos factory in Delft produced a series of blue-and-white plates illustrating biblical subjects with borders of clouds and cherubs. It used a rather inky blue and foliage was carefully delineated. Groups of vases to decorate cupboards were made in Chinese transitional Ming-Ch'ing style of the mid 17th century.

**Faience** Tin-glazed earthenware was made in Germany from the early 16th century, particularly in the form of stove tiles. The period of great innovation came with the settling of Dutch religious refugees in Hanau, and the founding of a faience factory there in 1661. This initially produced copies of Chinese-style delftware, but its products soon incorporated European influences. The *Vögelesdekor* pattern, consisting of scattered flowers, small dots and birds, was used to decorate wares such as the *Enghalskrug*, a bulbous narrow-necked jug. This style was also used at other German factories, such as Nuremberg and Ansbach. Another important factory was founded at Frankfurt in 1666; this produced slightly more decorative wares, based on both Chinese Wanli (1573–1620) and European designs. During the 18th century faience production became widespread in Germany.

Faience was produced in France from the 14th century, but it took the arrival of Italian immigrants in the early 16th century to stimulate large-scale production. In 1512, production began in Lyons of Italian-style wares decorated with biblical scenes based on locally published engravings, and Italian-style wares were similarly produced at Rouen from the 1520s. By the 1540s the strapwork style (interlacing bands) of the palace of Fontainebleau was also

**TULIP VASE**
*Dutch Delft, probably the Greek "A" factory*
**Tin-glazed earthenware; c. 1690**

By the 1690s the Greek "A" factory, under the directorship of Adrian Kocks, was producing wares of European baroque shape with Chinese-inspired blue-and-white decoration. Vases and cisterns of a height of more than three feet were made for the palace of William and Mary at Hampton Court. This particular example consists of three sections that fit together to form a single structure. 160 cm (64 in) high.

an influence. Rouen wares can be distinguished by their cumbersome potting, cool, sombre colours and simple motifs with heavy outlines. The second phase of Rouen dates from the late 17th century: designs based on silver shapes and decorated in a rather rigid, late Baroque style.

The most important faience factory in France was run by the Hannong family in Strasbourg. The first wares, in the 1720s, were similar to those of Rouen, but there was a dramatic change during the 1740s. The arrival of German porcelain-painters in 1748–9 led to the introduction of *petit feu* colours – colours painted on the body after an initial firing, then refired at a much lower temperature. This technique enabled very subtle colouring to be used, as opposed to the limited primary palette which resulted from only one, high-temperature firing (*grand feu* colours). *Deutsche Blumen* (German porcelain flower painting noted for its accuracy) was also introduced at this time. By the 1770s, however, flower painting was in the French-style. Strasbourg is also noted for its chinoiserie (Chinese-style decoration), finely modelled figures and animal-shaped tureens.

**DISH**
*Strasbourg*
Faience; 1750–51

This painted dish is from a service made for the Elector Clemens Augustus of Cologne. The technique of flower painting using *petit-feu* colours was adopted from porcelain manufacture. (*Right*)

**DISH**
*Rouen, Bertin workshop*
Faience; *c.* 1740

The colours, shape and decoration of this dish are typical of the emphatic Baroque phase of Rouen faience towards the end of the 17th century. This design is thought to have originated at the Guilibaud workshop. (*Below*)

THE SECRET OF MAKING PORCELAIN WAS CLOSELY GUARDED BY THE
CHINESE, BUT THE POPULARITY IN EUROPE OF ORIENTAL PORCELAIN
INEVITABLY LED TO IMITATION WHICH PRODUCED WARES OF
GREAT REFINEMENT AND CHARM.

# EUROPEAN PORCELAIN

The opening of maritime trade routes to the Far East during the 16th century led to a fashion for porcelain in Europe and stimulated numerous attempts to reproduce the material. In Florence an experimental, artificial soft-paste porcelain was produced, using powdered glass instead of the kaolin (china clay) and felspathic rock (china stone) used in true, hard-paste porcelain. Soft-paste porcelain has a more porous body, and, because of the ease with which it collapsed during firing, it tended to be thickly potted and to lack detail when compared with hard-paste.

By the late 17th century successful porcelain experiments were being carried out in France, and in 1673 a factory opened in Rouen. Very few pieces made there have survived, and attribution for those that have is complicated by their close similarity to those produced by the St Cloud factory.

### ST CLOUD
Production at St Cloud probably began during the 1690s. The porcelain produced there has a creamy body with a "wet-looking" glaze that tends to gather in hollows and soften any decoration. (In contradistinction, the ornamentation on hard-paste is crisp and precise.)

St Cloud wares generally have simple shapes and are thickly potted. The earliest decoration was nearly always in a very inky blue underglaze, with patterns of strapwork, lacework or pendants, and often with ornamental moulding or notching in imitation of silver decoration. Moulded and applied decoration, such as blossoms and leaves, was also used.

### CHANTILLY
In 1725 a factory was founded at Chantilly. For the first 10-15 years tin oxide was added to whiten the surface of the porcelain produced there, resulting in an almost opaque glaze resembling that on tin-glazed earthenware. Very simple shapes, imitating the 17th-

**"SEAU" (PAIL)**
*Chantilly*
Soft-paste porcelain;
**c. 1745**

The fascination for oriental porcelain is reflected in this simple pail. (*Right*)

**SUCRIER AND COVER**
*St Cloud*
Soft-paste porcelain; **2nd quarter 18th century**

The moulded prunus and wild cherry design is based on Chinese porcelain. (*Below*)

century Japanese Kakiemon style, were used and often mounted in silver. In 1740 the factory gradually abandoned the simple Kakiemon style in favour of more intricate sprays of flowers. The porcelain of the 1750s has a much more creamy appearance.

### MENNECY

The last established of the early French soft-paste factories was Mennecy, in 1748. It was founded under the patronage of the Duc de Villeroy and its wares bear the mark DV. The factory initially imitated Chantilly and particularly St Cloud, though by 1750 the purely French style of Vincennes-Sèvres was a greater influence. Mennecy wares are characterized by a Meissen-like colour scheme and loose flower painting. Because of a royal ban on the use of gilding, details were picked out in pink and occasionally blue. Cups with spiral reeding (raised lines) were a feature of the factory. The early production of chinoiserie figures was abandoned around mid-century in favour of figures in the Rococo style.

**COVERED BOWL AND STAND**
*Vincennes*
Soft-paste porcelain with moulded, enamel and gilded decoration; **c. 1750**

Bowls of this type were used for serving soup or broth in the boudoir, never at the dining table. The elaborate fish, shell and mushroom knop of this example suggests it was used for fish soup taken on Fridays or Holy Days. The crisp painting, delicate palette and fine moulding are typical of the factory's Rococo-style production of this date.

## FRENCH CERAMICS MANUFACTURERS TO 1820

| | | |
|---|---|---|
| **ROUEN** | 1520s–c. 1800 | Faience. Italian-style wares during the 1520s. By late 17th century, silver shapes decorated in Baroque style. |
| **NEVERS** | 1588– | Faience. Early wares in Italian style, later mixing of European and Chinese styles and shapes. |
| **STRASBOURG** | 1721–81 | Faience. Rococo-style wares with beautiful flower painting in *petit-feu* colours from the late 1740s. |
| **ROUEN** | 1673–c. 1700 | Very rare soft-paste porcelain. Similar to St Cloud. |
| **ST CLOUD** | 1690s–1766 | Soft-paste porcelain. Thickly potted, simple wares based on European silver or Chinese shapes. |
| **CHANTILLY** | 1725–c. 1800 | Soft-paste porcelain. Tin-oxide initially added to whiten the glaze. Until c. 1740 wares based on Japanese Kakiemon decoration, then European flowers. |
| **MENNECY** | 1734–1806 | Soft-paste porcelain. Early wares similar to St Cloud; by 1750 influence of Vincennes/Sèvres. Chinoiserie and European figures. |

## VINCENNES/SÈVRES

The Sèvres porcelain factory began as a modest workshop in the royal château of Vincennes in 1740. It was set up by a crown servant, Orry de Fulvy (1703–51), with the express purpose of improving both the quality and quantity of French porcelain. Key figures, Jean-Claude Duplessis (c.1695–1774) and Jean-Jacques Bachelier (1724–1806) arrived at Vincennes in 1748 and c.1750 respectively. Duplessis, a bronze-founder and goldsmith, was appointed the first artistic director and was responsible for the design of models. Bachelier, an artist, also held the title of artistic director from 1751 and was put in charge of the painters' workshop.

After de Fulvy's death in 1751 there followed a period of financial and political manoeuvring. Although during this time the company was selling more and more porcelain, it continued to operate at a loss. Its rapid expansion led it to move to a new site at Sèvres, south-west of Paris, where production began in 1756. Nevertheless, its financial situation continued to deteriorate, and in 1759 Louis XV bought the factory outright, and it remained Crown property until the Revolution.

**Painting and moulding at Vincennes** Because pieces were not marked, none can be firmly attributed before 1745. By the late 1740s table and tea wares, vases, flower and powder pots were all in production at Vincennes, the designs mostly based on Meissen. Although it can be difficult to distinguish early Vincennes from the products of other French soft-paste factories, it is easily distinguishable from hard-paste Meissen – in particular by the greater crispness and delicacy of its Meissen-style flower painting.

By c.1750 Duplessis had added many inventive new shapes and relief patterns – derived from rococo natural motifs and silver and pewter shapes – to the production at Vincennes.

**Figures and gilding at Vincennes** By the late 1740s a great variety of figures was being produced. Vincennes was unable to match the exquisitely painted Meissen figures, as the nature of the paste made glaze application difficult. To remedy this, Bachelier introduced biscuit porcelain; the first examples – children, animals, and reclining figures – appeared in 1751. The decorative painter François Boucher (1703–77) was an important source of designs.

In 1748 the secret of gilding porcelain was acquired at Vincennes and from 1749 it was commonly used on the more expensive pieces, often being built up in layers and carefully tooled to give additional richness. Gilding patterns included *caillouté* (pebble), *vermiculé* (worm-tunnel) and *mouches d'or* (gold spot).

**Ground colours at Vincennes/Sèvres** An important development at Vincennes/Sèvres dates from 1752, when the first ground colour, an underglaze blue (known as *bleu lapis*, after its resemblance to lapis lazuli) was introduced. A combination of dark-blue grounds and reserves (plain areas) edged with gilding and filled with gilded or painted birds is characteristic of late Vincennes. *Bleu lapis* was replaced in 1763 by an overglaze blue, *bleu nouveau*, which does not have the cloudiness of the underglaze blue.

Overglaze pink, turquoise, green and yellow grounds were added to the repertoire during the 1750s. These are seen to best effect on ornamental, pot-pourri and flower vases.

**Enamel painting at Sèvres** By the mid-1750s the emphasis had shifted to exuberant rococo forms with detailed enamel painting. Exotic birds, flower sprigs, chinoiserie, children and cherubs (again after Boucher) are the most common subjects.

The practice of filling reserves completely, in

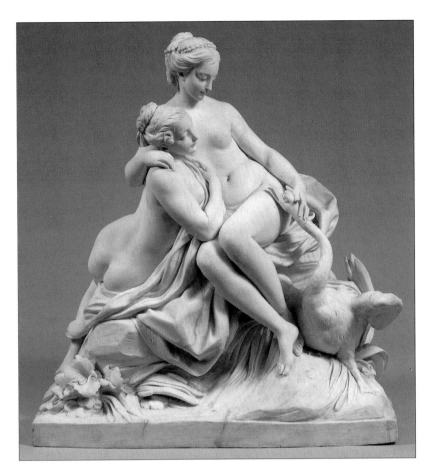

**LEDA AND THE SWAN**
*Sèvres*
Soft-paste biscuit porcelain;
**c. 1765**

A wide range of figure groups was produced in biscuit porcelain by the factory during the 1760s and 1770s. The unglazed, fired porcelain figures imitate free-standing marble sculpture, although they were actually cast in a series of plaster moulds. Mythological subjects were always popular, and this model was designed by Etienne-Maurice Falconnet after a painting by François Boucher. Falconnet was director of sculpture at the Sèvres factory from 1757–66.

the manner of miniature paintings, was common by the late 1750s. Especially popular were 17th-century Dutch peasant scenes borrowed from engravings after Teniers, Boucher pastoral subjects and military and harbour scenes.

**Neo-Classicism at Sèvres** In the late 1750s newly-fashionable Neo-Classical patterns, such as the Greek key (a maze-like pattern) and Vitruvian scrolls (repeated wave-like scrolls), were incorporated into rococo decorative schemes. And from 1763, new, sculptural porcelain with blue grounds and elaborate gilding showed the factory responding increasingly to avant-garde Neo-Classical taste. A manifestation of this in the 1770s and 1780s was the mounting of plain blue-ground vase bodies in gilt-bronze. A lighter version of Louis XVI taste can be seen in the porcelain plaques with floral decoration mounted in furniture of the period.

In the 1780s the prevalent Neo-Classical taste in the arts was refined under the influence of further archaeological discoveries at Herculaneum in Italy. Antiquity was clearly the source for two new services created for Queen Marie Antoinette: the "arabesque" decorated service designed by the architect Louis Le Masson c.1782 and the service for her dairy at Rambouillet designed by Jean-Jacques Lagrenée (1739–1821) in 1788.

**Hard-paste porcelain at Sèvres** Hard-paste porcelain was produced at Sèvres from c.1769. It proved much easier to manufacture than soft-paste, which was particularly susceptible to fluctuations in kiln temperature. However, the

factory was unable to apply the ground colours for which it was noted to hard-paste porcelain. Examples from the 1770s are usually white with elaborate gilding and enamel decoration. By the 1780s, however, new ground colours applicable to hard-paste, were developed. Because of the difficulty of applying ground colours to hard-paste, soft-paste production continued until 1804. Hard-paste Sèvres has a crown mark painted above the crossed *L*s of Louis XV's cipher.

**Marks at Vincennes/Sèvres** In 1753, when Louis XV owned a quarter-share of the factory at Vincennes, it was officially granted permission to call itself a *Manufacture Royale* and to use the crossed *L*s of the king's cipher as its mark (it had, in fact, been using the *L*s unofficially for some years). From 1753 date-letters were used with the *L*s, usually being placed between them. Beginning with *A* in 1753, these date-letters continue to the end of the alphabet (excluding

*W*), ending in 1777. Then a double-letter sequence starts in 1778 and ends with *qq* in July 1793, when the letters *RF* for *République Française* and the name *Sèvres* replace all previous marks until 1800.

The marks are usually painted over the glaze on the base of pieces. Painters' and gilders' marks, in the form of a symbol or letter, are also often painted above or below the *L*s. Many have been identified through reference to factory records. The absence of painted marks by no means excludes the possibility of a piece having been made at Vincennes or Sèvres: many pieces received no marks.

Incised symbols or letters, can often be found under the glaze on the base of Sèvres pieces. These identify moulders, throwers or modellers. Unlike painted marks, incised marks cannot be faked, and provide a secure way of attributing a porcelain body. But they are an unreliable guide to decoration because large quantities of Sèvres porcelain were later redecorated.

Another distinguishing feature of all saucers, shallow bowls, plates and trays produced at Vincennes/Sèvres after 1752 is a small hole in the inside of the foot-rim. This enabled the pieces to be hung from a metal spike in the kiln during enamel firing.

## MEISSEN

Experiments into the production of true, hard-paste porcelain were carried out in Germany during the late 17th century – at the behest of

Augustus the Strong, Elector of Saxony – by Count Ehrenfried Walter von Tschirnhausen (1651–1708) and the alchemist J. F. Böttger (1682–1719); and the porcelain was successfully produced by 1708–9.

In 1710 Augustus founded a ceramics factory at Meissen, near Dresden. Its first years are noted for the production of an extremely hard, dark reddish-brown stoneware known as Böttger stoneware. This was produced only until about 1717–18 and is avidly sought by collectors. The main output was wares modelled after Chinese originals (particularly Yixing ware), and after European baroque glass and silver shapes (an important modeller of wares based on silverwork was J. Irminger).

The earliest Meissen porcelain (termed *Böttgerporzellan*) has a rather creamy look, the colour of dirty ivory, and a thick, fizzy glaze. Shapes either replicate those of the stoneware or are based on Chinese originals. Most wares were left undecorated.

The 1720s and early 1730s saw the dominance of colourists at Meissen, of whom the most important was J. G. Höroldt. He introduced a new palette of bright colours, including iron red, rose-purple, turquoise and a yellowish leaf-green, and is best known for his distinctive style of chinoiserie – imaginative scenes of Chinese figures generally set within elaborate Baroque cartouches (shields or tablets) of leaves and strapwork. These were often filled with a pinkish-brown colour that has a slight sheen known as Böttger lustre.

Meissen ware is marked by a white, glassy body (unglazed areas have a chalky appearance),

**PLATE**
*Sèvres*
Hard-paste porcelain with enamel decoration; **1784**

This plate forms part of the Arabesque service, commissioned in 1782 by Louis XVI for Marie-Antoinette and designed by Louis Le Masson. Its avant-garde decoration is based on the newly excavated frescoes at Pompeii. The service was completed in 1787, but never delivered to Marie-Antoinette. (*Left*)

**TEAPOT**
*Meissen*
Böttger stoneware and silver; **1710–12**

This extremely rare example is decorated with *Muschelschliff*, cut and highly polished concave facets. Gem cutting and polishing had been a leading industry in Saxony since the late 16th century. It was revived by Böttger in 1710 at the instruction of Augustus the Strong. (*Below*)

and, in its decoration, a greyish, milky turquoise, a very clean yellow and sharply outlined painting. A favourite decorative motif was a highly stylized, brilliantly coloured, linear form of flower-painting (based on oriental sources) known as *indianische Blumen*. Coloured grounds were introduced in 1726–7 and experiments using underglaze blue were conducted from 1721.

The early 1730s saw a shift towards European subjects for decoration and during the early *indianische Blumen* were abandoned in favour of more naturalistic, European flowers (*deutsche Blumen*). In the 1740s there was also an increased reliance on French sources (Watteau, Greuze and Pater), continuing naturalism (particularly in flower painting, which became looser by the 1750s – as *Manierblumen*) and the use of battle scenes.

In 1756 Meissen was occupied by the Prussians during the Seven Years War and, although the factory recommended production in 1763, it never regained its pre-eminence. In the late 18th century wares were decorated in a Neo-Classical style copied from Sèvres.

**Modellers** After the dominance of the colourists at Meissen in the 1720s, the modellers came to the fore in the 1730s. The greatest was J. J. Kändler (1706–75). He began by modelling small animals from life, and by 1735 had progressed to the decoration of services and figures. The 1,000-piece Swan Service, the most important and magnificent service of the 18th century, was one of his masterpieces, created with the assistance of J. F. Eberlein. Kändler created over 900 models before his death. Perhaps the most famous were his series of *commedia dell'arte* (Italian Comedy) figures. His figures of the 1730s, painted in strong colours, were the most markedly baroque. During the late 1740s gilt-edged rococo scroll bases started to appear on his work, as did the famous "crinoline" group – figures of ladies with huge skirts. Kändler was reluctant to make concessions to the Rococo or to Neo-Classical styles, but models from the 1750s on do exhibit much paler colours and plain bases appear during the early 1770s. Among other Meissen modellers, F. E. Meyer (1723–85), is noted for his oddly proportioned figures of orientals playing instruments and his plump putti.

DU PAQUIER AND VIENNA
A porcelain factory was founded in Vienna by Claude du Paquier, a court official, and began

**FIGURE**
*Meissen*
Hard-paste porcelain;
**c. 1740**

This magnificent Harlequin was modelled by J. J. Kändler. The strong colours and sense of containment and stability exemplify the Baroque style of which Kändler was the greatest exponent. (*Left*)

**TEA AND COFFEE SERVICE**
*Meissen*
Hard-paste porcelain;
**1723–4**

Each piece is painted with chinoiserie scenes in the manner of J. G. Höroldt. He kept a sketchbook filled with such scenes as a source for the factory painters who imitated his style. The gold cartouches are typical of early Meissen. (*Below*)

production in 1719. Its wares are marked by the smoky hue of the body, as distinct from the creamy white of early Meissen. Early wares were principally based on Baroque silver shapes, often far more exaggerated or unusual than those of Meissen. Decorative styles relied heavily on foliar motifs, strapwork, trellis work and puce or iron-red monochrome decoration. Taken over by the State in 1744, the factory introduced large-scale figure production three years later. From about 1765 decorative styles were copied from Sèvres, and from 1784 wares were produced in Neo-Classical style.

**BOWL AND COVER**
*Du Paquier*
**Hard-paste porcelain;
c. 1725**

This linear style of black monochrome decoration, known as *Schwarzlot*, is typical of the Du Paquier factory. Here it is heightened with gilding. The angular handles, based on metalwork forms, are also characteristics of the factory. (*Left*)

# NORTH EUROPEAN MANUFACTURERS TO 1820

| | | |
|---|---|---|
| **SIEGBURG** | early 15th century–1630s | Elegant white-bodied stoneware such as the *Schnelle*, with crisply moulded decoration. |
| **RAEREN** | 16th century–1630s | Stoneware with brown or blue glaze; jugs with moulded frieze decoration. |
| **COLOGNE** | 16th century | Stoneware with glaze in shades of brown; bulbous jugs with moulded mask of a bearded man (*Bartmannskrug*). |
| **FRANKFURT** | 1662–1772 | Faience initially after Chinese blue and white, later with European subjects. |
| **MEISSEN** | 1710–63 | *Böttger* stoneware and hard-paste porcelain, chinoiserie decoration, flower painting (*indianische Blumen and deutsche Blumen*), harbour scenes, Watteau subjects, figures and groups. |
| | 1763–74 (Academic phase) | Rococo and Neo-Classical wares and figures. |
| | 1774–1814 (Marcolini period) | Mostly Neo-Classical wares and some figures. |
| **VIENNA** | 1719–44 (Du Paquier period) | Hard-paste porcelain. Exaggerated baroque silver shapes and decoration. |
| | 1744–1864 (State period) | Large-scale figure production, wares in French rococo and Neo-Classical style. |
| **HÖCHST** | 1746–96 | Hard-paste porcelain. Rococo figure groups based on sentimental subjects after artists such as Boucher. |
| **NYMPHENBURG** | 1747– | Hard-paste porcelain. Rococo figures by F.A. Bustelli, high-quality flower painting. |
| **FÜRSTENBERG** | 1753– | Hard-paste porcelain. Figures of miners and from the Italian Comedy, wares painted with flowers, birds and landscapes. |
| **LUDWIGSBURG** | 1759–1824 | Hard-paste porcelain. Simple, charming figures, rococo wares decorated with flowers. |
| **BERLIN** | 1751–7 (Wegely period) | Hard-paste porcelain. Figures, often in white. |
| | 1761–3 (Gotzkowsky period) | |
| | 1763– (State period) | Magnificent dinner services, high quality flower and landscape painting Neo-Classical style. |
| **FULDA** | 1764–89 | Hard-paste porcelain. Rococo tablewares with decoration copied from Meissen. |
| **ZURICH** | 1763–90 | Soft-paste 1763–5. Hard-paste 1765 onwards. Naive, rococo figures, wares with figures in landscapes and good flower painting. |
| **NYON** | c. 1780–1813 | Hard-paste porcelain. Wares in contemporary French style. |

## HÖCHST

Serious production had begun at Höchst in Germany by the early 1750s. The earliest pieces have a greyish, porous body covered by a white, fairly opaque glaze and tend to be heavily potted. By about 1753 finer models were being produced with hollowed bases, and rococo scrollwork and colours were introduced. Of this early period the most notable works are the series of *commedia dell'arte* figures, probably modelled by Simon Feilner.

By the early 1760s French taste had come to predominate, typified by the production of rather sentimental subjects – chiefly the work of Laurentius Russinger, master modeller between 1762 and 1767, and his successor, Johann Peter Melchior.

## NYMPHENBURG

Another German factory to commence production during the 1740s was that of Prince Maximilian II Joseph of Bavaria at Nymphenburg. Early Nymphenburg production was not of great quality, but around the mid-1750s brilliantly decorated wares that sometimes rank with the best Meissen were produced. The factory is, however, most famous for its figures, principally those modelled between 1754 and his death by Franz Anton Bustelli (1705–63), who epitomizes the rococo taste of the mid 18th century. His figures are characterized by exaggerated, elegant poses and embody graceful movement; the best-known are a set of 16 *commedia dell'arte* figures. His earlier work is more boldly coloured than his later output.

## FÜRSTENBERG

The Fürstenberg factory began producing porcelain in 1753. The earliest material, characterized by a grey body and yellowish, sometimes black-speckled glaze, was not successful. Even so, at least two noteworthy series of figures were produced during this time by Simon Feilner who arrived from Höchst in 1753: *commedia dell'arte* figures (1754) and miners (1757). After 1770 paste and glaze improved, and during the mid-1770s smaller versions of the earlier figures were reissued. Later, the factory is notable for its biscuit (unglazed) wares.

## FRANKENTHAL

In 1754 Louis XV issued an edict which forbade any competition against his porcelain factory

**FIGURE GROUP**
*Zürich*
Hard-paste porcelain;
**c. 1770**

Two lovers representing Summer comprise this rare allegorical group. The naïve modelling and pale colours are typical of the Zürich factory. (*Left*)

**FIGURE GROUP**
*Frankenthal*
Hard-paste porcelain;
**c. 1770**

This group is one of two versions of "The Good Mother" modelled by C. G. Lück and based on an engraving after Jean-Baptiste Greuze's painting, *La Mère de Famille*. (*Centre*)

**FIGURE GROUP**
*Höchst*
Hard-paste porcelain;
**c. 1770**

This rare group of Amythas and Sylvia was originally modelled in 1760–65 by Laurentius Russinger and remodelled by J. P. Melchior in 1770. (*Below*)

itself to modelling, and Ludwigsburg is best-known for its appealing, rather naïve rococo figures. Pastel colours were used up until *c.*1770, after which time they were to become progressively stronger.

### WEGELY AND BERLIN

The manufacture of porcelain at Berlin began in 1751 with the granting of a monopoly to Wilhelm Kaspar Wegely by Frederick the Great. The factory lasted only six years, and Wegely porcelain which has a good white body with a thin glaze, is fairly rare. A range of figures, including tradesmen, peasants and birds, were produced, often left uncoloured. Service wares were decorated with some colours, good gilding and a rare use of underglaze blue.

From 1761 to 1763 the factory was run by Johann Ernst Gotzkowsky and produced a slightly greyish, speckled porcelain bearing a G mark. Surviving examples have often been decorated at a later date. In 1763 the State assumed control of the factory, and for the rest of the century it was best-known for its magnificent dinner services. The material was very white (but after about 1771 acquired a slight bluish

at Vincennes, thereby compelling Charles-François Hannong to move his fledgling porcelain factory from Strasbourg to Frankenthal in Germany. The factory is best-known for its figures but also produced excellent service wares. Its porcelain had a creamy, soft white, sometimes yellowish-tinged glaze, but its quality declined from 1774. The often complex groups of figures exemplify the rococo taste of the period.

The most skilled modeller was K. G. Lück, (d. 1775) who from *c.*1756 to 1775 produced hunting groups, Chinese figures and everyday scenes. Wares were also decorated in Rococo style until *c.*1770, when Sèvres style tended to predominate.

### LUDWIGSBURG

One of the last of the larger German factories to commence producing porcelain was that of the Duke of Württemberg at Ludwigsburg in 1759. Its smoky-greyish, sometimes unevenly glazed porcelain is not of the highest quality but lent

**FIGURE OF A MUSICIAN**
*Ludwigsburg*
Hard-paste porcelain;
*c.* **1765**

The musician is one of a series of seven modelled by the Württemberg Court sculptor, Christian Wilhelm Beyer (1725–1806), and considered among his best work. The soft pastel colours, painted by D. Chr. Sausenhofer (*c.* 1727–1802), and the somewhat naïve modelling are characteristic of the Rococo-style figures produced by the Ludwigsburg factory during the 1760s.

tinge) and was skilfully decorated with *deutsche Blumen*, landscapes, and figures. From the mid-1760s the Sèvres factory was an influence, and after 1780 the antique style was fashionable. Figures were also produced, notably by F. E. Meyer, but they are of an inferior quality to his Meissen work.

## FULDA

From 1764 to 1789 a porcelain factory operated at Fulda, producing chiefly rococo wares and figures. The decorative styles of the pieces were copied from Meissen. The best figures, produced during the first 10 years by Wenzel Neu, bear a resemblance to those of the Höchst factory. Best-known today are the figures of the Fulda court orchestra and the *Cris de Paris* series by G. L. Bartolème.

## THURINGIAN FACTORIES

A number of factories began producing porcelain during the early 1760s in Thüringia. Their wares are generally characterized by a greyish, sometimes coarse porcelain and a provincial style of decoration copied mostly from Meissen. Those of Kloster-Veilsdorf are made of a fine, white paste; the best-known are *commedia dell'arte* figures of the 1760s, which have been attributed to Wenzel Neu.

## ZÜRICH AND NYON

A factory was founded near Zürich in 1763. Initially, it produced soft-paste porcelain but by 1765 it had switched to hard-paste. The wares have a distinctive smoky greenish-grey tone and a fairly thick, fizzy glaze. Those decorated in typical rococo style of the 1760s, with a "floating" landscape, are most common; but naturalistic flower painting of exceptional virtuosity was also a speciality of the factory. A large range of charming, mostly small-scale, uncomplicated figures was produced and is very popular with

collectors. Wares produced at the Swiss town of Nyon from *c.*1780 have a much whiter body than those from Zürich and are decorated in contemporary French style.

## DUTCH PORCELAIN

A factory was started at Weesp in 1757 and from 1759 produced hard-paste porcelain in contemporary European style. In 1771 the factory moved to Oude Loosdrecht and during the

**TEA AND COFFEE SERVICE**
*Wegely (Berlin)*
Hard-paste porcelain;
**1751–7**

A very rare example of a service, each piece has moulded decoration of oriental flower sprays.
*(Above)*

## NETHERLANDS CERAMICS MANUFACTURERS TO 1820

| | | |
|---|---|---|
| **ANTWERP** | 16th century | Tin-glazed earthenware decorated in Italian style. |
| **DELFT** | early 17th century onwards | Delftware, initially based on Chinese late Ming blue and white wares, then incorporating European subjects and shapes, and by the early 18th century, enamel colours. |
| **WEESP** | 1757–71 | Hard-paste porcelain. |
| **OUDE LOOSDRECHT** | 1771–82 | Good-quality flower painting, distinctive brown monochrome decoration. |
| **AMSTEL** | 1782–1820 | |
| **THE HAGUE** | 1776–90 | Hard-paste porcelain in the style of the Tournai factory. |

early 1780s to Amstel. Peasant scenes were a favourite subject for decoration, sometimes in a distinctive brown palette, and the factory produced very high-quality flower-painting.

In 1776 a factory was started at The Hague. It initially decorated Tournai porcelain, then produced wares in a similar style until its closure in 1790.

### SCANDINAVIAN FACTORIES

**Denmark** Soft-paste porcelain in the French style was produced at Copenhagen from 1759 by Louis Fournier, who had previously been at Vincennes and Chantilly. The main production of the factory was of tableware, usually decorated with flowers and, later, fruits, with restrained use of gilding.

In 1775 F. H. Müller founded a hard-paste factory in Copenhagen, employing staff from Meissen, Berlin and Fürstenberg. The factory was taken over by the King in 1779. The

earliest products had a greyish-blue tone and were decorated in underglaze blue. Silhouetted portrait heads and historical scenes were popular during the 1780s. Flower painting was also practised, the most famous example being on the *Flora Danica* service begun in 1789.

**Sweden** A soft-paste porcelain factory was founded at Marieberg in 1759, but it was not until the arrival of Pierre Berthevin as manager from Mennecy in 1776 that production began on a large scale. The porcelain closely resembled that of Mennecy in its creamy body and style of flower decoration. A spirally-fluted custard cup was a much-used shape. Hard-paste porcelain was briefly produced 1777–1782, the year of the factory's closure.

### ITALIAN PORCELAIN

Grand Duke Francesco I de' Medici is credited with instigating the first successful production of porcelain in Europe. His experimental factory operated in Florence from *c*.1575 to 1587, and about 64 examples of its output are known today. These various soft-paste ornamental objects are generally based on contemporary stoneware or metalwork shapes. A distinctive underglaze blue, sometimes edged in manganese, was used to decorate wares, which were often based on Near Eastern designs. The thick, fizzy glaze gives the blue a soft, unfocused look.

**Venice** The first Venetian factory was operated from 1720 to 1727 by Francesco Vezzi and C. C. Hunger of Meissen. In common with early Meissen, Vezzi material was sometimes creamy white, sometimes rather greyish, and it was fairly thinly potted. The factory produced mostly tableware – including a distinctive eight-sided teapot – with moulded decoration based on Baroque silver design. Painted subjects ranged from flowers to figures and were in strong reds, yellows and greens.

A much larger factory founded in Venice in

**A SOLITAIRE**
*Berlin*
Hard-paste porcelain;
*c.* **1764**

Each piece is painted with pairs of lovers, probably after Watteau, a favourite source for the factory.
(*Below*)

## SCANDINAVIAN CERAMICS MANUFACTURERS TO 1820

| **COPENHAGEN** | 1759–65 | Soft-paste tablewares in French style. |
|---|---|---|
| **COPENHAGEN** | 1775–9 | Hard-paste porcelain. Early wares based on German styles, later on Neo-Classical. |
| | 1779– | Good flower painting. |
| | (Royal Copenhagen) | |
| **MARIEBERG** | 1759–77 | Soft-paste. |
| | 1777–82 | Hard-paste. Early wares similar to Mennecy. |

1764 by G. Cozzi produced hard-paste porcelain with a greyish body. Designs were initially derived from German rococo porcelain and later incorporated Neo-Classical styles. Painted subjects included flowers, figures and landscapes. Figures, many of them left unpainted, included the *commedia dell'arte*, peasants and mythological scenes.

**Doccia** The Marchese Carlo Ginori founded a factory at Doccia, near Florence, in 1735, and it began sales to the public in 1746. Before *c.*1770 the paste was very grey and coarse with a smeared glaze; then a tin oxide was added to the glaze making it whiter. Most common are wares of the 1740s, which are sculptural, baroque and decorated in strong colours. Flesh tints were stippled in a very distinctive manner. Painted subjects included figures, landscapes and stylized Chinese-style fighting cocks. Among the figures were *commedia dell'arte*, contemporary and classical subjects.

**Capodimonte** This most famous of Italian factories, founded by Charles IV, King of Naples, in 1743 at Capodimonte, in Naples, produced an attractive, translucent soft-paste porcelain. The chief modeller was Giuseppe Gricci (d. 1770), who produced superbly modelled figures based on contemporary subjects and the *commedia dell'arte* and created the magnificent chinoiserie porcelain rooms of the palaces of Portici near Naples (1757–9) and Aranjuez, south of Madrid, in Spain (1763–5). In 1759 Charles IV succeeded his father to the Spanish throne and moved the factory to Buen Retiro near Madrid. The body of the Spanish porcelain is yellower than the Italian and resembles creamware.

Ferdinand IV revived porcelain manufacture in Naples in 1771, and the factory produced wares and figures in the then fashionable Neo-Classical style.

**PAIR OF FIGURES**
*Doccia*
**Hard-paste porcelain;**
**c. 1760**

These striking black and gold figures depict Scaramouche and Ragonda from the commedia dell'arte. (*Left*)

**FIGURE GROUP**
*Capodimonte*
**Soft-paste porcelain;**
**c. 1750**

Titled "The Rabbit Catchers", this group was modelled by Giuseppe Gricci. (*Top left*)

## ITALIAN PORCELAIN MANUFACTURERS

| | | |
|---|---|---|
| **MEDICI (Florence)** | 1575–87 | Extremely rare soft-paste porcelain. Underglaze blue decoration. |
| **VEZZI (Venice)** | 1720–27 | Hard-paste porcelain. Tableware decorated after baroque silver design. |
| **COZZI (Venice)** | 1764–1812 | Hard-paste porcelain. Rococo wares based on German porcelain, later in Neo-Classical style. |
| **DOCCIA** | 1746– | Hard-paste porcelain. Tablewares in Baroque style with strong colours. Figures from the Italian Comedy, contemporary and classical subjects. |
| **CAPODIMONTE** | 1743–59 (Sicily) 1759–1803 (Spain) | Soft-paste porcelain. Figures based on the Italian Comedy and contemporary subjects. The chinoiserie porcelain rooms of the palaces of Portici and Aranjuez. |
| **NAPLES** | 1771–1806 | Soft-paste porcelain. Wares and figures in Neo-Classical style. |

## PORCELAIN MARKS

The practice of regularly marking ceramics with the symbol of the factory began in Europe with porcelain produced at Meissen during the early 1720s. In imitation of the Chinese practice, marks were generally placed on the underside of the foot or base of the object. They could be painted under or over the glaze, or incised or impressed with a stamp into the clay. Marking was not compulsory for most of the 18th century, and factory marks alone are not necessarily a reliable guide to date and origin. Not all pieces were marked, and many marks, such as the crossed swords of the Meissen factory, were widely imitated, and have been convincingly forged. In addition to the mark of the factory, the numbers or symbols of modellers, painters and gilders are often marked, and more rarely, the date and signature of the artist.

1 Cozzi
2 Naples
3 Florence (Medici)
4 Capodimonte
5 Doccia
6 Marieberg
7 Copenhagen (1760–6)
8 Copenhagen (1775–1801)
9 The Hague
10 Oude Loosdrecht
11 Weesp
12 Meissen (1723–63)
13 Meissen (1763–74)
14 Meissen (1774–1814)
15 Nymphenburg
16 Ludwigsburg
17 Höchst (1750)
18 Höchst (1765–74)
19 Fürstenberg
20 Fulda (1765–80)
21 Fulda (1781–9)
22 Frankenthal
23 Wegely (Berlin)
24 Berlin
25 Vienna
26 Nyon
27 Zurich
28 St Cloud
29 Chantilly
30 Mennecy

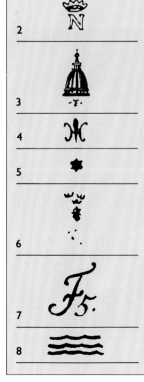

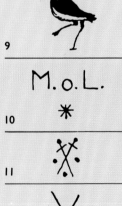

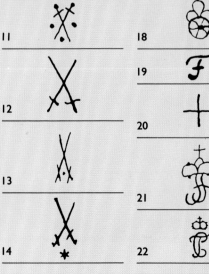

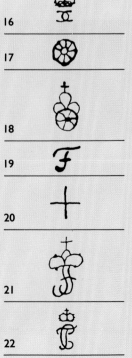

DURING THE 18TH CENTURY THE BRITISH CERAMICS INDUSTRY ENTERED
AN ERA OF CREATIVE DEVELOPMENT AS INVENTIVE CRAFTSMEN PRODUCED
WARES THAT HAVE PROVED ENDURINGLY POPULAR.

# BRITISH CERAMICS TO 1820

From humble origins British ceramic art developed into a thriving industry competing with, and finally excelling, wares produced in continental Europe and the Orient. Initially, the British potter concentrated on producing simple forms for basic day-to-day use. During the late medieval period (the 10th to the 15th century) common, coarse earthenware clays were employed, kilns and workshops being erected wherever suitable clay beds were found. Lead glazes (transparent or translucent glazes) were developed to counteract the porous nature of the clay and as a decorative device.

As British taste became more refined over the centuries and as British decorative arts followed changing European styles – Baroque (the late 16th to the early 18th century), Rococo (*c.*1720–60), Neo-Classical (*c.*1765–1804) and Empire (1804–*c.*1825) – so potters were forced to develop their skills and business acumen. Tin-glazed (opaque-white-glazed) wares began to be produced in the late 16th century by immigrant Flemish potters, and by the beginning of the next century fine-quality Chinese "hard-paste" porcelain (kaolinic porcelain fired at a temperature of 1300-1400°C) reached Britain. Hard-paste porcelain proved immensely popular. Durable, high-fired (1200–1400°C) German stoneware flooded into the country and by the end of the 17th century patents for its manufacture were being taken out.

Initially, in Britain, a fairly opaque "soft-paste" porcelain (imitation porcelain fired at *c.*1100°C) was manufactured; then came innumerable changes to the porcelain formulae until eventually translucent "hard-paste" porcelain was produced by William Cookworthy (1705–80) in 1768. Bone china (a paste incor-

**GROUP OF JUGS**
*Nottingham*
Partially glazed earthenware; **13th to 15th centuries**

Excavated during rebuilding work in Nottingham, the jugs are therefore attributed geographically, as well as stylistically, to the Nottingham area. These are typical examples of the unpretentious pottery vessels produced during the late medieval period.

# BRITISH POTTERY MANUFACTURERS

| | | | |
|---|---|---|---|
| **TOFT, family** | 17th century | Staffordshire | Domestic items in white "pipe-clay" and slip decoration. |
| **ELERS, John and David** | *fl. c.*1690-98 | London and Staffordshire | Red stoneware displaying high-quality craftsmanship. |
| **MALKIN, Samuel** | early 18th century | Staffordshire | Items with press-moulded detail filled with coloured slip. |
| **WHIELDON, Thomas** | 1719-95 | Staffordshire | Experimented with clays and glazes. |
| **WEDGWOOD, Josiah** | 1730-95 | Staffordshire | Experimented with clay refinement to produce a high-quality medium. Production included Jasperware, Queen's ware (creamware), and a large variety of stoneware. |
| **WOOD, family** | 1730s-1840s | Burslem | Earthenware ornamental figures and Toby jugs. |
| **PRATT, family** | 1730s-1830s | Staffordshire | Earthenware with distinctive glazes and bright underglazes. |

porating bone ash) was introduced at Bow in 1749 and standardized by Josiah Spode II (1754–1827).

Meanwhile, entrepreneurial potters like Josiah Wedgwood (1730–95) experimented with clay refinement and produced a lightweight medium that could be cast and moulded to a quality that competed with porcelain and tin-glazed wares. By the early 19th century manufacture of the latter in Britain had ceased.

### THE MIDDLE AGES

The earthenware vessels produced in Britain during the medieval period are marked by the unaffected simplicity and practicality of their form. The level of workmanship on them, however, is generally inferior to that on wares made during the Roman occupation.

Medieval forms were to influence the late 19th- and early 20th-century studio potters who drew inspiration from their simplicity. Medieval potters did, however, "show off" occasionally, producing some fascinating – and now expensive – jugs modelled with freehand reliefs of knights and beasts, and aquamaniles (water ewers) in the form of animals.

From the early 13th to the late 16th century reddish-brown earthenware tiles were used to pave floors in important buildings. Patterns were produced by mechanically stamping the "leather-hard" (hard enough to carve but not brittle) tiles and often filling the sunken areas with white slip (semi-liquid clay). Finished with a translucent lead glaze, the pattern stood out in

**JUG**
*Coventry*
Lead-glazed earthenware;
**13th–14th century**

Excavated in Coventry, this vessel displays the applied clay ornament technique predominant on medieval London and Midlands wares. The buff, sandy body has a mottled copper-green translucent glaze and the surface is decorated with hand-worked stylized branches with button-like pellet buds. The base is thumb-pressed all around, giving a "pie-crust" effect. A common decorative feature on medieval jugs, this also served to prevent the vessel from rocking on a flat surface as bases generally were slightly convex.

warm yellow against the dark background. Such tiles normally appear for sale only in small quantities, often individually; they are usually very worn, with indistinct patterns. Occasionally lightly-trodden, fresh-looking tiles become available – but at a high price.

### THE 17TH CENTURY

In the early 16th century, Italian maiolica (tin-glazed earthenware) had spread throughout Europe, potters everywhere seizing with enthusiasm on its opaque white glaze, which offered such a fine surface for richly coloured decoration. Tin-glazed earthenware production reached Britain in the mid 16th century via Antwerp in Flanders, when two sons of Guido da Savino (d. 1541), an Italian master potter working in Antwerp, came to England with Jacob Jansen (d. 1593) and set up a manufactory there. By the early 17th century production was on a large scale, mainly in London but also in Bristol and neighbouring Brislington.

Referred to in Britain as delftware (after the Dutch city of Delft), tin-glazed earthenware appealed to wealthy landowners and the urban middle classes. As well as providing a wide range of useful vessels, 17th-century "gallypotters", as tin-glaze potters were known (after the Dutch *geleyerspotbacker*), also produced boldly decorated chargers (large, shallow dishes) depicting royalty, fruit, flowers and religious themes for display purposes. Often the rims of such chargers were bordered with blue dashes, with a varying degree of control.

**Slipware** Alongside the development of tin-glazed pottery came refinements to wares decorated with slip (fire clay and water), whose roots dated from the medieval period. Such pieces were notably produced at Wrotham in Kent, and in Staffordshire. At Wrotham potters used chiefly a red clay for the body of the vessels, which were then ornamented with moulded white-clay reliefs, often incorporating the recipient's and potter's initials. Finally, a translucent lead glaze was applied, the fired vessel displaying bold yellow-tinged decoration on a chocolate-brown ground.

In Staffordshire the art of slip decoration reached a peak in the second half of the 17th century. Master potters, such as William Taylor, Ralph Simpson (1651–c.1724), John Wright and the Toft family, particularly Thomas and Ralph (b. 1638), made elaborate chargers, posset (milk curdled with wine or ale) pots and tygs (drinking vessels with two or more handles),

**CHARGER**
*London*
Tin-glazed earthenware;
**c. 1662**

The central medallion depicts Charles II and Catherine of Braganza in full regalia, shortly after their marriage. She holds a patriotic rose and around the pair are various military trophies. The rim is elaborately detailed with Italianate grotesque beasts.
*(Right)*

**CHARGER**
*Staffordshire*
Slip-decorated
earthenware; **c. 1675**

This spontaneous design shows Charles II standing in an ermine-lined ceremonial robe within a typical trellis-pattern border. The slip outlines are embellished with beaded "jewelling". The potter's name is emblazoned at the bottom.
*(Below)*

decorated with various designs, including royalty, birds and animals. A coarse, porous earthenware clay was coated with a white pipeclay slip or "engobe" (a slip coating that gives the base colour of the ground) and allowed to dry. Upon this prepared surface the design was trailed in orange and brown slip and beads of white were carefully dropped along the outlines. The full names of the decorators were often emblazoned on the rims of chargers.

Although slipware potters produced show

pieces for particular occasions, especially coronations, marriages and births, they made their main living from the sale of purely utilitarian ware such as mugs, cups and money boxes. Not surprisingly, these lowly items are uncommon today: while a broken commemorative piece might still be kept for sentimental reasons, a damaged everyday item was more likely to be discarded.

Eventually the slipware potters resorted to short cuts. By the early 18th century it was common practice for chargers to bear not freehand but press-moulded designs, made by pressing the slip into an incised mould. A notable exponent of this method was Samuel Malkin (*fl.* 1710–35).

### 18TH-CENTURY POTTERY

Nearly 1,000 years after the introduction of the tea ceremony in China (T'ang period, *c.* AD 700), the first Chinese teapots began to reach Britain. In the late 1680s two Dutch silversmith brothers, John and David Elers arrived in England and within two years were making red stoneware tea wares in the Chinese manner, first at Fulham, then in Staffordshire. In their short manufacturing career they managed, by means of the painstaking preparation of the clay, to produce exquisitely finished items, and the few surviving examples of their work which come on to the market today are always highly prized by collectors.

A lull in the production of tea wares in the early 18th century corresponded with a dip in the popularity of tea consumption. However, there was a resurgence of tea-drinking in the second quarter of the century, and tea (and coffee) wares were produced in profusion.

New materials and manufacturing processes introduced to the Potteries brought about the production of durable, lightweight and fashionable wares to satisfy the demands of "genteel" society. But by 1750 potters were battling against the popularity of both imported and home-produced porcelain. The struggle of potters to keep "one step ahead" had begun, and it continued with Britain's emergence as the frontrunner in the Industrial Revolution.

Staffordshire was well-served with local clay, coal and innovative potters, especially Thomas Whieldon (1719–95), William Greatbatch (1735–1813) and the Wood and Wedgwood families. Plaster of Paris, introduced around 1740, gave potters the ability to mass-produce elaborately detailed press-moulded and slip-

cast wares from moulds. Both processes depended upon the absorption of water from the liquid clay and required porous moulds, for which plaster of Paris was ideally suited.

The range of clay pottery in the North was enlarged to include creamware (fine lead-glazed pottery with a hard, light-coloured body usually containing flint); red earthenware and red stoneware; agate ware (two or more colours mixed together in imitation of agate); black ware (now generically termed "Jackfield" after the 18th-century pottery in Shropshire); tortoiseshell ware (earthenware clouded and mottled with manganese-brown and other colours); white and brown stoneware; and, from about 1770, pearlware (a bluish-white development of creamware).

Staffordshire is also noted for its white salt-glazed stoneware, on which a thin glaze was produced by the introduction of common salt into

**CAULIFLOWER-
MOULDED COFFEEPOT**
*Staffordshire*
Creamware with translucent green lead-glaze; *c.* 1765–70

Tea wares and coffee wares moulded in the form of vegetables and fruit were popular novelties in the 18th century and were produced by several Staffordshire potters. The lightweight creamware body was highly serviceable and proved a strong competitor with porcelain.

the kiln during firing. In many ways the somewhat fussy delicacy and decoration of this has more affinity with porcelain than pottery. Nottingham and Derbyshire are also renowned for the use of carefully controlled kiln salting to give their excellent brown stonewares an attractive lustrous finish.

## WOODS AND PRATTS

To pottery collectors the name Ralph Wood has always signified a master block-cutter, the person responsible for fine-quality ornamental figures and toby jugs (traditional English beer-mugs in the form of a toper in a three-cornered hat). In fact, there were three potters named Ralph Wood – father (1715–72), son (1748–95) and grandson (1775–1801). Production was restricted to the period c.1789–1801. Many of the figures were actually made by Ralph Wood II's brother, John (1746–97), and other potters.

The strongly coloured, relief-moulded creamware and pearlware that became popular in the early 1780s is referred to generically as Pratt ware after a Staffordshire family of potters whose impressed mark has been found on two pieces. Highly distinctive, with its limited palette of high-temperature metallic-oxide colours, and often commemorative in design, Pratt ware was made throughout the North of England as well as in Scotland and at Bovey Tracey in Devon.

**PAIR OF SWANS**
*Staffordshire*
Salt-glazed stoneware; **mid 18th century**

These figures are evidence of the strong influence that the Meissen porcelain factory had on the 18th-century English potters. (*Above*)

**PAIR OF SQUIRRELS**
*Staffordshire*
Creamware; **late 18th century**

The figures are based on an illustration in *The Ladies' Amusement*, an 18th-century decorators' handbook with engravings by various contemporary artists. (*Above left*)

**BEAR JUGS**
*Probably Nottingham*
Salt-glazed brown stoneware; **mid 18th century**

These figures depict the traditional "sport" of bear baiting. Each beast is covered with shredded clay to simulate fur. (*Left*)

**FIGURE OF A LADY**

**FIGURE OF A LADY**
*Staffordshire*
Creamware; **mid 18th
century**

A vertical seam, clearly
seen running the length of
this charmingly naïve press-
moulded figure, shows
where the back and front
have been luted together.
While the figure is
tentatively attributed to
Thomas Whieldon,
numerous Staffordshire
potters employed this
inexpensive method of
production. (*Right*)

**"RODNEY'S SAILOR"
FIDDLER TOBY JUG**
*Staffordshire*
Creamware; **late 18th
century**

This rare type of primitively
modelled Toby jug has
previously been attributed
to John Astbury and dated
to the early 1740s.
However, a dated example
proves that the group was
made much later in the
18th century. The features
are shared with portrait
mugs inscribed "Success to
Lord Rodney" and all
probably date from after
the admiral's famous
victory over the French
navy in 1782. "Toby Fillpot"
(and the ale jugs associated
with him) epitomizes the
eccentric, overindulgent
18th-century British toper.
(*Far right*)

## JOSIAH WEDGWOOD (1730-95)

Josiah Wedgwood is rightly considered the
father figure of industrial British pottery.
Born at Burslem in Staffordshire, he became
a pottery apprentice at the age of nine. In
1754, shortly after serving his apprenticeship,
he was taken on as a partner by Thomas
Whieldon, and from 1769 to 1780 he was in
business with the textile merchant Thomas
Bentley (1730–80), who, like Wedgwood,
was inspired by the revival of classical Greek
and Roman art. Wedgwood's constant aim
was perfection, and to this end he closely
supervised his loyal workforce. One of his
notable innovations was the issuing of
descriptive catalogues of his products.

Today the term Wedgwood is associated
almost exclusively with blue-and-white
jasperware (hard, fine-grained stoneware).
Although this did make up a proportion of his

output, Wedgwood also perfected
Queensware (the name he gave to his
creamware after it had received royal
patronage in 1765), variegated wares (in
imitation of decorative hard-stones),
pearlware, black basaltes (in imitation of
compact basalt rock), cane ware (a
straw-coloured body) and all kinds of
coloured and plain stoneware.

As well as having his own team of artists
and craftsmen, Wedgwood commissioned
talented outsiders such as the sculptors John
Flaxman (1755–1826) and John Bacon
(1740–99) and the painter George Stubbs
(1724–1806). He earned royal patronage by
undertaking work that other potters found
too difficult or not cost-effective. He also
made a point of clearly marking his products
for the world to see.

**Attribution** The provenance of 18th-century pottery is constantly being reassessed. Early in the century, makers' marks were uncommon and attribution to this period must be regarded as conjectural unless backed up by firm evidence or, perhaps, plausible tradition. The previously acceptable attributions of "Whieldon", "Ralph Wood" and many others are now being questioned. Today the names are used in a generic rather than a definitive sense. For example, some "Whieldon" pieces may well have been the work of William Greatbatch, a prolific potter who is currently drawing critical attention from scholars and collectors.

18TH-CENTURY PORCELAIN

During the 18th century many "soft-paste" porcelain factories started up in Britain. The Chelsea porcelain manufactory was in production by at least 1745 as is shown by wares marked with that date. Bow was certainly active by 1747 and issued several inkpots bearing dates of the period 1750–52. The earliest dated piece of British blue-and-white porcelain is a bowl waster (kiln failure) found at the unsuccessful Pomona Works at Newcastle under Lyme in Staffordshire and dating from 1746. In the same

**INKPOT**
*Bow*
Soft-paste bone-ash
porcelain; **1750**

Made to celebrate and advertise the opening of the new Bow factory building in 1750, this piece is decorated with the "banded hedge" pattern in the Japanese "Kakiemon"

style. The disfiguring brown specking around the base shows the difficulties that early British porcelain makers experienced controlling the ceramic bodies and kiln firings. (*Above*)

**"GOAT AND BEE" JUG**
*Chelsea*
Soft-paste "glassy"
porcelain; **c. 1745–50**

An example of Chelsea porcelain influenced by contemporary silver, the jug has an incised triangle mark on its base. (*Above*)

county, Longton Hall was in production by 1751. Bristol saw early successful attempts at porcelain production in the late 1740s. A reference to Derby cream jugs appears in a document dated 1750.

Recent discoveries have, however, made attribution less certain than it was. For example, it is now known that two categories of wares previously attributed to a factory in Liverpool were in fact made 200 miles further south. Pieces previously allocated to the Liverpool fac-

# BRITISH PORCELAIN MANUFACTURERS

| | | | |
|---|---|---|---|
| **COOKWORTHY, William** | 1705–80 | Plymouth and Bristol | First to produce hard-paste porcelain. |
| **CHELSEA PORCELAIN WORKS** | c. 1745–69 | London | Soft-paste production began at Chelsea. Ornamental wares. |
| **BOW FACTORY** | c. 1747–late 1770s | London | Soft-paste bone-ash pieces copying Chinese imports. |
| **VAUXHALL CHINA WORKS** | 1751–64 | London | Granted soaprock licence. |
| **WORCESTER PORCELAIN** | 1751 to present | Worcester | Experimental hard-paste pieces in the beginning, then changed to mainstream domestic and ornamental pieces of high quality. |
| **DERBY** | c. 1750–1848 | Derby | Soft-paste ornamental wares of high quality. |
| **LONGTON HALL** | c. 1751–60 | Staffordshire | Soft-paste, glassy porcelain. |
| **LOWESTOFT PORCELAIN** | c. 1757–c. 1800 | Lowestoft | Commemorative tourist ware, domestic ware, imitation Chinese style. |
| **CAUGHLEY** | c. 1772–1799 | Shropshire | Soft-paste steatitic porcelain. |

tories of William Ball (active *c.*1755–69) and William Reid (active *c.*1755–61) emanated from Vauxhall and Limehouse in London. Such reattributions usually lead to a change in the value of wares.

**London** The Chelsea factory, close to the Thames embankment, was managed in its early years by the Huguenot silversmith, Nicholas Sprimont (1716–71) and its first wares reflected contemporary silver work in style. Striving to equal the best imported products from France and Germany, Chelsea produced porcelain "calculated rather for ornament than for use". In 1769 the factory was sold to James Cox and in 1770 resold to William Duesbury (1725–86) of

**BOTANICAL PLATE**
*Chelsea*
Soft-paste "glassy" porcelain; **c. 1752–5**

This free style of decoration is known as "Hans Sloane" botanical, after the patron of the Chelsea Physic Garden, which was close to the porcelain manufactory. The designs were taken from contemporary prints (and possibly from life) and date to the "red anchor mark" period of the factory. The scattered insects often disguised slight blemishes in the porcelain body.

the Derby porcelain works. It closed in 1784.

The first manager of the Bow factory was Thomas Frye (1710–62), a mezzotint-engraver. Initially named New Canton, the factory deliberately set out to imitate and undercut Chinese imports. Next it challenged, like Chelsea, European competitors and extended its market as far afield as the USA. Bone china, using bone-ash mixed in the clay, originated at Bow, which thus became the forerunner of today's British porcelain industry. The factory survived into the late 1770s.

The Vauxhall China Works operated from 1751 to 1764, after a licence to use soapstone (a mineral used in soft-paste porcelain) had been granted to Nicholas Crisp and John Sanders (d. 1758). A factory announcement stated that the "essential properties of China-ware" were that it should "bear the hottest liquors without danger of breaking". John Bacon, the future sculptor, was bound to Nicholas Crisp in 1755, being "chiefly employed in forming shepherds, shepherdesses and such like small ornamental pieces". In 1763 Crisp became bankrupt. He later set up a porcelain manufactory at Bovey Tracey in Devon but, unfortunately with little apparent success.

Production at the Thameside porcelain factory at Limehouse appears to have been limited to 1745–8, and the history of the works is shrouded in a certain amount of mystery.

**Midlands** Soapstone was used by Benjamin Lund in the production of porcelain in Bristol in the late 1740s. In 1751 the factory was advertising wares imitating "foreign china". The following year it was taken over by the Worcester

Porcelain Company, established in 1751 by Dr John Wall (1708–76) and 14 partners.

Worcester wares remained somewhat experimental until 1755 but from then until 1760 pieces were decorated with fine painting. After that date the high-quality output became rela-

**MUG**
*Bow*
Soft-paste bone-ash porcelain; **c. 1750**

Domestic blue-and-white porcelain was far cheaper to produce than enamelled wares as it did not require further firings. This mug displays typical 18th-century chinoiserie decoration. (*Above*)

**BOWL**
*Worcester*
Soft-paste steatitic porcelain, **c. 1752–4**

The enamelled decoration is derived from Chinese *famille verte* porcelain but shows a Europeanized character. Soapstone was a characteristic ingredient at Worcester. (*Left*)

tively mainstream. The firm's London agent, Thomas Flight, bought the factory in 1783, and Martin Barr was taken into partnership in 1792. In 1840, the company merged with a rival Worcester factory founded by Robert Chamberlain. Further mergers resulted in the Worcester Royal Porcelain Company.

Thomas Turner, a former Worcester employee, founded a porcelain works at Caughley, Shropshire, in 1772. Not surprisingly, his products bear a strong resemblance to Worcester wares – some wares were sent to Worcester for decoration. The company was taken over by the Coalport factory in 1799, but porcelain continued to be produced there until 1814, when the two firms were amalgamated.

**Derby** The Derby porcelain factory was probably founded *c.*1750 by another Huguenot refugee, Andrew Planché (1727–1805) and a local banker, John Heath. Initially, they concentrated on making figures in competition with Chelsea and Europe, advertising them as "second Dresden" (in reference to the German city noted for its graceful porcelain). William Duesbury became a partner in 1756 and the factory expanded. From 1764 to 1769 the factory

**PIERCED BASKET**
*Worcester*
Soft-paste steatitic porcelain; **c. 1756**

The Worcester porcelain body was commercially very successful. (*Above*)

**PAIR OF CHOCOLATE CUPS**
*Worcester*
Steatitic porcelain; **c. 1804–13**

The Flight and Barr families ran the Worcester

Porcelain Company in various partnerships. These cups are exquisite examples of the Empire style of decoration. (*Below*)

**POTPOURRI VASE**
*Longton Hall*
Soft-paste "glassy"
porcelain; **c. 1755**

---

This is a technical *tour-de-force* in flamboyant Rococo style. The encrusted ornaments can be matched to other Longton Hall specimens.

glassy body were also produced.

**Lowestoft** Lowestoft in Suffolk housed an extremely successful porcelain manufactory from about 1757 to *c.*1800, producing commemorative tourist ware as well as serving the local population. One of the factory's partners, Robert Browne, is thought to have gained employment at Bow and practised industrial espionage there. The similarity of Lowestoft's early products to those of Bow lends support to this story. Emphasis was placed on useful, unpretentious wares, but some small decorative figures were also made.

**Liverpool** It was only during the first half of the 18th century that Liverpool began to develop as a major centre of ceramics production. Of the 20 or so pottery works in the city about half are thought to have made porcelain at some time. By 1760 the industry in Liverpool had already begun to decline in the face of competition from Wedgwood's creamware, which flooded into the port via the newly-built canal system.

Apart from William Ball and William Reid, known Liverpool porcelain manufacturers include Richard Chaffers (*fl.* 1732–65), Philip Christian (*fl.* 1765–76), Samuel Gilbody (*fl.* 1754–61), the Pennington family (*fl.* 1769–99) and Thomas Wolfe (*fl.* 1795–1800).

**"Hard-paste" porcelain** In the 1750s William Cookworthy, a Plymouth apothecary, discovered in Cornwall the two ingredients of "hard-paste" porcelain (the true, much admired Chinese kind) – china-clay (kaolin) and china-stone (a felspathic rock). In 1768 he opened a small factory in Plymouth and began producing this genuine porcelain. Two years later Cookworthy transferred production to Bristol, where Richard Champion (1743–91), became his manager and in 1773 bought him out. In 1781, Champion moved to Tunstall in Staffordshire to establish a new manufactory, the Staffordshire Company, but a year later he severed his links with ceramics. The company moved from Tunstall to Shelton, where it took on the name New Hall and continued in production until about 1830.

### THE EARLY 19TH CENTURY

The Regency period (1811–20) saw the mass-production of high-quality porcelain by such manufacturers as Coalport, Spode, Rockingham, Swansea and Worcester, the latter producing exquisite ornamental pieces.

used soapstone in its porcelain productions. From 1770 to 1784 Duesbury supervised experiments with new porcelain formulae and the production of excellent-quality ornamental wares. The original Nottingham Road factory closed in 1848.

**Longton Hall** The Longton Hall factory in Staffordshire lasted for a decade from 1750, under the guidance (from 1751) of William Littler (b.1724). Like Derby, it initially specialized in figures, but after Littler became manager many utilitarian wares were produced. Elaborate rococo designs in an unpredictable

THE COURTLY PATRONAGE OF CERAMICS FACTORIES HAD LARGELY ENDED
BY THE CLOSING YEARS OF THE 18TH CENTURY. HOWEVER, A NEW
MIDDLE CLASS MARKET WAS GROWING, AND DEMANDING GRAND
PORCELAIN AND POTTERY FOR DISPLAY.

# EUROPEAN CERAMICS 1820–1920

By 1820, the Industrial Revolution had transformed the manufacture of porcelain from a luxury art serving royal and wealthy patrons into a streamlined business activity. (Some of the larger Continental factories, however, still enjoyed Royal patronage.) Reliable hard-paste porcelain was developed on the Continent and bone china in England, and white earthenware was industrially produced. Factories were mechanized, labour was divided and centres of production moved from cities to provinces rich in raw materials, such as Limoges (kaolin) and Staffordshire (coal). Hence by 1830, when there was a general economic recovery after the Napoleonic wars, porcelain factories were to supply the ever-expanding middle classes with pieces at affordable prices.

### EMPIRE

The Empire style (c. 1800–30), a French development of the Neo-Classical, employed many of the latter's motifs but was generally more elaborate: cups became wider and had paw feet and caryatid handles, and vases were made in Egyptian and Etruscan shapes, often with exotic embellishments and large elaborate and colourfully painted surfaces.

The costs of manufacturing Empire wares were high, and by 1800 even the great porcelain factory of Sèvres could no longer afford the luxury of being unprofitable. In that year Alexandre Brongniart was appointed as the new director of Sèvres and, to cut costs, he abandoned the expensive and less reliable soft-paste manufacture in favour of hard-paste. This was used to produce both the prestige wares commissioned during the first half of the century by Louis XVIII, Charles X and Louis-Philippe and simpler wares for general sale.

In Germany the Königliche Porzellan Manufaktur (KPM) in Berlin received royal patronage until well into the 19th century, and royal presentation vases in Empire style were made right up until the 1870s, when most other

**BERLIN VASE**
Hard-paste porcelain;
**1840–50**

As its name "Französische Vase" indicates, this is probably not a direct copy from an antique prototype but comes via a French example.

factories had launched into a multitude of other revivalist styles.

In Russia the Imperial Porcelain Manufactory at St Petersburg was even more closely connected to the court, and under Nicholas I (1825–55) the Empire style was used to great effect to enhance his prestige.

The Royal Vienna Manufactory produced fine Empire porcelains but, despite its attempts to enter the mass market (it had even introduced printed decoration and gloss-gilding in 1853), the factory was forced to close in 1866.

### REGENCY

The English counterpart of the Empire style was Regency. But in England porcelain was made in markedly lesser quantities, because there was no state manufactory. The Flight and Barr partnerships at Worcester produced the best wares, but Derby, Nantgarw, Swansea and Liverpool also produced pieces of merit. By the late 18th century much English porcelain production had been run down because soft-paste porcelain had proved to be unreliable in the kiln and therefore costly. However, in about 1794, bone china was developed. This, England's answer to hard-paste – which had long been produced on the Continent – fulfilled the demands of ease and cheapness of manufacture, durability and translucency, and it had a fine white surface that was easily decorated. Even so, it took many years to perfect bone china; by the end of the 18th century few factories were experimenting with porcelain, and in Staffordshire, the centre of the Potteries, earthenware, in the form of creamware and the whiter pearlware, had become dominant.

**Earthenware** Between 1800 and 1845 the improved creamware of Josiah Spode was still important; so too were lustre wares (with a thin metallic film), especially copper lustre, produced mainly at Sunderland, Newcastle upon Tyne, Bristol, Liverpool and Yorkshire. Ironstone china, containing a by-product of iron smelting and characterized by a hard, white body, had its heyday during this period. Staffordshire portrait figures, as well as chimney-piece ornaments in the form of animals, were made throughout the 19th century, carrying on a tradition of the later 18th century.

After 1810, ceramics factories produced vast amounts of printed blue-and-white pottery; and other colours were developed. Subjects included American and English town and landscape scenes. Much of the production, by such firms

**PAIR OF STAFFORDSHIRE IRONSTONE VASES**
White earthenware;
**c. 1830**

Ironstone is a hard white earthenware primarily associated with Charles J. Mason, who took out a patent in 1813. Other makers include Davenport, T. & J. Ashworth, Meigh and Ridgway. Spode marketed a similar body as "stone china", and various other wares were marketed under the trade names Patent Stone China, Pearl Stone China, Imperial Ironstone, Royal Ironstone and Genuine Ironstone.

as Spode, Ridgway, Wedgwood, Adams and Pratt (the latter specialized in multicoloured printing) was for export.

### NEO-ROCOCO

England was the first country to embrace the revived Rococo style. Bone china, with its kiln stability and good modelling qualities, was an ideal medium for such an elaborate style, with its swirling asymmetrical rocaille (shell and rock) motifs, often in relief and gilded, together with applied flowers. Hence a product was manufactured which looked colourful, expensive and grand, meeting all the demands of the emerging middle classes' desire for ostentation. Tea-sets and other ornamental pieces of a slightly plainer nature were produced for the mass market, while Rockingham in Yorkshire, Coalport in Shropshire and the five Staffordshire makers Minton, Copeland & Garrett, Ridgway, Daniel and Davenport produced costly pieces with a greater area of painted surface and elaborate modelling.

The revived Rococo style made little impact on Sèvres but was taken up by other French manufacturers, especially Jacob Petit of Fontainebleau, founded 1834. Petit produced pieces in imitation of those of the major 18th-century porcelain factories and often mixed elements from several different eras. After 1830, Limoges developed into the major centre for French porcelain; its well-run factories employed the latest technology and were thus able to respond to the constant changes in fashion that epitomize the 19th century.

### GERMAN PORCELAIN 1830–80

Reorganization and modernization of the German porcelain factory, Meissen, in 1814 halted its decline, and by 1840 it was producing vast quantities of high-quality wares for a large middle- and upper-class market. Lithophanes (porcelain pieces with pictures showing through the porcelain) were mass-produced between 1830 and 1850. They drew on religious subjects and genre scenes from 17th- and 18th-century Dutch, French and Italian paintings. From the late 1840s Meissen revived many models from the 18th century, especially Rococo and Neo-Classical figures. Neo-Renaissance snake-handled vases were made from the mid 1860s and Limoges-style wares after 1862, the latter copied from Royal Worcester examples displayed at the London Exhibition of 1862.

Scores of smaller concerns in Bohemia, including Schlaggenwald and Pirkenhammer, and in Thuringia, including Sitzendorf, Gotha and Volkstedt, all produced historical revivals of inferior quality to those of Meissen but which presumably were cheaper.

**Berlin** This porcelain centre proved rather less adaptable than Meissen and was always one step behind; still producing during this period Neo-Classical pieces in small quantities and experimenting in the 1860s with Neo-Renaissance and Italian maiolica revivals which, by then, were already becoming unfashionable. Berlin is principally remembered during this period for the many porcelain plaques it made for decorating workshops throughout Central Europe. The German retailer Heinrich Bucker lists in his catalogue for the 1867 Paris Exhibition 11 different illustrated plaques, the subjects including La Madona di San Sisto, after Raphael, La Vierge, after Murillo, and Les Fils de Rubens, after Rubens.

### ENGLISH PORCELAIN 1830–80

At the Great Exhibition of 1851 the most important English ceramics manufacturer of the period, Minton, showed not only numerous revivals of Sèvres vases, fireplaces, tiles and

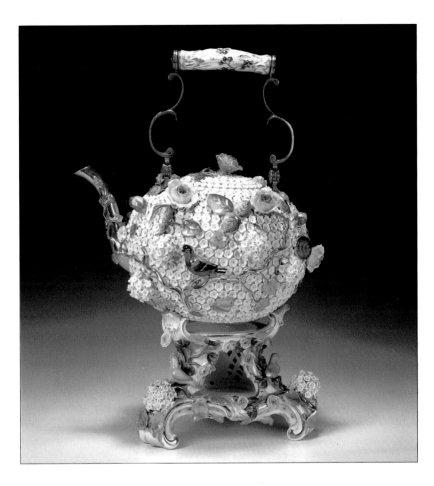

**"SCHNEEBALLEN" KETTLE AND STAND**
*Meissen*
Hard-paste porcelain;
**c. 1870–80**

With its surface entirely covered with may flowers, the piece is typical of the elaborate interpretations of mid-18th-century Meissen wares. In England the "Snowball" vase was copied at Chelsea in the 18th century and by Spode in the 19th century. (*Above*)

**BUST OF JUNO**
*Copeland*
Matt-white porcelain;
**c. 1851**

This example was modelled by the sculptor W. Thead, after an original in the Museo Nazionale in Rome, and was shown at the Great Exhibition of London in 1851. (*Right*)

**PÂTE-SUR-PÂTE VASE**
*Minton*
Tinted Parian; **c. 1878**

This vase, included in the Paris Exhibition of 1878, was decorated by Louis M. E. Solon and modelled by Albert Ernest Carrier de Belleuse. It was part of the Thomas Goode & Co. collection until 1989. (*Left*)

**ELEPHANT HEAD VASES**
*Minton*
Bone china; **c. 1889**

This vase, one of two versions copied from Sèvres originals, was designed by Jean-Claude Duplessis (1694–1774) and first made in 1757. It is one of the most successful copies produced by the 19th-century porcelain manufacturers. (*Above*)

**"MAJOLICA" JARDINIÈRE AND STAND**
*Minton*
Earthenware; **c. 1882**

This elaborate piece was designed by the artist and sculptor Albert Ernest Carrier de Belleuse, who moved to England in 1848 and began to work as a modeller for Minton. (*Right*)

Meissen-style wares but also majolica pieces and statues in Parian. Majolica was a richly-enamelled, relief-moulded earthenware, used to make vases, domestic wares, jardinières, garden ornaments and architectural pieces. Parian was an even more remarkable technical innovation; a non-porous, almost marble-like medium, it was a great improvement on the biscuit (unglazed) porcelain of the 18th century which

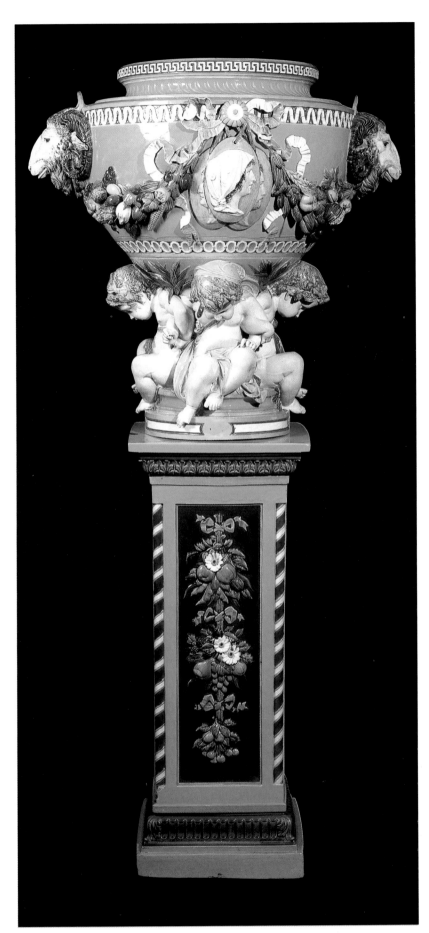

was easily chipped and stained. By the time of the Great Exhibition more than 20 manufacturers were displaying Parian statues and figures designed by leading contemporary sculptors.

Other notable wares of this period include copies of 16th-century lead-glazed earthenware – commonly known as Henry II ware – with inlaid coloured clays on a buff ground. These and painted dinner and dessert services were sold by the prestigious London firms of Morlock & Co, Phillips & Co, and Thomas Goode.

**Pâte-sur-pâte** The most important Victorian ceramics development was *pâte-sur-pâte*, (paste-upon-paste) in which designs were built up in low relief with layers of porcelain slip (clay and water). The varying thicknesses give the effect of shading in the design. The technique was introduced at Sèvres during the early 1850s and later explored commercially by the Minton artist L. M. E. Solon, who, from about 1870 to 1890, decorated Parian vases with tinted and glazed *pâte-sur-pâte*.

THE REACTION AGAINST INDUSTRIALIZATION
The first two-thirds of the 19th century produced great technical advances in ceramics, but factory-made goods were increasingly criticized for their lack of artistic innovation and their poor design. The English art historian and social critic John Ruskin (1819–1900) urged a return to individual craftsmanship, and the Arts and Crafts Movement and Aesthetic Movement sought ways to improve design. It was the designer and writer William Morris (1834–96) who developed these ideas of good design and craftsmanship with his craft workshops.

In France the reaction against industrialization had been tangibly expressed even earlier, art-potters having appeared in the 1840s. Théodore Deck (1823–91), who set himself up in Paris in 1856, can be considered the first of these craftsman. He was inspired principally by Near-Eastern and Persian designs. Others followed his example and experimented with a variety of oriental high-temperature glazes, shapes and designs. In England the work of the French potters was echoed in that of W. Howson Taylor (1876–1935), at his Ruskin Pottery near Birmingham, and that of Bernard Moore (1850–1935) in Staffordshire.

**English art-potters** In England the Doulton factory at Lambeth produced the first true art-potters in the late 1860s. William de Morgan (1839–1917), the potter most closely attuned to the principles of William Morris, produced

### JAPANESE INFLUENCES

Japanese influence was important not only on individual studio potters but also on designers at the larger factories, who controlled the execution of work by others. Japanese wares, including pieces decorated with cloisonné (a type of enamelling), ivories and bronzes, were shown at the Paris Exhibition of 1862, and the revelation of their simple shapes, sparse decoration and asymmetrically placed motifs made a dramatic impact on those who saw them.

From 1885, the Royal Copenhagen porcelain factory produced innovative wares based on Japanese styles and designed by the architect Arnold Krog (1856–1931), who used subtle blue and grey glazes. The Frenchman Félix Bracquemond (1833–1914) produced probably the best of the European japonaiserie in ceramics. Inspired by the discovery of a volume of sketches by the Japanese artist Katsushika Hokusai, he made a series of woodcuts that were copied on an earthenware service produced in 1866 by F. E. Rousseau. Bracquemond also designed for Deck and Sèvres, and designed the flowers and swirling ribbons on the Art Nouveau Service, a series of plates which were a precursor of the movement.

### ART NOUVEAU AND ART DECO

The Art Nouveau movement fought against revivalism and at the same time sought to remove the distinction between so-called fine arts and applied arts. The sinuous style of Art Nouveau based on forms from nature was essentially Continental – though the Staffordshire art-potter William Moorcroft (1872–1946) produced some excellent designs in tube-lined slip, known as Florian ware, between 1898 and 1906. With the exception of Sèvres, perhaps the greatest exponent of the Art Nouveau style in ceramics was the Rozenburg factory in The Hague, which in 1899 introduced its unique fine eggshell porcelains.

Art Nouveau continued into the early 20th century, but after the International Exhibition in Paris in 1900 the style deteriorated as manufacturers attempted a synthetic version for mass production. It was replaced by Art Deco, a group of styles that reached a peak at the Paris Exhibition of 1925. Whereas the emphasis of Art Nouveau had been on ornament that accentuated form, that of Art Deco was on broken or interrupted surface patterns that negated form. The inspiration for Art Deco came from various sources, including Cubism, architecture, tribal

**VASE**
*Ernst Chaplet*
Hard-paste porcelain;
**1885–1904**

Chaplet was inspired by oriental *sang-de-boeuf* glazes and in 1887, when he settled in Choisy-le-Roi, he perfected this and other techniques. (*Left*)

**VASE AND COVER**
*William de Morgan*
Earthenware; **c. 1890**

This vase is painted with a brightly coloured floral and foliate design, inspired by Iznik pottery of Persia. (*Above*)

earthenware pieces in lustre and bright Persian designs from the 1870s. Other manufacturers included the Barum Pottery in Devon, Minton's Kensington Gore Studios, the Della Robbia Pottery at Birkenhead and Pilkington's Royal Lancastrian ware.

Christopher Dresser (1834–1904), one of the ceramics champions of the Aesthetic Movement, produced designs for several North of England potteries as well as for Minton.

**"DE MONTFORT" VASE**
*Sèvres*
Porcelain; *c.* 1908

This vase is a fine example of the Art Nouveau style and features a typical foliate design.

art, Egyptian art and industrial design.

In Prague a group of architects heavily influenced by the Wiener Werkstatte founded the craft workshops known as the Artel organization in 1908. The group's ceramic artists included Vlatislav Hofman (b.1884) and Pavel Janak (b.1882). Artel figures in the Art Deco style were manufactured by leading factories, such as Meissen and Berlin.

Other makers of Art Deco ceramics included the Doccia factory in Italy, Royal Copenhagen in Denmark, Rosenthal in Bavaria and Wedgwood, Susie Cooper, Moorcroft, Carlton Ware, Clarice Cliff and Doulton in England.

### BRITISH STUDIO CERAMICS

British patterns took a different direction to that of the Continental studio potters, largely through the influence of Bernard Leach (1887–1979), who, in 1920, after teaching in Japan, set up a pottery in St Ives, Cornwall, with the Japanese potter Shoji Hamada. Leach emphasized the principles of what became known as the studio movements. The potter was responsible for every stage of production, from digging the clay to the final firing. Leach also believed that the ideal potter should seek an impersonal perfection of form and glaze rather

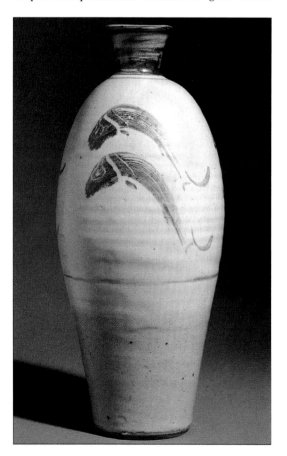

**VASE**
*René Buthaud*
Earthenware; **c. 1925**

Buthaud's work is characterized by simple massive shapes with firmly outlined designs. (*Above*)

**"FISH" BOTTLE VASE**
*Bernard Leach*
Stoneware; **c. 1930**

The vase combines a Chinese shape with spontaneous painted decoration. (*Left*)

than an expression of personal vision. At St Ives, where Leach and Hamada experimented with Japanese-style stoneware, Leach had a number of pupils who later became famous, including Michael Cardew (1901–83).

Other British potters were encouraged by the development of craft teaching in regional colleges of art. Apart from Leach, the two finest British potters of the 20th century, Lucie Rie (b.1902) and Hans Coper (1920–81), who emerged from the studio movement, 20th-century British ceramics will be mainly remembered not for the factory-produced wares that typify the previous century but for the work created by individual art- and studio potters.

COMPETITION FROM BRITISH POTTERIES HAMPERED THE DEVELOPMENT
OF AN AMERICAN CERAMICS INDUSTRY. BUT THE AMERICAN CHALLENGE,
WHEN IT CAME DURING THE 19TH CENTURY, WAS A VIGOROUS ONE.

# AMERICAN CERAMICS

To the newly arrived artisan-potters of the 17th century, the American colonies were lands rich in natural resources. But circumstances set limitations on the development of their craft. Both potters and their potential customers were scattered in small settlements around the countryside rather than located in large urban centres; and the chances of exchanging ideas or gaining apprenticeship under skilled masters were severely limited.

In addition, English governments sought to suppress all colonial attempts to establish manufacturing industries, a policy which seems to have been especially effective in the field of ceramics. The demand for everyday ware was met by local potters, but moneyed clients in the colonies looked to England for their best services.

Despite limited opportunities for potters in the first 200 years of American settlement, trained artisans were among the early arrivals to the newly settled colonies. Domestic potters were registered as arriving in New England in 1635, and several Dutch potters were practising their craft in New Amsterdam (now New York) by 1660. The successful establishment of potteries throughout the colonies is commemorated in such place names as Potter's Creek, Clay City, Pottertown, Jugtown – and in four states, Kaolin.

### POTTERY

Early American dishes and utensils were made from a low-fired earthenware called redware. This took its base colour from the iron oxide in the clay, which turned to a rich brown-red when fired. Its uses were simple and functional, and kitchen and dairy items, as well as tableware, were turned out in large numbers by potters.

The simplest form of decoration was the slip glaze. Obtained by diluting mineral-coloured clay (often lead-based) and trailing it over the piece to be fired, it would result either in abstract blotches of colour or in the delineation

**CHARGER OR LARGE PLATE**
Cream-slip earthenware with sgraffito decoration;
**1818**

This embellished peasant pottery was popular in Pennsylvania. (*Right*)

of simple words or names. The later technique of sgrafitto (made by scratching a design through the coloured glaze to expose the clay beneath) was a speciality of the Pennsylvania Germans from about 1760 to the 1830s.

**Stoneware** The first signed and dated piece of American stoneware (duller in colour than earthenware and ranging from greyish white to brown) was made by Joseph Thiekson of New Jersey in 1722, although there is evidence that stoneware was being made even earlier. The

**COFFEEPOT**
Glazed earthenware;
*c.* 1825

Folk wares like these were made all along the East Coast and into the Midwest from the earliest days of settlement. Little equipment was needed, and decoration was often rudimentary. (*Above*)

Corselius (later Crolius) family set up the first recorded stoneware kiln on Potbaker's Hill, Manhattan Island. From 1730 to 1870, 15 members of the family carried on the trade in a welter of name and factory changes. In the 1730s scattered stoneware centres were established along the rich clay vein which ran from South Amboy, New Jersey, northeast to Staten Island and Long Island, New York. Many of the small redware producers also set themselves up as stoneware manufacturers.

Records suggest that some fine-grade early stoneware was made, but most of the output was of a utilitarian thickness suited to the jugs, crocks, churns, whistles, decorative figurines and moneyboxes (called banks) that formed the mainstay of production. Decoration was usually simple – freehand painting of birds, animals, initials and dates in cobalt blue or brown. This remained almost unchanged until 1850, when the freehand painting changed to cheaper stencilling.

### THE RISE OF COMMERCIAL POTTERIES

The use of lead glazes on earthenware led to a lead-poisoning scare, which in the late 18th century encouraged even more redware manufacturers to invest in stoneware production. In addition, the embargo placed on British goods by the American government in 1807 spurred further the development of American stoneware producers. Small potteries from the Carolinas to Ohio were kept busy supplying their customers' needs. By the 1840s production was on a scale that could qualify as industrial.

**Creamware** In the 1770s an ex-employee of the English potter Josiah Wedgwood, John Bartlam, had a brief success with his imitation of Wedgwood's light, flint clay earthenware (known as Queensware) and factory production in Charleston, South Carolina. It was enough to inspire similar efforts in Philadelphia, Pittsburgh and New York. After independence, Pittsburgh became the creamware capital of the United States, while other centres of production sprang up in Louisville, Kentucky, and in Indiana during the 1830s.

### BRITISH DOMINANCE AND AMERICAN REACTION

British manufacturers saw no irony in selling to the rebel colonists and produced portrait busts of Washington and Franklin and plates and jugs with American slogans and scenes. Between

**ANGLO-AMERICAN CREAMWARE PLATE**
Frigate flying the Stars and Stripes, in transfer-printed brown; c. 1800

Wares such as this – made in Liverpool and Staffordshire – were exceptionally popular with American settlers before, during and after the American War of Independence. American makers excelled in commemorative glassware, but they never effectively challenged the early dominance of British potteries in the field.

American independence and the War of 1812, ordinary blue-and-white transfer-printed Staffordshire creamware became an American bestseller, while ornamental ceramics emblazoned with now-triumphant republican sentiments continued to be made specifically for the American market. After the War of 1812, and repeal of the embargo, British factories began producing an even wider selection of patterns and colours to meet demand.

It took many years for American manufacturers to respond. The challenge was led by David Henderson's American Pottery Manufacturing Company of Jersey City, New Jersey, founded in 1833. This produced plates with floral-printed designs as well as jugs and bowls with patriotic and historical themes or personalities. Many smaller, now unremembered, potteries fired unremarkable, floral-bordered, transfer-printed ware throughout the 19th century, but the popularity of this declined when fashions changed after the 1860s.

## BENNINGTON AND MAIOLICA

Bennington pottery, first produced at Bennington, Vermont, is a flint-enamel-glazed variety of tableware, figures and utility ware that forms part of a widespread production of folk pottery, much of it of the same type. An alternative name for Bennington pottery is Rockingham ware, since it was based on the mottled brown glaze produced at that English factory from the 18th century onwards. In fact, much of this sought-after pottery was not produced in Bennington at all but in kilns on the Ohio River or in Pittsburgh or Baltimore.

The first kiln at Bennington was built by

Captain John Norton in 1793, but it was not until around 1843 that it began the production of the flint-enamel-glazed wares with which it is mostly associated. As well as the common brown-glazed items, it produced whimsical animal figures – poodles, lions, deer and cows – and flasks in various colourful glazes. Distinctive hound-handled pitchers, printed with hunting scenes, are also typical pieces. Some of the best articles were produced between 1851 (two years before the company was re-named the United States Pottery Factory) and its closure in 1858.

The Great Exhibition held in London in 1851 set off a craze in Britain for maiolica, a modern lead-glazed version of an older tin-glazed version. Within two years American potters were producing their own maiolica: Edwin Bennett in Baltimore, and Carr & Morrison in New York (until 1855). By the 1880s, maiolica was being manufactured all over the eastern seaboard, from James Taft's Hampshire Pottery in Keene, New Hampshire, to the most famous producers, Griffin, Smith and Hill of Phoenixville, Pennsylvania, whose "Etruscan Majolica", modelled on vegetable, flower and shell shapes, remained in production until 1892.

## FROM CHELSEA TO ROOKWOOD

Intimations of a new breath of air in 19th-century American pottery, of a reaction against slavish copies and increasing mass production, were provided by the output of Robertson's Chelsea Keramic Art Works (founded 1866) in Chelsea, Massachusetts. By the 1880s their manufacture included a grey earthenware, red bisque (unglazed porcelain) and Oriental glazes, including the deep red *sang de boeuf*. By the 1890s they were chiefly known for dishes of fine crackleware (ceramics with deliberately produced fine cracks in their glaze) that had banded border designs with names such as "Rabbit", "Iris", "Turkey", "Grape" and "Swan". In 1895 the Chelsea works were renamed the Dedham Pottery, and blue-and-white tableware became a prime product.

The most notable initiative in art pottery, however, was taken by Maria Longworth Nichols (1849–1932), a prominent socialite and art patron who in 1880 established a kiln in Cincinnati, Ohio, naming it Rookwood after her family estate. Rookwood mainly produced display pieces – vases, bowls and plates. The "Standard Rookwood" of the early years – coloured slip (clay mixed with water) painting

**CROCK**
Salt glaze and slip with hand-painted decoration, **c. 1850–59**

Known as Burlington ware, such blue-painted crocks, pots and churns were produced throughout New England, New York and Ohio in the 19th century. (*Right*)

**DEDHAM POTTERY MARK, used 1929–43**

**SERVING BOWLS**
*Dedham Pottery*
Blue-and-white ceramic; **early 20th century**

Dedham Pottery is best known for its animal- and floral-bordered patterns. The clean-cut figured bands call to mind the works of Walter Crane and Kate Greenaway. (*Below*)

# PRINCIPAL AMERICAN CERAMICS MANUFACTURERS

|  |  |  |  |
|---|---|---|---|
| **THIEKSON, Joseph** | *fl.* 1720–30s | New Jersey | First recorded stoneware maker. |
| **DUCHÉ, Andre** | 1710–78 | Savannah, Georgia | First recorded porcelain maker in US, *c.* 1728 |
| **CORSELIEUS (Crolius), family** | *fl.* 1730–1870 | Manhattan, New York | Fifteen-member family producing stoneware for three generations. |
| **AUST, Gottfried Brother** | *fl.* 1756–88 | Bethabara and Salem, North Carolina | Maker of black-glazed Moravian ware. |
| **BONIN, George** | *fl.* 1770–72 | Southwark, Philadelphia, PA. | With George A. Morris founded first working porcelain company in US. |
| **BARTLAM, John** | *fl.* 1771–5 | Charleston, SC. | Entrepreneur potter who founded first US creamware factory. |
| **NORTON, John** | *fl.* 1793–1840s | Bennington, Vermont | Founded first pottery producing American "Rockingham". |
| **BELL, family** | *fl.* 1820–80 | | Peter Bell of Hagerstown, Maryland, Samuel Bell of Strasbourg, Virginia and Solomon Bell of Waynesboro, PA. Makers of Shenandoah pottery – redware and stoneware. |
| **TUCKER, William Ellis** | *fl.* 1825–32 | Philadelphia, PA. | Producer of American porcelain on commercial scale. |
| **HEMPHILL, Joseph Alexander** | 1770–1842 | Philadelphia, PA. | Partner of William Ellis Tucker (qv) 1831–8 in the porcelain company of Tucker and Hemphill (later the American China Manufacturing Co.). |
| **BENNETT, James** | *fl.* 1834 | East Liverpool, Ohio | Established stoneware factory. |
| **HENDERSON, David** | *fl.* 1833–40s | New Jersey | Founder of New Jersey Porcelain and Earthenware Company, latterly the American Pottery Manufacturing Co, New Jersey. |
| **BENNETT, Edwin** | *fl.* 1846–1890s | Baltimore, Maryland | Brother of James. Founder of factory at Baltimore, Maryland. |
| **CARTLIDGE, Charles** | *fl.* 1848–56 | Greenpoint, Conn. | Founder of biscuit porcelain factory under his name. |
| **BOCH, William** | *fl.* 1850–61 | Greenpoint, Conn. | Founder of bone-china company under his name. |
| **KNOWLES, Isaac W.** | *fl.* 1854–80s | East Liverpool, Ohio | Founder with Isaac Harvey in 1854 of what became Knowles, Taylor and Knowles in 1870. |
| **NICHOLS (Storer), Maria Longworth** | 1849–1932 | Cincinnati, Ohio | Amateur art potter who went on to found Rookwood Pottery in 1880. |

**PITCHER-SHAPED VASE**
*Tucker & Hemphill*
Hand-painted porcelain;
**c. 1833**

Tucker & Hemphill of Philadelphia was established by William Ellis Tucker and Alexander Hemphill in 1831; it was continued by Joseph Hemphill, Alexander's father, after Tucker's death in 1832. The decoration of pieces such as this owed much to Sèvres for their inspiration.

The most notable initiative in art pottery, however, was taken by Maria Longworth Nichols (1849–1932), a prominent socialite and art patron who in 1880 established a kiln in Cincinnati, Ohio, naming it Rookwood after her family estate. Rookwood mainly produced display pieces – vases, bowls and plates. The "Standard Rookwood" of the early years – coloured slip (clay mixed with water) painting under the glaze on a dark ground – evolved into more experimental styles: "Tiger Eye" – gold-speckled and adventurine-glazed – introduced in the mid-1880s; oriental body shapes displaying floral motifs on backgrounds called Iris, Sea Green and Aerial Blue; matt glazes introduced by designer Artus van Briggle in 1896; and transparent glazes after 1904. Now-valued signatures that appeared on pieces included those of Laura L. Fry, Van Briggle, Clara Chapman Newton, Kuitaro Shirayamadani and head decorator Albert R. Valentein.

**Other notable potteries** Ohio was the Mecca of art pottery, with Cincinnati as its focal point. In addition to Rookwood, the Avon Pottery, the Cincinnati Art Pottery, the Mary Louise McLaughlin Factory, the Matt Morgan Art Pottery and the T. J. Wheatley Pottery were all established there between the years 1879 and 1889. As always with craftsmen-potters, the turnover rate was high, with artisans leaving to found their own companies or to work in others. Laura Fry left Rookwood to found the Lonhuda Pottery in Steubensville, Ohio; in 1895 this merged with Samuel Weller's Pottery in Zanesville, Ohio, to become the Louwelsa Factory. The combination of Rookwood-derived work and iridescent lustreware produced by the Lonhuda/Louwelsa concern is highly prized by collectors. Two other Zanesville firms were the J. B. Owens Pottery, founded by William Long of the Lonhuda Pottery and producer of Utopian ware (derived from Rookwood) (1895–1907), and the Roseville Art Pottery, noted for their Rozanne and Rozanne Royal lines (*c*.1900).

### PORCELAIN
The development of porcelain manufacturers in Colonial America was even more adversely affected than proletarian earthenware by British protectionist policies. The import of Chinese porcelain via Britain was tolerated, however, and blue-and-white and polychrome "Lowestoft" ware in commissioned heraldic and commemorative sets was much favoured by affluent Americans.

The kaolin clay needed to produce true hard-paste porcelain was first found in America in 1738, by Andre Duché (1710–78), the son of a potter, who came across a thick vein running from Virginia through Georgia. After several false starts at porcelain manufacturing, he seems to have given up the enterprise and by 1743 his place had been taken by Samuel Bowen, who received a gold medal from the English Society for the Encouragement of the Arts, Manufactures and Commerce. Nonetheless, no work by him survives.

For authenticated surviving, if sparse, early American porcelain one must look to the fac-

**VASE**
*Rookwood Pottery*
Amber stoneware with transparent glaze and cameo decoration;
**c. 1890**

Rookwood items can be identified by the monogram "RP" (1880–86). From 1886 to 1900, a small flame was added for every year; from 1900, this was replaced by a Roman numeral, beginning with "I".

tory of George Bonin and George Anthony Morris in Southwark, Philadelphia, established in 1770. Their success lasted a mere two years, however, and today only some 20 blue-and-white pieces remain.

### A TRADITION ESTABLISHED
A more sustained achievement is represented by the Philadelphia company owned by William Ellis Tucker from 1800 to 1828. Later it was shared in partnership with John Hulme (1828–9), then with Alexander Hemphill, until Tucker's death in 1832, after which Hemphill continued the licence until 1838. The company's most famous products were fine white pitchers with gilt and floral decoration.

Though better known for its stoneware, the Bennington factory of Norton & Fenton also made Parian ware (unglazed, fine-grained biscuit porcelain) from 1843, as well as blue-and-white and gilded tableware from 1853. Two notable smaller companies working at the same period in Greenpoint (now Brooklyn), New York, were Charles Cartlidge & Company (1848–56), largely producing Parian ware, and the Union Porcelain Works (founded in 1862) of Thomas Smith.

The "Lotus Ware" of Knowles, Taylor & Knowles, produced during 1891-8, brought the aesthetics of the British Arts and Crafts Movement to the production of belleek porcelain (thin, iridescent Parian ware), which enjoyed a vogue after the US Centennial Exhibition of 1876 in Philadelphia.

THE ARTFUL TRICKS OF FORGERS, AND THE MORE HONEST EFFORTS THAT
CREATE REPRODUCTIONS, HAVE FREQUENTLY PROVEN HARD TO DETECT –
ESPECIALLY BY THOSE WHO WANT TO MAKE A GREAT DISCOVERY.

# FAKES, FORGERIES, AND REPRODUCTIONS

The collector of ceramics is plagued by a wide range of copies of original articles. Most of these are honest reproductions, made with no attempt at deception and often contemporary with the originals, such as Chelsea copies of Meissen figures. Some copies, however, are forgeries, deliberately intended to deceive the purchaser into thinking he or she is buying an original. Fakes are a sub-class of forgeries, genuine objects altered in some way.

From the time of the Tang dynasty (618–906), the Chinese have looked back to earlier periods as being worthy of copying. No deception has been intended: the Chinese have a strong sense of history, and by remaking pieces

**TWO DELFT WINE BOTTLES**

A 1930s forgery with false wear (left) and a genuine piece (right), 184 mm (7¼ in). (*Below*)

**TWO TEAPOTS**

Genuine Yongzheng ware, 175 mm (6⅞ in), (left) and a French imitation (right) made *c.* 1880, 108 mm (4¼ in). (*Bottom*)

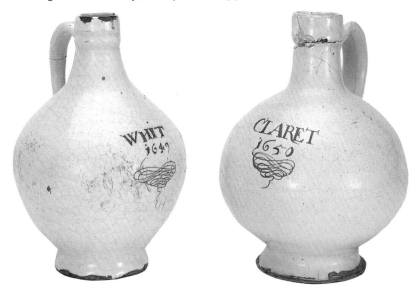

from former reigns they believe they link themselves to them. To this end, they have reproduced on their copies the appropriate reign marks.

However close a copy, it will contain clues in its shape, body, glaze, colour or painting that will enable it to be differentiated from the original. It is impossible for the copier to reproduce exactly all the ingredients and techniques that were available to the original creator: clay deposits become worked out, kilns change, glazes become standardized, formulae are lost. Most important of all, the eye of the imitator is unconsciously influenced by the styles of his own period and of earlier periods unknown to the craftsmen he is copying. These are almost impossible to shake off and subtle elements of them will appear in the forms or painting.

Judging the authenticity of a pot involves all the criteria mentioned above. Marks have been copied since Meissen first put its crossed-swords mark on its pieces *c.* 1724. This mark became a symbol of quality, and many of the first English factories in the mid 18th century added it to their pieces, Worcester, Derby, Lowestoft and Longton Hall among them.

The most numerous and, for the amateur, most confusing reproductions were made in Paris by Émile Samson in the second half of the 19th century. Most, particularly the Meissen copies, are close to the originals, but the hard-paste bodies of the English copies, which should have been of soft paste, enable these to be detected as reproductions. In most cases Samson added an impressed mould number or his own identifying mark or both. These have occasionally been erased, making deception more likely.

The most recent fakes of note have been old plates, mostly Meissen, Chinese or Japanese, which have had their original decoration replaced with that resembling the designs on more valuable ware. These fakes can be very hard to detect.

## TWO IZNIK TANKARDS

On the left is a copy by the Florentine Ullyse Cantagalli, made *c.* 1880, with the identifying mark removed to aid deception, 220 mm (9⅝ in). On the right is a genuine 16th-century example, 210 mm (8¼ in). Cantagalli specialized in copies of Italian maiolica, Persian and Turkish wares.

## FURTHER READING

The following list of materials for further reading offers a broad range of literature. Both specialist and general works are included. While every effort has been made to give the date of the most recent edition, new ones may have been published since this book went to press.

Adams, Len & Yvonne
**Meissen Portrait Figures**
London 1987

Atterbury, Paul (ed)
**History of Porcelain**
1982

Barber, Edwin and Atlee
**The Pottery and Porcelain of the United States and Marks of American Potters**,
(combined edition)
New York 1976

Battie, David (ed)
**Sotheby's Encyclopedia of Porcelain**
London 1990

Charleston, R.J. (ed)
**World Ceramics**
London 1968

Chewon, Kim, and G. St.G. M. Gompertz
**The Ceramic Art of Korea**
London 1961

Cushion, J.P., and W.B. Honey
**Handbook of Pottery and Porcelain Marks**
(revised edition)
London 1965

Dimond, M.S.
**A handbook of Muhammadan Art**
(Chapter X)
New York 1958

Dray, Rudolf E.
**Apothecary Jars**
London 1978

Fay-Halle, Antoinette, and Barbara Mundt
**Nineteenth Century European Porcelain**
London 1983

Frothingham, Alice Wilson
**Lustreware of Spain**
New York 1951

Garner, F.H.
**English Delftware**
London 1948

Godden, G.A.
**Encyclopaedia of British Porcelain Manufacturers**
London 1988

Honey, W.B.
**Old English Porcelain**
London 1977

Howard, D. and J. Ayers
**China for the West**
London and New York 1978

Jenyns, R.S.
**Later Chinese Porcelain**
London 1951

**– Japanese Porcelain**
London 1965

Kurz, O.
**Fakes – A Handbook for Collectors**
London 1948

Leach, Bernard
**A Potter's Book**
London 1977

Levin, Elaine
**The History of American Ceramics, 1607-Present**
New York 1981

Liverani, G.
**Five Centuries of Italian Majolica**
London 1960

Llewellyn, Jewitt
**The Ceramic Art of Great Britain**
London 1985 (Reprint of 1883 edition)

Medley, Margaret
**The Art of the Chinese Potter**
Oxford 1981

Miller, R.A.
**Japanese Ceramics**
Rutland 1960

Savage, George
**18th Century German Porcelain**
London 1958

**– 17th and 18th Century French Porcelain**
London 1960

Spargo, John
**The A B C of Bennington Pottery Wares**
Bennington, Vermont, 1948

Wallace Collection
**Catalogue of Ceramics, Pottery, Maiolica, Faience & Stoneware**
London 1976

Watkins, Lura Woodside
**Early New England Potters and Their Wares**
Cambridge, Massachusettes, 1950

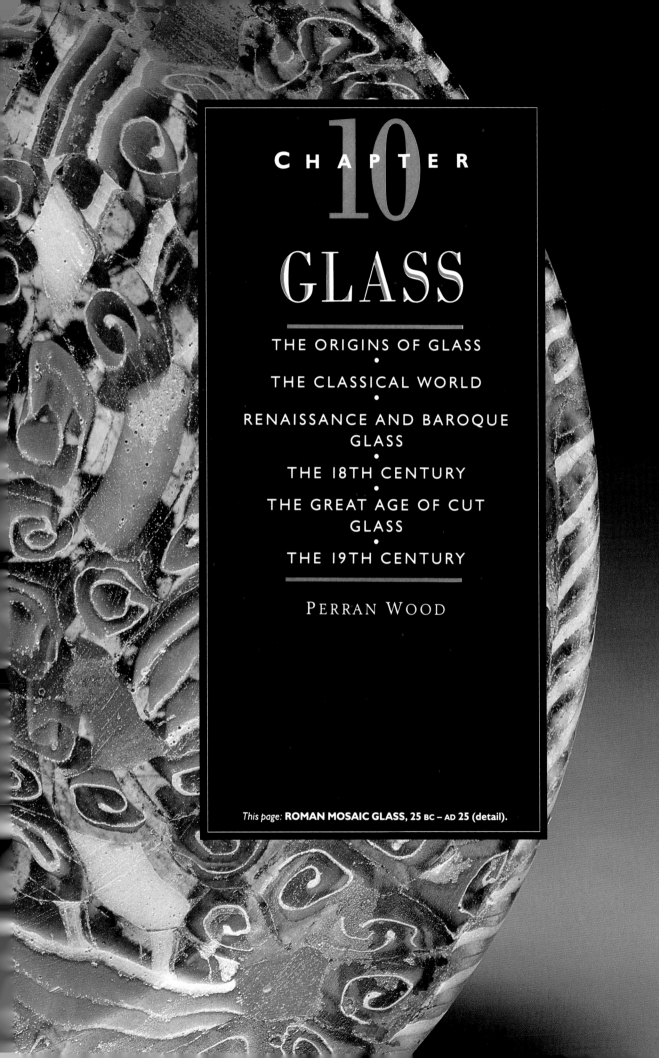

# CHAPTER 10

# GLASS

THE ORIGINS OF GLASS
·
THE CLASSICAL WORLD
·
RENAISSANCE AND BAROQUE
GLASS
·
THE 18TH CENTURY
·
THE GREAT AGE OF CUT
GLASS
·
THE 19TH CENTURY

PERRAN WOOD

*This page:* **ROMAN MOSAIC GLASS, 25 BC – AD 25 (detail).**

# 10
# GLASS

**T**HE EARLY HISTORY OF GLASS IS THE STORY OF A RARE AND COSTLY
MATERIAL THAT SURVIVED IN LIMITED QUANTITIES. **B**UT THIS FRAGILE PAST
LAID THE BASIS FOR THE VERSATILE PRODUCTS OF MORE RECENT HISTORY
THAT HAVE COMBINED UTILITY WITH BEAUTY.

**LAMP**
*Egypt;* **Late 14th century**

By the 14th century Syria
was renowned for its
production of enamelled
wares, particularly mosque
lamps. The art of enamelling
was to be adopted by the
Venetians, perhaps a by-
product of their extensive
trade with the Middle East.
(*Above*)

From the earliest times, glass has fascinated man. In areas of volcanic
activity, natural glass – obsidian – was used from prehistoric times
to make tools. Man-made glass first appeared in Mesopotamia (present-day Iraq) in the third millennium BC. Its ingredients are simple:
silica (sand) is melted in a furnace, together with alkaline fluxing agents
or salts (soda or potash), which lower the temperature at which the
mixture becomes molten (soda is obtained by burning seaweed, potash
from the ash of deciduous trees). The addition of certain chemicals
such as metallic oxides influences the colour and clarity of the glass:
iron turns it green; cobalt, blue; nickel or manganese, violet, while
colour is removed by counteracting one tint with another to produce
greatly prized "crystal" clear glass. When glass is molten it can be
manipulated with a series of special tools, many of which are
unchanged since Roman times.

Once glass-blowing had been discovered in the Near East around 50
BC, it was possible to produce large quantities and a wide range of

**BOWL**
*Eastern Mediterranean or
Italy;* **100 BC–AD 100**

A fine example of deeply
coloured luxury glassware
of this period. The bowl
would have been cast and
then polished to bring out
the depth of colour.

household vessels in glass at little cost, as long as a supply of the basic materials was available. Glassmaking centres tended to spring up in afforested areas with a ready supply of fuel, raw materials for the construction of the furnace and its pots, and preferably near a river, from which clean sand could be obtained and which allowed for easy trade and transport. Gradually tightly-knit dynastic communities of glassmakers settled permanently in areas like the forests of Bohemia and Silesia, Lorraine, the Spessart and in Stourbridge, England.

By the Renaissance, a glass house needed a considerable staff and teamwork to ensure efficient production. The glass house master directed the whole operation and workforce, which included the pot maker, the furnace builder, the smith (to maintain the iron tools), the clerk (to supervise the financial side) and the glassmakers: a head gaffer with various apprentices, gatherers, servitors, marverers and finishers.

From the humblest beginnings glassmaking has expanded over the centuries, in some epochs remaining a commonplace substance, in others treated as a rare material of mystical and financial value. The craft has continually been refined and adapted to current needs, and the various uses to which glass has been put have mushroomed. Besides its domestic uses for drinking and storage, its application in such areas as architecture has become standard procedure. Glass has also played an important role in science and technology, used in scientific instruments such as barometers and lenses, chemical experiments, medicine, fibre optics, communications and lighting.

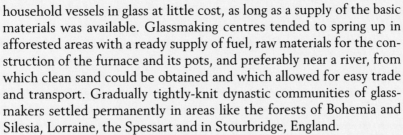

**CANDELABRUM**
*England;* **c. 1770**

The English first developed the use of faceted glass drops on chandeliers and candelabra to increase the reflected light of candles.
(*Above*)

**JUG**
*Joseph Locke*
**Amber glass and gold; 1883**

By the late 19th century, glassmakers in Europe and America were greatly expanding the range of effects that could be obtained by adding various chemicals to glass.

THE EARLIEST GLASS OBJECTS WERE NOT THE MUNDANE WINDOWPANES

OR TABLEWARE MOST OF US ARE USED TO TODAY, BUT BEADS WHOSE

RARITY ENSURED THEY WERE REGARDED AS PIECES OF GREAT VALUE.

# THE ORIGINS OF GLASS

The latest archaeological evidence pinpoints Mesopotamia as the birthplace of glassmaking, which seems to have developed out of the application of vitreous glazes to jewellery, tiles and pottery. The earliest known solid-glass objects are beads, which played an important role not only in personal adornment but also in trade and barter. One of the earliest techniques used to form glass vessels was the "sand-core" method, wherein glass, melted in a crucible, was wound around a "core" of sand, mud and straw wrapped around an iron bar, rather like making a "coil" pot. Small flasks for costly unguents and perfumes were manufactured, often in deep blue or green, onto which threads of glass in white or yellow were trailed and marvered, then combed into a zigzag pattern. Another important technique developed at this time was mould-casting. Either an open or two-part mould was used, into which molten glass or crushed frit was pressed and then reheated to

**KOHL FLASK**
*Egypt;* **c. 1500–1310 BC**

This flask in the shape of a palm column was constructed using the "core" technique and then decorated with applied white and yellow threads pressed into the glass and combed into a zigzag pattern. (*Above*)

**JUG AND ALABASTRON**
*Eastern Mediterranean:*
**400–300 BC**

These pieces were produced by the techniques used in Egypt nearly 1500 years before (*Left*)

fuse; the lost-wax process, too, was used. Moulds were employed to make "mosaic" glass, which consisted of tiny cross sections of drawn-out glass rods arranged in a pattern and then fused and polished when cooled. Objects were carved from solid blocks of glass with implements harder than glass, such as quartz or flint.

### EGYPT
During the reign of the Egyptian pharaoh Thutmosis III (1505–1430 BC), the knowledge of glassmaking was transferred from Mesopotamia to the courts of the New Kingdom at Thebes and elsewhere. Large numbers of small glass articles, including flasks and scent bottles, have been excavated from sites along the Nile. Glass was also used as a decorative element on the furnishings stocked in royal tombs, the most famous examples being from the tomb of Tutankhamen.

### BRONZE AND IRON AGE GLASS
The Bronze Age civilizations suffered decline and collapse c.1200 BC, and with them glassmaking centres in Crete, Cyprus, Anatolia, Syro-Palestine and the Peloponnese. Glassmaking only revived during the Iron Age (1100 BC) with the re-establishment of settled culture and trade. Over the centuries new peoples rose to prominence, including the Phrygians in Anatolia, the Phoenicians along the Levant, the Assyrians along the Tigris/Euphrates and the Greeks in the Aegean. The core technique was revived and vessels took on the shapes of Greek pottery. Tableware was also produced, usually of a pale green tint, but sometimes colourless and coloured. This technique was particularly popular in Persia from the 7th to the 4th century BC, when shallow, almost colourless bowls were decorated with deeply cut petal flutes copied from metalware. The Phoenicians were great traders, and through their activities glassmaking spread westwards across the Mediterranean basin.

IN SPITE OF ITS FRAGILE COMPOSITION, KNOWLEDGE OF THE GLASS MADE
AND USED BY THE ANCIENT GREEKS AND ROMANS IS REASONABLY
EXTENSIVE, AND GIVES A CLEAR PICTURE OF A SOPHISTICATED SOCIETY.

# THE CLASSICAL WORLD

The rise of Macedon's power and the campaigns of Alexander the Great had a convulsive effect on the eastern Mediterranean. The fragmentation of Alexander's empire at his death (323 BC) resulted in the establishment of Hellenistic centres in the Middle East, the most important and long-lasting being that of the Ptolemies at their capital, Alexandria, where a flourishing trade in luxury goods, including glass, grew up, attracting craftsmen from Mesopotamia, Syria and further afield. Techniques of cutting, enamelling and decorating on glass, such as placing gold leaf between two layers of glass (sandwich-gold glass), were perfected there and re-exported, mainly to Italy, where the Etruscans and later the Romans were gaining in influence. In about 50 BC one of the most revolutionary glassmaking techniques was discovered, probably in the Levant: the art of blowing glass. A blob of molten glass is gathered on the end of a hollow iron pipe that allows the glassmaker to blow a hollow receptacle of any size and shape, and to repeat the process cheaply and quickly.

### THE EARLY ROMAN WORLD

In the second half of the first century BC, the Mediterranean basin was for the first time under the control of one power and was united by a common language, communication lines and trade links. With the development of glassblowing at the start of this period, glassmaking reached a high point in its history. Not until Venetian supremacy in the 15th and 16th centuries was there such an explosion of new techniques and forms, such sophistication in luxury glass items and such vast amounts of commonplace, everyday, glass utensils being made. Glass in strong colours was popular. Mould fusion and mosaic techniques were reserved mainly for luxury glass, while blown glass served more functional purposes.

Over the first three centuries AD, glassmaking of considerable uniformity in style and

**SANDWICH-GLASS MEDALLION**
*Roman*
Etched gold leaf between two glass layers

The Latin inscription means "to Anatolius with thanks". (*Left*)

**THE LYCURGUS CAGE CUP**
*Roman*
**4th century AD**

Depicted is King Lycurgus being overwhelmed by the Maenads. (*Below*)

These little mould-blown flasks, probably intended for oils, unguents and scent, are found all over the eastern Mediterranean and were probably made in Syria.

technique spread to all parts of the Roman Empire, to Gaul, Germania and the Iberian Peninsula, mainly at the hands of Syrian or Syrian-influenced glassmakers. Mould-blowing was perfected during the first century AD, and a profusion of small bottles and flasks made by this technique has survived, some with masks or Janus heads, inscriptions and names, grapes and shells. At the same time overlaid, then carved cameo glass was developed, probably in Alexandria. Highly sophisticated murals and pavements were created by means of the mosaic technique: thousands of tiny multicoloured tesserae were cut from solid blocks of glass and assembled into patterns and pictorial scenes. By the time Vesuvius erupted in AD 72, burying Pompeii and Herculaneum, many houses had glass windowpanes, cast and polished and mounted in wooden or metal frames.

LATER ROMAN DEVELOPMENTS

From the end of the second century AD there was a trend away from coloured glass, and colourless glass became the norm for luxury glass. This tended to be cut, engraved or decorated with applied coiled threads, probably a

**CAGE CUP**
*Romano-Syrian*
**c. AD 300**

Cage cups were hanging lamps, their outer reticulated detail carved from the solid glass mass. They are the most prized relics of antique glassmaking. (*Left*)

**THE PORTLAND VASE**
*Roman*
**First century AD**

The epitome of Roman luxury glass, this famous vase is the most celebrated surviving piece of "cameo glass", wherein layers of glass were fused together and then carved. (*Below*)

pieces with coloured threads or blobs continued to be made for some time, but an accelerating decline in standards is noticeable as the western Roman Empire collapsed. There was a gradual stylistic transition towards what is now termed Frankish glass in Gaul and Germania. Shapes become more Teutonic in feeling, less sophisticated; the glass held greater natural impurities, the forms were less delicate, shapes were limited and less inventive. However, the Roman traditions of glassmaking, though stifled, survived the Dark Ages, taking their place among other crafts, whose practice was maintained and stimulated by the Church and Charlemagne and his descendants in what was to become medieval France, Burgundy and the German lands of the Holy Roman Empire. North of the Alps soda glass gradually disappeared after about AD 1000, replaced by potash glass or *waldglas* (forest glass), while glassmakers around the Mediterranean continued to use soda glass, whose raw materials were readily available.

Syrian fashion strongly taken up in Cologne and the Rhineland. The fourth century saw major political changes with the division of the empire into eastern and western halves, and the adoption of Christianity as the official religion. New shapes were introduced, such as small stemmed cups and hanging lamps. Sandwich-gold glass enjoyed a revival, with Christian and Jewish motifs now adorning inset medallions.

With the fragmentation of the Roman Empire, contact between glassmaking centres in the east and west waned, and separate styles and traditions developed. In the Rhineland clear

THE FASHION FOR SHOWY, THEATRICAL GLASSWARE THAT BEGAN IN
THE RENAISSANCE WAS CARRIED ON INTO THE BAROQUE AGE, AS
GLASSMAKING SPREAD MORE WIDELY TO CENTERS ACROSS
WESTERN EUROPE.

# RENAISSANCE AND BAROQUE GLASS

The origins of Venice as a glassmaking centre lay in the Middle Ages. Excavations on Torcello have revealed evidence of glassmaking activity from the sixth and seventh centuries. By the 11th and 12th centuries tesserae, bottles for wine and oil, cups and glass weights were produced, and in the 13th century there was a huge output of glass beads (made from various multi-coloured canes) used as currency in trade. By the late 14th century, there are records of the export of Venetian glass, ie, Richard II granting leave to Venetian merchants to sell their wares, including glass, on the Thames quayside. Through their trading links, Venetian craftsmen were influenced by Byzantium and Syria.

Prosperous, powerful Venice was founded on trade and the naval power to protect and further that trade. Geographically placed in a pivotal position between Byzantium, the Middle East and the western Mediterranean, it developed as the link between the increasingly important European centres and Byzantium and the emporia at the end of the Silk Route. In fact, the sudden surge in glassmaking in Venice only really took off as its trading empire in the Aegean and Levant came under increasing pressure from the Turks and it was forced to look westwards for trade links and allies. The 13th and ·14th centuries saw the glass industry organized through statutes into various sections making beads, flat glass (windowpanes), bottles and lenses. In 1292 all glassmaking activities were transferred to the islands of Murano, about 5 km (3 miles) from the city centre. This was partly to avoid the risk of serious fires, but also had the effect of moulding the glassmaking community (who by the end of the 16th century numbered about 3,000) into a close, secretive body.

Towards the end of the 15th century Venice produced a group of ceremonial glasses of great richness and vigour. The shapes of these goblets and covers, footed bowls and pilgrim flasks, mostly in deep, rich blues and greens, were still influenced by Gothic metalwork. The decora-

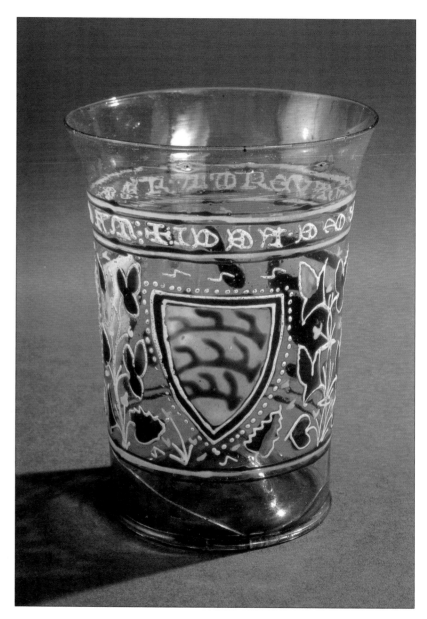

tion, however, reflected the revival of European power and influence, and the burgeoning interest in the roots of European culture in classical antiquity known as the Renaissance. Betrothal pieces, for instance were enamelled with portraits of the couple portrayed as classical busts or in contemporary dress in the manner of

**ENAMELLED BEAKER**
*Possibly Syrian*
**14th century**

Decorated with a Latin inscription and Germanic armorials, this piece was made for a Frankish client.

cameos and medals. Decorators were also inspired by the work of artists such as Mantegna, Gentile da Fabriano and Carpaccio, and used elements from these masters in their own interpretation of classical mythology and allegory. An important decorative element was the bands of dots, scrolls and foliate ornament often framing the main decoration.

At the same time the Venetians experimented with the production of glass in imitation of other materials such as porcelain and semi-precious stones. A small group of wares in opaque-white glass called *lattimo* has survived, reflecting the interest in Chinese porcelain, as well as pieces in *calcedonio*, whose dark marbled effects strove to imitate chalcedony and other materials highly prized at Renaissance courts.

This passion for gems included rock crystal, a natural quartz that, according to alchemists, held magic properties. Its clarity, particularly when carved and polished, was greatly admired, and Venetian glass technicians attempted to obtain these qualities in glass, adding lime to the soda/silica recipe to obtain *cristallo*, a clearer, more watery crystal-like metal than had hitherto been produced. While relatively robust, this improved clear glass could be blown wafer thin and, having a low cooling point, it was easily manipulated with pincers and other implements into an endless variety of shapes. No other European glassmaking centre produced glass of this type in the early 16th century, and the demand for Venetian luxury glass from the courts of Europe was insatiable.

As *cristallo* supplanted other types of coloured glass produced at Murano during the 16th century, glass decorators also adapted to the new material. Enamelling was gradually confined to the decorative borders, with multicoloured dots lined over gilding. Gold leaf was applied and scratched through with a needle to make patterns and inscriptions, and engraving with the point of a diamond was also effected, a technique that Vicenzo di Angelo dall Gall is credited with perfecting *c*.1549. Engraving was often combined with gilding and trailing, and the motifs were mostly foliate, such as acanthus-leaf scrolls, grotesques and occasionally armorials.

## MANNERISM

As the High Renaissance gave way to the more sophisticated and exaggerated style known in the fine arts as Mannerism, this was also reflected in the products of Murano. Paintings of the

**ENAMELLED PILGRIM FLASK**
*Venetian*
**c. 1500**

The earliest Venetian enamelled wares are often in rich dark blue and greens. The decoration is ebullient and favours Renaissance motifs. (*Left*)

**CALCEDONIO BOWL**
*Venetian*
**c. 1500**

The Venetians experimented with glass imitating semiprecious stones as well as rock crystal. (*Below*)

time show that simple but elegant *cristallo* tableware was produced. But the Muranese do not seem to have been able to restrain their inventiveness for long and even the most humdrum cruets and lamps tended to be embellished with coloured trails often ending in fanciful birds' or serpents' heads. The stems of goblets might be blown into a mould with satyrs' masks and the bowl shaped with fanciful curves and moulded detail, or the glass mass itself could be formed of white twisted tubes of glass fused together *(vetro a filigrana)*. This technique, which was to remain in fashion for over 200 years, was first recorded in Murano in 1527, when the Serena brothers applied for a monopoly to make "glass of stripes with twists of cane". From then on cups, beakers, goblets, salvers and tazzas appeared in a range of filigree techniques – lacy, twisting, criss-cross, spiralling etc. Another type of glass developed was "ice glass". A typical Mannerist conceit, it involved plunging a piece of *cristallo* into cold water to craze the surface.

### THE VENETIAN INFLUENCE

Despite efforts of the Venetian authorities to maintain a monopoly on glass, the demand was so great that glassmakers were lured abroad to the European courts, which were desperate for a more accessible supply. As early as 1490 the authorities were threatening glassmakers who divulged technical secrets with dire punishments and penalizing those who tried to return to Venice after working abroad. They seem to have had very little effect, however. The glass house established by Wolfgang Vitl at Hall in the Tyrol in 1534, was the scene of the first important efforts at *façon de Venise* glassmaking outside Italy. In 1570 Archduke Ferdinand II, Regent of the Tyrol, founded a glass house in Innsbruck under his own personal patronage and supervision. He persuaded the Signoria to send him a team of glassblowers, asking for those "with the greatest fantasy in them" and he even attempted blowing glass himself. A representative cross section of what was produced in the Tyrol has been preserved at his castle of Ambras and in the Kunsthistorisches Museum in Vienna. The glasses are usually distinct from Venetian examples in the greyish tint of the metal and the slightly heavier forms. Most popular were covered goblets on high feet with diamond-engraved decoration, often centred around armorial motifs such as the double-headed eagle of the Holy Roman Empire.

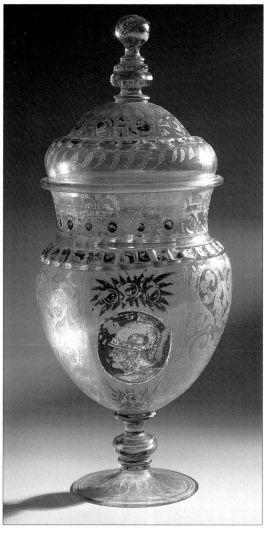

**ENGRAVED AND COLD-PAINTED GOBLET AND COVER**
*Court Glasshouse, Innsbruck*
**c. 1575**

Venetians working for the Archduke Ferdinand II produced distinctive engraved and painted wares in a greyish glass. (*Left*)

**FAÇON DE VENISE GOBLET**
*Antwerp*
**Late 16th century**

The stem with mould-blown masks and applied mask prunts was particularly popular with glassmakers working in the Venetian style in the Netherlands. (*Below*)

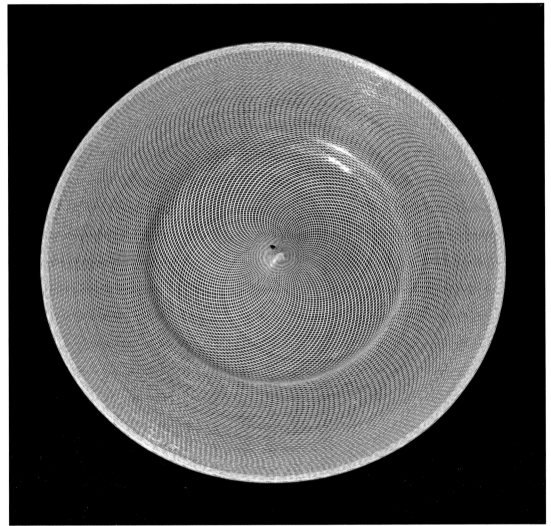

**FILIGREE PLATE**
*Venetian*
**Late 16th century**

The Venetians produced exuberant wares in *vetro di filigrana*. Rods of opaque-white glass and air bubbles were incorporated into the glass to achieve effects the Germans called "net" glass.

Besides shapes based on Venetian prototypes, there are Germanic forms like tall, cylindrical *stangen* and *humpen*.

Other glass houses producing Venetian-style glass were set up in the German lands, but none stayed in production for long. The ingredients for making *façon de Venise* glass were expensive and difficult to procure, and glassmakers tended to be restlessly peripatetic. Munich, Vienna, Kassel and Dessau, among others, could boast, if only briefly, of a glass house worked by Italians, and there is no doubt that Venetian-style glass had a considerable effect on the native forest glass production, leading to greater refinement and the adoption of some Venetian elements, especially enamelling.

### FRANCE

The greatest trading rival of Venice in the Mediterranean was the city-state of Genoa, among whose fiefdoms was Altare, whose glass-making expertise at first possibly developed via Syria and then in the 15th century received an infusion from Murano. As no piece from Altare has been identified, their products certainly must have been closely modelled on those of Venice. The Genoese authorities seem to have had a more broad-minded approach to the problems of monopoly and encouraged the Altarists to go abroad, hiring them out and only stipulating they did not pass on their secrets.

Although Venetians had been producing enamelled wares in Lyon from the second decade of the 16th century, it was the in-heritance of the Dukedom of Nevers by the Gonzaga Marquis of Monferrato (where Altare was situated) that led to the establishment of an important Venetian-style glassmaking centre in France. From Nevers Altarists moved on to Paris, Nantes, Rouen and Orléans. Over the next century this influx of Italians resulted in the establishment of an important body of *gentilhommes verriers* (gentlemen glassmakers), strong on the technical side of glassmaking, who continued making simple forms of glasses and bottles in the Venetian manner into the 17th century, but became increasingly expert in manufacturing flat glass as well.

### THE LOW COUNTRIES

From early on Italian glassmakers were attracted to the Low Countries, which had long maintained links with Italy and which it was overtaking as the trading powerhouse of Europe. In 1506 Engelbert Colinet, a native of the southern Netherlands, was allowed to set up a glass house at Beauwelz, near Mons, in which Italians were employed, and from 1541 there were Venetians working in Antwerp, which became the most important glassmaking centre in the Low Countries for the next hundred years, producing Venetian-style table glass of such quality that it is virtually indistinguishable from that of Venice. Ice glass and filigree glass were very popular, as were well-proportioned goblets with lion's-head mould-blown stems, the bowls often decorated with applied lion's-head prunts and diamond-point engraving. Many pieces from the Netherlands have sur-

vived with silver or gilt-metal mounts. Alongside more sober products exuberant glass was produced to satisfy the late Mannerist and early Baroque fashions for display and fantasy. Glass houses at Mons and Namur as well as Liège, which overtook Antwerp as the glassmaking centre of the Netherlands after the Thirty Years War, produced *nefs*, elaborate centrepieces in the form of fanciful boats, as well as "serpent-stem" goblets which were in demand well into the 17th century.

### ENGLAND

Records show that eight Italian glassblowers came to London from Antwerp in 1549. The "Parr Pot", a tankard with *lattimo* stripes and English silver-gilt mounts, may be an example of their work. Venetian glasses are mentioned in the inventories of Henry VIII at Nonesuch Palace, where they would have been regarded as requisite status symbols. Even in Scotland, at a banquet in honour of the Patriarch of Venice, the Earl of Moray ordered the table to be set with a number of crystal glasses and then for the cloth to be whipped off, smashing the glass,

**GROUP OF *FAÇON DE VENISE* "SERPENT-STEM" GOBLETS**
*Netherlands*
**Mid 17th century**

These goblets represent the heights of luxury and fantasy attained by "Venetian" craftsmen. Many of these pieces were made at the Beauwelz glasshouse in present-day Belgium.

which was immediately replaced with even better and costlier examples! England benefited greatly in terms of craftsmen and expertise from the religious upheavals of the mid 16th century on the Continent, particularly France and the Netherlands, whose glassmakers, among others, moved across the Channel in search of stability to practise their craft. Flat-glass makers from Normandy and Lorraine settled in the Sussex and Surrey Weald and in 1567 one Jean Carré (d 1572), a native of Arras, arrived in London and applied for a patent to produce glass *à la façon de Venise*. He established two furnaces at Alfold, producing window glass and simple forest glass utensils, and the Crutched Friars glass house in London, where he employed a team of glassblowers from the Netherlands and Venice, under the master Jacopo Verzelini (1522–1616). Ten glasses attributed to Carré are standard *façon de Venise* productions, of the type associated with northwestern Europe; apart from the English inscriptions identifying their source, their metal was of a greyish tint, their forms were on the plain side, with generous proportions and little manipulation, and their diamond-point decoration was of the foliate type like that produced in Hall or Antwerp. In 1592 Verzelini retired and left the running of the glass house to his son, having established the manufacture of glass in England on a sound footing that was to see it through well into the 17th century.

## SPAIN

In the 16th and 17th centuries, Spanish glass displayed the conjunction of Venetian and Islamic influences evident in all the country's arts and crafts. Early on an idiomatic style was forged, making Spanish glass easily identifiable in the way that glass from other centres further north is not. The monarchs Ferdinand and Isabella were keen collectors of Venetian wares, which would have encouraged the foundation of local industry. Indeed, by the beginning of the 16th century Barcelona was said to have had a reputation rivalling that of Venice. A small group of distinctively enamelled pieces has survived from the mid 16th century. The forms are often as idiosyncratic as the enamelling, with slim, flattened bottles vaguely resembling pilgrim flasks but with Islamic undertones. The decoration is almost always foliate with precise but simplistically drawn details of human figures, birds, cypresses and stylized foliage in predominantly apple green, yellow and white. In

the 17th century Catalan production started to combine Venetian techniques like filigree with traditional Catalan forms such as the *porrón* and *cantir*, drinking vessels for wine, and the *almorratxa*, its multiple spouts for sprinkling rosewater. Spouts and handles were often embellished with vigorous pincerwork, trailing and rings, ostensibly of Venetian influence but somehow more reminiscent of traditional Syrian decoration. Other glassmaking centres, particularly in southern Spain, seem to have

**FAÇON DE VENISE GOBLET**
*Jacopo Verzelini, London*
**1586**

At this date Verzelini was the only person in England allowed by Royal Patent to produce Venetian-style glass. It bears the English inscription: "In God is my trust".

made no efforts to produce Venetian-style crystal and turned out mainly green-tinted wares with indigenous shapes.

### GERMANY AND CENTRAL EUROPE

Venetian glass was largely confined to urban centres. However, from medieval times the vast tracts of Central European and Scandinavian forests such as Franconia, the Fichtelgebirge and the Riesengebirge (on the borders of Bohemia and Silesia), Lorraine, Thuringia, the Spessart and the valleys of the Meuse and Sambre rivers had facilitated the establishment of glassmaking centres within easy reach of abundant natural resources.

As the domestic use of glass became increasingly widespread, landlords, particularly in Bohemia, encouraged entrepreneurial glassmakers such as the Preusslers and Schurers to set up glass houses on their land. The contractual agreement would usually include rent and part of the output to the landlord. Soon, domestic glass ware was being produced in the thousands, and many distinctive shapes evolved. These ranged from the popular *roemer*, made in the Rhineland and the Spessart, to the suggestively-shaped 17th-century *angster*. The colours of some glass ware, which was originally unavoidably created by impurities, became, by the 17th century, a desirable attribute.

### ENAMELLING

A vital element of glass decoration the Germans borrowed from Venetians during the latter half of the 16th century and employed with enthusiasm right into the 18th century was the use of enamels painted on glass. The earliest enamelled glasses of German interest, all with German armorials, were executed in Murano for Teutonic customers. Towards the end of the century the situation is blurred, with a number of flared goblets on high feet extant that could have been made in Venice or a glass house over the Alps, such as Hall, Munich or Prague, which produced Venetian-style glass made by immigrant Italians. Another type of glass on which armorials were painted in the last quarter of the 16th and first quarter of the 17th centuries was the *stangen*, a tall, cylindrical beaker with everted folded foot. Many of the coats-of-arms belong to families from Nuremberg – an important independent city with trading links to Italy. Another group of *stangen* were decorated, probably in Bohemia, with low-fired enamel allegorical figures of Fame and Justice after

**FOREST-GLASS**
***KRAUTSTRUNK***
*German*
**Late 15th century**

This primitive green glass (coloured by the impurities in the recipe) had its roots in a long tradition of glassmaking in afforested areas in France and the German lands.

# GERMAN GLASS SHAPES

From medieval roots sprang the manufacture of a range of wares, mainly beakers of various forms and flasks in tones of green, hues coming about from impurities in the sand and/or ash flux. From Gothic glasses such as the *maigelein,* a low oval beaker with incurved sides, and the *nuppenbecher* (a squat beaker, the sides with applied blobs or prints), there had developed the *roemer,* a distinctive beaker with a barrel-shaped bowl on a cylindrical stem decorated with raspberry prunts and a high spun foot.

More primitive forms included the *daumenglas,* with intruded prunts with which to grip the stem, and the "unbreakable" beakers, a distinct group in the deepest emerald green and of identical heavy form with large raspberry prunts and a verse written in diamond-point around the rim, exhorting the drinker to "drain me, set me down and fill me up again". Other variants were the *passglas,* a tall, cylindrical beaker, and *stangen,* with applied horizontal trailed, engraved or enamelled rings, which drinkers in turn had to drain exactly from ring to ring; whoever missed the next ring had to keep going until he drained the glass to the exact level of a ring. As the 17th century progressed some of these glasses increased in sophistication, with assured handling of elements such as dimple moulding, trailing and prunts. There were also joke glasses such as *angsters* (flasks with multiple necks, probably developed from the *kuttrolf*) phallus flasks and flasks in the form of animals.

1 Maigelein

2 Nuppenbecher

3 Roemer

4 Daumenglas

5 Passglas

6 Stangen

7 Kuttrolf

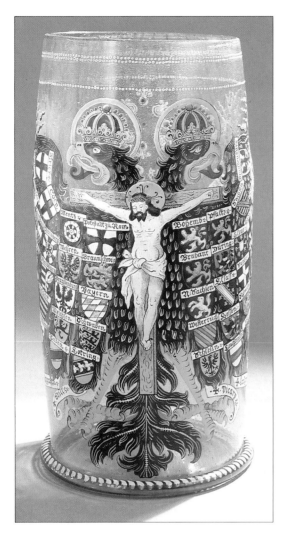

**ENAMELLED** *HUMPEN*
*German*
**Dated 1651**

This large cylindrical beaker was probably intended as a bumper for beer or wine. It is painted with the double-headed eagle of the Holy Roman Empire and the arms of the states comprising it arranged on its wings. (*Far left*)

**ENAMELLED** *HUMPEN*
*Franconia*
**Dated 1699**

A popular motif used by Franconian painters during the 17th and 18th centuries was the Ochsenkopf ("Oxhead") Mountain, a particularly fertile area and supposedly rich in hidden metals. (*Left*)

engraved sources. In these instances a Venetian and Germanic stylistic synthesis was taking place, the form Germanic in origin and the decoration, often engraving combined with enamelling, pointing to Venice.

Another large group of mainly *humpen* was painted with a Germanic nationalistic motif, the *reichsadler*, or double-headed eagle, symbol of the Holy Roman Empire. Based on an early 16th-century woodcut, the bird has outstretched wings decorated with lines of armorial shields representing the entire hierarchy of the empire, from the electors who chose the emperor at the top down to the humbler landgraves. The earliest known example of this variety of large *humpen* is dated 1572, and the type was produced into the 18th century, though by then in debased form. There were also "electors'" *humpen*, with the electors represented by rows of mounted horsemen; guild *humpen* and beakers, often commissioned by guild members and their friends; so-called *jagdhumpen* with painted views of stag, bear and boar hunts; and

betrothal pieces with names, dates and the two families' coats-of-arms.

A type of enamelled vessel popular in Franconia was the *ochsenkopf humpen*, its subject the magical Ochsenkopf Mountain in the Fichtelgebirge, symbolically depicted with an ox's head, forests, game, and sometimes a chapel on its summit, all bound with a padlock signifying the mineral riches it held.

The art of enamelling continued in the German lands, particularly Bohemia, far into the 18th century, but gradually declined into a folk craft. Surviving examples of this are thousands of little octagonal flasks in clear and coloured glass, painted in a limited range of colours with peasants and stylized foliage.

**Wash-Enamelling** A more sophisticated offshoot of these guild-oriented enamelling workshops was the art of painting in a thinner enamel – sometimes in colours, sometimes in a monochrome such as black or sepia, called *schwarzlot* in German. This was practised by artists working from home *(hausmaler)*, and with it a more painterly effect could be achieved. One of the earliest and greatest exponents of this technique was Johann Schaper (1621–70) who worked in Nuremberg. As a rule these decorators used prints for inspiration, concentrating on classical landscapes, armorials and figural scenes. This decorative tradition continued into the first half of the 18th century in Bohemia.

DEVELOPMENTS IN THE ART OF ENGRAVING
The Venetians had developed diamond-point engraving on glass during the 16th century, and

a decorative vocabulary of classical and foliate motifs had grown up wherever the Venetian style of glassmaking took root.

As a direct result of the passionate interest in and collecting of curiosities, minerals and other specimens, cameos and *preciosa*, engraving took off in a new direction. Emperor Rudolph II (reigned 1576–1612) transferred his capital from Vienna to Prague and set about attracting the most virtuoso craftsmen skilled at working rock crystal, agate, bloodstone and smoky topaz, either carving them into cameos (with raised decoration) or sculpting from the solid sub-

**SCHWARZLOT
ENAMELLED BEAKER**
*Johann Schaper, Nuremberg*
**c. 1660**

Schaper was perhaps the finest of the Nuremberg school of painters who used this technique of black or sepia wash enamel on both porcelain and glass. The scene of a gypsy cavalcade is after a print by Jacques Callot.

## PORTRAIT GOBLET
*Nuremberg; engraved by
Hermann Schwinger*
**c. 1680**

The portrait is of Paul
Albrecht Reiter, a
Nuremberg notable
depicted in typical Baroque
style in full-bottomed wig,
lace and armour. Schwinger
excelled at fine calligraphic
inscriptions, as on the
reverse of this example.
(*Right*)

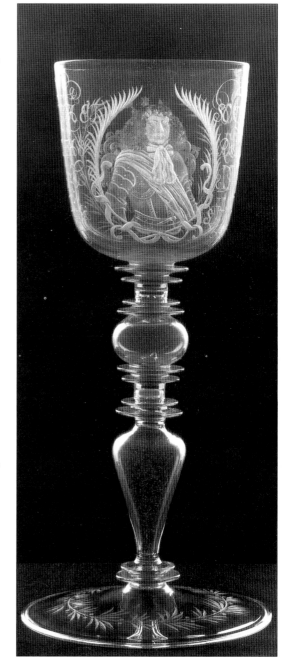

## PART-COLOURED
## GOBLET AND COVER
*Nuremberg*

Glassmakers at Nuremberg
specialized in producing
dramatic goblets with
elements in purple, green
and blue. (*Left*)

## LEHMANN PLAQUE
*Casper Lehmann, Prague*
**Engraved glass; 1620**

The simple depiction on
this plaque may well have a
hidden political meaning
drawn from the turbulent
history of 17th-century
Central Europe. The same
year the plaque was made
the Hapsburg ruler crushed
a rebellion of his Bohemian
subjects. The lion
traditionally symbolizes
Fortitude and Vengeance,
and the plaque may allude
to the recent Hapsburg
victory.

stance objects and vessels that were then ingeniously mounted in precious metals with further
accretions of jewels or enamelling. The skills of
Rudolph's craftsmen also involved the development of an efficient mechanism to work the
stonecutter's wheel, either with treadle, human
or, later, water power.

Caspar Lehmann (*c.* 1570–1622) was one of
the skilled artists attracted to Rudolph's court.
He is always credited with transferring the technique of wheel-engraving from gems and
hardstones to glass, but there were other contemporaries such as Zacharias Peltzer (*fl.*
1576–96), who may have taught Lehmann at

# IMPROVEMENTS IN GLASS TECHNOLOGY

Glass technology took a leap forward as wheel-engraved decoration on glass became popular. The Renaissance had provided a tremendous stimulus to all aspects of discovery, both geographical and scientific. Galileo, for instance, was refining the power of his telescopes with ground lenses, Descartes and Newton investigating the behaviour of light when passed through lenses. The manufacture of a heavier, more crystalline glass became increasingly important in the development of scientific and nautical instruments (it was also necessary to withstand the action of the engraving wheels). In 1612 Antonio Neri (1576–1614) published his famous treatise on glassmaking, *L'Arte Vetraria*, which included recipes for the making of crystal and coloured glass. In 1662 this was translated into English by Christopher Merrett and in 1679 into German by the glassmaker and chemist Johann Kunckel (1630–1703). Working for the great Elector of Brandenburg (d 1688), Kunckel claimed to have discovered the recipe for making ruby-red glass, or *goldrubinglas*. In Bohemia in the 1670s and 1680s glass masters such as Le Vasseur d'Ossimont and Müller were developing a heavier more "rock-crystalline" glass by adding chalk to the potash flux. In England George Ravenscroft, who had spent time in Venice, produced a different but improved type of heavy crystal with the use of lead oxide.

At the same time in France Louis XIV instigated a huge building programme, at Versailles and elsewhere, for whose furnishing he and his minister Colbert formulated a policy of stimulating the domestic production of the decorative arts, including glass. In 1688 Bernard Perrot (originally Perotto, d 1709), an Altarist from Orléans was granted the patent by the Académie des Sciences for the production of flat glass by a new method, that of casting. This was highly important for the development of the Baroque interior: it was now possible to produce large windowpanes not disfigured by the bull's-eye of the crown method, and it also led to the development of large wall mirrors in which chandeliers, with new twinkling glass drops, could be reflected. A manufactory for the production of cast flat glass under royal patronage was established at St-Gobain in the forest of La Thiérache.

**18TH CENTURY GLASSMAKING**
Engraving from Diderot's *Encyclopédie*

the court of Duke Wilhelm V of Bavaria. In 1609 Lehmann was granted a patent for engraving glass that mentions him as its inventor; only one signed piece of his survives, a footed beaker with allegorical figures in the Prague Museum. Lehmann's one recorded pupil was Georg Schwanhardt (1601–67), who was vital in the dissemination of the technique, returning as he did to Nuremberg where he trained his two sons, Georg (1625–76) and Heinrich (1640–93).

Thus an active, highly accomplished tradition of engraving was established in Nuremberg that lasted into the second quarter of the next cen-tury. The Nuremberg engravers' work is found mainly on small ovoid beakers with covers supported on hollow bun feet and on tall covered goblets with ovoid bowls, the stem made up of hollow knops and collars.

Engraved decoration at this time consisted mainly of armorials, portraits of the emperor or important Nuremberg dignitaries, and allegorical, biblical and mythological scenes. Engraver Johann (or Hans) Wolfgang Schmidt (1676–1710) specialized in battle scenes. By the end of the 17th century wheel-engraving had supplanted almost all other forms of decoration on glass and was practised throughout Europe.

GREAT IMPROVEMENTS IN THE QUALITY OF THEIR PRODUCTS WERE ACHIEVED BY GLASSMAKERS WORKING DURING THE 18TH CENTURY. NEW CENTERS OF PRODUCTION EMERGED, WHILE OLD ONES DECLINED.

# THE 18TH CENTURY

The roots of 18th-century prosperity and the expansion of glassmaking on a wider scale were found in the second half of the previous century. The cessation of religious upheavals in Europe, research into the production of a clearer and more robust type of glass and developments in France in flat glass, led to the establishment of new glassmaking centres by the early 1700s.

## ENGLAND

Present-day knowledge of 17th-century English glass is obscured by lack of proven examples. It seems that Italians and Dutch continued to work there, but in the current *façon de Venise* style practised throughout the Low Countries, which makes it almost impossible to pinpoint the origins of glasses that were mainly produced with funnel bowls, a simple hollow stem, often in the form of a knop, and a wide foot, its rim folded under for added strength.

There is evidence that English glass retailers ordered directly from Venice, which suggests that home production was lacking in quality and/or quantity. In 1674 the Glass Sellers' Company, a city guild that controlled the glass trade, appointed George Ravenscroft (1632–83) to carry out research into the feasibility of producing a better, tougher, more transparent indigenous glass. He achieved this

**ARMORIAL BOWL**
*Savoy Glasshouse, George Ravenscroft*
**c. 1674**

Engraved with the arms of the Butler Buggins family, the fact that it is "crizzled" suggests that it belongs to the period when Ravenscroft was still experimenting with lead glass. (*Below left*)

**GROUP OF TWIST WINE GLASSES**
*English*
**c. 1760**

During the mid 18th century English glassmakers excelled at producing a wide range of stems enclosing white and coloured enamel and air threads. The engraved motifs all express Jacobite sentiments. (*Below right*)

after adding lead oxide to the batch, producing a clear, highly refractive yet robust glass, which encouraged the use of simpler forms and styles that set off the material's splendid qualities.

Of the nine recorded pieces bearing Ravenscroft's seal – a prunt he placed on his work by permission of the Glass Sellers' Company after 1677 – many show Venetian influence via the Netherlands in the use of coiled and pincered stems, gadrooning and "nipped diamond waves", a form of pinched ribbing. By the end of the 17th century, a new type of drinking glass, the "baluster wine", appeared. Utilizing the new, heavier glass with its greater refractive qualities and coinciding, too, with a more sober, restrained fashion in the decorative arts during Queen Anne's reign, these glasses, some as tall as 30 cm (12 in), were often extremely simple, consisting of a deep ovoid bowl on a stem composed of a true or inverted baluster. There was a complete vocabulary of knops – ball, acorn, annulated – with or without the baluster, and the foot was wide and usually with a folded rim.

The fashion for these heavy balusters only lasted from about 1690 until the 1720s, by which time the glasses were getting smaller and the stems lighter, the knops now incorporating air bubbles and formed more as "buttons" or collars. This elegant glass type became known as

**ENGRAVED GOBLETS**
*Dutch*
**c. 1750**

Engraving was very popular in the Netherlands, both with a diamond point and the wheel. These two well-proportioned glasses, long called "Newcastle" light balusters but now thought to be Dutch in origin, are decorated with a scene, a toast to "Friendship" and the arms of the United Provinces.

the "Newcastle" baluster, although there is no evidence to prove that it originated or was produced exclusively there. A large number are engraved with Dutch motifs such as the arms of the United Provinces and the House of Orange, suggesting that some were exported to the Netherlands. However, it seems more likely that many were produced in the Low Countries (18th-century pattern-books from a glass house in Namur include drawings of what have traditionally been called "English" glasses), and that this and other types of "English" glass were made contemporaneously on both sides of the North Sea.

In 1745 the first of a series of taxes on glass by weight was introduced that is thought to have encouraged glassmakers to lighten their products. It also coincides, however, with the Rococo period in the decorative arts, which was fanciful and lighter in style. Glasses became smaller and less weighty: the bowls were of trumpet form drawn up on a slender plain stem with air bead or a very light baluster.

Probably toward the middle of the century English glassmakers started introducing air threads and then opaque-white and coloured threads into the stems – originally a Venetian technique, but now used in a Rococo manner. A relatively large number of these glasses have survived and give a good picture of the inventiveness of the glassmakers from the 1750s to the 1780s, and the variations and combinations of threading they achieved. Most are small, many probably designed to hold cordials and fortified wines. Some seem to have been made in large sets, indicating that uniformity on the dining table or at social occasions was desirable.

Engraving on glass in England never reached the heights that it did on the Continent. Many engraved glasses have survived, but most are of pedestrian quality. As elsewhere, the subjects tended to be armorial, toasts to popular heroes, and simple flowers and birds. In a group apart are the glasses engraved with Jacobite or the opposing Hanoverian sentiments. These date from after the 1745 rebellion and include the Jacobite rose, portraits of Bonny Prince Charlie, the group of "Amen" glasses and so-called "concealed" Jacobite emblems.

Coloured glass was also fashionable in the second half of the century. In centres like Bristol, London and South Staffordshire royal-blue, emerald-green and opaque-white wares were produced. Sets of decanters were particularly popular, many gilded with the names of the intended contents and kept in a metal or leather-bound stand. Decanters with ground-glass stoppers had only come into general use at the table around the 1760s. (Before that liquor was generally decanted into a serving bottle or jug from the "black" wine bottle).

Besides engraving, other forms of decoration on glass in England at this time included gilding and enamelling. The Beilby family in Newcastle-upon-Tyne had an enamelling studio in the 1760s and 1770s. Their work is distinctive and at its best of fine quality. Besides large numbers of wine glasses painted in opaque white with fruiting vine round the gilt rim, they also carried out a number of outstanding armorial pieces in coloured enamels.

### THE NETHERLANDS

Antwerp, as one of the great European trading centres of the 16th and 17th centuries, also developed a flourishing glassmaking trade, founded and for many years run by Italians. After this great city went into decline at the end of the Thirty Years War (1648), it was overtaken by Liège as the centre of glassmaking in the Low Countries. Right up to the end of the 17th century glass in the Netherlands was produced in the *façon de Venise* style, incorporating some aspects of Nuremberg and Bohemian shapes and designs.

As in the Holy Roman Empire, engraving on glass was very popular here; in the 17th and 18th centuries the United Provinces were the centre of a group of amateur engravers such as Anna Roemers (1583–1651) and her sister Maria Tesselschade (1595–1646), and the cloth merchant Willem van Heemskerk (1613–1692). They were extremely accomplished calligraphists, using the point of a diamond to delineate inscriptions and homilies on goblets

**CRUET BOTTLE**
*English*
**c. 1780**

Sets of deep blue, green and, more rarely, amethyst decanters, rinsers and cruet bottles (such as this one) became popular in England towards the end of the 18th century. They were placed in stands and marked in gilt with the contents. *(Above)*

**DIAMOND-ENGRAVED FLUTE**
*Monogramist "M",*
*The Netherlands*
**Dated 1657**

The infant Prince William III of Orange, later William III of England, is depicted here. The image is taken from a contemporary print, with the royal arms on the reverse. *(Above right)*

and bottles, no doubt as gifts amongst their circle of friends.

The tradition was continued by Frans Greenwood (1680–1763) of Rotterdam who perfected the art of stipple engraving, a technique of tapping the surface of the glass to leave areas of dots in greater or lesser concentration, creating a subtle effect only appreciated when the glass was held up to the light. He specialized in using paintings of the previous century as subjects. In his turn he influenced a number of other amateur engravers such as Aert Schouman (1710–1792), Jacobus van den Blijk and the atelier of David Wolff (1732–1798). Wolff and his

**SWEETMEAT BOWL AND COVER**
*Bohemian*
***c.* 1730**

The polygonal outline of this *konfektschale* is typical of German Baroque glass design of the period. Goblets and covers of matching shape and engraved detail would also have appeared on the table. The blue tint is unusual.

circle produced a large group of glasses with engravings of sentimental rococo subjects such as putti and children at play, as well as armorials and landscapes.

Wheel engraving had been practised in the Netherlands from the second half of the 17th century and remained popular for the next hundred years or so – as can be seen by the large number of Dutch engraved glasses that have survived. Subjects depicted include armorials, gifts, allegories, landscapes, views of houses, and endless variants of toasts to "Trade", "Love", "Agriculture", "the new mother", "Shipping", "the House of Orange" with appropriate

inscriptions. The most celebrated engraver whose name has survived is Jacob Sang, member of a large family of glass engravers originally from Thuringia.

### BOHEMIA AND GERMANY

The development of a heavy crystalline glass in Bohemia and Potsdam was contemporary with developments in England, and its possibilities as a vehicle for Baroque expression were especially exploited in three German centres over the turn of the century. The Elector of Brandenburg installed Martin Winter (d. 1702) in the glass house at Potsdam, while his brother Friedrich

(d. *c.*1712) worked for Count Schaffgotsch in Silesia, and Christoff Labhardt (d. 1695) and his pupil Franz Gondelach (1663–1726) worked for the Landgrave of Kassel. In all three places water power was used to drive the lathes and grinding wheels, facilitating the production of some of the finest examples of Baroque sculptural art. Gondelach particularly excelled at carving goblets and tazzas from solid blocks of glass in *hochschnitt* (high-relief cutting). This tradition was not long-lived and soon died out, except in Potsdam, where Gottfried Spiller (*c.*1663–1728), carried on the *hochschnitt* tradition into the 1720s.

By the end of the 17th century in Bohemia, a large number of glass houses had been set up on estates of local nobles, and so much glass was produced that entrepreneurs were encouraged to set up export links all over Europe and even the Americas, a phenomenon that lasted well into the 19th century. Depots were set up abroad, and there were travelling salesmen and journeymen engravers who distributed Bohemian glass around Europe on their backs in panniers or carts. Some glass was exported already decorated, or the glass-seller would engrave a piece for the purchaser on the spot with "personalized" motifs.

The first half of the 18th century saw the covered *pokal* at the height of its popularity. These were sturdy goblets with generous bowls supported on a variety of stem forms that were echoed in the finial of the cover, all grounded on a wide foot with plain rim. A common Bohemian stem formation consisted of shoulder knop and baluster stem enclosing spiralling red and gold threads. Invariably the base of the bowl and the stem are cut with facets, roundels or flutes. The wheel-engraved decoration on these goblets tends to be of middling quality, and the motifs limited to strapwork, foliate ornament and Bérainesque grotesques, all combined with the usual armorial devices, and mythological and biblical scenes, often inscribed with toasts. These glasses were used for display and for formal drinking as "bumpers" to be passed round the table.

### THE COURT GLASS ENGRAVER

To some extent glass houses at this time performed the same function as the 16th-century glass houses operated by expatriate Italians. They provided the best, most fashionable product for the many large and small German courts. Wherever there was a glass

**BLUE-TINTED TANKARD**
*German*
**17th century**

Of generous form, this piece represents the provincial German love of clear colours and applied decoration, in this case the blobs on the body, called "prunts". (*Above*)

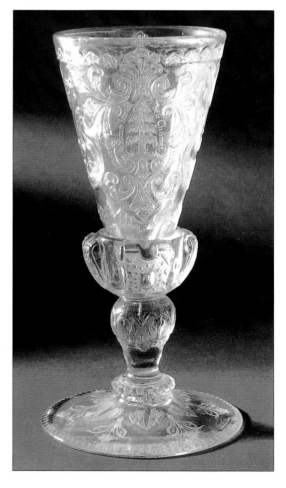

***HOCHSCHNITT* GOBLET**
*Silesian*
**c. 1700**

This goblet is an expression in glass of the baroque interest in grand objects of display in rock crystal. It was carved in the Petersdorf workshop of Friedrich Winter with water-powered grinding wheels and was intended for his patron Count Schaffgotsch. (*Right*)

house there would be the *hofglasschneider*, some of whose products can be identified from extant signed pieces.

Across the border from Bohemia, in Silesia (now part of modern Poland), some of the most sophisticated engraved work of the 18th century was produced in and around Warmbrunn during the 1740s and 1750s, when the influence of the Rococo resulted in a lightening of decorative motifs. Against the often high quality of the engraving must be placed the "horror vacui" attitude to the surfaces of the bowl, foot and cover, which were packed with a plethora of polished and matt engraved ornament, sometimes heightened with gilding. One of the foremost exponents of this school was Christian Gottfried Schneider (1710–73).

## VENICE

The history of Venice during the 18th century is one of sad decline. No longer a maritime power, the city now lived on its past glories and the tourist trade until the Veneto was annexed by the Austrians in 1797, a casualty of the Napoleonic upheavals. A good idea of what was still being produced at Murano in the early 18th century can be gleaned from the cache of glass offered to King Frederick IV of Denmark-Norway on the occasion of his visit in 1709, most of which is still preserved in Rosenborg Castle, Copenhagen. Techniques such as filigree and combed opaque-white threading are much to the fore, and there are also wares in a pale opalescent glass. There are simple glasses in *cristallo* and shapes that hark back to the late 16th century. There are even glasses engraved in the Bohemian style.

A high standard of decoration on glass was maintained in Murano, where at the Al Gesù

**ENGRAVED GOBLET**
*Silesian*
**c. 1760**

The engraving here is by one of the best Silesian engravers of this period, Christian Gottfried Schneider, of Warmbrunn. It displays lighter, more decorative aspects of the Rococo. (*Above*)

**ARMORIAL GOBLET AND COVER**
*Gottfried Spiller, Potsdam*
**c. 1695**

This is a fine example of the monumental style favoured by Spiller, a relation of the Winters, here applied to a goblet with the arms of the Elector Frederich III of Brandenberg. (*Right*)

**ENAMELLED *TREMBLEUSE* CUP AND SAUCER**
*Venetian*
**First half of 18th century**

White glass (*lattimo*) seems to have been especially popular with certain Murano glasshouses, such as the Miotti at Al Gesù. (*Left*)

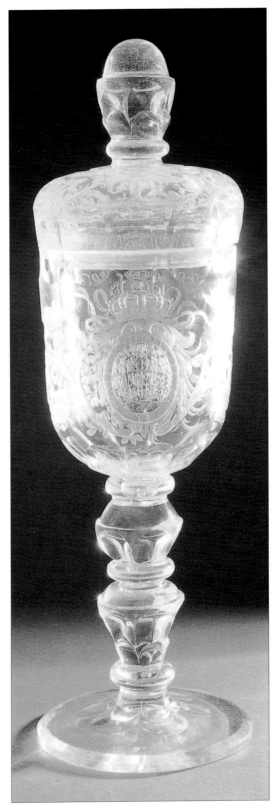

glass house the Miotti family produced series of views of Venice after engravings in monochrome on opaque-white glass for the tourist trade. However, by the end of the century the production at Murano had declined to a fraction of what it had been in its heyday.

THE GLITTERING, LUXURIOUS EFFECT OF CUT GLASS PROVED A
HANDSOME ORNAMENT ON THE DINING TABLES OF THE WEALTHY
DURING THE 18TH CENTURY, AND HAS PROBABLY NEVER GONE
OUT OF FASHION.

# THE GREAT AGE OF CUT GLASS

Curiously, nearly a century elapsed before the capabilities of the heavy English lead glass as a medium for cut decoration were appreciated. Early cutting was limited to shallow facets and blazes. Possibly the development of the cut-glass chandelier and a separate "eating room" (early dining rooms) was crucial. Although the Bohemians, for example, used glass for pendants on what were still basically metal chandeliers, and the Venetians created all-glass chandeliers that were blown, moulded and manipulated, the English developed the cut-glass chandelier, girandole and candelabrum composed of separate cast or blown sections that were facet-cut, and to which strings of cut beads and pendent drops were attached. The increased popularity of a separate eating room during the latter half of the 18th century, complete with a permanently positioned long mahogany table, also resulted in the increasing demand for large table services, particularly glittering cut ones. To serve this demand retail glass-selling and -cutting shops such as Blades and Akerman in London opened up, displaying (and advertising) the most up-to-date fashions in cut wares. Architects such as Robert Adam and James Wyatt disseminated the increasingly influential Neo-Classical style, which from the 1760s to the mid 19th century dominated the decorative arts.

**CUT SWEETMEAT
GLASS**
*English*
**c. 1785**

This glass, sometimes called a "top glass", would have stood on the top of a pyramid of salvers of decreasing size. In the 1780s cutting in England was confined to flat prisms and facets.

### IRELAND
The increased prosperity resulting from the introduction of free trade in 1780 encouraged English glassmakers to settle in Ireland. In Cork, Waterford and Dublin, glass houses were established that specialized in cut wares, as well as vast amounts of utilitarian glass exported to the Americas and the West Indies. A hallmark of Irish glass is the decanter blown into a ribbed mould, sometimes with the name of the glass house embossed around the base. Large shallow-cut canoe-shaped fruit bowls with moulded bases were also popular.

### NEO-CLASSICISM IN BOHEMIA
The influence of the Neo-Classical style in Europe was soon felt in the German lands, where the popularity of the Baroque *pokal* had declined by the 1770s. The appeal of engraving, too, waned, the technique being replaced by the Anglo-Irish fashion for cutting, often combined with gilding. A good example of the hybrid pieces of the late 18th century is the work of Johann Menzel of Warmbrunn in Silesia. He produced a series of Neo-Classical goblets with

deep bowls and sliced stems spreading on to a
square base and a matching low cover. The
bowls were decorated with *zwischengold* ovals
with silhouettes in black on a gold foil ground,
and the remaining decoration usually consisted
of facets and a little engraving.

A large amount of utilitarian table glass was
produced in Bohemia based on current English
styles. At the opposite end of the scale a studio
artist such as Johann Mildner, working at
Gutenbrunn in Lower Austria at the end of the
century, produced some of the most exquisite
*zwischengold*-revival beakers and carafes ever
made. He specialized in portraits, armorials and
elaborate monograms, and his pieces, rims and
bases were emphasized with gold and red foil
borders. These vessels were not for everyday use
and presage the fashion of the first quarter of
the 19th century for both porcelain and glass
"cabinet" pieces, which were elaborately decorated and intended for display.

## PAPERWEIGHTS

Paperweights first appeared in Venice in the
early 1840s and were perfected in the French
factories of Baccarat, Clichy and St Louis by
1848. At first the French concentrated on
*millefiori* weights, whose grounds are
composed of short lengths of multicoloured
canes arranged in patterns, sometimes with a
date, and enclosed within a mould in a ball of
fine lead crystal (thus magnifying the
appearance of the contents). Soon their
repertoire expanded to include fruit, elaborate
flower and serpent weights, all fashioned with
the aid of a lamp. Particularly popular were
pansies, clematis and dahlias. Paperweights
were produced over a period of only about
fifteen years.

**FRENCH PAPERWEIGHTS; 19th century**

THE APPLICATION OF INDUSTRIAL TECHNOLOGY TO GLASS-MAKING
DURING THE 19TH CENTURY DID NOT PREVENT A RENEWED TRADITION
OF INDIVIDUAL CRAFTSMANSHIP AND HIGH ARTISTIC STANDARDS.

# THE 19TH CENTURY

The influence of the Neo-Classical style extended well beyond the first quarter of the 19th century. As the century progressed, however, trends in glassmaking were towards increasingly complicated strands of production, ending with the complete separation in the 20th century of studio or "art" glass from domestic and utilitarian glass. Although the Industrial Revolution was in full swing, glass technology did not change significantly during this period. The technique of press-moulding was invented in the United States in the 1820s and steam power was applied to the process of glass-cutting. More important was an accelerating interest in the chemical composition of glass recipes and moves to increase the efficiency of firing. Stylistically it was an era of increasing eclecticism with a string of stylistic revivals; artistically little original work emerged until the Art Nouveau movement at the end of the 19th century.

## CUT GLASS

The importance of cut glass continued well into the 19th century, with Anglo-Irish fashions enthusiastically copied and elaborated on in France (at St Louis and Baccarat), Belgium (Vonêche and Val-St-Lambert), Bohemia, Russia and the United States (New England Glass Company, Boston). All these centres employed English and Irish cutters to instruct local craftsmen. Part of the Neo-Classical repertory included the use of sulphides as decorative elements in the composition. These were opaque-white ceramic paste medallions with raised cameo decoration, most often bust portraits of contemporary monarchs or public figures. The French particularly excelled at creating large vases with combinations of rich cutting and sulphides, the whole then elaborately mounted in gilt-bronze. The Imperial Glassworks at St Petersburg specialized in producing extraordinary objects in glass, including furniture. Cutting styles changed over the

**PRESSED GLASS TRAY**
*New England*
**c. 1840**

Pressed glass was invented in the United States in the 1820s as a way of producing the appearance of cut detail on a mass scale. (*Right*)

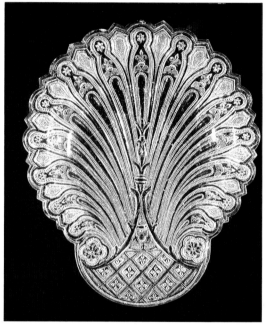

**SILHOUETTE BEAKER**
*Johann Sigismund Menzel, Warmbrunn*
**c. 1800**

This goblet combines typical characteristics of the Neo-Classical style in its simple urn form and classical silhouette. (*Right*)

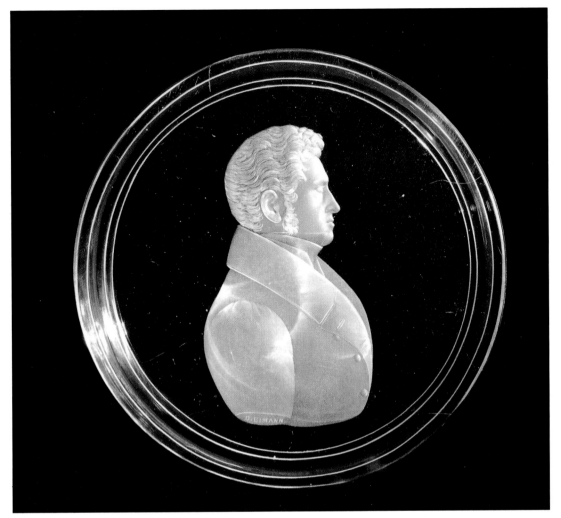

**ENGRAVED PORTRAIT PLAQUE**
*Dominik Biemann*
**c. 1820**

This classical portrait, treated like an antique medallion, was engraved by one of the best early 19th-century Bohemian engravers; he spent the summers at Franzensbad engraving portraits of visitors to the spa.

decades, moving from prisms and blazes in the 1820s to wide facets in the 1830s and 1840s, before reaching a peak of raised diamonds and other deep-cut decoration at the time of the Great Exhibition in 1851.

### AUSTRIAN AND BOHEMIAN GLASS DECORATION

Besides purely cut wares, glassmaking centres in the German lands and Bohemia continued the engraving traditions of their past, with various changes. The *pokal* and cover had long been out of fashion, and in the post-Napoleonic world – wary of the forces of "Revolution" – government was secretive and ultraconservative. Thus, there was a greater emphasis on sentimental, romantic "Biedermeier" virtues, such as domesticity and a love of the countryside. In porcelain a more feminine fashion for "cabinet" cups and vitrine objects was in vogue, which influenced glass as well. Particularly in northern Bohemia, glass-engraving studios developed, whose craftsmen used small beakers or goblets from local

glass houses, decorating them with mythological, allegorical and hunting scenes on a very much simpler scale than their 18th-century counterparts.

With the restoration of peace, travel once more became increasingly widespread; engravers supplied visitors to numerous Central European spas with beakers decorated with views of the spa and including monograms and

**THREE TUMBLERS**
*Bohemian*
**c. 1830–40**

These glasses reflected the interest in producing novel effects in glass, often striving to imitate semiprecious stones and new colours.

dates. Many of these were repetitive and pedestrian, but the work of some, such as Dominik Biemann (1800–57), was in a different class. Settled in Prague, for many years he spent his summers in Franzensbad where he engraved portraits and other scenes of exceptional skill on beakers and plaques. Many of these Bohemian "spa" glasses of the 1830s and 1840s are embellished with red or amber stain or overlay through which the engraved decoration was cut. This reflected the increasing interest of Bohemian factories in experimenting with coloured glass.

In the 1820s a type of black and brick-red glass called "hyalith" was perfected in the glass houses of Count Georg von Buquoy; this reflected renewed interest in obtaining lapidary effects with glass. Friedrich Egermann (1777–1864) experimented with acid washes on glass at Blottendorf to create *lithyalin* marbled effects. Other Bohemian centres specialized in pastel-coloured and opaline glass, probably influenced by the French in the 1830s, who produced small toiletry wares as well as larger urns in a variety of subtle opaline colours, often gilt-bronze mounted in Palais Royal workshops.

The Bohemians also experimented with casing ie, applying layers of coloured glass, sometimes as many as four or five, over a colourless or green base and cutting through them in different patterns to reveal the progressive layers. These techniques were adapted to paperweight manufacture in France in the 1850s and then reintroduced as "cameo" wares in England and elsewhere in the 1880s.

Contemporary with these trends were the studios of artists, many of them originally porcelain painters, who decorated mainly beakers in transparent wash enamels. This technique was perfected by Samuel Mohn (1762-1815) in Dresden and his son, Gottlob Mohn (1789-1825), who moved to Vienna in 1811. These cabinet pieces, with charming topographical views of and around Vienna and the Rhine, and rather sentimental allegories of Love and Faith, were mostly intended for those who flocked to Vienna for the Congress of 1815. Another important adherent of this technique was Anton Kothgasser (1769-1851).

In an era of increased facility of communication, the influence of Bohemian coloured glass spread quickly throughout Germany, France and Great Britain, to the extent that it is often difficult to tell the product of one country from

**TRANSPARENT-ENAMELLED BEAKER**
*Samuel Mohn*
**c. 1812**

Samuel Mohn of Saxony perfected the art of transparent-enamel painting on glass; he and his son produced some of the most skilful work in this medium, mainly small beakers with scenic views (such as this one), sold to tourists travelling in Europe after the Napoleonic wars.

another. Education, whether scientific or in the arts, was increasingly emphasized with the spread of design schools, the foundation of museums, the publication of books on ornament and design, and the staging of exhibitions.

### THE CLASSICAL REVIVAL

Around the middle of the century, as the excellence of the Bohemian schools of engraving came to be appreciated abroad, the emphasis in glass decorating started to shift away from cutting. Bohemian engravers themselves went abroad, much in the way of their Venetian predecessors. August Boehm (1812-90), who was from Meistersdorf, moved to Stourbridge and later to the United States, influencing local styles in the process. A number of Bohemians settled in London and worked for retailers such as Copeland and Dobson & Pearce. They specialized in classical and "Renaissance" motifs in deep-polished intaglio-engraving on blanks of classical form made by glassmakers such as Thomas Webb & Sons of Stourbridge and Whitefriars in London.

In the 1850s patents were taken out on a new decorating technique, acid-etching. This involved covering glass with a wax resist and drawing a design with a sharp point through the wax. The glass was then dipped in a solution of hydrofluoric acid, which ate into the exposed glass and left the waxed areas untouched. Various quite subtle effects could be achieved, depending on the strength of the acid and the length of time a piece was immersed in the solu-

**PAIR OF ENAMELLED
OPAQUE-WHITE VASES**
*Possibly French*
**c. 1850**

France, England and Bohemia all produced this type of ware, its decoration of varying quality. Here it is of the first order. (*Above*)

**ENAMELLED SCENT
BOTTLE**
*English*
**c. 1770**

The opaque-white glass is cut with facets and skilfully painted. (*Left*)

tion. Originally introduced as a quick, cheap alternative to wheel-engraving, in the hands of artists such as John Northwood (1836-1902) and his team of etchers at Wordsley near Stourbridge, the technique could be just as expensive and time-consuming as engraving. It was not until the later invention of etching and pantograph machines, which traced simple geometric patterns on glass, that the original intention was realized.

## CAMEO GLASS

Besides classical motifs on clear glass, John Northwood involved himself in efforts to resurrect the lost art of the ancients: cameo glass, of which the most famous surviving example was the Portland Vase in the British Museum, an *amphoriskos* in royal-blue translucent glass cased in a layer of opaque-white glass that was cut away to leave a frieze of classical figures. Once the technical difficulties of blowing a two-layered vessel that did not shatter in the annealing stage (ie, slow cooling in a special oven) had been overcome at the Red House Glassworks in Stourbridge, Northwood was able to produce a perfect reproduction of the vase between 1873 and 1876.

Other factories were quick to emulate Northwood's achievements, which had attracted considerable publicity. By the 1880s the three Stourbridge firms of Thomas Webb & Sons, Richardson and Stevens & Williams had studios of cameo-engravers producing large quantities of cameo glass into the 1890s, at which time demand slackened. At Webb's the team was led by George Woodall (1850-1925), the most gifted of Northwood's pupils. He continued Northwood's and other pioneers' work with classical figural scenes, many of which he signed. As in the case of Emile Gallé, in Nancy, France, large quantities of "commercial" cameo were produced – vases, biscuit barrels and scent bottles, mostly with floral decoration in two

**GROUP OF CAMEO WARES**
*Stourbridge*
**c. 1880–90**

Stourbridge cameo glass, unlike its more complex multicoloured and many-layered counterparts by the French glasshouses, generally comprised simple white-relief subjects against a dark ground. Occasionally, the outer layer was coloured, as on the yellow vase with pink-grape motif (second from right).

colours. The more elaborate pieces, such as Webb's "gem cameo", with as many as five layers, often featured Eastern motifs and designs influenced by the ornament of Owen Jones.

REVIVALS ON THE MAINLAND

In Germany and Central Europe the stylistic revivals developed along slightly different lines. By the 1860s the Neo-Renaissance style was in fashion and remained influential until the end of the century. One of the most important enthusiasts of this style was Ludwig Lobmeyr (1829-1917), who not only founded a glass retail outlet in Vienna, but also set up his own outlet and decorating links in Adolfov and Steinschönau in southern Bohemia. Engraving on Lobmeyr pieces is always technically of the finest quality, whether work by masters such as Karl Pietsch, who engraved large scale classical scenes, or the engraving on revival reproductions of Baroque early 18th-century goblets and covers.

With the creation of the German state in 1870, increased national consciousness led to the revival and imitation of earlier Germanic art forms. For example, the Rheinische Glashütten AG near Cologne produced pieces based on medieval *waldglas* prototypes such as the *roe-*

mer, *krautstrunk* and *humpen*. More than one centre at this time produced large quantities of imitations of 17th-century enamelled glass copied from the originals – sometimes these were executed so well that they are not readily distinguished as copies today.

## VENETIAN REVIVAL

Glassmaking activities had not ceased at the demise of the Venetian Republic at the end of the 18th century, but did appear to have sunk into a marked decline. There were occasional flashes of inspired work, such as the rediscovery of the art of *millefiori* by Pietro Bigaglia and the

**LATTICINIO GOBLET**
*Whitefriars*
**c. 1880**

The *latticinio* technique was revived in Britain in the 19th century. (*Above*)

**THREE "HISTORICAL REVIVAL" GOBLETS**
*German*
**c. 1890**

Early Bohemian glass inspired many 19th-century Europeans. (*Above right*)

Franchini brothers in the 1840s.

However, in 1859-60 Antonio Salviati (1816-1900) founded a glassworks at Murano, with British financial backing, which was to specialize in rediscovering the techniques of the 15th- and 16th-century masters who had made Venice supreme. At the International Exhibition in London in 1862, and again in Paris in 1867, Salviati glass attracted much favourable comment and did much to popularize the neo-Venetian style. Other Muranese glassworks followed Salviati's lead in producing mosaic wares in the manner of the first century AD as well as filigree, lampwork, serpent-stem goblets and *calcedonio* pieces. The elegance of form particularly attracted English glassmakers, such as Harry Powell (1853-1922) of Whitefriars.

### THE IMPACT OF THE EAST

With the forced opening up of trade with China and Japan by the United States and Europe from the 1850s onwards, the West came into contact for the first time with the entire gamut of oriental fine and decorative arts. Works of art were acquired by major national museums, exhibited at the major international exhibitions from 1862 onwards and illustrated in art publications. Glass decorators, whether in enamels or engraving, began to use a vocabulary of Eastern motifs such as the prunus, pine, chrysanthemum, carp and dragon.

In the 1870s a new type of "rock-crystal" style was developed. In the early 18th century the Winter brothers in Germany had based their experiments in "carving" glass on 16th- and 17th-century Italian and Bohemian Mannerist examples in rock crystal. The latter-day style of carving glass to resemble rock crystal was based on Eastern examples of carved quartzes, jades and other hardstones. Rock-crystal pieces were exhibited by Baccarat, Pantin and other French manufacturers at the 1878 Paris Exposition, while in England it was the Bohemian engravers such as Kny, Fritsche and Keller, employed by Webb and Stevens & Williams, who perfected the style at Stourbridge. In the case of the most dramatic pieces, such as the famous Corning Ewer, the effects were achieved through exaggeratedly deep carving, often with swirling movement and a plethora of raised detail, all highly polished to obtain the watery, rock-crystal effect. More "commercial" rock-crystal wares, often made up into large table services, relied on quieter effects of engraved and polished Eastern motifs. From the 1890s the demand for rock-crystal wares declined,

**"ROCK CRYSTAL" EWER**
*Stourbridge*
**1886**

This elaborate ewer with aquatic theme was engraved by William Fritsche. (*Left*)

***LES COPRINS* LAMP**
*Emile Gallé*
*c.* 1900

This table lamp illustrates three stages of mushroom growth (*Coprin* is a kind of mushroom). It stands on a

detailed wrought-iron mount and its stems and shades are of triple-overlay and engraved glass. (*Above*)

although services continued to be made by Webb as late as the 1920s.

## GALLÉ AND TIFFANY
To conclude this brief history of glassmaking, mention must be made of Emile Gallé (1846–1904) in France and Louis Comfort Tiffany (1848–1933) in America. In their different ways, these glassmakers used the whole range of new decorative techniques built up during the 19th century to lead glassmaking out of the doldrums of stylistic revivals. Their movement was termed the "Art Nouveau".

Gallé's father owned a glass and faience fac-

**DRAGONFLY LAMP**
*Tiffany Studios*
**c. 1900**

This superb lamp has a base of bronze, "turtleback" iridescent-glass tiles and tiny mosaics.

**TWO VASES**
*Louis Comfort Tiffany*
**Early 20th century**

The Favrile-glass vase on the left features the so-called paperweight technique, while the one on the right – with its rough, mottled surface – was called Cypriot glass by Tiffany.

tory at Nancy in the old glass-making centre of Lorraine. He grew up obsessed with the world of nature which is reflected in all his work. He is best known for his innovatory vases and perfume bottles using cameo and "marquetry" techniques. Here the influence of Chinese Ch'ien Lung cased glass is visible.

Gallé's own work in this field was of the greatest sophistication, relying on colour-change in the various layers of glass, the carving of inlaid or "marquetry" details and designs based on natural forms but often stylized to the point of abstraction. At the same time his

factory was producing large quantities of more mundane and repetitive commercial wares.

Besides the Daum atelier, also at Nancy, the other important figure in the Art Nouveau movement was Louis Comfort Tiffany of the New York jewellery firm founded in 1837. He trained as a painter and became increasingly interested in the decorative arts. In 1879 he founded his own company which became renowned for its interior designs, with particular emphasis on colourful and exotic stained glass and lighting in Art Nouveau style. Towards the end of the century, in collaboration with

Arthur Nash from Stourbridge, Tiffany concentrated on perfecting iridescent glass, producing his famous series of hand-blown art-glass vases called "Favrile". This successful series produced many imitators, amongst them the German firm of Loetz.

## LALIQUE

The most famous of all glass designers in this century must surely be René Lalique. He began his career as a brilliant designer of jewellery, experimenting with various materials which led to his work with glass. He set up a small workshop in 1902 making cast objects by means of the "lost wax" process. He was soon commissioned to design perfume bottles and after the First World War, he was commissioned to design the lighting and other decorative glass features for luxury liners and civic features in Paris. He designed a wide range of objects, usually moulded or cast, often in a distinctive opalescent glass with bluish tints. Although Lalique ceased production at the beginning of the Second World War, he has rarely been surpassed since in the sophisticated stylization of his designs.

## FURTHER READING

The following list of materials for further reading offers a broad range of literature. Both specialist and general works are included. While every effort has been made to give the date of the most recent edition, new ones may have been published since this book went to press.

Arwas, V.
**Glass – Art Nouveau to Art Deco**
London and New York 1977

Battie, David and Simon Cottle (eds.)
**Sotheby's Concise Encyclopedia of Glass**
London and New York 1991

Bayer, Patricia, and Mark Waller
**The Art of René Lalique**
London 1988

Charleston, Robert J. (ed.)
**English Glass**
Victoria and Albert Museum, London 1968

**— Masterpieces of Glass: A World History from the Corning Museum of Glass**
New York 1980

Corning Museum of Glass
**A Survey of Glassmaking from Ancient Egypt to the Present**
Chicago 1977

— and the Museum of Decorative Arts, Prague
**Czechoslovakian Glass, 1350–1980**
New York 1981

Drahotová, Olga and G. Urbanek
**Europäisches Glas**
Prague 1982

Hollister, Paul
**The Encyclopedia of Glass Paperweights**
New York 1969

Humphrys, L.G.
**Glass and Glassmaking**
London 1973

Kaempfer, F., and K. Beyer
**Glass – A World History**
London 1966

Klein, Dan
**The History of Modern Glass**
London 1984

— and Ward Lloyd
**The History of Glass**
London 1984

Koch, Robert
**Louis C Tiffany, Rebel in Glass**
New York 1964

**— Louis C Tiffany's Art Glass**
New York 1977

Lattimore, C.R.
**English 19th-Century Press-Moulded Glass**
London 1979

McKean, Hugh F.
**The Lost Treasures of Louis Comfort Tiffany**
Garden City, New York 1980

McKearin, George S. and Helen
**American Glass**
New York 1948

**— Two Hundred Years of American Blown Glass**
Garden City, New York, 1950

Madigan, Mary Jean
**Steuben Glass: An American Tradition in Crystal**
New York 1982

Marcilhac, Félix
**R. Lalique, catalogue raisonné de l'oeuvre de verre**
Paris 1989

Mariacher, Giovanni
**Glass from Antiquity to the Renaissance**
London 1977, 1988

Marshall, Jo
**Glass Source Book**
London 1990

Mehlman, Felice
**Phaidon Guide to Glass**
London 1982

Morris, Barbara
**Victorian Table Glass and Ornaments**
London 1978

Neuwirth, Waltraud
**Das Glas des Jugendstils**
Munich 1973

Newman, Harold
**An Illustrated Dictionary of Glass**
London 1981

Phillips, P. (ed.)
**Encyclopedia of Glass**
London 1981

Polak, Ada
**Modern Glass**
London 1962

**— Glass, its makers and its public**
London and New York 1975

Revi, Albert Christian
**American Art Nouveau Glass, Its Genesis and Development**
Camden, New Jersey, 1968

**— American Art Nouveau Glass**
Camden, New Jersey, 1968

Spillman, Jane Shadel
**Glassmaking: America's First Industry**
Corning, New York, 1976

**— American and European Pressed Glass in the Corning Museum of Glass**
Corning, New York, 1981

— and Susanne K. Frantz
**Masterpieces of American Glass**
New York 1990

Thorpe, W.A.
**A History of English and Irish Glass**
London 1929

Utt, Mary Lou and Glenn, with Patricia Bayer
**Lalique Perfume Bottles**
New York 1990 and London 1991

Vose, Ruth Hurst
**Glass**
London 1980

Wakefield, Hugh
**Nineteenth Century British Glass**
London 1961

Warmus, W.
**Emile Gallé: Dreams into Glass**
Corning, New York, 1984

Warren, Phelps
**Irish Glass**
London 1972

Weiss, Gustav (translated by Janet Seligman)
**The Book of Glass**
London and New York 1971

Wills, Geoffrey
**Victorian Glass**
London 1976

Wilson, Kenneth M.
**New England Glass and Glassmaking**
New York 1972

Zerwick, Chloë
**A Short History of Glass**
Corning, New York, 1980

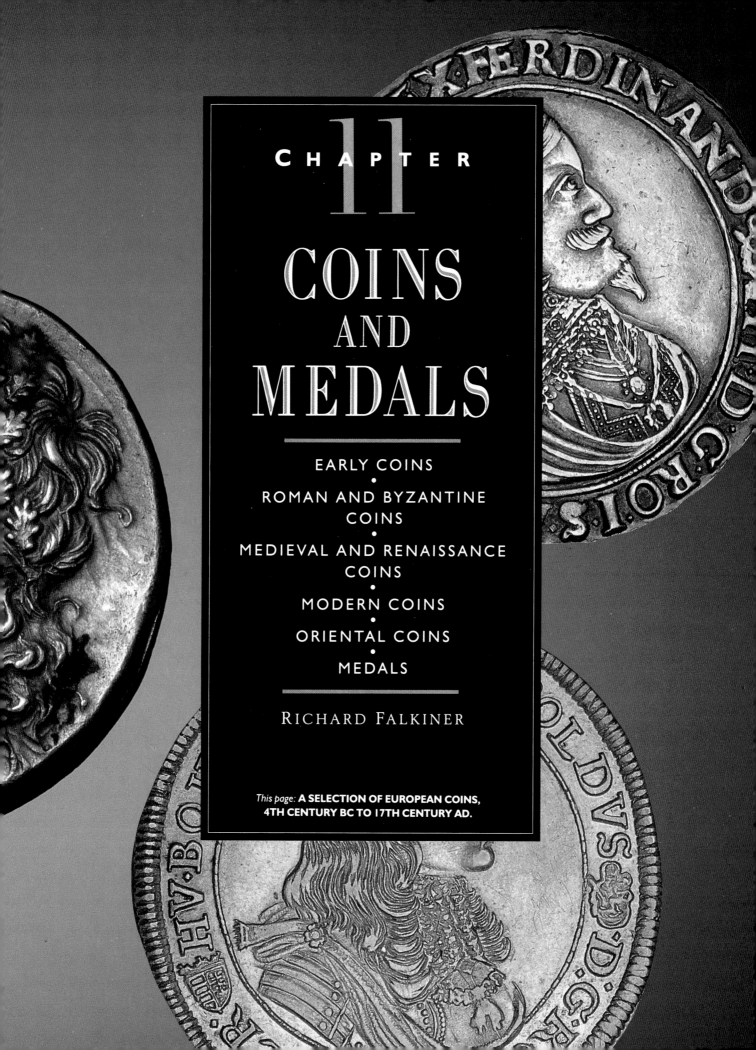

# CHAPTER
# 11
# COINS
# AND
# MEDALS

EARLY COINS
·
ROMAN AND BYZANTINE
COINS
·
MEDIEVAL AND RENAISSANCE
COINS
·
MODERN COINS
·
ORIENTAL COINS
·
MEDALS

RICHARD FALKINER

*This page:* **A SELECTION OF EUROPEAN COINS,
4TH CENTURY BC TO 17TH CENTURY AD.**

# COINS AND MEDALS

**W**HETHER POWERFUL OR WEAK, STATES AND RULERS HAVE ALWAYS USED COINS AND MEDALS TO TRANSMIT A SENSE OF PRESTIGE – IN QUANTITY – TO THEIR SUBJECTS, CITIZENS, OR NEIGHBORS. **O**NLY RARELY WAS EXPENSE SPARED IN TRYING TO CREATE OBJECTS OF THE FINEST APPEARANCE POSSIBLE.

**ROMAN AUREUS**
Gold; AD 161–169

Both obverse and reverse are shown, the obverse bearing a bust of Emperor Lucius Verus. (*Below centre*)

**ISLAMIC DINAR**
Gold; **early 8th century**

To avoid infringing the Islamic ban on images imposed in AD 696, this coin uses lettering rather than depictions. (*Below*)

Coins and medals have been used by practically every sophisticated society for about 2,500 years, covering a period and an area wider than those spawned by almost all other kinds of antiques. When they are in good condition, we see them just as they were seen by the societies who used them, and the designs they bear can tell us much about those societies and their rulers. In addition, analysis of their metals and the hoards in which they are found can provide information about alliances, migrations and economic, military and political history which would otherwise be lost.

From the 3rd century BC, coins were in everyday use in China, the Mediterranean basin and the Near East, even for the least well off, and were made in great quantities. The classical and medieval silver and gold coins that have come down to us were originally either lost or deposited in the ground, usually with a view to recovery when the political climate improved. Copper coins were either lost or, being of low value, discarded when they ceased to be functional – hence, large numbers have survived to satisfy the collector of today.

Unlike most other antique items, coins usually have the advantage for the collector that exactly what they are and when they were produced is actually written on them. True, the inscription may be in an unfamiliar lan-

**SOLIDUS**
Gold; **5th century** AD

This historically important coin is one of a hoard in the Ashmolean Museum, Oxford. It was found in the Crondall (Hampshire) hoard and was struck after the Romans had abandoned their British province. (*Below*)

guage or script, but a translation of this can usually be obtained by one means or another and the coin's identity thus revealed. The would-be collector who may be daunted by the prospect of dealing with apparently mysterious coins should remember that there has never been anything intrinsically arcane in the inscriptions on them. On the contrary, those minting them in every age have had to ensure that, to be acceptable to the public, they were clearly identifiable; and, with the right approach, so they remain to this day.

The medal is a natural offshoot of the coin. Medals have been used as prizes for sporting success, as awards for gallantry on the battlefield, or as tokens of one ruler's esteem for another – or for himself. Medals have also been struck to commemorate specific events, such as England's defeat of the Spanish Armada. While coins offer clues to the economic history of a people, medals can show a collector what events or accomplishments past generations found significant.

**SCUDO OF POPE INNOCENT XII (1691–1700)**
**Gold; 1694**

This coin of the Papal States reflects contemporary styles of architecture and goldsmiths' work. This is a characteristic of Italian coins from the Renaissance onwards. (*Below and below left*)

**ORDER OF THE GARTER**

The English Order of the Garter was founded in 1349. The badge is worn across the chest on a pale blue ribbon. (*Above*)

## CHIVALRIC INSIGNIA

Orders of Chivalry developed during the Middle Ages out of attempts by the Church and medieval monarchs to impose standards of behaviour and conduct on knights.

Over history many of these orders have vanished with the monarchies that founded them, victims of the modern world's preference for republican regimes. Those that survive, such as the several British orders, have developed into groups of citizens who have given signal service to their ruling monarch – yet there may still be a very strong, if unofficial, hereditary element.

The oldest surviving order is the Order of the Garter, founded by King Edward III of England. The exact date is not known; the records of the order before 1416 have perished. However, robes bearing the order's motto are mentioned in the

wardrobe accounts for September 1347 to January 1349, and the letter patent for the preparation of the Royal Chapel at Windsor are dated August 1348.

On the Continent the order of greatest prestige and longevity is the Order of the Golden Fleece. It was created by Philip the Good, Duke of Burgundy, in 1430.

Over time the forms of the chivalric orders became many and various, but a feature of them all was that members were entitled to wear a precious insignia on formal occasions. While the insignia have survived, the ribands that supported them have often perished. Much information about the ribands and where the insignia might be worn on the body can be gleaned from the portraits of past members, who would display their insignia with pride.

**ORDER OF THE GOLDEN FLEECE**

REFERENCES FROM THE BIBLE AND ON CUNEIFORM TABLETS INDICATE
THAT COINAGE HAS HAD AS PROFOUND AN INFLUENCE ON THE
DEVELOPMENT OF SOCIAL SYSTEMS AS THE INVENTION OF WRITING.

# EARLY COINS

The analysis of coin hoards is of crucial importance in numismatics, the study of coins and medals, and modern statistical methods of such analysis have reached a very sophisticated state. The larger the hoard being analysed, the more accurate the conclusions that can be drawn from it.

There are three main types of hoard: the war chest, personal savings and the "wishing well". In the first, most coins will have a narrow range of dates and their condition will have worsened in proportion to the length of time they have been in circulation. Also included will be a proportion of strays, with a wider range of dates, which might even be foreign. Such a hoard is characteristically very large and probably was the property of a retreating army or an overthrown government.

The personal savings hoard is obviously much smaller. If the date range is narrow, it might represent a single payment received by, for instance, a retiring soldier or official, but, if the range is wide – over a generation, say – the hoard might have been accumulated slowly. In the latter case, there will be a tendency for all the coins to be in the same state, saved either when new or because of their good condition and consequent full weight.

Typical characteristics of "wishing well" hoard coins are low denomination and a wide spread in both date and place of minting. Such a hoard usually indicates the location of a religious shrine. Similar to this type is the foundation deposit in an important civic building or royal burial place. These will tend to be of high value and to have been immured when new, in which case they can be used to date accurately the building or burial.

A coin found singly can be interpreted as a casual loss. A typical spot where such coins can be found is a ford.

### THE INVENTION OF COINAGE

For nearly 2,000 years before the introduction of coinage, in the late 7th century BC, trade was carried out by means of bullion. This long took the form of copper (notably in Cyprus) and lead, but since these were heavy to carry and had a tendency to corrode, they were eventually replaced with silver. The earliest known reference to weighed silver is on a Sumerian cuneiform tablet of about the 21st century BC.

The first currency appeared when a mutually accepted seal was applied to ingots with a punch to guarantee their quality, in much the same way as a hallmark is used today on vessels of precious metal. And when a similar seal (of an individual or institution), guaranteeing both weight and purity, was applied to portions of bullion of a size convenient to the trading public, coinage came into being.

The Greek historian Herodotus, writing in the late 5th century BC, informs us that the Lydians, a race living in the north-west of Turkey, were the first people known to use a gold and silver coinage and to introduce retail trade. In 1904-5 British archaeologists excavated around the central Basis of the Artemesion (Temple of Diana) at Ephesus in Turkey, to which the Lydian ruler Croesus contributed funds in the mid 6th century BC. Here, in what was obviously the foundation deposit, they found treasure which included a vessel containing 19 electrum (gold and silver

**BULLION AND THE FIRST COIN**
Ephesus; c. 630 BC

For centuries metal had been traded as bullion (*below left*). At Ephesus (now in modern Turkey) electrum was first parcelled out in units of fixed weight and marked. (*Below right*)

alloy) coins. Also found in this culturally historic deposit were 93 electrum coins. Nine were not strictly coins: they were unmarked lumps, perhaps randomly hammered with different tools. But all conformed to standard weights based on twelfths of a main unit. It is believed that the coins in this hoard, thought to date from the last decades of the 7th century BC, give us the time and place for the invention of coinage.

Electrum occurs naturally in the gravel of the River Paktolos which flowed through the Lydian capital, Sardis. It seems to have been accepted – at least, early on in the history of coinage – as a uniform commodity regardless of the ratio of the two metals.

**Early trading** To the trader the advantage of having coins was that transactions were made easier by having currency neatly parcelled into portions of fixed purity and weight. However, this benefit was a two-edged sword. From the very beginning the State claimed and rigidly enforced a monopoly on minting coins. This enabled the State to take a profit by creating coins which traded at a premium on the melt value of the bullion. At the same time, the State could demand that taxes should be paid in bullion or perhaps even in new coins rated only at their metal value. In the latter case, the State could use the coins to pay for goods and services without having the expense of turning bullion into coins. It is believed that initially bullion and coins were traded independently, side by side,

but that transactions involving the government certainly involved coins.

Eventually, and probably as the result of government legislation, coins almost completely replaced bullion as currency. At first, coins must have circulated only locally, because, to have been accepted, the seal on the coin would have to have been of a familiar, trusted individual or institution.

It is thought that about 700 BC merchants created their own coins: this is because the images they bear are many and various. Some are known today from unique examples or, at best, only a handful of specimens. Soon afterwards there appeared electrum coins that, as well as being of diverse types, were made in different sets of weight ratios to the Ephesus hoard presumably representing the different standards of various neighbouring cities.

STANDARDIZATION AND PURPOSE

After Alexander the Great (d. 323 BC), Greece, Egypt, and Asia from the eastern Mediterranean to the Indus River amounted to a Hellenic commonwealth. This gave rise to a standardized coin that greatly facilitated international trade, since there was now less need to negotiate local coinages far from home. These early Greek coins were not struck centrally and so there is a great diversity of style, but the basic design and the ostensible weight and purity were the same. In addition to symbols indicating these they

**HELLENISTIC COIN**
Silver; **4th/3rd century BC**

After the death of Alexander the Great (323 BC), the art of coinage flowered, particularly portrait coins. The output and variety is vast, and many compare well aesthetically with the art of any period, whether in miniature or not. (*Below left*)

**ATHENIAN TETRADRACHM**
Silver; **c. 440 BC**

So popular and trusted as a means of exchange did these "owls" become, that they remained in wide use until the sack of Athens by the Romans in 88 BC. Imitations, often crude, were made as far afield as Arabia. (*Below*)

bore a number of secondary ones denoting the mine and the officer who was responsible for running it.

On Alexander's death his vast empire was almost immediately taken apart by his generals, each grabbing a portion. This division gave rise to a series of four-drachm (tetradrachm) silver pieces bearing their idealized portraits. (A drachm of silver was the basic currency unit.) Another result of Alexander's conquests was that, due to the capitulation of the Persian king Darius III (336–330 BC), the vast quantity of pure gold, formerly held in the Persian treasury, spread throughout the Mediterranean. This gold, repeatedly remelted, formed the material for Celtic coinages as far north-west as the British Isles.

The earliest coins were not created for the convenience of the people but rather for merchants, and also perhaps temple authorities, who acted as very rudimentary banks, as a medium for the storage and movement of wealth. Soon after the invention of coinage, a drachm of silver was the cost of one scrawny sheep. And in the late 5th century BC such a coin was the daily wage of the architect of one of the finest buildings on the Acropolis, the Erechtheum. This reminds us that it is impossible to compare wages and prices over the centuries.

We have to look to the city-states of southern Italy, founded by Greek colonists, mainly in the 8th and 7th centuries BC, for the introduction of coins for the masses. These were tokens of bronze without intrinsic value and so their use depended entirely on public confidence in the issuing authority. Each city had its own distinctive currency design and it was, therefore, important that these designs were recognized and trusted. This was the beginning of coinage used purely as a convenient means for everyday small transactions.

However, the development of coinage was an opportunity for counterfeiters to show their skills. Accordingly gold and silver coins soon were not only differentiated by locality but had incorporated into their design an alphabetical device or symbol indicating who was responsible for minting them. Experts are grateful because close analysis of these symbols sometimes enables them to determine the order in which coins of a particular city were issued. At this time coins were not struck constantly but only as the need arose, perhaps once a decade. Occasionally, early Greek coins turn up with a name scratched on them, presumably when they had been pawned.

**GREEK COINS**
Silver

This is a random selection of some of the finest coins made in the ancient Greek world. The idealized portraits and emblems on each are peculiar to a specific city-state. The earlier pieces tended to be traded near to their place of minting, but later there was a move to less variety – but with individual issues differentiated by a tiny symbol in the field of the design on the reverse. (*Right*)

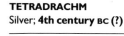

**TETRADRACHM**
Silver; **4th century BC (?)**

This is one of the most common coins of the ancient world, first issued by Alexander the Great (336–323 BC). He portrayed himself as Herakles (Hercules) wearing the pelt of the Nemean lion. These coins were struck at many mints from Greece to the Indus River. Many were struck in Alexander's name after his death. (*Left*)

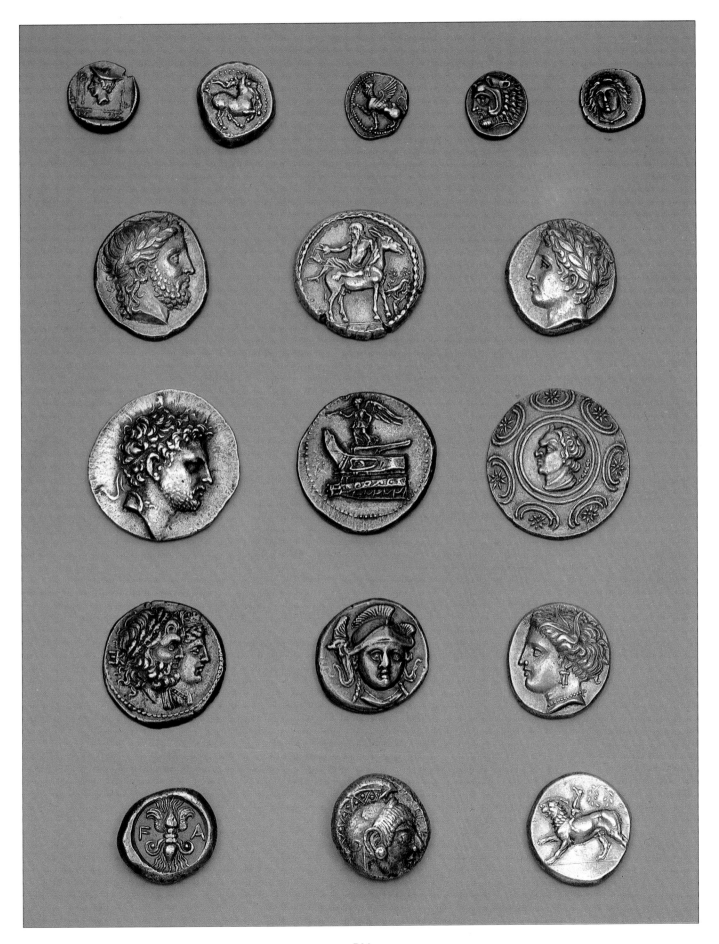

THE EMPIRES THAT DOMINATED THE NORTHERN MEDITERRANEAN FOR
SOME 1200 YEARS MAINTAINED A TRADITION OF COINAGE EMPHASIZING
THE POWER OF THE STATE AND THE BLESSINGS OF RELIGION.

# ROMAN AND BYZANTINE COINS

**SESTERTIUS**
Bronze; AD 117–138

The naturalistic portrait of
the Roman emperor
Hadrian on this coin
contrasts sharply with the
more idealized products of
the Hellenistic world.
(*Below*)

In the late 4th century BC coinage appeared in the central Italian peninsula. Bronze coins were initially traded by weight, but because bronze is a relatively bulky material, soon the coins were being traded in a more convenient token manner. Beginning as crude, chopped-up lumps of metal, the coins developed into rect-angular ingots marked with an image probably signifying the commodity of which it was intended to represent the value: an amphora, a cow, a shield, and so on. (In this way, it had affinities with the independently invented Chinese coinage.) But even these ingots were inconvenient, and they were short-lived.

The Romans then adopted a series of large bronze coins based on a duodecimal system (division of each unit into twelve parts). This development was out of step with the decimal system being used elsewhere and, as it was imperative that the coinage of Rome, her allies and her satellites should conform to the rest of the world, during the early Empire the duo-decimal system was abandoned.

Sicily and southern Italy had been colonized by Greeks during the previous centuries, and accordingly it was the provincial Greek coinages (far from provincial in style) that provided the prototypes for Roman coins.

In about 212 BC the Romans introduced the denarius a name which, abbreviated to d., was used to denote the penny of the UK's pre-deci-mal coinage abandoned in 1971 and which still survives in the dinar of today's Middle Eastern currencies. With this introduction, the empha-sis of the Roman monetary system switches from bronze to silver. The denarius was worth ten bronze Aes pieces, and early on bore the numeral X.

Soon after, during the war with Hannibal in 209 BC, Rome's gold reserves were called upon for the production of the first gold coins, the aurei. So was created a trimetallic coinage, in which the ratio of circulating gold to silver was about 1:9 and silver to bronze about 1:120.

## INFLUENTIAL PRACTICES
In Rome coinage was under the charge of a com-mittee of three junior magistrates. Production was not continual but carried out as the exigen-cies of war or public works demanded. The designs are many and various and mainly in-tended to glorify the families of the magistrates who signed the coins: a depiction of the exploits of an ancestor, perhaps, or of an episode from the history of Rome.

With the expansion of Rome's power, its coinage began to circulate outside the Empire. We learn from the Roman historian Tacitus, writing in the late 1st century AD, that Roman silver coinage had become popular with the Celts on the fringes of the imperial – and, as he

**AUREUS**
Gold; AD 117–138

The aureus was the standard Roman gold for the first three centuries of the empire, until it was replaced by the solidus. (*Above*)

between the consul Marius and the general Sulla, there was a change in the type of inscription on coinage, bringing about a new style that was to continue into the Middle Ages. During his period of office from 83 to 79 BC, when he became the first of a long line of dictators to rule Rome, Sulla struck coins bearing his own name, the first time this had been done. Julius Caesar took the process a stage further and shortly before his assassination in 44 BC, outraged tradition still further by actually having his own portrait stamped on coins.

### THE FACES OF EMPIRE

After the years of upheaval following the death of Caesar, his adopted son Octavian succeeded as Caeser in 29 BC and two years later became the first Roman emperor, taking the title of Augustus Caesar. Roman territories now stretched the length of the Mediterranean from Spain in the west to Asia Minor in the east. With this expansion coins had begun to be minted not only in Rome but outside it and, as Roman domination spread, in places ever further from the centre.

The ratio of gold to silver coins was now about 1:25; the minting of both was the prerogative of the emperor. From 24 BC, when Augustus recognized the people's need for small change for everyday transactions, bronze coinage became abundant. The provision of it was left to the senate and this was indicated by the inscription of S(enatus) C(onsulto).

**Changes in imagery** Over the next three centuries issues of coinage became larger and coins smaller as they became more ubiquitous. In addition, imperial portraits on coins gradually departed from the realism of those of the first 12 Caesars. The portraits become less of a likeness of the individual, more a portrait of the

saw it, civilized – world. However, the Celts had no reason to trust the Roman government and from about 200 BC had begun putting up to about a dozen nicks in the edge of the flan (the disc of metal used to make the coin) before striking their coins, to show that these were not bronze coins plated with silver. These coins, called serrati (from their serrated edges), were the first to use the milling common on coins of today. Its modern use has been to prevent a practice common in the Middle Ages – clipping, the paring of the edges of gold and silver coins to make bullion and afterwards passing on the coins at their full theoretical value.

In the early 1st century BC, which saw rivalry

## CELTIC COINS

Balkan Celts began producing their own coinage in the 3rd century BC, and Celts throughout Europe, reaching as far as Britain, followed suit. The first designs imitated those of the staters of Philip II of Macedonia (d. 337 BC), father of Alexander the Great. Usually, repeated copying of a design down the years leads to a degradation of it, but, uniquely, the Celts, though retaining the original basic design, managed to imbue it with an aesthetically fine style of their own.

emperor's office, attributes, costume and regalia. The face became little more than a representation of the spiritual and symbolic aspect of the ruler, his supreme detachment and serenity. This transformation from realism to idealization reaches its apogee in the upward-gazing head of Constantine the Great (AD 312–337), crowned with a diadem. This portrait we are told by the contemporary Greek historian Eusebius, is derived from the coins of Alexander the Great struck almost seven centuries previously, a resemblance undoubtedly intended to convey a political message.

On the reverse sides of coins figures of gods appeared constantly, and legends reflected the times: for example, in time of threat there appeared SALUS REPUBLICAE (Safety of the State) and when the threat receded FEL(icitae) TEMP(us) REP(aratio), which freely translated means "Happy days are here again". The reverse side was thus used to broadcast the hopes and achievements of the authorities.

By the end of the 3rd century the political relationship between the Augusti and their now-subordinate Caesars in the Roman Empire was very delicate, and so when an alliance was made it could lead to a legend on coins such as CON-CORDIA AUG(usti) (Peace among rulers).

**LATER ROMAN COINS**
Gold and Bronze; **4th century**

Following the adoption of Christianity as the official religion of the empire, the design of Roman coins took on a more abstract character. The portraits on these coins show the departure from the realism of the earlier empire, and the first signs of evolution to the Byzantine manner. These coins exemplify the era of continuously degrading weight standard and fineness characterizing the decline of the Roman empire.

The arrival of a Caesar or Augustus in a city would be celebrated by an inscription such as ADVENTUS CAESAR (or AUGUSTUS). Thus political aspirations and achievements were faithfully recorded. By this time, the mint was given on coins, in abbreviated form and usually below the inscription on the reverse.

BYZANTINE COINS

The turmoil of the very early 4th century was resolved when Constantine the Great became ruler of the whole Roman Empire in 324. Constantine moved the centre of the empire from Rome to a small town on the Bosphorus, Byzantium, and changed its name to Constantinople.

Within a century, emperors were being depicted on coins in military dress; these were times when the barbarian hordes were pressing on the empire. The military portraits show us a warrior emperor, at first in profile but soon full-face, with helmet, spear and cuirass, and with his shield embossed with the design of a horseman spearing and trampling a prostrate barbarian foot-soldier. This is the prototype of the St George and Dragon motif used in the 18th century by the engraver Benedetto Pistrucci on the sovereigns and crown pieces of the British king

(491-518) the Christian emblem had become
totally unambiguous: an angel standing purposefully supporting a full-length cross. Within half
a century this image had evolved into the angel
holding a staff surmounted by the Chi-Rho
monogram (the first two Greek letters of
Christ's name) and a globe surmounted by a
cross. The final development of this theme was
the depiction of just a plain cross on steps.

### THE INFLUENCE OF ISLAM

The early spread of Islam was to have an impact
on the imagery of Byzantine coins. Until then
the establishment of Christianity as the State
religion by Constantine had meant that the role
of the Saviour as titular head of state had been
taken for granted. Initially, relations between
Muslims and Christians were apparently cor-
dial. In 691 Justinian II sent a set of columns for
the building of the mosque at Mecca; and six-
teen years later the same emperor sent the
caliph 100,000 solidi (Byzantine coins), a hundred workmen and 40 loads of tesserae (mosaic
cubes) salvaged from ruined churches. Evidence
enough of initial friendship, but nevertheless
Christianity had to be proclaimed, and, as the
solidus circulated widely, it provided the perfect medium for the purpose. Accordingly,

George III. (As a general point, it can be said
that States tend to use safe, traditional motifs
and styles in order to maintain public confidence. For instance, the reverse design on the
half-crowns of Elizabeth II owes much to those
on the coins of her earlier namesake.)

The reverse sides of these Byzantine coins
were now exclusively Christian in content. Even
the traditional pagan personifications of cities
and the goddess Victory are tricked out with
Christian symbolism. By the reign of Anastasius

**BYZANTINE SOLIDUS**
Gold; **9th century**

During the Iconoclastic dispute of the 8th and 9th centuries, images of the emperor become more linear. (*Above*)

**BYZANTINE NOMISMA**
Gold; **11th century**

Once the artistic problems caused by Iconoclasm were resolved, Byzantine coinage settled down to a style

associated with the icons and art of the Orthodox churches. (*Below*)

between 692 and 695, solidi were issued bearing the Latin legend Christus Rex Regnum (Christ, King of Kings), and for the first time in art history there appears the now-familiar bearded, care-worn head of Christ. This was acceptable to Islam at the time because it did not proscribe images until 696.

The source of a haggard image of Christ remains obscure unless it was the vernicle (cloth bearing an image of Christ's face) recorded as being exhibited over the gate of the city of Edessa (modern Urfa, in Turkey). At the end of Justinian II's reign, after his exile and restoration, his coins reverted to showing what had previously been, since at least the 4th century, the traditional clean-shaven, youthful Christ.

**Iconoclasm** From the first quarter of the 8th century another religious development was to influence the style of Byzantine coinage: iconoclasm, an opposition to the use of images in worship. The representation of the emperor as ruler or military commander remained, as did the cross on the reverse, but the style became much more stylized, the cross starker and the bust of the emperor devoid of relief and reduced to a generalized type. This tendency is particularly well-marked in the coinage of Theophilus (829–842). He was the last officially iconoclast emperor, but even so, stylized images continued after him, only gradually becoming more realistic over the next two centuries. By the beginning of the 11th century the style had developed into something close to that of the painted icon. Indeed, these later coins show us what contemporary icons must have looked like.

At this time most coins began to be made in a cup-shape. This form of the flan enabled increasingly brittle metal to be used without reducing the diameter. To reduce the size would have reflected poorly on the State's prestige.

**The decline of Byzantine coinage** The last 200 years of the Byzantine Empire – from the mid-13th to the mid-15th century – saw a continual degradation of fineness, or purity, and design in the minting of coins. In 1453, when the thousand-year empire collapsed, its coinage was virtually non-existent.

Silver coins were issued only intermittently in the Byzantine Empire, in contrast with Islamic states whose main coinage was silver. Bronze coins were struck in huge quantities; they bore the emperor's portrait and on the reverse a much more elaborate system of letters indicating the denomination, the mint and often the date, and who was responsible for the issue.

THE STORY OF COINS IN WESTERN EUROPE OVER THE THOUSAND YEARS
AFTER THE FALL OF THE ROMAN EMPIRE IS ONE OF A GRADUAL RETURN TO
THE STANDARDS SET IN THE ANCIENT MEDITERRANEAN.

# MEDIEVAL AND RENAISSANCE COINS

The shift eastward of the capital of the late Roman Empire was to have profound effects on the political stability and culture of the West: the way was eventually left open for the migrations of Germanic tribes into the empire. The coinage becomes cruder and fewer were made of gold, because of an acute shortage. As time passed coins became increasingly debased.

At first, migratory warlords paid lip-service to the emperor in faraway Constantinople. The imagery on their coins was a crudely representative head of the emperor and a legend, often barely literate, giving a sometimes wrong, long-dead Byzantine emperor's name. Later, however, coins bore the names of local rulers.

In Britain the departure of the Roman legions in the early 5th century led to crude, small copies of Roman bronze coins by the native population. There were also, however, a few issues of coins made of relatively pure gold, which probably had only a very small circulation. Most of the extant examples come from the Crondall (Hampshire) hoard deposited in the 5th century and now in the Ashmolean Museum, Oxford. A few of these rare gold coins were still in limited circulation in the early 7th century, as demonstrated by the Sutton Hoo (Suffolk) find, in the British Museum.

South of the Alps the names of the invaders made their appearance on coins earlier, the designs were in general more accomplished, and gold coinage was more plentiful. The very deep south, Sicily and North Africa, was still, at least nominally, under the control of Byzantium and the coins of these areas reflect this, although, to the experienced eye, they appear somewhat provincial in style.

By the beginning of the 9th century the Frankish Empire of Charlemagne stretched, to judge from the mints, from Brittany to the Rhine and as far south as Beneventum, south of Rome. By this time coinage in the West was almost exclusively silver; only a few gold solidi

**IMITATION SOLIDUS**
**Gold; 5th century**

This coin imitates the solidi of the Roman emperor Licinius (ruler 308–324). It was found in Britain, in East Anglia, and shows how post-Roman authorities preserved traditional forms. (*Above*)

**DERNIER (PENNY)**
**Silver; late 9th century**

A shortage of gold bullion in western Europe during the "Dark Ages" affected its coinage. The empire ruled by Charlemagne (crowned by the Pope on Christmas Day, 800) adopted the silver dernier which remained the standard coin for seven centuries. (*Above*)

were struck. The Carolingian silver dernier (denarius) was produced in very large numbers and its weight and purity were well-maintained.

In 864 the Edict of Pitres decreed that the dernier was to be the standard currency throughout the Empire. The century was not over before local variations were issued by magnates with or without imperial authority. Also it was not long before abbeys and bishops had the royal monopoly of minting farmed out to them and the dernier was issued in a bewildering variety of forms. It did, however, become the staple currency of Western Europe for little short of the next 500 years.

As trade became more international, gold began, little by little, to reappear and in 1284 the first gold ducat was minted in Venice. The gold ducat was generally successful. From its origins in Venice it rapidly spread to the many and various small states, dukedoms and cities of Italy and the Mediterranean and was to remain in circulation, through various mutations of the weight standard, until the late 18th century. The Venetian ducat itself was used extensively as an international trading coin in the Levant and local imitations of it circulated as far afield as southern India.

## THE FIRST ECU
North of the Alps the reintroduction of a gold coinage after about a millennium got off to a more uncertain start. In England, Henry III struck a gold "penny" in 1272 (seven or eight survive) and in France Louis IX issued a similar coin bearing the royal arms (eight survive). This last was the first ecu, derived from the word escutcheon, the heraldic term for a shield. But in the absence of an extensive international trade there was not much use for gold coins. Edward III issued a short-lived gold coinage which was recalled in 1344.

In about 1290 Philip IV of France (1268–1314) began producing a series of splendid gold coins. In general, French royal policy was to use gold coinage as a medium to both enhance and advertise the splendour of their dynasty, and the designs mirror the architecture of the Gothic cathedrals being erected at the time. The English, not to be outdone, struck from 1351 the gold noble, minted at first in London and Calais.

In the West the gold florin became known under the general term gulden. Today the original name is reflected in the abbreviation Fl for the Netherlands guilder.

In silver coinage, the penny, or dernier, continued to be produced, and multiples of it were introduced. One was the gros (four pennies), which made its appearance in the reign of Louis IX (1214–70) and under Edward I in 1279. But this was not a popular coin, and most of the rare examples which survive must have been used as talismans, since many show signs of having been gilded or mounted as jewellery.

ROYAL FACES

There had been no representational portraits of rulers on coins since late Roman times. But when the art of portrait painting developed in Renaissance Italy in the 15th century, it was not long before the first modern portrait coin was issued – in Venice, by Doge Niccoló Tron, in 1472. This was an unpopular move, since the republican traditions of the city were quite as strong as in ancient Rome, when Julius Caesar caused similar offence. But such was the vanity of the Renaissance prince that the practice quickly spread in Italy, where such a coin became known as a testone (*testa* is Italian for head). The first royal coin portrait in a northern kingdom was that of James III of Scotland in 1485. In England the royal portrait was introduced in the last years of the reign of Henry VII (1485-1509) on dies engraved for the first shilling piece. States of a more republican turn of mind tended to employ the image of their patron saint.

The discovery of the Americas in the late 15th century upset the coinages of Europe because of the vast amount of gold discovered there and injected into the world economy. The influence of this proliferation of gold would have been even more profound had it not been for the simultaneous increase in silver mining in Europe. In 1498 Sigismund, ruler of the Tyrol, was short of gold but had silver mines in his domains. Accordingly, he issued a silver coin which had the same bullion value as the gulden (the medieval German gold coin). Naturally, as

**PAVILLON D'OR**
Gold; late 14th century

The name of this coin is derived from the image on its face of King Edward III of England in a pavilion. It was issued by his son Edward the Black Prince at Bordeaux. (*Left*)

**ECU**
Gold; 15th century

The French monarchy used a splendid series of gold coins in Gothic style to reinforce its prestige. King Charles VII (1422–61) issued this one. (*Right*)

**GROAT (4d.)**
Silver; c. 1498

The first realistic portrait on an English coin was of Henry VII on the silver groat. It established the tradition of portraying the monarch on English and British coins – a tradition still continued today. (*Left*)

silver is less valuable than gold, it was larger, and so was born the crown piece. This was popularly known in Germany as the thaler: from 1519 the Bohemian town of Joachimsthal operated a mint for these new coins (there were silver mines locally) and they soon became known as Joachimsthalers, then thalers. It is from this word that "dollar" evolved.

The rest of the 16th century and beyond was taken up with many attempts, often vain, to make the gold and silver coins of Europe compatible. This led to ever-changing designs and weight standards.

A NEW TYPE OF MASTERPIECE EMERGED WITH THE INTRODUCTION OF MINTING MACHINERY. THE QUALITY OF MODERN COINS ACHIEVED A CONSISTENCY THAT COMPENSATES FOR ANY LOSS OF INDIVIDUALITY.

# MODERN COINS

Until the 16th century coins had been more or less hand-made, despite the fact that mints had achieved some measure of primitive mass production, particularly when large amounts of coins were required. (In general, the greater the need for coinage the more hurriedly produced it is, and this shows in its quality.) The introduction of minting machinery made a profound change in the appearance of coins, which now began to take on the familiar appearance of modern coins.

In America the first coins struck at Massachusetts, in about 1650, were similar to siege pieces in appearance, simply being crudely punched N E for New England. They proved to be too easy to counterfeit and in 1652

were replaced with shillings bearing an oak, pine or willow tree and the inscription: IN MASATHUSETS, together with the date. These coins were struck over the next 30 years as occasion demanded but always marked with the original date of issue, 1652. Larger denominations were provided by Mexican pesos made from native silver.

Soon the owners of America plantations flouted the royal prerogative of minting coins and commissioned their own coins from London mints which they shipped out from home, a practice to which the easy-going Charles II apparently turned a blind eye.

In 1670 the French Compagnie de Indes Orientales was given the right to provide its

**ECU**
Silver; 1987

Only a few "European Currency Units" have been struck. They have little practical use. (*Below*)

**THALERS**
Silver; 17th and 18th centuries

A bewildering variety of coins was issued by the many states of Europe during the 17th and 18th centuries. A whole gallery of portraits of the many now-obscure rulers can be built up by collectors. The interests of topographers are served by those republican regimes which tended to show a view of their fine city. The coins of this time were really propaganda instruments. The group shown here were all struck to a fairly uniform size and weight. They circulated throughout Europe and eventually spread to the Americas, via colonization and adaptation. The US dollar has derived its name from the European thaler. (*Left*)

colonies with a coinage produced in Paris. During the 18th century the bulk of French–American coinage bore the comprehensive inscription: COLONIES FRANÇAISES and was also struck in Paris. Because of the dangers from shipwreck and piracy and because it represented almost all profit to the issuer, the coinage shipped out was mainly copper.

In post-revolutionary France a competition to design a new coinage was held in 1791. Judged by the painter Jacques-Louis David, it was won by Augustin Dupré. Although the design was revolutionary, the currency retained the old weight standards.

At this time the decimal system was gaining acceptance both in France and in America, and soon it became the norm in most of Europe, except England, which did not adopt it until 1971. The widespread use of the system led to the Latin Monetary Union, an arrangement closely adhered to until it was formalized in 1868. Its main effects were that a ratio of 15.5:1

for gold to silver was established by France in 1803 and adopted by Belgium, Italy and Switzerland; that gold coins were struck to a fineness of 900/1000; and that denominations were of uniform weight and value. As a result, there is a certain quality of sameness, of fabric if not of design, to 19th-century European and American coins.

The First World War seriously affected the currencies of many nations and gold coins were widely discontinued. The Latin Monetary Union was finally dissolved in 1926.

**US COINS
1976**

These coins mark the bicentennial of US independence. (*Above, left to right*)

**BRITISH SOVEREIGN
Gold; 19th century**

(*Below*)

## SIEGE COINS

In Europe the Thirty Years War (1618-48) and in England the Civil War (1642-9) gave rise to a specialized type of coin: the siege piece. Those beleaguered in a siege obviously had to continue paying their troops but had no access to bullion. As a result, the plate of the town and citizenry was appropriated and, in the absence of mint machinery, was sheared into pieces of convenient weight and identified with a punch. In England, when Charles I was headquartered in Oxford, the colleges lost most of their plate in this way.

IN ASIA DIFFERENT SYSTEMS OF COINAGE WERE EMPLOYED. THE MIDDLE

EAST AND INDIA FOLLOWED THEIR MEDITERRANEAN COUNTERPARTS,

WHILE CHINA DEVELOPED ITS UNIQUE, YET FAMILIAR, APPROACH.

# ORIENTAL COINAGE

The ancient Near East produced coinage that originally was of fine quality but over the centuries became ever cruder imitations. Copies of Athenian owl coins circulated in Arabia but lacked the flair of Celtic adaptations in the West.

The advent of the Sassanids, the dynasty that ruled Persia from AD 226 to 641, saw a change in the nature of Far Eastern coins. Mainly of silver, they were struck on wide flans. They begin by being stamped with a fine head of the king and can be identified by the change in design of the crown of each successive ruler; the reverse bears the Zoroastrian fire altar with two attendants. However, typically they become ever cruder as they are imitated by provincial regimes, who debased the metal until coins which were theoretically of silver were little better than brass. In turn, these coinages – along with the Sassanid dynasty – were swept away by the all-pervading influence of Islam after the mid 7th century.

## ISLAMIC COINAGE

Islamic coinage is excelled only by Chinese for stability of design. In the 7th century, Muhammadan conquerors, having no coinage of their own, struck imitations of the Byzantine-style coinages of their new subjects, eliminating their Christian symbolism.

In 696, 77 years after the death of Muhammed, image-making was formally proscribed and the effect on the design of Islamic coinage was immediate. Gold and silver coins now bore the bismillah, the Islamic declaration of faith, and continued to do so for some 1,200 years, with only rare exceptions. The coins also bore the date on which they were struck, the name of the mint and often the names of the local ruler by whose authority they were issued and of the caliph to whom he gave allegiance. In this way Islamic coins provide an exact record of political and military history over many centuries and over an area stretching from Spain

**PARTHIAN DRACHM**
Silver; **2nd century AD**

*(Right)*

**SASSANIAN DIRHAM**
Silver; **4th century AD**

The Pathians dominated what is today Iran and Iraq from *c.* 255 BC to AD 226. They were succeeded by the Sassanid kings. Both produced series of portrait coins of their rulers. *(Below)*

to the Pacific. Often the apparently insignificant copper coins prove to be the more historically interesting because they were issued by more local authorities and so give information which may not have been recorded elsewhere.

The weights of the gold coinage – at least, in the medieval period – tend to be erratic, implying that transactions were carried by weight, not standard value, of coin. Except early on and in outlying areas, silver coinage was maintained at a good level of purity. Over the entire period, copper coins were, as with other coinages, clearly intended as mere tokens.

## CHINESE COINAGE

From the beginning, Chinese coins were never anything but tokens, as are the coins of virtually every nation now.

From about the 12th century BC, commodities, animals and even household ornaments had been in use as currency. This was in advance of the West, since such goods, unlike bullion, could be measured easily and without dispute, and also lent themselves to small transactions. In addition, the standard design of tools, which were also used as currency, gave little room for haggling. Cowrie shells furnished the small change. By the late 6th century BC the Zhou

**ISLAMIC DIRHAM**
Silver; **early 8th century**

Many Islamic coinages were issued from the time of Mohammed in the mid 7th century right up to the present. They bear not only the date they were struck but also the name of the ruler who issued them. (*Above*)

**ISLAMIC DINAR**
Gold; **12th century**

The lion is a rare example of the use of an image. The coin dates from the time of the Crusades, when the Moslem world was influenced by western European culture brought to the Crusader kingdoms of the Middle East. The

extensive series of Islamic coins furnishes historians with details that chronicle the seemingly never-ending conflicts that are the hallmark of Middle Eastern history. (*Centre left*)

**COINS OF THE MOGHUL EMPEROR AKBAR (1542–1605)**
Gold

The Moghul empire of northern India established Islamic artistic conventions in the subcontinent. Its coins reflect their Moslem heritage. (*Far left and left*)

dynasty, which had ruled China since the late 11th century BC, was issuing inscribed miniature imitation bronze hoes as currency, and these were soon followed by token knives and token cowrie shells.

In the 3rd century BC the system of token objects was replaced by coinage, which took the form of inscribed, circular bronze coins with a central square hole. This was to be the basic model for Chinese and all Far Eastern coinage until it succumbed to Western influence some 2,000 years later. Thus it had a much longer life than any other type of coin.

### INDIAN COINAGE

The non-Islamic coinages of India are as many and varied as her peoples, and the images they bear follow the art and architecture of their time and place. Kushan and Gupta coinages are, for the most part, based on the Roman gold aureus but have Hindu iconography. At first, this is well-executed but as time passes it degenerates. Distinctive inscriptions clearly separate them from similar coins modelled on this series, although the dating of the relevant rulers is sometimes controversial.

Local imitations of central issues were made. On these the style of the original degenerates, without developing into anything aesthetic, as it did in Celtic coinages, and the metal also becomes less pure. The conclusion is that these imitations were mostly a token coinage.

In southern India the various local coinages were obviously derived from a central gold coinage. In order to adhere to a gold currency and yet meet the needs of small, everyday trans-actions, some gold coins were made that are scarcely larger than a pinhead. Although there seems to have been some sort of duodecimal weight standard, it appears that the purity of these southern Indian coins was judged by colour. Silver was also employed in the region. Many larger bronze coins were produced for the smallest marketplace transactions. From what little evidence there is, coins seem to have been used by tael (an Eastern bullion measure of weight). It is obvious from the worn condition of so many of them that they circulated over many centuries.

Beginning in the 17th century, the British and Dutch East India Companies imposed multi-language, European-style coinages on India. These in turn evolved into a British imperial coinage in use until the country's was granted independence in 1947.

**CHINESE COINS**
Bronze; **3rd century BC**
(*Above*) **and 13th century AD**

At first Chinese coins followed the principle of pictographic writing – they represented useful objects. But soon it was realized that a circular form with a central hole was more practical. The Chinese hardly ever used precious metals for coinage. (*Top*)

**GUPTA COIN**
Gold; **5th century AD**

(*Left*)

**INDIAN COINS**
Gold; **12th century** (*Below left*) **and 18th century**

(*Below*)

COMMEMORATIVE "COINS" HAVE ALWAYS BEEN STRUCK FOR SPECIAL
OCCASIONS. THESE MEDALS ARE USUALLY CRAFTED BETTER THAN COINS,
AND LESS SUBJECT TO THE WEAR AND TEAR OF EVERYDAY USE.

# MEDALS

Classical Greek times provide one of the earliest examples of a medal. The exceptionally high standard of design and execution of certain large denominations of coin produced by the Greek city of Syracuse in Sicily show that they had a commemorative function. Initially, the events commemorated were sporting, and presumably the coins were given as prizes – that is to say, as medals. The neighbouring city of Metapontum gives us the first definitive evidence, dating from about 450 BC. The coin in question bears the inscription "the prize of Achelous", indicating that it was given as a prize in the games held in honour of the person named. Supporting evidence is supplied by the fact that it is Greek and Roman coins of large denominations that have most tended to survive in good condition, implying that they were treasured for their own sake rather than used for financial transactions.

The Romans issued medals, to begin with in bronze, which were no more than particularly well-struck examples of the current coinage. The designs of late Roman medals, all of which are extremely rare, demonstrate that they were intended to be given by the ruler to those he wished to compliment. This practice had come into favour again by the early 16th century, soon after the revival of medals during the Renaissance. They were handed out as favours – presumably, much as signed photographs of presidents are today. This use of medals continued until the advent of photography.

Many medals of late antiquity have survived in almost mint state, and the places where they have been found point to their having been used to flatter the barbarian chieftains who were pressing upon the Roman Empire, in the same way as those medals sent by George III and Louis XVI to American Indian chiefs. Roman medals have been found as far away as Afghanistan, but those from such remote places tend to be in poor condition, indicating that they were more worn as trophies than preserved in

**MEDAL**
*Pisanello*
**1438**

This portrait medal of the Byzantine emperor, John VIII Palaeologus, was made when he visited Italy in 1438. (*Above*)

**MEDAL**
*Albrecht Dürer*
**1521**

This handsome silver portrait medal was intended for presentation by the city fathers of Nuremberg to the Holy Roman Emperor Charles V. (*Right*)

**MEDAL**
Benvenuto *Cellini*
**1534**

Many of the most-
celebrated artists of the
Renaissance turned their
hand to the design and
production of medals.
Cellini was commissioned
by Pope Clement VII to
produce this one depicting
Moses on the rock with his
staff to create miraculously
a spring during the Exodus.

honour of the donor. That these ancient medals were status symbols is shown by the fact that later imitations – crude, even though with a style of their own – are known from the Germanic races and the Vikings.

In 1438 the Byzantine emperor John VIII, Palaeologus, rode into Ferrara to seek support from the Christian West against the Muslim Turks. His exotic attire impressed the artist Antonio Pisano, familiarly known as Pisanello, who created a realistic portrait medal of the emperor, the first of the great Italian Renaissance medals.

Such medals quickly became very popular: up to about 1530 there are some 1,200 different types. No more than, say, 30 examples survive of any single type. They were cast by the lost-wax process, and the same process was used to make later copies from an existing specimen. Because of this it is not possible to be certain which of the medals that survive are originals and which after-casts. However, it is known that the mould to make an after-cast was about 1 percent smaller than the original, and so measurements are of crucial importance in evaluating these early medals. In the absence of a firm attribution, collectors have to be content with a judgement as to the quality of the medal and its closeness to the artist's intention.

It was not long before dies came to be used for medal production. The very rare gold and silver medals struck by the French to celebrate the ousting of the English from what they considered to be their territories in 1455 were struck from engraved dies. These pieces, which were in effect coins of multiple denominations, owe nothing in their design to the new art of the Renaissance but are Gothic in character.

The first German medal was cast from a stone model carved by Lucas Cranach in 1508.

**MEDAL**
*Italy*
**17th century**

This was issued in honour of Francesco Redi, the Italian physician, naturalist and poet. (*Above*)

**MEDAL**
*France*
**18th century**

The original tin case (shown) for this medal of Marie Antoinette has survived, ensuring that this portrait came down to us in immaculate condition. (*Left*)

hanced by the die. The flans would tend to reproduce the acquired dents and scratches of the struck original.

We are fortunate in having a very detailed description of the early striking of medals written by the 16th-century Italian sculptor Benvenuto Cellini, both in his autobiography and in his treatise on goldsmithery. One of the first Italian medals is that which Cellini struck to impress Pope Clement VII in 1532. His Holiness said that not even the ancients had coins such as these.

The German world tended to produce portrait pieces of their numerous princelings with elaborate heraldic reverses. The French, with their centralized monarchy, for the most part favoured larger medals which eulogized the king and had allegorical reverses. But nowhere were medals as popular as they were in Italy, where they were regarded more as a form of miniature sculpture.

There is some confusion as to what are the earliest English medals, but several 16th-century portrait medals of Henry VIII, dating from early in his reign and derived from German models attributed to Hans Schwarz, have a strong claim. We are on more certain ground with the medal proclaiming Henry as supreme head of the Church (1545).

The first Scottish medal was of Archbishop Schevez of St Andrews and was cast in the Netherlands in 1491. The first that can with certainty be ascribed to native talent was of John Stewart, Duke of Albany, struck in gold from Craufurd Moor (Ayrshire) and dated 1524.

Dutch medals, like Spanish, began with those by Italian artists attracted there by the great magnates of the day. Niccoló Spinelli was working at the court of Charles the Bold, Duke of Burgundy and of the Netherlands, in 1468, and Giovanni Candida was making medals of, among others, the young Emperor Maximilian and Mary of Burgundy from 1472. The first native Dutch medal designer of note was Quentin Metsyss, who may have produced the Scottish medal of Archbishop Schevez and was probably responsible for that of the Dutch scholar Erasmus, dated 1519.

In 1521 a portrait medal of the young Emperor Charles V was designed by Albrecht Dürer and struck in Nuremberg from dies prepared by Hans Kraaft. For both these larger medals a rough outline known as a blank was cast with the design's image and then finished by the application of the dies. Cast examples of these medals do exist and are usually considered comparatively late productions, but it could be that they are copies produced during the period of original striking or even the original cast flans unen-

### GALLANTRY AND CAMPAIGN MEDALS

Rewards for military heroism or long service are known from Roman times, when they usually took the form of masks of Medusa (perhaps in reference to Perseus's shield) and were made of agate. They have been found all over the Roman

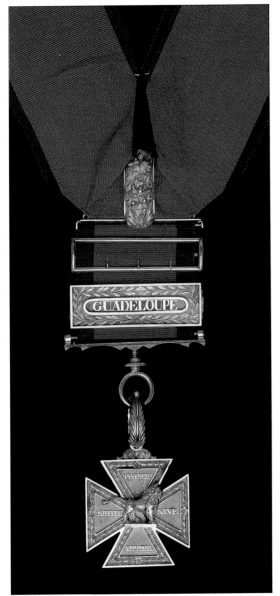

### PENINSULAR WAR GOLD CROSS
*Britain*
**19th century**

General officers who served under Wellington during the Peninsular War received this medal to honour their service. (*Left*)

### RAF MEDALS
*Britain*
**20th century**

The medal on the far left is an award for gallantry in the air during the Second World War. The others either reward service on various fronts of the war or commemorate the Queen's Coronation. (*Below*)

Empire, particularly along the Rhine. A few examples, made of Whitby jet, have been discovered in northern Britain. All the indications are that they were awarded informally.

Military rewards became more like those we know today during the Thirty Years War (1618-1648) and the English Civil War (1642-9). (The process may, however, have begun earlier, in England the previous century, with the awards given for the destruction of the Spanish Armada.) From this time on they took the form of medals as we know them, often made with an integral ring for suspension from a riband.

In the Thirty Years War the mercenary played a large part, and it has been suggested that medals of consistent form and of graduation in value furnished a means during the war of creating loyalty and cohesion in otherwise uncommitted and disparate groups.

It was not until the Napoleonic Wars that the issue and wearing of medals became strictly structured by military protocol.

## FURTHER READING

The following list of materials for further reading offers a broad range of literature. Both specialist and general works are included. While every effort has been made to give the date of the most recent edition, new ones may have been published since this book went to press.

American Numismatic Society
***America's Copper Coinage, 1783–1857***
New York 1985

*– America's Silver Coinage, 1794–1891*
New York 1987

Bradley, H.W.
***A Handbook of Coins of the British Isles***
London 1984

Breen, Walter
***Complete Encyclopedia of US and Colonial Coins***
New York 1988

Broome, Michael
***A Handbook of Islamic Coins***
London 1985

Carson, R.A.G.
***Coins, Ancient, Medieval and Modern***
London 1962

Cresswell, O.D.
***Chinese Cash***
1971

Cribb, J., B. Cook and I. Carradice
***The Coin Atlas***
London 1990

Doty, Richard G.
***The Encylopaedia Dictionary of Numismatics***
London 1982

Dyer, Graham P.
***The Royal Mint, an Illustrated History***
London 1986

Haxby, James
***Striking Impressions***
Ottawa 1984

Jones, John Melville
***A Dictionary of Ancient Roman Coins***
London 1990

Linecar, Howard
***The Observer's Book of Coins***
1977

McDonald, Gregg
***Australian Coins and Banknotes***
1985

Room, Adrian
***A Dictionary of Coin Names***
London 1987

Seaby, Peter
***Coins of Scotland, Ireland and the Islands***
London 1984

Whitting, P.D.
***Byzantine Coins***
London 1963

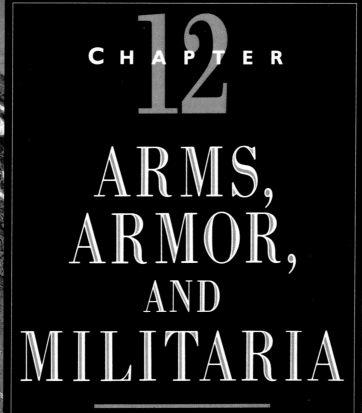

# 12

# ARMS, ARMOR, AND MILITARIA

ARMOR
·
EDGED WEAPONS
·
FIREARMS
·
MILITARIA

FREDERICK WILKINSON

*This page:* **INDIAN SHIELD, c. 1800 (detail).**

# ARMS, ARMOR, AND MILITARIA

HUMAN INGENUITY AND CRAFTSMANSHIP RECEIVED THEIR MOST VITAL TEST IN THE DESIGN AND DEVELOPMENT OF ARMS AND ARMOR, WHERE THE LIFE OF THE USER COULD DEPEND COMPLETELY ON THE RELIABILITY, ACCURACY OR STRENGTH OF THE WEAPONS.

**SHIELD**
*Indo-Persian*
Steel and brass; **c. 1820**

Engraved overall with sun motifs, this is typical of the form used throughout the Indian sub-continent.

Armour has been described as sculpture in steel, and a finely shaped breastplate, helmet or pair of gauntlets can indeed possess grace and beauty. Until the 17th century each piece of armour was the product of skilled craftsmen. The armourer delighted in his ability to cover the body in such a way that the wearer was able to move freely and yet was still protected against the point or edge of a weapon. The shape of the human body and its degree of movement are such that, to achieve his object, the armourer was called upon to exercise his skills to the limit. One of the finest examples of such skill is the foot combat armour of Henry VIII, which completely enclosed the entire body but still allowed him to move easily in combat. The armourer was also ready to decorate his armour, and in the 16th century he created steel copies of the current fashion in clothes.

For collectors with an appreciation of craftsmanship armour has an immense appeal; and for those with the least dash of romanticism in them armour must surely recall not simply war but the glamour of knights jousting in tournaments. For those who are more interested in

**LUFTWAFFE DRESS DAGGER**
*German*
**c. 1940**

This Second Model with sword knot was used by officers of the Third Reich. (*Below*)

investment good-quality armour has been one field of antiques that has appreciated fairly consistently over the years.

War is a grim affair, but the glamour of its trappings (known as militaria), such as uniforms, has enticed many people into collecting them. This is a field full of opportunities for collectors and one of the few which still enables those of moderate means to acquire a range of items at reasonable prices. Apart from uniforms, militaria includes helmets, badges, belts and many other types of equipment, medals (which can be expensive), flags, photographs, prints and other printed material, postage stamps and many other items. Militaria is also a field that offers considerable scope for the collector wishing to research a particular item: official records can yield the identity of the winner of a medal, the wearer of a uniform or the writer of a letter.

Weapons may seem a less attractive field of collecting, since they are so obviously associated with pain, injury and death. However, the collector of antique weapons usually sees them less in this light than as the

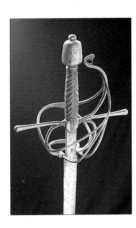

**HILT OF A SWEPT-HILT RAPIER**
*Spanish*
**c. 1620**

Such weapons were primarily intended for thrusting rather than cutting, and the bars were designed to protect the swordsman's hand. The top section of the blade is blunted so that the fingers could be looped over the quillons to ensure a firm grip. The solid pommel at the top of the wire-bound grip helped to balance the long blade. Other rapiers were fitted with bowl-shaped guards and are known as cup-hilted rapiers. Both types of rapier were often used with a dagger in the left hand, usually decorated in the same style as the sword. During the 16th and 17th centuries this style of fighting with the sword was taught at many fencing schools throughout Europe. During the 18th century the rapier was shortened and lightened and became the decorative smallsword. (*Above*)

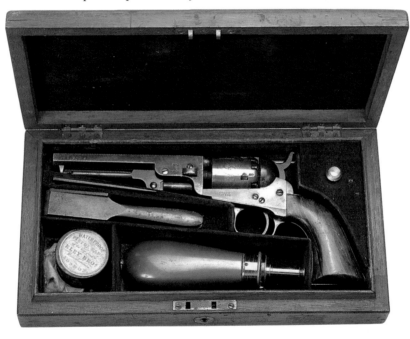

**CASED PERCUSSION REVOLVER POCKET MODEL**
*Colt*
**c. 1853**

The weapon fired a small bullet, calibre .31 in. and was produced with various barrel lengths. The cylinder was engraved with a stagecoach hold-up scene. American Samuel Colt visited the Great Exhibition of 1851 in London and later set up a factory in London, where this revolver was made. It carries English proof marks and the case, in the English style, holds a bullet mould, powder flask and tin of caps. In the top corner is a compartment for either bullets or paper cartridges. It is often claimed that Colt invented the revolver, but such weapons had been developed long before his patents in the 1830s. His major contribution to the arms trade, however, was his use of factory production. He was also an expert promoter of his product and presented samples to many leading public men. (*Left*)

work of skilled craftsmen; moreover, in the 17th and 18th centuries many swords were more costume items than weapons. Precious metals and fine-quality engraving, chiselling and etching make many swords works of art. The same is true of the sporting gun, for the owner was often a man who wished to flaunt his wealth and position and so would order one of the top gun-makers to produce a weapon of beauty. Inlaid decoration using ivory, bone, decorative woods and precious metals might all be used to embellish the stock, and the metal parts might be gilded, blued or chiselled into intricate or grotesque shapes. For the collector with an interest in mechanical curiosities, many of the patented modifications to firearms intended to make them shoot more rapidly or further are fascinating and often positively bizarre. High-quality weapons are expensive, but there are many types of weapon, such as bayonets, that are comparatively cheap.

Over the past few years there have been published a number of books invaluable to the new collector and expert alike and well worth study. For those with an eye for the unusual and often beautiful, arms, armour and militaria can prove a fascinating field of collecting.

FROM MEDIEVAL BREASTPLATES TO 19TH-CENTURY SHIELDS, THE ARMOR

WORN BY SOLDIERS THROUGH THE AGES CONVEYS VIVIDLY THE

DISCOMFORTS AND DANGERS OF WARFARE IN THE PAST.

# ARMOR

Certain forms of armour can be traced back to the ancient world of the Egyptians, Greeks and Romans, but surviving collectable armour seldom dates back further than the 16th century. The rare ancient pieces that do occasionally appear on the market, such as Greek helmets, are very expensive.

Mail, the defence composed of interlocking, circular metal links, was worn from Roman times but surviving European examples, mostly in museums, seldom go back to earlier than the

**ARMOUR**
**16th and 17th centuries**

At top is a tasset to protect the thigh, and next to it a couter or elbow piece. A tasset and poleyn to guard the left thigh and knee is below.

15th century. Mail was an efficient and flexible defence, but as the skill of the weapon-maker grew his products were able to pierce mail more easily. The warrior had to improve his defences and to do this he attached metal plates to the basic suit of mail shirt and leggings. By the late 14th century the entire body was covered by plate armour.

The main defence for the body was the cuirass, which comprised breast and backplate secured at the sides by leather straps, hooks and lugs or spring fittings. At the lower end of the breastplate were attached plates which formed a defence for the lower abdomen and thighs. The legs were protected by carefully shaped, hinged plates and the top of the foot was covered by a number of narrow, overlapping plates. The arms were similarly protected by a series of enclosing plates; vulnerable areas, such as the inside of the elbow, the armpit and the knee, were given extra protection with pieces of mail and ingeniously shaped plates. The hands were covered with leather gloves to which were fitted articulated plates allowing the free movement of fingers and thumb. The head was protected by a helmet and, over the centuries, a number of different types were worn.

Armour was worn by many troops from the 10th to the 17th centuries, but the introduction of firearms in the 14th century initiated a gradual decline in its use. The gun gradually replaced the bow as the main projectile weapon and the simplest musketeer's bullet could penetrate most plates. It was quite possible to manufacture armour thick enough to stop a bullet but it was then so heavy that it impeded the wearer and so limited the manoeuvrability of the troops. By the mid-18th century armour had largely disappeared from the battlefields of Europe, with the exception of some cavalry, such as the French cuirassiers, who retained their sturdy cuirasses.

In the 19th century armour came into use again. This was mainly for ceremonial occasions, but it was used for practical purposes during the American Civil War (1861–65). There was a further revival during the First World War, when the Germans equipped some of their more exposed troops with heavy body armour and reinforcing plates for the helmet. The same war saw the reintroduction of protective metal helmets in an attempt to reduce the large number of head wounds suffered by troops.

## FULL SUITS

Most people do not have the available room to display a full suit of armour – or complete harness, as it is technically known – on a dummy.

In addition, the scarcity of full suits means that prices are high. This was also the case in the last century, and to satisfy the market copies of various styles of armour were made. Some of these are unlikely to deceive collectors (their metal is usually too thin and pliable) but others can be difficult to identify as copies. The inside surface of the metal can be useful in indicating whether an item is old or not, Victorian and modern copies of armour tend to have rather smooth, even surfaces, whereas the originals were normally rough from the hammer. However, this is not a hard-and-fast rule: some modern craftsmen re-create the old roughness. In time the outer surface of armour tends to acquire small pits and scratches, giving it a slightly mottled appearance, and in some cases the metal laminates, splitting slightly into lay-

ers. The presence of either feature usually indicates that the metal is of some age.

Among makers who have tried to produce exact replicas of old armour, to deceive collectors, was Ernst Schmidt, who worked in Munich in the early 20th century. In addition, there have been a few unscrupulous dealers and collectors who have had pieces "restored" and

**CUIRASS**
*French*
**Mid 19th century**

Worn by the cavalry of the Second Empire, this cuirass, like much of the uniform and other equipment of the period, differs little from that worn by Napoleon's troops. (*Left*)

**FULL SUIT OF ARMOUR**
**19th century**

By the 19th century the supply of genuine armour was limited and expensive, but there was a demand for it to decorate the homes of the romantic rich. A large number of copies were made – this is in the style of the 16th century – and they vary in quality. Some from German workshops are of top quality. (*Below*)

**PIKEMAN'S POT**
*English*
**c. 1630**

Most 17th-century armies were made up of groups of musketeers and pikemen whose prime job was to protect the musketeers while they were reloading. Pikemen wore a cuirass and skirt of armour with this style of helmet. The helmet has a fitting mounted at the back to hold a plume. The line of brass rivets around the base of the skull secured the inside padded lining. Those worn by officers are often decorated with embossed patterns. (*Left*)

"refreshed". The collector should check every piece carefully.

### BREASTPLATES AND BACKPLATES

Because of the dearth of complete harnesses, and their high prices, many collectors concentrate on one particular component of armour, such as the breastplate, gauntlet or helmet.

Surviving breastplates of the 17th century are fairly common and are generally those worn either by mounted harquebusiers (soldiers armed with hand guns) or by pikemen. Harquebusiers' breastplates are usually substantial and are often marked with a bullet dent somewhere near the centre. This is not a souvenir of battle: when the armourer had completed the plate it was taken outside and a musket was fired at it to test its protective quality. Some helmets were similarly tested, but with a pistol rather than a musket.

The pikeman's breastplate is distinguished by

**CLOSE HELMET**
*German*
**c. 1580**

The helmet retains much of its original colouring. The visor could be raised by pressing the spring catch at the base, and it was then propped open by the pivoted bar at the side. The entire front could be swung up after undoing the hook. (*Right*)

**BREASTPLATE**
*Italian*
**Mid 16th century**

This anime-type breastplate is made up of overlapping plates riveted to leather straps. (*Below*)

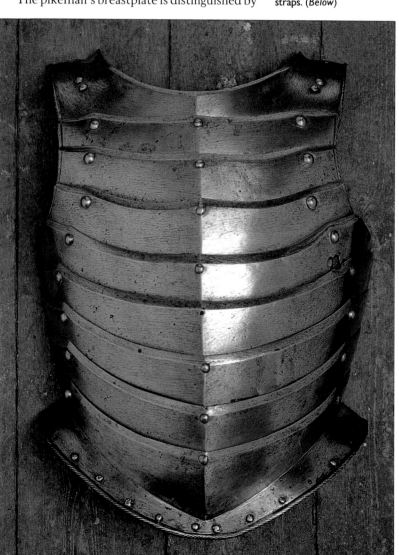

its centrally pointed shape and waist flange, and it often has two slightly overlapping plates suspended from the base.

Backplates matching the breastplates are normally of thinner metal and do not carry a test bullet dent. The backplate of the harquebusier has a slightly upstanding collar not found on that of the pikeman.

Most of these 17th-century breastplates and backplates are plain except perhaps for some simple incised line decoration. Many are stamped, usually near the neck, with the mark and possibly the initials of the armourer.

Cuirasses of the early 16th century are often in what is known as the Maximilian style – fluted (vertically grooved). This fluting was partly decorative but was primarily to strengthen the armour as well as helping to deflect a point away from vital areas of the body.

### HELMETS AND GAUNTLETS

During the early Middle Ages the helmet was often large and rather bucket-shaped. Such great helms, now extremely rare, were succeeded by the close helmet, known as an armet. The early form of this consisted of two side sections and a pivoted visor. The later form was made up of a skull section covering the back and sides of the head, a pivoted section that swung down to cover the lower part of the face and a visor, pierced with slits for vision and holes for ventilation, that could be lowered to cover the rest of the face.

Contemporary with the close helmet was the burgonet, which left the face uncovered and was commonly fitted with some form of peak (a projecting forepiece). One type, popular with horsemen during the Thirty Years War (1618–48) and the English Civil Wars (1642–60), had a skullpiece, a neck guard, two cheek pieces and a peak, which was sometimes fitted with a three-bar face guard and could be swung up clear of the face.

For ordinary foot soldiers helmets were simpler, in general consisting of a skull piece and brim only. Known as morions or cabassets, these are not uncommon.

One guide to assessing the age of helmets is to look inside: if the skullpiece is made of two sections hammer-welded together or united by rivets along the centre, the helmet is likely to be 17th- rather than 16th-century. Helmets are popular with armour collectors. Those of the 17th century can still be found and are reason-

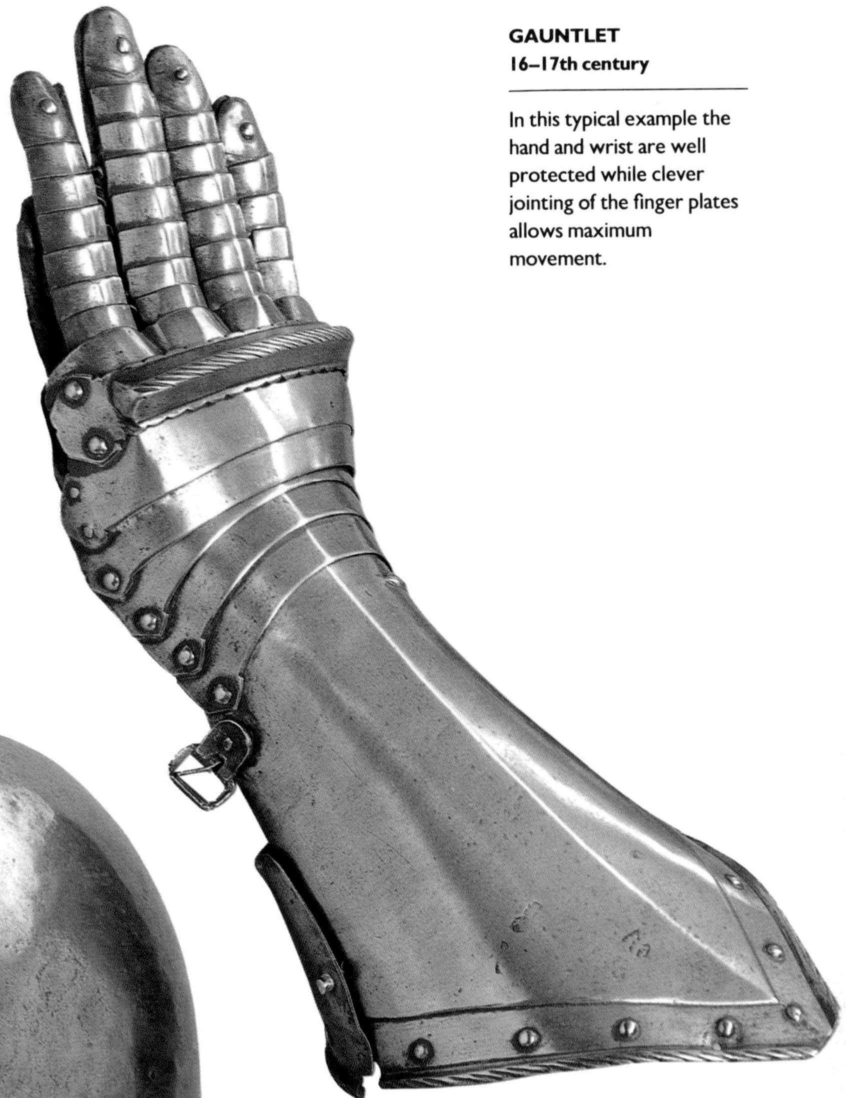

### GAUNTLET
### 16–17th century

In this typical example the hand and wrist are well protected while clever jointing of the finger plates allows maximum movement.

### HORSEMAN'S POT
### c. 1630

The skull is one piece and the neck guard has three overlapping plates known as lames. Later versions were often less well made, with the skull made in two pieces and the neck guard a single plate made to look as if it comprised several plates. The face was guarded against sword slashes by the bar or nasal, which could be adjusted. Another type of similar helmet has a three-bar face guard fitted to a peak pivoted at the sides. (*Left*)

ably priced; the same applies to steel helmets of the two World Wars.

Most gauntlets consist of a cuff, sometimes composed of two hinged pieces; a shaped plate, with overlapping knuckle strips, for the back of the hand; and a series of small rectangular plates to protect the fingers. Early examples sometimes have broad overlapping plates covering all the fingers. During the 17th century, when much armour had been discarded, the left forearm and hand of the cavalryman, which held the horse's reins, were protected by a bridle gauntlet, whose cuff extended as far as the elbow.

A few gauntlets were made of buff leather with reinforcing scales stitched to the main glove. Buff leather was also used in the 17th century as a body defence.

### EASTERN STYLES

Eastern armies retained armour for much longer than Western ones; Indian soldiers continued to wear it up to this century. Warriors of Turkey, Persia and India wore basically similar armour, a mixture of mail and plates. The Indo-Persian style generally consists of a body defence of four large plates worn over a mail shirt, plate defences for the arms, occasionally mail trousers

and the whole topped off with a dome-shaped helmet. The helmet is frequently fitted with a curtain of mail to protect the neck and the face is guarded by an adjustable nasal bar. Such armour was produced well into the 19th century but later examples are usually of slightly inferior quality.

The Japanese developed a special form of armour, which has acquired a strong following among collectors. Japanese armour makes great use of small, lacquered plates laced together to form larger, flexible plates. (However, some armourers did produce European-style armour incorporating large plates.) Helmets consist of a metal skullpiece and laced, lacquered strips to protect the neck; the front is often embellished with a crest. Japanese armour is not common and is invariably expensive.

Armour is a specialized study and many general dealers do not have the expertise to assess and value the various pieces. The best sources of supply are generally auction rooms, which employ specialist cataloguers, and specialist dealers. There are some excellent copies of pieces on the market, so the collector should use one of the available reference books to check any piece before buying.

**HELMET**
*Indo-Persian*
Metal, mail and gold; **late 18th century**

The face was protected by an adjustable bar and the two front fittings held tall plumes. (*Above*)

**SHIELD**
*Indian*
Animal hide;
**c. 1800**

Painted overall with a border of a gilt pattern, the shield is rather unusual in that a tuft of the animal hair has been left as added decoration. (*Right*)

FROM THE DASHING OFFICER'S RAPIER TO THE HUMBLE INFANTRYMAN'S BAYONET, EDGED WEAPONS HAVE BEEN A COMPONENT OF THE SOLDIER'S LIFE WHETHER IN THE BARRACKS OR ON THE BATTLEFIELD.

# EDGED WEAPONS

Some very early swords, axes and daggers survive and, considering their antiquity, are not expensive. The supply of bronze weapons of this kind from the Middle East has diminished recently and consequently prices have risen. Iron, which replaced bronze, improved the cutting edge of weapons but reduced their survival rate, and most swords and daggers from before the 15th century are in a poor, rusted condition. Swords of later date are fairly common and often of reasonable quality.

Among the most impressive swords are two-handed types of the 16th century. Most are 2 m (6 ft) long, and a few have a serpentine or flamboyant blade. Other large fighting swords of this period are known as bastard or hand-and-a-half swords, from the size of the hilt, which is big enough to permit a two-handed grip for a particularly powerful swing. Executioner's swords have a similar larger grip and are characterized by the broad, flat-tipped blade, which is often engraved with pious sentiments about justice, sin and punishment.

### RAPIERS

The late 16th century and early 17th century saw the increasing adoption of the rapier, with its long, fairly narrow blade intended primarily for thrusting. The hilts were designed to give protection to the hand and varied considerably

**HILT OF A TWO-HANDED SWORD**
*German*
**c. 1580**

Large swords were made as weapons, or as marks of status. (*Above*)

**SWORDS**
**14th century**

Early swords like these are rare and expensive. (*Below*)

**HILT OF A PAPPENHEIMER RAPIER**
*German*
**c. 1630**

The rapier resembles the swept-hilt type but has two pierced shell guards filling the space between the lower bars. The name derives from a cavalry general who fought during the Thirty Years War. Such weapons were often fitted with blades intended to cut and thrust. (*Above*)

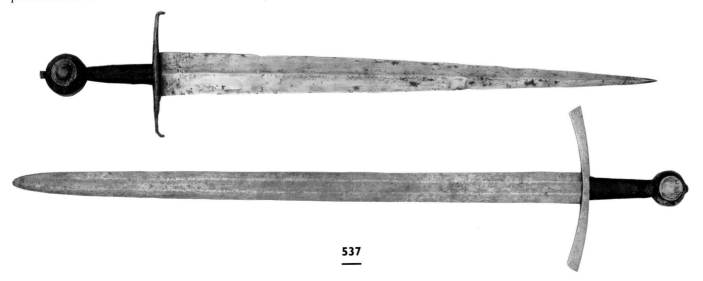

in design. The most common type is probably the swept hilt, on which the guard is made up of curved bars and a long crossguard. Later in the 17th century saw the introduction of the cup-hilted rapier, on which the barred guard was replaced by a hemispherical metal cup, often pierced with intricate patterns.

Rapiers were largely the weapons of the upper classes. The common soldiery were armed with much simpler swords, most having a straight blade and a simpler version of the rapier hilt. During the English Civil Wars a rapier with a basket guard was common; it is known today as a mortuary sword, from a chiselled bust on the guard taken to be that of the martyred Charles I.

### SMALL-SWORDS

As firearms played a bigger part in war, the sword was relegated in importance. The long-bladed rapier was gradually replaced by a lighter, shorter-bladed weapon known as a small-sword, which was as much a part of costume as a weapon. These swords were popular from the late 17th to the late 18th century. The blades are straight and usually double-edged, though some have a blade known as a coli-chemarde, which is broad near the hilt, then narrows abruptly to a normal width. The hilts are often elaborate and fashioned of iron, brass, silver and, occasionally, gold. The hilt is a useful approximate guide to the date of the weapon: in most cases, the smaller the two curved arms just above the shell guard of the hilt the later the sword. Some small-swords, known as mourning swords, have blackened hilts and were intended for formal wear at funerals.

The small-sword was abandoned as a costume item around the 1770s but continued in use as a status symbol. Simplified forms were evolved for diplomatic, court and official wear. The hilts of these are usually fairly basic and the blades, often decorated with an etched design, are substantial. American societies, such as the Knights of Columbus, seem to have developed a taste for similar pieces, especially during the late 19th century, and cruciform-hilted swords with elaborately decorated blades, often inscribed with the owner's name, were produced by firms such as the Ames Sword Company.

### REGULATION MILITARY SWORDS

Army swords of standard pattern began to appear in the 17th century, but in Britain there was little real standardization until 1796 when

**HILT OF A SMALL SWORD**
*English*
Silver; 1765

The rapier of the 17th century was gradually reduced in size and by the 18th century had become the smallsword. These were light and decorative, capable of serving as a weapon but more a piece of male decorative costume. Many were fitted with hilts of silver and this can help in dating the sword, for the silver will usually carry a hallmark and the identifying letter was changed annually. This example is fitted with a colichemarde blade which was much wider at the top near the hilt and narrowed abruptly about a third of the way to the point. The idea was to give strength without too much weight. Smallswords ceased to be worn as part of a gentleman's costume in about 1780.

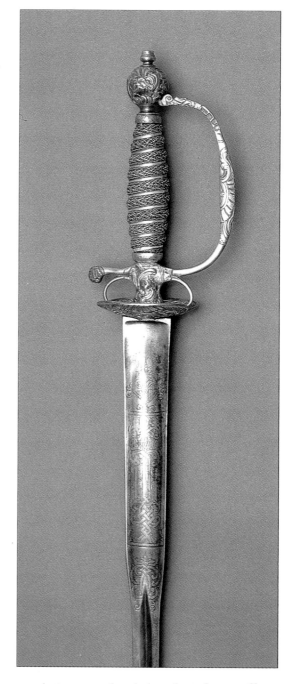

regulations stipulated that the infantry officer was to carry a straight-bladed weapon with a simple hilt consisting of a shell guard with knuckle bow, urn-shaped pommel and simple crossguard.

During the 19th century there were many changes in army sword patterns, which collectors enjoy studying. Most military issue swords are not expensive unless they happen to be presentation pieces, inscribed and given to an officer on retirement or in appreciation of some deed.

The British infantryman relinquished his sword in the mid-18th century. The infantry officer kept his as a weapon until the end of the

19th century, after which it became merely a symbol of rank. The cavalry, which relied on the sword much more than the infantry did, long debated whether its sword should be primarily a thrusting or a cutting weapon, an argument eventually decided in Britain with the issue of a straight-bladed thrusting sword. This, however, was not until 1908, when the cavalry had become largely superfluous.

### NAVAL SWORDS

These offer less scope for the collector than military swords and as a consequence they are less popular. The fighting sword of the seaman, the cutlass, tends to be substantial, workman-like and seldom decorated. The small dagger worn by many naval officers and known as a midshipman's dirk is more attractive. It has a short, straight or curved blade, and the hilt is often of ivory and the scabbard of black leather. Officers' regulation swords are not dissimilar from those of the infantry except for generally featuring the fouled anchor on the hilt or blades. The outstanding naval sword is the Lloyds Presentation sword, given by the Lloyds Company during the Napoleonic Wars to honour the bravery of naval officers. The swords, which came in 30-, 50- and 100-guinea models, have broad, curved blades decorated with blueing and gilding. Most swords carry an inscription detailing the action for which they were presented. Supplied in a wooden case complete with sword belt, they are rare and very expensive.

### DAGGERS AND KNIVES

Bronze Age daggers are not uncommon but, as with swords, there are few surviving examples of the iron daggers worn as part of everyday costume until about the 16th century. The type

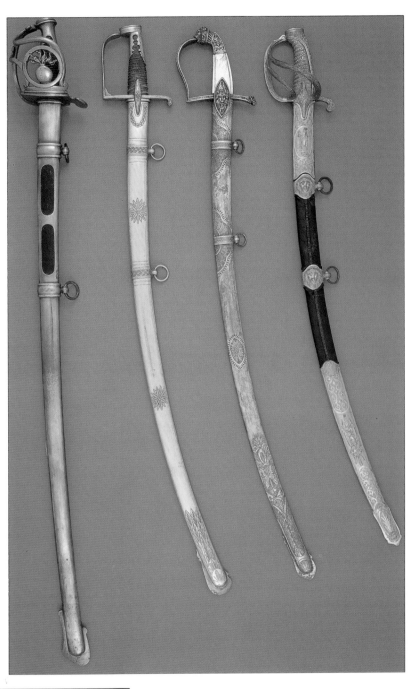

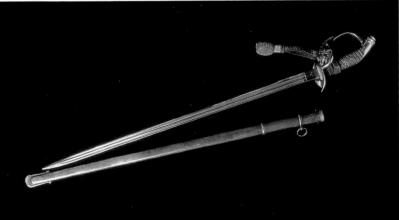

**OFFICER'S SWORD**
*Prussian*
**Late 19th century**

The angled grip is a common feature of these swords. The hilt has its portepee or knot, which originally was looped around the wrist to prevent loss of the sword if it were dropped in battle. The scabbard is metal. (*Left*)

**MILITARY SWORDS**
*French*
**Early 19th century**

From left to right are: a trooper's sabre of the Mounted Grenadier Guard, c. 1800; a sabre of a senior officer, possibly one of the Imperial Guard, c. 1805; a field officer's sabre, c. 1800; and a senior officer's sword, c. 1820. (*Above*)

most often seen on the antique market is the quillon dagger, which is more or less a miniature sword with a straight, pointed blade and a simple crossguard that often had a ring fitted to one side to protect the hand. In one kind of swordplay a rapier was used in the right hand and a dagger in the left. The Spanish favoured a dagger with a curved, triangular guard, and often manufactured and decorated rapier and dagger as a pair.

During the colonial expansion of the 19th century, exploration and big-game hunting brought about a revival in large multi-purpose knives. Probably the best known is that named after the American, Colonel James Bowie (d. 1836) and first produced in the 1830s. Ironically, this heavy-bladed, single-edged knife that epitomized the Wild West was manufactured mainly in Sheffield, England.

The next revival of knife and dagger production came during the First World War when trench knives were made for use in silent hand-to-hand combat. Similar weapons were produced during the Second World War for the

Commandos and other elite forces. The best known was the Fairbairn Sykes fighting knife.

There was another great revival of edged-weapon production in Germany during the Third Reich. Encouraged by the cutlers of Solingen, a long-established German centre of blade production, the Nazi leaders introduced a wide range of dress daggers and swords for the armed forces and political groups. When the Second World War had begun to recede into the past, collectors gradually became interested in these weapons, and today there is a considerable market for them. Some, such as those worn by SS officers, fetch very high prices, and even common army daggers still cost as much as an ordinary sword at least 100 years older.

## BAYONETS

Introduced in the 17th century, bayonets were intended to enable the musket to serve as a short pike. The early types, known as plug bayonets, had a tapered wooden hilt that was simply pushed into the muzzle of the gun barrel. Since they plugged the muzzle and prevented the

## PLUG BAYONETS
*English*
### c. 1680

Both bayonets have the blades stamped with bladesmith's marks; the one on the left is dated 1688 and inscribed "ANDREW RUDSBY". This type of bayonet was the first to be used by soldiers; its wooden grip was pushed into the muzzle of the musket to convert it into a short pike. When the bayonet was in place the musket could no longer be loaded or fired. By the latter part of the century new designs overcame this problem and bayonets have been part of most troops' equipment ever since. *(Right)*

## DAGGERS
*German*
### c. 1940

At left is a German Red Cross officer's pattern with its knot or portepee; in the centre is the dagger of an enlisted man of the Technical Emergency Corps, adopted in 1938, and at right is an SS officer's model of 1936, with its double chain hanger. These Third Reich dress daggers were ignored for some years after the Second World War, but interest grew and they are now keenly collected. Those of the SS are most highly prized. Large numbers of copies have been made and some are difficult to distinguish from the originals. *(Left)*

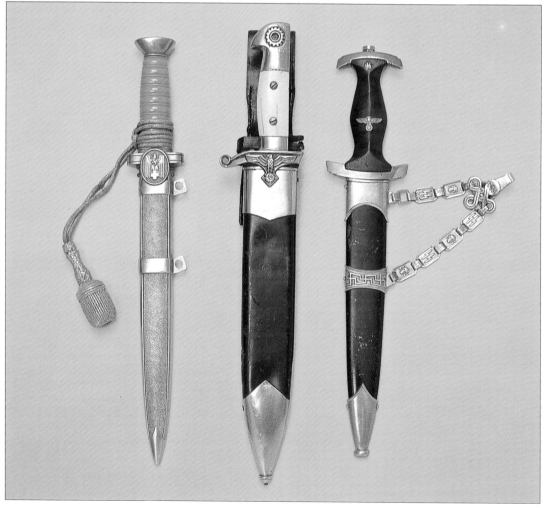

firearm being fired, alternative designs were sought. The answer was the socket bayonet, which had a tubular grip that slipped over the muzzle of the gun. This was used by most armies throughout the 18th century and well into the 19th.

As different muskets and rifles were adopted, bayonets of different patterns were introduced. The later, more common ones are still fairly cheap and even the rarest are not excessively expensive.

### EASTERN SWORDS AND KNIVES

The sword and dagger saw more service in the Orient than in Europe, and Indian swords are quite common at dealers and auctions. The most common type is the *talwar*, which is usually fitted with a single-edged, slightly curved blade. The style of hilt varies but often has a flat disc pommel at the top and a short, stubby cross-guard. The entire hilt is of metal, which on better quality examples is decorated. There are many other Asian swords of interest to the collector, ranging from the traditional, scimitar-shaped Turkish *kilij* to the strange hockey-stick-shaped Nepalese *kora*.

Among Asian knives and daggers are the kris from Malaya and the East Indies. The best-known type is that with a curving, serpentine blade, but many were straight-bladed. Most krises have grey-looking blades with a rough, furrowed, patterned surface. Many collectors have found this finish displeasing and have polished the blades, reducing the interest and value of the weapon.

The finest swords ever produced are Japanese, and they are highly prized. Many date back well into the Middle Ages and yet still look as good as new. The blade is single-edged and usually slightly curved, and often carries the maker's name, which aids dating. The small rectangular or oval guards (*tsuba*) fitted to these swords are collected in their own right, as are other fittings. Any collector interested in Japanese weapons is well advised to study the field before buying, since the snags and pitfalls are many!

Modern copies of old swords are produced and offered for sale as originals, but generally they are easy to spot. Another problem for the collector is that some edged weapons have been made up of a blade from one source and a hilt from another, something often carried out during the "working life" of the weapon. Such pieces have a much lower value than unaltered ones of the same period.

### KATANA
*Tane Tadahiro*
**Mid 17th century**

The Japanese swordsmiths produced the finest blades in the world. Their system was long and painstaking, and their secret was to produce a blade which had a very hard, sharp edge but which did not, like most such blades, shatter when struck. The finely polished blades should never be touched by the bare flesh as it may cause rusting. (*Right*)

### TALWAR
*Indian*
**Mid 19th century**

The hilt and the full length of the blade are chiselled and inlaid in gold. The shape is typical of so many Indian swords, with its curved, single-edged blade and hilt with short stubby quillons and flat disc pommel. The sheath is of wood and is covered with red velvet. (*Below*)

THE KIND OF WEAPON WITH WHICH MOST PEOPLE ARE LIKELY TO BE
FAMILIAR IS THE FIREARM, A CATEGORY THAT INCLUDES A VARIETY OF TYPES
DISTINGUISHED BY THEIR FIRING MECHANISMS.

# FIREARMS

Antique firearms are probably the most collected of all antique weapons, but they do present some problems. Most countries exclude antique firearms from strict control, but unfortunately the definition of an antique is often vague and it is as well for the collector to seek guidance. In general, it is with firearms dating from the mid-19th century that difficulties arise. An extremely rough guideline is that if the weapon takes a modern centre-fire metal-cased cartridge then it *may* require some form of certificate or licence. If in doubt, the collector should check with the dealer, auction house or local police. However, the latter may not have enough knowledge of the subject to answer queries and it is worth approaching specialist groups or magazines for informed advice.

## MATCHLOCKS

Gunpowder was known to the Chinese as far back as the 11th century but the first firearms did not appear in Europe until the 14th century. The earliest common form of firearm was the matchlock musket, which was long, heavy and cumbersome. It was fired by operating a trigger or lever which caused an arm, the serpentine, to swing forward to press the glowing tip of a piece of cord, the match, into a pan full of priming powder, mounted at the side of the barrel. As the powder flashed with fire, the

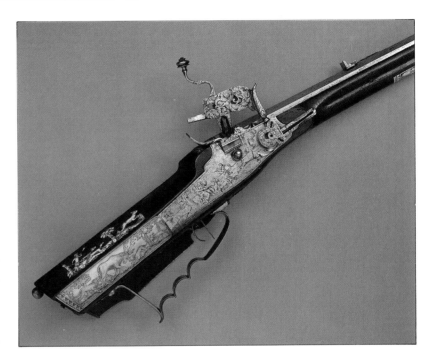

**WHEEL-LOCK RIFLE**
*German*
**c. 1680**

The wheel is set on the inside of the chiselled lock plate. The set trigger was adjusted so that only light pressure was needed to fire. (*Above*)

**MATCHLOCK MUSKET CONVERTED TO FLINTLOCK**
**c. 1620**

The shape of the butt and the mother-of-pearl inlay are typical of matchlock muskets of the early 17th century. However, the older lock has been replaced by a flintlock, thus extending the use of this weapon for a very small cost. (*Left*)

flame passed through a small hole in the side of the barrel, the touch hole, and ignited the main charge of powder inside the barrel.

In the Orient the matchlock continued in use until early this century but in Europe it was largely superseded by the end of the 17th century. It was very vulnerable to the weather and was dependent on a lighted match being ready at hand.

## WHEEL-LOCKS

In the early 16th century gun-makers designed a much more efficient ignition system: the powder in the pan was lit by sparks produced by friction between a piece of pyrites, a naturally occurring mineral, and the roughened edge of a steel wheel. The pyrites was held in a hinged arm that could be pulled back clear of the wheel to prevent unintentional ignition and discharge. This new mechanism, the wheel-lock – which enabled gun-makers to produce a smaller, portable firearm, the pistol – was to remain in use until the early 18th century.

Most wheel-lock pistols, guns and rifles were decorated with inlay, chiselling and carving, and their consistently high quality makes them very expensive to collect.

The cost of producing wheel-locks, even the relatively plain military versions, meant that they could not be issued to all troops, and they were generally restricted to bodyguards and some cavalry units.

### FLINTLOCKS

The complexity of the wheel-lock encouraged gun-makers to seek for simpler, less expensive methods of ignition, and the outcome in the early 17th century was the flintlock. In this system the sparks were produced by friction between a shaped piece of flint and a vertical steel plate, the frizzle or frizzen, positioned above the pan and united with its cover. The flint was held between the jaws of a curved metal arm known as the cock, and the whole mechanism, the lock, was mounted at the side of the wooden stock. A small quantity of priming powder was placed in the pan and the frizzle closed holding the priming in place. The cock was pulled back to an upright position, the half-cock, and in this position the trigger would not operate the mechanism, so rendering the weapon safe. To fire, the cock was pulled further back, the trigger was pressed and the cock swung forward, scraping the flint down the frizzle, creating sparks, and at the same time push-ing the frizzle forward so that the sparks fell into the priming.

With refinements, the flintlock remained popular for the next two centuries and is still in use today in some parts of the world. In addition to being used on guns and pistols, the mechanism was also fitted to some cannon.

Flintlock pistols are probably the most collected of all antique weapons and come in all sizes, conditions and prices. The cheapest are the small pocket pistols of the late 18th and early 19th centuries. Some, known as boxlock pistols, have the flintlock mechanism mounted centrally on top. Two-barrelled pistols were popular; some have two separate locks, while others have at the side a tap action that is turned to allow each barrel to be fired in turn.

The finest form of flintlock pistol was probably the duelling pistol. This was usually supplied in pairs in a wooden case complete with powder flask, bullet-making mould and cleaning rods. The maker's trade label is often stuck on the inside of the lid and this can be very useful as a dating guide. Such sets were mostly made from the late 18th century to the 1840s. Cased sets by famous London makers, such as Wogdon, Nock, Manton and Egg, are highly prized and fairly expensive.

A few pistols were made with a small spring-mounted bayonet attached to the barrel. Spring bayonets were also fitted to the barrel of many blunderbusses. These wide-muzzled weapons

**BOXLOCK FLINTLOCK POCKET PISTOL**
*Wallis*
**Late 18th century**

The cock holding the flint is mounted at the centre of the pistol rather than in the usual place at the side; this feature gives this type of weapon its name since the lock is box-shaped. A sliding safety catch is fitted behind the cock and was used to ensure the weapon could safely be carried, even when loaded. This type of pistol was loaded by unscrewing the barrel, pouring the powder into the breech, seating the bullet on top and then screwing back the barrel. This boxlock flintlock pocket pistol was very popular during the latter part of the 18th century and the early 19th century. (*Below*)

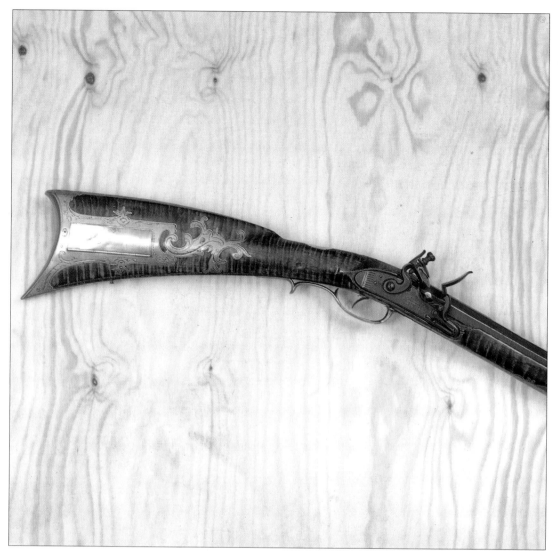

**FLINTLOCK RIFLE**
*Pennsylvania*
**Early 19th century**

The lock is engraved
"Rogers and Brothers
Philadelphia". These long-
barrelled, small-bore
weapons were noted for
their accuracy. The brass lid
in the butt covered a small
hollow used to store
patches for the bullets.
(*Left*)

**PAIR OF PERCUSSION
PISTOLS**
*Gastinne Renette of Paris*
**c. 1850**

In general, the pistols made
on the Continent were
more highly decorated than
those from Britain and
North America. These
pistols were made either
for target shooting or
duelling. When made as
duelling pistols such
weapons were supplied in a
case with all accessories.
(*Below*)

fired a charge of several balls and were popular
with mail-coach guards as well as for the
defence of private homes.

The flintlock was the firing mechanism fitted
on the British army's famous musket, the Brown
Bess, which saw service all over the world from
the 1720s to the 1840s. A flintlock mechanism
was also used on the Baker rifle issued by the
British army to the newly formed Rifle Corps in
the early 19th century.

The flintlock was refined and improved but
was always rather limited and there were many
attempts to improve its ignition system. The
combined times taken by each stage of ignition
– pulling the trigger, the cock swinging forward,
the priming being lit, then the main charge –
caused an appreciable delay between the decision to fire the weapon and its actual discharge. This hangfire, as it was called, made it
difficult for the hunter to aim accurately at a
moving target.

### THE PERCUSSION CAP

The cure for hangfire was devised by Alexander Forsyth, a Scottish clergyman, who replaced the frizzle and pan with a small amount of explosive chemicals known as fulminate. This charge was placed over the touch hole and struck by a solid-nosed hammer, which replaced the cock. The fulminate exploded and the resultant flash passed through the touch hole to ignite the main charge very much more quickly than under the old system. There were problems in handling the fulminate, but these were solved in the 1820s by the invention of the percussion cap, a small copper thimble with a layer of fulminate inside at the top. The cap was pushed on to the top of a small metal tube, the nipple, which connected with the touch hole. Struck by the hammer, the cap was banged against the nipple, the fulminate was detonated and the flash passed through the nipple to ignite the charge.

The adoption of the percussion cap simplified production, reduced costs and enabled manufacturing towns such as Birmingham in England and Liège in Belgium to produce considerable quantities of cheap pocket pistols, which are now among the most inexpensive of antique firearms.

Many flintlock weapons were adapted to take the new percussion systems, but today such weapons are not popular with collectors. It is not unknown for dealers, collectors and restorers to reconvert the lock of a weapon back to flint, but this does not restore its value, and most dealers and auction houses would point out the change to a purchaser.

### REVOLVERS

The percussion cap also simplified the production of multishot weapons. The pepperbox multi-barrelled revolver, common from the 1840s, incorporated a solid cylinder with six chambers drilled into it, each with its own nipple and percussion cap. Pressure on the trigger rotated the barrel, bringing each chamber in line with a hammer which struck the cap firing the shot.

In the 1830s a single-barrelled revolver was designed by the American, Samuel Colt (1814–62). (Despite many claims that Colt invented the revolver, this is not true, for versions of the weapon had been in use since the 16th century.) Colt dominated the revolver market, but his visit to England in 1851 stirred British gun-makers into producing their own percussion revolvers, and soon Adams, Tranter, Webley and other British makers challenged Colt's domination of the market. Like duelling pistols, many of the new weapons were sold in cases with various accessories.

### BREECH-LOADING GUNS

A limiting characteristic of firearms up to this date was how long it took to load and fire them. Most antique firearms were muzzle-loading, and even with the revolver, powder and ball had

**FLINTLOCK GUN**
*Wilson of London*
**c. 1800**

The style and decoration of this weapon suggest that it was made for the export market. (*Above*)

**FIREARMS**
*American*
**19th century**

From top to bottom are: a .31 Whitney percussion revolver; a percussion long rifle by W. Golcher, and a Remington .36 percussion revolver. (*Below*)

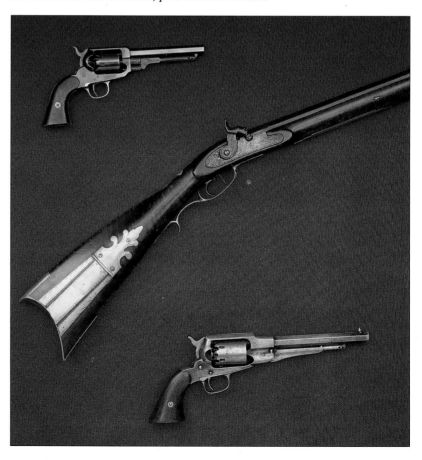

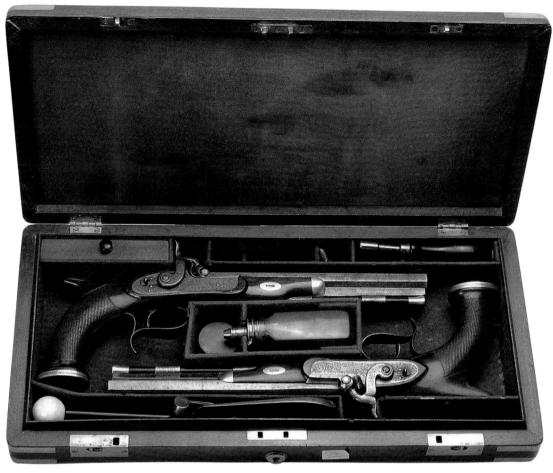

## CASED PERCUSSION DUELLING PISTOLS
*Thomas Broomhead*
**c. 1820**

These pistols are fitted with saw-handled butts and spurred trigger guards to enable a firmer grip. The locks are fitted with sliding-bolt safety catches, and like most such weapons are quite plain and designed to function quickly and accurately. The case contains a powder flask, bullet mould, nipple key and accessories. (*Left*)

## CASED PERCUSSION NAVY MODEL REVOLVER
*Colt*
**c. 1855**

The lid of the case has a trade label giving instruction on the care and use of the revolver. In the corner compartment are some of the paper cartridges containing the powder charge and bullet. This revolver was made in London at Colt's Pimlico factory and was a very popular model. It was a six-shot weapon firing a bullet of .36 in. diameter. This example retains much of its original colour, making it highly desirable, and as the case contains all the accessories it would be a very valuable collector's item. (*Right*)

to be rammed into the cylinder and a cap placed on the nipple. Paper cartridges, bringing powder and ball together, scarcely improved matters. Gun-makers constantly experimented to overcome this problem. The solution lay in a system whereby the charge could be loaded directly into the breech (chamber), but the problem was to find a way of sealing the breech so that gas generated by the explosion did not escape through any gaps and so reduce the pressure driving the projectile along the barrel.

The answer came with the brass cartridge case, perfected in the mid-19th century. The percussion cap was placed at the centre of the base of the brass case, which held the powder and projectile. The cartridge was simply placed in the breech, and as the cap was struck by a firing pin the exploding charge expanded the case and effectively sealed the chamber. The modern firearm had arrived, and Smith and Wesson produced the first commercial breech-loading metal-cartridge revolver in the 1850s. Others, such as Oliver Winchester (1810–80), followed in their footsteps and were soon producing repeating weapons.

**DRAGOON 3RD MODEL PERCUSSION REVOLVER WITH HOLSTER**
*Colt*
*c.* 1853/4

This weapon belonged to Captain Francis T. Bryan of the U.S. Army and saw service on the American frontier. A heavy weapon, it fired a bullet of .44 in. calibre. The cylinder was engraved with a scene of a fight with American Indians. All of Colt's early revolvers were single action, which means that the hammer had to be pulled back before the trigger could be pressed to fire the weapon. It fired six shots and was loaded by pouring powder into each chamber of the cylinder, seating a bullet and forcing it down with the lever fitted beneath the barrel and placing a percussion cap on the nipples.

## PRECAUTIONS

There are two precautions that every collector of antique firearms should always observe. Gunpowder retains its power for a long time, so it is as well to check that every weapon is unloaded. With muzzle-loading weapons a pencil or wooden rod should be dropped down the barrel and the depth of the barrel to the muzzle noted. The rod should then be withdrawn and placed against the exterior of the barrel. If the two lengths are the same it may be taken that the weapon is unloaded. If, however, the inner measurement is the shorter by more than a fraction of an inch or so, there may be powder still in the breech.

The other precaution to be observed is in operating the action of a firearm. Anyone wishing to check that the flintlock or percussion system is in working order should adopt the following procedure. The cock or hammer should be firmly grasped and pulled back; while this grip is maintained, the trigger can then be pressed. If the mechanism is working, the hammer or cock will try to swing forward. They should be allowed to do so only slowly – otherwise, the result may well be a broken nipple or cracked cock or hammer. Such faults can be repaired, but the intrinsic value of the piece will be reduced since it will no longer be in its original condition.

**A**S WELL AS HIS WEAPONS AND ARMOR, THE SOLDIER ALSO REQUIRES

CLOTHING AND OTHER EQUIPMENT. **T**HIS RANGE OF ITEMS HAS

EXPANDED GREATLY SINCE THE INTRODUCTION OF PROPER UNIFORMS.

# MILITARIA

I n general, militaria fetches lower prices than arms and armour. There are, of course, expensive items, such as early head-dress and rare medals, but for the most part militaria is a field of opportunity for the collector of more limited means.

### BADGES, BELT PLATES, UNIFORMS

Until the 17th century in Britain and most of Europe, armies were identified chiefly by means of coloured scarves or items such as twigs pushed into the hat band. Then the idea of a common uniform was adopted, and by the 18th century most countries had each its own style of uniform for its army. Distinction between regiments was achieved by badges or added areas of colour on the coat or hat.

The British wore the traditional red coat, with the various regiments indicated by different-coloured cuffs and lapels. Soon, regimental distinctions were marked by a range of badges. At first these were merely painted on the equipment, but later they were made separately, in metal. The size of badge has diminished over the ages and those of modern times are much smaller than those of the early 18th century.

Among collectors of militaria, badges are very popular. The subject is complex: there are many variations, patterns and styles within each regiment. The price of badges ranges from very cheap to quite high for rarer examples. A number of reliable books on the subject has been published and they are invaluable to all collectors, both beginners and veterans. The popularity of badges has led, over the past few years, to the production of first-class copies, known as restrikes, often of the more desirable badges. It is becoming increasingly difficult to identify these modern reproductions.

In the British army the troops almost all carried a sword and bayonet until the mid-18th century, when the sword was withdrawn from service. The weapons were carried in scabbards suspended from a belt. At first the belt encircled the waist, but from the later part of the 18th century it was worn over the shoulder and secured on the chest by a large metal plate. Originally a simple oval, these shoulder belt plates, which are popular with collectors, became progressively more decorative until 1855, when they were abandoned by most regiments.

Collecting uniforms is not particularly popular because of the problems of display: dummies are expensive and space-consuming and a fine tunic dangling from a hanger loses some of its

**SHOULDER BELT PLATE**
*Highland Light Infantry Militia*
**19th century**

Abandoned by the British army in 1855, these plates were kept by Scottish units. This example lacks the battle honour of Assaye, indicating it was for a militia officer.

**HELMET**
*Norfolk Yeomanry*
**Leather; early 20th century**

Raised in 1901 the Norfolk Yeomanry had four squadrons, with King Edward VII as its Honorary Colonel. He became Colonel in Chief in 1905, when the unit became the King's Own Royal Regiment of Imperial Yeomanry.

appeal. Most available uniforms date from the second half of the 19th century and are generally offered at very reasonable prices. Military uniforms are more popular than naval, which attract little interest. Neither do diplomatic uniforms, despite their magnificent decoration. Accessories, such as waist belts, holsters and packs, are also collected in their own right.

**Third Reich uniforms** As with weapons, there has been a growth of interest in uniforms of the Third Reich. Unfortunately, very many copies have been made by costumiers to dress the casts of all the cinema and TV films that have been made about the Second World War, and quantities of these have found their way on to the collectors' market. The copies are so good that it is often difficult to know what is real and what is not. Collectors therefore need to be very careful and buy with discrimination, advice which applies to all Third Reich items.

## HEAD-DRESS

Military head-dress has undergone many changes in style over the centuries, and each style has affected the design of the head-dress badge. In the early 19th century most British troops wore a shako, a tall, cylindrical hat with a small peak and carrying a large brass plate on the front. Later the cylindrical form was changed to one which widened at the crown, but in mid-century the cylinder was reintroduced. The next style was a low-crowned, small-peaked shako which could only accommodate a smaller badge.

In 1873 a spike-topped helmet in the style of the Prussian pickelhaube was adopted, together with a new, large badge. The pickelhaube is one of the most popular items of head-dress with collectors. Fashioned in leather or metal, it inspired other armies to adopt similar styles as the Prussian army swept from victory to victory. Elaborate ceremonial forms, surmounted by an eagle with outswept wings, were worn by the bodyguards of the German

**OTHER RANKS SHAKO**
*12th Royal Lancers (Prince of Wales's)*

The plate has the Queen's crown, indicating it must predate 1902. (*Below*)

**OFFICER'S SHAKO**
*Highland Light Infantry*
*c. 1890*

The shako was abandoned by most units of the British army in 1879 but retained by this unit. (*Left*)

## SELECTION OF ARMY CAP BADGES
*British*

Such badges still represent an attractive and reasonably priced field of collecting. (*Above*)

## PURPLE HEART MEDAL
*American*
**20th century**

The medal's design is based on George Washington's Badge of Military Merit, created during the Revolutionary War in 1782. Resurrected in 1932, since 1942 the medal can only be given to those wounded in action. Its ancient origin is marked by the profile of Washington's head; the shield carries his coat of arms. (*Right*)

emperor and a similar style was worn by the Russian tsar's bodyguards.

The pickelhaube was abandoned by the British for a variety of small, round pillbox caps for the cavalry and a peaked cap for the infantry, but, with full-dress uniform, the old style helmet continued to be worn until well into the 20th century. Eventually, the pillbox and peaked cap were replaced by the field service cap and the beret, which became general wear for the British and many other armies. For all these the badge was once again made smaller.

### MEDALS

From ancient Egyptian times rulers have rewarded their loyal troops with awards of various kinds, and from the 17th century it became increasingly common to present some kind of medal to mark a campaign, battle or some specific act of bravery. Medal-collecting is enormously popular in most countries but probably more so in Britain and America than elsewhere.

In Britain the regular issue of campaign

medals started with the battle of Waterloo. Following the Napoleonic Wars, British troops took part in campaigns all over the world, and there is therefore a large selection of medals for the collector to choose from. In addition to campaign medals there are awards for bravery, long service, good conduct and even some for temperance. American awards are fewer in type but are keenly collected, especially the rare early awards for bravery.

The value of medals is affected by many factors, such as rarity, condition, the rank of the recipient and the unit in which he served. There are fakes, on which units or names have been altered, but these are uncommon, and if the medal is acquired from a reputable source there is little risk of being caught out.

### MISCELLANEA

War has always generated an enormous amount of attention on the part of civilians and great quantities of prints, paintings, books and other printed material have been devoted to the subject. Prints are available in quantity and range from 16th-century woodcuts to modern mass-produced colour prints. During the last century the published sheet music for popular songs and dances with a military theme often carried luridly coloured representations of battles and their heroes, and this forms a small but popular field for militaria collectors.

British tobacco companies were quick to recognize popular interest in the military, and until the middle of this century it was common to include in each packet of cigarettes a picture card depicting armies of the world, uniforms, badges, weapons and similar topics. Early cigarette cards are rare and expensive but later ones are still available at reasonable prices. The value of a card plummets as soon as it is stuck in an album, so specimens should always be kept clean and loose.

Instruction booklets for weapons and pamphlets on military subjects have been produced from the 16th century onwards. The earlier publications, though sought after, are not too highly priced, and many of the late 19th-century examples are common and inexpensive.

Militaria is probably one of the last collecting fields that holds out the hope of a marvellous find amid junk, and no boot fair, jumble sale, house-contents sale or street market should be ignored. Any such find is unlikely to be worth a fortune but will be enough to delight the fortunate collector.

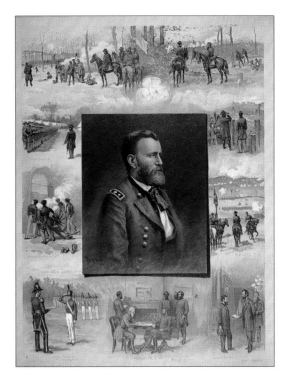

**LITHOGRAPH**
*L. Prarg & Co., Boston* **1885**

From the middle of the 19th century every war and campaign generated a flood of printed material: song sheets, patriotic illustrations and commemorative pieces. This example honours General (later President) Ulysses S. Grant, one of the heroes of the North from the American Civil War (1861–5). It shows his life from his training at West Point to his final victory at Appomattox, where he took the final surrender of the Confederacy.

## FURTHER READING

The following list of materials for further reading offers a broad range of literature. Both specialist and general works are included. While every effort has been made to give the date of the most recent edition, new ones may have been published since this book went to press.

Angolia, J.
**Swords of Germany 1900–1945**
San Jose, California, 1988

Bearse, R.
**Sporting Arms of the World**
New York 1975

Blackmore, H.
**British Military Firearms**
London 1961

Blair, C.
**European Armour**
London 1979

**– European and American Arms c. 1100–1850**
London 1983

Blair, C., and L. Tarrasuk
**The Complete Encyclopaedia of Arms and Weapons**
London 1979

Ezell, E.
**Handguns of the World**
Harrisburg, Pennsylvania, 1981

Fuller, R., and R. Gregory
**Military Swords of Japan**
New York 1986

Grancsay, S.
**Arms and Armour**
New York 1968

Kipling, A., and H. King
**Head-Dress Badges of the British Army** (2 vols)
London 1972 and 1978

Myatt, F.
**Modern Smallarms**
London 1978

Neumann, G.
**Swords and Blades of the American Revolution**
Newton Abbot 1973

Norman, A.V.
**The Rapier and Small Sword**
London 1980

Rawson, P.
**The Indian Sword**
London 1968

Robinson, H.
**Oriental Armour**
London 1967

Robson, B.
**Swords of the British Army**
London 1975

Stone, G.C.
**A Glossary of the Construction and Use of Arms and Armour**
New York 1961

Taylerson, A., and W. Chamberlain
**Adams' Revolvers**
London 1976

**Wilkinson, F.
Battle Dress**
London 1970

**– Collecting Military Antiques**
London 1978

**– Edged Weapons**
London 1970

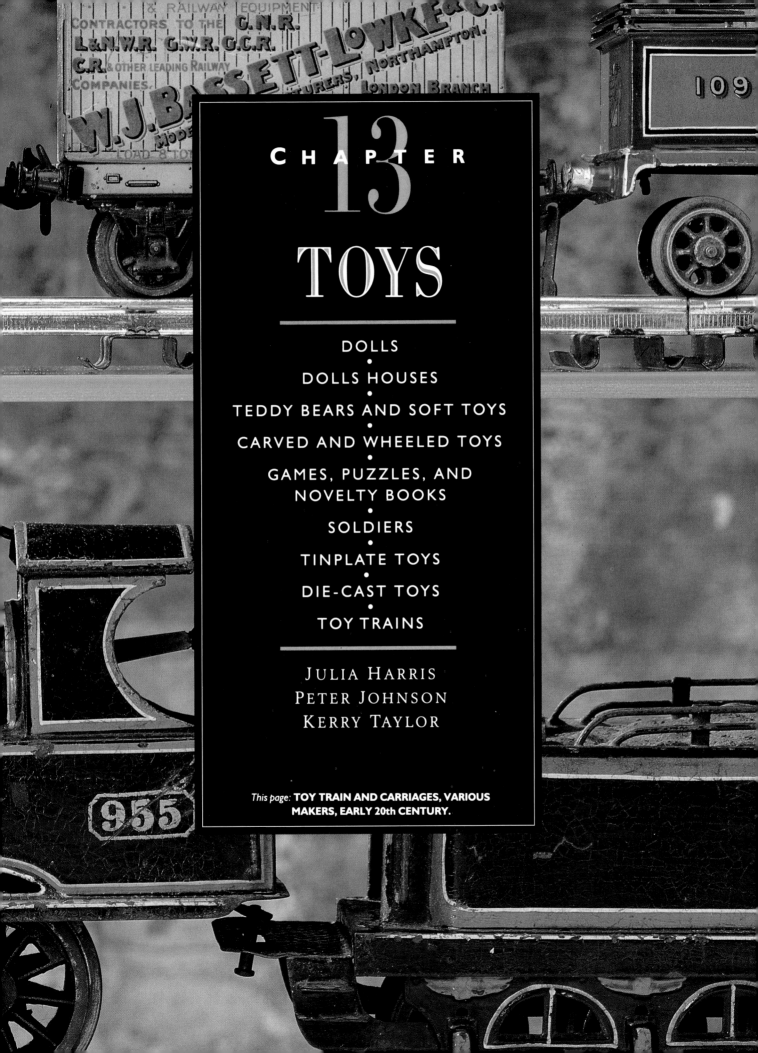

# CHAPTER 13

# TOYS

DOLLS
•
DOLLS HOUSES
•
TEDDY BEARS AND SOFT TOYS
•
CARVED AND WHEELED TOYS
•
GAMES, PUZZLES, AND
NOVELTY BOOKS
•
SOLDIERS
•
TINPLATE TOYS
•
DIE-CAST TOYS
•
TOY TRAINS

JULIA HARRIS
PETER JOHNSON
KERRY TAYLOR

*This page:* **TOY TRAIN AND CARRIAGES, VARIOUS
MAKERS, EARLY 20th CENTURY.**

# 13
# TOYS

THE CRAFTSMANSHIP AND EXCELLENCE OF DESIGN INVOLVED IN MAKING

MANY TOYS OF THE PAST HAS LARGELY BEEN LOST TO THE MASS-

PRODUCTION MENTALITY OF MODERN TIMES, BUT TODAY THE IDEA OF

REGARDING A TOY AS A FORM OF ART HAS GAINED MUCH WIDER

RECOGNITION AND ACCEPTANCE.

Collecting toys, dolls and games is a relatively recent activity, one which has largely evolved since the 1960s. After an initial refusal by many in the antiques business to take it seriously, it is now widely regarded as a bona fide area of collecting. Many books on the subject have been published, international auction rooms have set up specialist departments to deal with teddy bears, dolls, tinplate toys, trains, soldiers and games, and some prices have attained levels rivalling those achieved by more traditional antiques.

The late Victorian and Edwardian period was the golden age for toys and dolls. Rich families provided their children with trains powered by steam, fragile porcelain dolls dressed in the latest French fashions and other expensive, elaborate playthings. Even the cheap toys mass-produced from stamped-out and lithographed tinplate possess a charm and quality sadly lacking in modern toys. However, because toys by

**TOY SLEIGH**
*Lutz*
**Late 19th century**

The bright, primary colours and the combination of plaster figures with tinplate vehicle are characteristic of early German toys. It is unusual to find the figures, which are subject to cracking, in such pristine condition.

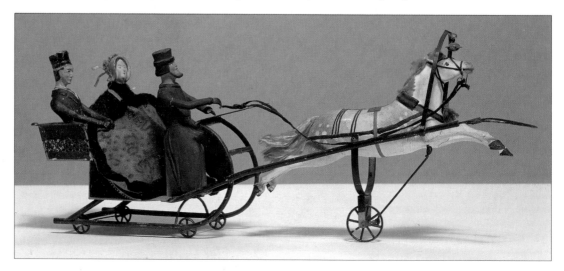

their very nature are subjected to wear and tear, it is difficult to find any from the past in good condition.

Condition is paramount to collectors – metal fatigue in a Dinky toy, a hairline crack on the face of a porcelain doll, badly chipped paintwork on a soldier, rust on an old toy battleship, worn pads and bare patches on a teddy bear lower value considerably. But restoration of damage like this is something to be undertaken only as a last resort and only by an expert. Numerous pieces have been ruined by well-intentioned owners who have replaced original costumes with smart nylon imitations or painted their Dinky toys to brighten them up. It is better to have a bit of honest rust rather than a new finish that completely obliterates the quality of the original.

**JAPANESE INFANTRY**
*Britain's*
**Lead hollow cast; 1930s**

A group of one of the hundreds of sets the firm produced of foreign armies.

**TINPLATE PHAETON**
*Lutz*
**Late 19th century**

The superb quality of the painting, and fine detailing such as the candle-powered lighting and painted rose swags to the foot plate suggest that the piece was made by Lutz for the French market. It bears the original retailer's label "Passage de l'Opera, Paris" From the large number of French toy carriages which have survived it is evident that this type of toy appealed in particular to French buyers. It is an unusually large size and would originally have come complete with plaster horses and possibly passengers.

Part of the allure and charm of antique toys is that they often reflect in miniature the times in which they were made. Dolls, for example, accurately chart the changes in fashion, make-up and hair-styles from the 18th century (when they began to be made on a large commercial basis) to the present day. It is interesting to compare an early 18th-century doll, with its large, gesso-covered head, hard, black eyes, small, painted mouth, slim, angular-jointed, wooden body and fine brocades, with a late 19th-century French bisque (unglazed porcelain) *bébé* (infant doll), with its peaches-and-cream complexion, realistic eyes, chubby proportions and wine-coloured velvets; ideals of beauty changed radically over the two centuries.

Tinplate and diecast toys often incorporated technological advances not only in their design but in their construction: steam and electricity, for example, were both common, if hazardous, methods of powering trains, magic lanterns and other moving toys around 1900.

The Industrial Revolution saw an enormous mass-production of toys and dolls, as new processes allowed factories to produce goods quickly and efficiently. By the 20th century gone were the myriad outworkers paid by the piece; their place had been taken by the production line, with pieces made, assembled and boxed all under one roof.

In recent years, as the prices of early toys have soared beyond the reach of the average pocket, some collectors have looked to the best of 20th-century toy production. In particular, space- and TV-related toys of the 1960s have become extremely sought after. Modern toys seem set to grow in popularity, and the scope is endless.

THE ENDEARING FACE OF THE CHILD'S DOLL HAS BEEN WITH US IN

HANDMADE FORM SINCE THE 17TH CENTURY. MORE RECENT

COMMERCIAL PRODUCTION HAS CREATED ITS OWN BRAND OF CHARM.

# DOLLS

Dolls are known to have existed in ancient Egypt and ancient Greece, but they were then made mainly for religious purposes rather than as children's toys. These dolls are sought after by antiquaries, but for most collectors it is only children's dolls, dating from the 17th century onwards, that are of real interest.

During the past 20 years collecting dolls has become enormously popular and, to judge by the prices dolls fetch in salerooms, they are also a sound investment.

### WOODEN DOLLS

Few wooden dolls from earlier than the 17th century have survived. Perhaps the most charming ever made were those known as "Queen Anne" dolls, dating from c.1700–1800. They cannot be attributed to any particular maker, but it is believed that most originated in England. The earlier of these dolls tend to be more finely carved and painted than later ones. The head and torso were usually turned on a lathe, and the better dolls had ball-and-socket jointing, realistically carved limbs and even an indication of breasts. A wig of flax or real hair was nailed to the gessoed (plastered) head. Some examples had forearms and legs of leather, with fork-like fingers.

The eyes were of black or brown and spaced well apart; on later dolls they were blue and more close-set. Some rare dolls had eyes and black beauty patches (a cosmetic fashion of the 18th century) painted on the face. Brows were painted on in a stitch-like or dotted style, the

**PEDLAR DOLL**
*German*
**Gessoed wood and painted features; 1830** (*Above*)

---

**WOODEN DOLL**
**c. 1740** (*Below*)

---

nose was normally a triangle of wood and the cheeks were painted red. On the finest examples of wooden dolls the hips were well-rounded and the waist small.

**Grödnertal dolls** By the 19th century a much more basic type of wooden doll had emerged. Dolls of the Regency period were of the German Grödnertal type. These had a gessoed head, painted black hair in the period style and painted features. The body was carved, peg-jointed at the elbow and hip and had block feet; some of the better dolls had a jointed waist and/or swivel neck. Costume was usually in the French Empire style, but later versions had a fuller, lower-waisted skirt.

By the middle of the century craftsmanship had declined and the dolls became more skittle-like. Developments of the Grödnertal included the penny wooden, which had a simpler, rounded head, and the wooden top (still in production), marked by a sturdy body, spoon-shaped head and carved rather than painted features. "Dutch" dolls of Grödnertal type were in fact made in Germany but so-named because they were imported into Britain via Amsterdam.

**American manufacturers** In the mid-19th century wooden dolls of a distinctive, non-European style, were mass-manufactured in the United States. Joe Ellis of Springfield, Vermont, which continued until 1879, made dolls with a fully articulated body. One of the most famous American makers was the Schoenhut Co. of Philadelphia, which produced a spring-jointed doll, patented c.1909, with

## PRINCIPAL MANUFACTURERS OF WOODEN DOLLS

| | | | |
|---|---|---|---|
| **ELLIS, Joe** | c. 1869–73 | Springfield | All-wooden dolls with fully articulated bodies. |
| **MASON AND TAYLOR, firm of** | c. 1881 | Springfield | All-wooden dolls. |
| **SCHOENHUT, A.** | c. 1872–1930 | USA | Spring-jointed dolls. |

# FRENCH MANUFACTURERS OF BISQUE HEAD DOLLS

| | | | |
|---|---|---|---|
| **BARROIS, E.** | *c.* 1844–77 | Paris | Bisque shoulder head parisiennes. |
| **BRU, Jne, firm of** | *c.* 1866–99 | Paris | Bisque parisiennes and bébés. |
| **DANEL, firm of** | *c.* 1889–1895 | Paris | Consistently high-quality bisque head bébés. |
| **GAULTIER, Francois** | *fl. c.* 1860–75 | Paris | Parisiennes and bébés. The firm continued until *c.* 1899. |
| **MAISON HURET** | *c.* 1850– | Paris | Bisque or china shoulder head dolls. |
| **JULLIEN, Jne** | *c.* 1875–1904 | Paris | Bisque head bébés. |
| **MAISON JUMEAU** | *c.* 1842– | Paris | Bisque parisiennes and bisque head bébés. |
| **MARQUE, A.** | *c.* 1910–16 | | A sculptor. His dolls are now very rare. |
| **RABERY & DELPHIEU** | *c.* 1856–99 | Paris | Bébé dolls. |
| **ROHMER, Madame** | *c.* 1857–80 | Paris | China or bisque head parisiennes. |
| **SCHMITT ET FILS** | *c.* 1851–1891 | Paris | Bébé dolls. |
| **SFBJ (Societe Français de Fabrication des Bébés et Jouets)** | *c.* 1899– | Paris | Child and character dolls. |
| **STEINER, Jules** | *c.* 1855–1908 | Paris | Bébé dolls and mechanical dolls. |

an enamel-painted, carved head, sometimes crowned with a mohair wig.

## BISQUE-HEAD DOLLS

In France, from about 1860 to 1880, there appeared what are known as Parisienne, or *poupée*, dolls with a bisque (fired but unglazed ceramic) head. Made for children of the affluent and often supplied with accompanying trousseau-trunk, these are among the most beautiful and collectable of all dolls. Most had a swivel neck and a stuffed kid leather body. The head usually had a wig of real hair or mohair wig on a cork pate, glass eyes in colours ranging from pale blue to brown and two-tone pale pink lips. Ears are sometimes pierced, and some dolls have a suggestion of breasts. As with all other types of French bisque-headed doll, the mould number, and/or maker's initials, was usually incised on the back of the head or stamped on the body; but there are some good-quality Parisiennes with no markings.

Among makers known to have produced Parisiennes are: Mme Huret, Mme Rohmer, Léon Casimir Bru, Jumeau, Terrène, Verry Fils, Simonne, Metayer, F. Gaultier, Guiton, and

**BÉBÉ DOLL**
*Léon Casimir Bru*
**Bisque with paperweight eyes; 1880**

Phenix. Reproductions have since been made and authentication is not always easy.

**The *bébé*** A development from the Parisienne was the *bébé*, a luxury doll representing an idealized girl between the ages of eight and twelve. The bisque of the best-quality *bébés* is pale, the brows are often heavy and feathered, the large eyes are made of blown glass, and the moulded or applied ears are pierced. Those having a closed mouth are more sought-after. The sturdy body is of wood or wood and composition, but late models have a composition body, which from about 1904 onwards is in five pieces.

Manufacturers (all Parisian) who produced consistently high-quality *bébés* include the famous Jumeau firm, 1850–1900; Léon Casimir Bru, 1860–1900; Jules Nicholas Steiner, 1860–1910; and A. Marque, 1910–16. Other Parisian firms of note were Rabery et Delphieu, 1856–1900; Schmitt et Fils, 1851–91; Fleischmann et Bloedel, 1873–1900; Jullien, 1827–1904; Pintel et Godschaux, 1887–1900; Danel et Cie, 1889–95.

Many of these firms incorporated talking and kiss-throwing mechanisms in their *bébés*. And

## GERMAN MANUFACTURERS OF BISQUE HEAD DOLLS

| | | | |
|---|---|---|---|
| **ALT, BECK & GOTTSCHALK** | c. 1854 onwards | Thuringia | Child and character dolls. |
| **DRESSEL, Cuno & Otto** | est. 1730 | Sonneberg | Bisque heads by various makers. Composition dolls. |
| **FLEISHMANN & BLOEDEL** | c. 1873<br>c. 1890 | Bavaria<br>Paris | Bisque head bébés. |
| **HEUBACH, firm of** | c. 1820–1940 | Thuringia | Bisque head character dolls. (Confused with firm of Ernst Heubach, Koppelsdorf.) |
| **KAMMER & REINHARDT** | c. 1870–1940 | Waltershausen | Heads mostly by Simon and Halbig. Child and character dolls with wood and composition bodies and ball-and-socket joints. |
| **KESTNER, J. D.** | c. 1800–1940 | Waltershausen | Child and character dolls. |
| **KLING, firm of** | c. 1836 onwards | Thuringia | Bisque or china shoulder head dolls. |
| **MARSEILLE, Armand** | 1880–1940 | Koppelsdorf | Very prolific doll-maker. Bisque head child and character dolls. |
| **SIMON & HALBIG** | c. 1869–1930 | Thuringia | Child and character dolls. |

other variations upon the standard doll were invented by makers such as Bru-Bébé la Teteur and Jumeau-Bébé Phonograph; the latter included with their dolls a Lioret phonograph and records of chatter and singing.

By the end of the century the competition from Germany had forced many of the major Parisian firms to form a syndicate known as SFBJ (Société Francaise de Fabrication des

**LADY COSTUME DOLL**
*François Gaultier*
**Bisque shoulder head on a kid-leather body; 1870**

A vast number of costume dolls have survived and form a collecting field of their own. This fine-quality doll wears the costume of a provincial French woman and is made of black felt.

**JUMEAU "TRISTE"**
*Emile Jumeau*
**Bisque head; 1880**

This rare doll is known as the "Long-faced Jumeau" in the United States, because of its wistful expression. The head was marked with a number only and has very full cheeks. The rarest of this type of doll has a heart-shaped face. (*Right*)

Bébés et Jouets). This combination continued until well into the 1920s.

From the turn of the century the quality of *bébés* generally declined. (For identification purposes, the most common SFBJ mould numbers of these inferior dolls is 60 and 301.) However, from about 1909 onwards, a successful line of character dolls, thought to have been modelled on real children, was produced in both

France and Germany. SFBJ character dolls represented both boys and girls and had child, toddler or baby bodies. One of the rarest had three interchangeable heads of different expression. (The mould numbers of the SFBJ dolls are mostly in the 200s.)

**German dolls** By the end of the 19th century German production of bisque-headed dolls, in Thüringia and Bavaria, had overtaken the French output. Early German models were copies of the French, but with thicker bodies.

The better manufacturers included Armand Marseille (a Russian émigré), 1880–1940, the most prolific maker of all time. Moulds 370 (shoulder head – that is, head and shoulder made in one piece) and 390 (socket head – a separate head fitting into a socket in the shoulder plate) are the most commonly found. (As with French dolls, the markings are found on the back of the head or the body.) Marseille also made a range of character and baby dolls which are now widely collected.

Another German firm, Kammer and

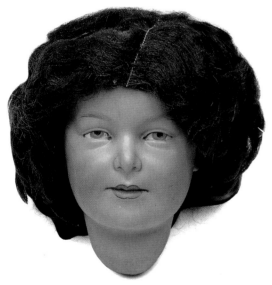

Reinhardt, 1870–1940, produced not only standard dolls but, from about 1909, a range of character dolls (heads made by Simon and Halbig, 1869–1930), which today are much sought after because of their realistic modelling. Often named after the child who modelled for the doll, they have a wood and composition body (child, toddler or baby) with ball-and-socket joints. Mould numbers range from 100 (the famous "Kaiser Baby") to the 120s.

J. D. Kestner, 1800–1940, produced a variety of dolls. Their character baby dolls (mould numbers 200s) are much sought after.

Other manufacturers of note include

**"MORITZ" CHARACTER DOLL**
*J. D. Kestner*
**Bisque head with moulded hair; 1910**

Moritz is a famous German folk-tale character. (*Above*)

**CHARACTER DOLL**
*Kammer and Reinhardt*
**Bisque head; 1910**

This doll has "intaglio" eyes, with concave-cut, painted pupils give the illusion of depth and realism. (*Left*)

**LENCI DOLL**
*Italian*
**Moulded felt; 1930s**

Cloth dolls by the Lenci firm have recently enjoyed much popularity, forming a collecting area all of their own. Illustrated is a large-sized example. Fakes, copies and reproductions abound, so the purist should buy only attributable examples.

Gerbruder Heubach, 1820–1940, which produced many character dolls and small novelty figures such as "snow babies" (reproductions abound); Cuno and Otto Dressel, established 1730; Heinrich Handwerk, 1876–1930; Max Handwerk, 1900 to the present; and Schoenau & Hoffmeister, c.1901–63. Fritz Bartenstein produced novelty dolls with two or three faces on one head (as opposed to three interchangeable heads), as did Carl Bergner, 1880–1910, who created one with Little Red Riding Hood, Grandmother and Wolf faces.

## DOLLS OF OTHER MATERIALS

Glazed china was another material used in the 19th century to make shoulder heads. The better-quality examples date from the first half of the century and were made by porcelain manufacturers such as Meissen, KPM (Königliche Porzellan Manufactur), Dressel and Kister. (They are, however, difficult to attribute.) They are of fine, pink-tinted porcelain with painted blue (occasionally brown) eyes and pink lips and sometimes a swivel neck. The hair was commonly black, sometimes fair, but rarely in other colours. From about 1845, the head, and often the footwear, were decorated with lustre. The body was either sawdust-filled leather, peg-jointed wood or cloth. By the end of the century, standards had declined and hairstyle and facial decoration had become simpler.

**Parian heads** The shoulder head of some dolls was made from unpainted, white bisque,

## MANUFACTURERS OF OTHER DOLLS

| | | | |
|---|---|---|---|
| **PIEROTTI, family of** | c. 1770–1930 | London | Wax dolls with real fair hair and slim body. |
| **MONTANARI** | c. 1849–80 | London | Wax dolls with realistic details. |
| **GREINER, Ludwig** | c. 1858–74 | Philadelphia | Papier-mâché dolls. |
| **MEECH, Herbert** | c. 1865–1917 | London | Poured wax dolls. Doll-maker to the Royal Family. |
| **CHASE, Martha Jenks** | c. 1889 onwards | Rhode Island | Rag dolls. |
| **ADAMS, E. & A.** | c. 1891–c. 1910 | New York | Columbian rag dolls. |
| **PECK, Lucy** | c. 1891–1930 | London | Poured wax dolls. |
| **STEIFF, firm of** | c. 1894 | Giengen-am-Brenz | Felt, plush, velvet character dolls. |
| **HORSMAN & CO** | c. 1909 onwards | New York | Rag dolls. |
| **KRUSE, Kathe** | c. 1910 onwards | Bad Kosen | Cloth character "art" dolls. |
| **LENCI (E. & E. Scavini)** | 1920 onwards | Turin | Felt character dolls. |

which is termed Parian because of its resemblance to Parian porcelain. Such heads were usually mounted on a stuffed cloth body. The heyday of Parian dolls was about 1855–85. Most originated from Germany, but a number of French factories, including Sèvres, made them. Such dolls usually had simply moulded hair, painted eyes and no neck articulation; but there are rare examples with an ornate hairstyle, glass eyes and swivel neck.

**Wax dolls** The finest examples of wax dolls – which originated in Italy and had their roots in religious effigy-making – were made in Britain during the 19th century. From about 1850, the Pierotti family of London, 1770–1930, made dolls noted for the slight turn of their head, real, fair hair and slim body, which usually bore the distributor's stamp.

Dolls made by the Montanari company, 1849–80, had a soft-toned wax, short neck with a distinctive roll of fat, real brown hair, lashes and brows and often violet-coloured eyes. They are now rare.

**Waxed papier-mâché heads** The earliest dolls with a head of papier mâché dipped in wax date from the 18th century and were mostly made in Germany. They were known as slit-head dolls, as the hair was inserted into a gap in the crown; early 19th-century examples had the "sausage-curl" hairstyle typical of the period. The eyes, of blue or black enamel and without pupils, are sometimes movable. The shoulder head was mounted on a sawdust-filled body that

**AUTOMATA DOLL**
*Gustav Vichy*
**Bisque shoulder head with swivel neck; 1870**

Automata are among the most valuable dolls, and were really novelties for adults instead of toys for children. This lady with a mandolin has retained her costume in excellent condition and the mechanism is in good working order.

had leather forearms.

As the century progressed standards declined. However, "pumpkin head" dolls, which have a large round face and moulded fair hair, often decorated with a coloured plume or ribbon, are worth collecting if in good condition.

**Papier-mâché heads** During the same period German manufacturers also used unwaxed papier mâché for dolls' heads. In Britain such dolls reached their height of popularity during the Regency period, when they were characterized by their elaborate hairstyles. The rarest examples are those with real hair and glass eyes and Biedermeier dolls (so-called after the informal style then current in German furniture and other decorative arts), which had a bald spot on the crown.

"Milliners" models, 1800–40, thought to be of German origin, have skilfully moulded hair and are particularly sought after. Papier–mâché dolls made in Sonneberg have distinctive bamboo teeth and a kid leather body; those of C. Motschmann, c.1850–70, have "floating" joints derived from Japanese dolls. Other notable German manufacturers included: Cuno and Otto Dressel and Adolf Fleischmann. The most famous American manufacturer was the German-born L. Greiner.

By the late 19th century papier-mâché for dolls' heads had been replaced by a (usually lower-quality) mixture of wood pulp and glue termed composition.

VALUED BOTH FOR EDUCATION AND ENTERTAINMENT, DOLL'S HOUSES
HAVE BEEN A SOURCE OF ENJOYMENT FOR ADULTS AND CHILDREN FROM
THE 16TH CENTURY TO THE PRESENT DAY.

# DOLLS' HOUSES

Miniature houses made for children's play did not appear until about 1800, when they were termed dolls' houses. Before that they were intended more for adults than children and were called baby-houses or cabinet houses. It is generally difficult to date both types, since the architectural style of so many does not correspond to that of the period in which they were made.

The miniature inhabitants of baby-houses were made of wood or wax and costumed in the same period style as that of the house. Several fine 17th-century Dutch baby-houses have survived, such as the Petronella Dunois, Petronella Oortman and Petronella de la Court houses, and also a splendid 18th-century house. They are lavishly equipped with household chattels of the period. However, such fully furnished baby-houses are extremely rare, and, like most others, these Dutch examples are now in museums.

The earliest of the surviving German baby-houses, known as Dockenhauser, is one made *c*.1611 for the daughter of Albrecht V of Bavaria, which is now held in the Germanisches Museum in Nuremberg.

Nineteenth-century dolls' houses proper are the most commonly collected type today (though some early 20th-century models are also highly prized). The long, low architectural lines of 17th- and 18th-century baby-houses continued in early 19th-century models, but windows changed: 12 panes gave way to two or four, in keeping with the architectural style of the time.

## GERMANY AND FRANCE

Germany excelled in the production of dolls' houses and exported them to many countries. German firms also made models of shops, kitchens (the Nuremberg type, named after its centre of distribution, was characterized by its profusion of utensils), cooking ranges and three-sided room settings. Model rooms concealed within the skirts of lady dolls were also made

**CHILD'S WARDROBE**
*Edmund Joy*
**Wood; 1709**

This is an extremely rare early William and Mary piece in the form of a house of Anglo-Dutch style. The interior consists of an arrangement of drawers and shelves.

during the first quarter of the century.

Of particular interest to collectors are the houses made by the firm of Christian Hacker (established 1870), which were decorated using lithographic techniques to decorate both houses and furniture.

French manufacturers concentrated more on room settings than on complete houses. Like the Germans and Dutch, they also produced Nuremberg kitchens. Two particularly French types of dolls' house were the Deauville type, which had a colourfully lithographed exterior and a marbled base, and the house with a mansard roof, which could be opened to reveal storage space inside.

# MANUFACTURERS OF DOLLS' HOUSES AND MINIATURE FURNITURE

| | | | |
|---|---|---|---|
| **BESTELMEIER, G. H.** | c. 1793–1854 | Nuremberg | Distributor of dolls' kitchens, shops, houses, toys, etc. |
| **HACKER, C.** | c. 1875–20th century | Nuremberg | Dolls' houses, shops etc. Used lithographic techniques to decorate houses and furniture. |
| **ROCK AND GRANER** | 1837–89 | Biberach an der Riss | Tin furniture, room settings, equipment. (Taken over by Märklin). |
| **SCHNEEGASS** | c. 1830s–1900 | Waltershausen bei Gotha | Fine simulated rosewood furniture, also Regency, Art Nouveau style; called "Waltershausen" furniture. |
| **MAISON HURET** | c. 1849–1920 | Paris | Fine quality wood and metal furniture. |
| **BANNEVILLE ET AULANIER** | 19th-early 20th century | Paris | Metal and "Tiffany" miniature furniture. |
| **AVERY, W. & SONS** | 19th and 20th century | Redditch | Painted or gilded metal furniture. |
| **MORRELL'S** | c. 1820–1900 | London | Fine miniatures in ivory, silver, porcelain and wood. |
| **LINES, G. & J. LTD** | 1858–1919 | London | Dolls' houses and furniture. Architectural mouldings were a characteristic of their work. (Lines Bros, London, c. 1919–70; Triang dolls' houses and furniture post c. 1927.) |
| **ALTOF, BERGMANN & CO** | c. 1867–1900 | New York | Fine tin dolls' houses, furniture and chattels. |
| **OUSIUS, M.** | post c. 1860 | Paris | Fretwork furniture and room settings. |
| **DOL–TOI PRODUCTS** | post c. 1940 | Stamford (UK) | Furniture. |
| **SILBER & FLEMING** | c. 1850–1907 | London | Dolls' houses. |
| **BLISS, R. MANUFACTURING CO** | 1832– | Rhode Island | Lithographed houses and furniture. |
| **CONVERSE, Morton E.** | c. 1878 | Massachusetts | Lithographed wood dolls' houses and buildings. |
| **DOWST MANUFACTURING CO** | c. 1875 onwards | Chicago | Metal furniture, houses, room settings. c. 1920 "Tootsie Toy". |
| **FRANCIS, FIELD AND McLOUGHLIN** | c. 1838 onwards / c. 1855 onwards | Philadelphia / New York | Good furniture, metal houses and tin toys. / Lithographed folding houses. |
| **STEVENS & BROWN, firm of** | c. 1868 onwards | Connecticut | Tin-plate and cast iron furniture and room settings. |
| **TYNIE TOY** | c. 1920 | Rhode Island | Good dolls' houses and furniture. |

BRITAIN AND THE UNITED STATES

By the 1850s lithography was the main technique for exterior decoration on British dolls' houses. Popular designs included middle-class town houses and villas in the architectural style of the day. Houses for children to construct at home were also produced.

Some of the most commonly found yet well-constructed houses were made by the firm of G. and J. Lines, 1858–1919 (afterwards Lines Bros, then Triang). Typical examples of their work incorporate architectural mouldings. They are extremely difficult to date as early styles were reproduced for many years. Other manufacturers included Silber and Fleming, c.1850–1907, and J. Sillett, established 1850. Folding houses

and rooms were made in the early 20th century by L. G. Slocum, founded 1912. In 1911 E. Wintle manufactured a house formed from boxes and lids.

There are very few surviving American dolls' houses from the first quarter of the 19th century. The industry developed slowly, and the greatest number were made after 1870. One of the best-known makers was the Tower Shop, founded 1830 and later becoming the Tower Toy Company.

Of particular interest to collectors are the houses made by R. Bliss, established 1832. The firm's first paper-on-wood houses were produced from 1889 and use lithography for their detailed decoration. Lithographed houses were also made by Morton E. Converse. These had a much simpler appearance and a rustic, Germanic charm. Dolls' houses made by McLoughlin from c.1855 are notable for their vivid colour lithography; attractive folding models were produced c.1875–86.

The wooden dolls' houses, with lithographed exterior and a range of painted furniture, manufactured by the Schoenhut company in 1917 are widely collected.

### MINIATURE FURNITURE

The finest miniature furniture was made during the 17th and 18th centuries. Silver was a particularly favoured medium, but porcelain, wood, glass and even gold was used. Pewter was mainly used in Nuremberg kitchens. Some superb miniature furniture was also made from papier mâché, from straw work (small strips of coloured straws) and from wood in Art Nouveau style. One notable French manufacturer of miniature furniture was Banneville et Aulangier, which made metal pieces, including the Tiffany (simulated gilt) type.

In Germany simple painted furniture was made in the Berchtesgaden area. The earlier pieces have a more classical line, and as the century progresses the quality diminishes.

**DOLLS' HOUSE FURNITURE**
*Waltershausen, Germany*
Wood with simulated rosewood and "Boulle" decoration; **1860**

Sets of "Duncan Phyfe" furniture such as that shown are very sought after. Particularly rare items are the piano and games table. (*Above*)

**CHILD'S TIN STOVE**
*Various German Manufacturers*
Tin with copper-covered utensils; **1890**

Tin stoves are always worthwhile acquisitions for collectors, provided that their condition is good. This example is of relatively simple design and much more decorative examples do exist.

Lithographed-paper-on-wood furniture was also very popular by the late 19th century. Common designs featured children or the alphabet or were in Gothic Revival style. Manufacturers included Schweitzer – late 18th century to the present – which also produced metal-filigree furniture; Rock und Graner, 1837–89, established 1837, which also made metal miniatures; and Märklin, established 1840. Ceramic miniature furniture was also made in Germany, by the 19th-century firms of C. B. Casper and Enger Sohn, and in the Meissen (traditional "onion-pattern") style.

**Britain** The furnishings of the early British baby- and cabinet houses are of the finest quality; much of it, especially the silver items, was imported from the Netherlands. In 1790, Thomas Jaques was making miniature furniture in hardwood and Tunbridge ware (objects with coloured wood-inlay decoration). During the 19th century miniature furniture in brass, tin and pewter was made in quantity.

In the 1920s Lines Bros marketed a range called "Period dolls' Furniture", offering furnishings in Tudor, Queen Anne, Regency and Victoria styles.

**United States** In the United States R. Boyle, was producing pewter miniature furniture as early as c.1781. In the 19th century manufacturers included the Philadelphia Toy Manufacturing Co, established 1858; Ellis; Britton, which produced cast-iron miniature pieces; the Tower Guild, which made wooden furniture; and R. Bliss, which used lithographs for decoration. Among 20th-century manufacturers were Dowst Bros, which produced a range called "Tootsie Toy", and Perleins and Vernon, which marketed "Tynietoy".

THE TEDDY BEAR HAS ATTAINED AN APPEAL THAT IS WORLDWIDE. IT ALSO
YIELDED A HOST OF OTHER SOFT TOYS, EACH TRYING TO EARN AN
EQUIVALENT PLACE IN PEOPLE'S AFFECTIONS.

# TEDDY BEARS AND SOFT TOYS

Soft toys were first made commercially
in the late 19th century but the most
popular of them all, the teddy bear, was not
introduced until the beginning of this century.
Who can lay claim to producing the first teddy
bear is still a matter of dispute: in the United
States Clifford Berriman's cartoon depicting
Theodore ("Teddy") Roosevelt refusing to shoot
a bear on a hunting trip inspired Morris Mitchom
of New York to make the first American teddy
bear c.1902, but in Germany at about the same
time Margaret Steiff was also manufacturing a
soft toy bear.

Certain manufacturers' bears have their own
distinctive characteristics, but even so attributing and dating teddy bears is in general
extremely difficult.

### GERMAN TEDDY BEARS
Before the introduction of the teddy bear, the
German firm of Margaret Steiff was already producing brown burlap bears on wheels and "dancing" bears (upright, motionless bears with forelegs chained to a bar behind the head). Richard
Steiff, Margaret's son, drafted the initial designs
for the first teddy bear. These early examples
had a triangular head, wide-apart, rounded ears,
button eyes, a pronounced stitched snout,
mouth and "claws", swivel joints, long arms and
tapering legs, elongated flat paw pads, excelsior
(wood shavings) filling and often a growling box,
all covered in mohair plush.

From 1904 every Steiff bear had attached to
its left ear a metal button, whose design, size and
colour changed over the years. The earliest buttons were small, made of pewter and blank.
Later, the firm's name was inscribed in Roman
capitals. Then came script lettering, first on a
chrome button, then a brass one then, before
the Second World War, a grey-painted one.
However, for reasons of economy, stocks of earlier buttons were sometimes used up by the
manufacturer at a later date, thus confusing
date-attribution for the modern collector. In

addition, it is not unknown for dealers to add a
button to a bear to increase its value.

Beneath the Steiff button is a label, which has
changed over the years from white, on pre-1926
bears to red (1926-34), yellow (1934–50) and
white-and-yellow or black-and-white (since
1950). The label gives in code the size, posture,
material and other information about the bear.

Most commonly produced in a range of gold
and beige shades, Steiff bears have also, rarely,
been made in black, white, cinnamon, apricot,
red, rose, silver, smoky grey, dark brown and
dual tone. Their mohair material also varied
from long straight pile to long curly plush and
short plush. From 1920 the company used glass
eyes as well as the existing button ones.

Steiff's are considered the finest of all teddy
bears, and the firm still produces a line.

Gebruder Bing of Nuremberg, 1865–1932,
also made teddy bears. Especially collectable are

**TEDDY BEAR**
*Steiff*
Black mohair plush with
button eyes; 1912

One of the rarest colours
produced by this German
firm was black. Examples of
this type with button eyes
mounted on red felt discs
number only 494.

the mechanical types that climb, walk or tumble. The bears were made in white, dark gold or brown mohair and had swivel joints and excelsior filling. They bore a metal tag, marked GBN before 1919 and BW (Bing Werke) after. The keyhole of the mechanical bears was also marked in the same way.

Gebruder Hermann KG, 1907 to the present day, produced teddy bears similar to both Steiff and Bing. Early examples, made in gold, brown, beige or dual-tone plush, are rare.

Schreyer and Co of Nuremberg, 1912–36, produced some interesting novelties, such as lipstick holders, powder compacts and scent bottles in the form of a teddy bear. Bearing a tag labelled Schuco, these were produced in various colours, including lilac, scarlet and gold. Schreyer also manufactured mechanical bears, including the "Yes/No" teddy in 1920 and walking and tumbling bears. One of the rarest is the "Skating Bear", and also sought after are the "Bell-Hop" bears (dressed as hotel pages). The keys to all these are marked "Schuco".

### BRITISH AND AMERICAN TEDDY BEARS
Recently, British teddy bears have been given the recognition they deserve. Chad Valley, established 1823, made teddy bears from 1920 onwards in a range of 13 sizes and six qualities. The rarest are those in bold colours. Early bears had a tinplate button, inscribed with "Chad Valley Hygienic Toys", attached to the body and had a woven label, marked in black (later in red) "Hygienic Toys Made In England By Chad

Valley Co. Ltd", sewn to the foot. Bears produced after 1938, carry the Royal Warrant, and present-day examples are labelled "By appointment Toy makers to HM Queen Elizabeth the Queen Mother".

Merrythought Toys have produced an attractive range of bears from 1930 to the present day. The earliest were made of mohair plush and had swivel joints and glass eyes. Attached to one ear was a metal button, inscribed with "Hygienic

**TEDDY BEAR**
*German*
**Curly mohair plush; 1920**

Identifying bears can be difficult if examples are unmarked, and many are unattributable. This teddy is of a rather unusual ginger colour.

# MANUFACTURERS OF TEDDY BEARS AND SOFT TOYS

| | | | |
|---|---|---|---|
| **CHAD VALLEY** | 1823 to present | Birmingham | Bears in 13 sizes and 6 qualities. Royal Warrant since c.1938. |
| **GEBRUDER BING** | 1865–1923 | Nuremberg | Rare mechanical and standard bears. |
| **STEIFF, firm of** | Late 19th century to present | Giengen-am-Brenz | Fine plush teddy bears, mechanical and miniature types. |
| **IDEAL TOY & NOVELTY CO** | 1903 onwards | New York | Unmarked bears: early examples confused with Steiff. |
| **GEBRUDER HERMAN KG** | 1907 to present | Sonneberg | Teddy bears, often dual-plush. |
| **SCHUCO (Schreyer & Co)** | 1912–36 | Nuremberg | Mechanical, yes/no bears and miniature bears. |
| **MERRYTHOUGHT** | c. 1930 to present | Ironbridge | Teddy bears. |
| **CHILTERN TOYS** | c. 1930s onwards | | Teddy bears with velvet pads. |
| **FARNELL, J. K.** | 20th century | | Teddy bears. |

Merrythought Toys. Made in England", and a wishbone symbol. Examples after 1950 are marked "Merrythought, Ironbridge, Shrops. Made in England".

Early teddy bears made by Dean's Rag Book Co are sought after by collectors. Established in 1903, the company produced gold plush bears with glass eyes and cloth pads, part-filled with kapok as well as excelsior. They had a tag sewn to the foot, marked "Dean's Rag Book Co. Ltd". Chiltern Toys also made fine teddy bears in the 1930s. These had a round, flattish head, glass eyes, and a flattish nose.

In the United States the outstanding manufacturer of teddy bears was the Ideal Toy and Novelty Co of New York, established in 1903. The earliest examples, in mohair, are not marked, but they do have distinguishing charac-teristics, such as large round ears. The bodies were swivel-jointed.

GERMAN AND ITALIAN SOFT TOYS

In Germany Steiff started making soft toys from felt in 1893 and subsequently developed a range of models in other materials. Schreyer also produced various soft toys of interest to the collector. The earliest were clockwork and included dogs, monkeys, rabbits and, in 1935, Mickey Mouse. They all carried a tag marked with the Schuco logo.

Gebruder Bing made soft toys in plush, velvet and felt and from 1920 produced a range of all-cloth dolls with painted features. Two other notable German soft-toy makers, both in production from 1900, were Lindler and Sons, and Button and Loening, which made a

## TEDDY BEAR SHAPES

The basic form of the Teddy Bear has undergone significant changes since 1903, that can broadly be categorized decade by decade. The earliest teddy bears can be distinguished by general statistics: long limbs, pronounced snout, prominent back hump and small, wide apart ears. By 1920, the limbs, especially arms, became much shorter, whilst the torso still retained roughly the same proportions as before. Feet also became smaller, although firms such as Steiff still used elongated pads.

By 1930 many bears were introduced with more rounded head and a less accentuated snout, larger ears, often not so widely spaced as in earlier examples. In the 1940s and 1950s an altogether chubbier and less life-like bear evolved, the limbs being much "stumpier" and the head was disproportionately large compared to the body and had a smaller snout. Limbs were even less tapering than ever in outline and the back hump disappeared in virtually all cases.

1900s

1920s

1930s

After 1945

Struwwelpeter (Shock-headed Peter), a model of a German storybook character with his conspicuous mop of red hair.

In Italy, Lenci, established 1920, made felt ethnic dolls, pierrots, harlequins, long legged lady dolls and others. They were marked on the foot and also had either a label or a button attached to the body. There are plenty of copies of these dolls around.

### AMERICAN AND BRITISH SOFT TOYS

In the United States, Art Fabric Mills, 1899–1910, made character dolls, such as Topsy-Turvy dolls and Buster Brown in 1904; Uncle Billy, and the Newly Weds, both from 1907; and a variety of soft-toy animals from 1908. All these were marked "Art Fabric Mills".

Arnold Print Works, 1876–1919, made cloth dolls with lithographed features, and other soft toys, from 1892. Sets of the Brownies, 12 figures printed per yard of fabric, were marketed from c.1892, and full sets are rare. The mark on all these toys was "Arnold Print Works, North Adams, Massachusetts".

Other American manufacturers of soft toys included the Ideal Toy and Novelty Co; Albert Bruckner, founded 1901, which made a Topsy-

**TWO TEDDY BEARS**
*Steiff, Germany*
**Mohair plush; c. 1910**

Steiff teddy bears in gold mohair plush command high prices only if the condition is good and they are early in date. Gold and beige tones are the most common colours to be found for all teddy bears.

Turvy doll; Mrs Beecher, which made Missionary Rag Babies in silk jersey from 1893 to 1910; Columbian Dolls, founded in 1891, which produced cloth dolls, marked "Columbian Doll Emma E. Adams, Oswego Center, New York", until 1900.

In Britain Chad Valley made a variety of soft toys, which included Bobby Penguin, Grotesque Cat and in the late 1920s Peter Pan, Bambina dolls, Mabel Lucie Attwell dolls, Bonzo, Buster Bunny and Niggers. Few Chad Valley toys were marked until 1920. Dean's Rag Book Co produced until 1936 colourful rag dolls of great appeal to collectors, such as Mr Puck, Golliwogs and Alice in Wonderland figures. From 1912 glove puppets and Polchinello (Punch) rattles were made and in 1930 clowns, Dancing Darkies and Dickie Blob the Inkwell Fairy. Dolls of Mickey and Minnie Mouse, manufactured in 1933, are much sought after by collectors.

Merrythought Toys have made a range of soft toys since 1930, the most collectable of which are felt-costumed characters, which carry a textile or paper tag. Merrythought's Golliwog, based on Florence Upton's storybook character, was one of the most popular toys ever made.

ROCKING HORSES, TOY COACHES, NOAH'S ARKS – THESE ARE SOME OF
THE MOST NOSTALGIC OF TOYS, WHICH OFFER A REMINDER OF NURSERIES
FROM AN AGE WHEN EVERYTHING SEEMED SIMPLER.

# CARVED AND WHEELED TOYS

Some of the earliest surviving toys are of wood. From the Middle Ages to the 19th century, this aspect of toy-making was dominated by Germany, where the industry was concentrated in and around Nuremberg and Sonneberg.

### ROCKING HORSES, HOBBY HORSES, VELOCIPEDES

The rocking horse, a carved wooden galloping horse atop parallel curved rockers, dates from 1650. It became immensely popular in the 19th century, when fine examples were produced in Germany by W. Graeffer and in Switzerland by Erste Schweizerische Spielwarenfabrik.

The hobby horse, popular since the 16th century, is also made of carved wood and consists of a horse's head mounted on a body from which two hoops are hung. Falsely called hobby horses are certain wooden horses made after *c*.1870, which were mounted on a wooden trestle base and safety "rockers", which made the toy swing rather than rock. Many dapple-painted examples dating from *c*.1900 survive, including "Bronko", sold in 1913 by Gamages, London, in four sizes.

The velocipede, which became a popular toy

in the mid-19th century, was a carved wooden horse mounted on a tricycle base, with a twin handled bar in the head and sometimes decorative ironwork on the undercarriage. The earliest examples had a slim body and wooden wheels. Dunkeleys of London is known to have taken out a patent *c*.1880. The collector should be aware that modern reproductions are common.

**British and American manufacturers** In Britain, from *c*.1895, G. and J. Lines produced rocking horses marked with a thistle emblem, those pre-1919 also marked "G. and J. Lines", those post-1919 "Triang". Star Manufacturing Co produced rocking horses after 1900 and in 1919 began making hobby horses.

In the United States, in the 19th century, B. Crandall manufactured skin-covered rocking horses and bare wood velocipedes; and Morton E. Converse produced both bare wood and skin-

**WHEELED WOODEN HORSE**
*Germany*
**Painted and carved wood;
late 19th century**

The small iron wheels are typical of those to be found on German toys of this period. This horse was sturdily built but needs a new harness, mane and tail. However, too much restoration would spoil its value to collectors.

## PRINCIPAL MANUFACTURERS OF WOODEN TOYS

| | | | |
|---|---|---|---|
| **CHAD VALLEY** | 1823 to present | Birmingham | Noah's arks. |
| **BLISS, R.** | c. 1832– | Rhode Island | Toy stables. |
| **CONVERSE, Morton E.** | c. 1878 | Massachusetts | Bare wood and skin covered rocking horses. |
| **ERSTE SCHWEIZERISCHE SPIELWARENFABRIK** | Late 19th and 20th centuries | Switzerland | Rocking horses. |
| **LINES, J. & G.** | c. 1895– | London | Rocking horses, marked with a thistle. |
| **LINDLER, Louis** | c. 1900 | Germany | Rocking horses. |

covered rocking horses. Other American manufacturers included A. Christian of New York and E. W. Bushnell.

### WHEELED TOYS

A variety of wheeled toys, in both wood and papier mâché, were produced from the 18th century onwards. The finest were made in Germany, where the industry was centred on Thüringia. Among the types of wheeled toy made were horses, coaches, other horse-drawn vehicles, boats, trains and animals. Some of the latter, such as the French papier-mâché bulldogs of c.1870, were fitted with bellows to emit a cry when pulled along. Very popular in the 19th century were bisque-headed clown dolls mounted on a wheeled wooden base covered with lithographed paper.

In the United States Schoenhut produced its

**NOAH'S ARK**
*Erzebirge, Germany*
**Painted wood; 1850**

Such arks are highly desirable toys, and this example has all the characteristics typical of German work. Here the dove has been painted on the roof, other examples have a separately carved bird. Hundreds of exotic pairs of animals were cut from the cross section of each log.

Humpty Dumpty Circus of carved wooden figures in c.1903; the sets before 1913 comprised 26 figures, those after 1913 totalled 33.

### NOAH'S ARKS

The first toy Noah's Arks were produced in Germany, in Erzebirge, Oberammergau, Sonneberg and Berchtesgaden. Early arks were mounted on a boat-hull base, later versions on a flat base. They were often decoratively painted and were produced in a range of sizes. The basic shape was rectangular with either a roof that opened or a side panel that slid back. Colourfully lithographed examples were made and after c.1900 the occupants were also lithographed. The more costly arks were supplied with many animal species.

In Britain Chad Valley made arks from the turn of the century.

THE PRINTING PRESS WAS FIRST USED TO MAKE TOYS – BOARD GAMES –
DURING THE 18TH CENTURY. FROM SMALL BEGINNINGS THERE EMERGED
A HOST OF COLORFUL, INEXPENSIVE PARLOR TOYS.

# GAMES, PUZZLES, AND NOVELTY BOOKS

Printed board games originated in the 18th century as publishers' sidelines. The earliest consisted simply of printed paper, but this was later linen-backed and eventually reinforced with card. The games were often marked with the maker's name and date. Towards the end of the 19th century, toy-makers began producing games, primarily of a moral nature and often based on social, geographical or political themes. Few were marked and so these games are more difficult to attribute to a manufacturer and date.

British firms included John Harris, which in *c*.1802 took over E. Newbury; William Spooner, which published lithographed games from *c*.1831: J. Wallis, which began making map-based games as early as *c*.1794; and J. Betts, taken over by A. N. Myers after *c*.1875.

In the United States the well-known Parker Brothers, still in business, began manufacturing board games from 1883. W. and B. Ives published games from *c*.1843, and Selchow and Richter from *c*.1864.

The mid-19th century saw the production of educational playing cards for children. By 1870 these had given way to amusement cards. One leading manufacturer was C. W. Faulkner and Son, *c*.1890-1900.

### TOY THEATRES

The first toy theatres date from the early 19th century. The earliest known manufacturer, J. F. Schreiber of Esslingen, began production in 1800. The toy merchant G. H. Bestelmeier of Nuremberg, 1793-1825, sold shadow theatres and glove puppet theatres, and in France, late in the century, Pellerin produced toy theatres, with such titles as L'Opéra and Théâtre Français.

The toy theatre did not develop in Britain until after *c*.1810. Probably the first manufacturer was William West, 1783-1854, who *c*.1811 produced 12 sets of characters, and props printed on sheets of paper, which were sold "A penny plain, twopence coloured".

J. K. Green also produced a toy stage and figures in *c*.1812. Following a decline from *c*.1830, toy theatres in Britain enjoyed a brief revival at the end of the century. One manufacturer was Benjamin Pollock (its sheets are still being printed), which in 1876 took over John Redington, founded *c*.1850. Others included W. Webb, founded 1847, and Martin Skelt, founded 1835.

In the United States, from the last quarter of the 19th century, toy theatres were made by Scott and Co and J. H. Singer.

In the early 18th century the British cartographer J. Spilbury invented the dissected puzzle (forerunner of the 20th-century jigsaw), which consisted of a picture engraved on squares and cut into pieces for reassembly. These puzzles had religious, geographical or ethical subjects but gradually gave way to lithographed types intended mainly for amusement and depicting animals and historical events. Makers of dissected puzzles also produced picture-block puzzles (wooden cubes with a different image

**TOY THEATRE**
*German*
**Chromolithographed paper on wood; 1850–60**

Toy theatres are very decorative collector's items and make an interesting addition to most interiors. Those dating from the 19th century or earlier are the most valuable and of course the condition of the paper is extremely important.

## PRINCIPAL MANUFACTURERS OF GAMES, PUZZLES AND NOVELTY BOOKS

| | | | |
|---|---|---|---|
| **HARRIS, John** | c. 1746–1856 | London | Board and table games; dissected puzzles and picture blocks. |
| **KNICKERBOCKER CO** | c. 1850 | New York | Dissected puzzles and picture blocks. |
| **IVES, W. & S. B.** | c. 1843 | Massachussetts | Board and table games. |
| **BRADLEY, Milton** | from 1860 | Massachussetts | Board and table games; dissected puzzles and picture blocks. |
| **PEACOCK, William** | c. 1850 | London | Dissected puzzles and picture blocks. |
| **TUCK, Raphael & Sons** | c. 1870 | London | Dissected puzzles and picture blocks. |
| **NEWBERY, E.** | | London | Board and table games; dissected puzzles and picture blocks. |
| **PARKER BROS** | est. 1883 | Massachussetts | Board and table games. |

segment on each face). These probably originated in Germany c.1800. Those produced from c.1850 were lithographed.

American manufacturers of dissected and picture-block puzzles included Milton Bradley, from 1860 (taken over later in the century by McLoughlin Bros); S. L. Hill, from c.1858; and Knickerbocker Co, from c.1850. British firms included J. Wallis, from c.1775; W. Peacock, from c.1850; and Raphael Tuck and Sons, from 1870 to the present.

Novelty "pop-up" books for children are much sought after by collectors. The earliest was published c.1760 by Sayer of London. This provided a model much later for S. and J. Fuller of London, who in 1860 published *History of Little Fanny*. Later manufacturers included Dean and Son.

In Germany in the late 19th century J. F. Schreiber produced "tab" books (picture-story books whose characters were animated by moving a tab projecting from the page). Nister pro-

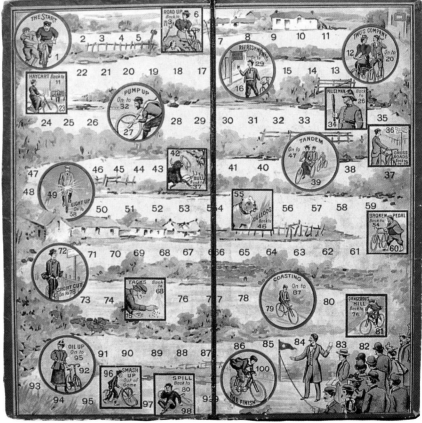

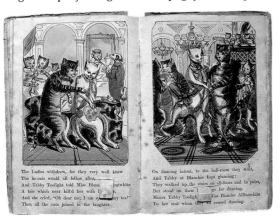

duced "pop-up" books and books in various shapes, such as that of a cat or a house; these are of great interest to collectors. Also dating from the same period, and very collectable, are German "speaking picture" and "musical" books, which incorporated mechanisms that emitted animal-like sounds or tunes when operated by a pull string.

THE TOY SOLDIER, WITH ITS BRIGHT COLORS AND FREQUENTLY
HIGHLY-SKILLED MODELING, CAN EVOKE CHILDHOOD MEMORIES AS WELL
AS THE PAGEANTRY OF THE MILITARY PARADE.

# SOLDIERS

For collectors of toy soldiers, antiquity means the 18th century. Painted wooden warriors have been found in Egyptian tombs of 2300 BC (perhaps intended to protect the dead), but these are museum pieces. It is also known that Louis XIV of France possessed a miniature army in silver, designed by Georges Chassel of Nancy and Paris and made by the silversmith Merlin, but these troops disappeared, and, anyway, should any be discovered today they would have more relevance as examples of the silversmith's art for a museum than as toy veterans for a collector's shelves. It was only relatively late in history that toy soldiers – and especially commercially made figures, the heart of modern collecting – were produced in any appreciable numbers. Collectors recognize several clearly defined, main genres of toy soldiers. Flats (Zinnfiguren) – the epitome of "the little tin soldier", thin, almost two-dimensional figures, which grew out of the 18th-century

**FREDERICK THE GREAT**
*Probably Aloys Ochel of Kiel, Germany, after Johann Gottfried Hilpert of Nuremberg*
**Early 20th century**

The conquering "Old Fritz" is characteristically mounted on a fine grey in a classic pose painted by several artists in the late 18th century. This pose was successfully copied by Hilpert, "the father of the tin soldier", in flat, almost two-dimensional form and several sizes. It became the model for many German flat-makers who followed. The version seen here is in the 30mm size, the standard "Nuremberg scale" popularized by Ernst Heinrichsen in the mid 19th century. The victories of Frederick the Great stimulated the commercial tin-soldier industry more than any other historical events in the second half of the 18th century; his figure is to be found in many vignette sets for specific battles.

pewter industry in southern Germany ("tin" soldiers are in fact made of pewter, an alloy of tin and lead). This type is still made today in modest quantities by small, specialized firms catering for a collectors' market. Solid – fully rounded, lead-alloy figures from France and Germany, whose heyday lasted from the mid-19th century to the 1930s. The lighter, hollow-cast models of William Britain, the United Kingdom's premier toy-soldier factory dominated the lead-soldier market from 1893 to the early 1960s. The splendidly "animated" figures made from composition (a putty-like material) in Germany between 1904 and the Second World War were led by the Elastolin and Lineol marks and supported by an armoury of model vehicles and other tinplate "hardware" of war.

Sub-divisions of interest include French and Austrian variations of flats; solid soldiers from Denmark and Sweden; British emulators and copyists of William Britain; and Belgian and Dutch forays into composition.

### THE AMERICAN DIMENSION

American collectors are notably bereft of a home source of toy soldiers, apart from a range of heavy castings manufactured in the first half of this century, which, for all their crudeness of design, nevertheless have a "toyshop" charm. From their position at the lower end of the retail market, these figures are known as dimestore soldiers. Rarity rules, even in this area, and dimestore specialists will pay high prices for a scarce figure of the 1930s or 1940s. The leading European manufacturers actively targeted the United States' juvenile market from the late 19th century onwards.

The present wave of collecting interest has its origin in the mid-1960s. At this time health and marketing considerations finally phased out the use of lead products in the toy industry, which was increasingly concentrating on plastics and diecast metals, and as a result, base lead, hallowed by obsolescence, was transmuted to gold.

Tin Soldiers

Johann Gottfried Hilpert (1732-1801), master pewterer, is credited with having been "the father of the tin soldier". Born in Coburg, central Germany, where he had spent four years learning the basic trade of making kitchen utensils under his tinsmith father, Andreas, he moved in 1750 some 60 miles south to Nuremberg, where he completed his apprenticeship and was soon set up as a tinsmith in his own right.

By 1760, Europe was in the fourth year of what was to become known as the Seven Years' War. But around Nuremberg, neighbouring Fürth and Augsburg, 80 miles to the south, the tin mines flourished despite the war, and the tinsmiths they supplied were finding new wares to market. They saw commercial possibilities in the flat, tin figures they had traditionally made for their own children from the pewterer's "flash", the excess metal remaining from their kitchen-ware manufacture. Among the pewterers was Hilpert, who became the first known commercial maker of toy soldiers.

Initially, however, Hilpert's output was characterized by pacific themes: theatrical, farming, hunting and exploration subjects, with figures and animals engraved on the slate master-moulds after contemporary drawings. Joined in his rapidly growing business by his younger brother and his son, Hilpert, inspired by the war victories of Frederick the Great and his Prussian legions, developed one of his most successful lines, a series of 40 types of Frederick's troops together with detachments of their enemies, French, Russian and Turkish soldiers. These figures were produced in scales ranging from 50mm to 60mm. (The scale of toy soldiers is invariably denoted by the height in millimetres of a hatless, unmounted figure.) One outstanding Hilpert creation, probably a special commission in about 1777, was a 150mm high flat figure

# MAKERS OF TOY-SOLDIERS

| | | | |
|---|---|---|---|
| **HEINRICHSEN, Ernst** | *fl.* 1839–88 | Nuremberg | Flats. Popularized 30mm standard figures which became known as the *Nuremberg scale*. (Heirs active throughout first half of 20th century.) |
| **LUCOTTE** | *fl. c.* 1830s | Paris | Maker of highest-quality full-round solid figures. Taken over by Cuperly, Blondel and Gerbeau in 1838 and soldiers marketed under the name Mignot: latter active to modern times. |
| **HEYDE, George, firm of** | *fl. c.* 1870–1945 | Dresden | Solid figures in rich range of sizes and activities. Factory and records destroyed in wartime bombing. |
| **BRITAIN, firm of** | *fl.* from 1893 | London | Mechanical toys from 1840s, then revolutionary hollow-cast figures of soldiers from 1893. William Britain Jr (1860–1933) was the architect of firm's success. |
| **JOHILLCO, (John Hill & Co)** | *fl.* first half 20th century | London | Successful manufacturer of hollow-casts. |
| **ELASTOLIN** | First half 20th century | Southern Germany | Large-scale composition figures. |
| **LINEOL** | First half 20th century | Berlin | Large-scale composition figures. |
| **MANOIL, firm of, and BARCLAY, firm of** | First half 20th century | New York New Jersey | Principal American makers of dimestore soldiers. |
| **OCHEL, Aloys** | *fl.* 1920s–30s | Kiel | World's largest producer of flats. Finest production during 1920s and 1930s. |
| **HILPERT, Johann Gottfried** | *fl. c.* 1770–1801 | Nuremberg | "The father of the tin soldier". Flats. Moulds taken over first by Stahl of Nuremberg, to 1822, and Haring, of Furth, 19th and early 20th centuries. Successors' work inferior to that of the master. |

of Frederick astride a favourite horse, a portrait that was subsequently copied time and again by other makers of flats.

Hilpert survived both his brother and his son, and after his death in 1801 his stock, including his precious moulds, was bought by Johann Ludwig Stahl, a dealer, who exploited the Hilpert legacy in lacklustre style for another 17 years. Stahl eventually sold out to Arthur Haring, a Fürth tinsmith, whose firm made workmanlike but undistinguished figures until the 20th century, disposing of the Hilpert moulds somewhere along the way.

Few of Hilpert's figures have come down to us, but his example stimulated the growth of a 19th-century industry of flat-makers – not only in Nuremberg but in Fürth, Augsburg, Saxony to the north-west and, farther afield, Hanover, Brunswick, Würzburg and Hildesheim – and many of their tin soldiers have survived.

### TECHNIQUES & STANDARDIZATION

Moulds for tin soldiers were traditionally made of two small blocks of Thüringian slate. One surface of each was finely polished so that the two parts fitted snugly together when clamped for pouring the molten metal. The engraver, often a highly skilled artist, made an image representing one side of his soldier figure on one face, then produced a complementary image on the other face. When the blocks were clamped together, a conical opening in the top gave access to a channel down which molten metal was poured to reach the engraved area of the mould's interior. After almost instantaneous setting, the mould was unclamped and the surplus metal scraped off the figure.

Pure tin is expensive; furthermore, it would be too brittle to stand up to nursery wars. Therefore, the makers of flats used pewter, in a mix of 2 parts lead to 3 parts tin, with agents of bismuth and antimony added to control various reactions. Some manufacturers employed skilled painters to decorate their wares; others sent them off to the distributors unpainted, in their oval or round split-pine boxes. A third option was partial painting: a hussar, for example, would have his flesh, uniform and equipment painted, but his horse left in its silvery state.

Skilled 19th-century practitioners of the art of soldier-making include Lorenz, Schradin, Gottschalk, Ammon, Allgeyer, Schweigger, Haffner and many more (several of whom progressed to making *semi-round* and *full-round* figures). Identification of a manufacturer is often

made difficult by the confusing trade practices of the time: boxes were frequently labelled by the distributor simply with their area of origin or with the distributor's own name; some manufacturers "signed" their metal products with initials, which, however, were constantly changing; and the confusion is sometimes compounded by an engraver's mark. Consequently, a collector relies heavily on old catalogues and experience of handling figures.

An important name in the history of flats is Ernst Heinrichsen (1806-88), who standardized the size of toy armies, thus allowing children to mix the wares of different makers realistically. This Nuremberg manufacturer, who set up business in 1839, had significant success with his main range of 30mm figures; and by example as a prospering manufacturer, and by dint of subtle campaigning, he persuaded makers in many parts of Germany to change from their larger scales to his, which, after the mid-19th century, became known as the Nuremberg scale. It was principally in this scale that Aloys Ochel of Kiel, one of many distinguished 20th-century makers, became during the 1920s and 1930s the world's largest manufacturer of tin figures. Ochel's products were packed in cardboard boxes trademarked Kilia (superior painted models) and Oki (inferior unpainted).

### SOLIDS

Solid figures require more metal in their manufacture than do flats, some of which were less than 1.5mm thick. Therefore it was commercially out of the question to consider mass-producing solids from alloys similar to those developed by the Nuremberg pewterers, with their high and expensive content of tin. The answer was an alloy of lead and antimony, and so was born the lead soldier.

Experiments with lead by several German flat-makers, including Ammon, Allgeyer, Haffner and Heinrichsen, resulted in an unsatisfactory hybrid known as the semi-round, or semi-solid, figure. From above, it looked elliptical, with a maximum thickness of about 5mm. (Its height was about 45mm.) Such figures, although still produced as secondary lines by some German factories until well into this century, lacked realism and found little allegiance in France and practically none in Britain.

France won the honours for introducing the first successful commercial examples of the truly three-dimensional solid figure. This was the achievement of a Parisian company called

Lucotte, which probably made its début in lead around the time of the French Revolution in 1789. In the early 19th century, Lucotte was taken over by another company, CBG (Cuperly, Blondel and Gerbeau), which in 1838 took the name of Mignot, the banner under which the best French toy soldiers have been made ever since. Records of precise ownership and documentation of factory practices are notoriously patchy, but 19th-century Lucottes and Mignots, as the mainly 54mm soldiers are known to collectors, are highly prized. The former enjoy a substantial premium in value and among them the fine models of Napoleonic armies are particularly popular. During the 19th century the United States (its memory of Lafayette, the French hero of the American War of Independence, ever green) extended a warm welcome to the toy soldiers of France. Abraham Lincoln played with Mignots with his son Tad.

Just as Lucotte and Mignot ruled in France, so the company of George Heyde eventually came to dominate German full-round solids. Heyde is believed to have begun production shortly before 1872, the date of his first catalogue. Nothing more precise is known because the company he founded, its factory, records and moulds, and all personal clues to Heyde himself, were obliterated in February 1945 by the Allied bombing of Dresden. This city was the source of some of the most imaginative toy soldiers the world has ever known. And imaginative is the word: Heyde's widely exported wares abounded in glorious inaccuracies – British Household Cavalry on brown horses, not black, North American Indians carrying Zulu shields. Even so, no other maker has produced figures in such a variety of poses. They not only march, shoot, charge and stand guard; they bivouac with cups of coffee and bottles of

**NAPOLEON'S CEREMONIAL COACH**
*Mignot of Paris*
54mm, full-round solids;
**early 20th century**

The coach is an example of skilfully modelled ceremonial "realism" in three-dimensional form, which displaced the flats in popularity from the middle of the 19th century onwards.

**3rd REGIMENT DES VOLTIGEURS DE LIGNE**
*Mignot of Paris*
54mm, full-round solid;
**modern manufacture**

The standard-bearer represents the glory of the Napoleonic era, a period given enormous attention in the toy-soldier range from the leading French maker. This "cabinet" figure of the 1970s was one of a series from the old moulds. Mignot foot-soldier sets of 12 pieces traditionally included officer and colours, and often a bugler.

schnapps, coil wire, study maps, feed cavalry mounts, sweep decks, climb look-out posts and lie mortally and gorily wounded. When they shoot, they do so with a metal blob of flame and smoke at the rifle muzzle, a trick Heyde borrowed from the **Zinnfiguren**-makers.

**NODDING-HEAD
PORTRAIT FIGURES**
*Heyde of Dresden*
90mm, full-round solids;
**c. 1914**

The three figures represent
contemporary characters
on the world stage: King
George V (left), the Kaiser
and his son, "Little Willi".
Their socket heads nod
when the floor is tapped.
(*Top*)

**BRITISH CAMEL CORPS**
*Heyde of Dresden*
65mm; **early 20th
century**

The set is an example of
those made by the premier
German "solids" factory
with sights on the British
toy market. (*Above*)

Enormous quantities of Heyde soldiers were
produced, representing the troops of many
nations and made in a bewildering variety of
scales, ranging from 43mm to 120mm. For the
modern collector they constitute a vast and rich
legacy of single-factory specialization.

## HOLLOW-CASTS

No genre of toy soldiers has a greater following
among collectors, on both sides of the Atlantic,
than the lead, full-round models of William
Britain of London, a firm which was founded
about 1845 and which still flourishes in the toy
market today, as Britains Limited. Under
William Britain, sen. (1826-1906), the firm's
early production consisted of ingenious
mechanical toys, such as a kilted Scotsman who
raised a whisky bottle to his lips and a Chinese
coolie pulling a rickshaw. Lead soldiers became
the mainstay of the company's commercial success in the last decade of the 19th century,
thanks to a revolutionary invention, the hollow-
cast figure. This is credited to William Britain,
jun. (1860-1933), the eldest of the founder's

five sons involved in the enterprise.

William Britain, jun., poured his molten
metal (lead with 12½ percent antimony, a
"stiffening" element) into the mould, as did his
Continental competitors, but he added a quick
spinning movement to the operation, thus forcing much of the innermost lead out through a
hole which every one of these soldiers has, normally in the top of the head. The result was that
the remaining lead set inside the mould like a
shell. This hollow-cast figure became the basis
of the family fortune: using considerably less
metal than the solid figures of French and
German makers, it was both cheaper to make
and lighter to ship.

William Britain began manufacturing hollow-
casts in 1893, and his first products were
mounted soldiers of the Life Guards. This was
set Number 1 in what was to become a catalogue
list running into thousands of military and civil-
ian types of figure in the next 70 years, during
which Britains emerged as the world's premier
supplier of toy soldiers.

Collectors recognise two "golden" periods in
the firm's production: the years to the outbreak
of war 1914, models from which are known as
*"ancient Britains"*; and the 1930s, when the
issue of new sets was most prolific. Soldiers are
mainly in the 54mm scale, with some 45, 47 and
70mm exceptions. Other British firms (notably
John Hill and Co, known as Johillco) followed
Britains into the hollow-cast market, with varying degrees of success.

Britains phased out the production of its
lead-based models in the 1960s. But it did not
quit the toy soldier market – in addition to a
wide variety of other toys, a range of soldiers
made from non-toxic metal is currently produced by the firm.

## COMPOSITION

Collectors of composition toy soldiers, finely
modelled figures generally in the 70mm scale,
revere the products of Elastolin and Lineol, two
names which give clues to the nature of the
material used. This type of soldier, popular in
Germany, was traditionally manufactured from
sawdust and glue, leavened with kaolin and
linseed oil. Into this putty-like mix a wire skeleton was inserted, and the whole was lightly
cooked in a brass mould until hard. Painting by
hand followed the cooling process.

Elastolin was the name chosen for its range of
soldiers by the firm of Hausser, founded
by the brothers Otto and Max Hausser at

### MULE BATTERY OF MOUNTAIN ARTILLERY
*William Britain*
54mm, hollow-cast; **1930s**

This is one of Britain's most attractive sets. The gun, when its three pieces are assembled, fires matchsticks or metal shells. (*Above*)

### COMPOSITION AND TINPLATE
*German*
**c. 1930–40**

The clockwork searchlight lorry and its trailer are by Hausser. The soldiers are by Elastolin and the shellburst comes from the rival firm, Lineol. (*Below*)

### WEHRMACHT BANDSMAN
*Elastolin*
70mm, composition;
**c. 1939**

An Army figure of the Third Reich, part of a set of bandsmen, carries a typical German bell-banner. It represents the excellence

of modelling achieved by German manufacturers at this period. The process employed a mixture of sawdust, glue, kaolin and linseed oil. Hitler encouraged the manufacture of such toys for at least two years after the war began. (*Right*)

Ludwigsburg, near Stuttgart in southern Germany, in 1904. The firm resumed production of toy figures in post-war West Germany. Lineol, based in the Berlin area, enjoyed its most successful period during the 1930s. Both firms excelled in models of the army of the Third Reich, including its vehicles and artillery, and produced portrait figures of German and other world leaders.

Emulators of the German composition success sprang up in Belgium, The Netherlands, Denmark, Austria and Italy.

THE TINPLATE TOY WAS A PRODUCT OF THE INDUSTRIAL REVOLUTION.

MADE IN LARGE QUANTITIES, THEY WERE AFFORDABLE, AND PLACED

SHOP-BOUGHT TOYS WITHIN REACH OF ORDINARY WAGE EARNERS.

# TINPLATE TOYS

One factor that makes tinplate toys so appealing to collectors is that they mirror many of the technical, social and economic developments of the late 19th and the 20th centuries. For example, the period 1895-1914 – when mass-production enabled the tinplate toy industry to grow enormously – was also a time of revolution in transport, and tinplate toys of the time reflect this in miniature: the change-over from horse-drawn carriages to motor transport, the development of the motor car, bus, and tram, the first aeroplanes, and, more sinisterly, the development of submarines, gun boats, armoured trains and tanks.

### BEFORE 1918

Until about 1880 tinplate-toy-making had been very much a cottage industry with home-based workers assembling and hand-finishing products on a piece-rate. With the widespread adoption of the factory system, every stage of production, from pressing to assembly, decoration and

**EXPRESS WAGON**
*Althof Bergmann*
**c. 1880**

This toy incorporates some of the best features of American toys – the strong contrasting colours, stencilled decoration and name plate with rather naive but galloping "Dexter" horses which are so redolent of American weather vanes. Ives' toys often incorporate a plaster-headed boy, but these are more commonly found on their clockwork velocipedes.

packing, was carried out under one roof, thus giving management more quality and distribution control.

To manufacture tinplate toys, a thin sheet of steel was coated with tin; this sheet was then embossed and cut into the desired forms and shapes and these were then assembled by soldering or by the use of tabs and slots. Early toys tended to be rather naïve and whimsical in design and construction and their decoration was either hand-painted or stencilled. On fine-quality toys specially skilled finishers added hand-painted or enamelled details.

In the late 19th century there were experiments with other methods of decoration: direct printing (using two non-absorbent surfaces, which had the disadvantage that the ink did not take properly), transfer printing (transferring a design via an intermediary medium, which was messy and time-consuming) and, more satisfactorily, offset lithography (printing the design on a rubber-coated roller which was then offset on

the tinplate). Toy-makers, however, seem to have been slow to take advantage of lithography, as, despite its availability from the end of the 19th century, toys produced as late as *c.*1908 are still either entirely hand-painted or enamelled or only partly lithographed.

**United States** Some of the earliest, and most appealing, tinplate toys were produced in the USA. Relying on American folk-art tradition, they include hoop toys, paddle-steamers, carpet trains and horse-drawn vehicles. Francis Field began tinplate toy production in the 1830s, but the major growth period was the 1860s, when Althof Bergmann, Hull & Stafford, James Fallows, Edward Ives, Stevens and Brown and other firms were founded. Toys by these makers are extremely scarce and highly prized among collectors.

**France** In France the 1880s saw the founding of the toy firms of F. Martin, Radiguet and G. Dessin. Late-19th-century horse-and-carriage toys and simple spray-painted carousels and ferris wheels are commonly found but unfortunately have no trade labels. Novelty toys by F. Martin – clockwork Parisian-streetlife figures with weighted feet, such as buskers and street vendors – are still relatively easy to find.

**Germany** One of the first major German tinplate-toy-makers was Ludwig Lutz, established *c.*1846 in Ellwangen an der Jagst. In 1883, Ludwig's son August continued the family tradition and produced brightly enamelled ships and trains. Lutz products were later marketed by two giant toy producers, Bing and Märklin, under their own names before ultimately being taken over by Märklin in 1891. Early German toys by Lutz and others, such as Hess, *c.*1826,

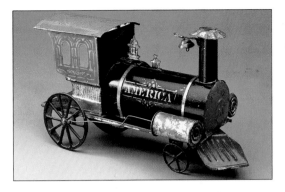

are seldom marked (they probably carried paper labels, since destroyed or lost) and are very scarce. However, the very fact that the pieces are unmarked can enable the knowledgeable collector to pick them up in general sales, where they are sometimes overlooked. These early toys, which occasionally incorporate wood, are normally in the form of horse-drawn carriages, sleighs, simple trains or paddle-steamers. They are brightly painted in primary colours, often contrasted with black, and are transporting

**FERRIS WHEEL**
*Marklin*
**c. 1898**

The central ticket booth houses a simple musical mechanism. The central wheel of stamped and scrolling tinplate is inset with stained-glass panels.

well-modelled, hand-painted, composition or china-headed passengers.

A rapid expansion of the German toy industry took place in the 1890s, and by the turn of the century German products could be found in toy shops throughout Europe and the USA. And between 1895 and 1945 Germany's production of tinplate toys was greater and of higher quality than that of any other country. Their popularity was due not only to their quality but to their being tailored for specific export markets. For example, Bing produced a gunboat, the *Brandenburg*, which for the British market became *HMS Terrible* and for the American *New York*. The Germans were also quick to respond to new developments. For example, if a new style of bus was brought into service in a major city, a toy model of it would be in production within weeks.

The two finest German tinplate-toy manufacturers were Gebruder Bing and Märklin. Gebruder Bing, founded in Nuremberg by the brothers Ignaz and Adolf Bing in 1865,

produced vast quantities of toys. Until 1923 these bear the initials GBN in various styles; then the mark changes to BW (Bing Werke). The company ceased trading in 1932, during the worldwide Depression, a bleak time for most manufacturing industries.

Märklin was founded in Göppingen by Theodor Wilhelm and his wife Caroline in 1859. Their earliest tinplate toys were dolls, kitchenware and spirit-fired cooking ranges (endur-

**SPIRIT-FIRED STEAM LOCOMOTIVE AND COACHES**
*Marklin*
**c. 1905**

"The Tsar's Train" is reputed to have been a gift to Tsar Nicholas II.

ingly popular and still strong sellers in the 1910s). However, the business did not really thrive until their sons took over in 1888 and introduced the latest technological advances and mass-production methods. Their earlier toys bear the GM (Gebruder Märklin) monogram, in a range of styles, the later ones "Märklin" combined with a speeding bicycle logo. The firm is still in production today, having successfully survived two world wars and the post-war demand for plastic toys. It proudly asserts that it is the oldest manufacturer of trains in the world.

Other tinplate-toy manufacturers include Lehmann (whose novelty toys are particularly prized), founded 1875; Schoenner, 1875; Gunthermann, 1877; and Carette, 1886.

### 1918-39

In the aftermath of the First World War, most established manufacturers resumed production. Initially, tinplate toys were produced to pre-war designs – for example, hand-enamelled limousines with bevelled-glass windows and hard rubber tyres. However, these were quickly discarded as, for economic reasons, manufacturers used cheaper pressings, clock-work motors and poorer-quality lithography. Imaginative, more stylized designs combined with bright new colours and gimmicky mechanisms resulted in delightful, lightweight toys. An exception to this trend, however, was tin-plate boats, which continued to be produced in the old-fashioned way – that is, with soldered tinplate hulls, the only satisfactory method of making a vessel watertight.

Constructional kits became big sellers. The most famous were made by Meccano in England; those of Märklin were also notable.

The 1920s saw the introduction of toys as a marketing tool: Singer Sewing Machines shrewdly believed that a child playing with a good-quality miniature working replica of an adult's sewing machine would, on reaching adulthood, buy a full-sized one of the same brand. The French were particularly keen on this idea. For example, André Citroën produced fine-quality toy cars which were almost scale models of his full-sized vehicle. Following this, two French toy manufacturers quickly saw the commercial potential of model cars: JEP (Jouets en Paris) produced model prestige cars such as the Rolls Royce and Hispano-Suiza; and CIJ (Compagnie Industrielle des Jouets) made one of the most collectable of toy racing cars – the

P2 Alfa Romeo, complete with leather bonnet straps, finely meshed radiator and accurate bonnet louvres and suspension. These cars – most commonly found finished in scarlet, occasionally in white, silver or blue – appeal not only to

the toy collector but also to the automobile enthusiast, who appreciates their accurate depiction of detail.

The cinema was also a major influence on toy-making in the 1930s. The cartoon figures of Mickey Mouse and Felix the Cat were reproduced in tinplate by German manufacturers, and in the United States in 1934 Louis Marx made the first toy spaceship in imitation of film character Buck Rogers' "25th-century" screen rocket. Always a considerable importer of tinplate toys, the United States did not become major exporters until Marx, who made a wide range of humorous novelty toys, and Kingsbury, best remembered today for their series of land-speed-record cars.

**"WHEEL A GEAR" ROBOT**
*Taiyo*
**1960**

This battery-operated toy boasts moving eyes, sparks, moving gears, walking mechanism and a horrid noise, just the thing to captivate the space-crazed 1960s child! Its value to a collector is enhanced by the fact that it still retains its original box.

# PRINCIPAL METAL TOY-MAKERS

| | | | |
|---|---|---|---|
| **ROCK UND GRANER** | 1813–1913 | Biberach an der Riss | Fine-quality clockwork trains. |
| **LUTZ, Ludwig** | c. 1846–91 | Ellwangen an der Jagst | Surviving products are rare and revered by collectors. |
| **BERGMAN, Althof** | Founded 1856 | New York | Floor trains, wheeled bell toys, boats, and horsedrawn transport. |
| **GEORGE W. BROWN & CO.** | Founded 1856 | Connecticut | Merged in 1869 with J & E Stephens to form Stephens and Brown. Clockwork toys, hooped toys, velocipede, paddle boats. |
| **LINES BROTHERS** | Founded 1858 | London | Tri-ang trains, mini cars, Spot-On die-cast toys. |
| **MARKLIN** | Founded 1859 | Göppingen | Fine quality tinplate trains, cars and gunboats. |
| **EDWARD IVES** | 1860s–1920s | Connecticut | Tinplate, iron, and composition-headed figures. |
| **GEBRUDER BING** | c. 1863–1932 | Nuremberg | Tinplate-toy manufacturer. |
| **MARTIN, Fernand** | 1878–1912 | Paris | Clockwork novelty toys and automata. |
| **GEBRUDER FLEISCHMANN** | Founded 1887 | Nuremberg | Tinplate boats and ships. |
| **CHAD VALLEY** | Founded 1897 | Birmingham, UK. | Large tinplate 1930s limousines. |
| **BASSET-LOWKE** | Founded 1899 | Northampton | Toy-train manufacturer. |
| **JOUETS EN PARIS** | 1899–1965 | Paris | Good, large, well-made cars. |
| **HORNBY** | 1901–64 | Liverpool | Maker of Meccano, Hornby trains, speedboats, Dinky toys. |
| **LIONEL** | Founded 1901 | USA | Toy trains. |

# DIE-CAST TOYS

THE MODERN WORLD ENTERED THE PLAYROOM IN THE 20TH CENTURY
WITH PRODUCTION OF DIE-CAST MODELS.

Die-cast toys are produced by pouring molten metal (normally a lead alloy) into moulds and subjecting them to pressure. It is an inexpensive and fast method of production, ideal for producing inexpensive toys for supplying the mass market.

Die-cast toys were first produced in the early 20th century, by both the Dowst Manufacturing Co of America, which in 1914 introduced the "Tootsie Toys" range of cars, and by Simon & Rivollet of France, which made a series of horse-drawn vehicles (now rare). However, Britain was to become the largest manufacturer of die-cast toys in the world, and the name of Dinky, the leading maker, was to become synonymous with the die-cast toy.

### DINKY

Dinky was just one of many successful lines initiated by the Liverpool entrepreneur Frank Hornby. In 1901 he began producing constructional toys and registered the name Meccano in 1907. His 'O' gauge Hornby train sets of the 1920s and 30s were enormously popular and it was the accessories for these that gave rise to the Dinky toy. The "Modelled Miniatures", as they were initially called, were at first in the form of railway staff, passengers and signals, farm animals, and so on. It was not until 1934 that the first cars were made and the name changed to "Dinky Toys". Their scales were 1/48 and 1/43.

The first series of Dinkies produced was the 22 and comprised motor truck, delivery van, tractor, tank and two sports cars. These early vehicles were made from a predominantly lead alloy, unlike the later Zamak alloy of mainly aluminium and zinc. Unfortunately, the earlier models are therefore prone to metal fatigue, which makes them rare and therefore valuable. The pre-war vehicles tended to have dished wheels (sloping towards each other at the top) and smooth (often white) rubber tyres and had applied tinplate radiators and solid alloy underframes. These characteristics help to date-

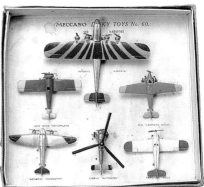

differentiate pre-war models from similar ones reintroduced after the war.

During the war the only Dinkies produced were small quantities for sale at Christmas. After 1945 new lines were introduced alongside the old ones, and in 1947 the new 1/36 scale Dinky Supertoy was born. Some of the most sought-after models are the Guy and Foden lorries bearing decorative advertisement transfers on their sides. In 1961 the company was taken over by Lines Brothers (Triang), which continued to produce Dinkies until 1979.

### CORGI AND LESNEY

In 1956 Corgi toys started making cars with jewelled headlights, insertable passengers, opening doors and bonnets revealing detailed cast engines. Later they produced screen and TV tie-in cars such as the Chitty Chitty Bang Bang, James Bond, Captain Scarlet, Thunderbirds and Batman models. Corgi toys are still in production today.

Lesney was another giant of the die-cast toy world. Their familiar Matchbox Toys and Models of Yesteryear were made to the scales of 1/25 and 1/30. Financial troubles caused the company to cease production in 1987.

One of the finest constructed and most expensive of die-cast toys was the Spot On vehicle, introduced by Triang in 1959 to compete with Dinky and Corgi and produced until 1967.

**AEROPLANE GIFT SET
No 60**
*Dinky*
**c. 1935-41**

This is quite a rarity. Many of these small, early Dinky pieces suffer from metal fatigue. (*Above*)

**CARS**
*Dinky*

These brightly coloured post-war cars are still relatively easy to obtain, unlike the 1930s pieces. (*Below*)

THE PLAYROOMS OF THE PAST WERE CRISS-CROSSED BY THE TINPLATE
CLOCKWORK OR LIVE-STEAM TOY TRAINS THAT SUMMONED TANTALIZING
FANTASIES OF GROWING UP TO BE A TRAIN DRIVER.

# TOY TRAINS

In the 19th century the railroad opened up hitherto isolated tracts of the United States and united this enormous country. It is not surprising therefore that some of the earliest toy trains were American. In 1856 George Brown of Forestville, Connecticut, began producing brightly coloured trains with stencilled decoration and simple clockwork mechanisms. At this date trains ran along the floor without the aid of rails. It is believed that the German manufacturer Issmayer of Nuremberg was the first to introduce rails – in 1866, when he provided a circular track for his trains.

As the century progressed, steam was used as motive power for toy trains, and Piddlers or Dribblers – as they have come to be known for the spluttering mess they made – were popular nursery toys. In Britain scientific-instrument-makers such as Newton produced beautiful and highly finished Piddlers made almost entirely of brass. They were fitted with spirit-fired burners to heat the water in the boiler, which powered oscillating driving cylinders.

At this time there was no standard measurement for each toy-train gauge (distance between opposite wheels and rails), and trains came in multitudinous sizes. This meant that an engine made by one company could not be used to pull carriages from another and caused problems with exporting.

By 1900 German manufacturers had taken a strong hold of the toy-train market. The three finest German makers were Gebruder Bing, Carette and, perhaps best known of all, Märklin. It is Märklin which is credited with standardizing most of the gauges (following an exhibition of Märklin sectional tracks at the Leipzig Fair of 1891), as follows: gauge 0: 32mm (1¼ in); gauge 1: 45mm (1¾ in); gauge 2: 51mm (2 in). The only gauge in which there remained a variation was gauge 3: 64mm (2½ in) for all manufacturers with the exception Märklin, which used 75mm (3 in).

The American company Ives adopted gauge 0, and French manufacturers, of whom the most important were Radiguet and JEP (Jouets en Paris), adopted gauges 0 and 1.

The most popular gauges in the early 1900s

## TINPLATE TRAIN SET
*German*
**c. 1835**

The 2-2-2 locomotive with matching tender, complete with original plaster passengers in 1830s costume. This is one of the earliest commercially made train sets and was possibly made by Lutz. (*Above left*)

## LIVE-STEAM LOCOMOTIVE AND TENDER (GAUGE III)
*Marklin*
**c. 1909**

The painted simulated rivets to the locomotive which are often found on early large-gauge Marklin locomotives. (*Left*)

were 2 and 3. It is astonishing that the enormous trains of these gauges were intended for use indoors. However, it should be realised that these were toys for children of the rich, whose homes would have very large rooms. Gradually, toy trains became smaller and cheaper as manufacturers made them accessible to a wider range of income groups.

The beginning of the 20th century saw the introduction of electrically driven model trains. These were large, messy and potentially dangerous: mains electricity not being generally available in the home, large wet batteries were needed to provide the charge, which could give a considerable jolt.

In Britain two railway enthusiasts W. J. Bassett-Lowke and Harry Franklin set out to make affordable, good-quality model trains to feed the growing demand from both children and adults. In 1900 Bassett-Lowke and his chief designer Henry Greenly, visited the Paris Exposition, where both men were impressed by the wares of Carette, Marklin and Bing. Bassett-Lowke and Bing entered into a contract whereby Bing would produce trains to Greenly's designs in British liveries – the first British commercial scale model trains were born. By 1902 these models were in the shops and were extremely successful. A year later Bassett-Lowke had begun to produce their own trains in their Northampton workshops, the first one being a 2-2-2 (two wheels at the front, two in the middle, and two at the back) gauge 1 locomotive and tender, "Lady of the Lake".

The First World War saw a halt in the production of model trains everywhere. Production got under way again in the 1920s, with new names appearing in the field. The most important was Hornby, which introduced a very simple clockwork 0-4-0 locomotive, tender and open wagon. It was initially bolted together in the same way as Hornby's other constructional toys but was later soldered together in more traditional style. Hornby introduced its first electric train set in 1927, and by the mid-1930s this had developed into their famous 20-volt sets with large headlamps inserted into the smoke boxes at the front.

In the United States the Lionel Company, founded in 1901, produced highly realistic, powerful trains to its own gauge – $2\frac{1}{8}$ in. (54mm) which it cheekily named "Standard Gauge". Other American competitors such as Ives and American Flyer had to adopt this new gauge, as their trains, made to European sizes, were regarded as non-standard. Although 0 gauge was also still in production, standard gauge was by far the most popular. German manufacturers, whose products had reigned supreme in the United States until about 1910, now found their American markets declining as their trains ceased to be assimilable into the American railway systems. Lionel continued with great success until the Wall Street Crash of 1929, when it ceased trading.

The 1920s also saw changes in the popularity of the various gauges in Europe. Early in the decade gauge 0 was the most favoured, gauge 1 played a declining role and gauges 2 and 3 had virtually disappeared. However, in the 1930s gauge 0 began to be supported by a new gauge, 00, which was so much smaller in scale that an entire railway layout could be fitted into a small room. This smaller 00 gauge had been introduced on a commercial basis by Bing in 1922, by special commission of Bassett-Lowke, who described his sense of achievement:

When builders were steadily putting up more compact houses, with smaller rooms, I visualised the demand for a still narrower gauge than 0, and I brought over from Germany the first model railway outfit of just half that size, on a gauge of $\frac{5}{8}$ inch. It was a crude affair made of tin, but this introduction to Great Britain of gauge 00 marked an important milestone in model railway history.

By 1935 Bassett-Lowke had introduced the Twin Train Railway, or Trix Twin Railway, which ran two 00 electric trains along the same lines but at different speeds. Initially made in Nuremberg, it was, after its outstanding success, manufactured in Northampton. In 1938, in direct competition with its own Trix line, Hornby also launched its well-known Dublo train sets, with a wide range of accessories.

## FURTHER READING

The following list of materials for further reading offers a broad range of literature. Both specialist and general works are included. While every effort has been made to give the date of the most recent edition, new ones may have been published since this book went to press.

Bartholomew, Charles
**Mechanical Toys**
London 1979

Coleman, Dorothy
**The Collector's Encyclopaedia of Dolls**
New York 1968

**The Collector's Encyclopaedia of Dolls Houses, Dolls and Miniatures**
London 1983

Johnson, Peter
**Toy Armies**
London and New York

Opie, James
**Britain's Toy Soldiers 1893–1932**
London and New York

Speaight, George
**Juvenile Drama: The History of the Toy Theatre**
1946

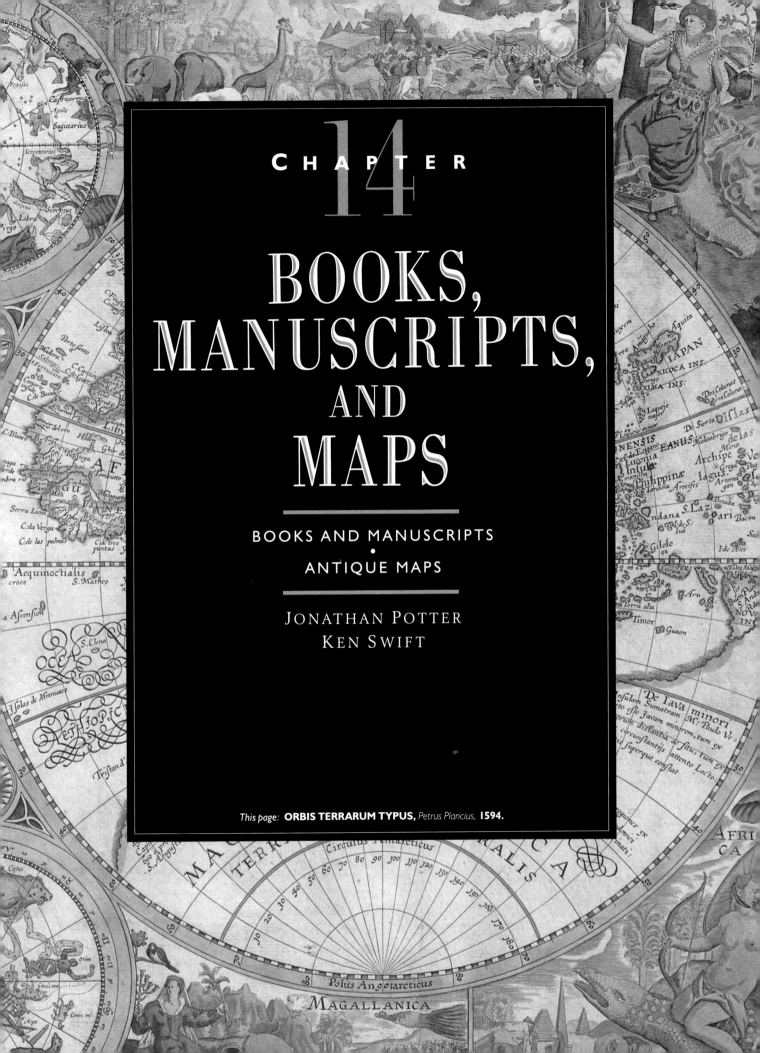

# CHAPTER 14

# BOOKS, MANUSCRIPTS, AND MAPS

BOOKS AND MANUSCRIPTS
·
ANTIQUE MAPS

Jonathan Potter
Ken Swift

*This page:* **ORBIS TERRARUM TYPUS,** *Petrus Plancius,* **1594.**

# BOOKS, MANUSCRIPTS, AND MAPS

THE VARIETY OF MANUSCRIPTS, BOOKS, AND MAPS ENCOMPASS ANYTHING FROM EPHEMERA SUCH AS WORKS OF ENTERTAINMENT TO WEIGHTY LITERARY, RELIGIOUS, AND SCIENTIFIC PUBLICATIONS.

This chapter attempts to cover what is perhaps the largest of all categories of antique artefacts: books and maps produced by hand, or reproduced mechanically. This covers a vast range of material. The very success of printing, the first modern example of mass-production techniques, has led to the survival of a huge amount of unconsidered items. The durability of early materials and cultural and religious changes since the 15th century, has meant that many examples of early printing still exist, yet go uncollected because their quality and importance are not sufficiently regarded.

Prices of maps drawn or printed before the 19th century are comparable to those of other antique objects of the same periods, but

**ARTHUR RACKHAM**
*A Midsummer Night's Dream*
**1908**

The pre-eminent illustrator of early-20th-century high quality children's books with colour plates was Rackham, whose goblins and fairies enhance the magical atmosphere of the text. (*Above*)

**WILLEM JANSZOON BLAEU**
*Americae nova Tabula*
**1618**

The Dutch maritime empire of the early 17th century required accurate sea charts, and inspired a generation of mapmakers in the Netherlands to produce superb terrestial atlases. The latest discoveries were recorded in richly decorated and hand-coloured printed maps whose superb quality has never been surpassed. (*Left*)

**ILLUSTRATED
CHILDREN'S BOOKS**
*Mabel Lucie Attwell, Louis
Wain and W. F. Thomas,
(illustrators)*

Picture books and comic
papers for small children
are among the most difficult
items to find in fine
condition, because of their
sometimes rough
treatment at the hands of
their young owners.

only the minority of manuscripts, or books containing illustrated
material, and the first editions of major literary and scientific texts,
fetch similar prices.

## RARE QUALITIES

Whatever the value or rarity of items in a chosen field, experienced
collectors will usually limit their purchases even further: a particular
author, illustrator, binder, printer, publisher, topic within a general
subject, or any combination of these. Some collectors always prefer the
first impression, while others are satisfied with the first edition.

An edition is, strictly speaking, all copies of a book printed at any
time from one setting-up of type; an impression comprises the whole
number of copies of that edition printed at one time (i.e., without the
type or plates being removed from the presses). This may seem to be
a very fine distinction, but there are very many instances in which
a mistake has been discovered in the text early on in the printing,
and corrected on the spot; if all the printed sheets are then used in
producing the bound book, then some copies will contain the earlier,
corrupt text, and some the later, corrected text. The irony here is that
a purist collector of first editions will prefer the former to the later; this
preference will be reflected in the price.

"Trade" editions such as these, are sometimes preceded by large-
paper or limited editions, which may contain extra illustrations or the
signatures of the author or illustrator, or be printed on finer paper, or
bound in more expensive materials.

It is usually the case that an author's first book, printed before
the publisher is confident of a large sale, is the most difficult to find of
his works. Sometimes censorship, fire, flood or bombing consume a
publisher's stock before it reaches the bookseller, and make what
should have been a quite common title very difficult to find. Books that
contain manuscript emendations or presentation inscriptions from the
author, especially to another notable person, are highly prized.

**LITTLE SISTER TO THE
WILDERNESS, LILLIAN
BELL**
*Stone and Kimball*
**1895**

This binding was designed
by Bruce Rogers, the
American typographer,
who believed that mass-
produced cloth or paper-
covered bindings could
approach the beauty of
hand-printed Private Press
books.

BOOKS AND MANUSCRIPTS OFFER MANY ATTRACTIONS, SUCH AS THE
HANDSOME ILLUSTRATIONS OF HAND-COLORED PLATES, OR THE WELL-
CRAFTED APPEARANCE OF A ROW OF LEATHER BINDINGS.

# BOOKS AND MANUSCRIPTS

The classical world contained great libraries and had an established book trade, but much of this was lost when literacy declined during the last centuries of the Roman Empire. We owe the survival of the few classical works we have to the Christian monasteries of Europe. St Benedict made it one of the rules of the order of monks he founded at Monte Cassino in Italy in 531 that each monk spend part of his day in the scriptorium, copying and decorating ancient texts, and, as the ideal of the monastic life spread throughout Europe, so too did the book-making tradition.

Ultimately all of Western Europe was over-run by barbarians, and it was the monks of Ireland and the Byzantine Empire who kept learning alive, producing in the 7th and 8th centuries some of the most beautiful books ever made. The monastery at Iona produced, probably in the 8th century, the supreme masterpiece of the Celtic school, *The Book of Kells*, still surviving in the library of Trinity College, Dublin, and from the monastery at Lindisfarne came *The Lindisfarne Gospels* (*c.*700), now housed in the British Library, London and one of the nation's greatest treasures.

After the revival of monasticism in southern England, the principal medieval scriptoria were the monasteries of Winchester, St Albans, Canterbury, Durham, Peterborough, Glastonbury and Bury St Edmunds. These mainly copied liturgical, musical and other works for their own use but also produced books of hours (manuals of private devotion) for the laity, especially for ladies. For wealthy patrons these were illuminated with decorations and illustrations, and they often included a calendar with an illustration for each month, showing the details of medieval life. The greatest examples, such as the Bedford Hours, produced for John, Duke of Bedford, in France *c.*1423 (now in the British Library) have been preserved in fine condition. But there were also more humble specimens, which now show signs of their regular use.

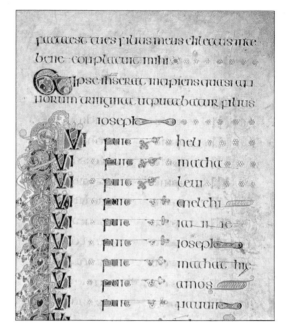

**BOOK OF KELLS**
*Iona*
**8th century**

The half-uncial script of the Book of Kells shows the distinctive wedge-shaped terminals at the tops of the letters, characteristic of the Irish tradition. The complex interlace patterns incorporating human and animal forms, which recur throughout the book, are the highest expression of Celtic ornament. (*Left*)

**BENTIVOGLIO BOOK OF HOURS**
Italy
**c. 1500**

Manuscripts and the earliest printed books did not have separate title pages. Instead, the beginning of the text was marked with the word *Incipit* (meaning "here begins"), followed by the title. The title here is *Officium Beatae Virginis Mariae* (the Hours of the Holy Virgin Mary), an example of what is commonly known as a book of hours. (*Left*)

## PRINCIPAL EUROPEAN PRINTERS 1450–1550

| | | | |
|---|---|---|---|
| **AMERBACH, Johannes** | 1443–1513 | Basle | Scholarly printer. |
| **BLADO, Antonio** | *fl.* 1515–67 | Rome | Printer. |
| **CAXTON, William** | 1422–92 | Westminster | First printer in England. |
| **FROBEN, Johannes** | 1460–1527 | Basle | Printer to Erasmus. |
| **GARAMOND, Claude** | 1480–1561 | Paris | Type designer. |
| **ESTIENNE family (Latin form, Stephanus)** | | Paris | Scholarly printers. |
| **Henri** | 1460–1520 | | |
| **Robert** | 1503–59 | | |
| **Henri II** | 1528–98 | | |
| **GUTENBERG, Johannes** | *fl.* 1436–62 | Mainz | Inventor of printing. |
| **JENSON, Nicolas** | d 1480 | Venice | French printer and type designer. |
| **KOBERGER, Anton** | 1445–1513 | Nuremberg | Printer of the *Nuremberg Chronicle*. |
| **MANUTIUS, Aldus** | 1450–1515 | Venice | First printer of pocket-sized classics. |
| **SCHÖFFER, Peter** | d 1503 | Mainz | Printer of the 42-line Bible. |
| **SWEYNHEYM and PANNARTZ** | *fl.* 1465 – | Subiaco | First printers in Italy. |
| **TORY, Geofroy** | 1480–1533 | Paris | Influential French typographer and designer. |

Most of these books were made of vellum, produced from the skin of sheep, goats and calves.

Professional scriptoria were also established in university towns to supply texts for students, and in addition professional scribes set up shop in the precincts of great cathedrals.

The transition from manuscripts to printed books was far from clear-cut. After the invention of printing it was still quite common for printed books to be copied by hand, especially if only part of the text was required, and manuscript book production – especially for particular genres such as poetry – remained important in Western Europe until as late as the 17th century.

### THE FIRST PRINTED BOOKS

What brought about the printing revolution of the mid-1400s was the invention of movable type, a method of mass-producing individual metal letters that could be rearranged into any combination and used over and over again. The credit for this invention is given to the German Johann Gutenberg (*c.*1399–1468), who began printing with it in Mainz in 1439. Very little of Gutenberg's output is known, and the only complete book that can definitely be ascribed to him is the 36-Line Bible (1457). Nevertheless, Gutenberg's technical efficiency has never been surpassed, and his Bible remains one of the most beautiful books ever produced.

Books had been printed before Gutenberg, from wood-blocks. The importance of his invention was twofold: it made possible the editing or correcting of texts, and increased enormously the speed with which large numbers of identical texts could be produced.

In 1455 the partnership between Gutenberg and the lawyer who financed him, Johann Fust, broke down. Most of Gutenberg's presses and types passed to Fust's son-in-law, Peter Schoeffer of Gernsheim, who set up a rival printing enterprise and produced the 42-Line Bible (*c.*1456). This was produced on at least four presses, and many copies were printed on vellum. Fust and Schoeffer followed their Bible

And haue a mantel rially J bore
A Cook they hadde with hem for the nonys
To boylle the chekens & the mary bonys
And powder marchaunt tart and galingale
Wel knew he a draughte of london ale
He coude roste sethe boyle and frye
Make mortrellys and wel bake a pye
But gret harm was it as it thoughte me
For on his shynne a Marmoyl hadde he
And blank Manger made he with the best
A Shipman was ther that woned fer be west
For ought J woot he was of dertemouth
He rood vp a rouncy as he couthe
In a gowne foldynge to the kne
A dagger and a lace hangynge had he
Aboute his necke vnder his arm adoun
The hote somer hadde made his hewe al broun
And certaynly he was a good felawe
Ful many a draughte wyn he hadde drawe
Fro burdeux ward whyle the chapman slepe
Of conscience took he no kepe
At ful many abatoylle in that londe
He faught and hadde the higher honde
But of his craft to reken wel his tyde
His stremys and his daungers hym be syde
Ther was non suche from hul in to Cartage
For wyse he was though he were ful of corage
Hardy he was and waar to vndertake
With many a tempest his berd hath quake

**GEOFFREY CHAUCER:**
**CANTERBURY TALES**
William Caxton
**1478**

Caxton used types in the "bastarda", or informal, style (with tapering ascenders and descenders) to print the first vernacular English texts. The red initials were added by hand.

with their 1457 Psalter, printed on vellum in black and red, with decorated initials printed in red and blue. This was a considerable technical achievement: before this – and for many years afterwards – colour was only added to printed books by hand. This was also the first printed book with a colophon, a tail-piece stating where and when the book was printed.

Books produced during the first 50 years of printing are known as incunabula (literally meaning "in swaddling-clothes"). Such books were hardly distinguishable from manuscripts: the types were copied from the hands in which manuscript books were written, and text layout was closely modelled on manuscript exemplars. Some printers, however, had their own identifying device, or trademark; Fust and Schoeffer had one by 1463, and the Venetian printer Aldus Manutius by 1501. The title page, giving title, author and place and date of printing, did not come into general use until after 1500.

Presses were soon established in all the important commercial centres; and by 1480 more than 110 towns had one. After the sack of Mainz in 1462, Italy, and in particular Venice, became the new centre of book production. By 1500 the city contained no fewer than 150 presses.

The first English printer was William Caxton (c. 1422–c. 1491). Having learned to print in Cologne, he produced there the first book in the English language, *Recuyell of the Historyes of Troye* (1474). In 1476 he set up a press in Westminster and the following year produced the first book to be printed in England, the *Dictes and Sayengis of the Philosophers*.

**Paper** Clearly, vellum was too costly a material for the vastly increased number of books being produced by the printing presses. Paper manufacture, unknown in the West until the 12th century, increased considerably during the 15th century, and this made the material cheaper and encouraged its use for book production. Whereas in 1400 only one-fifth of books were produced using paper, by 1500 the proportion had risen to half. Paper-making did not reach England until the late 15th century, and even then for several hundred years afterwards England remained dependent upon supplies from the Continent.

THE EMERGENCE OF PUBLISHING

Apart from some minor improvements in presses, there was virtually no technical progress in printing from the mid 16th century to the end of the 18th. But the period did see increasing sophistication in the organization of the book trade, with type-founder, printer, editor, publisher and bookseller becoming separate functions. The publisher gradually became the central figure of the trade, and the professional author entered the field.

In England the content of books gradually changed. In the early years of printing it was theological texts that had predominated, but by the mid 17th century they were easily outstripped by historical, scientific and fictional titles. The range of marketing techniques also expanded: advertisements, prospectuses, stock lists and book catalogues, book reviews, pub-

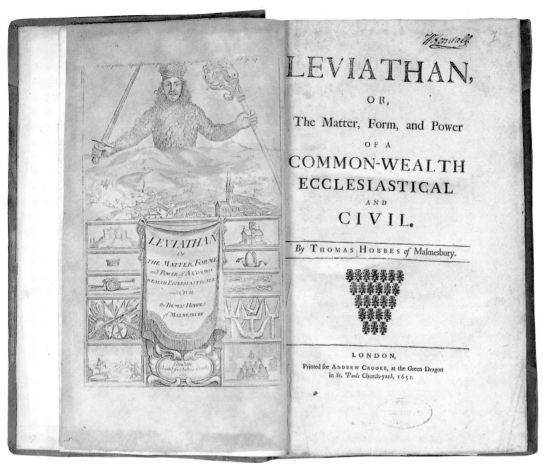

**THOMAS HOBBES:
LEVIATHAN**
London
**1651**

The engraved frontispiece is emblematic of the relationship between Church and State: on the left the temporal power of castles, weapons and war, and on the right the spiritual power of the Church represented by cathedrals, logic and disputation. Above, the State is shown to be made up of the people, who hold the emblems of both Church and State. Emblems were much in vogue in the 16th and 17th centuries, and whole books of them were printed.

## PRINCIPAL EUROPEAN PRINTERS 1550–1800

| | | | |
|---|---|---|---|
| **BASKERVILLE, John** | 1707–75 | Birmingham | Printer and type designer. |
| **BODONI, Giambattista** | 1740–1813 | Parma | Printer and type designer. |
| **CASLON, William** | 1692–1766 | London | First English typefounder. |
| **DIDOT, family** | | Paris | Printers and type designers. |
| **François** | 1689–1758 | | |
| **François-Ambrose** | 1730–1804 | | |
| **Firmin** | 1764–1836 | | |
| **ELZEVIER, family** | | Leiden | Scholarly printers. |
| **Louis** | d 1617 | | |
| **Bonaventura** | 1583–1652 | | |
| **Abraham** I | 1592–1652 | | |
| **Izaak** | 1596–1651 | | |
| **Daniel** | 1626–80 | | |
| **FOURNIER, family** | | Paris | Typefounders. |
| **Jean Pierre,** *l'aîné* | 1706–83 | | |
| **Pierre Simon,** *le jeune* | 1712–68 | | |
| **IBARRA, Joachim** | 1725–85 | Madrid | Printer. |
| **PLANTIN, Christophe** | c. 1520–89 | Antwerp | Printer. |

PUBLII VIRGILII

MARONIS

BUCOLICA,

GEORGICA,

ET

AENEIS.

BIRMINGHAMIAE:

Typis JOHANNIS BASKERVILLE.

MDCCLVII.

**VIRGIL: AENEID**
John Baskerville
**1757** '

Baskerville experimented with new materials and new styles of both type and layout, producing the first Neo-Classical books. He rejected ornament, relying entirely on type for his effects. The new types he designed show a much greater contrast between thick and thin strokes than earlier types.

The French Bibliothèque Nationale evolved from the library of Charles V, the Italian Mediceo-Laurenziana combined the collections of Cosimo and Lorenzo de' Medici, and the Prussian State Library grew out of that of Frederick William, the Great Elector. In England, the collections of the British Museum (now the British Library) began with the library of Sir Robert Cotton (1571–1631) and the Bodleian Library in Oxford was founded by Sir Thomas Bodley (1545–1613).

MASS PUBLISHING

In the early 19th century the whole printing process, from letter-founding to book-binding, became mechanized and production increased. In England during the period 1802–27 the number of titles produced each year remained stable at about 850, but by 1835 it had climbed to 2,530 and by 1880 had reached 9,000. New fiction was published in three-decker format: three volumes at 31s.6d. for the set. This was a prohibitively high price for many people, and the demand for fiction was met partly by the new circulating libraries, such as Mudie's, established 1842, and partly by the various uniform series of reprints, introduced from 1830 onwards, at a fifth of the price of the three-decker format. As the century progressed, reprints became progressively cheaper: the "yellowbacks" introduced in 1853 (so-called because of their illustrated glazed, paper-covered boards, usually with a yellow background) were sold at 1s.6d. each.

The increased literacy and disposable income of the masses, together with the new demands of railway travellers, led to various series of cheap, discardable books: Constable's Miscellany (1827–35), Murray's Family Library (1829–34), Colburn & Bentley's Novels (1831–54) and W. H. Smith's Railway Editions, sold at railway stations from 1848.

On the Continent, the same trend towards cheap reprints was followed by the Leipzig printer Christian Bernhard Tauchnitz (1816–95), who in 1837 started to produce his small-format paperback reprints in the English language. By 1935 the company had produced over 5,000 titles. Although, strictly speaking, these were pirated editions, Tauchnitz gained the goodwill of English-speaking authors and publishers by voluntarily paying royalties and by agreeing not to sell the books in England or the Empire. Typographically, however, the Tauchnitz books were dreary. In contrast, the

lishing in instalments and the first book auctions all date from this period.

In the Netherlands the two leading printing firms were Plantin and Elzevier. During the great period of Dutch mercantile power in the 16th and 17th centuries, their books were sent all over the world. Plantin specialized in bibles, and Elzevier became famous for their pocket-sized editions of the Greek and Latin classics. The first American press was established at Cambridge, Massachusetts, in 1639. Its earliest extant book is *The Bay Psalm Book* (1640). Printing in Australia started in Sydney in 1795, and in South Africa at Cape Town in 1784.

The period 1550–1800 also saw the creation of the great private book collections which now form the nucleus of Europe's national libraries.

## PRINCIPAL PRINTERS –
## THE 19TH CENTURY AND AFTER

| | | | |
|---|---|---|---|
| **COBDEN-SANDERSON, T.J.** | 1840–1922 | London | Co-founder of The Doves Press. |
| **DWIGGINS, William Addison** | 1880–1956 | Hingham, Mass. | Typographer. |
| **GILL, Eric** | 1882–1940 | Ditchling | Stone carver, type designer and wood engraver. |
| **GOUDY, Frederick** | 1865–1947 | Chicago and New York | Printer and type designer. |
| **VAN KRIMPEN, Jan** | 1892–1958 | Haarlem | Type designer and typographer. |
| **MARDERSTEIG, Hans (Giovanni)** | 1892–1977 | Verona | Printer and typographer. |
| **MORISON, Stanley** | 1889–1967 | London | Type historian and typographer. |
| **MORRIS, William** | 1834–96 | London | Type designer and founder of The Kelmscott Press. |
| **ROGERS, Bruce** | 1870–1957 | Boston and New York | Type designer and typographer. |
| **TSCHICHOLD, Jan** | b 1902 | Basle | Type designer and typographer. |
| **UPDIKE, Daniel Berkeley** | 1860–1941 | Boston, Mass. | Type historian and founder of The Merrymount Press. |
| **WALKER, Emery** | 1851–1933 | London | Typographer and co-founder of The Doves Press. |

**COLUMBIAN PRESS**
George Clymer
**1821**

The earliest presses were made of wood and could print only a small area of type at one time. The iron presses introduced at the beginning of the 19th century could print a larger area, but, lacking the natural spring of wood, required a counterweight to make the work of raising the plate less demanding for the pressmen. The counterweight on the Columbian press – made in the United States – is in the form of an American Eagle.

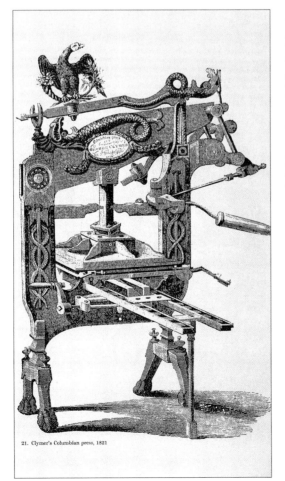

21. Clymer's Columbian press, 1821

Insel-Bücherei, launched in 1912 at 6d. each, had high standards of typography and well-designed covers and were often illustrated in colour. By 1937 25 million copies of 500 titles had been sold.

In England mass publishing at a very low price arrived in 1935, when Allen Lane founded his Penguin paperback series. His success led other publishers to produce popular titles in paper covers. In the 20th century the rise of the paperback has been the most important development in publishing.

### BIBLES

During the Middle Ages, virtually the only available text of the Bible was the Vulgate, whose Latin text had become very corrupt through the processes of translation and copying. In 1514, in order to produce a more accurate text, Cardinal Ximenes, the primate of Spain, commissioned the first polyglot Bible known as *The Complutensian Polyglot* from its place of printing (Complutum being the Latin name for Alcalá in Spain). *The Complutensian Polyglot* printed the Hebrew, Chaldee, Greek and Latin texts of the Old Testament, and contained the first edition of the New Testament to be set in Greek as well as in Latin. However, publication

**THE BIBLE**
London
**1611**

This page from the second folio edition of the Authorised Version of the Bible shows the heavy woodcut border typical of Elizabethan and Jacobean book design. The same motifs of interlaced leather or carved wood or stone are found also in contemporary bookbindings and architectural detail. *(Below)*

**THE BIBLE**
London
**1630**

The technique of engraving on wood blocks was used during this period to produce elaborate double-page illustrations such as this representation of the family tree of Noah. *(Right)*

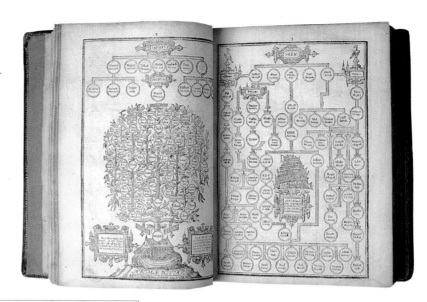

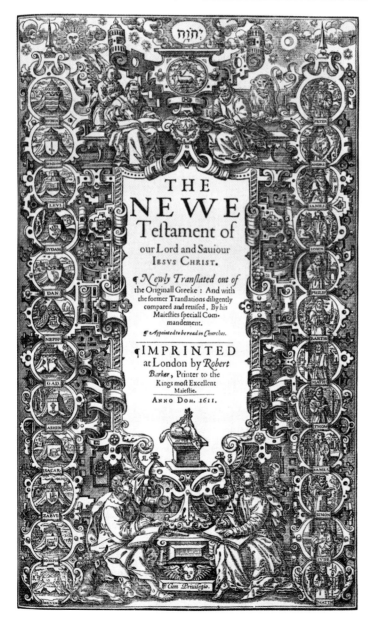

of the New Testament volume was delayed to give precedence to the Dutch scholar Erasmus's edition of the Greek New Testament (1516), which had been given exclusive rights for four years. Erasmus's edition, which gave the Latin and Greek texts side by side, was the first to treat the Vulgate critically. It was enormously influential and formed the basis for Luther's German translation of 1522.

The ideas of the leading thinkers in the Reformation promoted a desire among common people to read the Bible for themselves in their own language, but this was fiercely resisted by the Catholic authorities. The first vernacular translation into English was by William Tyndale (c. 1494–1536), who was forced by opposition to his work to leave England. Publication of his New Testament began in Cologne in 1525 but was interrupted by the local magistrates and had to be finished in Worms. He had published only part of the Old Testament before he was arrested near Brussels and executed.

Miles Coverdale's version (1535) represents the first complete Bible in English; like Tyndale's New Testament, it had to be printed abroad. The first officially sanctioned Bible in English was the Great Bible, begun in Paris but completed in London in 1539. The title page shows God blessing King Henry VIII, and it was decreed that a copy should be set up in every English parish church.

The Geneva (or "Breeches") Bible (1560), so-called from its rendering of Genesis 3.7 ("they...made themselves breeches", where the later Authorised Version has "aprons"), was published in a handy portable format, and for the next 50 years was the Bible most commonly owned by private individuals. It was the first

## TYPE DESIGNS

The three main classes of type design all appeared during the first 50 years of printed book production: Gothic (or black letter, so-called because of the dense black effect given by a page set in this type), roman (upright non-Gothic letters) and italic. All early books printed in northern Europe were in Gothic types, but by 1570–80 these had been displaced by roman type for most books other than theology and law, except in Germany, where a form of black letter type remained in everyday use for all subjects until the end of the Second World War.

Roman type was based upon the formal book hand used by the humanists of the Renaissance, who had imitated it from 8th-century French copies of the classical manuscripts they studied. Roman types were first used in Italy and were further refined in France, where Claude Garamond (c.1480–1561) became one of the first specialists in the designing, cutting and casting of type. His typefaces, known as Garamond, are particularly beautiful and still in use today.

Italic types were based upon the informal cursive or "running" hand used by the Italian humanists for letters and private writing, as opposed to the formal book hand they used for copying texts. The Venetian printer Aldus Manutius (1450–1515), a scholar with a passion for Greek and Roman classics, was the first to use italics. He set his pocket editions of classical texts – known as Aldines – in the type. However, from such use as a text face for whole books, italic was rapidly relegated to a subsidiary textual position, being used solely for emphasis or for subsidiary matter in texts set principally in roman type.

Whereas Gothic and italic virtually ceased to evolve after the 16th century, roman type has continued to develop down to the present day. The principal later additions to the range of roman types were the modern face, which was developed in the later 18th and early 19th centuries by designers such as the Englishman John Baskerville (1706–75) and the Italian Giambattista Bodoni (1740–1813), and sans serif, which was perfected in the 20th century by the English designer Eric Gill (1882–1940).

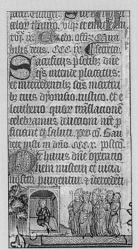

Humanistic Minuscule, 15th century (*Above*)

Humanistic Italic, 16th century (*Above*)

Gothic black letter, 13th-15th century (*Top and above*)

ABCDEFGHIJKLMN
OPQRSTUVW
XY&Z

abcdefghijklmnopqrstuvwxyz

Baskerville Roman

A B C D E F G H I J
K L M N O P Q R S
T U V W X Y & Z

abcdefghijklmnopqrst

Garamond Italic

Bible in Roman type and the first English Bible with numbered verses. Between 1560 and 1640 140 editions were published. The Authorised Version (1611) involved 54 scholars and had as its patron James I. A refinement and synthesis of the earlier work of Tyndale, Coverdale and others, rather than a completely new translation, it soon supplanted all previous English versions.

The first Bible printed in America was John Eliot's Indian Bible (Cambridge, Massachusetts, 1663) and the first American Bible to be printed in English was produced in Philadelphia in 1782.

### NATURAL HISTORY PUBLICATIONS

The first printed herbal (compendium of plants with medicinal properties) in English is John Gerard's *Herball* (1597), with 2,200 illustrations. Like Nicholas Culpeper's *Complete Herbal* (1652), it contains many folk beliefs, along with more scientific observations. Both were illustrated with woodcuts. Copperplates were used to illustrate later botanical works, such as Oliver Goldsmith's *History of the Earth and Animated Nature* (1711).

The *Botanical Magazine*, founded in 1787 by William Curtis (1787 onwards), was notable for both the excellence of its text and the accuracy and beauty of its illustrations. A very different sort of work was Thornton's *Temple of Flora* (1799–1807), which contained aquatints and mezzotints of great beauty, showing flowers in a variety of romantic and dramatic settings.

Some of the most beautiful botanical illustrations ever were produced in France in the early 19th century by Pierre Joseph Redouté, using stipple engraving (dots instead of lines). His masterpieces include *Les Liliacées* (8 volumes, 1802–16), *Les Roses* (1817–24) and *Choix des Plus Belles Fleurs* (1827–33).

The same variety of techniques was also applied to ornithological works. Among the finest examples of beautifully hand-coloured copperplates were Edward Donovan's *The Natural History of British Birds* (1794–1819). In *The Birds of North America* (1827–38) by the American naturalist John James Audubon, hand-coloured ·aquatints, mostly by Robert Havell, a London engraver, were used to reproduce Audubon's magnificent paintings. Less than 200 copies of the book were published, and it remains one of the most expensive natural history books in the world.

The 19th century was the golden age

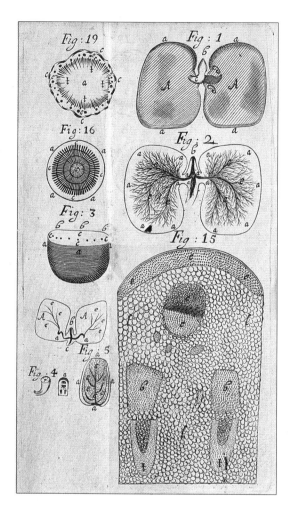

**NEHEMIAH GREW: THE ANATOMY OF PLANTS**
London
**1682**

With this book Grew inaugurated the new sciences of plant physiology and morphology. Using the microscope, he was able to compare different plants and examine the same plant at different stages of its development. He also made the first scientific investigation of the significance of tree rings, and was one of the first scientists to put forward the theory of sexual reproduction in plants.

of natural history. Technical advances led to cheaper mass-produced, colour-printed books, such as William Jardine's *Naturalist's Library* in 40 volumes, aimed at the mass market. At the other end of the scale, nature printing (printing direct from natural specimens, such as ferns and sea weeds) had a relatively limited distribution, since few copies could be made from each specimen.

### TRAVEL BOOKS

One-third of all volumes printed in Europe before 1500 were illustrated, but many of these illustrations were crude, all-purpose woodcuts used over and over again in different books. This is especially true of early depictions of towns and cities. From the late 17th century, travel books exploited the advances in illustrative techniques to provide maps and accurate views as visual evidence of the geographical discoveries of their authors.

The 18th century was the great age of exploration, which was chronicled in such works as Captain Cook's *An Account of a Voyage Round the World* (1773), Mark Catesby's *The Natural*

## DAVID ROBERTS: HOLY LAND, SYRIA, IDUMEA, ARABIA, &C
London
**1842–5**

David Roberts was a painter of architectural subjects, whose travels in the Middle East were recorded in a series of drawings reproduced as tinted lithographs. (*Above*)

## JOHN HANNING SPEKE: JOURNAL OF THE DISCOVERY OF THE SOURCE OF THE NILE
**1863**

Speke published an account of his travels traversing equatorial eastern Africa, which led to his discovery of the Nile's source. (*Right*)

*History of Carolina, Florida and the Bahama Islands* (1731–43) and Lord Anson's *A Voyage Round the World* (1748). African exploration was documented in Mungo Park's *Travels in the Interior Districts of Africa* (1799), Richard Burton's *First Footsteps in East Africa* (1856), John Speke's *Journal of the Discovery of the Source of the Nile* (1863) and David Livingstone's *Missionary Travels in South Africa* (1857).

Lewis and Clark's accounts of their east-to-west overland crossing of North America were first printed in a pirated London edition in 1809; the first official version was published in Philadelphia in 1814. The Australian counterpart was Charles Sturt's *Two Expeditions into the Interior of South Australia,* which was first published in 1833.

Increasing anthropological interest in the indigenous populations encountered by the explorers and the early pioneers is exemplified by George Catlin's series of books illustrating his travels among the native population of North America: *Manners, Customs and Condition of the North American Indians* (1841), *North*

# ILLUSTRATION PROCESSES

The processes employed to illustrate books fall into three categories: relief processes, such as woodcut, where the design to be printed is left in relief on the printing surface; intaglio processes, such as copperplate engraving, etching, aquatint and steel engraving where the lines of the design are sunk into the surface of a thin plate, and planographic processes, such as lithography, where the design is borne on a flat printing surface. For book production the differences are important, since relief processes can be printed along with the text, whereas intaglio and planographic processes must be printed on different kinds of presses, and often on different kinds of paper, and added to the printed book at a later stage, thus tending to make the book more expensive to produce.

Woodcuts were in use before the invention of movable type and continued to be used by early printers to provide decoration as well as illustrations. But by the end of the 16th century, copper-engravings were being used to illustrate fine books, and woodcuts were relegated to more popular works for which continued to be used until the end of the 18th century. In England Thomas Bewick (1753–1828), noted for his natural history illustrations, revolutionized the technique of printing from wooden blocks by using a graver (a sharp metal tool) on the hard end-grain of boxwood to engrave his designs on wood, thus combining the convenience and cheapness of the woodcut with the greater delicacy of the intaglio process. The technique was used throughout the early 19th century by many popular publications, such as *The Illustrated London News*.

**Copperplate engraving** Engraving on copperplate allows effects of half-tone and shadow to be conveyed by cross-hatching, which is not possible in woodcut. The technique reached its peak in the Netherlands during the 16th and 17th centuries. Etching involves coating copperplate with wax, through which the design is drawn with a needle. This makes the artist's hand less constricted and the lines freer than if directly cut into the copper with a graver, as in an engraving. The plate is then

immersed in a bath of acid, which eats the metal away where the artist's needle has penetrated the wax. Some of the lines can then be re-waxed to prevent further action by the acid and the plate re-immersed, producing a softer effect than that of an engraving.

Another variation of copperplate engraving is stipple engraving, in which the engraved line is replaced by a series of small dots, creating a more delicate effect. Mezzotint is a further variation: the plate is worked all over with a rocking tool, to produce thousands of minute dents, this rough surface is inked (so that it would print completely black if not treated further) and

**WOOD ENGRAVING**
From Thomas Bewick's *A General History of Quadrupeds*; **1740** (*Top*)

**LITHOGRAPH**
From David Roberts' *Holy Land, Syria, Idumea, Arabia &c*; **1842-45** (*Above*)

**WOODCUT**
Wood-block print of St Christopher; **1423** (*Above right*)

is then scraped away where half-tones and highlights are required. Mezzotint was widely used for reproducing oil paintings, especially portraits.

In aquatint engraving, developed by Le Prince in 1787, copperplate is first coated with resin, which is then baked hard, the design is scratched through the resin and acid is applied. In this technique not only the engraved lines are etched away but also the minute spaces between the resin grains, giving an effect similar to that of wash drawings and watercolours. Aquatint was used extensively from about 1790 to 1830 to illustrate travel and topographical books.

In lithography, invented by the German engraver Alois Senefelder (1771–1834) in Munich in 1798, the design is drawn with a greasy wax crayon directly on to a block of limestone. The stone is then dampened, only the unwaxed areas absorbing the water. When ink is rolled over the surface, the wet areas repel, the waxed design attracts it. After the invention of photography in the early 19th century, the principle of lithography was used in various mechanical processes for directly printing an artist's work for book illustration.

## BOOK ILLUSTRATORS OF THE 19TH AND EARLY 20TH CENTURIES

| | | |
|---|---|---|
| **BEARDSLEY, Aubrey** | 1872–98 | Contributor to *The Yellow Book*. |
| **BEWICK, Thomas** | 1753–1828 | Wood engraver. |
| **BLAKE, William** | 1757–1827 | Illustrator and engraver of his own poems. |
| **BROWNE, Hablot Knight "Phiz"** | 1815–82 | Illustrator of Dickens. |
| **CALDECOTT, Randolph** | 1846–86 | Children's book illustrator. |
| **CRANE, Walter** | 1845–1915 | Designer and book illustrator. |
| **CRUIKSHANK, George** | 1792–1878 | Caricaturist. |
| **DORÉ, Gustave** | 1832–83 | Illustrator of *The Bible*, *The Ancient Mariner*, *Don Quixote*, etc. |
| **DOYLE, John "HB"** | 1797–1868 | Political satirist. |
| **DOYLE, Richard** | 1824–83 | Fairy illustrator and humorist. |
| **DULAC, Edmund** | 1882–1953 | Art Deco book illustrator. |
| **GILLRAY, James** | 1757–1815 | Political satirist. |
| **GREENAWAY, Kate** | 1846–1901 | Illustrator of children's books. |
| **HEATH ROBINSON, William** | 1872–1944 | Portrayer of mad inventions. |
| **KING, Jessie M.** | 1876–1949 | Illustrator in the Glasgow Art Nouveau style. |
| **LEECH, John** | 1817–64 | Comic illustrator, especially of hunting scenes. |
| **NICHOLSON, William and PRYDE, James** | 1872–1949 1866–1941 | "The Beggarstaff Brothers". Poster artists and book illustrators. |
| **PELLEGRINI, Carlo "Ape"** | 1838–89 | *Vanity Fair* caricaturist. |
| **POTTER, Beatrix** | 1866–1946 | Writer and illustrator of her own children's stories. |
| **RACKHAM, Arthur** | 1867–1939 | Illustrator of children's books. |
| **ROBERTS, David** | 1796–1864 | Painter of the Holy Land. |
| **TENNIEL, John** | 1820–1914 | Best known as illustrator of *Alice in Wonderland*. |
| **WARD, Leslie Matthew "Spy"** | 1851–1922 | *Vanity Fair* caricaturist. |

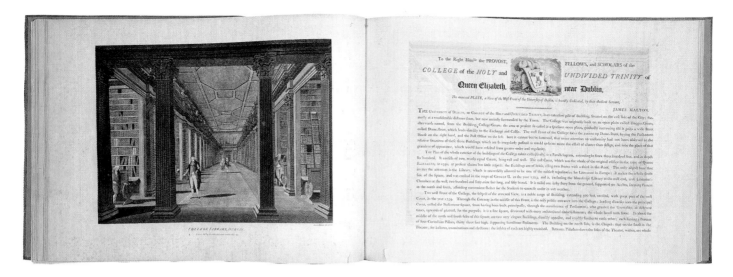

American Portfolio (1844) and Last Rambles Amongst the Indians of the Rocky Mountains and the Andes (1868).

In the late 19th and early 20th centuries, handbooks for the general traveller became popular, with the publication of Baedeker's, Murray's and A. & C. Black's extensive series of guide-books. These were liberally illustrated with wood and steel engravings or half-tone colour plates. The field of exploration includes two accounts of polar expeditions: Admiral Robert E. Peary's North Pole (1910) and Leonard Huxley's edition of Scott's Last Expedition (1922).

### TOPOGRAPHICAL BOOKS

Although antiquaries had always been interested in local history, old buildings and archaeological remains, it was not until the later part of the 18th century that a wider public came to appreciate such things. This shift was also linked with a growing appreciation of picturesque scenery. To cater for this taste various series of books were produced, such as those by two English publishers, James Malton (d. 1803) and Rudolf Ackermann (1764–1834), who both commissioned watercolour paintings of local scenes, some by such famous artists as J. M. W. Turner and John Sell Cotman, which were reproduced by the aquatint process. Among Malton's fine publications were Picturesque Tour through the Cities of London and Westminster (1792) and Picturesque and Descriptive View of the City of Dublin (1794–5). Ackermann co-ordinated the work of artists, engravers and colourists, and organized a vast market for the sale and distribution of the engravings which they produced. Among his many successful publications were

The Microcosm of London (1808–10), with 104 coloured plates by A. C. Pugin and Thomas Rowlandson , The University of Oxford (1814), with 82 coloured plates, The University of Cambridge (1815), with 79 coloured plates and The History of the Colleges (public schools) (1816), with 79 coloured plates.

Thomas Rowlandson (1756–1827), the great English caricaturist and illustrator of Regency life, generally etched and aquatinted his own plates. His best-known work was the series illustrating Dr Syntax's tours: originally produced at the rate of two plates per month for Ackermann's Poetical Magazine, with text supplied by William Combe, they were subsequently published in three volumes as The Tour

**JAMES MALTON: PICTURESQUE AND DESCRIPTIVE VIEW OF THE CITY OF DUBLIN 1794–5**

The aquatint plates reflect the style of late 18th-century architecture. (Top)

**RUDOLPH ACKERMANN: THE MICROCOSM OF LONDON 1808–10**

Drawings by Pugin and Rowlandson. (Above)

# BOOKBINDING

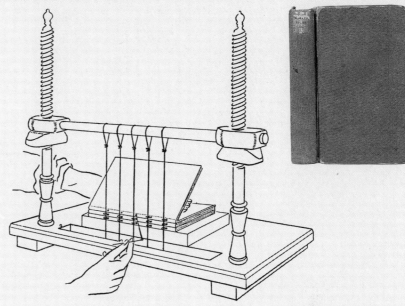

In the classical world, a book consisted of a roll of parchment or papyrus, formed by pasting together end to end sheets of the material. The inconvenience of moving from one part of the text to another in this arrangement led, by AD c.400 to the development of the codex, or modern form of the book, in which sheets are bound together at one edge.

The typical manuscript book was bound by first quiring (inserting one inside the other) folded vellum pages; stitching together the pairs through the fold, sewing together the quires across the spine; and finally encasing the whole in wooden boards, then leather. In essence, this is the technique which survives to the present day, although in modern bookbinding vellum has been replaced by paper, wood by pasteboard and leather by cloth.

The decoration of bindings is a skilled art, which over the centuries has borrowed motifs, and even materials, from many other art forms, including jewellery, textiles and architecture. The finest illuminated manuscripts were decorated with jewels or enamels and kept in shrines. The form of decoration usually applied to early printed books, which were less costly, was blind-stamping (or decoration "in blind" – that is, without gold leaf). Gold-tooling was not introduced until after the mid 15th century. In this technique heated brass tools were applied to a sheet of paper holding the required design, fixed over the cover of the book, to produce "blind" impressions on the cover. These were then treated with a solution of egg-white and vinegar, gold leaf was laid on them, and the heated tools were applied again.

Each period of European book production had its characteristic styles of decoration, and there were recognizable regional variations. Each binder had his own unique set of tools, and it is therefore possible not only to identify the country and period of a binding, but often the binder who made it.

**SEWING FRAME**

The vertical cords attach the book to the boards and produce the raised bands on the spine. (*Above left*)

**CLOTH BINDINGS**

Publishers introduced cloth-bound books in the early 19th century. (*Above*)

---

*of Dr Syntax in Search of the Picturesque* (1812), *The Tour of Dr Syntax in Search of Consolation* (1820) and *The Tour of Dr Syntax in Search of a Wife* (1821).

After the late 1820s, topographical works tended increasingly to be illustrated with steel engravings. Among the most impressive works of this type are the numerous books of draughtsman William Henry Bartlett (1809–54), who travelled extensively in the British Isles, Europe, North America and the Near East.

### CHILDREN'S BOOKS

Books produced specifically for children were rare until the mid 18th century, and those that were published were overtly educational and often moralizing in tone. Some of the earliest were in the form of chapbooks (little illustrated books sold by itinerant pedlars).

In 1744 John Newberry began publishing children's books that eschewed the oppressive morality of earlier texts. His wood engravings marked a considerable advance in the quality of illustrations used; he even employed copperplates in some books.

The 19th century saw a great proliferation of books written for children. Many of them now aimed principally to entertain their young readers, though a moral was often not far below the surface. Translations were also important, as in The Brothers Grimm's *German Popular*

*Stories*, first published in English in 1824 with George Cruikshank's illustrations, and Hans Christian Andersen's *Wonderful Stories for Children*, the first English translation of which appeared in 1846.

Perhaps the most famous 19th-century children's book was Lewis Carroll's *Alice in Wonderland* (1865), illustrated, as was its sequel *Through the Looking Glass* (1872), by Sir John Tenniel. Many American children's books have also become world favourites, including Washington Irving's *Sketch Book* (1819), Samuel Griswold Goodrich's *Tales of Peter Parley about America* (1827), Nathaniel Hawthorne's *Wonder Book for Boys and Girls* (1852) and *Tanglewood Tales* (1853), Louisa Alcott's *Little Women* (1868), Mark Twain's *Adventures of Tom Sawyer* (1876) and *Adventures of Huckleberry Finn* (1885) and Joel Chandler Harris's *Nights with Uncle Remus* (1880).

Illustration has always been important in children's books. Colour printing for children was first successfully used by Edmund Evans, who published the illustrations of Walter Crane, as in *Baby's Opera* (1877), of Kate Greenaway,

as in *Under the Window* (1878) and of Randolph Caldecott, as in *John Gilpin* (1878).

The early 20th century was the golden age of English colour-printed children's books, ranging from the charming books of Beatrix Potter, such as *The Tale of Peter Rabbit* (1901), to splendidly produced books for older children, such as *Peter Pan in Kensington Gardens* (1906), illustrated by Arthur Rackham, and *Fairy Tales* (1910), illustrated by Edmund Dulac.

### PRIVATE PRESS BOOKS

The private press movement was a reaction, at the end of the 19th century, against the poor standards of contemporary commercial book production. Its pioneering figure was the English designer and essayist William Morris (1834–96), leader of the Arts and Crafts Movement. When Morris determined to print his own books himself his priorities were the harmonization of type, illustration, ink and paper, and the importance of the opening (the two adjacent pages when a book lies open), rather than the single page, as the unit of typographic design. To further his aesthetic aims, he designed his own types: the Golden, based on

**LEWIS CARROLL:
ALICE'S ADVENTURES
IN WONDERLAND
1865**

This private nonsense tale by an Oxford academic, written for a young female friend, was published ten years later with Tenniel's black and white illustrations. The popularity of the work, and of its companion piece, *Through the Looking-Glass* (1872), derived as much from Tenniel's skill in depicting the characters as from Carroll's in describing them.

### SHAKESPEARE: A MIDSUMMER NIGHT'S DREAM
Arthur Rackham
**1908**

Rackham began his career in the late 19th century as a book illustrator in black and white, but it is for his colour plates for many children's books of the first three decades of the 20th century that he is now best remembered. His greatest forte is the depiction of grotesque creatures and woodland scenes (many adult book collectors of his work testify to the childhood terrors which his illustrations engendered). The handsome quarto format of these books, and the high quality of paper and decorated cloth bindings, represent the golden age of children's book production.

**GEOFFREY CHAUCER: WORKS**
Kelmscott Press
**1896**

The woodcut borders and decorations by Edward Burne-Jones impart great richness and density to the pages. Each opening (or pair of pages) was conceived as a unity.

the roman letter of the 15th-century French printer Nicolas Jenson, and the Troy and Chaucer, both of a simplified Gothic character.

The 53 books Morris produced at his Kelmscott Press from 1890 to 1898 display high standards of press-work, but to some tastes Morris's attempt to revive medieval standards of book design is misconceived: the Gothic type is sometimes hard to read, and the thick hand-made paper makes the bound books heavy and bulky as well as expensive to produce. The importance of Morris lies more in the inspiration he gave to contemporary enthusiasts, who set up their own private presses. These include the Merrymount Press (founded in Boston, Massachusetts, 1893), the Ashendene Press

(1894–1935), the Eragny Press (1894–1914), the Vale Press (1896–1904), the Essex House Press (1898–1909), the Doves Press (1900–16), the Grabhorn Press (founded in San Francisco, 1919) and the Gregynog Press in Wales (1922–40).

Francis Meynell's Nonesuch Press (1923 onwards) showed that the ideals of the private press enthusiast could be adapted to the constraints of the commercial publisher: beautiful books did not have to be hand-made, given adequate standards of design and detailed instructions to printers. The Limited Editions Club (founded in New York, 1929) followed the same principles.

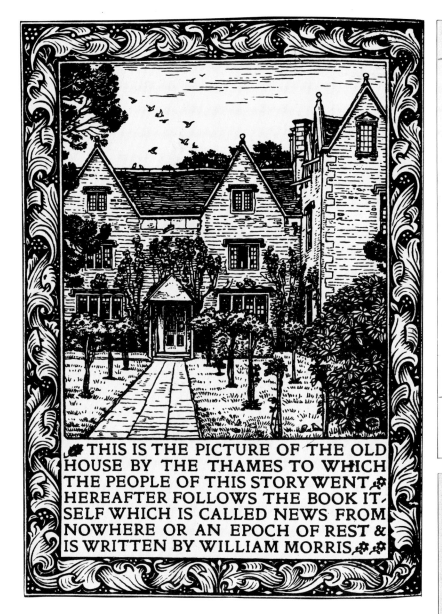

**WILLIAM MORRIS: NEWS FROM NOWHERE**
Kelmscott Press
**1893**

Morris was a social theorist as well as a book designer, and he wished for a return to handcraft techniques which would restore dignity and creativity to manual labour. (*Above*)

**THE BIBLE**
Doves Press
**1903–5**

The books produced by Walker and Cobden-Sanderson at the Doves Press are the antithesis of Kelmscott medievalism. The first line and the long descender of the initial "I" were added by hand by Edward Johnston. (*Top right*)

**A ROYCROFT ANTHOLOGY**
c. 1905

One of the American followers of the English private press movement was Elbert Hubbard at the Roycroft Press. Also known as Fra Elbertus, he went back to Italian 15th-century models for this anthology. (*Right*)

THE BEST WAY OF TRACING THE DEVELOPMENT OF GEOGRAPHY IS
THROUGH THE MANY DIFFERENT MAPS – EACH SUCCESSIVE ONE TENDING
TO GREATER ACCURACY – PUBLISHED OVER THE YEARS.

# ANTIQUE MAPS

The history of printed maps produced over the past five centuries shows the expansion of both European knowledge of and influence over the whole world during that period. Initially, Renaissance interest in the classics saw a dependence on the ancient *Geographia* of the Alexandrian astronomer and geographer Ptolemy (2nd century AD) and other classical theorists; within a few years, however, the great voyages of the Portuguese explorers Bartholomew Diaz (*fl.* 1481–1500) and Vasco da Gama (*c.*1460–1524), the Italian-born Christopher Columbus (1451–1506) and others showed the inadequacy of classical cartography. Between the early 16th century and 1850 we see this development graphically illustrated in maps which are some of the finest collaborations of science and art ever produced.

Over the centuries, as techniques for transmitting information improved, map-making changed dramatically in style and today presents collectors with a fascinating array of visual alternatives for conveying the configurations of land, sea and stars. Sixteenth-century woodblock maps, for example, have a bold, dramatic appearance that contrasts with the elegantly artistic work of a century later; a style subsequently subdued in the 18th century by precise, documentary cartography.

Although maps existed before the first printed atlases, today's collector has to concentrate on maps published in atlases and occasionally, in more recent times as separate broadsheets or multi-sheet productions. Manuscripts – that is, hand-drawn maps – are often attractive but are extremely rare.

### THE FIRST HUNDRED YEARS
The earliest printed maps were produced in the late 15th century in the great European centres of learning and culture – chiefly in northern Italy and central Europe – and were based on Ptolemy's *Geographia*, a compilation of nearly 8,000 place names and co-ordinates.

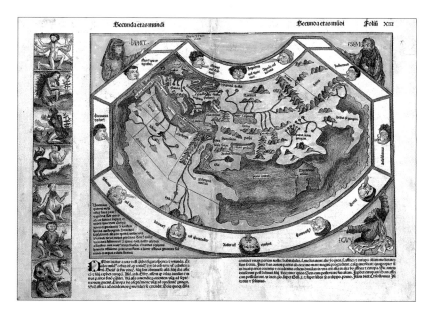

(Manuscript copies of the *Geographia*, containing maps compiled from the information in it, were often beautifully illustrated, but they never appear on the open market now.) These early maps, though sometimes finely engraved, have little to recommend them as decorative items, with the sole exception of the 1482 Ulm edition of *Geographia*.

In 1487 Diaz voyaged along the west African coast and around the Cape; in 1492 Columbus made his celebrated landfall; in 1496 the Italian navigator John Cabot (1450–98) discovered Newfoundland; in 1499 da Gama reached the

**MAP OF THE WORLD, 1493**
*Hartmann Schedel*
Approx. 52 × 38 cm (21 × 15 in)

Published in Schedel's *Nuremberg Chronicle*, this map, with its fantastic world "inhabitants", shows the traditional Ptolemaic land-form concept. A few years later post-Columbian knowledge had reconstructed the world map. (*Above*)

**THE BRITISH ISLES, 1482**
Approx. 46 × 39 cm (18 × 16 in)

From *Geographia*, this map illustrates the standard Ptolemaic shape for the islands. The E-wards slant of Scotland and the northerly placement of Ireland are particularly noticeable. The vivid colouring is typical of this edition. (*Right*)

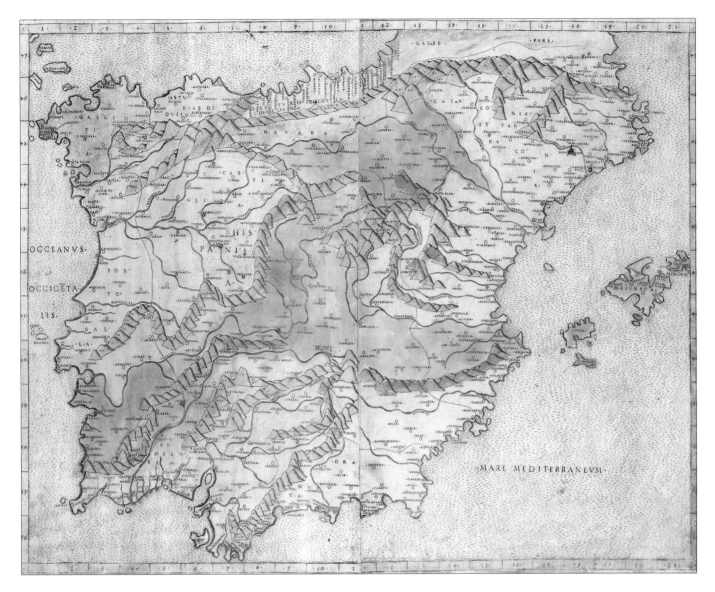

west coast of India; and in 1520 the Portuguese explorer Ferdinand Magellan (c.1480–1521) rounded South America; two years later one of his ships reached Spain, being the first to circumnavigate the world. As a result of these epic voyages, the ancient view of the world became defunct: it was now known that the Indian Ocean was not land-locked and the Atlantic was not limitless, that a previously unknown "New World" lay westwards between Europe and the Orient, that a great new ocean, the Pacific, existed and that the world was definitely not flat. However, cartography was very much in its infancy and consequently rather slow to assimilate all this new knowledge. Indeed, it was not until 1570, when the *Theatrum Orbis Terrarum*, of the Flemish cartographer Abraham Ortelius (1527–98) was published, that an atlas was produced which did not lean heavily on Ptolemaic geography.

**Notable early maps** Despite the basic dependence on Ptolemy during the first hundred years of printed maps, some geographical progress was made, as the following list of some notable map publications shows:

| | |
|---|---|
| 1472 | The first map printed in Bologna, Italy: a woodcut representing the world. |
| 1477 | The first edition of Ptolemy's *Geographia* with maps. |
| 1482 | The first edition of *Geographia* to include modern maps. |
| 1492 | A world map by Francesco Rosselli, the first to dispel the notion of a land-locked Indian Ocean. |
| 1506–7 | Three world maps of great significance by Giovanni Contarini, Johann Ruysch, and the German Martin Waldseemuller (c. 1470–c. 1518), the first of the New World. |

**TABULA MODERNA HISPANIAE, 1507/8**
Approx. 50 × 39 cm (20 × 16 in)

This is one of the earliest modern, as opposed to classical, maps of the Iberian Peninsula and appeared in editions of *Geographia* published in Rome. The group of islands placed erroneously off the northwest coast is the Azores, one of the major ports of call for ships bound for the New World.

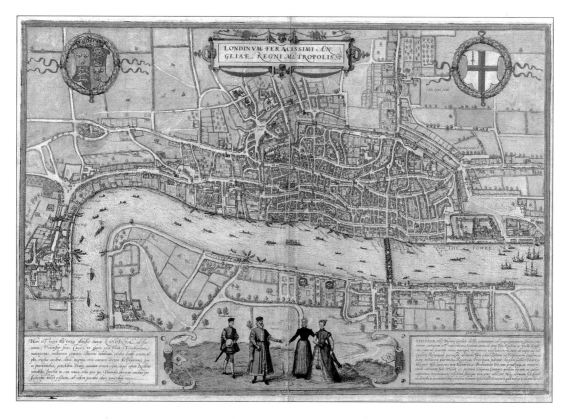

**LONDINUM, 1572**
Approx. 48 × 32 cm (19 × 13 in)

First issued in 1572 this, the first printed plan of the cities of London and Westminster, is typical in style and format of those in the *Civitates Orbis Terrarum* of Braun and Hogenberg. Most major European cities and ports were illustrated within the six volumes, many appearing in print for the first time. British towns displayed included Bristol, Cambridge, Canterbury, Chester, Edinburgh, Exeter, Norwich, Oxford and Windsor (on one plate). York, Shrewsbury, Lancaster and Richmond-upon-Thames appeared on one engraving, as did the Irish towns of Dublin, Galway, Limerick and Cork.

1513    Martin Waldseemuller's edition of Ptolemy, incorporating the first maps of North-west and South Africa and the first atlas map to focus on Central America.

1540    Edition of Ptolemy by the German Sebastian Münster (1489–1552), and subsequently his own *Cosmography*, incorporating many new maps, including the first of each continent as a separate geographic entity.

1548    The *Geografia* of Giacomo Gastaldi, the first pocket-sized atlas.

1570    Abraham Ortelius's *Theatrum Orbis Terrarum*, regarded as the first modern atlas, comprising 53 map plates.

### THE BIRTH OF REGIONAL CARTOGRAPHY, 1570–1600

Ortelius's *Theatrum Orbis Terrarum* was the first of several major atlases published at the end of the 16th century. Many of the maps in these atlases derived from separately issued originals, of which in many cases only a few copies, or perhaps only a single copy, survives. As a result, the atlases are the sole source of these maps now available to collectors. The *Theatrum* comprised maps of all parts of the world. Ortelius himself drew some of the maps and also those in the *Parergon*, the historical addendum to the atlas. His associations with cartographers across Europe led to constant additions to the atlas, so that between the first edition and that of 1595, current at his death, the number of maps in the atlas more than doubled, to over 100. Although many of the regional maps were not amended, those of the world and of the Americas are very noticeably improved from the originals of 1570.

Among Ortelius's associates was the Flemish map-maker and geographer Gerhard Kremer (1512–94), better known as Mercator. The most influential cartographer of the period, Mercator produced his own *Atlas* (the first use of the word to describe a collection of maps), the first section issued in 1585, the third and last in 1595 by his son. Mercator's maps are cartographically superior to, and more finely engraved than, Ortelius's but are generally regarded as less decorative.

Mercator's name is probably the best known in cartography, for the World map projection he conceived and published in 1569. Despite its superiority over other maps of the period, allowing navigators to plot a straight course for the first time, it was many years before the Mercator projection became regularly used.

# PROMINENT MAP-MAKERS

| | | | | |
|---|---|---|---|---|
| **PTOLEMY, C.** | fl. 2nd century AD, Alexandria; maps published in numerous cities (1477–1730). | **BLAEU, family** | fl. c. 1600–72, Amsterdam; map-, atlas- and globe-makers. |
| **MUNSTER, S.** | 1489–1552, Basle; published woodblock maps 1540–1628. | **SPEED, J.** | 1552–1629, London; English county maps (1610–c. 1770) and world maps (1627–76). |
| **MERCATOR, family** | fl. 1537–95, Duisberg; many influential maps. | **SANSON, N.** | 1600–67, Paris; various atlases from 1650. |
| **ORTELIUS, A.** | 1527–98, Antwerp; published maps from first "modern" atlas (1570–1612). | **CORONELLI, V.** | 1650–1718, Venice; globe- and atlas-maker. |
| **HONDIUS, family** | fl. 1588–c. 1640, London and Amsterdam; map engravers and publishers. | **DE L'ISLE, G.** | 1675–1726, Paris; influential maps of great accuracy. |

The *Speculum Orbis Terrarum*, an atlas produced in 1578 by Gerard de Jode, rivalled the *Theatrum* in its conception and also used the work of many respected cartographers, but its two editions (the second in 1593) never threatened the other's success. De Jode's maps, attractively designed and well engraved, are consequently much more rare than those of Ortelius and Mercator and are particularly sought after by collectors.

The *Civitates Orbis Terrarum*, published by two Germans, Georg Braun, canon of Cologne cathedral, and Frans Hogenberg, appeared in six volumes, from 1572 to 1617. This collection of over 450 plans, views and panoramas showed all the major European towns and ports, many of Africa and Asia and two New World cities – Mexico and Cusco.

The atlas of Christopher Saxton, published in 1579, consisted of 34 maps of the English and Welsh counties and is regarded as the first specifically national atlas. Saxton compiled his maps mainly from his own surveys, having them engraved by some of the finest English and Flemish engravers. In many instances the counties are grouped together, and the first maps of some individual counties do not appear until the publication, in 1607, of re-engraved versions of Saxton's maps, in the *Britannia* of the English historian William Camden (1551–1623). Of the originals, all but one are dated between 1574 and 1578, the years of their engraving, and have the Royal Coats of Arms and those of Thomas Seckford, under whose patronage the maps were produced.

The *Spieghel der Zeevardt* (1584) produced by Lucas Janszoon Waghenaer, was the first atlas of detailed navigational charts of the north and west coasts of Europe.

**Dutch cartography** During the 16th century the northwards shift in maritime power from the Iberian peninsula and the Spanish Netherlands to Amsterdam was accompanied by a demand for detailed maps and charts from Dutch merchants and seamen. One of the most influential publications of this period was the *Itinerario* (1594) of the Dutch Cartographer Hugo van Linschoten (1563–1611). This included finely engraved, detailed and decorative charts of the coastlines of Africa south of Sierra Leone, the Indian Ocean and Asia as far as Japan and New Guinea; and also a colonial map of South and Latin America. All these maps are now much sought after, both in the original

**CORNWALL, 1579**
*Christopher Saxton*
**Approx. 51 × 38 cm (20 × 15 in)**

From Saxton's atlas of the English and Welsh counties, this is one of the most attractive and famous of early maps. Decorative features such as sea monsters, ships and cartouches surround the land. The map bears the signature of the Dutch engraver, Leonart Terwoort. Saxton's maps were reissued in 1645, 1689/93 and 1720.

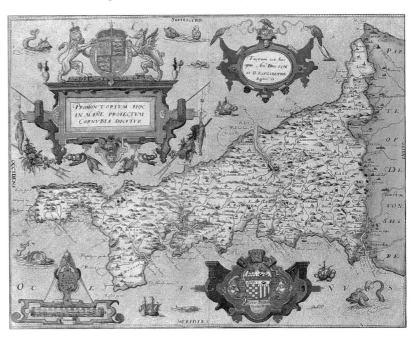

edition and the English re-engraving of 1598. This included an extra map, of the Moluccas, or Spice Islands, illustrated with diagrams showing local produce.

A notable world map, one of the first to utilize Mercator's projection, was made by the English cartographer Edward Wright. In Germany, mainly in Cologne, Matthias Quad, Johann Bussemacher and others were producing copies of work by contemporary map-makers in the Low Countries. However, Dutch dominance of the map industry was such that most major publications over the next 100 years emanated from Amsterdam.

### EARLY 17TH CENTURY: THE GOLDEN AGE OF CARTOGRAPHY

The first half of the 17th century saw some of the finest cartographic publications of any period. The most artistic work was produced by the map-makers, engravers and printers of Amsterdam. In the 1590s Willem Janszoon Blaeu (1571–1638) founded a cartographic family dynasty in the city, initially producing manuscript and printed sailing charts, pilot books, navigational instruments and globes. In 1630 his first world atlas appeared, then in 1662 the *Atlas Maior*, the most sumptuous atlas of its age, or probably of any age. In its completed form – 12 volumes containing about 600 maps, often finely hand-coloured and heightened with gold, and luxuriously bound in velvet or rich morocco leather – it made a superb official presentation piece to visiting dignitaries. Maps by the Blaeus can still be found but are scarce, the demand for those of the world and the Americas being particularly great.

Also in Amsterdam Jodocus and Henricus Hondius reissued Mercator's *Atlas*, with additional maps, from 1606. From 1638 Jan Jansson continued this development to the point when the 10-volume *Atlas Major* (as it was now called) of 1658 rivalled – though with little commercial success – the work of the Blaeus.

Apart from the great atlas-makers, other notable Dutch cartographers of the time in-

**AFRICAE, 1630**
*Willem Blaeu*
Approx. 52 × 41 cm (21 × 16 in)

Blaeu's series of Continental *cartes à figures* were engraved by 1620 but did not appear in atlas form until 1630, when the *Atlantis Appendix* – his first terrestrial atlas – appeared. They were subsequently used in all Blaeu world atlases. This design format, showing towns, ports, harbours and portraits of inhabitants, was employed by other Dutch and some English map-makers throughout the 17th century.

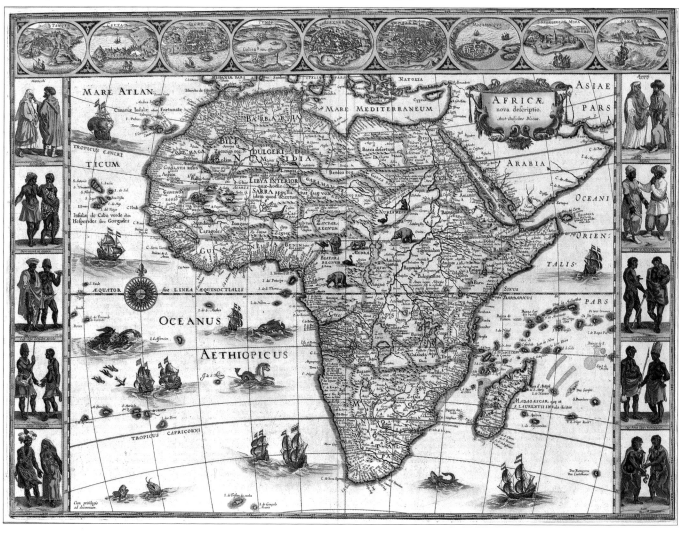

# DECORATIVE MAPS

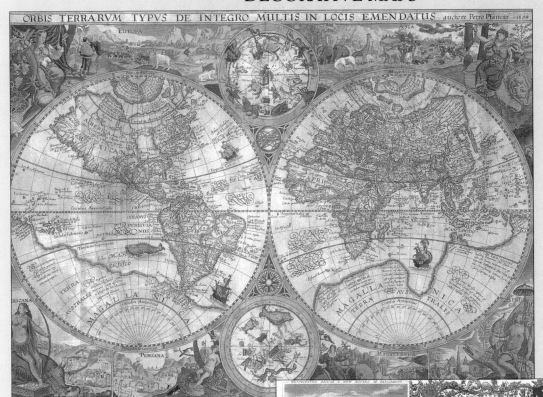

ORBIS TERRARVM TYPVS DE INTEGRO MULTIS IN LOCIS EMENDATVS auctore Petro Plancio 1594

Many 17th-century maps incorporate town views and illustrations of local inhabitants, dwellings, and flora and fauna. The first illustrated world map of this type was produced by Petrus Plancius in 1594 – a double hemisphere with celestial diagrams in the corners, representing each continent. Usually in such decoration the continents were represented by symbolic female figures – for example, Europe might be shown as an opulently dressed figure, surrounded by scientific instruments and set against a pastoral background; Asia as veiled and jewel-bedecked, in the midst of boxes of trinkets and spices and against a backcloth of minarets or pagodas; Africa as a naked figure astride an exotic animal with a background of native huts or the Pyramids; America as an Amazonian type armed for hunting, against background scenes of gold- or silver-mining or perhaps cannibalism.

World maps often also included classical figures and scenes symbolizing the seasons or the elements. Maps of continents and regions were often portrayed in a style known as

*cartes à figures*: panels at the sides showing inhabitants from different areas or citizens of different classes, and along the top, and sometimes the bottom, depicting plans or panoramic views of the area's major cities or ports. In this way, not only the shape and physical nature of a country but also the appearance of its inhabitants and their dwellings could be seen, often for the first time, by Europeans.

**MIDDLESEX, *c.* 1850**
*Thomas Moule*
**Approx. 26 × 20 cm (10 × 8 in)**

cluded Petrus Plancius; Pieter van den Keere, probably best known for his set of English county maps commonly known now as "miniature Speeds", a reference to the work of the English cartographer John Speed; and Claes Janszoon Visscher.

**Sea charts** As a result of Dutch merchant marine activity, Amsterdam became in the 17th century the centre of sea-chart publishing. Loose charts, sometimes printed on vellum for longevity, and atlases of charts were produced around 1600 by Waghenaer, Blaeu, and Willem Barentsz. By mid-century Jacob Colom's chart-books in Dutch, French and English were much in demand. The finest productions, in terms of design, engraving, paper quality and presentation, were the *Zee-Spieghel* and *Zee Atlas* of Pieter Goos.

Many of the chart-books are finely engraved and often decorated with large cartouches (ornamental scrolled tablets or shields) and scenes of naval battles; they are much sought after by collectors. Among the most regularly encountered are those by Goos and Frederic de Wit, whose charts of *c.*1675 were reissued, with some revisions, by Louis Renard in 1715 and 1730. However, the most important and prolific chart-making business in the Netherlands, for more than a hundred years from about 1680 onwards, was that of the van Keulen family, whose 6-part *Zee-Fakkel* included large-scale charts of all known coasts of the world.

MID-17TH TO MID-18TH CENTURY:
THE FRENCH INFLUENCE

By the early 17th century a number of maps and atlases had been published in France, primarily in Paris. These were however, mainly copies of Dutch originals and, apart from Jean Le Clerc's atlas of the French provinces, showed little innovation. But by mid-century European cartography was advanced by the work of Nicolas Sanson, whose maps, especially of North America, adopted a more precise, documentary approach to mapmaking.

Sanson died in 1667 but his sons, Guillaume and Adrian, together with Alexis Hubert Jaillot, had his maps re-engraved to a larger format than any before and in a flamboyant, decorative style. Published in Paris in 1681, and later in Amsterdam until about 1730, they are among the most attractive maps ever produced.

Paris became increasingly important as a cartographical centre, as a result of the activities of French explorers, Jesuit missionaries and mer-

chants. In 1700 Guillaume de L'Isle published his first atlas, a precise, disciplined work that is a milestone in the progress of map-making from predominantly an art form to a science. De L'Isle's work was reprinted over the next several decades, often, after his death in 1726, with additional or amended information by his successors, Philippe and Jean Nicolas Buache and Jean Dezauche. The interest of Philippe Buache in scientific cartography led him to produce

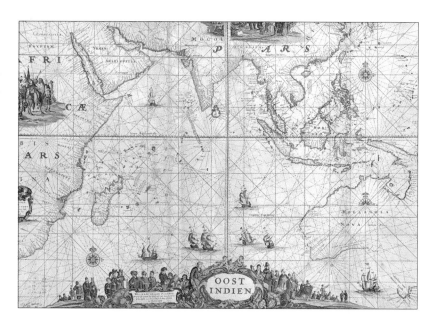

**THE INDIAN OCEAN,**
*c.* 1680
Approx. 61 × 37 cm (24 × 15 in)

This Dutch chart clearly shows the extent of 17th century European knowledge of the Australian coastline. (*Above*)

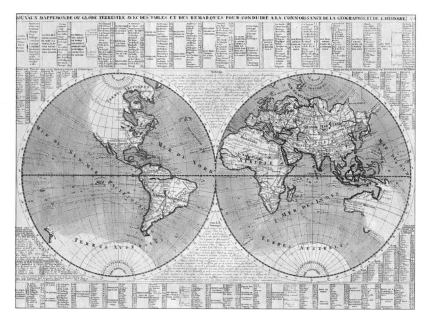

**"NOUVELLE MAPPEMONDE",**
*c.* 1720
*Henri Abraham Chatelain*
Approx. 61 × 46 cm (24 × 18 in)

This map, from Chatelain's *Atlas Historique,* shows a more precise view of the world than many others of the time.

physical and geological maps, among them some of the earliest mineralogical surveys. His work also included, however, some bizarre cartographic theorizing.

The *Atlas Historique* (*c.*1720) of Henri Abraham Chatelain, contains one of the most spectacular maps of any period, the *Carte Très Curieuse*, which concentrates on the New World and includes the coastlines of eastern Asia, western Europe and Africa. On an exceptionally large scale, it incorporates a wealth of illustration and information.

### Late 18th Century:
### British Map-Making
Before the 18th century British map-making was predominantly of atlases of county maps whose content was derived mainly from the surveys of Christopher Saxton. John Speed's *Prospect of the Most Famous Parts of The World* (1627) was conceived as a supplement to his already successful atlas of county maps and was the first world atlas produced by an Englishman; its cartography was, in the main, based on earlier Dutch work but, especially for the New World, Speed's maps were original. A later edition of the atlas (1676) included maps of Russia, Palestine, New England, Virginia and Maryland, and the Carolinas, which are now sought after by collectors. An additional feature of interest on Speed's maps is that they invariably have, printed on the reverse, an English text describing the area shown.

It was not until the mid-18th century that the British contribution to map-making became significant. As Britain's increasing maritime and

**MEXICO AND FLORIDA**
*T. C. Lotter, after de L'Isle*
Approx. 58 × 48 cm (23 × 19 in)

This German version, by T. C. Lotter, of the Frenchman de L'Isle's map shows strong French characteristics in the accuracy of its cartography. It incorporates a Germanic style in its bolder engraving, large vignette decoration and the addition of inset plans to utilize the entire engraved area.

military importance spread across the globe the necessity for large-scale maps and accurate charts of foreign areas became paramount, and this demand was met through the practised techniques of the domestic estate surveyor. In addition, the survey of British coastal waters by Captain Greenville Collins, published in 1693, had led the way in the development of a hydrographic department at the Admiralty and the production of pilot books, published by Richard and William Mount and Thomas Page, covering the coasts of the whole world.

British interest at this time was centred on the North American colonies and southern Asia where, in both cases, the principal European rival was the French. John Mitchell's detailed, accurate map of 1755 of "The British and French Dominions in North America" was used at the Treaty of Paris in 1783 to settle the rival British and French territorial claims. The coastlines of the Atlantic and Indian Oceans and the Orient were accurately surveyed for the first time by expert hydrographers, including William Herbert, Joseph Speer, Alexander Dalrymple, William Heather, Frederic Wallet

des Barres and James Cook (1728–79). The Indian subcontinent, under the East India Company's Surveyor-General, Captain James Rennell, was mapped by 1780. Many of these surveys, especially those of coastal areas, form the basis of today's Admiralty charts.

In the late 18th century the map-makers of London and Edinburgh, interpreting the findings of Cook and other explorers and surveyors, gradually filled in the gaps on world maps. And in the work of the Arrowsmiths in London and William and Alexander Keith Johnston in Edinburgh can be seen the foundations of the atlases of today.

## MAP COLLECTING

Map collections may consist of a particular cartographer's work; of maps of a specific period; or of a particular type of printing, such as woodblock or copperplate. The most popular type of map collection, however, is that based sequentially on a single area. By such concentration, the collector can observe the increase in knowledge of the area, the development of its settlements and communications, and the

**BRITAIN, 17th century**

*John Speed*

Approx. 51 × 38 cm (20 × 15 in)

Speed's famous map, first published in 1612 and subsequently copied by Blaeu and Jansson, shows Britain during the Saxon kingdoms. Border portraits and scenes illustrate people and events of the period. *(Right)*

**CELESTIAL SPHERES, c. 1690**

Approx. 92 × 63 cm (37 × 25 in)

Published by de Wit, this is a magnificent double hemisphere surrounded by six smaller diagrams of planetary, lunar and solar theory. *(Below)*

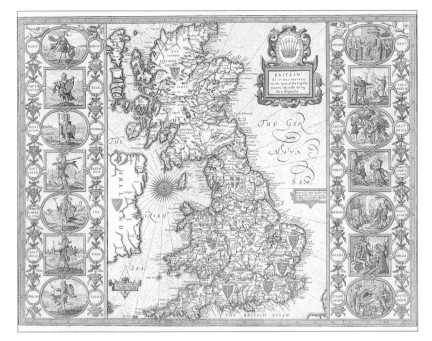

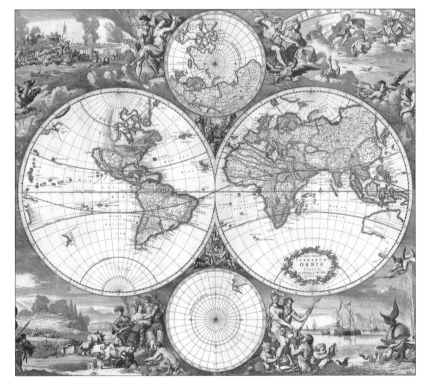

**TERRARUM ORBIS,**
*c.* 1670

Approx. 55 × 48 cm (22 × 19 in)

De Wit's finely engraved double hemisphere shows California as an island, but is also very notable for its use of mythological and symbolic characters as decoration. (*Above*)

ing individual counties; it is theoretically possible to collect almost 100 maps of one county, each showing notable differences. Among some of the finest county atlases are: William Camden's *Britannia* of 1607; John Speed's *Theatre of the Empire of Great Britain* of 1610 onwards; the so-called "miniature Speed" maps from a pocket size atlas of 1627 onwards; elegantly engraved maps of each county by Blaeu and Jansson from 1645; John Ogilby's "strip" road maps from his atlas of 1675; T. Kitchin and E. Bowen's detailed, informative maps of the mid 18th century.

Many old maps of the British Isles, or of England and Wales, can be found. Certain 16th-century maps, showing developments from the ancient Ptolemaic outline of Britain, and some of the decorative 17th-century maps are very much in demand now. Although some are very rare, others of significance and decorative appeal can readily be found.

Scotland and Ireland are less well served than England and Wales. The first atlas of individual Scottish county maps was published by Blaeu in 1654 and the first of Ireland by Sir William Petty in 1685. Before this some fine maps of the whole of each country and of groups of counties had appeared, including sectional maps by Mercator of both countries; four separate province maps of Ireland by Speed, subsequently copied by Blaeu and Jansson; and the Orkneys and the area around Edinburgh by Hondius. During the 18th century a number of county atlases of both countries appeared, though never as many as of England.

**Maps of the world** Throughout history not only have more maps of the world been produced than those of any single region but the world map has also been treated with greater artistry and embellishments than any other. It is not surprising then that world maps are still among the most sought-after by collectors as well as by those looking for a single dramatic decorative piece. Despite the high demand, interesting rare maps of the world, from the 16th century onwards, can still be found. Eighteenth-century maps are easier to get than earlier ones and, if not as decorative, have greater cartographic interest.

**Maps of Europe** Many maps of western European countries from the mid-16th century are available. With the exception of Scandinavia, where regional mapping started about 1630, European countries have always produced regional maps of greater detail and

changing cartographic styles in representing these features.

**Maps of the British Isles** The collector of regional British maps is well served by the large production of county atlases, following on from Saxton's of 1579, unparalleled in any other country. Consequently, a collection of English county maps can be built up from the Elizabethan period to mid-Victorian times, when the detailed national sectional maps of the Ordnance Survey took the place of those show-

**ITALIA, 1631**
*Jodocus Hondius*

A decorative and well engraved map, this was incorporated into the series of atlases commenced by Mercator and ultimately published by Jansson. (*Above*)

**IAPONIA, 17th century**
Approx. 48 × 35 cm (19 × 14 in)

Used by Ortelius in his *Theatrum . . .* from 1595, this was the first relatively accurate Western depiction of the islands of Japan. The map was originally compiled by the Portuguese Jesuit, Luis Teixeira, cartographer to the Spanish Crown. This map was reissued in various forms until 1655, when Blaeu published the map of another Jesuit, Father Martino Martini, whose map proved to be the best until the 19th century, when European access to the interior again became possible. (*Above right*)

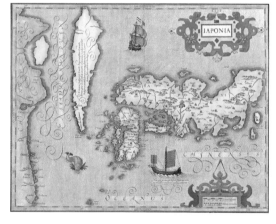

larger scale than those of their national maps. A worthwhile collection of old European maps would include those from standard French and Dutch atlases and perhaps separately issued larger-scale maps.

**Maps of Asia** Maps of southern Asia appeared in Martin Waldseemuller's 1513 edition of Ptolemy, reissued until 1541, by which time Sebastian Munster's map of the Asian continent had been published. An Italian map *c.*1560, by Giacomo Gastaldi, provided much of the detail for Ortelius and Mercator, whose atlases ultimately included individual maps of the Holy Land, the Turkish Empire, Persia, South-east Asia, China, Japan, Ceylon and Tartary. There is a good selection of maps of these areas available for collectors.

**Maps of Africa** Until Martin Waldseemuller's atlas of 1513 the only maps of Africa were on the (now rare) world maps of the time and Ptolemaic maps of northern Africa. And before the appearance of the atlases of Ortelius

and Mercator in the late 16th century, there were only a few regional maps. Among the Italian publications of this period is the first atlas of the continent of Africa, Livio and Giulio Sanuto's set of 12 finely engraved maps, published in Venice in 1588. Beautifully engraved maps of the greater part of the continent and the Congo by Filippo Pigafetta also appeared about this time.

During the 17th century fine maps of the continent appeared by all the major mapmakers. Among the most sought after are those by Blaeu, Hondius, Speed, John Overton and Vincenzo Coronelli.

**Maps of North America** No other continent can trace its history, over the last 500 years, on maps as clearly as North America. The collector can find pre-Columbian maps showing no hint of a New World, 16th-century maps giving only uncertain indications of the north and south American landmasses, and subsequently a succession of maps showing those masses in ever greater detail.

Among the finest of the maps and atlases most likely to be found by collectors today are: Waldseemuller, Ortelius, Mercator, Speed, Sanson, Coronelli and Mitchell.

**Maps of the West Indies and South America** These areas had, of course, been well-travelled and exploited by the Spanish and Portuguese. Gastaldi's 1548 atlas had included the first map of South America alone, along with others of Cuba and Hispaniola. Spectacular maps of South America were issued in de Bry's publication of 1592 and Linschoten's of 1596; and in 1606 Hondius' version of Mercator's *Atlas* includes a much improved map of South America, one of the Magellan Straits, and another of the more important West Indian islands. By 1630 maps of Colombia, Venezuela, Guiana, Brazil, Chile and Peru had been published by De Laet and Hondius.

During the 18th century the attentions of the French and English ensured the detailed surveying of most of the West Indian islands and some fine maps of this period can be found.

**Maps of Australasia and the Pacific** Detailed maps of the southern and north-western Pacific regions did not begin to appear until after the voyages of Cook and others from 1768. Separate maps of Japan, of many other areas of south and east Asia and of the South American coast exist from the early 1600s. However, only a few maps before 1770 concentrate on today's Australia or New Zealand, and most of these show little, or incorrect, detail. As a result of Cook's voyages, relatively correct map outlines were provided for New Zealand, the east coast of Australia and numerous Pacific island groups.

From the early 1800s maps of Australia as a single entity began to appear in most atlases, and from around 1830 maps of individual regions, especially the south and east, Tasmania and Western Australia became available. The vast interior of Australia remained little known throughout the 19th century, but many fascinating maps can be found which show the tracks of the hinterland's explorers.

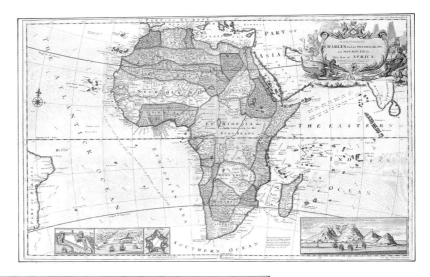

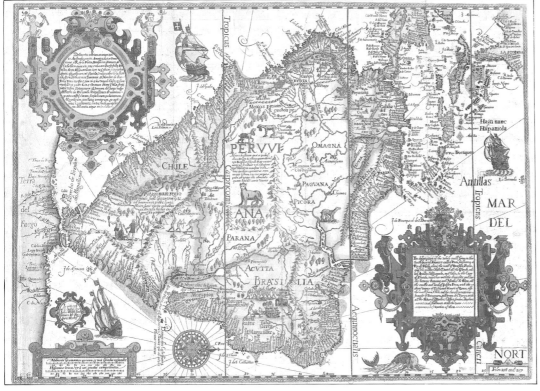

**AFRICA, early 18th century**
*Herman Moll*
Approx. 97 × 58 cm (39 × 23 in)

Moll's *Atlas*, published in London from about 1715, included large detailed maps of each continent. In this instance the cartouche is surrounded by creatures and scenes from the "Dark Continent". (*Above*)

**SOUTH AMERICA, 1598**
*Linschoten*
Approx. 53 × 37 cm (21 × 15 in)

This is a spectacular map of the continent "on its side". Tierra Del Fuego occupies the entire southern section, and large rococo cartouches surround panels giving details of the area shown. (*Left*)

## FURTHER READING

The following list of materials for further reading offers a broad range of literature. Both specialist and general works are included. While every effort has been made to give the date of the most recent edition, new ones may have been published since this book' went to press.

Bland, David
*A History of Book Illustration: The Illuminated Manuscript and the Printed Book*
London 1958

Brownrigg, L.L. (ed.)
*Medieval Book Production: Assessing the Evidence*
Los Altos Hills, California, 1990

Darnton, F.J. Harvey
*Children's Books in England* (3rd Edition)
Cambridge 1982

Day, Kenneth (ed.)
*Book Typography 1815–1965 in Europe and the United States of America*
London 1966

Diehl, Edith
*Bookbinding: its Background and Technique*
New York 1980

Hunter, Dard
*Papermaking: the History and Technique of an Ancient Craft*
New York 1978

Moran, James
*Printing Presses: History and Development from the Fifteenth Century to Modern Times*
London 1973

Needham, Paul
*Twelve Centuries of Bookbindings: 400–1600*
New York 1979

Slythe, R. Margaret
*The Art of Illustration 1750–1900*
London 1970

Steinberg, S.H.
*Five Hundred Years of Printing* (2nd Edition)
Harmondsworth 1961

Updike, Daniel Berkeley
*Printing Types: their History, Forms and Use*
(2 vols – 3rd Edition)
Cambridge, Massachusetts, 1962

# GLOSSARY

**acanthus** Stylized carving of the acanthus leaf commonly used to ornament furniture.

**ancient Britains** The term collectors use for William Britain's soldiers manufactured 1893–1914.

**anthemion** Ornamental motif of a radiating pattern based on the honeysuckle flower.

**apostle** A generic term used to describe a cast figure of Christ or one of the apostles soldered on to the ends of spoons.

**applied decoration** Ornaments made separately and then fixed to the body of an object. Also known as applied relief or applied ornament.

**apron** See *skirt*.

**aquatint** A method of giving texture to a copper plate prior to etching, characterized by an all-over crackle. It was much used in the late 18th and early 19th centuries.

**arabesque** An intricate interwoven design of scrolling foliage and flowers.

**armorial** Objects decorated with a coat of arms.

**as bought** A term used for pieces the date and origins of which are unknown.

**as found** A term for pieces that are damaged or defective.

**baluster** (1) A rounded shape that swells out at the bottom used for vases and the legs of furniture. (2) A slender pear-shape used for *finials*, knife handles and other silverware. (3) A type of glass stem that resembles an architectural or furniture baluster.

**beading** An ornamental edging made from a series of half spheres soldered into position.

**bébé** A French child doll.

**bent-limb body** A baby doll's body, jointed at the shoulder and the hip.

**Biedermeier** (1) A style of furniture and interior decoration popular in Germany during the 19th century. (2) Porcelain dolls made between *c*.1805 and 1840; also those with a black spot on their pate.

**bisque** Unglazed porcelain, also known as biscuit.

**blind** The decoration of a book binding made by impressing a pattern into the covering material without the use of gold leaf.

**bobbin-turning** Decoration for furniture legs and supports consisting of a row of spheres or bobbins. Turning refers to its manufacture on a lathe.

**bombé** A term for the outwardly curving shape of a piece of furniture.

**boss** A small circular or oval ornament used to cover a join between mouldings.

**Böttger lustre** A pinkish-brown colour with a slight metallic sheen used by the Meissen factory and named after its founder.

**Böttgerporzellan** The first *hard-paste porcelain* manufactured in Europe, developed by J. F. Böttger at Meissen in 1708–9. It has a creamy, smoky look with a thick, fizzy glaze.

**Böttger stoneware** An extremely hard, reddish-brown stoneware produced at the Meissen factory. It was often highly polished, and cut or facetted using glass-cutting techniques.

**boulle** A variety of marquetry using tortoiseshell and a metal (usually brass) inlay. For further information, see page 76.

**breaker** A word collectors use to describe furniture that is worth less in one piece than broken up as raw material.

**bright-cut** A technique using a special tool to create angled facets that sparkle.

**Britannia standard** A silver alloy of 958 parts silver to a thousand of metal introduced in England in 1697. In 1720 the old sterling standard was restored. For further information, see page 355.

**brocade** A form of textile decoration in which yarn is woven into fabric.

**bun foot** A round, turned foot used on furniture of the late 17th century.

**bygones** Objects made obsolete by newer technology. It is most commonly used for kitchenware and agricultural tools.

**cabriole** A double-curved and tapering furniture leg, often ending in a stylized paw. The design was derived from animal hind legs.

**caqueteuse** The French gave the name "gossip's chair" to those with a tall back and widely-splayed arms. These could accommodate the voluminous dresses of 16th century women.

**carat** (1) A unit of weight for gemstones. (2) A measure of the fineness of gold, pure gold being 24 carats.

**carcase** The main body or framework of a piece of furniture, over which veneer might be stuck.

**cartouche** An ornamental motif, usually oval in shape, with curved or rolled edges resembling a scroll. A coat of arms or inscription is often placed within it.

**caryatid** A standing female figure used to decorate or support in the place of a column.

**casting** The manufacture of coins and objects in a mould into which is poured molten metal.

**castor** A small wheel placed on furniture to make pieces easier to move.

**certosina** A Moorish-influenced style of inlay decoration with mother-of-pearl popular in Venice during the 16th and 17th centuries.

**champlevé** A type of enamelling in which the powdered glass is put into hollowed-out areas in the surface of the piece before firing.

**chinoiserie** The European style of decoration, occasionally fanciful, influenced by Chinese originals and extremely popular during the 18th century.

**cire perdue** See *lost-wax technique*.

**cloisonné** A type of enamelling in which compartments separated by thin metal strips are filled with powdered glass before firing.

**codex** A text in rectangular book form, where the sheets are folded into pages and stitched together along one edge.

**colophon** The tail piece of a manuscript or early book giving details of the date of completion, place of printing or writing, and often the name of the scribe or printer.

**commedia dell'arte** A tradition of Italian popular theatre, often comedies, dating from 16th to 18th centuries. The stock characters, such as Punch or Harlequin, were favourite subjects for porcelain painters and modellers.

**compendario** A sketchy style of decoration on Italian maiolica from the 16th and 17th centuries that utilizes only a limited palette, and leaves much of the white body undecorated.

**composite set** A group of chairs similar in style but not, properly speaking, a matched set.

**coopering** The name for the process of curving timbers for coopered joints on furniture.

**countermark** An additional punched mark applied to a coin to revalidate it or change its face value.

**crackle** Deliberate hairline fractures in ceramics.

**crazing** Hairline fractures, usually unintentional, in ceramics.

**creamware** A white or cream earthenware with a transparent glaze, imitative of porcelain. Developed in Britain about 1750.

**cup-and-cover** A style of decoration on some Elizabethan table legs and bed posts. A bulbous turned leg is given carved embellishments.

**cut-card** Decoration created from cut-out thin sheet silver that has been soldered into place.

**damascene** An ornamental inlay of narrow silver or gold strips set in a metal surface.

**Delftware** *Tin-glazed* earthenware from the Netherlands.

**deutsche Blumen** "German flowers". A decorative floral pattern used by German potters during the 18th century. Its accurate depictions were highly regarded.

**diaper ornament** A pattern of repeated design features such as diamond-shapes or lozenges, each enclosing a motif. Used to decorate silverware.

**die-stamping** A method of decorating silver using a die to create an impression on a sheet of the metal. The design on the die appears in relief.

**dimestore** Toy soldiers that appeared in American stores between the First and Second World Wars.

**duodecimo.** See *format*.

**earthenware** Pottery fired at a lower temperature than stoneware. It is a porous material and therefore generally covered with a glaze – which can be decorative – to make it impervious to liquids.

**ébéniste** French for a cabinet-maker, first used in the 17th century. It was derived from the fashion for the extensive use of ebony veneer. See page 78.

**ebonizing** The staining of wood or the painting of a gesso base over wood black to mimic ebony veneer.

**eggshell porcelain** The Japanese produced the first examples of this almost paper-thin porcelain during the 19th century, to capitalize on the enormous demand for Oriental ceramics in the West.

**embossing** The decoration of silver by raising a design from behind with the aid of a blunt punch.

**enamelling** (1) The covering of a metal surface with a thin sheet of translucent coloured glass. (2) Ceramic decoration in which the pigments are painted over the glaze.

**en camaieu** A method of painting porcelain in shades of a single colour.

**engine-turning** The manufacture of wooden objects by rotating them on a lathe.

**engraving** (1) A kind of illustration used in books. The design is incised as a negative image on the printing surface (wood, copper, steel). (2) Decoration cut into the surface of metal, such as on silverware.

**etching** A decorative or printing technique in which acid is used to "eat" the design into a copper printing plate or the surface of a metal object.

**exergue** The space below the main design, such as the monarch's head, on a coin.

**facets** The small polished planes of a cut gem, or the similarly small and polished planes in cut glass.

**faience** A term usually applied to tin-glazed earthenware produced in France, Germany, Switzerland and Scandinavia.

**famille-rose** The "pink family". A palette of colours used on Chinese porcelain in the 18th century. Opaque pinks and carmine predominate.

**famille-verte** The "green family". A palette of colours used for Chinese porcelain characterized by the brilliant green enamel used.

**finial** (1) An ornamented knob on the opposite end to the bowl of a spoon. (2) An ornamental knob or spire on the highest point of any vertical projection.

**flan** The plain piece of metal on which a coin is struck by a pair of dies.

**flash** Excess metal from a tinsmith's production of domestic ware.

**flat** The earliest type of toy soldier, about 1.5mm thick, having an almost two-dimensional appearance.

**flatware** Items of tableware that are flat, such as spoons, forks or plates (but excluding knives).

**flint-enamel glazing** Glaze to which silica has been added to achieve a glass-like finish. A method patented in the United States in 1849 involved dusting the glaze before firing with a metallic powder incorporating manganese.

**fluting** A series of ridges extending over part or all of an object. The ridges may be straight or spiralling. Fluting is used to decorate glass, silver and furniture.

**folio** See *format*.

**format** The number of pages printed together on each side of a sheet of paper which when folded determines the size and shape of the book: as in folio (2 leaves), quarto (4 leaves), octavo (8 leaves), duodecimo (12 leaves).

**framed construction** A technique of making furniture using horizontal and vertical timbers in a framework. It is characteristic of joinery from the 15th and 16th centuries.

**fretwork** An intricate decorative border pattern of lines used on wood and silver.

**fusee** A cone-shaped pulley and chain linked to the spring of a clock which counteracts the declining strength of the mainspring.

**gadroon** (1) The application of a repetitive series of small vertical, diagonal or twisted flutes commonly as a border decoration on silverware. (2) To apply a series of convex curved lobes or repeated spiral ribs as a decorative border on furniture. (Gadrooning is the word for such decoration.)

**gallery** A vertical band pierced with openings encircling the rim of silver objects.

**gesso** A plaster-like compound applied to wooden furniture or dolls to facilitate painting or gilding.

**gilding** The decoration of an object with a thin layer of gold, gold foil or gold leaf.

**girandole** (1) The first type of mirror, usually with a heavily ornamented frame, that could be hung on the wall. (2) Type of earring with three pendant drops suspended from a bow-shaped setting.

**gore** A piece of triangular paper or cloth used for sections of a globe's map or to make a dress wider or the desired shape.

**grand feu colours** The limited palette of earthy colours used on wares fired only once at high temperature.

**gros point** A kind of embroidery stitch worked over double-thread canvas.

**grotesque** Fantastic ornament or decoration composed of mythical creatures (satyrs, centaurs), outlandish vegetation and bizarre faces.

**hard-paste porcelain** Porcelain made from clay (*kaolin*) and feldspathic rock (petuntse). True porcelain as opposed to the *soft-paste* variety.

**harewood** Also known as silverwood. The wood of the sycamore tree stained green.

**Holbein patterns** The term used for some Turkish carpets from the 15th and 16th centuries characterized by octagonal and other geometric ornament with borders of highly complex interlace decoration. The design has similarities with those shown in the works of European painters, especially Holbein the Younger (1497?–1543).

**hollow-cast** A type of toy soldier pioneered by William Britain which has a hollow body.

**hollow ware** Tableware of a rounded, hollow shape, such as salt cellars, bowls, cups.

**incunabulum** (pl. incunabula) A book printed before 1500.

**indianische Blumen** "Indian flowers". A linear, highly stylized form of flower painting with a brilliant palette developed at Meissen during the 1720s.

**inlay** A decoration in a contrasting colour, material or metal set into wood or metal. Most commonly used to decorate furniture.

**intaglio** Decoration incised into an object, in contrast to *relief*.

**intarsia** Inlaid panelling on furniture that creates an elaborate picture or design.

**istoriato** The style of colourful narrative scenes found on some Italian maiolica. The best examples date from the 16th century.

**japanning** A European alternative to Oriental lacquerwork. The wood was covered with a skin of *gesso*, followed by many layers of gum lac, seed lac or shellac varnish to create a hard, smooth ground which was then polished. A variety of background colours were produced, and the decorations were usually outlined in gold or silver.

**kaolin** A white clay essential to the manufacture of *hard-paste porcelain*.

**knop** A small, round protuberance in a wineglass stem.

**lacca** A lacquer developed in Italy and used extensively on 18th-century Italian furniture.

**laid paper** Paper made in a mould of vertical and horizontal wires that leave characteristic marks in the finished paper.

**laminated wood** Wood pieces made up of thinner layers and frequently bent or moulded to produce curved shapes such as bed footboards or headboards.

**laub- und bandelwerk** "Leaf and strapwork". A baroque form of ornament generally used for gilt or enamel borders or cartouches enclosing painted scenes.

**lead glazed** The earliest type of transparent glaze used in European pottery.

**lead soldier** A general term for a figure made of lead-antimony alloy.

**legend** The inscription on a coin.

**lignum vitae** Hard and extremely heavy wood imported from the West Indies. It is dark brown with streaks of black.

**linenfold** Carving on furniture that mimics folded linen.

**lion sejant** A kind of finial in the shape of a lion sitting with straight forelegs found on silver spoons. They were made in Britain between the 15th and 17th centuries.

**lock** The part of a firearm activated by the trigger to fire the weapon.

**lost-wax technique** A method of casting metal. A clay-coated wax model is fired in a kiln. The heat causes the wax to disappear, leaving a hollow clay mould into which the molten metal can be poured.

**lustre decoration** Shiny, metallic decoration used on glass, earthenware and sometimes on porcelain.

**lustreware** Ceramics painted with a metallic pigment before firing, which produces a fine metallic, often iridescent, film.

**maidenhead knop** A spoon's finial in the shape of the bust of a woman rising out of a calyx. Spoons with this were made in England between *c*.1450 and *c*.1650.

**maiolica** *Tin-glazed* earthenware, usually of Italian origin. Majolica is a corrupted version of the term adopted by 19th-century potters to describe their maiolica.

**manierblum** A naturalistic style of flower painting employed at Meissen and elsewhere during the 1750s.

**marquetry** Shaped pieces of wood or other material used as a veneer on furniture to create decorative mosaics, and floral, landscape or other patterns.

**mezzotint** A method of applying tone to a copper plate prior to engraving. The surface of the plate is roughened, then burnished away to produce tones and highlights.

**milling** The striation or lettering on the side of a coin employed to discourage clipping.

**moulding** A length of shaped wood applied to the surface of a piece of furniture. Frequently, the shape is of architectural origin.

**mudéjar** A Spanish furniture style with strong Moorish elements, such as decorative, geometric-pattern inlay.

**niello** A powdered black metal alloy inlay used to decorate silver. A pattern would be engraved on an object, then filled with the alloy. The piece would then be fired and the alloy would fuse with the silver. After firing the piece was cleaned and polished, with the niello black design contrasting against the silver.

**Nuremberg scale** A 30mm size for *flats* (soldier), popularized by Ernst Heinrichsen in the mid 19th century.

**objets de vertu** Small decorative objects displaying the very best craftsmanship.

**obverse** The face of a coin or medal with the main image, in most cases "heads".

**octavo** See *format*.

**ogee** A continuous succession of two curves, one convex and the other concave, shaped like a shallow "S". The ogee was frequently used as a decoration on 18th-century silver and furniture. It is also known as "the line of beauty".

**ormolu** A term derived from the French for ground gold. It refers to gilded bronze or brass furniture mounts.

**overglaze** Decoration added to ceramics that have already been fired by painting or transfer printing before the piece is fired again.

**overlay** The top layer of cased glass, frequently engraved so that a different coloured layer underneath is revealed.

**pad foot** A type of foot on a furniture leg that is rounded and resting on an integral disc.

**parcel-gilt** Partially-gilded wood.

**parchment** A white material made from untanned lamb's skin used as writing surface or binding material.

**Parian ware** A kind of *bisque* porcelain of a very white colouring resembling that of Parian marble. It was commonly used for Classical reproduction and Neo-Classical figures of the 19th century.

**parquetry** Furniture veneering in shaped pieces of wood or other material contrived in such a way as to produce a decorative geometric pattern.

**passementerie** Decorative textile trimming made of braid, cord, beads or similar material.

**patera** A circular or oval ornament often incorporating leaf or leaf-like decoration, used on silver and furniture.

**paw foot** A variety of foot on a furniture leg that is shaped like an animal's paw.

**peg jointed** The type of joint for a doll's limbs using a round dowel to connect the two parts.

*petit feu* **colours** The broad range of colours (including pastels) that can be used to decorate porcelain or *faience* by painting the object after an initial firing, and then refiring it a lower temperature.

**petit point** Tent stitch embroidery work over single-thread canvas.

**petuntse** A granitic stone that fuses with *kaolin* at about 1300–1400°C to make *hard-paste porcelain*.

**piedfort** A coin struck on a flan thicker than the issued coin.

*pietre dure* Decorative work (also known as *pietra dura*) using inlaid semi-precious stones to depict scenes, coats of arms, geometric patterns, etc.

**pilasters** A flat decorative (instead of supportive) pillar projecting from a façade. Some furniture (for example, cabinets) employs pilasters.

**pontil** A rod used by glass-blowers to take the finished object off the blow pipe.

*poupée* A female doll.

**printer's device** A design or trademark used on the title page or *colophon*, identifying the printer of a given book.

**proof** A special striking of a coin using specially polished dies and blanks. Such pieces are not intended for circulation.

**prunt** A coloured glass blob used to decorate glass bodies. Sometimes these are shaped.

**putto** (pl. putti) A cupid or cherub used as a decorative motif.

**quarto** See *format*.

**rail** An horizontal piece in furniture frameworks that supports vertical elements.

**redware** Early American *earthenware* pottery of a rich brown-red colour achieved by the presence of iron oxide in the clay.

**reeding** Relief decoration of carved parallel convex lines.

**relief** Decoration that rises above the surface around it.

**reserve** A term in ceramics denoting on ceramics an area that is set apart in a coloured ground from the rest of the decoration.

**ripple moulding** A form of decoration consisting of wavy moulded lines on picture and mirror frames and on the panelling of furniture.

**rocaille** Stylized rococo rock and shell decoration applied to furniture.

**romayne heads** Decorative carved heads in profile set in *roundels*, possibly with additional ornamentation (for example, scrollwork).

**rosewood** A reddish-brown, black-streaked wood from tropical trees.

**roundels** A type of circular ornament that may incorporate additional decorations, such as *romayne heads*.

**sabre leg** A furniture leg curved and tapered like a sabre.

**satinwood** A close-grained, yellow wood popular in Britain after *c*.1750.

**scagliola** An imitation marble made from plaster and marble chips used on table tops during the 18th century.

*schwarzlot* A linear style of ceramics decoration using shades of black.

**scrimshaw** Objects carved and engraved from walrus tusks, whalebone and teeth by sailors.

**semi-round** A transitional type of toy soldier between the flat and the full-round.

**serpentine** Furniture decoration shaped like an undulating curve, with a convex centre and concave sides.

**sgraffito** A technique of decorating ceramics (also known as sgraffiato). A design is incised through the glaze or slip to reveal the colour of the body beneath.

**shagreen** Untanned leather with a grainy surface made from the skin of sharks, ray fish, horses, etc.

**shoulder heads** Dolls with the head and shoulders moulded in one substance.

**skirt** A piece of furniture's bottom front edge. Also known as an apron.

**soft-paste porcelain** A type of porcelain consisting of clay and powdered glass or frit. It is more gritty and porous than *hard-paste porcelain*, and is usually more thickly potted and holds less detail.

**solid** A toy soldier cast full-round, as opposed to flat.

**spelter** Zinc given the appearance of bronze by a special process. Used as a substitute for the more expensive bronze on Art Nouveau and Art Deco objects.

**splat** A flat central support on a chair's back.

**square-cut** Furniture legs, stiles or rails that are a square or rectangular shape, as opposed to rounded.

**sterling standard** A silver and copper alloy made of 925 parts out of a thousand of silver.

**stiles** Upright supporting posts or legs on a piece of furniture.

**stoneware** A ceramic body made of clay and ground-up fusible rock that vitrifies between 1200° and 1400°C. It does not require glazing to become impervious to liquids.

**strapwork** A decorative motif of interlaced bands used on silverware and furniture.

**stretcher** A strut connecting the legs of a piece of furniture.

**striking** The most usual method of making coins, using a pair of dies pressed on to a flan.

**swivel neck** An articulated neck on a doll, normally the bisque *shoulder head* variety.

**tambour work** Embroidery done in a circular frame made out of two hoops, one inside the other, in which the cloth to be worked has been stretched.

**thumbpiece** That part of a drinking vessel with a hinged lid where the user applied pressure with the thumb to lift the lid.

**tin-glaze** A glaze used in *maiolica*, *delft* and *faience* to which tin oxide has been added, giving a white, opaque surface ideal for decoration.

**tin soldier** A popular term for a flat, made from a mixture of tin, lead, bismuth and antimony.

**tinware** Domestic objects made of beaten and soldered tin. Cheaper and less robust than pewter.

**toleware** Tinware decorated with japanning.

**touchmark** A stamped mark attesting to the quality of the silver used to make an object.

**treen** Small domestic objects made of wood.

**trefoil** A common decorative motif in the shape of three symmetrical leaves.

**trestle table** A table held up by horizontal beams with inverted, v-shaped legs.

**tube-lined slip** Liquid clay applied directly on to the surface of ceramics using a pipette to create lines, circles or other controlled forms of decoration.

**turkeywork** An English knotted woollen pile textile used for seat covers and hangings.

**turning** The shaping of legs, *rails* or *stiles* on a lathe. It is possible to achieve many different shapes using turning.

**type** The design of a coin.

**underframing** The structure supporting a piece of furniture. It includes legs, *stretchers* and any other braces.

**underglaze** Colouring or design applied to a ceramic body before the glaze.

**vellum** Fine white skin used as a writing or printing material and for binding books; made from the untanned skin of calves or kids.

**veneer** A very thin, usually wood, layer affixed to the surface of a piece of furniture for decorative effect and to hide cheaper woods beneath.

**verre églomisé** A method of decorating mirrors popular *c.*1700. Gold or silver foil affixed to the back of the mirror was engraved with a needle. Then a contrasting colour was placed behind the foil, and enclosed in a layer of glass or a coating of varnish.

**Vitruvian scroll** A kind of boarder ornament consisting of a repeated pattern of scrolling. It was modelled on Classical originals and popular during the 18th century.

**wheel-engraving** A method of decorating glass and jewellery using an abrasive paste and a set of small metal wheels.

**woodcut** An illustrated process where parts of a wooden block are cut away, leaving a relief.

**wood engraving** An illustrative process where the design is incised into a wooden block with a graver on the hard cross-section or end-grain of the wood.

**wove paper** Paper made on a mould of woven wire, and therefore without the pattern of chain lines and wire lines seen in *laid paper*.

**x-chair** A chair supported by an x-shaped leg structure. Folding chairs are frequently x-chairs.

**yao** A suffix meaning ware sometimes added to the names of types of Chinese ceramics (for example, Junyao or Ruyao).

**yellowback** A nickname for cheap editions of fiction produced in the middle of the 19th century, with illustrated glazed paper-covered boards, usually with a yellow background.

***Zinnfigur*** German for tin soldier.

# INDEX

# U

# V

# W

# X

# Y

# Z

# CREDITS

Quarto would like to thank the following for their help with this publication and for permission to reproduce copyright material.

ABBREVIATIONS USED:

CCL     – Christie's Colour Library.
S         – Sotheby's.
FAAP  – Phillip de Bay, Fine Art & Archival Photography.
ATC    – Antique Textile Company.
BM     – British Museum, London.
V & A  – Victoria & Albert Museum, London.

KEY:

a – above
b – below
c – centre
l – left
r – right

p.2 CCL; p.3 Barry Davies Oriental Art; p.10 al American Clock and Watch Museum, b CCL, p.11 al S, br CCL; p.12 al S, br Ian Bennett; p.13 a CCL, cr CCL; p.14 ac CCL, cl S, bc Quarto/Arthur Middleton of Covent Garden, cr Phillips Fine Art Auctioneers; p.15 c Ian Bennett, br CCL; p.16–17 Phillips Fine Art Auctioneers; p.18 a Phillips Fine Art Auctioneers, c Angelo Hornak; p.19 a S, b Angelo Hornak; p.20 a Christie's, New York, b FAAP; p.21 Pilgrim Press; p.22 al Angelo Hornak, ar CCL; p.23 cr FAAP, b Angelo Hornak; p.24 Sotheby's, New York; p.25 FAAP; p.26 a V & A, b Martin Saunders; p.27 Private Collection; p.28 Musée de Cluny, Paris; p.29 a National Museum of Ancient Art, Lisbon, b Private Collection; p.30 bl Accademia, Venice, ar Metropolitan Museum of Art, New York, br Musée des Beaux Arts, Lille; p.31 Phillips Fine Art Auctioneers; p.32 a V & A; p.33 a S; p.36 b Pilgrim Press/Newbury Smith Associates; p.37 Angelo Hornak; p.38 & 39 CCL; p.40 a & b CCL; p.41 a CCL, b V & A; p.42 a & b CCL; p.44 CCL; p.46 a CCL; p.46 b CCL; p.47 a Trustees of the Chatsworth Settlement; p.49 t National Trust Waddesdon Manor; p.50 CCL; p.51 al, ar, al, c & bl Angelo Hornak, br Phillips Fine Art Auctioneers; p.52 S; p.53 t CCL, bl Country Antiques Dyfed, br Noël Riley; p.54 Gerald Kenyon; p.55 a Gerald Kenyon, cr Robin Butler, c & b Peter Apraharmian; p.56 ar & bl Blairman's; p.57 br CCL; p.58 al Temple Newsam House/Christopher Hutchinson, br Blairman's; p.59 a & b CCL; p.61 a Blairman's, c & b CCL; p.62 ar Blairman's, br CCL; p.63 al Quarto/Blairman's, br CCL; p.64 a FAAP, b Quarto/Blairman's; p.65 ar Quarto/Blairman's, bl Quarto/Blairman's, br Blairman's; p.66 ac Quarto, ar Blairman's, bl CCL br

Blairman's; p.67 a & b Blairman's; p.68 S; p.69 a S, b Blairman's; p.70 a FAAP, b S; p71 a FAAP; p.72 bl S, r Louvre, Paris; p.73 a Bresset, b Prudence Cumming; p.74 al CCL, b Raymond Fortt; p.75 Jonathan Harris; p.76 CCL; p.77 a Christie's, Monaco, b Jonathan Harris; p.78 b Minneapolis Institute of Arts; p.80 a CCL; p.81 a CCL, b FAAP; p.82 a CCL, b FAAP; p.83 CCL; p.84 Musées des Nationaux, Paris; p.85 a & b Gloucester House Antiques; p.86 ar S, bl Angelo Hornak; p.87 a CCL, b S; p.88 ar Christie's, Rome; p.89 a & b Angelo Hornak; p.90 CCL; p.91 Christie's, Rome; p.93 al CCL, cr S, br S; p.94 Partridge Fine Art; p.95 a CCL; p.97 a & b Angelo Hornak; p.98 Partridge Fine Art; p.99 a CCL, b FAAP; p.100 FAAP; p.101 a FAAP, b S; p.103 al Mallett & Son (Antiques) Ltd., br Partridge Fine Art; p.104 Wallace Collection; p.105 b Bukowskis Sweden; p.106 S; p.107 a & b CCL; p.108 Christie's, Amsterdam; p.109 S; p.110 r S, b Bridgeman; p.111 r S, l Angelo Hornak; p.112 a V & A, b S, b Paul Reeves, c S, b Haslam & Whiteaway; p.114 S; p.115 Angelo Hornak, bl V & A; p.116 S; p.117 r & l Musée des Arts Decoratifs; p.118 r Hubert Josse, Paris; p.119 John Vaughan; p.120 S, Musée des Arts Decoratifs; p.122 a & b V & A, a S, b Design Council; p.123 a S, b Wittmann; p.124 CCL; p.125 Museum of Applied Arts, Helsinki; p.126 Colonial Williamsburg Foundation; p.127 American Museum Bath/Derek Balmer; p.128 bl Bernard and S.Dean Levy, Inc, New York, tr Robert O. Stuart; p.129 tr American Museum, Bath, br Quarto; p.130 bl Wayne Pratt and Company; p.131 a Metropolitan Museum of Art, New York, br American Museum, Bath; p.133 Quarto; p.134 Metropolitan Museum of Art, New York, b. American Museum, Bath; p.135 Abby Aldrich Rockerfeller Folk Art Centre; p.138 Barlings of Mount St, p.139 al Barlings of Mount St, ar S; b Quarto/Barlings of Mount St; p.140 al Barlings of Mount St, ar Quarto/Gregg Baker; p.141 al Quarto/Barlings of Mount St, bl Barlings of Mount St; p.142 bl Barlings of Mount St; p.144–145 Ian Bennett; p.146 al Ian Bennett, b Quarto; p.147 a, l & r Ian Bennett; p.148 Novosti Press Agency; p.149 Hispanic Society of America; p.150–161 Ian Bennett; p.162 C. John; p.163 Ian Bennett; p.164 a & b Ian Bennett; p.165 Ian Bennett; p.166–167 Angelo Hornak; p.168 c FAAP; p.169 cl Paul Reeves, r ATC; p.170 ATC, t Mayorcas Ltd, St. James's, b Quarto; p.171 a & b Quarto; p.172 a Mayorcas Ltd, St. James's, b Quarto; p.173 Quarto; p.174 a Quarto, b Mayorcas Ltd, St. James's; p.175 a & b Mayorcas Ltd, St. James's; p.176 t Quarto, b Mayorcas Ltd, St. James's; p.178 a Quarto, b Mayorcas Ltd, St. James's; p.179 ATC; p.180–188 ATC; p.189 FAAP; p.190 a & b ATC; p.191 al, ar, & br FAAP; p.192–193 FAAP; p.194 FAAP; p.195 l ATC, r V & A; p.196–199 ATC; p.200–201 CCL; p.202 c R. Garnier; p.203 a CCL, b Derek Roberts; p.204 tl CCL; bl CCL, br CCL; p.205 Derek Roberts; p.206 R. Garnier; p.207 bl, br & ar Derek Roberts; p.209 Strike One Ltd, Islington; p.210 l Strike One Ltd, Islington, tr & br Derek Roberts; p.211 al & r John Charlton Smith; bl CCL; p.212 Derek Roberts; p.214 ar & bl Derek Roberts, c CCL; p.215 a, cr & cl Derek Roberts; p.216 a & bl Derek Roberts, br CCL: p.217 bl & br Derek

Roberts; p.218–221 CCL; p.222–223 Robert Brandt Oriental Antiques; p.224 Spink & Son Ltd; p.225 a Barry Davies Oriental Art, b Wartski; p.226 l Spink & Son Ltd, b Barry Davies Oriental Art; p.227 l & r Spink & Son Ltd; p.228 & 229 CCL; p.230 a & b S; p.231 CCL; p.232–233 Spink & Son Ltd; p.234 a Barry Davies Oriental Art, bl & br Spink & Sons Ltd; p.235 r Spink & Son Ltd, l Barry Davies Oriental Art; p.236 S; p.237 l & r CCL; p.238 & 239 S; p.241 a & b Dr Charles Avery, r Cyril Humphris; p.242 l Dr Charles Avery, r Cyril Humphris; p.243 CCL; p.244 al, ac, ar & b CCL, al The Sladmore Gallery; p.245 a A.L. Barye; p.246 & 247 Bluett & Sons; p.248 bl & ar Barry Davies Oriental Art; p.249 a Spink & Son Ltd, b Robert Brandt Oriental Antiques; p.250 Wartski; p.251 a CCL, bl Wartski, br CCL; p. 252–254 Christie's South Kensington; p.255 a & b Claire Ayres; p.256–259 Quarto/Simon Castle; p.260 a Quarto/Simon Castle, b Quarto/Peter Hornsby; p.261 a & b Quarto/Simon Castle; p.262–263 Quarto/Simon Castle; p.264–265 Quarto/Michael German; p.266–267 Peter Hornsby; p.266–295 Quarto/Arthur Middleton of Covent Garden; p.296 cl & cr Quarto/Arthur Middleton of Covent Garden, a Quarto; p.297 & 298 Quarto/Arthur Middleton of Covent Garden; p.299 lc Christie's, South Kensington, r Quarto/Arthur Middleton of Covent Garden; p.300–305 Quarto/Arthur Middleton of Covent Garden; p.308 Quarto/Arthur Middleton of Covent Garden; p.309 Christie's South Kensington; p.310–311 Mick O'Shea; p.312 a Mick O'Shea, p.313 Mick O'Shea; p.314 Bingham; 315 a & b David Miles; p.316 ar CCL, br Bingham; p.317 bl CCL; p.318 ar, bl, & br Mick O'Shea; p.319 c & b Mick O'Shea; p.320–328 Bingham; p.330 a & r S; p.331–334 Bingham; p.335 David Miles; p.336–338 S; p.339 Quarto; p.340 a CCL, b Stephen Helliwell; p.341 a Bentley & Co, b Stephen Helliwell; p.342–353 Diana Scarisbrick; p. 354 CCL; p.356 Stephen Helliwell; p.360 CCL; p.361 a CCL, b S; p.362 a Quarto, b CCL; p.363 CCL; p.364 a & b CCL; p.365 S; p.366 a CCL, p.367 ar CCL, bl S; p.368 ar S, br CCL, p.369 a & b S; p.370 al & br CCL; p.371 a & b S; p.372 al CCL, br S; p.373 S; p.374 a & b S; p.375 CCL; p.379 al Mabel Brady Garvan Collection, Yale University Art Gallery, bc Christie's, New York, cr American Museum, Bath; p.380 Metropolitan Museum of Art, New York; p.381 b Design Council; p.382 Calouste Gulbenkian Museum, Lisbon, b Royal Copenhagen; p.383 a Virginia Museum of Fine Arts, Richmond, c S, b Design Council; p.384 b Royal Copenhagen; p.385 c S, b Design Council; p.388–389 S; p.390 a S, cl & br British Museum; p.391 al British Museum, br Quarto; p.392 a & b S; p.393 a S, b Bridgeman Art Library; p.394 S; p.395 bl S; p.396 a & b CCL; p.397 S; p.398 a Percival David Foundation, b S; p.399 bl S, ar CCL; p.400 al Percival David Foundation, br CCL; p.401 a CCL, b S; p.402 Percival David Foundation; p.403 a, c & b S; p.404 a & b S; p.405 a & b Percival David Foundation; p.406 S; p.407– 408 l Tokyo National Museum/International Society for Educational Information Inc., ar V & A, br S; p.409 al Tokyo National Museum/Society for Educational Information Inc.; br Bridgeman Art Library; p.410–413 S; p.414 CCL; p.415 a & b S; p.416 CCL; p.417 al CCL, r Sotheby's Billingshurst, b S; p.418–421 BM; p.422 bl Quarto, r S; p.423 a & b S; p.424 bl CCL, ar S; p.425 CCL; p.426 b S, a CCL; p.427–428 a S; p.429 CCL; p.430 al CCL, br S; p.431 al S, b S; p.432 a CCL; b S; p.433–437 S; p.438 a & b S; p.440 S; p.441 Bridgeman Art Library; p.442 a S, b S; p.443 CCL; p.444 tr CCL, c & b S; p.445 S; p.446 l S; r Quarto; p.447 S; p.448 a Quarto; b S; p.449 a Quarto; b S; p.450 S; p.451–454 S; p.455 CCL; p.456 a CCL, b Quarto; p.455 Quarto; p.456 bl Musée de Sèvres, ar CCL; p.457 Quarto/Musée de Sèvres; p.458 a & b CCL; p.459 ar American Museum, Bath; br Metropolitan Museum of Art, New York; p.460 American Museum, Bath; p.461 al Dedham Historical Society, r Bennington Museum; bl Dedham Historical Society; p.462 Everson Museum of Art; p.463 Henry Francis du Pont Winterthur Museum; p.464 S; p.465 l & r S; p.466–467 Sheppard & Cooper Ltd; p.468 ca Angelo Hornak, b CCL; p.470 bl, p.469 a Delamouse Ltd, b Angelo Hornak; ar CCL; p.471 t Sheppard and Cooper Ltd, London; b B M; p.472 Sheppard and Cooper Ltd, London; p.473 l The Corning Museum of Glass, New York; r B M; p.474 B M; p.475 t CCL, b S; p.476 t & b S; p.477 Sheppard and Cooper Ltd, London; p.478 S; p.479 B M; p.480 l The Corning Museum of Glass, New York, r S; p.482 l & r S; p.483 S; p.484 al & r S; bl CCL; p.485 Sheppard and Cooper Ltd, London; p.486 l The Corning Museum of Glass, New York, r S; p.487 Phillips Fine Art Auctioneers; p.488 l V & A, r CCL; p.489 S; p.490 t & b S; p.491 tl & r S, b B M; p.492 V & A; p.493 a V & A; b Phillips Fine Art Auctioneers; p.494 t The Corning Museum of Glass, New York; b S; p.495 a The Corning Museum of Glass, New York; b S; p.496 The Corning Museum of Glass, New York; p.497 b Delamosne; t S; p.498 Phillips Fine Art Auctioneers; p.499 l The Bridgeman Art Library; r S; p.500 l The Corning Museum of Glass, New York; r CCL; p.501 CCL; p.502 S; p.504–505 Quarto; p.506 br Quarto others S; p.507 –508 l Quarto; p.509 l & r Quarto; p.510 Quarto; p.511–512 Phillips Fine Art Auctioneers; p.513 a & b Quarto; p.514 Quarto; p.515 a S, b Quarto; p.516 a & b Quarto; p.517 a Sotheby's, b Quarto; p.518 Quarto; p.519 a Quarto, b Phillips Fine Art Auctioneers; p.520 & p.521 Quarto; p.522–523 Quarto; p.524 Quarto; p.525 Quarto; p.526 a & b Quarto; p.527 l & r Phillips Fine Art Auctioneers; p.528–529 Quarto/Michael German; p.530 a & cl Quarto/ Michael German; b Imperial War Museum, London; p.531 a Gunshots; c Quarto/Michael German; p.532 Gunshots; p.533 a, bl & br Quarto/Michael German; p.534 a & b Gunshots; p. 535 a Gunshots, b Quarto/Michael German; p.536 a & c Quarto/Michael German; p.537 c & ar Gunshots, b Sotheby's; p.538 Quarto/Michael German; p.539 a Sotheby's, b Imperial War Museum; p.540–541 Gunshots; p.542 l & r Quarto/Michael German; p.543 a & b Gunshots; p.544 Quarto/Michael German; p.545 a Gunshots, b Peter Newark's Historical Pictures; p.546 a Quarto/Michael German, b Gunshots; p.547 a & b Quarto/Michael German; p.548 Peter Newark's Historical Pictures; p.549 Quarto/Michael German; p.550 Gunshots; p.551 l & r Quarto/Michael German; p.552 a Quarto/Michael German; b Peter Newark's Historical Pictures; p.553 Peter Newark's Historical Pictures; p.554–555 The Dunk Collection; p.556 b S; p.557 l Mint & Boxed, r Peter Johnson; p.558–567 Phillips Fine Art Auctioneers; p.569–572 Phillips Fine Art Auctioneers; p.573 bl & r Robert Opie; p.574–579 Peter Johnson; p.580 Mint & Boxed; p.581 a Mint & Boxed, c & b S; p.582 Mint & Boxed; p.583 a Mint & Boxed, b S; p.584 a S, b Mint & Boxed; p.585 al Robert Opie, ar & b S; p.586 S; p.587 S; p.588–589 Jonathan Potter Ltd, Mayfair; p.590 a Quarto, b Jonathan Potter Ltd, Mayfair; p.591 a Phillips Fine Art Auctioneers; p.592 a The Board of Trinity College, Dublin, b V & A; p.594–597 Quarto; p.600 Quarto; p.601 a Quarto, b S; p.602 Quarto; p.603 John Rylands Library, Manchester; p.604 a & b FAAP; p.605 al & ar Quarto; p.606–608 Quarto, p.609 al William Morris Gallery, ar Angelo Hornak, br Lenswork; p.610–621 Jonathan Potter Ltd, Mayfair.

Every effort has been made to trace and acknowledge all copyright holders. Quarto would like to apologise if any omissions have been made.